CHRYSLER FULL 1967-88 REPAIR MANUAL

CEO	Rick Van Dalen
President	Dean F. Morgantini, S.A.E.
Vice President–Finance	Barry L. Beck
Vice President–Sales	Glenn D. Potere
Executive Editor	Kevin M. G. Maher, A.S.E.
Manager–Consumer Automotive	Richard Schwartz, A.S.E.
Manager–Professional Automotive	Richard J. Rivele
Manager–Marine/Recreation	James R. Marotta, A.S.E.
Production Specialists	Brian Hollingsworth, Melinda Possinger
Project Managers	Thomas A. Mellon, A.S.E., S.A.E., Christine L. Sheeky, S.A.E., Ron Webb
Schematics Editors	Christopher G. Ritchie, A.S.E., S.A.E., S.T.S., Stephanie A. Spunt
Editor	Dawn M. Hoch, S.A.E.

CHILTON *Automotive Books*
PUBLISHED BY **W. G. NICHOLS, INC.**

Manufactured in USA
© 1995 W. G. Nichols, Inc.
1025 Andrew Drive
West Chester, PA 19380
ISBN 0-8019-8662-1
Library of Congress Catalog Card No. 94-069445
7890123456   9876543210

Chilton is a registered trademark of Cahners Business Information, a division of Reed Elsevier, Inc., and has been licensed to W. G. Nichols, Inc.

www.chiltononline.com

Contents

1 GENERAL INFORMATION AND MAINTENANCE

- 1-2 HOW TO USE THIS BOOK
- 1-2 TOOLS AND EQUIPMENT
- 1-4 SERVICING YOUR VEHICLE SAFELY
- 1-5 FASTENERS, MEASUREMENTS AND CONVERSIONS
- 1-7 SERIAL NUMBER IDENTIFICATION
- 1-12 ROUTINE MAINTENANCE
- 1-27 FLUIDS AND LUBRICANTS
- 1-41 PUSHING AND TOWING
- 1-41 JACKING
- 1-42 MAINTENANCE AND LUBRICATION CHARTS

2 ENGINE PERFORMANCE AND TUNE-UP

- 2-2 TUNE-UP PROCEDURES
- 2-8 FIRING ORDERS
- 2-9 POINT TYPE IGNITION
- 2-11 ELECTRONIC IGNITION
- 2-20 IGNITION TIMING
- 2-21 VALVE LASH
- 2-22 IDLE SPEED AND MIXTURE ADJUSTMENTS

3 ENGINE AND ENGINE OVERHAUL

- 3-2 ENGINE ELECTRICAL
- 3-10 ENGINE MECHANICAL
- 3-57 EXHAUST SYSTEM

4 EMISSION CONTROLS

- 4-2 EMISSION CONTROLS
- 4-8 ELECTRONIC ENGINE CONTROLS
- 4-12 VACUUM DIAGRAMS

5 FUEL SYSTEM

- 5-2 BASIC FUEL SYSTEM DIAGNOSIS
- 5-2 CARBURETED FUEL SYSTEM
- 5-27 CARBURETED SPECIFICATIONS CHARTS
- 5-36 THROTTLE BODY FUEL INJECTION SYSTEM
- 5-41 DIESEL FUEL SYSTEM
- 5-43 FUEL TANK

6 CHASSIS ELECTRICAL

- 6-2 UNDERSTANDING AND TROUBLESHOOTING ELECTRICAL SYSTEMS
- 6-8 HEATER AND AIR CONDITIONER
- 6-15 RADIO
- 6-16 WINDSHIELD WIPERS AND WASHERS
- 6-18 INSTRUMENTS AND SWITCHES
- 6-21 LIGHTING
- 6-24 TRAILER WIRING
- 6-24 CIRCUIT PROTECTION
- 6-28 WIRING DIAGRAMS

Contents

7 DRIVE TRAIN

- **7-2** MANUAL TRANSMISSION
- **7-6** CLUTCH
- **7-11** TRANSFER CASE
- **7-13** AUTOMATIC TRANSMISSION
- **7-18** DRIVELINE
- **7-21** FRONT AXLE DRIVE
- **7-33** REAR AXLE

8 SUSPENSION AND STEERING

- **8-2** WHEELS
- **8-3** FRONT SUSPENSION
- **8-19** REAR SUSPENSION
- **8-21** STEERING

9 BRAKES

- **9-2** HYDRAULIC BRAKING SYSTEM
- **9-9** FRONT DRUM BRAKES
- **9-11** FRONT DISC BRAKES
- **9-16** REAR DRUM BRAKES
- **9-20** PARKING BRAKE

10 BODY AND TRIM

- **10-2** EXTERIOR
- **10-6** INTERIOR

GLOSSARY

- **10-11** GLOSSARY

MASTER INDEX

- **10-15** MASTER INDEX

See last page for information on additional titles

SAFETY NOTICE

Proper service and repair procedures are vital to the safe, reliable operation of all motor vehicles, as well as the personal safety of those performing repairs. This manual outlines procedures for servicing and repairing vehicles using safe, effective methods. The procedures contain many NOTES, CAUTIONS and WARNINGS which should be followed, along with standard procedures to eliminate the possibility of personal injury or improper service which could damage the vehicle or compromise its safety.

It is important to note that repair procedures and techniques, tools and parts for servicing motor vehicles, as well as the skill and experience of the individual performing the work vary widely. It is not possible to anticipate all of the conceivable ways or conditions under which vehicles may be serviced, or to provide cautions as to all possible hazards that may result. Standard and accepted safety precautions and equipment should be used when handling toxic or flammable fluids, and safety goggles or other protection should be used during cutting, grinding, chiseling, prying, or any other process that can cause material removal or projectiles.

Some procedures require the use of tools specially designed for a specific purpose. Before substituting another tool or procedure, you must be completely satisfied that neither your personal safety, nor the performance of the vehicle will be endangered.

Although information in this manual is based on industry sources and is complete as possible at the time of publication, the possibility exists that some car manufacturers made later changes which could not be included here. While striving for total accuracy, Nichols Publishing cannot assume responsibility for any errors, changes or omissions that may occur in the compilation of this data.

PART NUMBERS

Part numbers listed in this reference are not recommendations by Nichols Publishing for any product brand name. They are references that can be used with interchange manuals and aftermarket supplier catalogs to locate each brand supplier's discrete part number.

SPECIAL TOOLS

Special tools are recommended by the vehicle manufacturer to perform their specific job. Use has been kept to a minimum, but where absolutely necessary, they are referred to in the text by the part number of the tool manufacturer. These tools can be purchased, under the appropriate part number, from your local dealer or regional distributor, or an equivalent tool can be purchased locally from a tool supplier or parts outlet. Before substituting any tool for the one recommended, read the SAFETY NOTICE at the top of this page.

ACKNOWLEDGMENTS

Nichols Publishing expresses appreciation to Chrysler Corporation for their generous assistance.

Nichols Publishing would like to express thanks to all of the fine companies who participate in the production of our books:
- Hand tools supplied by Craftsman are used during all phases of our vehicle teardown and photography.
- Many of the fine specialty tools used in our procedures were provided courtesy of Lisle Corporation.
- Lincoln Automotive Products (1 Lincoln Way, St. Louis, MO 63120) has provided their industrial shop equipment, including jacks (engine, transmission and floor), engine stands, fluid and lubrication tools, as well as shop presses.
- Rotary Lifts (1-800-640-5438 or www.Rotary-Lift.com), the largest automobile lift manufacturer in the world, offering the biggest variety of surface and in-ground lifts available, has fulfilled our shop's lift needs.
- Much of our shop's electronic testing equipment was supplied by Universal Enterprises Inc. (UEI).
- Safety-Kleen Systems Inc. has provided parts cleaning stations and assistance with environmentally sound disposal of residual wastes.
- United Gilsonite Laboratories (UGL), manufacturer of Drylock® concrete floor paint, has provided materials and expertise for the coating and protection of our shop floor.

No part of this publication may be reproduced, transmitted or stored in any form or by any means, electronic or mechanical, including photocopy, recording, or by information storage or retrieval system, without prior written permission from the publisher.

HOW TO USE THIS BOOK 1-2
WHERE TO BEGIN 1-2
AVOIDING TROUBLE 1-2
MAINTENANCE OR REPAIR? 1-2
AVOIDING THE MOST COMMON MISTAKES 1-2
TOOLS AND EQUIPMENT 1-2
SPECIAL TOOLS 1-4
SERVICING YOUR VEHICLE SAFELY 1-4
DO'S 1-4
DON'TS 1-5
FASTENERS, MEASUREMENTS AND CONVERSIONS 1-5
BOLTS, NUTS AND OTHER THREADED RETAINERS 1-5
TORQUE 1-6
 TORQUE WRENCHES 1-6
 TORQUE ANGLE METERS 1-6
STANDARD AND METRIC MEASUREMENTS 1-7
SERIAL NUMBER IDENTIFICATION 1-7
VEHICLE IDENTIFICATION NUMBER (VIN) 1-7
 1967–69 MODELS 1-7
 1970–73 MODELS 1-7
 1974–79 MODELS 1-8
 1980–88 MODELS 1-8
EQUIPMENT IDENTIFICATION PLATE 1-9
ENGINE 1-9
TRANSFER CASE 1-12
MANUAL TRANSMISSIONS 1-12
AXLES 1-12
ROUTINE MAINTENANCE 1-12
AIR CLEANERS 1-12
 REMOVAL & INSTALLATION 1-12
FUEL FILTER 1-13
 REMOVAL & INSTALLATION 1-13
POSITIVE CRANKCASE VENTILATION SYSTEM 1-14
 TROUBLESHOOTING 1-15
 REPLACEMENT 1-15
EVAPORATIVE CANISTER 1-15
 SERVICING 1-15
BATTERY 1-16
 PRECAUTIONS 1-16
 GENERAL MAINTENANCE 1-16
 BATTERY FLUID 1-16
 CABLES 1-17
 CHARGING 1-18
 REPLACEMENT 1-18
BELTS 1-18
 INSPECTION 1-18
 ADJUSTMENTS 1-19
 REMOVAL & INSTALLATION 1-20
HOSES 1-21
 REMOVAL & INSTALLATION 1-21
HEAT RISER 1-22
 SERVICING 1-22
COOLING SYSTEM 1-22
 INSPECTION 1-22
 FLUID RECOMMENDATIONS 1-23
 DRAINING & REFILLING THE SYSTEM 1-23
 FLUSHING & CLEANING THE SYSTEM 1-23
AIR CONDITIONING SYSTEM 1-23
 SYSTEM SERVICE & REPAIR 1-23
 PREVENTIVE MAINTENANCE 1-24
 SYSTEM INSPECTION 1-24
WINDSHIELD WIPERS 1-24
 ELEMENT (REFILL) CARE & REPLACEMENT 1-24
TIRES AND WHEELS 1-24
 TIRE ROTATION 1-25
 TIRE DESIGN 1-25
 TIRE STORAGE 1-25
 INFLATION & INSPECTION 1-25

FLUIDS AND LUBRICANTS 1-27
FLUID DISPOSAL 1-27
FUEL AND ENGINE OIL RECOMMENDATIONS 1-27
 GASOLINE ENGINES 1-27
 DIESEL ENGINES 1-27
ENGINE 1-27
 OIL LEVEL CHECK 1-28
 OIL AND FILTER CHANGE 1-28
MANUAL TRANSMISSION 1-29
 FLUID RECOMMENDATIONS 1-29
 LEVEL CHECK 1-30
 DRAIN AND REFILL 1-30
AUTOMATIC TRANSMISSION 1-31
 FLUID RECOMMENDATIONS 1-31
 LEVEL CHECK 1-31
 DRAIN AND REFILL 1-31
TRANSFER CASE 1-32
 FLUID RECOMMENDATIONS 1-32
 LEVEL CHECK 1-33
 DRAIN AND REFILL 1-33
DRIVE AXLES 1-34
 FLUID RECOMMENDATIONS 1-34
 LEVEL CHECK 1-34
 DRAIN AND REFILL 1-34
STEERING GEAR 1-34
 FLUID RECOMMENDATIONS 1-34
 LEVEL CHECK 1-35
POWER STEERING PUMP 1-35
 FLUID RECOMMENDATIONS 1-35
 LEVEL CHECK 1-35
BRAKE MASTER CYLINDER 1-36
 LEVEL CHECK 1-36
 FLUID RECOMMENDATIONS 1-36
HYDRAULIC CLUTCH RESERVOIR 1-37
CHASSIS GREASING 1-37
 STEERING LINKAGE 1-38
 PARKING BRAKE LINKAGE 1-38
 AUTOMATIC TRANSMISSION LINKAGE 1-38
BODY LUBRICATION AND MAINTENANCE 1-38
 CARE OF YOUR TRUCK 1-38
 HOOD LATCH AND HINGES 1-38
 TAIL GATE AND DOOR HINGES 1-39
FRONT WHEEL BEARINGS 1-39
 REMOVAL, REPACKING, & INSTALLATION 1-39
PUSHING AND TOWING 1-41
PUSHING 1-41
TOWING 1-41
 COOLING 1-41
JACKING 1-41
1967–69 MODELS 1-41
1970 AND LATER MODELS 1-41
MAINTENANCE AND LUBRICATION CHARTS 1-42
SPECIFICATIONS CHARTS
 ENGINE IDENTIFICATION SPECIFICATIONS 1-10
 MAINTENANCE INTERVALS SPECIFICATIONS 1-43
 DIESEL MAINTENANCE INTERVALS SPECIFICATIONS 1-43
 CAPACITIES 1-44

1

GENERAL INFORMATION AND MAINTENANCE

HOW TO USE THIS BOOK 1-2
TOOLS AND EQUIPMENT 1-2
SERVICING YOUR VEHICLE SAFELY 1-4
FASTENERS, MEASUREMENTS AND CONVERSIONS 1-5
SERIAL NUMBER IDENTIFICATION 1-7
ROUTINE MAINTENANCE 1-12
FLUIDS AND LUBRICANTS 1-27
PUSHING AND TOWING 1-41
JACKING 1-41
MAINTENANCE AND LUBRICATION CHARTS 1-42

1-2 GENERAL INFORMATION AND MAINTENANCE

HOW TO USE THIS BOOK

This Chilton's Total Car Care manual for Dodge and Plymouth Trucks is intended to help you learn more about the inner workings of your vehicle while saving you money on its upkeep and operation.

The beginning of the book will likely be referred to the most, since that is where you will find information for maintenance and tune-up. The other sections deal with the more complex systems of your vehicle. Systems (from engine through brakes) are covered to the extent that the average do-it-yourselfer can attempt. This book will not explain such things as rebuilding a differential because the expertise required and the special tools necessary make this uneconomical. It will, however, give you detailed instructions to help you change your own brake pads and shoes, replace spark plugs, and perform many more jobs that can save you money and help avoid expensive problems.

A secondary purpose of this book is a reference for owners who want to understand their vehicle and/or their mechanics better.

Where to Begin

Before removing any bolts, read through the entire procedure. This will give you the overall view of what tools and supplies will be required. So read ahead and plan ahead. Each operation should be approached logically and all procedures thoroughly understood before attempting any work.

If repair of a component is not considered practical, we tell you how to remove the part and then how to install the new or rebuilt replacement. In this way, you at least save labor costs.

Avoiding Trouble

Many procedures in this book require you to "label and disconnect . . ." a group of lines, hoses or wires. Don't be think you can remember where everything goes—you won't. If you hook up vacuum or fuel lines incorrectly, the vehicle may run poorly, if at all. If you hook up electrical wiring incorrectly, you may instantly learn a very expensive lesson.

You don't need to know the proper name for each hose or line. A piece of masking tape on the hose and a piece on its fitting will allow you to assign your own label. As long as you remember your own code, the lines can be reconnected by matching your tags. Remember that tape will dissolve in gasoline or solvents; if a part is to be washed or cleaned, use another method of identification. A permanent felt-tipped marker or a metal scribe can be very handy for marking metal parts. Remove any tape or paper labels after assembly.

Maintenance or Repair?

Maintenance includes routine inspections, adjustments, and replacement of parts which show signs of normal wear. Maintenance compensates for wear or deterioration. Repair implies that something has broken or is not working. A need for a repair is often caused by lack of maintenance. for example: draining and refilling automatic transmission fluid is maintenance recommended at specific intervals. Failure to do this can shorten the life of the transmission/transaxle, requiring very expensive repairs. While no maintenance program can prevent items from eventually breaking or wearing out, a general rule is true: MAINTENANCE IS CHEAPER THAN REPAIR.

TOOLS AND EQUIPMENT

▶ See Figures 1 thru 15

Without the proper tools and equipment it is impossible to properly service your vehicle. It would be virtually impossible to catalog every tool that you would need to perform all of the operations in this book. It would be unwise for the amateur to rush out and buy an expensive set of tools on the theory that he/she may need one or more of them at some time.

The best approach is to proceed slowly, gathering a good quality set of those tools that are used most frequently. Don't be misled by the low cost of bargain tools. It is far better to spend a little more for better quality. Forged wrenches, 6 or 12-point sockets and fine tooth ratchets are by far preferable to their less expensive counterparts. As any good mechanic can tell you, there are few worse experiences than trying to work on a vehicle with bad tools. Your monetary savings will be far outweighed by frustration and mangled knuckles.

Two basic mechanic's rules should be mentioned here. First, whenever the left side of the vehicle or engine is referred to, it means the driver's side. Conversely, the right side of the vehicle means the passenger's side. Second, screws and bolts are removed by turning counterclockwise, and tightened by turning clockwise unless specifically noted.

Safety is always the most important rule. Constantly be aware of the dangers involved in working on an automobile and take the proper precautions. Please refer to the information in this section regarding SERVICING YOUR VEHICLE SAFELY and the SAFETY NOTICE on the acknowledgment page.

Avoiding the Most Common Mistakes

Pay attention to the instructions provided. There are 3 common mistakes in mechanical work:

1. Incorrect order of assembly, disassembly or adjustment. When taking something apart or putting it together, performing steps in the wrong order usually just costs you extra time; however, it CAN break something. Read the entire procedure before beginning. Perform everything in the order in which the instructions say you should, even if you can't see a reason for it. When you're taking apart something that is very intricate, you might want to draw a picture of how it looks when assembled in order to make sure you get everything back in its proper position. When making adjustments, perform them in the proper order. One adjustment possibly will affect another.

2. Overtorquing (or undertorquing). While it is more common for overtorquing to cause damage, undertorquing may allow a fastener to vibrate loose causing serious damage. Especially when dealing with aluminum parts, pay attention to torque specifications and utilize a torque wrench in assembly. If a torque figure is not available, remember that if you are using the right tool to perform the job, you will probably not have to strain yourself to get a fastener tight enough. The pitch of most threads is so slight that the tension you put on the wrench will be multiplied many times in actual force on what you are tightening.

There are many commercial products available for ensuring that fasteners won't come loose, even if they are not torqued just right (a very common brand is Loctite®). If you're worried about getting something together tight enough to hold, but loose enough to avoid mechanical damage during assembly, one of these products might offer substantial insurance. Before choosing a threadlocking compound, read the label on the package and make sure the product is compatible with the materials, fluids, etc. involved.

3. Crossthreading. This occurs when a part such as a bolt is screwed into a nut or casting at the wrong angle and forced. Crossthreading is more likely to occur if access is difficult. It helps to clean and lubricate fasteners, then to start threading the bolt, spark plug, etc. with your fingers. If you encounter resistance, unscrew the part and start over again at a different angle until it can be inserted and turned several times without much effort. Keep in mind that many parts have tapered threads, so that gentle turning will automatically bring the part you're threading to the proper angle. Don't put a wrench on the part until it's been tightened a couple of turns by hand. If you suddenly encounter resistance, and the part has not seated fully, don't force it. Pull it back out to make sure it's clean and threading properly.

Be sure to take your time and be patient, and always plan ahead. Allow yourself ample time to perform repairs and maintenance.

Begin accumulating those tools that are used most frequently: those associated with routine maintenance and tune-up. In addition to the normal assortment of screwdrivers and pliers, you should have the following tools:

• Wrenches/sockets and combination open end/box end wrenches in sizes 1/8–3/4 in. and/or 3mm–19mm 13/16 in. or 5/8 in. spark plug socket (depending on plug type).

➡If possible, buy various length socket drive extensions. Universal-joint and wobble extensions can be extremely useful, but be careful when using them, as they can change the amount of torque applied to the socket.

• Jackstands for support.
• Oil filter wrench.
• Spout or funnel for pouring fluids.

GENERAL INFORMATION AND MAINTENANCE 1-3

Fig. 1 All but the most basic procedures will require an assortment of ratchets and sockets

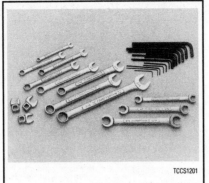
Fig. 2 In addition to ratchets, a good set of wrenches and hex keys will be necessary

Fig. 3 A hydraulic floor jack and a set of jackstands are essential for lifting and supporting the vehicle

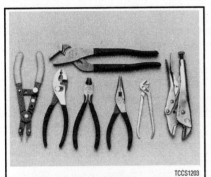
Fig. 4 An assortment of pliers, grippers and cutters will be handy for old rusted parts and stripped bolt heads

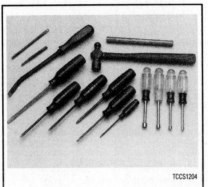
Fig. 5 Various drivers, chisels and prybars are great tools to have in your toolbox

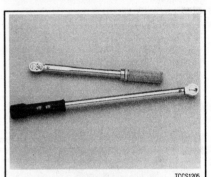
Fig. 6 Many repairs will require the use of a torque wrench to assure the components are properly fastened

Fig. 7 Although not always necessary, using specialized brake tools will save time

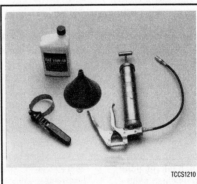
Fig. 8 A few inexpensive lubrication tools will make maintenance easier

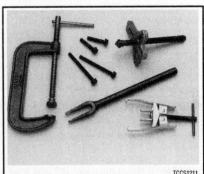
Fig. 9 Various pullers, clamps and separator tools are needed for many larger, more complicated repairs

Fig. 10 A variety of tools and gauges should be used for spark plug gapping and installation

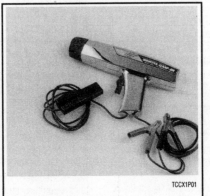
Fig. 11 Inductive type timing light

Fig. 12 A screw-in type compression gauge is recommended for compression testing

1-4 GENERAL INFORMATION AND MAINTENANCE

Fig. 13 A vacuum/pressure tester is necessary for many testing procedures

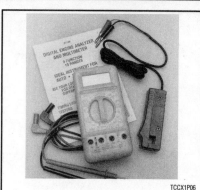

Fig. 14 Most modern automotive multimeters incorporate many helpful features

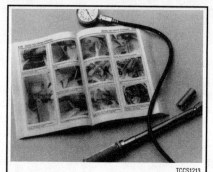

Fig. 15 Proper information is vital, so always have a Chilton Total Car Care manual handy

- Grease gun for chassis lubrication (unless your vehicle is not equipped with any grease fittings)
- Hydrometer for checking the battery (unless equipped with a sealed, maintenance-free battery).
- A container for draining oil and other fluids.
- Rags for wiping up the inevitable mess.

In addition to the above items there are several others that are not absolutely necessary, but handy to have around. These include an equivalent oil absorbent gravel, like cat litter, and the usual supply of lubricants, antifreeze and fluids. This is a basic list for routine maintenance, but only your personal needs and desire can accurately determine your list of tools.

After performing a few projects on the vehicle, you'll be amazed at the other tools and non-tools on your workbench. Some useful household items are: a large turkey baster or siphon, empty coffee cans and ice trays (to store parts), a ball of twine, electrical tape for wiring, small rolls of colored tape for tagging lines or hoses, markers and pens, a note pad, golf tees (for plugging vacuum lines), metal coat hangers or a roll of mechanic's wire (to hold things out of the way), dental pick or similar long, pointed probe, a strong magnet, and a small mirror (to see into recesses and under manifolds).

A more advanced set of tools, suitable for tune-up work, can be drawn up easily. While the tools are slightly more sophisticated, they need not be outrageously expensive. There are several inexpensive tach/dwell meters on the market that are every bit as good for the average mechanic as a professional model. Just be sure that it goes to a least 1200–1500 rpm on the tach scale and that it works on 4, 6 and 8-cylinder engines. The key to these purchases is to make them with an eye towards adaptability and wide range. A basic list of tune-up tools could include:

- Tach/dwell meter.
- Spark plug wrench and gapping tool.
- Feeler gauges for valve adjustment.
- Timing light.

The choice of a timing light should be made carefully. A light which works on the DC current supplied by the vehicle's battery is the best choice; it should have a xenon tube for brightness. On any vehicle with an electronic ignition system, a timing light with an inductive pickup that clamps around the No. 1 spark plug cable is preferred.

In addition to these basic tools, there are several other tools and gauges you may find useful. These include:

- Compression gauge. The screw-in type is slower to use, but eliminates the possibility of a faulty reading due to escaping pressure.
- Manifold vacuum gauge.
- 12V test light.
- A combination volt/ohmmeter
- Induction Ammeter. This is used for determining whether or not there is current in a wire. These are handy for use if a wire is broken somewhere in a wiring harness.

As a final note, you will probably find a torque wrench necessary for all but the most basic work. The beam type models are perfectly adequate, although the newer click types (breakaway) are easier to use. The click type torque wrenches tend to be more expensive. Also keep in mind that all types of torque wrenches should be periodically checked and/or recalibrated. You will have to decide for yourself which better fits your pocketbook, and purpose.

Special Tools

Normally, the use of special factory tools is avoided for repair procedures, since these are not readily available for the do-it-yourself mechanic. When it is possible to perform the job with more commonly available tools, it will be pointed out, but occasionally, a special tool was designed to perform a specific function and should be used. Before substituting another tool, you should be convinced that neither your safety nor the performance of the vehicle will be compromised.

Special tools can usually be purchased from an automotive parts store or from your dealer. In some cases special tools may be available directly from the tool manufacturer.

SERVICING YOUR VEHICLE SAFELY

♦ See Figures 16, 17 and 18

It is virtually impossible to anticipate all of the hazards involved with automotive maintenance and service, but care and common sense will prevent most accidents.

The rules of safety for mechanics range from "don't smoke around gasoline," to "use the proper tool(s) for the job." The trick to avoiding injuries is to develop safe work habits and to take every possible precaution.

Do's

- Do keep a fire extinguisher and first aid kit handy.
- Do wear safety glasses or goggles when cutting, drilling, grinding or prying, even if you have 20–20 vision. If you wear glasses for the sake of vision, wear safety goggles over your regular glasses.
- Do shield your eyes whenever you work around the battery. Batteries contain sulfuric acid. In case of contact with, flush the area with water or a mixture of water and baking soda, then seek immediate medical attention.
- Do use safety stands (jackstands) for any undervehicle service. Jacks are for raising vehicles; jackstands are for making sure the vehicle stays raised until you want it to come down.
- Do use adequate ventilation when working with any chemicals or hazardous materials. Like carbon monoxide, the asbestos dust resulting from some brake lining wear can be hazardous in sufficient quantities.
- Do disconnect the negative battery cable when working on the electrical system. The secondary ignition system contains EXTREMELY HIGH VOLTAGE. In some cases it can even exceed 50,000 volts.
- Do follow manufacturer's directions whenever working with potentially hazardous materials. Most chemicals and fluids are poisonous.
- Do properly maintain your tools. Loose hammerheads, mushroomed punches and chisels, frayed or poorly grounded electrical cords, excessively worn screwdrivers, spread wrenches (open end), cracked sockets, slipping ratchets, or faulty droplight sockets can cause accidents.
- Likewise, keep your tools clean; a greasy wrench can slip off a bolt head, ruining the bolt and often harming your knuckles in the process.

GENERAL INFORMATION AND MAINTENANCE

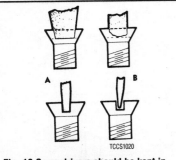

Fig. 16 Screwdrivers should be kept in good condition to prevent injury or damage which could result if the blade slips from the screw

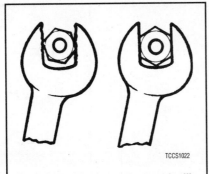

Fig. 17 Using the correct size wrench will help prevent the possibility of rounding off a nut

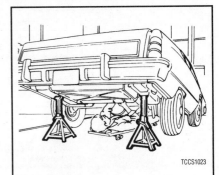

Fig. 18 NEVER work under a vehicle unless it is supported using safety stands (jackstands)

- Do use the proper size and type of tool for the job at hand. Do select a wrench or socket that fits the nut or bolt. The wrench or socket should sit straight, not cocked.
- Do, when possible, pull on a wrench handle rather than push on it, and adjust your stance to prevent a fall.
- Do be sure that adjustable wrenches are tightly closed on the nut or bolt and pulled so that the force is on the side of the fixed jaw.
- Do strike squarely with a hammer; avoid glancing blows.
- Do set the parking brake and block the drive wheels if the work requires a running engine.

Don'ts

- Don't run the engine in a garage or anywhere else without proper ventilation—EVER! Carbon monoxide is poisonous; it takes a long time to leave the human body and you can build up a deadly supply of it in your system by simply breathing in a little at a time. You may not realize you are slowly poisoning yourself. Always use power vents, windows, fans and/or open the garage door.
- Don't work around moving parts while wearing loose clothing. Short sleeves are much safer than long, loose sleeves. Hard-toed shoes with neoprene soles protect your toes and give a better grip on slippery surfaces. Watches and jewelry is not safe working around a vehicle. Long hair should be tied back under a hat or cap.
- Don't use pockets for toolboxes. A fall or bump can drive a screwdriver deep into your body. Even a rag hanging from your back pocket can wrap around a spinning shaft or fan.
- Don't smoke when working around gasoline, cleaning solvent or other flammable material.
- Don't smoke when working around the battery. When the battery is being charged, it gives off explosive hydrogen gas.
- Don't use gasoline to wash your hands; there are excellent soaps available. Gasoline contains dangerous additives which can enter the body through a cut or through your pores. Gasoline also removes all the natural oils from the skin so that bone dry hands will suck up oil and grease.
- Don't service the air conditioning system unless you are equipped with the necessary tools and training. When liquid or compressed gas refrigerant is released to atmospheric pressure it will absorb heat from whatever it contacts. This will chill or freeze anything it touches.
- Don't use screwdrivers for anything other than driving screws! A screwdriver used as an prying tool can snap when you least expect it, causing injuries. At the very least, you'll ruin a good screwdriver.
- Don't use an emergency jack (that little ratchet, scissors, or pantograph jack supplied with the vehicle) for anything other than changing a flat! These jacks are only intended for emergency use out on the road; they are NOT designed as a maintenance tool. If you are serious about maintaining your vehicle yourself, invest in a hydraulic floor jack of at least a 1½ ton capacity, and at least two sturdy jackstands.

FASTENERS, MEASUREMENTS AND CONVERSIONS

Bolts, Nuts and Other Threaded Retainers

♦ See Figures 19 and 20

Although there are a great variety of fasteners found in the modern car or truck, the most commonly used retainer is the threaded fastener (nuts, bolts, screws, studs, etc.). Most threaded retainers may be reused, provided that they are not damaged in use or during the repair. Some retainers (such as stretch bolts or torque prevailing nuts) are designed to deform when tightened or in use and should not be reinstalled.

Whenever possible, we will note any special retainers which should be replaced during a procedure. But you should always inspect the condition of a retainer when it is removed and replace any that show signs of damage. Check all threads for rust or corrosion which can increase the torque necessary to achieve the desired clamp load for which that fastener was originally selected. Additionally, be sure that the driver surface of the fastener has not been compromised by rounding or other damage. In some cases a driver surface may become only partially rounded, allowing the driver to catch in only one direction. In many of these occurrences, a fastener may be installed and tightened, but the driver would not be able to grip and loosen the fastener again.

If you must replace a fastener, whether due to design or damage, you must ALWAYS be sure to use the proper replacement. In all cases, a retainer of the same design, material and strength should be used. Markings on the heads of most bolts will help determine the proper strength of the fastener. The same material, thread and pitch must be selected to assure proper installation and safe operation of the vehicle afterwards.

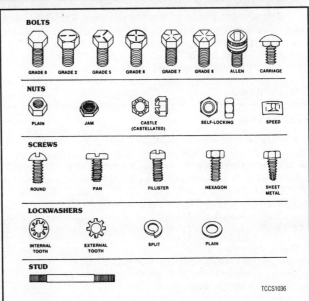

Fig. 19 There are many different types of threaded retainers found on vehicles

1-6 GENERAL INFORMATION AND MAINTENANCE

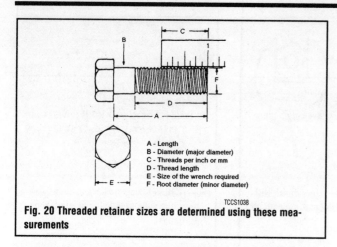

Fig. 20 Threaded retainer sizes are determined using these measurements

A - Length
B - Diameter (major diameter)
C - Threads per inch or mm
D - Thread length
E - Size of the wrench required
F - Root diameter (minor diameter)

Thread gauges are available to help measure a bolt or stud's thread. Most automotive and hardware stores keep gauges available to help you select the proper size. In a pinch, you can use another nut or bolt for a thread gauge. If the bolt you are replacing is not too badly damaged, you can select a match by finding another bolt which will thread in its place. If you find a nut which threads properly onto the damaged bolt, then use that nut to help select the replacement bolt.

※※ WARNING

Be aware that when you find a bolt with damaged threads, you may also find the nut or drilled hole it was threaded into has also been damaged. If this is the case, you may have to drill and tap the hole, replace the nut or otherwise repair the threads. NEVER try to force a replacement bolt to fit into the damaged threads.

Torque

Torque is defined as the measurement of resistance to turning or rotating. It tends to twist a body about an axis of rotation. A common example of this would be tightening a threaded retainer such as a nut, bolt or screw. Measuring torque is one of the most common ways to help assure that a threaded retainer has been properly fastened.

When tightening a threaded fastener, torque is applied in three distinct areas, the head, the bearing surface and the clamp load. About 50 percent of the measured torque is used in overcoming bearing friction. This is the friction between the bearing surface of the bolt head, screw head or nut face and the base material or washer (the surface on which the fastener is rotating). Approximately 40 percent of the applied torque is used in overcoming thread friction. This leaves only about 10 percent of the applied torque to develop a useful clamp load (the force which holds a joint together). This means that friction can account for as much as 90 percent of the applied torque on a fastener.

TORQUE WRENCHES

▶ See Figure 21

In most applications, a torque wrench can be used to assure proper installation of a fastener. Torque wrenches come in various designs and most automotive supply stores will carry a variety to suit your needs. A torque wrench should be used any time we supply a specific torque value for a fastener. Again, the general rule of "if you are using the right tool for the job, you should not have to strain to tighten a fastener" applies here.

Beam Type

The beam type torque wrench is one of the most popular types. It consists of a pointer attached to the head that runs the length of the flexible beam (shaft) to a scale located near the handle. As the wrench is pulled, the beam bends and the pointer indicates the torque using the scale.

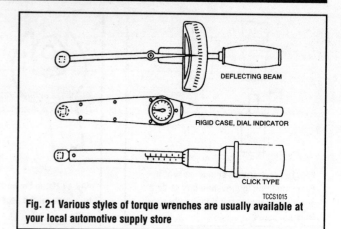

Fig. 21 Various styles of torque wrenches are usually available at your local automotive supply store

Click (Breakaway) Type

Another popular design of torque wrench is the click type. To use the click type wrench you pre-adjust it to a torque setting. Once the torque is reached, the wrench has a reflex signaling feature that causes a momentary breakaway of the torque wrench body, sending an impulse to the operator's hand.

Pivot Head Type

▶ See Figure 22

Some torque wrenches (usually of the click type) may be equipped with a pivot head which can allow it to be used in areas of limited access. BUT, it must be used properly. To hold a pivot head wrench, grasp the handle lightly, and as you pull on the handle, it should be floated on the pivot point. If the handle comes in contact with the yoke extension during the process of pulling, there is a very good chance the torque readings will be inaccurate because this could alter the wrench loading point. The design of the handle is usually such as to make it inconvenient to deliberately misuse the wrench.

➡ **It should be mentioned that the use of any U-joint, wobble or extension will have an effect on the torque readings, no matter what type of wrench you are using. For the most accurate readings, install the socket directly on the wrench driver. If necessary, straight extensions (which hold a socket directly under the wrench driver) will have the least effect on the torque reading. Avoid any extension that alters the length of the wrench from the handle to the head/driving point (such as a crow's foot). U-joint or wobble extensions can greatly affect the readings; avoid their use at all times.**

Rigid Case (Direct Reading)

A rigid case or direct reading torque wrench is equipped with a dial indicator to show torque values. One advantage of these wrenches is that they can be held at any position on the wrench without affecting accuracy. These wrenches are often preferred because they tend to be compact, easy to read and have a great degree of accuracy.

TORQUE ANGLE METERS

Because the frictional characteristics of each fastener or threaded hole will vary, clamp loads which are based strictly on torque will vary as well. In most applications, this variance is not significant enough to cause worry. But, in certain applications, a manufacturer's engineers may determine that more precise clamp loads are necessary (such is the case with many aluminum cylinder heads). In these cases, a torque angle method of installation would be specified. When installing fasteners which are torque angle tightened, a predetermined seating torque and standard torque wrench are usually used first to remove any compliance from the joint. The fastener is then tightened the specified additional portion of a turn measured in degrees. A torque angle gauge (mechanical protractor) is used for these applications.

GENERAL INFORMATION AND MAINTENANCE   1-7

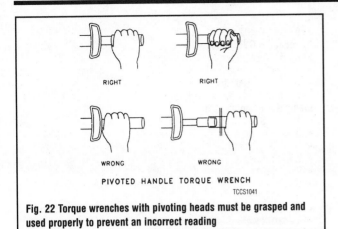

Fig. 22 Torque wrenches with pivoting heads must be grasped and used properly to prevent an incorrect reading

Standard and Metric Measurements

♦ See Figure 23

Throughout this manual, specifications are given to help you determine the condition of various components on your vehicle, or to assist you in their installation. Some of the most common measurements include length (in. or cm/mm), torque (ft. lbs., inch lbs. or Nm) and pressure (psi, in. Hg, kPa or mm Hg). In most cases, we strive to provide the proper measurement as determined by the manufacturer's engineers.

Though, in some cases, that value may not be conveniently measured with what is available in your toolbox. Luckily, many of the measuring devices which are available today will have two scales so the Standard or Metric measurements may easily be taken. If any of the various measuring tools which are available to you do not contain the same scale as listed in the specifications, use the accompanying conversion factors to determine the proper value.

The conversion factor chart is used by taking the given specification and multiplying it by the necessary conversion factor. For instance, looking at the first line, if you have a measurement in inches such as "free-play should be 2 in." but your ruler reads only in millimeters, multiply 2 in. by the conversion factor of 25.4 to get the metric equivalent of 50.8mm. Likewise, if the specification was given only in a Metric measurement, for example in Newton Meters (Nm), then look at the center column first. If the measurement is 100 Nm, multiply it by the conversion factor of 0.738 to get 73.8 ft. lbs.

CONVERSION FACTORS

LENGTH–DISTANCE				
Inches (in.)	x 25.4	= Millimeters (mm)	x .0394	= Inches
Feet (ft.)	x .305	= Meters (m)	x 3.281	= Feet
Miles	x 1.609	= Kilometers (km)	x .0621	= Miles
VOLUME				
Cubic Inches (in3)	x 16.387	= Cubic Centimeters	x .061	= in3
IMP Pints (IMP pt.)	x .568	= Liters (L)	x 1.76	= IMP pt.
IMP Quarts (IMP qt.)	x 1.137	= Liters (L)	x .88	= IMP qt.
IMP Gallons (IMP gal.)	x 4.546	= Liters (L)	x .22	= IMP gal.
IMP Quarts (IMP qt.)	x 1.201	= US Quarts (US qt.)	x .833	= IMP qt.
IMP Gallons (IMP gal.)	x 1.201	= US Gallons (US gal.)	x .833	= IMP gal.
Fl. Ounces	x 29.573	= Milliliters	x .034	= Ounces
US Pints (US pt.)	x .473	= Liters (L)	x 2.113	= Pints
US Quarts (US qt.)	x .946	= Liters (L)	x 1.057	= Quarts
US Gallons (US gal.)	x 3.785	= Liters (L)	x .264	= Gallons
MASS–WEIGHT				
Ounces (oz.)	x 28.35	= Grams (g)	x .035	= Ounces
Pounds (lb.)	x .454	= Kilograms (kg)	x 2.205	= Pounds
PRESSURE				
Pounds Per Sq. In. (psi)	x 6.895	= Kilopascals (kPa)	x .145	= psi
Inches of Mercury (Hg)	x .4912	= psi	x 2.036	= Hg
Inches of Mercury (Hg)	x 3.377	= Kilopascals (kPa)	x .2961	= Hg
Inches of Water (H_2O)	x .07355	= Inches of Mercury	x 13.783	= H_2O
Inches of Water (H_2O)	x .03613	= psi	x 27.684	= H_2O
Inches of Water (H_2O)	x .248	= Kilopascals (kPa)	x 4.026	= H_2O
TORQUE				
Pounds–Force Inches (in-lb)	x .113	= Newton Meters (N·m)	x 8.85	= in–lb
Pounds–Force Feet (ft-lb)	x 1.356	= Newton Meters (N·m)	x .738	= ft–lb
VELOCITY				
Miles Per Hour (MPH)	x 1.609	= Kilometers Per Hour (KPH)	x .621	= MPH
POWER				
Horsepower (Hp)	x .745	= Kilowatts	x 1.34	= Horsepower
FUEL CONSUMPTION*				
Miles Per Gallon IMP (MPG)	x .354	= Kilometers Per Liter (Km/L)		
Kilometers Per Liter (Km/L)	x 2.352	= IMP MPG		
Miles Per Gallon US (MPG)	x .425	= Kilometers Per Liter (Km/L)		
Kilometers Per Liter (Km/L)	x 2.352	= US MPG		

*It is common to covert from miles per gallon (mpg) to liters/100 kilometers (1/100 km), where mpg (IMP) x 1/100 km = 282 and mpg (US) x 1/100 km = 235.

TEMPERATURE	
Degree Fahrenheit (°F)	= (°C x 1.8) + 32
Degree Celsius (°C)	= (°F – 32) x .56

Fig. 23 Standard and metric conversion factors chart

SERIAL NUMBER IDENTIFICATION

♦ See Figures 24 and 25

Vehicle Identification Number (VIN)

The vehicle data plate on all models through 1969 is located on the top inside surface of the left wheel-well opening. On models through 1980 the plate is located on the rear face of the driver's side door. On 1981 and later models it is located on the upper left corner of the instrument panel, near the windshield.

1967–69 MODELS

A typical serial number for these years might be 2082–158000. The first 2 digits indicate the model code. The third digit indicates the number of cylinders; a 6 would mean six-cylinder, while an 8 would mean eight-cylinder. The fourth digit indicates the assembly plant, as follows:

- 1 or 2 Warren Truck Assembly
- 6 Windsor Truck Assembly
- 7 Missouri Truck Assembly

The fifth to tenth digits are the sequential serial number.

1970–73 MODELS

The vehicle identification number consists of a combination of 13 digits. The first seven characters identify the model, body type, GVW, engine model year and assembly plant. The last 6 digits are the sequential serial number, always starting from 000001. A typical serial number might be D24AE3U000001.

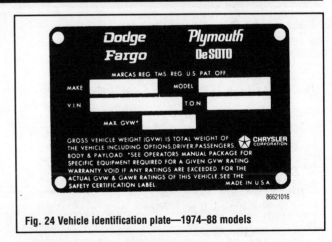

Fig. 24 Vehicle identification plate—1974–88 models

The first letter indicates the model
- D = 2 Wheel Drive
- W = 4 Wheel Drive

The second character indicates the series
- 1 = 100 (½ ton) series
- 2 = 200 (¾ ton) series
- 3 = 300 (1 ton) series

The third number is the body code
- 1 = Conventional Cab

1-8 GENERAL INFORMATION AND MAINTENANCE

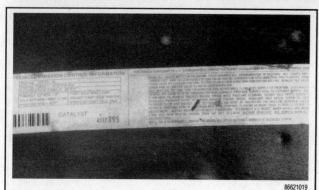

Fig. 25 The Vehicle Emission Control Information (VECI) label is normally found in the engine compartment

- 2 = Crew Cab
- 3 = Conv. Cab Utiline
- 4 = Conv. Cab Sweptline
- 5 = Crew Cab Utiline
- 6 = Crew Cab Sweptline

The fourth character indicates the GVW
- A = 6,000 lbs. or less
- B = 6,000–10,000 lbs

The fifth character indicates the engine
- B = 225–1 Series
- C = 225–2 Series
- E = 318–1 Series
- F = 360
- G = 318–3 Series
- J = 383 (1970–71)
- J = 400 (1972–73)
- K = 361–2 Series
- L = 361–3 Series
- M = 361–4 Series
- N = 413–1 Series
- P = 413–2 Series

The sixth digit gives the model year
- 0 = 1970 F series
- 1 = 1971 G series
- 2 = 1972 H series
- 3 = 1973 J series

The seventh digit gives the assembly plant.
- J = Windsor
- N = Burt Road
- S or V = Warren
- U or X = Missouri

The last six digits are the sequential serial number

1974–79 MODELS

Dodge and Plymouth VIN's are interpreted in a similar manner. An example follows:

Element (1st 1 or 2 letters) = Model Designation
- D = 2 Wheel Drive pickup
- AD = 2 Wheel Drive Ramcharger
- PD = 2 Wheel Drive Trail Duster
- W = 4 Wheel Drive pickup
- AW = 4 Wheel Drive Ramcharger
- PW = 4 Wheel Drive Trail Duster

Element 2 = Body Type
- 1 = Conventional Cab, Sport Utility
- 2 = Crew Cab
- 3 = Conventional Cab, Utiline
- 4 = Conventional Cab, Sweptline
- 5 = Crew Cab, Utiline
- 6 = Crew Cab, Sweptline
- 7 = Club Cab, Sweptline
- 8 = Club Cab
- 9 = Club Cab Utiline

Element 3 = GVW Class
- A = 6,000 lbs. or less
- J = 6,001–8,500 lbs.
- K = 8,501–10,000 lbs.
- C = 10,001–14,000 lbs.

Element 4 = Engine Type
- A = 440–3
- B = 225–1 Series
- D = 440–1 Series
- E = 318–1 Series
- F = 360 2–bbl.
- G = 318–3 Series
- H = 243 Diesel
- J = 400–1 Series
- K = 360–3 Series
- M = 361–4 Series
- R = 413–3 Series
- T = 360 4–bbl.
- X = Special 6
- Y = Special 8

Element 5 = Model Year
Indicates the last number of the model year. Example "4" indicates 1974.

Element 6 = Assembly Plant
- C = Jefferson
- J = Windsor
- K = Windsor
- T&S = Warren
- X = Missouri

Element 7 = Sequential Serial Number
Every year this number starts at 000,001.

1980–88 MODELS

The vehicle identification number consists of a combination of 17 elements (numbers and letters). Use the following example as a key:
1 B 4 F 5 1 3 E 1 B K 000001

Element or Position 1 — Country of Origin
- 1 = U.S.
- 2 = Canada
- 3 = Mexico

Element or Position 2 — Make
- B = Dodge
- P = Plymouth
- E = Fargo

Element or Position 3 — Type of Vehicle
- 4 = Multipurpose
- 5 = Bus
- 6 = Incomplete
- 7 = Truck

Element or Position 4 — GVWR (lbs.) and Hydraulic Brakes
- D = 1000–3000
- E = 3001–4000
- F = 4001–5000
- G = 5001–6000
- H = 6001–7000
- J = 7001–8000
- K = 8001–9000
- L = 9001–10000
- M = 10001–14000
- W = Bus or Incomplete Vehicle

Element or Position 5 — Truck Line
- D = Ramcharger 4x2 or Pick-up 4x2 or Chassis Cab 4x2
- W = Ramcharger 4x4 or Pick-up 4x4 or Chassis Cab 4x4

Element or Position 6 — Series
- 0 = 100
- 1 = 150
- 2 = 250
- 3 = 350

GENERAL INFORMATION AND MAINTENANCE

Element or Position 7 — Body
- 1 = Wagon
- 2 = Sport Utility
- 4 = Conventional Cab
- 8 = Front Section

Element or Position 8 — Engines (CID/Liters)
- E = 225/3.7L 1–bbl. (1980–82)
- H = 225/3.7L 1–bbl. (1983–88)
- W = 225/3.7 2–bbl. (1982)
- M = 225/3.7L 2–bbl. (1983)
- X = 238/3.9L EFI
- P = 318/5.2L 2–bbl.
- T = 318/5.2L 2–bbl.
- M = 318/5.2L 4–bbl.
- Y = 318/5.2L EFI
- S = 360/5.9L 2–bbl. (1982)
- T = 360/5.9L 4–bbl. (1982)
- U = 360/5.9L 4–bbl. Heavy duty, Single exhaust
- V = 360/5.9L 4–bbl. Heavy duty, Dual exhaust
- I = 360/5.9L 4–bbl. (Cal.)
- W = 360/5.9L 4–bbl. (Fed.)

Element or Position 9
Check digit

Element or Position 10 — Model Year
- A = 1980
- B = 1981
- C = 1982
- D = 1983
- E = 1984
- F = 1985
- G = 1986
- H = 1987
- J = 1988

Element or Position 11 — Assembly Plant
- K = Pillette Road (Windsor)
- M = Lago Alberto
- S = Dodge City
- T = Sherwood
- X = Missouri

Element or Position 12 through 17
Sequence Number

Equipment Identification Plate

▶ See Figure 26

The equipment identification plate is located on the inner surface of the hood or the front surface of the air conditioning or heater housing. It contains the model, wheelbase, VIN, Truck Order Number (TON) and all production or special equipment on the vehicle when it was shipped from the factory.

Engine

▶ See Figures 27, 28, 29 and 30

The engine that the factory installed can be identified by one of the digits of the Vehicle Identification Number (VIN) as explained earlier in this section. The engine itself can be identified by the engine serial number. The cubic in. displacement is given by the second, third, and fourth, or the third, fourth, and fifth digits of the engine serial number. This will vary depending on the year and engine.

Inline 6–cylinder engines have their serial number stamped on the joint face of the block, just below the No. 6 spark plug.

318 and 360 cu. in. V8s have the number on the front of the block, just below the left cylinder head.

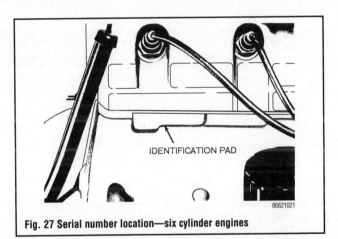

Fig. 27 Serial number location—six cylinder engines

Fig. 26 Equipment ID label—1979 vehicles

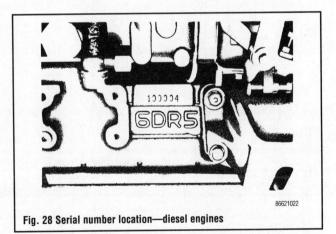

Fig. 28 Serial number location—diesel engines

1-10 GENERAL INFORMATION AND MAINTENANCE

ENGINE IDENTIFICATION

Year	Engine Displacement cu. in. (liters)	Engine Series (ID/VIN)	Fuel System	No. of Cylinders	Engine Type
1967	225 (3.7)	①	1-bbl	6	OHV
	251 (4.1)	①	1-bbl	6	L-head
	318 (5.2)	①	2-bbl	8	OHV
	383 (6.3)	①	2-bbl	8	OHV
	413 (6.8)	①	2-bbl	8	OHV
	413 (6.8)	①	4-bbl	8	OHV
1968	198 (3.2)	①	1-bbl	6	OHV
	225 (3.7)	①	1-bbl	6	OHV
	251 (4.1)	①	1-bbl	6	L-head
	318 (5.2)	①	2-bbl	8	OHV
	383 (6.3)	①	2-bbl	8	OHV
	413 (6.8)	①	2-bbl	8	OHV
	413 (6.8)	①	4-bbl	8	OHV
1969	225 (3.7)	①	1-bbl	6	OHV
	318 (5.2)	①	2-bbl	8	OHV
	383 (6.3)	①	2-bbl	8	OHV
1970	225 (3.7)	B	1-bbl	6	OHV
	318 (5.2)	E	2-bbl	8	OHV
	383 (6.3)	J	2-bbl	8	OHV
1971	225 (3.7)	B	1-bbl	6	OHV
	318 (5.2)	E	2-bbl	8	OHV
	383 (6.3)	J	2-bbl	8	OHV
1972	225 (3.7)	B	1-bbl	6	OHV
	225 (3.7)	C	2-bbl	6	OHV
	318 (5.2)	E	2-bbl	8	OHV
	360 (5.9)	F	2-bbl	8	OHV
	360 (5.9)	F	4-bbl	8	OHV
	400 (6.6)	J	2-bbl	8	OHV
1973	225 (3.7)	B	1-bbl	6	OHV
	318 (5.2)	E	2-bbl	8	OHV
	360 (5.9)	F	2-bbl	8	OHV
	360 (5.9)	F	4-bbl	8	OHV
	400 (6.6)	J	2-bbl	8	OHV
	440 (7.2)	A, D	4-bbl	8	OHV

ENGINE IDENTIFICATION

Year	Engine Displacement cu. in. (liters)	Engine Series (ID/VIN)	Fuel System	No. of Cylinders	Engine Type
1974	225 (3.7)	C	1-bbl	6	OHV
	318 (5.2)	E	2-bbl	8	OHV
	360 (5.9)	F, K	2-bbl	8	OHV
	360 (5.9)	T	4-bbl	8	OHV
	400 (6.6)	J	2-bbl	8	OHV
	440 (7.2)	D	4-bbl	8	OHV
1975	225 (3.7)	C	1-bbl	6	OHV
	318 (5.2)	E	2-bbl	8	OHV
	360 (5.9)	F, K	2-bbl	8	OHV
	360 (5.9)	T	4-bbl	8	OHV
	400 (6.6)	J	2-bbl	8	OHV
	440 (7.2)	D	4-bbl	8	OHV
1976	225 (3.7)	C	1-bbl	6	OHV
	318 (5.2)	E	2-bbl	8	OHV
	360 (5.9)	F	2-bbl	8	OHV
	360 (5.9)	T	4-bbl	8	OHV
	400 (6.6)	J	2-bbl	8	OHV
	440 (7.2)	D	4-bbl	8	OHV
1977	225 (3.7)	C	1-bbl	6	OHV
	318 (5.2)	B	2-bbl	8	OHV
	318 (5.2)	E	2-bbl	8	OHV
	360 (5.9)	F	2-bbl	8	OHV
	360 (5.9)	T	4-bbl	8	OHV
	400 (6.6)	J	2-bbl	8	OHV
	440 (7.2)	D	4-bbl	8	OHV
1978	225 (3.7)	C	1-bbl	6	OHV
	225 (3.7)	B	2-bbl	6	OHV
	243 (4.0)	H	D	6	OHV
	318 (5.2)	E, G	2-bbl	8	OHV
	360 (5.9)	F, K	2-bbl	8	OHV
	360 (5.9)	R, T	4-bbl	8	OHV
	400 (6.6)	—	2-bbl	8	OHV
	440 (7.2)	A, D	4-bbl	8	OHV

GENERAL INFORMATION AND MAINTENANCE

ENGINE IDENTIFICATION

Year	Engine Displacement cu. in. (liters)	Engine Series (ID/VIN)	Fuel System	No. of Cylinders	Engine Type
1985	225 (3.7)	H	1-bbl	6	OHV
	318 (5.2)	T	2-bbl	8	OHV
	360 (5.9)	1-Cal W-Fed	4-bbl	8	OHV
1986	225 (3.7)	H	1-bbl	6	OHV
	318 (5.2)	T	2-bbl	8	OHV
	360 (5.9)	1-Cal W-Fed	4-bbl	8	OHV
1987	225 (3.7)	H	1-bbl	6	OHV
	318 (5.2)	T	2-bbl	8	OHV
	360 (5.9)	1-Cal W-Fed	4-bbl	8	OHV
1988①	238 (3.9)	X	EFI	6	OHV
	318 (5.2)	Y		8	OHV
	360 (5.9)	W	4-bbl	8	OHV

① The engine code is not found in the VIN. The engine is instead represented by cubic inches.

ENGINE IDENTIFICATION

Year	Engine Displacement cu. in. (liters)	Engine Series (ID/VIN)	Fuel System	No. of Cylinders	Engine Type
1979	225 (3.7)	C	1-bbl	6	OHV
	225 (3.7)	B	2-bbl	6	OHV
	243 (4.0)	H	D	6	OHV
	318 (5.2)	E, G	2-bbl	8	OHV
	318 (5.2)	P	4-bbl	8	OHV
	360 (5.9)	F, K	2-bbl	8	OHV
	360 (5.9)	R, T	4-bbl	8	OHV
	400 (6.6)	—	2-bbl	8	OHV
	440 (7.2)	A, D	4-bbl	8	OHV
1980	225 (3.7)	C	1-bbl	6	OHV
	243 (4.0)	H	D	6	OHV
	318 (5.2)	E, G	2-bbl	8	OHV
	318 (5.2)	P	4-bbl	8	OHV
	360 (5.9)	F, K	2-bbl	8	OHV
	360 (5.9)	R, T	4-bbl	8	OHV
1981	225 (3.7)	E	1-bbl	6	OHV
	318 (5.2)	P	2-bbl	8	OHV
	318 (5.2)	M	4-bbl	8	OHV
	360 (5.9)	S	2-bbl	8	OHV
	360 (5.9)	T, U, V	4-bbl	8	OHV
1982	225 (3.7)	E	1-bbl	6	OHV
	225 (3.7)	W	2-bbl	6	OHV
	318 (5.2)	P	2-bbl	8	OHV
	318 (5.2)	R	4-bbl	8	OHV
	360 (5.9)	S	2-bbl	8	OHV
	360 (5.9)	T, U, V	4-bbl	8	OHV
1983	225 (3.7)	H	1-bbl	6	OHV
	225 (3.7)	M	2-bbl	6	OHV
	318 (5.2)	T	2-bbl	8	OHV
	318 (5.2)	U	4-bbl	8	OHV
	360 (5.9)	V	2-bbl	8	OHV
	360 (5.9)	1-Cal W-Fed	4-bbl	8	OHV
1984	225 (3.7)	H	1-bbl	6	OHV
	318 (5.2)	T	2-bbl	8	OHV
	318 (5.2)	U	4-bbl	8	OHV
	360 (5.9)	1-Cal W-Fed	4-bbl	8	OHV

1-12 GENERAL INFORMATION AND MAINTENANCE

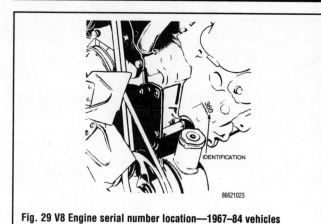

Fig. 29 V8 Engine serial number location—1967–84 vehicles

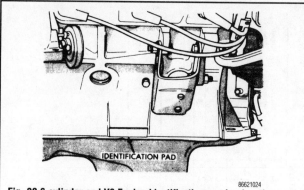

Fig. 30 6-cylinder and V8 Engine identification number location—1985–88 vehicles

The 225 cu. in. and the 238 cu. in. 6-cylinders have the serial number stamped on a pad at the right side of the block.

400 cu. in. V8s have the number on the right side of the block ahead of the distributor base.

440 cu. in. V8s are numbered on the left bank front tappet rail.

There is a quick way of telling the small block 318 and 360 cu. in. V8s from the 400 and 440s. On the 318 and 360s, the distributor is at the rear of the engine, while the 400 and 440 cu. in. V8s have it at the front.

Transfer Case

The New Process transfer cases have a build date tag attached to the front of the case.

Manual Transmissions

The transmission identification number is located on a tag secured by 2 bolts to the power take-off cover.

Axles

The drive axle code is stamped on a flat surface of the axle tube (next to the differential housing), or on a tag secured by one of the differential housing cover bolts.

ROUTINE MAINTENANCE

Please refer to the Maintenance Intervals charts found in this section in order to determine the appropriate maintenance intervals for these operations.

Air Cleaners

Different types of air cleaners are used. The standard type is the traditional dry paper element, but an oil bath air cleaner could be included on some vehicles as special equipment.

REMOVAL & INSTALLATION

Gasoline Engines

DRY TYPE

♦ See Figures 31 thru 37

Remove the top from the air cleaner, then remove the element and wrapper (if equipped). If the filter is equipped with a wrapper, remove and wash it in kerosene or similar solvent. Shake or blot it dry. Saturate the foam wrapper (through 1973) in 10W–30 oil and squeeze it tightly in an absorbent towel to remove excess oil. Leave the wrapper moist. The 1974 and later models use an optional white polyester outer wrapper which should be left dry.

Carefully clean the filter element by blowing it out with compressed air (from the inside out). Do not immerse the paper element in liquid. If the paper element is saturated for more than ½ of its circumference by oil from the wrapper, the element should be replaced and the rest of the crankcase ventilating system checked for proper function.

Wash the top of the air cleaner and housing with a suitable solvent, then wipe dry.

➡Do not immerse the temperature sensor, located in the housing, in cleaning solvent.

Install the paper element and wrapper (if equipped), then install the air cleaner cover.

Fig. 31 Release the fastener(s) and remove the air cleaner cover for access to the element

Fig. 32 With the cover removed, lift the element from the air cleaner housing

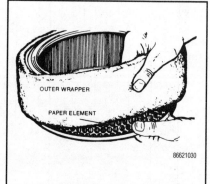

Fig. 33 Removing the outer wrapper—some 1974 and later engines

GENERAL INFORMATION AND MAINTENANCE 1-13

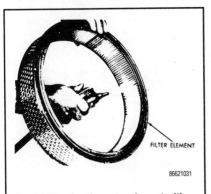

Fig. 34 Cleaning the paper element with compressed air

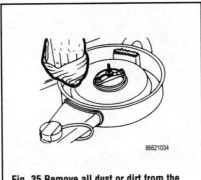

Fig. 35 Remove all dust or dirt from the air cleaner housing before installing the new filter

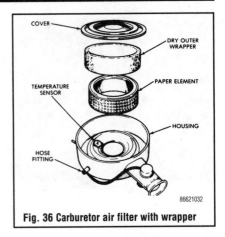

Fig. 36 Carburetor air filter with wrapper

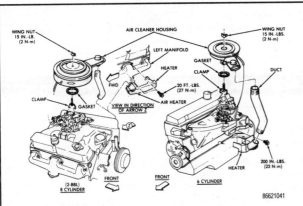

Fig. 37 Exploded view of typical air cleaner and preheater assemblies

OIL BATH TYPE

♦ See Figure 38

Oil bath air cleaners should be inspected for sediment level and correct oil level at every oil change. Cleaning is recommended more often for use in extremely dusty or off-road areas. Under extreme conditions, the filter may have to be serviced each day. Sediment should not exceed a build up beyond ⅜ in. (9.5mm) below the ledge on the oil reservoir.

✳✳ CAUTION

Be careful when working with kerosene, it is a very flammable substance, and can cause substantial injuries.

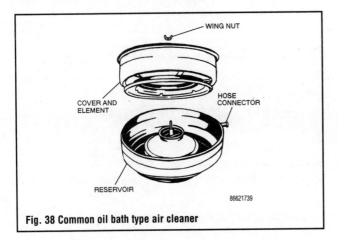

Fig. 38 Common oil bath type air cleaner

To service the air cleaner, remove the cover, filter element, and empty the oil from the reservoir. Wearing a pair of gloves, thoroughly clean the air filter element and air cleaner assembly in a suitable container using kerosene, then drain. Make sure to properly dispose of the used kerosene. Pay particular attention to the sump in the reservoir. Refill the reservoir to the arrow with fresh SAE 10W–30 engine oil and install the assembled air cleaner.

Diesel Engines

The diesel engine air filter should be cleaned every 6,000 miles and replaced every 18,000 miles. Remove the air cleaner assembly, then remove the paper element and the outer wrapper, if so equipped. Wash the wrapper in kerosene and shake it dry, then blow compressed air through the paper element to removed any dirt. If the filter element is saturated with oil for more than ½ it's circumference, replace the filter element and wrapper.

Fuel Filter

✳✳ CAUTION

Never smoke when working around gasoline! Avoid all sources of sparks or ignition. Gasoline vapors are EXTREMELY volatile!

REMOVAL & INSTALLATION

Carbureted Gasoline Engines

CANISTER TYPE

Some 1967–78 models had a cartridge type filter enclosed in a canister located in the fuel line. To replace the filter, unscrew the body of the canister, discard the gasoline safely and install a new cartridge. Screw the canister body on securely.

THROW-AWAY TYPE

♦ See Figures 39, 40 and 41

On some 1967–78 vehicles and all carbureted models thereafter, the fuel filter is a disposable type sealed paper element located in the fuel line.

On 1967 models, the filter is located in the line just before it enters the carburetor. In all other years, it is located in the line near the fuel pump. Later models also have another filter located on the fuel tank in the end of the fuel suction tube. This filter does not normally require service, although it is replaceable.

1. Remove the hose clamps on the fuel filter.

➥**Make sure to wrap a shop towel around the filter before removal in order to absorb any fuel spillage.**

2. Remove the filter and discard.
3. Inspect all hoses leading to the filter for any cracks or damage. If they are damaged replace them immediately. Never put a cracked or damaged hose back on, this could cause a fire.

1-14 GENERAL INFORMATION AND MAINTENANCE

Fig. 39 In–line fuel filter

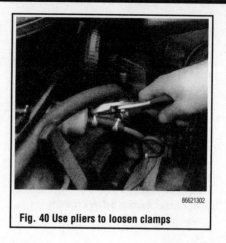

Fig. 40 Use pliers to loosen clamps

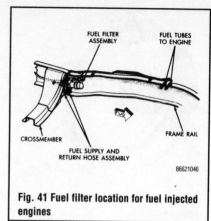

Fig. 41 Fuel filter location for fuel injected engines

To install:
4. Replace the fuel filter with new hose clamps, making sure they are tight and secure.
5. Be sure none of the fuel hoses are kinked or pinched in route to the filter. This could cause poor fuel distribution. Also check for fuel lines touching any heat surfaces.
6. Start engine, and check for leaks!

➥Position a container to catch and spilled fuel.

Fuel Injected Gasoline Engines

The fuel filter is located in the fuel line on the inside of the left frame rail, just ahead of the crossmember. To change the filter:
1. Relieve the fuel system pressure as described in Section 5.
2. Remove the filter retaining screw and remove the filter from the frame rail.
3. Wrap a shop towel around the hose connections to catch fuel spillage. Loosen the fuel hose clamps and disconnect the hoses from the filter.
4. Remove old fuel filter and replace it with a new one.
5. Connect the fuel hoses and tighten hose clamps. Position the filter on frame rail and tighten the retaining screw to 75 inch lbs. (8.4 Nm).

Diesel Engines

♦ See Figure 42 and 43

A gauze filter, located at the inlet port of the fuel feed pump, is designed to catch large particles of dirt in the fuel line. This filter must be cleaned every 12,000 miles (19,000 km) in kerosene. This system also uses another in-line fuel filter, which must be inspected every 12,000 miles (19,000 km). Replace the in-line filter element if it appears dirty or clogged. It should also be replaced at least every 24,000 miles (38,600 km).
1. Loosen the air plug at the top of the fuel filter. Remove the plug or open the draincock at the bottom and allow fuel to drain.
2. Remove the center bolt and separate the case from the cover.
3. Inspect the paper element for sediment buildup, if it appears clogged, replace it.
4. Clean the inside of the case thoroughly before installing the new element.

To install:
5. Install a new cover gasket "O-ring", reassemble the case to the cover.
6. Reinstall drain plug or close the draincock.
7. Bleed air from the system before starting vehicle.

Positive Crankcase Ventilation System

♦ See Figures 44 and 45

➥All gasoline engines covered by this manual are equipped with PCV systems.

The crankcase emission control equipment consists of a Positive Crankcase Ventilation (PCV) valve, a closed oil filler cap and the hoses that connect this equipment.

When the engine is running, a small portion of gases which are formed in the combustion chamber leak by the piston rings entering the crankcase. Since these gases are under pressure they tend to escape the crankcase and enter into the atmosphere. If the gases are allowed to remain in the crankcase for any length of time, they would contaminate the engine oil and cause sludge to build. If the gases are allowed to escape into the atmosphere, they would pollute the air, as they contain unburned hydrocarbons. The crankcase ventilation system recycles these gases back into the combustion chambers, where they are burned.

Crankcase gases are recycled in the following manner. While the engine is running, clean filtered air is drawn into the crankcase through the intake air filter and then through a hose leading to the oil filler cap. As the air passes through the crankcase it picks up the combustion gases and carries them out of the crankcase, up through the PCV valve and into the intake manifold. After they enter the intake manifold they are drawn into the combustion chamber and are burned.

The most critical component of the system is the PCV valve. This vacuum-controlled valve regulates the amount of gases which are recycled into the combustion chamber. At low engine speeds the valve is partially closed, limiting the

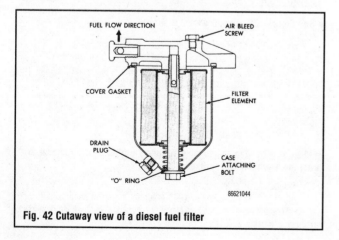

Fig. 42 Cutaway view of a diesel fuel filter

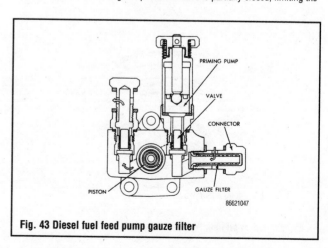

Fig. 43 Diesel fuel feed pump gauze filter

GENERAL INFORMATION AND MAINTENANCE 1-15

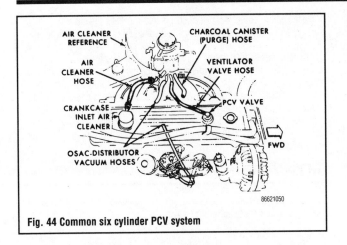

Fig. 44 Common six cylinder PCV system

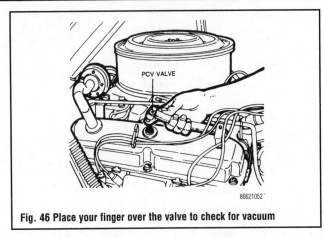

Fig. 46 Place your finger over the valve to check for vacuum

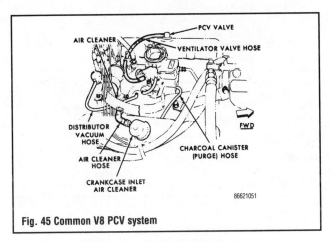

Fig. 45 Common V8 PCV system

Fig. 47 Common PCV location

flow of gases into the intake manifold. As engine speed increases, the valve opens to admit greater quantities of the gases into the intake manifold.

If the valve should become blocked or plugged, the gases will be prevented from escaping the crankcase by the normal route. Since these gases are under pressure, they will find their own way out of the crankcase. This alternate route is usually a weak oil seal or gasket in the engine. As the gas escapes by the gasket, it also creates an oil leak. Besides causing oil leaks, a clogged PCV valve also allows these gases to remain in the crankcase for an extended period of time, promoting the formation of sludge in the engine.

TROUBLESHOOTING

♦ See Figures 46 and 47

With the engine running, pull the PCV valve and hose from the valve rocker cover rubber grommet.

A hissing noise should be heard as air passes through the valve. If the valve is working properly, a strong vacuum should be felt when you place a finger over the valve inlet. While you have your finger over the PCV valve inlet, check for vacuum leaks in the hose and at the connections.

If the PCV valve is disconnected from the engine, a metallic clicking noise should be heard when it is shaken. This indicates that the metal check ball inside the valve is still free and is not gummed up. If no noise is heard, clean or replace the valve. Since these valves are normally inexpensive components, it would probably be smartest to replace the valve if it is suspect.

REPLACEMENT

1. Pull the PCV valve and hose from the rubber grommet in the rocker cover.
2. Remove the PCV valve from the hose.
3. Inspect the inside of the valve hose. If it is dirty, disconnect it from the intake manifold and clean it in a suitable, safe solvent.

To install:
4. If the PCV valve hose was removed, connect it to the intake manifold.
5. Connect the PCV valve to its hose.
6. Install the PCV valve into the rubber grommet in the valve rocker cover.

Evaporative Canister

♦ See Figures 48, 49 and 50

The Vapor Saver Evaporation Control System (VSECS) was originally used on 1970 vehicles sold in California and on most vehicles sold in the U.S. thereafter. The system is designed to prevent evaporated gasoline vapors from escaping into the atmosphere.

The carburetor is either vented internally or through the charcoal canister. Vapors are routed to the canister which is filled with activated charcoal, providing temporary storage. On some models you can replace the filter element located at the bottom of the canister. This should be done every 30,000 miles (48,000 km) on light duty trucks, 18,000 miles (29,000 km) on heavy duty trucks, or sooner in dusty conditions.

On fuel injected engines, a bi-level system is used in which vapors are drawn into the engine at idle and off-idle as well. The source of idle vacuum is a tee in the PCV system. The only service associated with the system is a replaceable filter element in the base of the canister.

SERVICING

The vapor storage canister is located on the left frame rail, behind steering gear, on models through 1972. On 1973–87 models it is located under the truck, next to the right side frame rail, and behind the transmission support crossmember.

On 1988 models, the canisters for all engines are located in the wheel-well area of the engine compartment. Some models are equipped with two storage tanks. These are identical and should be serviced together.

1-16 GENERAL INFORMATION AND MAINTENANCE

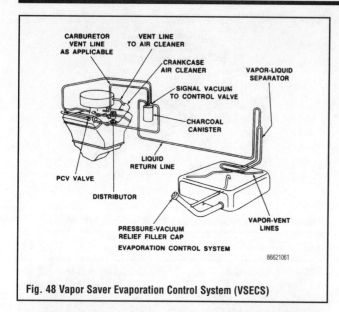

Fig. 48 Vapor Saver Evaporation Control System (VSECS)

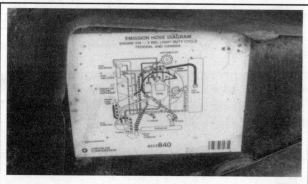

Fig. 49 An emission hose diagram should be found on a label in the engine compartment

Fig. 50 The vapor canister is easily removed after releasing the retainer(s)

Battery

PRECAUTIONS

Always use caution when working on or near the battery. Never allow a tool to bridge the gap between the negative and positive battery terminals. Also, be careful not to allow a tool to provide a ground between the positive cable/terminal and any metal component on the vehicle. Either of these conditions will cause a short circuit, leading to sparks and possible personal injury.

Do not smoke or all open flames/sparks near a battery; the gases contained in the battery are very explosive and, if ignited, could cause severe injury or death.

All batteries, regardless of type, should be carefully secured by a battery hold-down device. If not, the terminals or casing may crack from stress during vehicle operation. A battery which is not secured may allow acid to leak, making it discharge faster. The acid can also eat away at components under the hood.

Always inspect the battery case for cracks, leakage and corrosion. A white corrosive substance on the battery case or on nearby components would indicate a leaking or cracked battery. If the battery is cracked, it should be replaced immediately.

GENERAL MAINTENANCE

Always keep the battery cables and terminals free of corrosion. Check and clean these components about once a year.

Keep the top of the battery clean, as a film of dirt can help discharge a battery that is not used for long periods. A solution of baking soda and water may be used for cleaning, but be careful to flush this off with clear water. DO NOT let any of the solution into the filler holes. Baking soda neutralizes battery acid and will de-activate a battery cell.

Batteries in vehicles which are not operated on a regular basis can fall victim to parasitic loads (small current drains which are constantly drawing current from the battery). Normal parasitic loads may drain a battery on a vehicle that is in storage and not used for 6–8 weeks. Vehicles that have additional accessories such as a phone or an alarm system may discharge a battery sooner. If the vehicle is to be stored for longer periods in a secure area and the alarm system is not necessary, the negative battery cable should be disconnected to protect the battery.

Remember that constantly deep cycling a battery (completely discharging and recharging it) will shorten battery life.

BATTERY FLUID

▶ See Figure 51

Check the battery electrolyte level at least once a month, or more often in hot weather or during periods of extended vehicle operation. On non-sealed batteries, the level can be checked either through the case (if translucent) or by removing the cell caps. The electrolyte level in each cell should be kept filled to the split ring inside each cell, or the line marked on the outside of the case.

If the level is low, add only distilled water through the opening until the level is correct. Each cell must be checked and filled individually. Distilled water should be used, because the chemicals and minerals found in most drinking water are harmful to the battery and could significantly shorten its life.

If water is added in freezing weather, the vehicle should be driven several miles to allow the water to mix with the electrolyte. Otherwise, the battery could freeze.

Although some maintenance-free batteries have removable cell caps, the electrolyte condition and level on all sealed maintenance-free batteries must be checked using the built-in hydrometer "eye." The exact type of eye will vary. But, most battery manufacturers, apply a sticker to the battery itself explaining the readings.

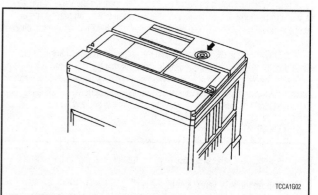

Fig. 51 Maintenance-free batteries usually contain a built-in hydrometer to check fluid level

➥ Although the readings from built-in hydrometers will vary, a green eye usually indicates a properly charged battery with sufficient fluid level. A dark eye is normally an indicator of a battery with sufficient fluid, but which is low in charge. A light or yellow eye usually indicates that electrolyte has dropped below the necessary level. In this last case, sealed batteries with an insufficient electrolyte must usually be discarded.

Checking the Specific Gravity

♦ See Figures 52, 53 and 54

A hydrometer is required to check the specific gravity on all batteries that are not maintenance-free. On batteries that are maintenance-free, the specific gravity is checked by observing the built-in hydrometer "eye" on the top of the battery case.

✳︎✳︎ CAUTION

Battery electrolyte contains sulfuric acid. If you should splash any on your skin or in your eyes, flush the affected area with plenty of clear water. If it lands in your eyes, get medical help immediately.

The fluid (sulfuric acid solution) contained in the battery cells will tell you many things about the condition of the battery. Because the cell plates must be kept submerged below the fluid level in order to operate, the fluid level is extremely important. And, because the specific gravity of the acid is an indication of electrical charge, testing the fluid can be an aid in determining if the battery must be replaced. A battery in a vehicle with a properly operating charging system should require little maintenance, but careful, periodic inspection should reveal problems before they leave you stranded.

At least once a year, check the specific gravity of the battery. It should be between 1.20 and 1.26 on the gravity scale. Most auto stores carry a variety of inexpensive battery hydrometers. These can be used on any non-sealed battery to test the specific gravity in each cell.

The battery testing hydrometer has a squeeze bulb at one end and a nozzle at the other. Battery electrolyte is sucked into the hydrometer until the float is lifted from its seat. The specific gravity is then read by noting the position of the float. If gravity is low in one or more cells, the battery should be slowly charged and checked again to see if the gravity has come up. Generally, if after charging, the specific gravity between any two cells varies more than 50 points (0.50), the battery should be replaced, as it can no longer produce sufficient voltage to guarantee proper operation.

CABLES

♦ See Figures 55, 56, 57 and 58

Once a year (or as necessary), the battery terminals and the cable clamps should be cleaned. Loosen the clamps and remove the cables, negative cable first. On top post batteries, the use of a puller specially made for this purpose is recommended. These are inexpensive and available in most parts stores. Side terminal battery cables are secured with a small bolt.

Clean the cable clamps and the battery terminal with a wire brush, until all corrosion, grease, etc., is removed and the metal is shiny. It is especially important to clean the inside of the clamp thoroughly (an old knife is useful here), since a small deposit of oxidation there will prevent a sound connection and inhibit starting or charging. Special tools are available for cleaning these parts, one type for conventional top post batteries and another type for side terminal batteries. It is also a good idea to apply some dielectric grease to the terminal, as this will aid in the prevention of corrosion.

After the clamps and terminals are clean, reinstall the cables, negative cable last; DO NOT hammer the clamps onto battery posts. Tighten the clamps securely, but do not distort them. Give the clamps and terminals a thin external coating of grease after installation, to retard corrosion.

Check the cables at the same time that the terminals are cleaned. If the cable insulation is cracked or broken, or if the ends are frayed, the cable should be replaced with a new cable of the same length and gauge.

Fig. 52 On non-sealed batteries, the fluid level can be checked by removing the cell caps

Fig. 53 If the fluid level is low, add only distilled water until the level is correct

Fig. 54 Check the specific gravity of the battery's electrolyte with a hydrometer

Fig. 55 The underside of this special battery tool has a wire brush to clean post terminals

Fig. 56 Place the tool over the battery posts and twist to clean until the metal is shiny

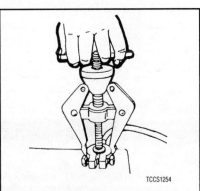
Fig. 57 A special tool is available to pull the clamp from the post

1-18 GENERAL INFORMATION AND MAINTENANCE

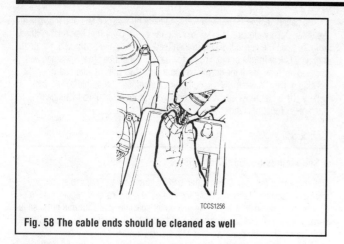

Fig. 58 The cable ends should be cleaned as well

CHARGING

> ⁂ **CAUTION**
>
> The chemical reaction which takes place in all batteries generates explosive hydrogen gas. A spark can cause the battery to explode and splash acid. To avoid personal injury, be sure there is proper ventilation and take appropriate fire safety precautions when working with or near a battery.

A battery should be charged at a slow rate to keep the plates inside from getting too hot. However, if some maintenance-free batteries are allowed to discharge until they are almost "dead," they may have to be charged at a high rate to bring them back to "life." Always follow the charger manufacturer's instructions on charging the battery.

REPLACEMENT

When it becomes necessary to replace the battery, select one with an amperage rating equal to or greater than the battery originally installed. Deterioration and just plain aging of the battery cables, starter motor, and associated wires makes the battery's job harder in successive years. This makes it prudent to install a new battery with a greater capacity than the old.

Belts

INSPECTION

▸ See Figures 59, 60, 61, 62 and 63

Once a year or at 12,000 mile (19,000 km) intervals, the tension (and condition) of the alternator, power steering, air conditioning, and Thermactor air pump drive belts (as equipped) should be checked. If necessary, the belts should be replaced or adjusted. Loose accessory drive belts can lead to poor engine cooling and diminish alternator, power steering pump, air conditioning compressor or air pump output. A belt that is too tight places a severe strain on the components it is driving which will lead to early component failure.

Replace any belt that is so glazed, worn or stretched that it cannot be tightened sufficiently. There are two different types of belts that may be found on your truck, v-belts (single ribbed) and serpentine type (multi-ribbed). Both of these types may drive one or more accessories.

➡ The material used in late model drive belts is such that the belts do not show wear as readily. Replace belts at least every three years.

On vehicles with matched belts, replace both belts. New ½, ⅜ and ¹⁵⁄₃₂ in. wide belts are to be adjusted to a tension of 140 lbs. and ¼ in. wide belts are adjusted to 80 lbs. (as measured on a belt tension gauge). Any belt that has been operating for a minimum of 10 minutes is considered a used belt. In the first 10 minutes, the belt should stretch to its maximum extent. After 10 min-

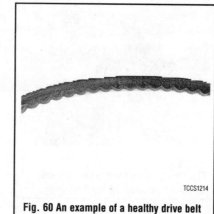

Fig. 59 There are typically 3 types of accessory drive belts found on vehicles today

Fig. 60 An example of a healthy drive belt

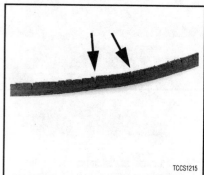

Fig. 61 Deep cracks in this belt will cause flex, building up heat that will eventually lead to belt failure

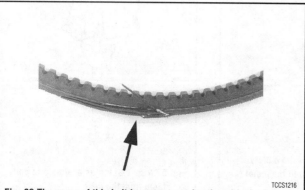

Fig. 62 The cover of this belt is worn, exposing the critical reinforcing cords to excessive wear

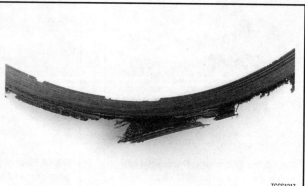

Fig. 63 Installing too wide a belt can result in serious belt wear and/or breakage

GENERAL INFORMATION AND MAINTENANCE

utes, stop the engine and recheck the belt tension. Belt tension for a used belt should be maintained at 110 lbs. for all except ¼ in. wide belts or at 60 lbs. for ¼ in. wide belts. If a belt tension gauge is not available, the following procedures may be used.

ADJUSTMENTS

▶ See Figures 64 thru 69

✴✴ CAUTION

If equipped, the electrically operated cooling fan may come on under certain circumstances, even though the ignition is OFF. Be sure to disconnect the negative battery cable before servicing your vehicle.

Alternator Belt

1. Position a ruler perpendicular to the drive belt at its longest straight run. Test the tightness of the belt by pressing it firmly with your thumb. The deflection should be between ¼–5/16 in. (6–8mm).
2. If the deflection exceeds these limits, loosen the alternator mounting and adjusting arm bolts.
3. Place a 1 in. (25mm) open-end or adjustable wrench on the adjusting ridge cast on the body, and pull on the wrench until the proper tension is achieved.
4. Holding the alternator in place to maintain tension, tighten the adjusting arm bolt. Recheck the belt tension. When the belt is properly tensioned, tighten the alternator mounting bolt.

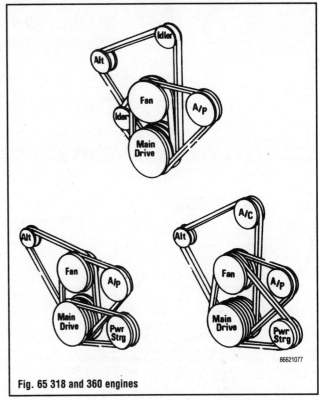

Fig. 65 318 and 360 engines

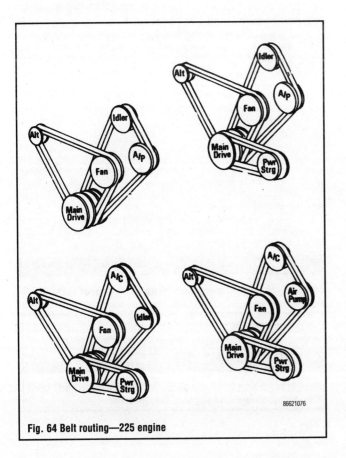

Fig. 64 Belt routing—225 engine

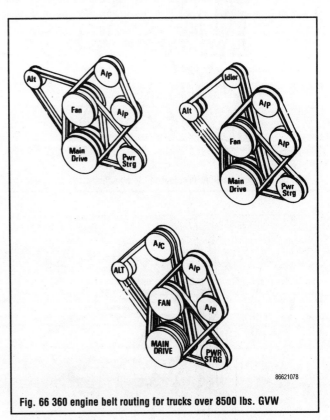

Fig. 66 360 engine belt routing for trucks over 8500 lbs. GVW

1-20 GENERAL INFORMATION AND MAINTENANCE

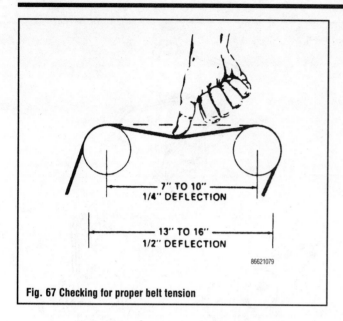

Fig. 67 Checking for proper belt tension

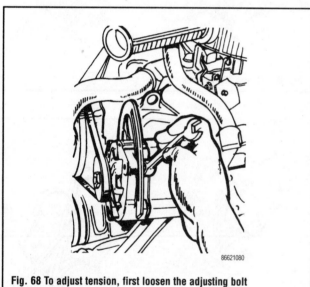

Fig. 68 To adjust tension, first loosen the adjusting bolt

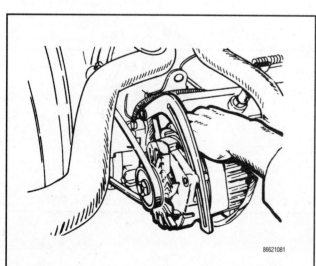

Fig. 69 Then move the component or idler pulley in the bracket to obtain the proper tension and hold it while you tighten the bolt

Power Steering

INLINE 6–CYLINDER ENGINES

1. Hold a ruler perpendicular to the drive belt at its longest run, test the tightness of the belt by pressing it firmly with your thumb. The deflection should be within ¼ in. (6mm), and ⁵⁄₁₆ in. (8mm).
2. To adjust the belt tension, loosen the adjusting and mounting bolts on the front face of the steering pump cover plate (hub side).
3. Using a large wooden dowel or a pry bar wrapped with a rag to protect the pump hub from damage, carefully pry on the hub in order to move the power steering pump toward or away from the engine until the proper tension is reached. Do not pry against the reservoir as it is relatively soft and easily deformed.
4. Holding the pump in place, tighten the adjusting arm bolt and then recheck the belt tension. When the belt is properly tensioned tighten the mounting bolts.

6-CYLINDER AND V8 ENGINES

1. Position a ruler perpendicular to the drive belt at its longest run. Test the tightness of the belt by pressing it firmly with your thumb. The deflection should be between ¼–⁵⁄₁₆ in. (6–8mm).
2. To adjust the belt tension, loosen the three bolts in the three elongated adjusting slots at the power steering pump attaching bracket.
3. Turn the steering pump drive belt adjusting nut as required until the proper deflection is obtained. Turning the adjusting nut clockwise will increase tension and decrease deflection; counterclockwise will decrease tension and increase deflection.
4. Without disturbing the pump, tighten the three attaching bolts.

Air Conditioning Compressor

1. Position a ruler perpendicular to the drive belt at its longest run. Test the tightness of the belt by pressing it firmly with your thumb. The deflection should be between ¼–⁵⁄₁₆ in. (6–8mm).
2. If the engine is equipped with an idler pulley, loosen the idler pulley adjusting bolt, insert a pry bar wrapped with a rag, between the pulley and the engine (or in the idler pulley adjusting slot), and adjust the tension accordingly. If the engine is not equipped with an idler pulley, the alternator must be moved to accomplish this adjustment, as outlined under Alternator Belt.
3. When the proper tension is reached, tighten the idler pulley adjusting bolt or the alternator adjusting and mounting bolts, as equipped.

Air Pump

1. Position a ruler perpendicular to the drive belt at its longest run. Test the tightness of the belt by pressing it firmly with your thumb. The deflection should be between ¼–⁵⁄₁₆ in. (6–8mm).
2. To adjust the belt tension, loosen the adjusting arm bolt slightly. If necessary, also loosen the mounting belt slightly.
3. Using a large wooden dowel or a pry bar wrapped with a rag to protect the pump from damage, carefully pry against the pump rear cover to move the pump toward or away from the engine as necessary.

✴✴ CAUTION

Do not pry against the pump housing itself, as damage to the housing may result.

4. Holding the pump in place, tighten the adjusting arm bolt and recheck the tension. When the belt is properly tensioned, tighten the mounting bolt.

✴✴ WARNING

Check to make sure that the V-ribbed belt is located properly in all drive pulleys before applying tensioner pressure.

REMOVAL & INSTALLATION

▶ See Figure 70

On most vehicles, to remove and install a new belt, you will need to loosen the mounting bracket bolts of the component. Using a suitable pry tool wrapped with a towel or rag, carefully pry the component forward slightly to give easy access to slide the belt off and on. You may need to do this an additional com-

GENERAL INFORMATION AND MAINTENANCE

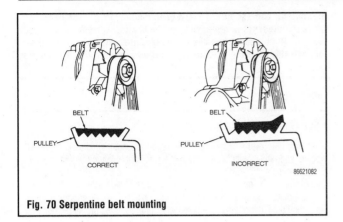

Fig. 70 Serpentine belt mounting

ponent(s) in order to make removal or installation easier. Some models have a few belts running different accessories, if you must replace a belt in the rear, you will first have to remove the belt(s) that are in your way. Look at your truck first to decide how many belts require removal to access the belt in need of replacement.

Hoses

♦ See Figures 71, 72, 73 and 74

✱✱ CAUTION

On models equipped with an electric cooling fan, disconnect the negative battery cable, or fan motor wiring harness connector before replacing any radiator/heater hose. The fan may come on, under certain circumstances, even though the ignition is OFF.

Inspect the condition of the radiator and heater hoses periodically. Early spring and at the beginning of the fall or winter, when you are performing other maintenance, are good times. Make sure the engine and cooling system are cold. Visually inspect for cracking, rotting or collapsed hoses, replace as necessary. Run your hand along the length of the hose. If a weak or swollen spot is noted when squeezing the hose wall, replace the hose.

REMOVAL & INSTALLATION

♦ See Figures 75 and 76

1. Drain the cooling system into a suitable container (if the coolant is to be reused, make sure the container is clean) by loosening the draincock on the bottom of the radiator.

✱✱ CAUTION

When draining the coolant, keep in mind that cats and dogs are attracted by ethylene glycol antifreeze, and are quite likely to drink any that is left in an uncovered container or in puddles on the ground. This will prove fatal in sufficient quantity. Always drain the coolant into a sealable container. Coolant should be reused unless it is contaminated or several years old.

2. Loosen the hose clamps at each end of the hose that requires replacement.
3. Twist, pull and slide the hose off the radiator, water pump, thermostat or heater connection.
4. Clean the hose mounting connections.

To install:

5. Position the clamps on the new hose.
6. Coat the connection surfaces with a water resistant sealer and slide the hose into position. Make sure the hose clamps are located beyond the raised bead of the connector (if equipped) and centered in the clamping area of the connection.

Fig. 71 The cracks developing along this hose are a result of age-related hardening

Fig. 72 A hose clamp that is too tight can cause older hoses to separate and tear on either side of the clamp

Fig. 73 A soft spongy hose (identifiable by the swollen section) will eventually burst and should be replaced

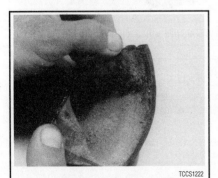

Fig. 74 Hoses are likely to deteriorate from the inside if the cooling system is not periodically flushed

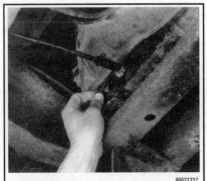

Fig. 75 Turn the radiator draincock to open and drain the engine cooling system

Fig. 76 Be CAREFUL When pulling hoses from component necks as many of the connections are easily damaged

1-22 GENERAL INFORMATION AND MAINTENANCE

7. Tighten the clamps to 20–30 inch lbs. (2–3 Nm). Do not overtighten.
8. Fill the cooling system.
9. Start the engine and allow it to reach normal operating temperature. Check for leaks.

Heat Riser

SERVICING

♦ See Figure 77

Every 30,000 miles (48,000 km), the heat riser valve should be checked for free operation and then lubricated with penetrating oil. The valve is located on the exhaust manifold near the exhaust pipe attachment point. Try to turn the valve counterweight by hand. If it's stuck, tap the end of the shaft a few times with a hammer. Apply penetrating oil to the shaft ends, then work the valve back and forth a few times. If the valve is still stuck and can't be loosened with oil and/or heat, it will have to be replaced.

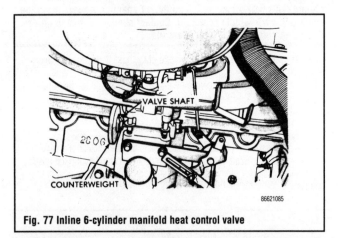

Fig. 77 Inline 6-cylinder manifold heat control valve

Cooling System

♦ See Figure 78

✷✷ CAUTION

Never remove the radiator cap under any conditions while the engine is running! Failure to follow these instructions could result in damage to the cooling system or engine and/or in personal injury. To avoid having scalding hot coolant or steam blow out of the radiator, DO NOT remove the cap from a hot radiator. Wait until the engine has cooled sufficiently, then wrap a thick cloth around the radiator cap and turn it SLOWLY to the first stop. Step back while the pressure is released from the cooling system. When you are sure the pressure has been released, press down on the radiator cap (still have the cloth in position) turn and remove the radiator cap.

INSPECTION

♦ See Figures 79 and 80

At least once every 2 years, the engine cooling system should be inspected, flushed, and refilled with fresh coolant. If the coolant is left in the system too long, it loses its ability to prevent rust and corrosion. If the coolant has been diluted with too much water, it won't protect against freezing.

The radiator cap should be examined for signs of age or deterioration. Fan belts should be inspected and, if necessary, adjusted to the proper tension (please refer to Belt Tension Adjustment in this section).

Hose clamps should be tightened, and soft or cracked hoses replaced. Damp spots, or accumulations of rust or dye near hoses, the water pump or other areas, indicate possible leakage. This must be corrected before filling the system with fresh coolant.

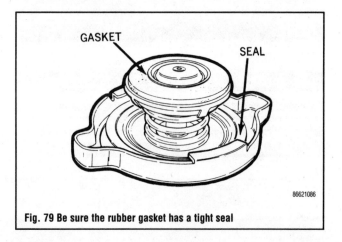

Fig. 79 Be sure the rubber gasket has a tight seal

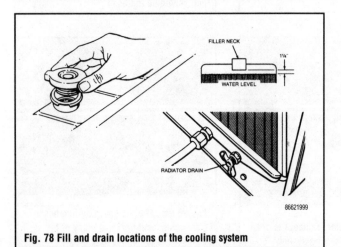

Fig. 78 Fill and drain locations of the cooling system

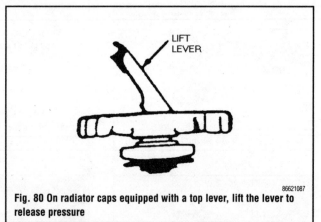

Fig. 80 On radiator caps equipped with a top lever, lift the lever to release pressure

Checking The Radiator Cap

While you are checking the coolant level, check the radiator cap for a worn or cracked gasket. If the cap doesn't seal properly, fluid will be lost in the form of steam and the engine will overheat. If necessary, replace the cap with a new one.

Radiator Debris

♦ See Figure 81

Periodically clean any debris (leaves, paper, insects, etc.) from the radiator fins. Pick the large pieces off by hand. The smaller pieces can be washed away with water pressure from a hose.

GENERAL INFORMATION AND MAINTENANCE

Carefully straighten any bent radiator fins with a pair of needle nose pliers. Be careful; the fins are very soft! Don't wiggle the fins back and forth too much. Straighten them once and try not to move them again.

FLUID RECOMMENDATIONS

Coolant found in late model trucks is normally a 50/50 mixture of ethylene glycol and water which can be used year round. Always use a good quality antifreeze with water pump lubricants, rust and other corrosion inhibitors, and acid neutralizers. Also available is another type of anitfreeze, Propylene Glycol, which is non-toxic. Keep in mind that should you decide to use a Propylene Glycol antifreeze, you should follow the antifreeze manufacturer's instructions closely. Do not mix Ethyene and Propylene Glycol together, as the benefits of the non-toxic Propylene Glycol would be lost. In the event you decide to change to Propylene Glycol, make sure to completely flush the cooling system of all Ethyene Glycol traces.

DRAINING & REFILLING THE SYSTEM

♦ See Figure 82

The system should be completely drained and refilled at least every two years in order to remove accumulated rust, scale and other deposits.

FLUSHING & CLEANING THE SYSTEM

♦ See Figure 83

1. Remove the radiator cap. Drain the existing coolant by opening the radiator draincock and engine draincock (if equipped, located on the water pump housing) or by disconnecting the bottom radiator hose at the radiator outlet.

➡ **Before opening the radiator draincock, spray it with some penetrating lubricant.**

2. Close the draincock or re-connect the lower hose and fill the system with water.
3. Add a can of quality radiator flush.
4. Idle the engine until the upper radiator hose gets hot.
5. Drain the system again.
6. Repeat this process until the drained water is clear and free of scale.
7. Close all draincocks and connect all the hoses.
8. If equipped with a coolant recovery system, flush the reservoir with water and leave empty.
9. Determine the capacity of your cooling system (see the Capacities Chart). Add a 50/50 mix of quality antifreeze and water to provide the desired protection.
10. Run the engine to operating temperature.
11. Stop the engine and check the coolant level.
12. Check the level of protection with an antifreeze tester, replace the cap and check for leaks.

Air Conditioning System

SYSTEM SERVICE & REPAIR

➡ **It is recommended that the A/C system be serviced by an EPA Section 609 certified automotive technician utilizing a refrigerant recovery/recycling machine.**

The do-it-yourselfer should not service his/her own vehicle's A/C system for many reasons, including legal concerns, personal injury, environmental damage and cost.

According to the U.S. Clean Air Act, it is a federal crime to service or repair (involving the refrigerant) a Motor Vehicle Air Conditioning (MVAC) system for money without being EPA certified. It is also illegal to vent R-12 and R-134a refrigerants into the atmosphere. State and/or local laws may be more strict than the federal regulations, so be sure to check with your state and/or local authorities for further information.

➡ **Federal law dictates that a fine of up to $25,000 may be levied on people convicted of venting refrigerant into the atmosphere.**

When servicing an A/C system you run the risk of handling or coming in contact with refrigerant, which may result in skin or eye irritation or frostbite. Although low in toxicity (due to chemical stability), inhalation of concentrated refrigerant fumes is dangerous and can result in death; cases of fatal cardiac arrhythmia have been reported in people accidentally subjected to high levels of refrigerant. Some early symptoms include loss of concentration and drowsiness.

➡ **Generally, the limit for exposure is lower for R-134a than it is for R-12. Exceptional care must be practiced when handling R-134a.**

Also, some refrigerants can decompose at high temperatures (near gas heaters or open flame), which may result in hydrofluoric acid, hydrochloric acid and phosgene (a fatal nerve gas).

It is usually more economically feasible to have a certified MVAC automotive technician perform A/C system service on your vehicle.

R-12 Refrigerant Conversion

If your vehicle still uses R-12 refrigerant, one way to save A/C system costs down the road is to investigate the possibility of having your system converted to R-134a. The older R-12 systems can be easily converted to R-134a refrigerant by a certified automotive technician by installing a few new components and changing the system oil.

The cost of R-12 is steadily rising and will continue to increase, because it is no longer imported or manufactured in the United States. Therefore, it is often possible to have an R-12 system converted to R-134a and recharged for less than it would cost to just charge the system with R-12.

If you are interested in having your system converted, contact local automotive service stations for more details and information.

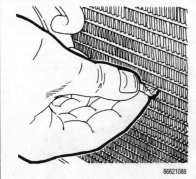

Fig. 81 Remove debris from the radiator fins

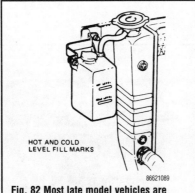

Fig. 82 Most late model vehicles are equipped with a coolant recovery system

Fig. 83 Filling the cooling system

1-24 GENERAL INFORMATION AND MAINTENANCE

PREVENTIVE MAINTENANCE

Although the A/C system should not be serviced by the do-it-yourselfer, preventive maintenance should be practiced to help maintain the efficiency of the vehicle's A/C system. Be sure to perform the following:

• The easiest and most important preventive maintenance for your A/C system is to be sure that it is used on a regular basis. Running the system for five minutes each month (no matter what the season) will help ensure that the seals and all internal components remain lubricated.

→Some vehicles automatically operate the A/C system compressor whenever the windshield defroster is activated. Therefore, the A/C system would not need to be operated each month if the defroster was used.

• In order to prevent heater core freeze-up during A/C operation, it is necessary to maintain proper antifreeze protection. Be sure to properly maintain the engine cooling system.

• Any obstruction of or damage to the condenser configuration will restrict air flow which is essential to its efficient operation. Keep this unit clean and in proper physical shape.

→Bug screens which are mounted in front of the condenser (unless they are original equipment) are regarded as obstructions.

• The condensation drain tube expels any water which accumulates on the bottom of the evaporator housing into the engine compartment. If this tube is obstructed, the air conditioning performance can be restricted and condensation buildup can spill over onto the vehicle's floor.

SYSTEM INSPECTION

Although the A/C system should not be serviced by the do-it-yourselfer, system inspections should be performed to help maintain the efficiency of the vehicle's A/C system. Be sure to perform the following:

The easiest and often most important check for the air conditioning system consists of a visual inspection of the system components. Visually inspect the system for refrigerant leaks, damaged compressor clutch, abnormal compressor drive belt tension and/or condition, plugged evaporator drain tube, blocked condenser fins, disconnected or broken wires, blown fuses, corroded connections and poor insulation.

A refrigerant leak will usually appear as an oily residue at the leakage point in the system. The oily residue soon picks up dust or dirt particles from the surrounding air and appears greasy. Through time, this will build up and appear to be a heavy dirt impregnated grease.

For a thorough visual and operational inspection, check the following:

• Check the surface of the radiator and condenser for dirt, leaves or other material which might block air flow.

• Check for kinks in hoses and lines. Check the system for leaks.

• Make sure the drive belt is properly tensioned. During operation, make sure the belt is free of noise or slippage.

• Make sure the blower motor operates at all appropriate positions, then check for distribution of the air from all outlets.

→Remember that in high humidity, air discharged from the vents may not feel as cold as expected, even if the system is working properly. This is because moisture in humid air retains heat more effectively than dry air, thereby making humid air more difficult to cool.

Windshield Wipers

ELEMENT (REFILL) CARE & REPLACEMENT

♦ See Figures 84, 85 and 86

For maximum effectiveness and longest element life, the windshield and wiper blades should be kept clean. Dirt, tree sap, road tar and so on will cause streaking, smearing and blade deterioration if left on the glass. It is advisable to wash the windshield carefully with a commercial glass cleaner at least once a month. Wipe off the rubber blades with the wet rag afterwards. Do not attempt to move wipers across the windshield by hand; damage to the motor and drive mechanism will result.

To inspect and/or replace the wiper blade elements, place the wiper switch in the **LOW** speed position and the ignition switch in the **ACC** position. When the wiper blades are approximately vertical on the windshield, turn the ignition switch to **OFF**.

Examine the wiper blade elements. If they are found to be cracked, broken or torn, they should be replaced immediately. Replacement intervals will vary with usage, although ozone deterioration usually limits element life to about one year. If the wiper pattern is smeared or streaked, or if the blade chatters across the glass, the elements should be replaced. It is easiest and most sensible to replace the elements in pairs.

If your vehicle is equipped with aftermarket blades, there are several different types of refills and your vehicle might have any kind. Aftermarket blades and arms rarely use the exact same type blade or refill as the original equipment.

Regardless of the type of refill used, be sure to follow the part manufacturer's instructions closely. Make sure that all of the frame jaws are engaged as the refill is pushed into place and locked. If the metal blade holder and frame are allowed to touch the glass during wiper operation, the glass will be scratched.

Tires and Wheels

Common sense and good driving habits will afford maximum tire life. Make sure that you don't overload the vehicle or run with incorrect pressure in the tires. Either of these will increase tread wear. Fast starts, sudden stops and sharp cornering are hard on tires and will shorten their useful life span.

→For optimum tire life, keep the tires properly inflated, rotate them often and have the wheel alignment checked periodically.

Inspect your tires frequently. Be especially careful to watch for bubbles in the tread or sidewall, deep cuts or underinflation. Replace any tires with bubbles in the sidewall. If cuts are so deep that they penetrate to the cords, discard the tire. Any cut in the sidewall of a radial tire renders it unsafe. Also look for uneven tread wear patterns that may indicate the front end is out of alignment or that the tires are out of balance.

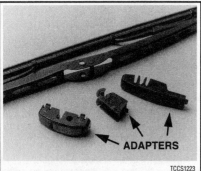

Fig. 84 Most aftermarket blades are available with multiple adapters to fit different vehicles

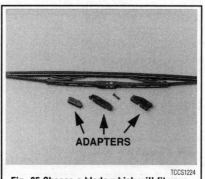

Fig. 85 Choose a blade which will fit your vehicle, and that will be readily available next time you need blades

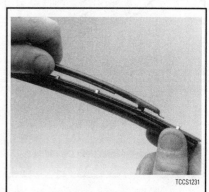

Fig. 86 When installed, be certain the blade is fully inserted into the backing

GENERAL INFORMATION AND MAINTENANCE

TIRE ROTATION

► See Figure 87

Tires must be rotated periodically to equalize wear patterns that vary with a tire's position on the vehicle. Tires will also wear in an uneven way as the front steering/suspension system wears to the point where the alignment should be reset.

Rotating the tires will ensure maximum life for the tires as a set, so you will not have to discard a tire early due to wear on only part of the tread. Regular rotation is required to equalize wear.

When rotating "unidirectional tires," make sure that they always roll in the same direction. This means that a tire used on the left side of the vehicle must not be switched to the right side and vice-versa. Such tires should only be rotated front-to-rear or rear-to-front, while always remaining on the same side of the vehicle. These tires are marked on the sidewall as to the direction of rotation; observe the marks when reinstalling the tire(s).

Some styled or "mag" wheels may have different offsets front to rear. In these cases, the rear wheels must not be used up front and vice-versa. Furthermore, if these wheels are equipped with unidirectional tires, they cannot be rotated unless the tire is remounted for the proper direction of rotation.

➡ The compact or space-saver spare is strictly for emergency use. It must never be included in the tire rotation or placed on the vehicle for everyday use.

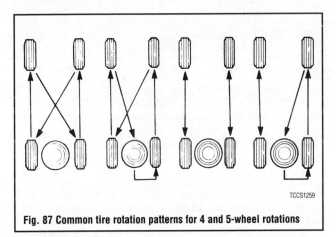

Fig. 87 Common tire rotation patterns for 4 and 5-wheel rotations

TIRE DESIGN

► See Figure 88

For maximum satisfaction, tires should be used in sets of four. Mixing of different brands or types (radial, bias-belted, fiberglass belted) should be avoided. In most cases, the vehicle manufacturer has designated a type of tire on which the vehicle will perform best. Your first choice when replacing tires should be to use the same type of tire that the manufacturer recommends.

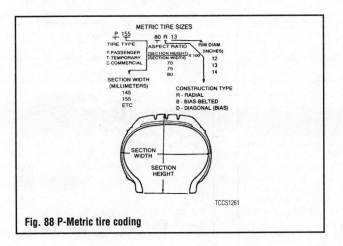

Fig. 88 P-Metric tire coding

When radial tires are used, tire sizes and wheel diameters should be selected to maintain ground clearance and tire load capacity equivalent to the original specified tire. Radial tires should always be used in sets of four.

✷✷ CAUTION

Radial tires should never be used on only the front axle.

When selecting tires, pay attention to the original size as marked on the tire. Most tires are described using an industry size code sometimes referred to as P-Metric. This allows the exact identification of the tire specifications, regardless of the manufacturer. If selecting a different tire size or brand, remember to check the installed tire for any sign of interference with the body or suspension while the vehicle is stopping, turning sharply or heavily loaded.

Snow Tires

Good radial tires can produce a big advantage in slippery weather, but in snow, a street radial tire does not have sufficient tread to provide traction and control. The small grooves of a street tire quickly pack with snow and the tire behaves like a billiard ball on a marble floor. The more open, chunky tread of a snow tire will self-clean as the tire turns, providing much better grip on snowy surfaces.

To satisfy municipalities requiring snow tires during weather emergencies, most snow tires carry either an M + S designation after the tire size stamped on the sidewall, or the designation "all-season." In general, no change in tire size is necessary when buying snow tires.

Most manufacturers strongly recommend the use of 4 snow tires on their vehicles for reasons of stability. If snow tires are fitted only to the drive wheels, the opposite end of the vehicle may become very unstable when braking or turning on slippery surfaces. This instability can lead to unpleasant endings if the driver can't counteract the slide in time.

Note that snow tires, whether 2 or 4, will affect vehicle handling in all non-snow situations. The stiffer, heavier snow tires will noticeably change the turning and braking characteristics of the vehicle. Once the snow tires are installed, you must re-learn the behavior of the vehicle and drive accordingly.

➡ **Consider buying extra wheels on which to mount the snow tires. Once done, the "snow wheels" can be installed and removed as needed. This eliminates the potential damage to tires or wheels from seasonal removal and installation. Even if your vehicle has styled wheels, see if inexpensive steel wheels are available. Although the look of the vehicle will change, the expensive wheels will be protected from salt, curb hits and pothole damage.**

TIRE STORAGE

If they are mounted on wheels, store the tires at proper inflation pressure. All tires should be kept in a cool, dry place. If they are stored in the garage or basement, do not let them stand on a concrete floor; set them on strips of wood, a mat or a large stack of newspaper. Keeping them away from direct moisture is of paramount importance. Tires should not be stored upright, but in a flat position.

INFLATION & INSPECTION

► See Figures 89 thru 94

The importance of proper tire inflation cannot be overemphasized. A tire employs air as part of its structure. It is designed around the supporting strength of the air at a specified pressure. For this reason, improper inflation drastically reduces the tire's ability to perform as intended. A tire will lose some air in day-to-day use; having to add a few pounds of air periodically is not necessarily a sign of a leaking tire.

Two items should be a permanent fixture in every glove compartment: an accurate tire pressure gauge and a tread depth gauge. Check the tire pressure (including the spare) regularly with a pocket type gauge. Too often, the gauge on the end of the air hose at your corner garage is not accurate because it suffers too much abuse. Always check tire pressure when the tires are cold, as pressure increases with temperature. If you must move the vehicle to check the tire inflation, do not drive more than a mile before checking. A cold tire is generally one that has not been driven for more than three hours.

1-26 GENERAL INFORMATION AND MAINTENANCE

Fig. 89 Tires with deep cuts, or cuts which bulge, should be replaced immediately

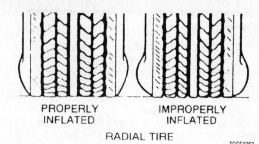

Fig. 90 Radial tires have a characteristic sidewall bulge; don't try to measure pressure by looking at the tire. Use a quality air pressure gauge

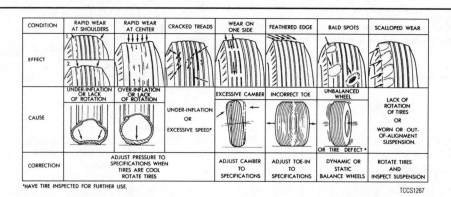

Fig. 91 Common tire wear patterns and causes

A plate or sticker is normally provided somewhere in the vehicle (door post, hood, tailgate or trunk lid) which shows the proper pressure for the tires. Never counteract excessive pressure build-up by bleeding off air pressure (letting some air out). This will cause the tire to run hotter and wear quicker.

✺✺ CAUTION

Never exceed the maximum tire pressure embossed on the tire! This is the pressure to be used when the tire is at maximum loading, but it is rarely the correct pressure for everyday driving. Consult the owner's manual or the tire pressure sticker for the correct tire pressure.

Once you've maintained the correct tire pressures for several weeks, you'll be familiar with the vehicle's braking and handling personality. Slight adjustments in tire pressures can fine-tune these characteristics, but never change the cold pressure specification by more than 2 psi. A slightly softer tire pressure will give a softer ride but also yield lower fuel mileage. A slightly harder tire will give crisper dry road handling but can cause skidding on wet surfaces. Unless you're fully attuned to the vehicle, stick to the recommended inflation pressures.

All automotive tires have built-in tread wear indicator bars that show up as ½ in. (13mm) wide smooth bands across the tire when 1/16 in. (1.5mm) of tread remains. The appearance of tread wear indicators means that the tires should be replaced. In fact, many states have laws prohibiting the use of tires with less than this amount of tread.

You can check your own tread depth with an inexpensive gauge or by using a Lincoln head penny. Slip the Lincoln penny (with Lincoln's head upside-down) into several tread grooves. If you can see the top of Lincoln's head in 2 adjacent grooves, the tire has less than 1/16 in. (1.5mm) tread left and should be replaced. You can measure snow tires in the same manner by using the "tails" side of the Lincoln penny. If you can see the top of the Lincoln memorial, it's time to replace the snow tire(s).

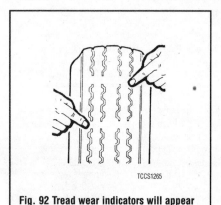

Fig. 92 Tread wear indicators will appear when the tire is worn

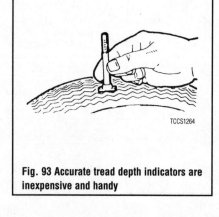

Fig. 93 Accurate tread depth indicators are inexpensive and handy

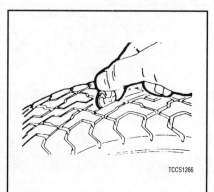

Fig. 94 A penny works well for a quick check of tread depth

GENERAL INFORMATION AND MAINTENANCE

FLUIDS AND LUBRICANTS

Fluid Disposal

Used fluids such as engine oil, transmission fluid, antifreeze and brake fluid are hazardous wastes which must be disposed of properly. Before draining any fluids, consult with local authorities; in many cases, waste oil, etc., is accepted in recycling programs. A number of service stations and auto parts stores are also accepting waste fluids for recycling.

Be sure of the recycling center's policies before draining the fluids, as many will not accept mixed fluids such as oil and antifreeze.

Fuel and Engine Oil Recommendations

GASOLINE ENGINES

♦ See Figures 95 and 96

All 1967–74 Dodge Trucks are designed to run on leaded gasoline. From 1975, any truck originally equipped with a catalytic converter MUST use unleaded gasoline.

The recommended oil viscosities for sustained temperatures ranging from below -10°F (-23°C) to above 100°F (38°C) are listed in this section. They are broken down into multiviscosities and single viscosities. Multiviscosity oils are recommended because of their wider range of acceptable temperatures and driving conditions.

When adding oil to the crankcase or when changing the oil and filter, it is important that oil of an equal quality to original equipment be used in your truck. The use of inferior oils may void the warranty, damage your engine, or both.

The Society of Automotive Engineers (SAE) grade number indicates the oil's viscosity (its ability to lubricate at a given temperature). The lower the SAE number, the lighter the oil; the lower the viscosity, the easier it is to crank the engine in cold weather but the less the oil will lubricate and protect the engine in high temperatures. This number is marked on every oil container.

Oil viscosities should be chosen from those oils recommended for the lowest anticipated temperatures during the oil change interval. Due to the need for an oil that embodies both good lubrication at high temperatures and easy cranking in cold weather, multigrade oils have been developed. Basically, a multigrade oil is thinner at low temperatures and thicker at high temperatures. For example, a 10W–40 oil (the W stands for winter) exhibits the characteristics of a 10 weight (SAE 10) oil when the truck is first started and the oil is cold. Its lighter weight allows it to travel to the lubricating surfaces quicker and offer less resistance to starter motor cranking than, say, a straight 30 weight (SAE 30) oil. But after the engine reaches operating temperature, the 10W–40 oil begins acting like straight 40 weight (SAE 40) oil, its heavier weight providing greater lubrication with less chance of foaming than a straight 30 weight oil.

The American Petroleum Institute (API) designations, also found on the oil container, indicates the classification of engine oil used under certain given operating conditions. Only oils designated for use Service SF (or a later superceding designation) heavy duty detergent should be used in your truck.

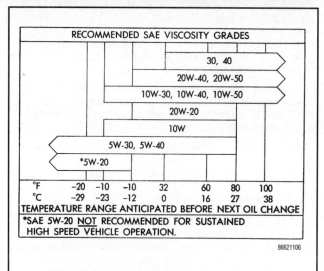

Fig. 96 Gasoline engine viscosity grades

Oils of the SF type perform may functions inside the engine besides their basic lubrication. Through a balanced system of metallic detergents and polymeric dispersants, the oil prevents high and low temperature deposits, while keeping sludge and dirt particles in suspension. Acids, particularly sulfuric acid, as well as other by products of engine combustion, are neutralized by the oil. If these acids are allowed to concentrate, they can cause corrosion and rapid wear of the internal engine parts.

✱✱✱ WARNING

Non-detergent motor oils or straight mineral oils should not be used in your Dodge gasoline engine.

DIESEL ENGINES

♦ See Figure 97

Diesel engines require different engine oil from those used in gasoline engines. Besides providing the protection that gasoline engine oil does, diesel oil must also deal with increased engine heat and the diesel blow-by gases, which create sulfuric acid, a highly corrosive substance.

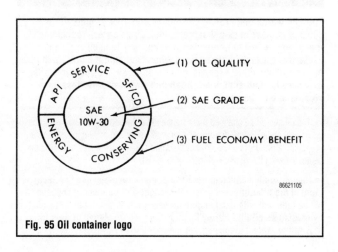

Fig. 95 Oil container logo

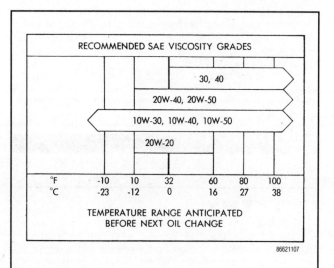

Fig. 97 Diesel engine viscosity grades

1-28 GENERAL INFORMATION AND MAINTENANCE

Under the American Petroleum Institute (API) classifications, gasoline engine oil codes begin with an **S**, and diesel engine oil codes begin with a **C**. This first letter designation is followed by a second letter code which explains what type of service (heavy, moderate, light) the oil is meant for. For example, the label of a typical oil bottle may well include: API SERVICES SF, CD. This means the oil is a superior, heavy duty engine oil and can be used in a diesel engine.

Many diesel manufacturers recommend an oil with both gasoline and diesel engine API classifications.

➡**Chrysler Corp. specifies the use of an engine oil conforming to API service categories of BOTH SG and CD (or the latest superceding codes). DO NOT use oils labeled as only SG or only CD as they could cause engine damage.**

Fuel makers commonly produce two grades of diesel fuel for use in automotive diesel engines No. 1 and No. 2. Generally speaking, No. 2 fuel is recommended over No. 1 for driving in temperatures above 20°F (7°C). In fact, in many areas, No. 2 diesel is the only fuel available. By comparison, No. 2 diesel fuel is less volatile than No. 1 fuel, and gives better fuel economy. Also, No. 2 fuel is a better injection pump lubricant.

The cetane number of a diesel fuel refers to the ease with which a diesel fuel ignites. High cetane numbers mean that the fuel will ignite with relative ease or that it ignites well at low temperatures. Naturally, the lower the cetane number, the higher the temperature must be to ignite the fuel. Most commercial fuels have cetane numbers that range from 35–65. No. 1 diesel fuel generally has a higher cetane rating than No. 2 fuel.

As the temperature goes down, diesel fuel tends to thicken. Diesel fuel contains paraffins (wax) and at low ambient temperatures, wax crystals begin forming in the fuel. The temperature at which this occurs is known as the cloud point. The cloud point for diesel fuel varies due to its composition and that information should be available from your fuel supplier or gas station. A typical cloud point temperature is 10°F (-12°C). This is an important piece of information as is extremely cold weather, diesel fuel can stop flowing altogether. This can result in no start condition or poor engine performance.

Depending on local climate, most fuel manufacturers make winterized No. 2 fuel available seasonally. The manufacturers often winterize No. 2 diesel fuel using various fuel additives and blends (No. 1 diesel fuel, kerosene, etc.) to lower its winter time viscosity. Generally speaking, though, No. 1 diesel fuel is more satisfactory in extremely cold weather.

➡**No. 1 and No. 2 diesel fuels will mix and burn with no ill effects, although the engine manufacturer will undoubtedly recommend one or the other. Consult the owner's manual for information.**

Many automobile manufacturers publish pamphlets giving the locations of diesel fuel stations nationwide. Contact a local dealer for information.

When planning a trip with a diesel powered vehicle, take into account the temperature of your destination. While your local temperature may be high enough for good running, lower temperatures at the destination may cause clouding and plugging.

Do not substitute home heating oil for automotive diesel fuel. While in some cases, home heating oil refinement levels equal those of diesel fuel, many times they are far below diesel engine requirements. The result of using dirty home heating oil will be a clogged fuel system, in which case the entire system may have to be dismantled and cleaned.

One more word on diesel fuels. Don't thin diesel fuel with gasoline in cold weather. The lighter gasoline, which is more explosive, will cause rough running at the very least, and may cause extensive damage to the fuel system if enough is used.

Engine

OIL LEVEL CHECK

▸ **See Figures 98 and 99**

Check the engine oil level every time you fill the gas tank. The oil level should be above the ADD mark and not above the FULL mark on the dipstick. Make sure that the dipstick is inserted into the crankcase as far as possible and that the vehicle is resting on level ground. Also, allow a few minutes after turning off the engine for the oil to drain into the pan or an inaccurate reading will result.

1. Open the hood and remove the engine oil dipstick.
2. Wipe the dipstick with a clean, lint-free rag and reinsert it. Be sure to insert it all the way.
3. Pull out the dipstick and note the oil level. It should be between the **SAFE/FULL** (MAX) mark and the **ADD** (MIN) mark.
4. If the level is below the lower mark, insert the dipstick and add fresh oil to bring the level within the proper range. Do not overfill.
5. Recheck the oil level and close the hood.

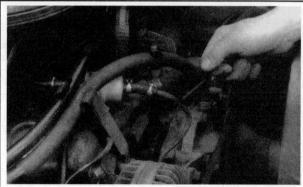

Fig. 98 Remove the engine dipstick to check the oil level

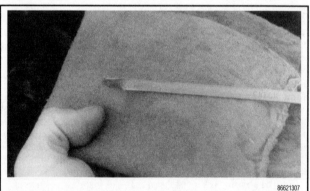

Fig. 99 Wipe the dipstick clean of oil and reinsert it, then withdraw it again (holding it horizontally) in order to read the oil level

OIL AND FILTER CHANGE

▸ **See Figures 100, 101 and 102**

✽✽✽ CAUTION

The EPA warns that prolonged contact with used engine oil may cause a number of skin disorders, including cancer! You should make every effort to minimize your exposure to used engine oil. Protective gloves should be worn when changing the oil. Wash your hands and any other exposed skin areas as soon as possible after exposure to used engine oil. Soap and water, or waterless hand cleaner should be used.

The oil should be changed more frequently if the vehicle is being operated in very dusty areas. Before draining the oil, make sure that the engine is at operating temperature. Hot oil will hold more impurities in suspension and will flow better, allowing the removal of more oil and dirt.

➡**Though some manufacturers have at times recommended replacement of the filter at every other oil change, Chilton recommends the filter be replaced with each engine oil service. The small amount saved by reusing an oil filter rarely justifies the risk. A clogged or dirty filter may fail to protect the expensive internal parts of your engine.**

GENERAL INFORMATION AND MAINTENANCE   1-29

Fig. 100 Loosen the drain plug using a wrench or a ratchet and socket

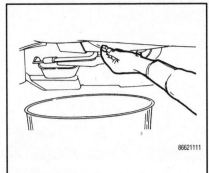

Fig. 101 Remove the plug by hand, keeping an inward pressure on it to keep oil from escaping past the threads

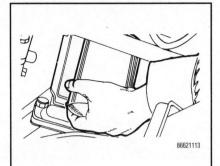

Fig. 102 A new spin-on filter should ONLY be installed by hand, DO NOT use a filter wrench for installation

➡ You will need a container which is capable of holding a minimum of 7 quarts of oil for gasoline engines or 9 quarts for the diesel. A container which is larger than the oil capacity is recommended so that it can be easily slid out from underneath the truck without the danger of spillage.

Loosen the drain plug with a wrench. Unscrew the plug using a rag to shield your fingers from the heat. Push in on the plug as you unscrew it (this should prevent oil from escaping past the threads until the plug is removed). Once the plug is unthreaded, quickly pull it and your arm back, away from the hot oil. Watch the oil drain and, if necessary, move the pan to keep underneath the stream of oil. Be careful of the oil. If it is at operating temperatures it is hot enough to burn you.

Give the oil sufficient time to drain in order to assure you have removed the most oil and dirt possible, then carefully install the drain plug. Make sure the plug is properly tightened, but DO NOT overtighten the plug as the threads are easily stripped. It would be better to leave the plug a little loose, than to overtighten and strip the threads, just be sure to check the plug for looseness or seepage after the engine has been fully warmed.

Cartridge Filter Replacement

♦ See Figure 103

Some early models were equipped with a cartridge type filter located in a canister on the side of the engine.
1. Place a drain pan under the filter housing.
2. Remove the filter housing bolt and lower the housing containing the cartridge.

※ CAUTION

The housing is full of hot oil! Be careful!

3. Remove the cartridge from the housing and dispose it.

Fig. 103 Exploded view of the dual cartridge type oil filters mounted on a 413 engine

➡ There are springs and washers located on the bolt. Be careful to avoid losing them.

4. Insert the new cartridge in the housing. It's a good idea to replace the housing O-ring or gasket.
5. Make sure that the old O-ring or gasket is not still partially on the housing or mounting bolt. Scrape the housing and bolt with a suitable tool, for better seating of the new gasket/ring.
6. Position the housing on the base and install the mounting bolt.
7. Fill the crankcase, then start the engine, let it idle for a few minutes, shut it off and recheck the oil level.
8. Check the floor beneath the vehicle for any leaks.

Spin-On Filter Replacement

♦ See Figures 104 thru 109

To remove the filter, you may need an oil filter wrench since the filter is often fitted tightly and the heat from the engine may make it even tighter. A filter wrench can be obtained at an auto parts store and is well worth the investment, since it will save you a lot of grief. Loosen the filter with the filter wrench. With a rag wrapped around the filter, unscrew the filter from the boss on the side of the engine. Be careful of hot oil that will run down the side of the filter.

➡ The diesel has 2 oil filters. Change both at the same time.

1. Make sure that you have a pan under the filter before you start to remove it from the engine; should some of the hot oil happen to get on you, you will have a place to dump the filter in a hurry.
2. Wipe the base of the mounting boss with a clean, dry cloth.

➡ Make sure the old filter gasket was removed with the filter and is not left on the engine adapter. If the old gasket is left in place, you are almost assured to have an oil leak.

3. When you install the new filter, smear a small amount of oil on the gasket with your finger, just enough to coat the entire surface, where it comes in contact with the mounting plate.
4. When you tighten the filter follow the part manufacturer's instructions. If none are provided, tighten it about ½–¾ a turn after it comes in contact with the mounting boss.

Manual Transmission

FLUID RECOMMENDATIONS

New Process A–230, A–250, A–390, A–745, and 2500:
• Dexron®III ATF
New Process NP–420:
• Below 32°F—SAE 30 engine oil
• 32–100°F—SAE 50 engine oil or SAE 90 gear oil
• 100+°F—SAE 140 gear oil
New Process NP–435:
• Below 32°F—SAE 30 engine oil

1-30 GENERAL INFORMATION AND MAINTENANCE

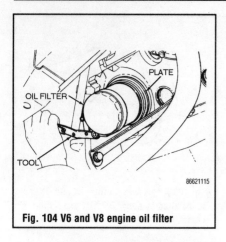

Fig. 104 V6 and V8 engine oil filter

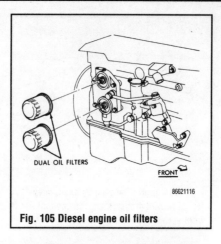

Fig. 105 Diesel engine oil filters

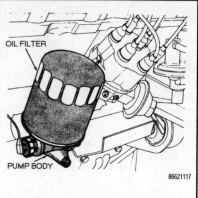

Fig. 106 Inline 6-cylinder engine oil filter

Fig. 107 Before installing the new spin-on filter, lightly coat the gasket with fresh engine oil

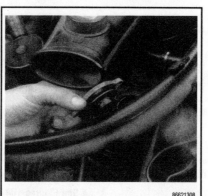

Fig. 108 Remove oil cap from valve cover

Fig. 109 Carefully refill the crankcase with fresh engine oil—a funnel cuts down on the mess

- 32–100°F—SAE 50 engine oil or SAE 90 gear oil
- 100+°F— SAE 140 gear oil

New Process NP-445:
- Below 32°F—SAE 30 engine oil
- 32–100°F—SAE 50 engine oil or SAE 90 gear oil
- 100+°F—SAE 140 gear oil

New Process NP-2500:
- SAE 10W-30 engine oil

Borg-Warner T-87E:
- Below 32°F—SAE 30 engine oil
- 32–100°F—SAE 50 engine oil or SAE 90 gear oil
- 100+°F—SAE 140 gear oil

A-833 Overdrive-4
- Dexron® III ATF

➡ If gear noise or rattle is experienced with the A-230/A-250/A-390/A-833, SAE 90 gear oil may be used in place of the ATF.

LEVEL CHECK

♦ See Figure 110

The fluid level should be checked every 6 months/6,000 miles (9500 km), whichever comes first.

1. Park the truck on a level surface, turn the engine **OFF**, apply the parking brake and block the wheels.
2. Remove the filler plug from the side of the transmission case with a proper size wrench. The fluid level should be even with the bottom of the filler hole.
3. If additional fluid is necessary, add it through the filler hole using a siphon pump or squeeze bottle.
4. Install the filler plug; do not overtighten.

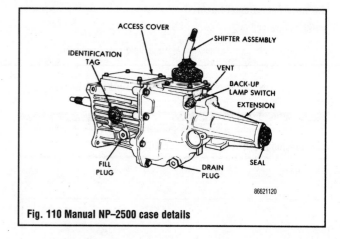

Fig. 110 Manual NP-2500 case details

DRAIN AND REFILL

1. Position the truck on a level surface.
2. Place a pan of sufficient capacity under the transmission and remove the upper (fill) plug to provide a vent opening.
3. Remove the lower (drain) plug and allow all of the fluid to drain from the transmission. On the A-390 top-cover three speed, remove the lower extension-to-case mounting bolt to drain the transmission.
4. Reinstall the drain plug.
5. Pump in sufficient lubricant to bring the level to the bottom of the filler plug opening.

GENERAL INFORMATION AND MAINTENANCE   1-31

Automatic Transmission

FLUID RECOMMENDATIONS

All Automatic Transmissions, use Dexron®III ATF.

LEVEL CHECK

♦ See Figure 111

It is very important to maintain the proper fluid level in an automatic transmission. If the level is either too high or too low, poor shifting operation and internal damage are likely to occur. For this reason a regular check of the fluid level is essential.

1. Drive the vehicle for 15–20 minutes to allow the transmission to reach operating temperature.
2. Park the truck on a level surface, apply the parking brake and leave the engine idling. Shift the transmission and engage each gear, then place the gear selector in **P** (PARK).
3. Wipe away any dirt in the area of the transmission dipstick to prevent it from falling into the filler tube. Withdraw the dipstick, wipe it with a clean, lint-free rag and reinsert it until it seats.
4. Withdraw the dipstick and note the fluid level. It should be between the upper (FULL) mark and the lower (ADD) mark.
5. If the level is below the lower mark, use a funnel and add fluid in small quantities through the dipstick filler neck. Keep the engine running while adding fluid and check the level after each small amount. Do not overfill.

DRAIN AND REFILL

♦ See Figures 112, 113, 114 and 115

➥A running production change was made in January of 1977 which eliminated the converter drain plug from the automatic transmission. This means that the transmission must be removed in order to drain the converter on models manufactured after this date.

With Converter Drain Plug

♦ See Figures 116 thru 121

1. Jack up the front of the vehicle and support it on jackstands.
2. Remove the converter access plate and turn the converter using the starter, until the converter drain plug is accessible.
3. Remove the converter drain plug and allow it to drain completely. Late 1972 and 1973–77 models use a 5/16 in. (8mm) hex head bolt, instead of the previously used 7/16 in. (11mm). A six-point socket must be used in the 5/16 in. (8mm) head.
4. Reinstall the converter drain plug.
5. Remove the bolts securing the transmission pan and carefully remove the pan to drain the fluid.
6. Clean the transmission pan thoroughly.
7. Remove the screws from the fluid filter in the bottom of the valve body; remove the filter and discard it.
8. Install a new filter using the screws.
9. Install the pan using a new gasket. Tighten the pan screws to 150 inch lbs. (17 Nm) of torque in a criss-cross pattern.
10. Install the torque converter access plate.
11. Carefully remove the jackstands and lower the vehicle, then immediately (so as not to forget) pour 6 quarts of DEXRON®III automatic transmission fluid through the filler tube.
12. Start the engine.
13. Let the engine idle for 2 minutes and move the gear selector through all the drive positions, pausing momentarily in each position.
14. Leave the gear selector in Neutral (making sure the parking brake is firmly set) and check the fluid level. If necessary, add enough fluid to bring the level to the "ADD ONE PINT" mark on the dipstick.
15. Test drive the vehicle to warm the fluid to normal operating temperature, then re-check the fluid level. Add fluid as necessary to properly fill the transmission to the upper (FULL) mark on the dipstick.

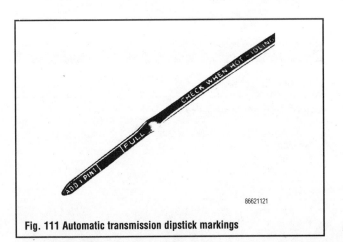

Fig. 111 Automatic transmission dipstick markings

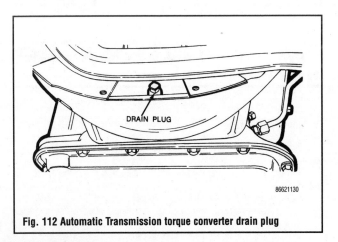

Fig. 112 Automatic Transmission torque converter drain plug

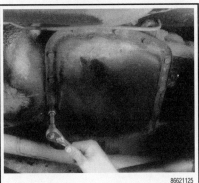

Fig. 113 Loosen, but do not remove the pan attaching bolts

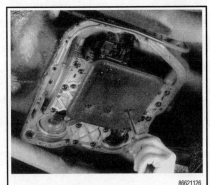

Fig. 114 Remove the filter attaching screws

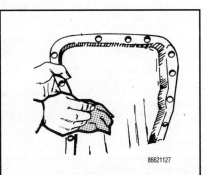

Fig. 115 Clean the pan with a suitable solvent and a rag—but be sure it is completely dry before installation

1-32 GENERAL INFORMATION AND MAINTENANCE

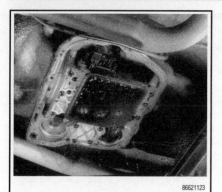
Fig. 116 The automatic transmission pan must be removed for access to the filter

Fig. 117 Remove old filter

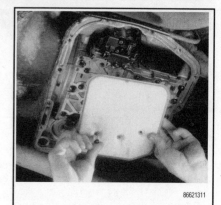
Fig. 118 Install new filter with screws

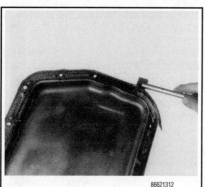
Fig. 119 Remove all traces of the old gasket from the transmission fluid pan

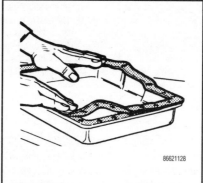
Fig. 120 Position a new gasket before installation

Fig. 121 Fill the transmission with a funnel through the transmission dipstick

⚠ WARNING

Do not overfill the transmission!

16. When you are finished, make sure the dipstick is fully seated.

Without Drain Plug

1. Raise the front of the truck and support it on jackstands. Place a large drain pan under the transmission.
2. Loosen the pan attaching bolts and tap the pan at one corner to break it loose.
3. Allow the fluid to drain into the drain pan.
4. Loosen the pan attaching bolts, then tap the pan at one corner to break it loose.
5. Allow the fluid to drain into the drain pan.
6. After most of the fluid has drained, carefully remove the attaching bolts, lower the pan and drain the rest of the fluid.
7. Remove the filter attaching screws and remove the filter.
8. Install a new filter. Tighten the screws to 35 inch lbs. (4 Nm).
9. Thoroughly clean the fluid pan with safe solvent and allow it to dry.
10. Using a new gasket, install the pan to the transmission. Tighten the attaching bolts to 150 inch lbs. (17 Nm).
11. Pour 4 quarts of DEXRON®II automatic transmission fluid in through the dipstick tube.
12. Lower the vehicle, start the engine and allow it to run for a few minutes. With the parking brake set, slowly move the gear selector to each position. Return it to the Neutral position.
13. Check the fluid level. Add more fluid as necessary to bring it up to the "ADD ONE PINT" level.
14. Drive the truck to bring the fluid up to normal operating temperature. Check the level again. It should be between the "Add" and "Full" marks.

Transfer Case

FLUID RECOMMENDATIONS

♦ See Figures 122, 123 and 124

The following lubricants should be used:

NP–200
GL–5 Gear Oils:
- Above 90°F—SAE 140W
- 10–90°F—SAE 90W
- Below 10°F—SAE 80W

SF Engine Oils:
- Above 32°F—50W
- Below 32°F—30W

NP–201
GL–5 Gear Oils:
- Above 90°F—SAE 140W
- 10–90°F—SAE 90W
- Below 10°F—SAE 80W

SF Engine Oils:
- Above 32°F—50W
- Below 32°F—30W

NP–203
- SAE 10W/30

NP–205—Through 1987
GL–5 Gear Oils:
- Above 90°F—SAE 140W
- 10–90°F—SAE 90W
- Below 10°F—SAE 80W

SF Engine Oils:
- Above 32°F—50W
- Below 32°F—30W

GENERAL INFORMATION AND MAINTENANCE   1-33

LEVEL CHECK

Position the vehicle on level ground. Remove the transfer case fill plug located on the left side of the transfer case. The fluid level should be up to the fill hole. If lubricant doesn't flow from the hold when the plug is removed, add lubricant until it does run out, then install the plug.

DRAIN AND REFILL

▶ See Figures 125, 126, 127, 128 and 129

The transfer case is serviced at the same time and in the same manner as the transmission. Clean the area around the filler and drain plugs and remove the filler plug on the side of the transfer case. Remove the drain plug on the bottom of the transfer case and allow the lubricant to drain completely.

Clean and install the drain plug. Add the proper lubricant. See the section on level checks.

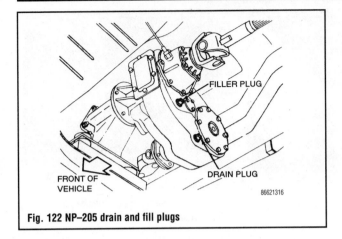

Fig. 122 NP-205 drain and fill plugs

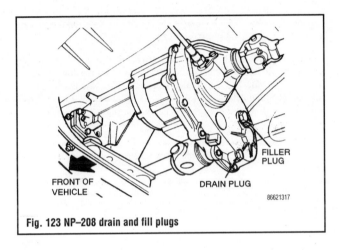

Fig. 123 NP-208 drain and fill plugs

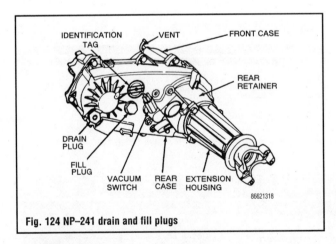

Fig. 124 NP-241 drain and fill plugs

NP-205—1988
- SAE SF 10W-30 Engine Oil

NP-208
- Dexron®III ATF

NP-241
- Dexron®III ATF

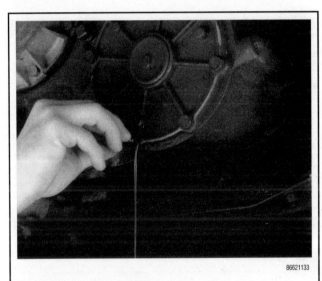

Fig. 125 Remove the lower plug to drain

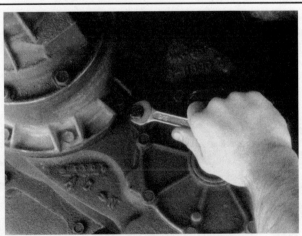

Fig. 126 Loosen the upper (fill) plug using a wrench, pliers or another suitable tool

1-34 GENERAL INFORMATION AND MAINTENANCE

Fig. 127 Remove upper (fill) plug in order to refill the transfer case

Fig. 128 Fill with gear oil specified for your vehicle

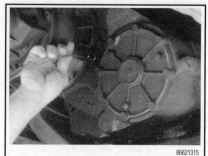

Fig. 129 If there is not enough room to fill with a bottle, use a special filler pump (which can usually be purchased from your parts store)

Drive Axles

FLUID RECOMMENDATIONS

♦ See Figure 130

Multipurpose gear lubricant meeting API GL–5 requirements or MOPAR hypoid lubricant can be used in conventional differential axles. Limited slip units, except in the 9¾ in. and 10½ in. axles, must use MOPAR hypoid lubricant. A MOPAR friction modifier additive is available to cure chatter and noise in these units.

The 9¾ in. and 10½ in. limited slip units must use MOPAR Sure-Grip lubricant. Gear lubricant viscosity depends on the anticipated temperatures: SAE 140 for above 90°F, SAE 90 for normal conditions (10°–90°F (12°–32°C)), and SAE 80 for below 10°F (-12°). The factory fill is normally SAE 90. Multiviscosity lubricants may be used. For more information on rear axle identification, please refer to the serial number identification information earlier in this section.

LEVEL CHECK

♦ See Figures 131 and 132

To check the axle lubricant level, remove the axle filler plug with the truck parked on a level surface.

➡The 9¾ in. and 10½ in. axles used from 1976–80 (300 series) have a pressed in rubber filler plug instead of the usual screw in plug.

You can use a finger for a dipstick, being careful of sharp threads. If necessary, add lubricant with a suction gun. The lubricant level should be ½ in. (13mm) below the filler plug hole on 8¼ in., 8⅜ and 8¾ in. axles, or at the bottom of the filler plug hole on all the rest.

DRAIN AND REFILL

♦ See Figures 133, 134, 135 and 136

➡Axles on Dodge and Plymouth trucks are not equipped with drain plugs. The old lubricant must be drained by removing the differential housing cover. Most 1972 and later models no longer use a paper gasket under the rear axle cover. Instead of the paper gasket, a bead of RTV silicone sealant is now used in production. The sealant is available for service.

Sealant should be applied as follows:
1. Scrape away any remains of the paper gasket or old traces of sealant, as applicable.
2. Clean the cover surface with mineral spirits. Any axle lubricant on the cover or axle housing will prevent the sealant from taking.
3. Apply a 1/16–3/32 in. (1.59–2.38mm) bead of sealant to the clean and dry cover flange. Apply the bead continuously along the bolt circle of the cover, looping inside the bolt holes as shown.
4. Allow the sealant to air dry.
5. Clean the carrier gasket flange (if solvent is used, allow it to air dry). Install the cover. If, for any reason, the cover is not installed within 20 minutes of applying the sealant, remove the sealant and start over.

Steering Gear

FLUID RECOMMENDATIONS

If it is necessary to add lubricant, use SAE 90 Gear Oil. In extremely cold weather use SAE 80 Gear Oil or dilute SAE 90 Gear oil with a small amount of SAE 10W engine oil to decrease steering effort. Install the filler plug.

Fig. 130 Fill the front axle with gear oil

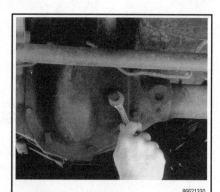

Fig. 131 Loosen the filler plug using a suitable wrench—front axle shown

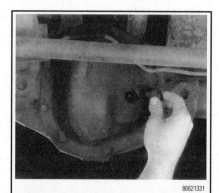

Fig. 132 Remove the fill plug to check fluid level

GENERAL INFORMATION AND MAINTENANCE   1-35

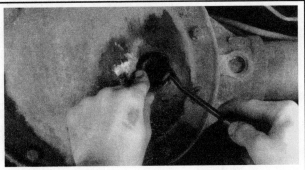

Fig. 133 To remove the rear axle push-in type plug carefully lever it out with a small prybar

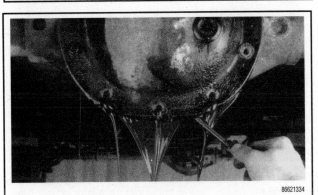

Fig. 134 Fluid is normally drained by unbolting the cover and breaking the gasket seal—rear axle shown

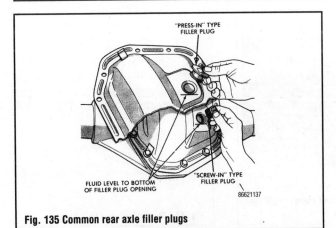

Fig. 135 Common rear axle filler plugs

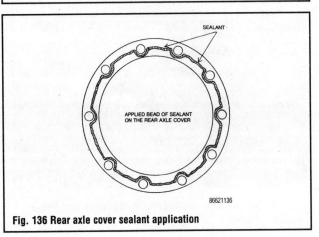

Fig. 136 Rear axle cover sealant application

LEVEL CHECK

➡ This check is only required on models through 1973; later models are permanently lubricated.

Clean the area around the filler plug, and remove the plug. The level of lubricant should just cover the worm gear.

Power Steering Pump

♦ See Figure 137

FLUID RECOMMENDATIONS

If it is necessary to add lubricant, use Chrysler Power Steering Fluid or its equivalent.

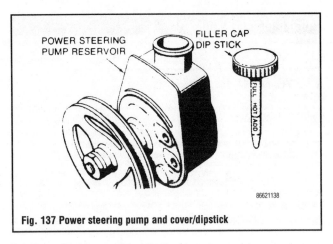

Fig. 137 Power steering pump and cover/dipstick

LEVEL CHECK

♦ See Figures 138, 139, 140 and 141

➡ Always clean the outside of the reservoir cover before removal.

1. Clean and remove the cover from the reservoir.
2. When the fluid is HOT, the level will be approximately ½–1 in. (13–25mm) below the top of the filler next or at the level indicated on the dipstick.
3. If the fluid is at ROOM TEMPERATURE (approx. 70°F (21°C)), the level will be about 1½–2½ in. (38–63mm) below the top of the filler neck.

✳✳ WARNING

Never add gear oil or automatic transmission fluid!

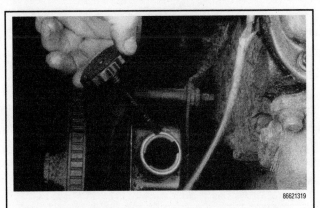

Fig. 138 The pump reservoir cover is usually a dipstick as well

1-36 GENERAL INFORMATION AND MAINTENANCE

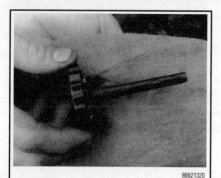

Fig. 139 Fluid should be at the appropriate level for the engine operating condition (the Full-HOT mark is higher on the dipstick)

Fig. 140 The Full-COLD mark is lower on the dipstick

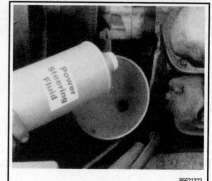

Fig. 141 A funnel is handy when topping off the power steering fluid

Brake Master Cylinder

LEVEL CHECK

♦ See Figures 142, 143, 144 and 145

The master cylinder reservoir is located under the hood, on the left side firewall. Make sure the vehicle is resting on level ground. Before removing the reservoir cap, clean all dirt away from the top of the master cylinder. Pry off the retaining clip or unscrew the hold-down bolt and remove the cap. The brake fluid level should be within ¼ in. (6mm) of the top of the reservoir.

There is a rubber diaphragm in the top of the master cylinder cap. As the fluid level lowers in the reservoir due to normal brake shoe wear or leakage, the diaphragm takes up the space. This is to prevent the loss of brake fluid out the vented cap and/or contamination by dirt. Make sure to inspect this cap for any tears or cracks, it will require replacement if any damage has occurred.

After refilling the master cylinder to the proper level (using heavy duty brake fluid), but before installing the cap, be sure to fold the rubber diaphragm up into the cap. Then install the cap in the reservoir and tighten the retaining bolt or snap the retaining clip into place.

FLUID RECOMMENDATIONS

♦ See Figure 146

Always use brake fluid which is supplied at any of your local parts stores, or even some of your local department stores with an auto parts department. Top off your truck with Dot-3 fluid only. DO NOT use Dot-5 silicone based fluids or rubber parts (seals) in the system will be damaged.

If the level of the brake fluid is less than half the volume of the reservoir, it is advised that you check the brake system for leaks. Leaks in the hydraulic brake system most commonly occur at the wheel.

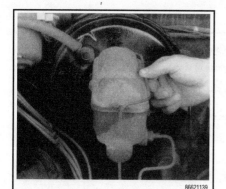

Fig. 142 Brake master cylinder with one piece cover and metal retainer bar

Fig. 143 To open the master cylinder cap, pry the bar off the top and carefully lift the cover

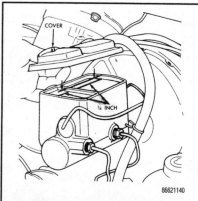

Fig. 144 Master cylinder fluid level

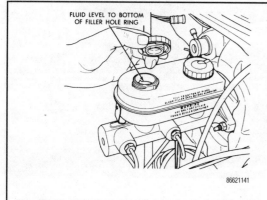

Fig. 145 Master cylinders with screw on caps, 1979 and later

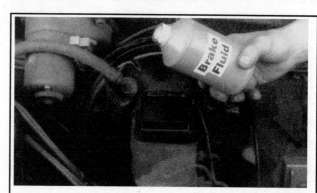

Fig. 146 ONLY refill the master cylinder with FRESH fluid from a sealed container

GENERAL INFORMATION AND MAINTENANCE   1-37

Hydraulic Clutch Reservoir

♦ See Figure 147

The clutch master cylinder is very similar to the brake master cylinder. The hydraulic fluid reservoirs on these systems are mounted on the firewall. Fluid level checks are performed like those on the brake hydraulic system. The system should be inspected periodically when other underhood services are performed. The proper fluid level is indicated by a step on the reservoir. To prevent contamination of the system with dirt, ALWAYS clean the top and sides of the reservoir before opening. Remove the reservoir diaphragm before adding fluid, and replace after filling. Keep the reservoir topped up with DOT-3; do not overfill.

✱✱ WARNING

Do not allow any petroleum base fluids to enter the clutch hydraulic system, this could cause seal damage.

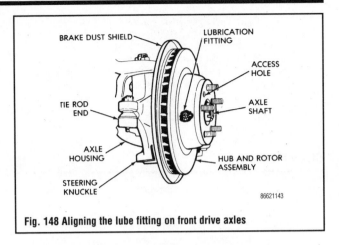

Fig. 148 Aligning the lube fitting on front drive axles

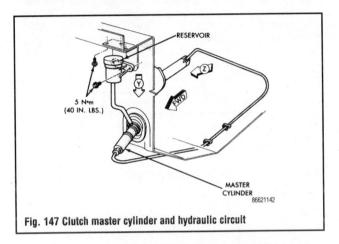

Fig. 147 Clutch master cylinder and hydraulic circuit

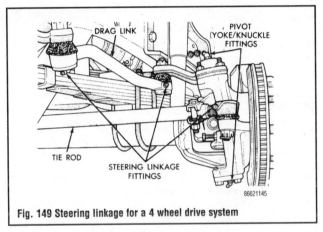

Fig. 149 Steering linkage for a 4 wheel drive system

Chassis Greasing

♦ See Figures 148, 149 and 150

The lubrication chart indicates where the grease fittings are located. The vehicle should be greased according to the intervals in the Preventive Maintenance Schedule at the end of this section.

Water resistant EP chassis lubricant (grease) conforming to Mopar specification NLGI Grade 2 should be used for all chassis grease points.

Every year or 7,500 miles (12,000 km) the front suspension ball joints, both upper and lower on each side of the truck, must be greased. Most trucks covered in this guide should be equipped with grease nipples on the ball joints, although some may have plugs which must be removed and nipples fitted. These nipples can be obtained through your local parts distributor.

✱✱ WARNING

Do not pump so much grease into the ball joint that excess grease squeezes out of the rubber boot. This destroys the watertight seal.

Jack up the front end of the truck and safely support it with jackstands. Block the rear wheels and firmly apply the parking brake. If the truck has been parked in temperatures below 20°F for any length of time, park it in a heated garage for an hour or so until the ball joints loosen up enough to accept the grease.

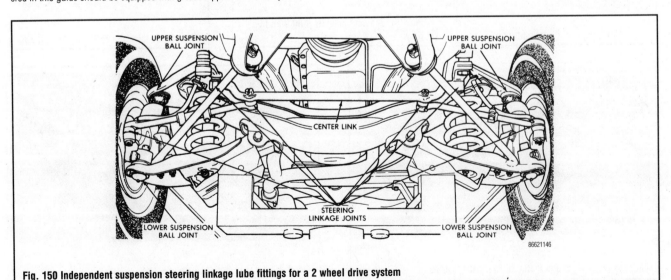

Fig. 150 Independent suspension steering linkage lube fittings for a 2 wheel drive system

1-38 GENERAL INFORMATION AND MAINTENANCE

Depending on which front wheel you work on first, turn the wheel and tire outward, either full-lock right or full-lock left. You now have the ends of the upper and lower suspension control arms in front of you; the grease nipples are visible pointing up (top ball joint) and down (lower ball joint) through the end of each control arm. If the nipples are not accessible, remove the wheel and tire. Wipe all dirt and crud from the nipples or from around the plugs (if installed). If plugs are on the truck, remove them and install grease nipples in the holes (nipples are available in various thread sizes at most auto parts stores). Using a hand operated, low pressure grease gun loaded with a quality chassis grease, lubricate the ball joint only until the rubber joint boot begins to swell out. DO NOT OVER GREASE!

STEERING LINKAGE

The steering linkage should be greased at the same interval as the ball joints. Grease nipples are installed on the steering tie rod ends on most models. Wipe all dirt and crud from around the nipples at each tie rod end. Using a hand operated, low pressure grease gun loaded with a suitable chassis grease, lubricate the linkage until the old grease begins to squeeze out around the tie rod ends. Wipe off the nipples and any excess grease. Also lubricate the nipples on the steering idler arms.

PARKING BRAKE LINKAGE

♦ See Figures 151, 152 and 153

Use chassis grease on the parking brake cable where it contacts the cable guides, levers and linkage.

AUTOMATIC TRANSMISSION LINKAGE

♦ See Figures 154 and 155

Apply a small amount of clean engine oil to the kickdown and shift linkage points at 7,500 mile (12,000 km) intervals.

Body Lubrication and Maintenance

CARE OF YOUR TRUCK

Glass Surfaces

All glass surfaces should be kept clean at all times for safe driving. You should use a window cleaner, the same cleaner you use on windows in your home. Use caution and never use an abrasive cleaners, this will cause scratching to the window surfaces.

Exterior Care

Your truck is exposed to all kinds of corrosive effects from nature and chemicals. Some of these are road salt, oils, rain, hail and sleet just to name a few. To protect not only the paint and trim, but also the many exposed mounts and fixtures, it is important to wash your vehicle often and thoroughly. After washing, allow all surfaces to drain and dry before parking in a closed garage. Washing may not clean all deposits off your truck, so you may need additional cleaners. When using professional cleaners, make sure they are suitable for acrylic painted surfaces, chrome, tires etc.. These supplies can be purchased in your local auto parts store. You also should wax and polish your vehicle every few months to keep the paint in good shape.

HOOD LATCH AND HINGES

♦ See Figure 156

Clean the latch surfaces and apply clean engine oil to the latch pilot bolts and the spring anchor. Also lubricate the hood hinges with engine oil. Use a chassis grease to lubricate all the pivot points in the latch release mechanism.

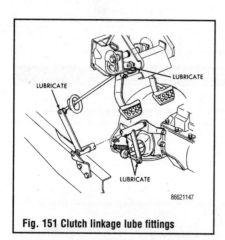

Fig. 151 Clutch linkage lube fittings

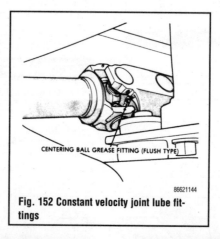

Fig. 152 Constant velocity joint lube fittings

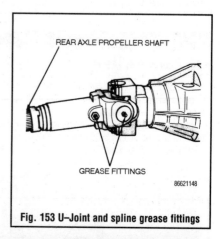

Fig. 153 U–Joint and spline grease fittings

Fig. 154 Location of automatic transmission linkage

Fig. 155 Linkage friction points should be lubricated

GENERAL INFORMATION AND MAINTENANCE

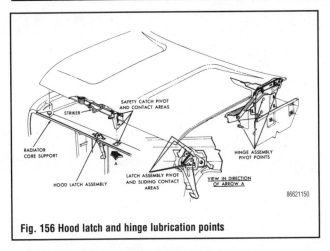

Fig. 156 Hood latch and hinge lubrication points

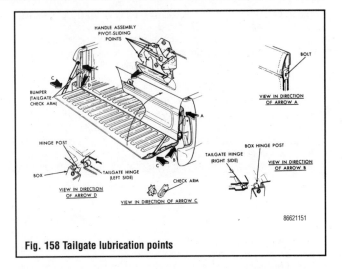

Fig. 158 Tailgate lubrication points

TAIL GATE AND DOOR HINGES

▶ See Figures 157, 158 and 159

The gas tank filler door and truck doors should be wiped clean and lubricated with clean engine oil once a year. The door lock cylinders and latch mechanisms should be lubricated periodically with a few drops of graphite lock lubricant or a few shots of silicone spray.

Front Wheel Bearings

REMOVAL, REPACKING, & INSTALLATION

Before handling the bearings, there are a few things that you should remember to do and NOT to do.

Remember to DO the following:
- Remove all outside dirt from the housing before exposing the bearing.
- Treat a used bearing as gently as you would a new one.
- Work with clean tools in clean surroundings.
- Use clean, dry canvas gloves, or at least clean, dry hands.
- Clean solvents and flushing fluids are a must.
- Use clean paper when laying out the bearings to dry.
- Protect disassembled bearings from rust and dirt. Cover them up.
- Use clean rags to wipe bearings.
- Keep the bearings in oil-proof paper when they are to be stored or are not in use.
- Clean the inside of the housing before replacing the bearing.

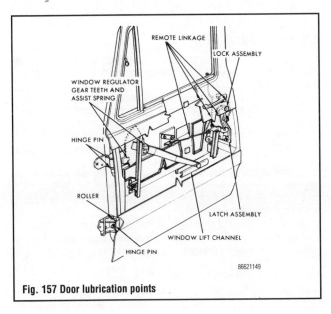

Fig. 157 Door lubrication points

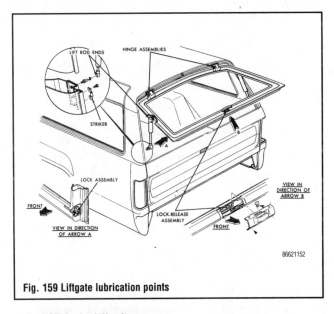

Fig. 159 Liftgate lubrication points

Do NOT do the following:
- Don't work in dirty surroundings.
- Don't use dirty, chipped or damaged tools.
- Try not to work on wooden benches or use wooden mallets.
- Don't handle bearings with dirty or moist hands.
- Do not use gasoline for cleaning; use a safe solvent.
- Do not spin-dry bearings with compressed air. They will likely be damaged.
- Do not spin dirty bearings.
- Avoid using cotton, waste, or dirty cloths to wipe bearings.
- Try not to scratch or nick bearing surfaces.
- Do not allow the bearing to come in contact with dirt or rust at any time.

2 Wheel Drive

▶ See Figures 160, 161 and 162

1. Raise and support the front end on jackstands.
2. Remove the wheel cover. Remove the wheel.
3. On vehicles equipped with drum brakes:
   a. Loosen the star adjusting wheel, remove the brake drum.
   b. Remove the grease cap from the spindle. Then, remove the cotter pin, locknut, adjusting nut along with the bearing assembly from the spindle.
   c. Clean the roller assembly with solvent and shake dry. If the roller assembly shows excessive wear or damage, replace the bearing.
   d. It is imperative that all old grease be removed from the bearings and

1-40 GENERAL INFORMATION AND MAINTENANCE

surrounding surfaces before repacking. The new lithium-based grease is not compatible with the sodium base grease used in the past.

    e. Clean the spindle with solvent to thoroughly remove all old grease.

    f. Covering the spindle with a clean cloth, brush all loose dirt and dust from the brake assembly. Remove the cloth carefully so as to not get dirt on the spindle.

    g. Install the brake drum and outer bearing to proper preload.

    h. With the wheel rotating to seat the bearing, adjust the wheel bearings by torquing the adjusting nut to 17–25 ft. lbs. (23–34 Nm). Then back off the adjusting nut ½ turn. Retighten the adjusting nut finger-tight. Install the locknut, aligning the castellations with the hole, then install a new cotter pin. Bend the ends of the cotter pin around the castellations (not over top) to prevent interference with the radio static collector in the grease cap. Install the grease cap.

    i. Install the wheels.

    j. Lower the vehicle, tighten lug nuts.

    k. Install the wheel cover.

4. On vehicles equipped with disc brakes:

    a. Remove the caliper from the disc and wire it to the underbody to prevent damage to the brake hose. See Section 9.

    b. Remove the grease cap from the hub. Then, remove the cotter pin, nut lock, adjusting nut and flat washer from the spindle. Remove the outer bearing assembly from the hub.

    c. Pull the hub and disc assembly off the wheel spindle.

    d. Remove and discard the old grease retainer. Remove the inner bearing cone and roller assembly from the hub.

    e. Clean all grease from the inner and outer bearing cups with solvent.

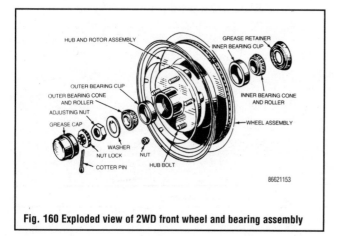

Fig. 160 Exploded view of 2WD front wheel and bearing assembly

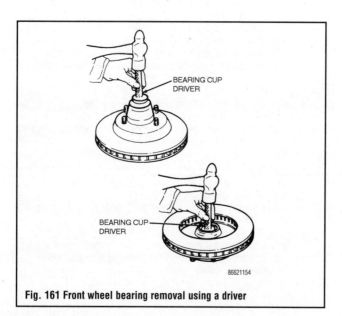

Fig. 161 Front wheel bearing removal using a driver

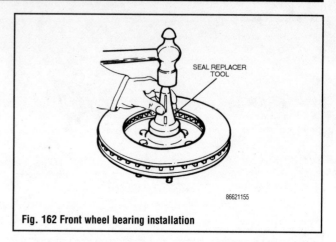

Fig. 162 Front wheel bearing installation

Inspect the cups for pits, scratches, or excessive wear. If the cups are damaged, remove them with a drift.

    f. Clean the inner and outer cone and roller assemblies with solvent and shake them dry. If the cone and roller assemblies show excessive wear or damage, replace them with the bearing cups as a unit.

    g. Clean the spindle and the inside of the hub with solvent to thoroughly remove all old grease.

    h. Covering the spindle with a clean cloth, brush all loose dirt and dust from the brake assembly. Remove the cloth carefully so as to not get dirt on the spindle.

    i. If the inner and/or outer bearing cups were removed, install the replacement cups on the hub. Be sure that the cups seat properly in the hub.

    j. It is imperative that all old grease be removed from the bearings and surrounding surfaces before repacking. The new lithium-based grease is not compatible with the sodium base grease used in the past.

    k. Install the hub and disc on the wheel spindle. To prevent damage to the grease retainer and spindle threads, keep the hub centered on the spindle.

    l. Install the outer bearing cone and roller assembly, along with the flat washer, on the spindle. Install the adjusting nut.

    m. With the wheel rotating to seat the bearing, adjust the wheel bearings by torquing the adjusting nut to 30–40 ft. lbs. (41–54 Nm). Then back off the adjusting nut ½ turn. Retighten the adjusting nut finger-tight. Install the nut lock, aligning the castellations with the hole, then install a new cotter pin. Bend the ends of the cotter pin around the castellations (not over top) to prevent interference with the radio static collector in the grease cap. Install the grease cap.

    n. Install the wheels.

    o. Lower the vehicle, tighten lug nuts.

    p. Install the wheel cover.

DRUM BRAKE ADJUSTMENT

The front wheels each rotate on a set of opposed, tapered roller bearings. The grease retainer at the inside of the hub prevents lubricant from leaking into the brake drum.

1. Raise and support the front end on jackstands.
2. Remove the grease cap and remove excess grease from the end of the spindle.
3. Remove the cotter pin and nut lock.
4. Rotate the wheel, hub and drum assembly while tightening the adjusting nut to 17–25 ft. lbs. (23–34 Nm) in order to seat the bearings.
5. Back off the adjusting nut ½, then retighten the adjusting nut finger-tight.
6. Install the new cotter pin, bending the ends of the cotter pin around the nut lock castellated flange (not over top).
7. Check the wheel for proper rotation, then install the grease cap filled with lubricant. If the wheel still does not rotate properly, inspect and clean or replace the wheel bearings and cups.
8. Install the wheels.
9. Lower the vehicle, tighten lug nuts.
10. Install the wheel cover.

GENERAL INFORMATION AND MAINTENANCE

DISC BRAKE ADJUSTMENT

1. Raise and support the front end on jackstands.
2. Remove the grease cap and remove excess grease from the end of the spindle.
3. Remove the cotter pin and nut lock.
4. Rotate the wheel, hub and disc assembly while tightening the adjusting nut to 30–40 ft. lbs. (41–54 Nm) in order to seat the bearings.
5. Back off the adjusting nut ½, then retighten the adjusting nut finger-tight.
6. Locate the nut lock on the adjusting nut so that the castellations on the lock are aligned with the cotter pin hole in the spindle.
7. Install the new cotter pin, bending the ends of the cotter pin around the castellated flange of the nut lock.
8. Check the wheel for proper rotation, then install the grease cap filled with lubricant. If the wheel still does not rotate properly, inspect and clean or replace the wheel bearings and cups.

❄ WARNING

New bolts must be used when servicing floating caliper units. The upper bolt must be tightened first. For floating caliper units, see Disc Brake Caliper Service in the Brake Section.

9. Install the wheels.
10. Lower the vehicle, tighten lug nuts.
11. Install the wheel cover.

4 Wheel Drive

Please refer to Section 7 for these procedures.

PUSHING AND TOWING

Pushing

Dodge and Plymouth trucks equipped with manual transmission can be push started, although this is not recommended if you value the appearance of your truck.

To push start, make sure that the bumpers of both vehicles are in reasonable alignment. Bent sheet metal and inflamed tempers are both predictable results from misaligned bumpers when push starting. Turn the ignition key to **ON** and engage high gear. Depress the clutch pedal. When a speed of about 10 mph is reached, slightly depress the gas pedal and slowly release the clutch. The engine should start. Never get an assist by having the vehicle towed. There is too much risk of the towed vehicle ramming the towing vehicle once it starts.

Vehicles equipped with automatic transmission cannot be started by pushing or towing.

Towing

Tow only in Neutral and at speeds not over 30 mph and distances not exceeding 15 miles (24 km). If either the transmission or rear axle is not functioning properly, or if the vehicle is to be towed more than 15 miles (24 km), the driveshaft should be disconnected or the truck should be towed with the rear wheels off the ground.

COOLING

Engine

One of the most common, if not THE most common, problems associated with trailer towing is engine overheating. If you have a standard cooling system, without an expansion tank, you'll definitely need to get an aftermarket expansion tank kit, preferably one with at least a 2 quart capacity. These kits are easily installed on the radiator's overflow hose, and come with a pressure cap designed for expansion tanks.

Another helpful accessory for vehicles using a belt-driven radiator fan is a flex fan. These fans are large diameter units, designed to provide more airflow at low speeds, with blades that have deeply cupped surfaces. The blades then flex, or flatten out, at high speed, when less cooling air is needed. These fans are far lighter in weight than stock fans, requiring less horsepower to drive them. Also, they are far quieter than stock fans. If you decide to replace your stock fan with a flex fan, note that if your truck has a fan clutch, a spacer will usually be needed between the flex fan and water pump hub.

Aftermarket engine oil coolers are helpful for prolonging engine oil life and reducing overall engine temperatures. Both of these factors increase engine life. While not absolutely necessary in towing Class I and some Class II trailers, they are recommended for heavier Class II and all Class III towing. Engine oil cooler systems consists of an adapter, screwed on in place of the oil filter, a remote filter mounting and a multi-tube, finned heat exchanger, which is mounted in front of the radiator or air conditioning condenser.

Transmission

An automatic transmission is usually recommended for trailer towing. Modern automatics have proven reliable and, of course, easy to operate, in trailer towing. The increased load of a trailer, however, causes an increase in the temperature of the automatic transmission fluid. Heat is the worst enemy of an automatic transmission. As the temperature of the fluid increases, the life of the fluid decreases.

It is essential, therefore, that you install an automatic transmission cooler. The cooler, which consists of a multi-tube, finned heat exchanger, is usually installed in front of the radiator or air conditioning compressor, and hooked in-line with the transmission cooler tank inlet line. Follow the cooler manufacturer's installation instructions.

Select a cooler of at least adequate capacity, based upon the combined gross weights of the truck and trailer.

Cooler manufacturers recommend that you use an aftermarket cooler in addition to, and not instead of, the present cooling tank in your radiator. If you do want to use it in place of the radiator cooling tank, get a cooler at least two sizes larger than normally necessary.

➥ **A transmission cooler can, sometimes, cause slow or harsh shifting during cold weather, until the fluid has a chance to come up to normal operating temperature. Some coolers can be purchased with or retrofitted with a temperature bypass valve which will allow fluid flow through the cooler only when the fluid has reached above a certain operating temperature.**

JACKING

A jack is a tire change tool only. If it is necessary to work under the vehicle, place the vehicle on jackstands. Do not operate the engine when the vehicle is raised on a jack.

1967–69 Models

An axle type jack is provided for emergency road service. When raising the front end of the vehicle, place the jack under the front spring, forward of the axle. When raising the rear end, place the jack under the axle next to the spring hanger.

❄ CAUTION

Do not attempt to raise one side of the truck with a floor jack midway between the front and rear wheels. This will result in a permanent damage to the body.

1970 and Later Models

A jack may used under the rear axle at the spring U-bolts or under the front suspension crossmember in the reinforced area inboard and next to the lower control arm pivot.

❄ CAUTION

Never use a floor jack under any part of the underbody. Do not attempt to raise one entire side of the vehicle by placing a jack midway between the front and rear wheels. This may result in permanent damage to the body!

For models supplied with a bumper jack, notches are provided in the bumper for raising the vehicle.

1-42 GENERAL INFORMATION AND MAINTENANCE

MAINTENANCE AND LUBRICATION CHARTS

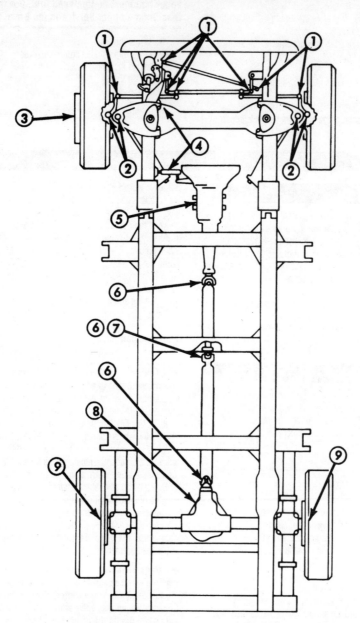

1. Steering linkage ball joints
2. Front suspension ball joints
3. Front wheel bearings
4. Clutch torque shaft
5. Transmission
6. U-joints
7. Slip spline (if equipped)
8. Rear axle
9. Rear wheel bearings

Fig. 163 Common chassis lubrication points

GENERAL INFORMATION AND MAINTENANCE

MAINTENANCE INTERVALS (in Thousands of Miles)* - GASOLINE

Item	'67	'68-'69	'70-'71	'72	'73-'74	'75	'76	'77	'78 (except diesel)	'79-'80 (except diesel)	'81-'88
Check, grease, and adjust rear wheel bearings on full-floating axles	—	—	50/12 mo	50/12 mo	50/12 mo	50/12 mo	50/12 mo	48/12 mo	48/12 mo	48/12 mo	48/12 mo
Check transmission and rear axle fluid level	2	2	—	4/3 mo	4/3 mo	5/6 mo LD/ 4/6 mo HD	5/6 mo LD/ 4/6 mo HD	6	6	6	6

*Minimum intervals for a van driven the average 12,000 miles per year under ideal conditions. Intervals given only in thousands of miles, or months, can be roughly converted to months, or miles: 12,000 mi = 12 mo. Reduce service intervals for severe use such as trailer towing, commercial service, or off-road driving. If both months and miles are given, use whichever interval elapses first.
LD—Light duty emission cycle vehicles, 6000 lb. GVW or less
HD—Heavy duty emission cycle vehicles, over 6000 lb. GVW
① No service required on passenger models in normal use, at 20,000 mi. for severe use at 16,000 mi. for motor home
② First at 36,000 miles or 2 years, then every 18,000 miles or 1 year
③ Check at least once a year and during brake service
④ Light duty—First at 52,000 miles or 3 years, then every 30,000 miles or 2 years
  Heavy duty—First at 48,000 miles or 3 years, then every 30,000 miles or 2 years
⑤ Chrysler Corp. does not recommend regularly scheduled oil changes for rear axles for normal service operation

MAINTENANCE INTERVALS (in Thousands of Miles)* - GASOLINE

Item	'67	'68-'69	'70-'71	'72	'73-'74	'75	'76	'77	'78 (except diesel)	'79-'80 (except diesel)	'81-'88
Clean air cleaner element or oil bath	8/6 mo	8/6 mo	8/6 mo	8/6 mo	8/6 mo	15 LD/ 12 HD	12 HD	12 HD	12 HD	12 HD	12 HD
Replace air cleaner paper element	24	24	24	24	24	30 LD/ 24 HD	30 LD/ 24 HD	30 LD/ 24 HD	30 LD/ 24 HD	22 LD/ 24 HD	30 LD/ 24 HD
Check PCV valve	6 mo	6 mo	3 mo	6 mo	12 mo	15 LD/ 12 HD	15 LD/ 12 HD	15 LD/ 12 HD	15 LD/ 12 HD	15 LD/ 12 HD	15 LD/ 12 HD
Replace PCV valve	12 mo	12 mo	12 mo	12 mo	24	30 LD/ 24 HD	30 LD/ 24 HD	30 LD/ 24 HD	30 LD/ 24 HD	30 LD/ 24 HD	30 LD/ 24 HD
Clean crankshaft intake air cleaner	12 mo	6 mo	6 mo	24 mo	12 mo	15/12 mo LD/12 HD	30 LD/ 12 HD	30 LD/ 12 HD	30 LD/ 12 HD	12/12 mo HD	30 LD/ 12 HD
Replace vapor storage canister filter	—	—	—	12 mo	12 mo	15 LD/ 12 HD	15 LD/ 12 HD	15 LD/ 12 HD	15 LD/ 18 HD	22 LD/ 18 HD	30 LD/ 18 HD
Lubricate exhaust manifold heat riser	4	4/3 mo	4/3 mo	6 mo	6	30 LD/ 16 HD	30 LD/ 16 HD	30 LD/ 18 HD	30 LD/ 18 HD	30 LD/ 18 HD	30 LD/ 18 HD
Rotate tires	8	8	8	8	8	8	8	6	6	6	6
Replace fuel filter	20	20	24	24	24	15 LD/ 12 HD	30 LD/ 16 HD	30 LD/ 18 HD	30 LD/ 18 HD	7/12 mo LD/ 6/12 mo HD	7.5/12 LD/ 6/12 HD
Change engine oil	4/3 mo	4/3 mo	4/3 mo	4/3 mo	4/3 mo	5/6 mo LD/ 4/6 mo HD	5/6 mo LD/ 4/6 mo HD	6/6 mo	6/6 mo	Every oil change	Every oil change
Change engine oil filter	8/6 mo	8/6 mo	8/6 mo	8/6 mo	8/6 mo	10/12 mo LD/ 8/12 mo HD	10/12 mo LD/ 8/12 mo HD	Every oil change	Every oil change	Every oil change	Every oil change
Change engine coolant	12 mo	12 mo	12 mo	12 mo	12 mo	15/12 mo	15/12 mo	②	②	②	②
Change manual transmission and/or transfer case lubricant	32	32	32	32	32	30	30	30	36	36	36
Change automatic transmission fluid and filter, adjust bands	32	32	32	32	32	30②	30	36	36	⑤	⑤
Change Front and/or rear axle lubricant	32	32	32	32	32	30②	30	30	24	⑤	⑤
Grease chassis and steering linkage	2	2	4/3 mo	4/3 mo	4/3 mo	5/6 mo LD/ 4/6 mo HD	5/6 mo LD/ 4/6 mo HD	6	6	22/24 mo LD/ 24/24 mo HD	22/24 mo LD/ 24/24 mo HD
Check, grease, and adjust front wheel bearings③	as needed	as needed	as needed	12	12	15 LD/ 12 HD	15 LD/ 12 HD	24	24	22 LD/ 24 HD	22.5 LD/ 24 HD
											37 LD/ 24 HD

Diesel Maintenance Intervals (in Thousands of Miles)

Clean air clean filter	6
Replace air cleaner filter	18
Change engine coolant	①
Change engine oil	6/12 mo
Change engine oil filter	6/12 mo
Replace fuel filter	24
Clean fuel feed pump strainer	12
Grease steering linkage	24/24 mo
Grease U-joints	24/24 mo
Grease ball joints	24/24 mo
Change manual transmission fluid	36
Change automatic transmission fluid	24/24 mo
Check, grease and adjust front wheel bearings	24
Change rear axle fluid	36
Check axle and transmission fluids	6
Rotate tires	6

① First at 36,000 miles or 2 years, then every 18,000 miles or 1 year.

1-44 GENERAL INFORMATION AND MAINTENANCE

CAPACITIES

Years	Engine cu. in. (liters)	Crank-case Inc. Filter (qts.)	Transmission (pt.) 3-sp	4-sp	5-sp	Auto	Transfer Case (pts.)	Drive Axle Front (pts.)	Rear (pts.)	Fuel Tank (gal.)	Cooling Systems w/AC (qts.)	wo/AC (qts.)
1967	225 (3.7)	6.0	⑭	7.0	—	18.5	⑪	⑧	⑬	N.A.	—	12.0
	251 (4.1)	6.0	—	5.5	—	—	5.0	6.0	6.0	N.A.	—	23.0
	318 (5.2)	6.0	⑭	7.0	—	18.5	⑪	⑧	⑬	N.A.	—	16.0
	383 (6.3)	7.0	⑭	7.0	—	—	⑪	⑧	⑬	N.A.	—	15.0
	413 (6.8)	9.0	⑭	7.0	—	—	⑪	⑧	⑬	N.A.	—	24.0
1968	198 (3.2)	6.0	㉘	7.5	—	18.5	⑪	⑧	⑬	N.A.	—	12.0
	225 (3.7)	6.0	㉘	7.5	—	18.5	⑪	⑧	⑬	N.A.	㉗	㉘
	318 (5.2)	6.0	㉘	7.5	—	18.5	⑪	⑧	⑬	N.A.	—	16.0
	383 (6.3)	7.0	㉘	7.5	—	—	⑪	⑧	⑬	N.A.	—	15.0
	413 (6.8)	9.0	㉘	7.5	—	—	⑪	⑧	⑬	N.A.	—	27.0
1969	225 (3.7)	6.0	3.25	7.0	—	18.5	⑪	⑧	⑨	N.A.	14.0	⑩
	318 (5.2)	6.0	3.25	7.0	—	18.0	⑪	⑧	⑨	N.A.	19.0	18.0
	383 (6.3)	7.0	3.25	7.0	—	—	⑪	⑧	⑨	N.A.	—	17.0
1970	225 (3.7)	6.0	3.25	7.0	—	18.5	⑪	⑧	⑨	N.A.	14.0	⑩
	318 (5.2)	6.0	3.25	7.0	—	18.0	⑪	⑧	⑨	N.A.	19.0	18.0
	383 (6.3)	7.0	3.25	7.0	—	—	⑪	⑧	⑨	N.A.	—	17.0
1971	225 (3.7)	6.0	3.25	7.0	—	18.5	⑪	⑧	⑨	N.A.	14.0	⑩
	318 (5.2)	6.0	3.25	7.0	—	18.0	⑪	⑧	⑨	N.A.	19.0	18.0
	383 (6.3)	7.0	3.25	7.0	—	—	⑪	⑧	⑨	N.A.	—	17.0
1972	225 (3.7)	6.0	⑯	⑰	—	⑱	4.5	⑧	⑨	N.A.	14.0	⑩
	318 (5.2)	6.0	⑯	⑰	—	⑱	4.5	⑧	⑨	N.A.	18.5	17.0
	360 (5.9)	6.0	—	⑰	—	⑱	4.5	⑧	⑨	N.A.	17.0	16.0
	400 (6.6)	6.0	—	⑰	—	⑱	—	—	⑨	N.A.	㉓	㉔
1973	225 (3.7)	6.0	⑯	⑰	—	⑱	4.5	⑧	⑨	N.A.	14.0	⑩
	318 (5.2)	6.0	⑯	⑰	—	⑱	4.5	⑧	⑨	N.A.	18.5	17.0
	360 (5.9)	6.0	—	⑰	—	⑱	4.5	⑧	⑨	N.A.	17.0	16.0
	400 (6.6)	6.0	—	⑰	—	⑱	—	—	⑨	N.A.	㉓	㉔
	440 (7.2)	6.0	—	⑰	—	⑱	—	—	⑨	N.A.	㉕	㉖
1974	225 (3.7)	6.0	⑯	⑰	—	⑱	4.5	⑧	⑨	N.A.	14.0	⑩
	318 (5.2)	6.0	⑯	⑰	—	⑱	4.5	⑧	⑨	N.A.	18.5	17.0
	360 (5.9)	6.0	—	⑰	—	⑱	4.5	⑧	⑨	N.A.	17.0	16.0
	400 (6.6)	6.0	—	⑰	—	⑱	—	—	⑨	N.A.	㉓	㉔
	440 (7.2)	6.0	—	⑰	—	⑱	—	—	⑨	N.A.	㉕	㉖

CAPACITIES

Years	Engine cu. in. (liters)	Crankcase Inc. Filter (qts.)	Transmission (pt.) 3-sp	4-sp	5-sp	Auto	Transfer Case (pts.)	Drive Axle Front (pts.)	Rear (pts.)	Fuel Tank (gal.)	Cooling Systems w/AC (qts.)	wo/AC (qts.)
1975	225 (3.7)	6.0	⑯	⑰	—	⑱	9.0	⑮	⑨	N.A.	14.0	⑩
	318 (5.2)	6.0	⑯	⑰	—	⑱	9.0	⑮	⑨	N.A.	18.5	17.0
	360 (5.9)	6.0	⑯	⑰	—	⑱	9.0	⑮	⑨	N.A.	17.0	16.0
	400 (6.6)	6.0	—	⑰	—	⑱	—	—	⑨	N.A.	㉓	㉔
	440 (7.2)	6.0	⑯	⑰	—	⑱	9.0	⑮	⑨	N.A.	17.0	16.0
1976	225 (3.7)	6.0	⑯	⑰	—	⑱	9.0	⑮	⑨	N.A.	14.0	⑩
	318 (5.2)	6.0	⑯	⑰	—	⑱	9.0	⑮	⑨	N.A.	18.5	17.0
	360 (5.9)	6.0	⑯	⑰	—	⑱	9.0	⑮	⑨	N.A.	17.0	16.0
	400 (6.6)	6.0	—	⑰	—	⑱	—	—	⑨	N.A.	㉓	㉔
	440 (7.2)	6.0	⑯	⑰	—	⑱	9.0	⑮	⑨	N.A.	17.0	16.0
1977	225 (3.7)	6.0	⑯	⑰	—	⑱	9.0	⑮	⑨	N.A.	14.0	⑩
	318 (5.2)	6.0	⑯	⑰	—	⑱	9.0	⑮	⑨	N.A.	18.5	17.0
	360 (5.9)	6.0	⑯	⑰	—	⑱	9.0	⑮	⑨	N.A.	17.0	16.0
	400 (6.6)	6.0	—	⑰	—	⑱	—	—	⑨	N.A.	㉓	㉔
	440 (7.2)	6.0	⑯	⑰	—	⑱	9.0	⑮	⑨	N.A.	17.0	16.0
1978	225 (3.7)	6.0	⑲	⑳	—	16.5	9.0	④	⑤	㉑	14.0	12.0
	243 (4.0)	9.0	—	⑳	—	—	9.0	④	⑤	㉑	14.0	13.0
	318 (5.2)	6.0	4.25	⑳	—	16.5	9.0	④	⑤	㉑	17.0	16.0
	360 (5.9)	6.0	4.25	⑳	—	16.5	9.0	④	⑤	㉑	15.5	14.5
	400 (6.6)	6.0	—	⑰	—	⑱	—	—	⑨	N.A.	㉓	㉔
	440 (7.2)	6.0	⑯	⑰	—	⑱	9.0	⑮	⑨	N.A.	17.0	16.0
1979	225 (3.7)	6.0	⑲	⑳	—	16.5	9.0	④	⑤	㉑	14.0	12.0
	243 (4.0)	9.0	—	⑳	—	—	9.0	④	⑤	㉑	14.0	13.0
	318 (5.2)	6.0	4.25	⑳	—	16.5	9.0	④	⑤	㉑	17.0	16.0
	360 (5.9)	6.0	4.25	⑳	—	16.5	9.0	④	⑤	㉑	15.5	14.5
	400 (6.6)	6.0	—	⑰	—	⑱	—	—	⑨	N.A.	㉓	㉔
	440 (7.2)	6.0	⑯	⑰	—	⑱	9.0	⑮	⑨	N.A.	17.0	16.0
1980	225 (3.7)	6.0	—	①	—	㉒	③	④	⑤	㉑	13.0	12.0
	243 (4.0)	9.0	—	⑳	—	—	9.0	④	⑤	㉑	14.0	13.0
	318 (5.2)	6.0	—	①	—	㉒	③	④	⑤	㉑	17.0	16.0
	360 (5.9)	6.0	—	①	—	㉒	③	④	⑤	㉑	15.5	14.5
1981	225 (3.7)	6.0	—	①	—	②	③	④	⑤	⑥	13.0	12.0
	318 (5.2)	6.0	—	①	—	②	③	④	⑤	⑥	17.0	16.0
	360 (5.9)	6.0	—	①	—	②	③	④	⑤	⑥	15.5	14.5
1982	225 (3.7)	6.0	—	①	—	②	③	④	⑤	⑥	13.0	12.0
	318 (5.2)	6.0	—	①	—	②	③	④	⑤	⑥	17.0	16.0
	360 (5.9)	6.0	—	①	—	②	③	④	⑤	⑥	15.5	14.5

GENERAL INFORMATION AND MAINTENANCE

CAPACITIES

Years	Engine cu. in. (liters)	Crankcase Inc. Filter (qts.)	Transmission (pt.) 3-sp	4-sp	5-sp	Auto	Transfer Case (pts.)	Drive Axle Front (pts.)	Drive Axle Rear (pts.)	Fuel Tank (gal.)	Cooling Systems w/AC (qts.)	Cooling Systems wo/AC (qts.)
1983	225 (3.7)	6.0	—	①	—	②	③	④	⑤	⑥	13.0	12.0
	318 (5.2)	6.0	—	①	—	②	③	④	⑤	⑥	17.0	16.0
	360 (5.9)	6.0	—	①	—	②	③	④	⑤	⑥	15.5	14.5
1984	225 (3.7)	6.0	—	①	—	②	③	④	⑤	⑥	13.0	12.0
	318 (5.2)	6.0	—	①	—	②	③	④	⑤	⑥	17.0	16.0
	360 (5.9)	6.0	—	①	—	②	③	④	⑤	⑥	15.5	14.5
1985	225 (3.7)	6.0	—	①	—	②	③	⑦	⑤	⑥	13.0	12.0
	318 (5.2)	6.0	—	①	—	②	③	⑦	⑤	⑥	17.0	16.0
	360 (5.9)	6.0	—	①	—	②	③	⑦	⑤	⑥	16.0	15.0
1986	225 (3.7)	6.0	—	①	—	②	③	⑦	⑤	⑥	13.0	12.0
	318 (5.2)	6.0	—	①	—	②	③	⑦	⑤	⑥	17.0	16.0
	360 (5.9)	6.0	—	①	—	②	③	⑦	⑤	⑥	16.0	15.0
1987	225 (3.7)	6.0	—	①	—	②	③	⑦	⑤	⑥	13.0	12.0
	318 (5.2)	6.0	—	①	—	②	③	⑦	⑤	⑥	17.0	16.0
	360 (5.9)	6.0	—	①	—	②	③	⑦	⑤	⑥	16.0	15.0
1988	238 (3.9)	4.0	—	7.0	4.0	②	4.5	⑦	⑤	⑫	15.1	15.1
	318 (5.2)	5.0	—	7.0	4.0	②	4.5	⑦	⑤	⑫	17.0	17.0
	360 (5.9)	5.0	—	7.0	4.0	②	4.5	⑦	⑤	30.0	15.5	15.5

N.A.: Information not available
① Overdrive-4: 7.5
   NP-435: 7.0
② A-904T/A-999: 17.1
   A-727: 16.8
③ NP-205: 4.5
   NP-208: 6.0
④ Dana 44F-BJ: 3.5
   Dana 60F: 6.5
⑤ Chrysler axles: 4.5
   Dana 60: 6.0
   Dana 70: 6.5
⑥ Standard: 20
   Optional: 30
   Ramcharger/Trail Duster: 35
⑦ Dana 44-8FD: 5.6
   Dana 60F: 6.5
⑧ Dana 44F: 3.0
   Dana 70F: 6.0
⑨ Chrysler axles: 4.0
   Dana 60: 6.0
   Dana 70: 7.0
   Dana 70HD: 7.25
⑩ 100 and 200 series: 13.0
   300 series: 14.0
⑪ US models: 4.5
   Canadian models: 6.6
⑫ Standard: 22.0
   Optional: 30.0
   Ramcharger/Trail Duster: 35

⑬ Chrysler axles: 3.75
   Dana 60: 5.5
   Dana 70: 6.0
⑭ A-745: 3.25
   T-87E: 6.9
⑮ Dana 44F-BJ: 3.0
   Dana 60F: 5.0
   Dana 70F: 6.0
⑯ A-250, exc. Club Cab: 4.5
   A-250 w/Club Cab: 5.25
   A-230, exc. Club Cab: 4.25
   A-230 w/Club Cab: 5.0
⑰ NP-435: 7.0
   NP-445: 7.5
⑱ A-727 w/11.75 in. torque converter: 19.0
   A-727 w/10.75 in. torque converter: 16.25
   A-345: 28.5
⑲ A-230: 5.0
   A-390: 3.6
⑳ NP-435: 7.0
   NP-445: 7.5
   Overdrive-4: 7.5
㉑ Forward of axle: 18.0
   Rear of axle: 21.0
㉒ w/o Lock-up Torque Converter: 16.5
   w/Lock-up Torque Converter: 17.1
㉓ D100, D200 w/air cond.: 17.0
   D100, D200 w/o air cond.: 16.0

㉔ D300 w/air cond.: 18.0
   D300 w/o air cond.: 17.0
㉕ D100 w/air cond.: 17.0
   D100 w/o air cond.: 16.0
㉖ D200, D300 w/air cond.: 18.0
   D200, D300 w/o air cond.: 17.0
㉗ D/W100, D/W200 w/air cond.: 13.0
   D/W100, D/W200 w/o air cond.: 12.0
   D/W300 w/air cond.: 15.0
   D/W300 w/o air cond.: 13.0
㉘ A-250: 4.0
   A-230 w/W100, W200, & D200 Crew Cab: 5.0
   A-230, all others: 4.25

ENGLISH TO METRIC CONVERSION: MASS (WEIGHT)

Current mass measurement is expressed in pounds and ounces (lbs. & ozs.). The metric unit of mass (or weight) is the kilogram (kg). Even although this table does not show conversion of masses (weights) larger than 15 lbs, it is easy to calculate larger units by following the data immediately below.

To convert ounces (oz.) to grams (g): multiply th number of ozs. by 28
To convert grams (g) to ounces (oz.): multiply the number of grams by .035

To convert pounds (lbs.) to kilograms (kg): multiply the number of lbs. by .45
To convert kilograms (kg) to pounds (lbs.): multiply the number of kilograms by 2.2

lbs	kg	lbs	kg	oz	kg	oz	kg
0.1	0.04	0.9	0.41	0.1	0.003	0.9	0.024
0.2	0.09	1	0.4	0.2	0.005	1	0.03
0.3	0.14	2	0.9	0.3	0.008	2	0.06
0.4	0.18	3	1.4	0.4	0.011	3	0.08
0.5	0.23	4	1.8	0.5	0.014	4	0.11
0.6	0.27	5	2.3	0.6	0.017	5	0.14
0.7	0.32	10	4.5	0.7	0.020	10	0.28
0.8	0.36	15	6.8	0.8	0.023	15	0.42

ENGLISH TO METRIC CONVERSION: TEMPERATURE

To convert Fahrenheit (°F) to Celsius (°C): take number of °F and subtract 32; multiply result by 5; divide result by 9
To convert Celsius (°C) to Fahrenheit (°F): take number of °C and multiply by 9; divide result by 5; add 32 to total

Fahrenheit (F)		Celsius (C)		Fahrenheit (F)		Celsius (C)		Fahrenheit (F)		Celsius (C)	
°F	°C	°C	°F	°F	°C	°C	°F	°F	°C	°C	°F
−40	−40	−38	−36.4	80	26.7	18	64.4	215	101.7	80	176
−35	−37.2	−36	−32.8	85	29.4	20	68	220	104.4	85	185
−30	−34.4	−34	−29.2	90	32.2	22	71.6	225	107.2	90	194
−25	−31.7	−32	−25.6	95	35.0	24	75.2	230	110.0	95	202
−20	−28.9	−30	−22	100	37.8	26	78.8	235	112.8	100	212
−15	−26.1	−28	−18.4	105	40.6	28	82.4	240	115.6	105	221
−10	−23.3	−26	−14.8	110	43.3	30	86	245	118.3	110	230
−5	−20.6	−24	−11.2	115	46.1	32	89.6	250	121.1	115	239
0	−17.8	−22	−7.6	120	48.9	34	93.2	255	123.9	120	248
1	−17.2	−20	−4	125	51.7	36	96.8	260	126.6	125	257
2	−16.7	−18	−0.4	130	54.4	38	100.4	265	129.4	130	266
3	−16.1	−16	3.2	135	57.2	40	104	270	132.2	135	275
4	−15.6	−14	6.8	140	60.0	42	107.6	275	135.0	140	284
5	−15.0	−12	10.4	145	62.8	44	112.2	280	137.8	145	293
10	−12.2	−10	14	150	65.6	46	114.8	285	140.6	150	302
15	−9.4	−8	17.6	155	68.3	48	118.4	290	143.3	155	311
20	−6.7	−6	21.2	160	71.1	50	122	295	146.1	160	320
25	−3.9	−4	24.8	165	73.9	52	125.6	300	148.9	165	329
30	−1.1	−2	28.4	170	76.7	54	129.2	305	151.7	170	338
35	1.7	0	32	175	79.4	56	132.8	310	154.4	175	347
40	4.4	2	35.6	180	82.2	58	136.4	315	157.2	180	356
45	7.2	4	39.2	185	85.0	60	140	320	160.0	185	365
50	10.0	6	42.8	190	87.8	62	143.6	325	162.8	190	374
55	12.8	8	46.4	195	90.6	64	147.2	330	165.6	195	383
60	15.6	10	50	200	93.3	66	150.8	335	168.3	200	392
65	18.3	12	53.6	205	96.1	68	154.4	340	171.1	205	401
70	21.1	14	57.2	210	98.9	70	158	345	173.9	210	410
75	23.9	16	60.8	212	100.0	75	167	350	176.7	215	414

ENGLISH TO METRIC CONVERSION: LENGTH

To convert inches (ins.) to millimeters (mm): multiply number of inches by 25.4

To convert millimeters (mm) to inches (ins.): multiply number of millimeters by .04

Inches			Decimals	Milli-meters	Inches to millimeters		Inches		Decimals	Milli-meters	Inches to millimeters	
					inches	mm					inches	mm
		1/64	0.051625	0.3969	0.0001	0.00254		33/64	0.515625	13.0969	0.6	15.24
	1/32		0.03125	0.7937	0.0002	0.00508	17/32		0.53125	13.4937	0.7	17.78
		3/64	0.046875	1.1906	0.0003	0.00762		35/64	0.546875	13.8906	0.8	20.32
1/16			0.0625	1.5875	0.0004	0.01016	9/16		0.5625	14.2875	0.9	22.86
		5/64	0.078125	1.9844	0.0005	0.01270		37/64	0.578125	14.6844	1	25.4
	3/32		0.09375	2.3812	0.0006	0.01524	19/32		0.59375	15.0812	2	50.8
		7/64	0.109375	2.7781	0.0007	0.01778		39/64	0.609375	15.4781	3	76.2
1/8			0.125	3.1750	0.0008	0.02032	5/8		0.625	15.8750	4	101.6
		9/64	0.140625	3.5719	0.0009	0.02286		41/64	0.640625	16.2719	5	127.0
	5/32		0.15625	3.9687	0.001	0.0254	21/32		0.65625	16.6687	6	152.4
		11/64	0.171875	4.3656	0.002	0.0508		43/64	0.671875	17.0656	7	177.8
3/16			0.1875	4.7625	0.003	0.0762	11/16		0.6875	17.4625	8	203.2
		13/64	0.203125	5.1594	0.004	0.1016		45/64	0.703125	17.8594	9	228.6
	7/32		0.21875	5.5562	0.005	0.1270	23/32		0.71875	18.2562	10	254.0
		15/64	0.234375	5.9531	0.006	0.1524		47/64	0.734375	18.6531	11	279.4
1/4			0.25	6.3500	0.007	0.1778	3/4		0.75	19.0500	12	304.8
		17/64	0.265625	6.7469	0.008	0.2032		49/64	0.765625	19.4469	13	330.2
	9/32		0.28125	7.1437	0.009	0.2286	25/32		0.78125	19.8437	14	355.6
		19/64	0.296875	7.5406	0.01	0.254		51/64	0.796875	20.2406	15	381.0
5/16			0.3125	7.9375	0.02	0.508	13/16		0.8125	20.6375	16	406.4
		21/64	0.328125	8.3344	0.03	0.762		53/64	0.828125	21.0344	17	431.8
	11/32		0.34375	8.7312	0.04	1.016	27/32		0.84375	21.4312	18	457.2
		23/64	0.359375	9.1281	0.05	1.270		55/64	0.859375	21.8281	19	482.6
3/8			0.375	9.5250	0.06	1.524	7/8		0.875	22.2250	20	508.0
		25/64	0.390625	9.9219	0.07	1.778		57/64	0.890625	22.6219	21	533.4
	13/32		0.40625	10.3187	0.08	2.032	29/32		0.90625	23.0187	22	558.8
		27/64	0.421875	10.7156	0.09	2.286		59/64	0.921875	23.4156	23	584.2
7/16			0.4375	11.1125	0.1	2.54	15/16		0.9375	23.8125	24	609.6
		29/64	0.453125	11.5094	0.2	5.08		61/64	0.953125	24.2094	25	635.0
	15/32		0.46875	11.9062	0.3	7.62	31/32		0.96875	24.6062	26	660.4
		31/64	0.484375	12.3031	0.4	10.16		63/64	0.984375	25.0031	27	690.6
1/2			0.5	12.7000	0.5	12.70						

ENGLISH TO METRIC CONVERSION: TORQUE

To convert foot-pounds (ft. lbs.) to Newton-meters: multiply the number of ft. lbs. by 1.3

To convert inch-pounds (in. lbs.) to Newton-meters: multiply the number of in. lbs. by .11

in lbs	N-m	in lbs	N-m	in lbs	N-m	in lbs	N-m	in lbs	N-m
0.1	0.01	1	0.11	10	1.13	19	2.15	28	3.16
0.2	0.02	2	0.23	11	1.24	20	2.26	29	3.28
0.3	0.03	3	0.34	12	1.36	21	2.37	30	3.39
0.4	0.04	4	0.45	13	1.47	22	2.49	31	3.50
0.5	0.06	5	0.56	14	1.58	23	2.60	32	3.62
0.6	0.07	6	0.68	15	1.70	24	2.71	33	3.73
0.7	0.08	7	0.78	16	1.81	25	2.82	34	3.84
0.8	0.09	8	0.90	17	1.92	26	2.94	35	3.95
0.9	0.10	9	1.02	18	2.03	27	3.05	36	4.0

GENERAL INFORMATION AND MAINTENANCE

ENGLISH TO METRIC CONVERSION: TORQUE

Torque is now expressed as either foot-pounds (ft./lbs.) or inch-pounds (in./lbs.). The metric measurement unit for torque is the Newton-meter (Nm). This unit—the Nm—will be used for all SI metric torque references, both the present ft./lbs. and in./lbs.

ft lbs	N-m	ft lbs	N-m	ft lbs	N-m	ft lbs	N-m
0.1	0.1	33	44.7	74	100.3	115	155.9
0.2	0.3	34	46.1	75	101.7	116	157.3
0.3	0.4	35	47.4	76	103.0	117	158.6
0.4	0.5	36	48.8	77	104.4	118	160.0
0.5	0.7	37	50.7	78	105.8	119	161.3
0.6	0.8	38	51.5	79	107.1	120	162.7
0.7	1.0	39	52.9	80	108.5	121	164.0
0.8	1.1	40	54.2	81	109.8	122	165.4
0.9	1.2	41	55.6	82	111.2	123	166.8
1	1.3	42	56.9	83	112.5	124	168.1
2	2.7	43	58.3	84	113.9	125	169.5
3	4.1	44	59.7	85	115.2	126	170.8
4	5.4	45	61.0	86	116.6	127	172.2
5	6.8	46	62.4	87	118.0	128	173.5
6	8.1	47	63.7	88	119.3	129	174.9
7	9.5	48	65.1	89	120.7	130	176.2
8	10.8	49	66.4	90	122.0	131	177.6
9	12.2	50	67.8	91	123.4	132	179.0
10	13.6	51	69.2	92	124.7	133	180.3
11	14.9	52	70.5	93	126.1	134	181.7
12	16.3	53	71.9	94	127.4	135	183.0
13	17.6	54	73.2	95	128.8	136	184.4
14	18.9	55	74.6	96	130.2	137	185.7
15	20.3	56	75.9	97	131.5	138	187.1
16	21.7	57	77.3	98	132.9	139	188.5
17	23.0	58	78.6	99	134.2	140	189.8
18	24.4	59	80.0	100	135.6	141	191.2
19	25.8	60	81.4	101	136.9	142	192.5
20	27.1	61	82.7	102	138.3	143	193.9
21	28.5	62	84.1	103	139.6	144	195.2
22	29.8	63	85.4	104	141.0	145	196.6
23	31.2	64	86.8	105	142.4	146	198.0
24	32.5	65	88.1	106	143.7	147	199.3
25	33.9	66	89.5	107	145.1	148	200.7
26	35.2	67	90.8	108	146.4	149	202.0
27	36.6	68	92.2	109	147.8	150	203.4
28	38.0	69	93.6	110	149.1	151	204.7
29	39.3	70	94.9	111	150.5	152	206.1
30	40.7	71	96.3	112	151.8	153	207.4
31	42.0	72	97.6	113	153.2	154	208.8
32	43.4	73	99.0	114	154.6	155	210.2

1-50 GENERAL INFORMATION AND MAINTENANCE

ENGLISH TO METRIC CONVERSION: FORCE

Force is presently measured in pounds (lbs.). This type of measurement is used to measure spring pressure, specifically how many pounds it takes to compress a spring. Our present force unit (the pound) will be replaced in SI metric measurements by the Newton (N). This term will eventually see use in specifications for electric motor brush spring pressures, valve spring pressures, etc.

To convert pounds (lbs.) to Newton (N): multiply the number of lbs. by 4.45

lbs	N	lbs	N	lbs	N	oz	N
0.01	0.04	21	93.4	59	262.4	1	0.3
0.02	0.09	22	97.9	60	266.9	2	0.6
0.03	0.13	23	102.3	61	271.3	3	0.8
0.04	0.18	24	106.8	62	275.8	4	1.1
0.05	0.22	25	111.2	63	280.2	5	1.4
0.06	0.27	26	115.6	64	284.6	6	1.7
0.07	0.31	27	120.1	65	289.1	7	2.0
0.08	0.36	28	124.6	66	293.6	8	2.2
0.09	0.40	29	129.0	67	298.0	9	2.5
0.1	0.4	30	133.4	68	302.5	10	2.8
0.2	0.9	31	137.9	69	306.9	11	3.1
0.3	1.3	32	142.3	70	311.4	12	3.3
0.4	1.8	33	146.8	71	315.8	13	3.6
0.5	2.2	34	151.2	72	320.3	14	3.9
0.6	2.7	35	155.7	73	324.7	15	4.2
0.7	3.1	36	160.1	74	329.2	16	4.4
0.8	3.6	37	164.6	75	333.6	17	4.7
0.9	4.0	38	169.0	76	338.1	18	5.0
1	4.4	39	173.5	77	342.5	19	5.3
2	8.9	40	177.9	78	347.0	20	5.6
3	13.4	41	182.4	79	351.4	21	5.8
4	17.8	42	186.8	80	355.9	22	6.1
5	22.2	43	191.3	81	360.3	23	6.4
6	26.7	44	195.7	82	364.8	24	6.7
7	31.1	45	200.2	83	369.2	25	7.0
8	35.6	46	204.6	84	373.6	26	7.2
9	40.0	47	209.1	85	378.1	27	7.5
10	44.5	48	213.5	86	382.6	28	7.8
11	48.9	49	218.0	87	387.0	29	8.1
12	53.4	50	224.4	88	391.4	30	8.3
13	57.8	51	226.9	89	395.9	31	8.6
14	62.3	52	231.3	90	400.3	32	8.9
15	66.7	53	235.8	91	404.8	33	9.2
16	71.2	54	240.2	92	409.2	34	9.4
17	75.6	55	244.6	93	413.7	35	9.7
18	80.1	56	249.1	94	418.1	36	10.0
19	84.5	57	253.6	95	422.6	37	10.3
20	89.0	58	258.0	96	427.0	38	10.6

2 ENGINE PERFORMANCE AND TUNE-UP

TUNE-UP PROCEDURES 2-2
SPARK PLUGS 2-2
   HEAT RANGE 2-2
   REMOVAL & INSTALLATION 2-2
   INSPECTION & GAPPING 2-3
SPARK PLUG WIRES 2-4
   TESTING 2-4
   REMOVAL & INSTALLATION 2-4
FIRING ORDERS 2-8
POINT TYPE IGNITION 2-9
BREAKER POINTS AND CONDENSER 2-9
   GENERAL INFORMATION 2-9
   INSPECTION 2-10
   REMOVAL & INSTALLATION 2-10
   DWELL ADJUSTMENT 2-10
ELECTRONIC IGNITION 2-11
DESCRIPTION AND OPERATION 2-11
   1972–83 MODELS 2-11
   1984 V8 ENGINES WITH DUAL PICKUP DISTRIBUTORS AND VACUUM ADVANCE 2-12
   1987–88 ENGINES WITH SINGLE PICKUP DISTRIBUTORS AND NO VACUUM ADVANCE; 1984–88 ENGINES WITH DUAL PICKUP DISTRIBUTORS AND ON VACUUM ADVANCE 2-12
DIAGNOSIS AND TESTING 2-12
   1972–83 MODELS 2-12
   1984 V8 ENGINES WITH DUAL PICKUP DISTRIBUTORS AND VACUUM ADVANCE 2-12
   1987–88 ENGINES WITH SINGLE PICKUP DISTRIBUTORS AND NO VACUUM ADVANCE; 1984–88 ENGINES WITH DUAL PICKUP DISTRIBUTORS AND ON VACUUM ADVANCE 2-15
ADJUSTMENTS 2-16
   1972–83 MODELS 2-16
   1984 V8 ENGINES WITH DUAL PICKUP AND VACUUM ADVANCE 2-18
   1984–88 V8 ENGINES WITH DUAL PICKUP AND NO VACUUM ADVANCE 2-18
COMPONENTS 2-18
   1984–88 CARBURETED ENGINES 2-18
   1988 FUEL INJECTED ENGINES 2-19
IGNITION TIMING 2-20
GENERAL INFORMATION 2-20
TIMING 2-20
   INSPECTION AND ADJUSTMENT 2-20
VALVE LASH 2-21
ADJUSTMENT 2-21
   GASOLINE ENGINES 2-21
IDLE SPEED AND MIXTURE ADJUSTMENTS 2-22
CARBURETED ENGINES 2-22
   ALL 1967 MODELS 2-22
   ALL 1967–76 MODELS AND 1977 CALIFORNIA MODELS 2-23
   HOLLEY 6145 CARBURETOR 2-23
   HOLLEY 2280/6280 CARBURETOR 2-25
   CARTER BBD CARBURETOR 2-26
   CARTER THERMO-QUAD CARBURETOR 2-29
   ROCHESTER QUADRAJET CARBURETOR 2-30
   HOLLEY 2210 CARBURETOR 2-32
   HOLLEY 2245 CARBURETOR 2-33
   HOLLEY 1945 CARBURETOR 2-34
FUEL INJECTED ENGINES 2-36
   MINIMUM IDLE SPEED ADJUSTMENT 2-36
SPECIFICATIONS CHARTS
TUNE-UP SPECIFICATIONS 2-5

2-2 ENGINE PERFORMANCE AND TUNE-UP

TUNE-UP PROCEDURES

♦ See Figure 1

In order to extract the full measure of performance and economy from your engine, it is essential that it be properly tuned at regular intervals. A regular tune-up will keep your vehicle's engine running smoothly and will prevent the annoying minor breakdowns and poor performance associated with an untuned engine.

A complete tune-up should be performed every 12,000 miles (20,280 km) or twelve months, whichever comes first. This interval should be halved if the vehicle is operated under severe conditions, such as trailer towing, prolonged idling, continual stop-and-start driving, or if starting or running problems are noticed. It is assumed that the routine maintenance described in Section 1 has been kept up, as this will have a decided effect on the results of a tune-up. All of the applicable steps of a tune-up should be followed in order, as the result is a cumulative one.

If the tune-up specifications on the vehicle emission control information sticker (located in the engine compartment) disagree with the Tune-Up Specifications chart in this section, the figures on the sticker must be used. The sticker often reflects changes made during the production run.

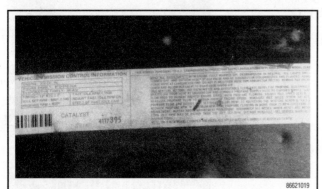

Fig. 1 Common vehicle emission control information sticker containing tune-up specifications

Spark Plugs

A common spark plug consists of a metal shell surrounding a ceramic insulator. A metal electrode extends downward through the center of the insulator and protrudes a small distance. Located at the end of the plug and attached to the side of the outer metal shell is the side electrode. The side electrode bends in at a 90° angle so that its tip is even with, and parallel to, the tip of the center electrode. The distance between these two electrodes (measured in thousandths of an inch) is called the spark plug gap. The spark plug in no way produces a spark, but merely provides a gap across which the current can arc. The coil produces anywhere from 20,000 to 40,000 volts which travels to the distributor, where it is distributed through the spark plug wires to the spark plugs. The current passes along the center electrode and jumps the gap to the side electrode; in so doing, it ignites the air/fuel mixture in the combustion chamber.

HEAT RANGE

♦ See Figure 2

Spark plug heat range is the ability of the plug to dissipate heat. The longer the insulator (or the farther it extends into the engine), the hotter the plug will operate; the shorter the insulator, the cooler it will operate. A plug that absorbs little heat and remains too cool will quickly accumulate deposits of oil and carbon, since it is not hot enough to burn them off. This leads to plug fouling and consequently to misfiring. A plug that absorbs too much heat will have no deposits, but, due to the excessive heat, the electrodes will burn away quickly and in some instances, pre-ignition may result. Pre-ignition takes place when plug tips get so hot that they glow sufficiently to ignite the fuel/air mixture before the actual spark occurs. This early ignition will usually cause a pinging during low speeds and heavy loads.

```
  1   2   3   4   5
 ‾‾‾ ‾‾‾ ‾‾‾ ‾‾‾ ‾‾‾
  R   4   5   T S  X
```

1 — R--INDICATES RESISTOR-TYPE PLUG.
2 — "4" INDICATES 14 mm THREADS.
3 — HEAT RANGE
4 — TS--TAPERED SEAT
    S--EXTENDED TIP
5 — SPECIAL GAP

Fig. 2 Example of a decoded spark plug number

The general rule of thumb for selecting the correct heat range when choosing a spark plug is: if most of your driving is long distance, high speed travel, use a colder plug; if most of your driving is stop-and-go, use a hotter plug. Original equipment plugs are compromise plugs, but most people never have occasion to change their plugs from the factory-recommended heat range.

REMOVAL & INSTALLATION

♦ See Figures 3 thru 8

➡ SPARK PLUGS DO NOT FOUL BY THEMSELVES! Check for what has caused the plug to foul. Installing new spark plugs will not correct a fouling condition.

A set of spark plugs usually requires replacement after about 20,000–30,000 miles (32,180–48,270 km), depending on your style of driving. In normal operation, plug gap increases about 0.001 in. (0.025mm) for every 1,000–2,500 miles (1,690–4,022 km). As the gap increases, the plug's voltage requirement also increases. It requires a greater voltage to jump the wider gap and about two-to-three times as much voltage to fire a plug at high speeds than at idle.

When you're removing spark plugs, you should work on one at a time. Don't start by removing the plug wires all at once, because unless you number them, they may become mixed up. Take a minute before you begin and number the wires with tape. The best location for numbering is near where the wires come out of the cap.

1. Twist the spark plug boot to remove the boot and wire from the plug. Do not pull on the wire itself, as this will ruin the wire.
2. If possible, use a brush to clean the area around the spark plug. Make sure all the dirt is removed so that none will enter the cylinder after the plug is removed.
3. Remove the spark plug using the proper size socket: either a ⅝ in. (16mm) or $FR13/16 in. (21mm) size socket depending on the engine. Fully seat the socket straight on the plug to avoid breakage or rounding off of the hexagonal wrenching portion, then turn the socket counterclockwise.
4. Once the plug is out, check it against the plugs shown to determine whether the plug is good or not. (This is crucial since plug readings are vital signs of engine condition.) A plug that is in good condition may be filed and re-used.
5. Check the plug gap.

To install:

6. Squirt a drop of penetrating oil on the threads of the new plug and install it. Don't oil the threads too heavily. Turn the plug in clockwise by hand until it is snug.
7. When the plug is finger-tight, tighten it with a wrench. If you don't have a torque wrench, tighten the plug firmly until the crush gasket seats, but be careful not to strip the threads of the plug or cylinder head.

➡ On some models equipped with electronic ignition, a small amount of silicone dielectric compound should be applied to the inside of the terminal boots whenever an ignition wire is disconnected from the spark plug or coil/distributor cap terminal.

8. Install the plug boot firmly over the plug. Proceed to the next plug.

ENGINE PERFORMANCE AND TUNE-UP   2-3

Fig. 3 A variety of tools and gauges are needed for spark plug service

Fig. 4 Mark spark plug wires prior to tune-up for easy replacement

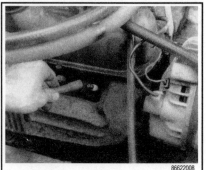

Fig. 5 Twist and pull on the rubber boot to remove the spark plug wires; never pull the wire itself

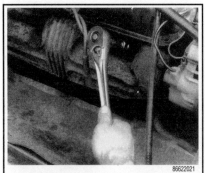

Fig. 6 Use the proper size socket to remove spark plugs; otherwise, you could damage threads in the cylinder head, or break the plugs

Fig. 7 After loosening, you may remove the plug with your hands as long as the engine is cold

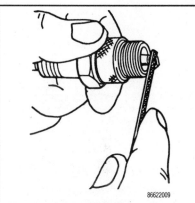

Fig. 8 A spark plug that is in good condition may be filed down and re-used

Fig. 9 Checking the spark plug gap with a feeler gauge

Fig. 10 Adjusting the spark plug gap

Fig. 11 If the standard plug is in good condition, the electrode may be filed flat— WARNING: do not file platinum plugs

INSPECTION & GAPPING

♦ See Figures 9, 10, 11, and 12

Check the plugs for deposits and wear. If they are not going to be replaced, clean the plugs thoroughly. Remember that any kind of deposit will decrease the efficiency of the plug. Plugs can be cleaned on a spark plug cleaning machine, which can sometimes be found in service stations, or you can do an acceptable job of cleaning with a stiff brush. If the plugs are cleaned, the electrodes must be filed flat. Use an ignition points file, not an emery board or the like, which will leave deposits. The electrodes must be filed perfectly flat with sharp edges; rounded edges reduce the spark plug voltage by as much as 50%.

Check spark plug gap before installation. The ground electrode (the L-shaped one connected to the body of the plug) must be parallel to the center electrode and the specified size wire gauge (please refer to the Tune-Up Specifications chart for details) must pass between the electrodes with a slight drag.

➡ NEVER adjust the gap on a used platinum type spark plug.

Always check the gap on new plugs as they are not always set correctly at the factory. Do not use a flat feeler gauge when measuring the gap on a used plug, because the reading may be inaccurate. A round-wire type gapping tool is the best way to check the gap. The correct gauge should pass through the electrode gap with a slight drag. If you're in doubt, try one size smaller and one larger. The smaller gauge should go through easily, while the larger one shouldn't go through at all. Wire gapping tools usually have a bending tool attached. Use that to adjust the side electrode until the proper distance is obtained. Absolutely never attempt to bend the center electrode. Also, be careful not to bend the side electrode too far or too often as it may weaken and break off within the engine, requiring removal of the cylinder head to retrieve it.

2-4 ENGINE PERFORMANCE AND TUNE-UP

A normally worn spark plug should have light tan or gray deposits on the firing tip.

A carbon fouled plug, identified by soft, sooty, black deposits, may indicate an improperly tuned vehicle. Check the air cleaner, ignition components and engine control system.

This spark plug has been **left in the engine too long,** as evidenced by the extreme gap- Plugs with such an extreme gap can cause misfiring and stumbling accompanied by a noticeable lack of power.

An oil fouled spark plug indicates an engine with worn poston rings and/or bad valve seals allowing excessive oil to enter the chamber.

A physically damaged spark plug may be evidence of severe detonation in that cylinder. Watch that cylinder carefully between services, as a continued detonation will not only damage the plug, but could also damage the engine.

A bridged or almost bridged spark plug, identified by a build-up between the electrodes caused by excessive carbon or oil build-up on the plug.

Fig. 12 Inspect the spark plug to determine engine running conditions

Spark Plug Wires

TESTING

Visually inspect the spark plug cables for burns, cuts, or breaks in the insulation. Check the spark plug boots and the nipples on the distributor cap and coil. Replace any damaged wiring. If no physical damage is obvious, the wires can be checked with an ohmmeter for excessive resistance.

REMOVAL & INSTALLATION

1. Mark all the spark plug wires near the cap with their cylinder number for identification purposes.
2. Grasp and twist the spark plug boot until the boot comes free of the plug. Do not pull on the wire.
3. Repeat for the other spark plug wires.
4. When installing a new set of spark plug cables, replace the cables one at a time so there will be no mix-up. Start by replacing the longest cable first. Install the boot firmly over the spark plug. Route the wire exactly the same as the original. Insert the nipple firmly into the tower on the distributor cap.
5. Repeat the process for each cable.

ENGINE PERFORMANCE AND TUNE-UP

TUNE-UP SPECIFICATIONS
Gasoline Engines

Years	Engine	Engine Displacement Liters	Spark Plugs Type	Spark Plugs Gap (in.)	Distributor Point Gap (in.)	Distributor Dwell (deg.)	Ignition Timing (deg.) Man. Trans.	Ignition Timing (deg.) Auto. Trans.	Valve* Clearance In.	Valve* Clearance Exh.	Idle Speed Man. Trans.	Idle Speed Auto. Trans.
1972	225	3.7	N11Y	0.035	Electronic		ⓡ	ⓡ	0.012	0.024	800	ⓡ
	318	5.2	N11Y	0.035	Electronic		ⓡ	ⓡ	Hyd.	Hyd.	750	750
	360	5.9	N12Y	0.035	Electronic		TDC	ⓡ	Hyd.	Hyd.	750	750
	400	6.6	ⓡ	0.035	Electronic		ⓡ	ⓡ	Hyd.	Hyd.	750	750
1973	225	3.7	N11Y	0.035	Electronic		ⓡ	ⓡ	0.012	0.024	800	ⓡ
	318	5.2	N11Y	0.035	Electronic		TDC	ⓡ	Hyd.	Hyd.	750	750
	360	5.9	N12Y	0.035	Electronic		ⓡ	ⓡ	Hyd.	Hyd.	750	750
	400	6.6	ⓡ	0.035	Electronic		ⓡ	ⓡ	Hyd.	Hyd.	750	750
	440	7.2	J11Y	0.035	Electronic		7.5B	ⓡ	Hyd.	Hyd.	700	700
1974	225	3.7	N11Y	0.035	Electronic		ⓡ	ⓡ	0.012	0.024	800	ⓡ
	318	5.2	N11Y	0.035	Electronic		ⓡ	ⓡ	Hyd.	Hyd.	750	750
	360	5.9	N12Y	0.035	Electronic		TDC	ⓡ	Hyd.	Hyd.	750	750
	400	6.6	ⓡ	0.035	Electronic		ⓡ	ⓡ	Hyd.	Hyd.	750	750
	440	7.2	J11Y	0.035	Electronic		7.5B	ⓡ	Hyd.	Hyd.	700	700
1975	225	3.7	RBL11Y	0.035	Electronic		ⓡ	ⓡ	0.010	0.020	ⓡ	ⓡ
	318	5.2	RN11Y	0.035	Electronic		TDC	ⓡ	Hyd.	Hyd.	ⓡ	ⓡ
	360	5.9	RN12Y	0.035	Electronic		ⓡ	ⓡ	Hyd.	Hyd.	750	750
	400	6.6	RJ11Y	0.035	Electronic		TDC	ⓡ	Hyd.	Hyd.	700	700
	440	7.2	RJ11Y	0.035	Electronic		2B	2B	Hyd.	Hyd.	—	700
1976	225	3.7	BL11Y	0.035	Electronic		TDC	TDC	0.012	0.024	800	750
	318	5.2	N11Y	0.035	Electronic		ⓡ	ⓡ	Hyd.	Hyd.	ⓡ	ⓡ
	360	5.9	N12Y	0.035	Electronic		ⓡ	ⓡ	Hyd.	Hyd.	ⓡ	ⓡ
	400	6.6	J11Y	0.035	Electronic		8B	8B	Hyd.	Hyd.	700	700
	440	7.2	RJ11Y	0.035	Electronic		2B	2B	Hyd.	Hyd.	—	700
1977	225	3.7	RBL11Y	0.035	Electronic		TDC	TDC	0.012	0.024	800	750
	318	5.2	RN11Y	0.035	Electronic		ⓡ	ⓡ	Hyd.	Hyd.	ⓡ	ⓡ
	360	5.9	RN12Y	0.035	Electronic		TDC	ⓡ	Hyd.	Hyd.	750	700
	400	6.6	RJ11Y	0.035	Electronic		2B	2B	0.010	0.020	750	700
	440	7.2	RJ11Y	0.035	Electronic		—	8B	Hyd.	Hyd.	—	700
1978	225	3.7	RBL11Y	0.035	Electronic		TDC	TDC	0.010	0.020	800	750
	318	5.2	RN11Y	0.035	Electronic		ⓡ	ⓡ	Hyd.	Hyd.	ⓡ	ⓡ
	360	5.9	RN12Y	0.035	Electronic		TDC	ⓡ	Hyd.	Hyd.	750	700
	400	6.6	RJ11Y	0.035	Electronic		2B	2B	Hyd.	Hyd.	750	700
	440	7.2	RJ11Y	0.035	Electronic		—	8B	Hyd.	Hyd.	—	700
1979	225	3.7	RBL15Y	0.035	Electronic		TDC	ⓡ	0.010	0.020	ⓡ	ⓡ
	318	5.2	N12YC	0.035	Electronic		ⓡ	ⓡ	Hyd.	Hyd.	ⓡ	ⓡ
	360	5.9	N12YC	0.035	Electronic		ⓡ	ⓡ	Hyd.	Hyd.	ⓡ	ⓡ
	400	6.6	RJ11Y	0.035	Electronic		2B	2B	Hyd.	Hyd.	700	700
	440	7.2	RJ11Y	0.035	Electronic		—	8B	Hyd.	Hyd.	—	700

TUNE-UP SPECIFICATIONS
Gasoline Engines

Years	Engine	Engine Displacement Liters	Spark Plugs Type	Spark Plugs Gap (in.)	Distributor Point Gap (in.)	Distributor Dwell (deg.)	Ignition Timing (deg.) Man. Trans.	Ignition Timing (deg.) Auto. Trans.	Valve* Clearance In.	Valve* Clearance Exh.	Idle Speed Man. Trans.	Idle Speed Auto. Trans.
1967	225	3.7	N11Y	0.035	0.017-0.023	40-45	ⓡ	ⓡ	0.012	0.024	ⓡ	ⓡ
	251	4.1	J7	0.035	0.017-0.023	36-42	5B	—	0.010	0.014	550	—
	318	5.2	ⓡ	0.035	0.014-0.019	28-32	5B	ⓡ	Hyd.	Hyd.	ⓡ	ⓡ
	383	6.3	J13Y	0.035	0.014-0.019	28-32	ⓡ	ⓡ	Hyd.	Hyd.	ⓡ	ⓡ
	413	6.8	N6	0.035	0.014-0.019	28-32	5B	—	Hyd.	Hyd.	500	—
1968	198	3.2	N11Y	0.035	0.017-0.023	42-47	ⓡ	—	0.012	0.024	ⓡ	—
	225	3.7	N11Y	0.035	0.017-0.023	42-47	TDC	TDC	0.012	0.024	ⓡ	ⓡ
	251	4.1	J7	0.035	0.017-0.023	36-42	5B	—	0.010	0.014	550	—
	318	5.2	N11Y	0.035	0.014-0.019	30-35	ⓡ	ⓡ	Hyd.	Hyd.	ⓡ	ⓡ
	383	6.3	J13Y	0.035	0.014-0.019	30-35	TDC	7.5B	Hyd.	Hyd.	ⓡ	ⓡ
	413	6.8	N6	0.035	0.014-0.019	28-32	5B	—	Hyd.	Hyd.	700	—
1969	225	3.7	N11Y	0.035	0.017-0.023	42-47	TDC	TDC	0.012	0.024	ⓡ	ⓡ
	318	5.2	N11Y	0.035	0.014-0.019	30-35	5B	5B	Hyd.	Hyd.	ⓡ	ⓡ
	383	6.3	J13Y	0.035	0.014-0.019	30-35	TDC	7.5B	Hyd.	Hyd.	700	600
1970	225	3.7	N11Y	0.035	0.017-0.023	42-47	TDC	TDC	0.012	0.024	ⓡ	ⓡ
	318	5.2	N11Y	0.035	0.014-0.019	30-35	5B	5B	Hyd.	Hyd.	ⓡ	ⓡ
	383	6.3	J13Y	0.035	0.014-0.019	30-35	TDC	7.5B	Hyd.	Hyd.	700	600
1971	225	3.7	N11Y	0.035	0.017-0.023	42-47	TDC	TDC	0.012	0.024	ⓡ	ⓡ
	318	5.2	N11Y	0.035	0.014-0.019	30-35	5B	5B	Hyd.	Hyd.	ⓡ	ⓡ
	383	6.3	J13Y	0.035	0.014-0.019	30-35	TDC	7.5B	Hyd.	Hyd.	700	600

2-6 ENGINE PERFORMANCE AND TUNE-UP

TUNE-UP SPECIFICATIONS
Gasoline Engines

Years	Engine	Engine Displacement Liters	Spark Plugs Type	Spark Plugs Gap (in.)	Distributor Point Dwell (deg.)	Distributor Point Gap (in.)	Ignition Timing (deg.) Man. Trans.	Ignition Timing (deg.) Auto. Trans.	Valve* Clearance In.	Valve* Clearance Exh.	Idle Speed Man. Trans.	Idle Speed Auto. Trans.
1980	225	3.7	RBL16Y	0.035	Electronic		12B	12B	0.010	0.020	①	②
	318	5.2	RN12YC	0.035	Electronic		③	④	Hyd.	Hyd.	⑤	⑥
	360	5.9	RN12YC	0.035	Electronic		⑦	⑧	Hyd.	Hyd.	⑨	⑩
1981	225	3.7	RBL16Y	0.035	Electronic		12B	16B	Hyd.	Hyd.	⑪	⑫
	318	5.2	RN12YC	0.035	Electronic		⑬	⑭	Hyd.	Hyd.	⑮	⑯
	360	5.9	RN12YC	0.035	Electronic		12B	16B	Hyd.	Hyd.	⑰	⑱
1982	225	3.7	RBL16Y	0.035	Electronic		12B	16B	Hyd.	Hyd.	⑲	⑳
	318	5.2	RN12YC	0.035	Electronic		㉑	㉒	Hyd.	Hyd.	750	750
	360	5.9	RN12YC	0.035	Electronic		㉓	㉔	Hyd.	Hyd.	㉕	㉖
1983	225	3.7	RBL16Y	0.035	Electronic		12B	16B	Hyd.	Hyd.	㉗	㉘
	318	5.2	RN12YC	0.035	Electronic		㉙	㉚	Hyd.	Hyd.	㉛	㉜
	360	5.9	RN12YC	0.035	Electronic		㉝	16B	Hyd.	Hyd.	725	750
1984	225	3.7	RBL16Y	0.035	Electronic		12B	16B	Hyd.	Hyd.	㉞	㉟
	318	5.2	RN12YC	0.035	Electronic		㊱	㊲	Hyd.	Hyd.	㊳	㊴
	360	5.9	RN12YC	0.035	Electronic		—	㊵	Hyd.	Hyd.	—	㊶
1985	225	3.7	RBL16Y	0.035	Electronic		12B	16B	Hyd.	Hyd.	㊷	725
	318	5.2	RN12YC	0.035	Electronic		㊸	㊹	Hyd.	Hyd.	㊺	㊻
	360	5.9	RN12YC	0.035	Electronic		6B	16B	Hyd.	Hyd.	800	㊼
1986	225	3.7	RBL16Y	0.035	Electronic		12B	16B	Hyd.	Hyd.	725	750
	318	5.2	RN12YC	0.035	Electronic		㊽	㊾	Hyd.	Hyd.	㊿	④
	360	5.9	RN12YC	0.035	Electronic		㊽	16B	Hyd.	Hyd.	①	②
1987	225	3.7	RBL16Y	0.035	Electronic		12B	16B	Hyd.	Hyd.	⑧	⑧
	318	5.2	RN12YC	0.035	Electronic		⑥	⑤	Hyd.	Hyd.	⑤	⑥
	360	5.9	RN12YC	0.035	Electronic		13B	⑦	Hyd.	Hyd.	800	800
1988	238	3.9	RN12YC	0.035	Electronic		10B	10B	Hyd.	Hyd.	750	750
	318	5.2	RN12YC	0.035	Electronic		10B	10B	Hyd.	Hyd.	700	700
	360	5.9	RN12YC	0.035	Electronic		10B	10B	Hyd.	Hyd.	800	⑨

*Valves are adjusted HOT
① Exc. high altitude: 12B
② High altitude: 8B
③ Exc. high altitude, Calif. and heavy duty Canada: 12B
④ Exc. high altitude, Calif. and heavy duty Canada: 8B
⑤ Exc. high altitude: 700
⑥ Exc. high altitude, Calif. and California: 650
  Heavy duty Canada: 750
⑦ Light duty: 12B
⑧ Light duty: 16B
⑨ Heavy duty: 10B

TUNE-UP SPECIFICATION FOOTNOTES

① 49 states and Canada: 800
② High altitude: 750
③ 49 states heavy duty: 750
④ Calif. and Canada heavy duty: 800
⑤ 49 states and Canada: 800
⑥ High altitude: 710
⑦ 49 states and Canada heavy duty: 750
⑧ California heavy duty: 800
⑨ Exc. Calif.: 750
⑩ Calif.: 775
⑪ High altitude and Calif.: 8B
⑫ 49 states and Canada: 12B
⑬ Heavy duty Canada: 8B
⑭ High altitude: 650
⑮ Calif.: 725
⑯ 49 states and Canada: 700
⑰ Heavy duty Canada: 750
⑱ High altitude and Calif.: 650
⑲ 49 states: 700
⑳ Canada: 750
㉑ Light duty: 16B
㉒ Heavy duty: 6B
㉓ High altitude: 800
㉔ w/o Clean Air System: 550
㉕ w/Clean Air System: 650
㉖ w/Clean Air System: 500
㉗ Carb. #WW3-300—650
㉘ Carb. #WW3-302—650
㉙ Carb. #WW3-304—500
㉚ Carb. #WW3-299—600
㉛ Carb. #WW3-301—600
㉜ Exc. Calif.: 725
㉝ Calif.: 775
㉞ Exc. heavy Canada: 8B
㉟ Canada heavy: 6B
㊱ Exc. heavy Canada: 650
㊲ Heavy duty: 12B
㊳ Heavy duty, exc. distributor #4145399: 10B
㊴ Heavy duty, w/distributor #4145399: 13B
㊵ High altitude: 750
㊶ 49 states light duty: 710
㊷ All others: 800
㊸ All light duty: 12B
㊹ Heavy duty w/distributor #4111950: 10B
㊺ All other heavy: 13B
㊻ Without Clean Air Package: 5B
㊼ With Clean Air Package: TDC
㊽ With distributor #2444256: J14Y
㊾ All others: N11Y
㊿ With distributor #2642718: 10B
① All others: 5B
② Without Clean Air Package: 12.5B
③ With Clean Air Package: TDC

① US, exc. high altitude and heavy duty: 800
② Without Clean Air Package: 12.5B
③ With Clean Air Package: 5B
④ 49 states heavy duty: 550
⑤ Without Clean Air Package: 650
⑥ With Clean Air Package: 550
⑦ Without Clean Air Package: 600
⑧ With Clean Air Package: 650
⑨ Without Clean Air Package: 500
⑩ With Clean Air Package: 600
⑪ 49 states: 600
⑫ Calif.: 800
⑬ 49 states: 600
⑭ Calif.: 800
⑮ Canada: 725
⑯ 49 states: 600
⑰ Calif.: 800
⑱ Canada: 750
⑲ Light duty 2-bbl 49 states and Canada: 10B
⑳ Calif. light duty 4-bbl: 12B
㉑ Light duty 2-bbl Canada: 2A
㉒ Light duty 2-bbl US: 16B
㉓ Light duty 4-bbl Canada: 10B
㉔ Heavy duty 4-bbl: 12B
㉕ Light duty 2-bbl 49 states: 650
㉖ Light duty 2-bbl Canada: 750
㉗ Light duty 4-bbl Canada: 750
㉘ Light duty 4-bbl 49 states: 650
㉙ Light duty 2-bbl Canada: 750
㉚ Light duty 4-bbl: 750
㉛ Heavy duty 2-bbl Canada: 4B
㉜ Heavy duty 4-bbl: 4B
㉝ Light duty 4-bbl 49 states US: 16B
㉞ Light duty 4-bbl 49 states: 600
㉟ Heavy duty 2-bbl Canada: 6B
㊱ Light duty 4-bbl Calif.: 750
㊲ Calif. 4-bbl: 10B
㊳ Light duty 4-bbl 49 states: 625
㊴ 49 states and Canada: 2B
㊵ Light duty 49 states and Canada: 750
㊶ Heavy duty Calif.: TDC
㊷ Light duty Calif.: TDC
㊸ Light duty Canada: 800
㊹ Heavy duty Calif.: 700
㊺ Light duty: 750
㊻ Heavy duty 49 states and Canada: TDC
㊼ 49 states and Canada: 750
㊽ Canada: 725
㊾ US: 700
㊿ US: 725
① Canada: 750

① With ESA spark system: 16B
② With ECU spark system: 12B
③ Heavy duty Canada with ECU spark system: 2A
④ Calif. with ESA spark system: 740
⑤ With ECU spark system: 760
⑥ 49 states with ESA spark system: 800
⑦ 49 states with ECU spark system: 700
⑧ Calif. with ESA spark system: 760
⑨ Canada with ECU spark system: 760
⑩ Light duty: 14B
⑪ Heavy duty without catalyst: 10B
⑫ Light duty with catalyst: 760
⑬ Light duty w/thout catalyst: 725
⑭ Heavy duty: 700
⑮ Except Calif.: 12B
⑯ Calif.: 8B
⑰ Except Calif.: 675
⑱ Calif.: 800
⑲ 49 states and Canada 2-bbl: 2A
⑳ Light duty Calif. 4-bbl: 6B
㉑ 49 states and Canada 2-bbl: 12B
㉒ Medium duty Calif. 4-bbl: 8B
㉓ Light duty Canada 4-bbl: 8B
㉔ 49 states and Canada 4-bbl: 8B
㉕ Medium duty Calif. 4-bbl: 6B
㉖ 49 states and Canada 2-bbl: 750
㉗ Calif. 4-bbl: 6B
㉘ 49 states and Canada 2-bbl: 680
㉙ All others: 6B
㉚ Heavy duty Canada 2-bbl: 4B
㉛ Calif. 4-bbl: 10B
㉜ 40 states and Canada 4-bbl: 4B
㉝ 49 states and Canada 4-bbl: 10B
㉞ 49 states 4-bbl: 4B
㉟ Calif. medium duty 4-bbl: 10B
㊱ Canada 4-bbl: 10B
㊲ Calif. heavy duty 4-bbl: 4B
㊳ All 2-bbl and Calif. medium duty 4-bbl: 750
㊴ All other heavy duty 4-bbl: 700
㊵ 49 states: 600
㊶ Calif.: 675
㊷ Canada: 800
㊸ 49 states and Canada 2-bbl: 12B
㊹ Light duty 2-bbl: 2A
㊺ 49 states 4-bbl: 8B
㊻ 49 states US 4-bbl: 8B
㊼ Canada 2-bbl: 12A
㊽ Canada light duty 4-bbl: 10B
㊾ Calif. medium duty 4-bbl: 10B
㊿ Heavy duty US 4-bbl: 8B

TUNE-UP SPECIFICATION FOOTNOTES

(73) 49 states and Canada 2-bbl: 600
Heavy duty Canada 2-bbl: 750
US 4-bbl: 750
(74) 49 states and Canada 2-bbl: 600
Heavy duty Canada 2-bbl: 750
Canada 4-bbl: 750
Calif. medium duty 4-bbl: 750
Heavy duty US 4-bbl: 750
(75) Calif. medium duty 4-bbl: 10B
49 states and Canada light duty 4-bbl: 12B
Heavy duty Calif. 4-bbl: 10B
49 states and Canada heavy duty 4-bbl: 4B
(76) 2-bbl heavy duty Canada: 4B
Calif. medium duty 4-bbl: 10B
49 states and Canada light duty 4-bbl with air pump: 12B
Heavy duty Calif. 4-bbl: 10B
49 states and Canada heavy duty 4-bbl: 4B
49 states and Canada heavy duty with aspirator: 10B
(77) Calif. medium duty 4-bbl: 750
49 states and Canada light duty 4-bbl: 650
Calif. heavy duty 4-bbl: 750
49 states and Canada heavy duty 4-bbl: 700
(78) Heavy duty Canada 2-bbl: 750
Calif. medium duty 4-bbl: 750
49 states and Canada light duty 4-bbl with air pump: 650
Calif. heavy duty 4-bbl: 750
49 states and Canada heavy duty 4-bbl: 700
49 states and Canada light duty with aspirator: 750
(79) 49 states 1-bbl: 600
Calif. 1-bbl: 800
Canada 1-bbl: 725
49 states and Canada 2-bbl: 700
(80) 49 states 1-bbl: 600
Calif. 1-bbl: 800
Canada 1-bbl: 725
(81) 49 states and Canada 2-bbl: 12B
Heavy duty Canada 2-bbl: 2A
US light duty 4-bbl: 12B
US heavy duty 4-bbl: 8B
(82) 49 states and Canada 2-bbl: 12B
Heavy duty Canada 2-bbl: 2A
US light duty 4-bbl: 16B
US heavy duty 4-bbl: 8B
(83) 2-bbl Canada: 4B
4-bbl US and Canada: 4B
4-bbl Calif.: 10B
(84) 2-bbl Canada: 750
4-bbl US and Canada: 700
4-bbl Calif.: 750
(85) Light duty: TDC
Heavy duty: 2.5A
(86) Holley 1945: 750
Carter BBS: 800
(87) Light duty: TDC
Heavy duty: 2.5A
(88) Light duty: 2.5B
Heavy duty: TDC
(89) Light duty: J13Y
Heavy duty: J11Y
(90) Light duty: 7.5B
Heavy duty: 2.5B
(91) 49 states: 10B
Calif. light duty: 5B
Calif. heavy duty: 7.5B
(92) With Clean Air System: 5A
Without Clean Air System: 5B
(93) 49 states 1-bbl: 2B
Canada 2-bbl: 2A
49 states and Canada 2-bbl: TDC
Calif. manual trans.: TDC
Calif. automatic trans.: 2A
(94) 49 states and Canada 1-bbl: 750
49 states and Canada 2-bbl: 700
Calif.: 750
(95) Light duty: 2B
Heavy duty: 2A
(96) Light duty: 2B
Heavy duty: 2A
High altitude: 6B
(97) Light duty: 6B
Heavy duty: TDC
Calif.: TDC
(98) Light duty: 700
Heavy duty: 750
Calif.: 700
(99) Heavy duty Calif.: 700
All others: 750

866220E1

TUNE-UP SPECIFICATIONS

Diesel Engines

Years	Engine	Engine Displacement Liters	Inject. Timing	Nozzle Opening Pressure (psi)	Curb Idle Speed (rpm)	Maximum Speed (rpm)	Valve Clearance Cold (in.) Int.	Valve Clearance Cold (in.) Exh.	Maximum Compress Pressure (psi)
1978	243	4.0	18B	1706–1848	600–700	3950–4050	0.012	0.012	426
1979	243	4.0	18B	1706–1848	600–700	3950–4050	0.012	0.012	426

866220A2

2-8 ENGINE PERFORMANCE AND TUNE-UP

FIRING ORDERS

▶ See Figures 13 thru 18

➡ To avoid confusion, remove and tag the spark plug wires one at a time, for replacement.

If a distributor is not keyed for installation with only one orientation, it could have been removed previously and rewired. The resultant wiring would hold the correct firing order, but could change the relative placement of the plug towers in relation to the engine. For this reason it is imperative that you label all wires before disconnecting any of them. Also, before removal, compare the current wiring with the accompanying illustrations. If the current wiring does not match, make notes in your book to reflect how your engine is wired.

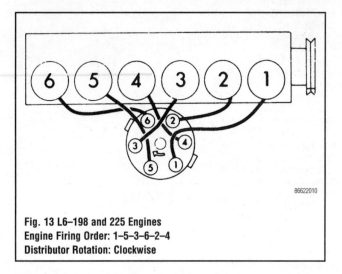

Fig. 13 L6-198 and 225 Engines
Engine Firing Order: 1-5-3-6-2-4
Distributor Rotation: Clockwise

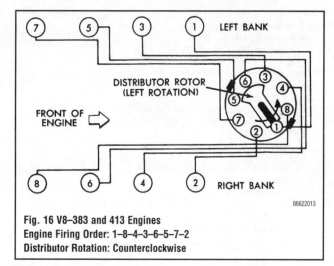

Fig. 16 V8-383 and 413 Engines
Engine Firing Order: 1-8-4-3-6-5-7-2
Distributor Rotation: Counterclockwise

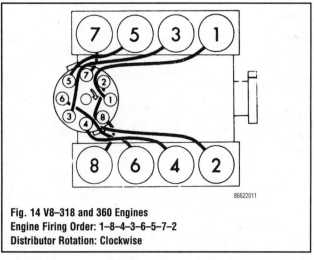

Fig. 14 V8-318 and 360 Engines
Engine Firing Order: 1-8-4-3-6-5-7-2
Distributor Rotation: Clockwise

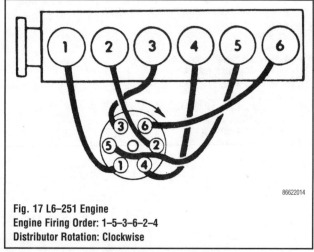

Fig. 17 L6-251 Engine
Engine Firing Order: 1-5-3-6-2-4
Distributor Rotation: Clockwise

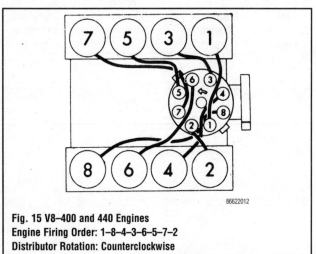

Fig. 15 V8-400 and 440 Engines
Engine Firing Order: 1-8-4-3-6-5-7-2
Distributor Rotation: Counterclockwise

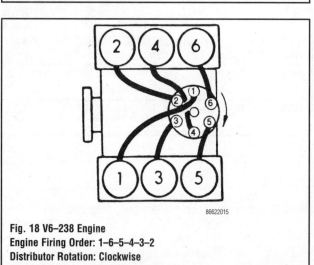

Fig. 18 V6-238 Engine
Engine Firing Order: 1-6-5-4-3-2
Distributor Rotation: Clockwise

ENGINE PERFORMANCE AND TUNE-UP

POINT TYPE IGNITION

All 1967–71 and some 1972 trucks use breaker point type ignition systems.

Breaker Points and Condenser

GENERAL INFORMATION

♦ See Figure 19

The points function as a circuit breaker for the primary circuit of the ignition system. The ignition coil must boost the 12 volts of electrical pressure supplied by the battery to as much as 25,000 volts in order to fire the plugs. To do this, the coil depends on the points and the condenser to make a clean break in the primary circuit.

The coil has both primary and secondary circuits. When the ignition is turned **ON**, the battery supplies voltage through the coil to the points. The points are connected to ground, completing the primary circuit. As the current passes through the coil, a magnetic field is created in the iron center core of the coil. As the cam in the distributor turns, the points open and the primary circuit collapses. The magnetic field in the primary circuit of the coil cuts through the secondary circuit winding around the iron core. Because of the scientific phenomenon called electromagnetic induction, the battery voltage is increased to a level sufficient to fire the spark plugs.

When the points open, the electrical charge in the primary circuit jumps the gap created between the two open contacts of the points. If this electrical charge were not transferred elsewhere, the metal contacts of the points would melt and the gap between the points would start to change rapidly. If this gap is not maintained, the points will not break the primary circuit. If the primary circuit is

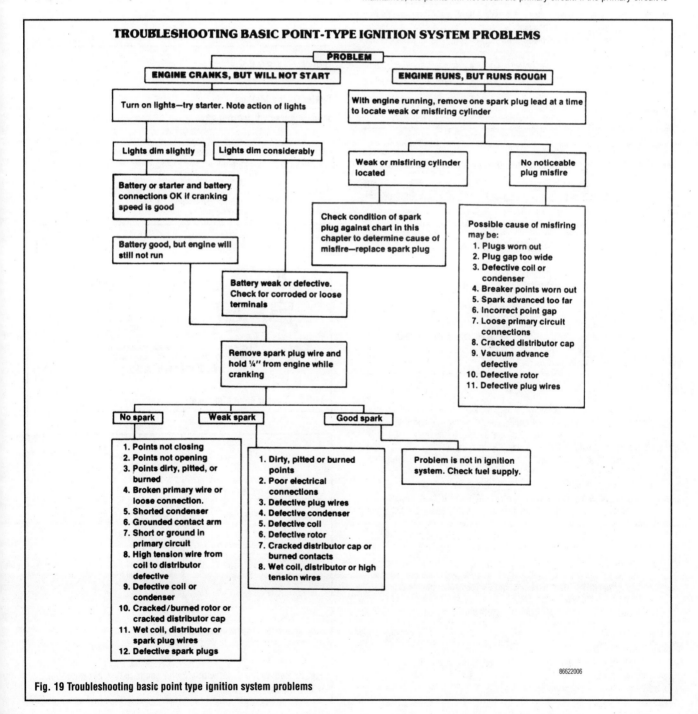

Fig. 19 Troubleshooting basic point type ignition system problems

2-10 ENGINE PERFORMANCE AND TUNE-UP

not broken, the secondary circuit will not have enough voltage to fire the spark plugs.

The function of the condenser is to absorb excessive voltage from the points when they open and, thus, prevent the points from becoming pitted or burned. For this reason, it is recommended that whenever you replace a set of points, you always replace the condenser at the same time.

It is interesting to note that the above cycle must be completed by the ignition system every time spark occurs. In a V8 engine, all of the spark plugs fire once for every two revolutions of the crankshaft. That means that in one revolution, four spark plugs fire. So, when the engine is at an idle speed of 800 rpm, the points are opening and closing 3,200 times a minute.

There are two ways to check the breaker point gap: it can be done with a feeler gauge or a dwell meter. Either way you set the points, you are basically adjusting the amount of time that the points remain open. The time is measured in degrees of distributor rotation. When you measure the gap between the breaker points with a feeler gauge, you are setting the maximum amount the points will open when the rubbing block on the points is on a high point of the distributor cam. When you adjust the points with a dwell meter, you are adjusting the number of degrees that the points will remain closed before they start to open as a high point of the distributor cam approaches the rubbing block of the points.

When you change the point gap or dwell, you will also affect the ignition timing. So, if the point gap or dwell is changed, the ignition timing must also be adjusted.

INSPECTION

1. Disconnect the coil high tension wire from the top of the distributor.

➡It should not be necessary to remove the spark plug wires in order to remove the cap.

2. Remove the distributor cap by prying off the spring clips on the sides of the cap.
3. Inspect the cap for any cracks, burn marks or excessive wear. If there are any signs of this, replace the cap.
4. Remove the rotor from the distributor shaft by pulling it straight up. Examine the condition of the rotor. If it is cracked or the metal tip is excessively worn or burned, it should be replaced.
5. Pry open the contacts of the points with a suitable tool and check the condition of the contacts. If they are excessively worn, burned or pitted, they should be replaced.
6. If the points are in good condition, adjust them, then install the rotor and the distributor cap. If the points need to be replaced, follow the procedure below.

REMOVAL & INSTALLATION

♦ See Figure 20

1. Remove the coil high tension wire from the top of the distributor cap, then remove the cap and rotor, as described in the preceding inspection procedure.
2. Loosen the screw that holds the condenser lead to the body of the breaker points, then remove the condenser lead from the points.
3. Remove the screw that holds and grounds the condenser to the distributor body. Remove the condenser from the distributor and discard it.
4. Remove the points assembly attaching screws and adjustment lockscrews. A tool with a magnetic tip will come in handy, to help prevent dropping a screw into the distributor. (A dropped screw could necessitate distributor removal.)
5. Remove the points, then wipe off the cam and apply new cam lubricant. Discard the old set of points.

To install:

6. Position the new set of points with the locating peg in the hole on the breaker plate, then install the screws that hold the assembly onto the plate. Do not tighten them all the way.
7. Attach the new condenser to the plate with the ground screw.
8. Attach the condenser lead to the points at the proper location.
9. Apply a small amount of cam lubricant to the shaft where the rubbing block makes contact.
10. Perform a dwell adjustment, as described below, before attaching the rotor and distributor cap.

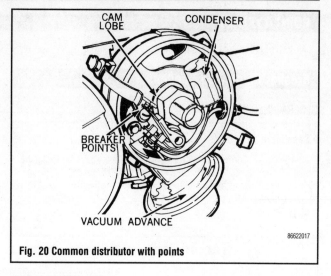

Fig. 20 Common distributor with points

DWELL ADJUSTMENT

Feeler Gauge Method

♦ See Figures 21, 22 and 23

1. If the contact points of the assembly are not parallel, bend the stationary contact to provide alignment across the entire surface of the contacts. Bend only the stationary bracket part of the point assembly, not the movable contact.
2. Turn the engine until the rubbing block of the points is on one of the high points of the distributor cam. You can do this by either turning the ignition switch to the **START** position and releasing it quickly (bumping the engine), or

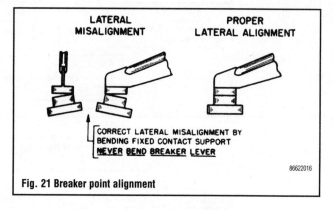

Fig. 21 Breaker point alignment

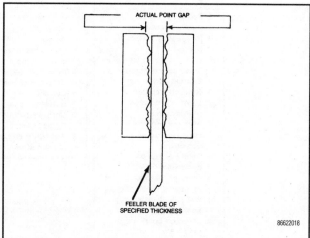

Fig. 22 Setting the dwell with a feeler gauge is less accurate than with a meter

ENGINE PERFORMANCE AND TUNE-UP

by using a wrench on the bolt that holds the crankshaft pulley to the crankshaft. Be sure to remove the wrench before starting the engine!

3. Place the correct size feeler gauge between the contacts. Make sure it is parallel with the contact surfaces.

4. With your free hand, insert a suitable tool into the notch provided for adjustment or into the eccentric adjusting screw, then twist it to either increase or decrease the gap to the proper setting.

5. Tighten the adjustment lockscrew and recheck the contact gap to make sure that it didn't change when the lockscrew was tightened.

6. Install the rotor, making sure it is firmly seated on the distributor shaft.

7. Install the distributor cap. Align the tab in the base of the distributor cap with the notch in the distributor body. Make sure that the cap is firmly seated on the distributor and that the retainer springs are in place.

8. Install the high tension wire. Make sure that the end of the high tension wire is firmly placed in the top of the distributor and the coil.

Dwell Meter Method

1. Adjust the points with a feeler gauge, as previously described, then attach the rotor and distributor cap.

2. Connect the dwell meter to the ignition circuit according to the manufacturer's instructions. One lead of the meter is connected to a ground and the other lead is connected to the distributor post on the coil. An adapter is usually provided for this purpose.

3. If the dwell meter has a set line on it, adjust the meter to zero the indicator.

4. Start the engine.

➡ **Be careful when working on any vehicle while the engine is running. Make sure that the transmission is in Neutral and that the parking brake is applied. Keep hands, clothing, tools, and test instrument wires clear of the rotating fan blades.**

5. Observe the reading on the dwell meter. If the reading is within the specified range, turn the engine **OFF**, then remove the meter.

6. If the reading is above the specified range, the breaker point gap is too small. If the reading is below the specified range, the gap is too large. In either case, the engine must be stopped and the gap adjusted in the manner previously described. After making the adjustment, start the engine and check the reading on the dwell meter. When the correct reading is obtained, stop the engine, then disconnect the dwell meter.

7. Check the ignition timing, and adjust if necessary, as detailed later in this section.

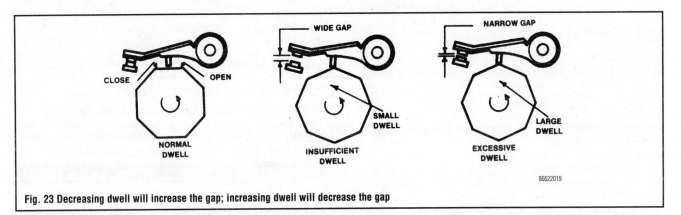

Fig. 23 Decreasing dwell will increase the gap; increasing dwell will decrease the gap

ELECTRONIC IGNITION

Description and Operation

1972–83 MODELS

♦ See Figures 24 and 25

Electronic ignition was optional in 1972–73 and became standard in 1974. This unit functions basically the same as a breaker point distributor, although the parts used are different.

The distributor housing, cap, rotor and advance mechanism are the same as on the conventional distributor; both systems also use the same spark plugs and ignition coil. A magnetic pickup and control (reluctor) replace the breaker points and rotor. A condenser is no longer necessary. The only maintenance required on electronic ignition systems is inspection of the wiring, as well as cleaning and changing of the spark plugs.

As a result of the elimination of breaker points, the dwell on electronic ignition units is non-adjustable. It can be read on a dwell meter, but cannot be adjusted.

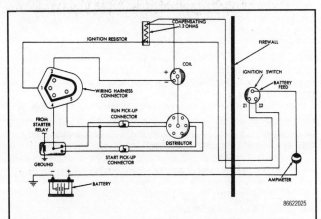

Fig. 24 Common electronic ignition system

Fig. 25 Electronic ignition schematic—6-cylinder engine with dual pickup distributor

2-12 ENGINE PERFORMANCE AND TUNE-UP

> ### ✷✷ WARNING
>
> Don't fool with the reluctor. The reluctor teeth may appear ragged at the edges, but no attempt should be made to clean them. A sharp edge is needed to quickly decrease the magnetic field and induce negative voltage in the pickup coil. If the teeth are rounded, the voltage signal to the control unit may be erratic.

1984 V8 ENGINES WITH DUAL PICKUP DISTRIBUTORS AND VACUUM ADVANCE

The system consists of the battery, ignition switch, ignition resistor control unit, coil, dual pickup distributor with vacuum advance mechanism, dual pickup start/run relay, spark plugs and necessary components for the routing of primary and secondary current.

During engine cranking, the dual pickup start/run relay is energized through the starter solenoid circuit, which allows the start pickup to adjust the timing for starting purposes only. As soon as the starter solenoid is de-energized, the start/run relay switches the sensing function back to the run pickup.

The pickup circuit is used to sense the proper timing for the control unit switching transistor. The reluctor rotating with the distributor shaft produces a voltage pulse in the magnetic pickup each time a spark plug should be fired. This pulse is transmitted through the pickup coil to the power switching transistor in the control unit, and causes the transistor to interrupt the current flow through the primary circuit. This break in the primary circuit induces a high voltage in the secondary coil circuit and fires the appropriate spark plug.

The length of time the switching transistor allows the current to flow in the primary circuit is determined by the electronic circuitry in the control unit. This determines the dwell.

➥ Dwell is not adjustable and there is no means to change it, since changes are not required.

1987–88 ENGINES WITH SINGLE PICKUP DISTRIBUTORS AND NO VACUUM ADVANCE; 1984–88 ENGINES WITH DUAL PICKUP DISTRIBUTORS AND NO VACUUM ADVANCE

The computer provides the engine with Ignition Spark Control during starting and engine operation, providing an infinitely variable spark advance curve. Input data is fed instantaneously to the computer by a series of sensors located in the engine compartment which monitor timing, water temperature, air temperature, idle/off-idle operation and intake manifold vacuum. The program schedule module of the Spark Control Computer receives the information from the sensors, processes it, then directs the ignition control module to advance or retard the timing as necessary. This whole process goes on continuously as the engine is running, taking only milliseconds to complete a circuit from sensor to distributor. The main components of the system are a modified carburetor and Spark Control Computer, which is responsible for translating input data and which transmits data to the distributor to advance or retard the timing.

There are two functional modes of the computer: start and run. The start mode only functions during engine cranking and starting. The run mode only functions after the engine starts and during engine operation. The two modes never operate together.

Should a failure of the run mode of the computer occur, the system will go into a "limp-in" mode. This will enable the operator to continue to drive the vehicle until it can be repaired. However, while in this mode, very poor engine operation will result. Should failure of the pickup coils or the start mode of the computer occur, the engine will not start.

The pickup coil signal is a reference signal. When the signal is received by the computer, the maximum amount of timing advance is made available. Based on the data from all the sensors, the computer determines how much of this maximum advance is needed at that instant.

The amount of spark advance is determined by two factors: engine speed and engine vacuum. However, when it happens depends on the following conditions:

1. Spark advance based on engine vacuum is determined by the computer when the carburetor switch is open. The amount is programmed into the computer, and is proportional to the amount of engine vacuum and rpm.
2. Spark advance based on engine speed is determined by the computer when the carburetor switch is open, and is programmed based on engine rpm.

Diagnosis and Testing

1972–83 MODELS

♦ See Figure 26

The magnetic pickup and control unit replace the functions of the breaker points. Unlike the breaker points, the magnetic pickup and control unit normally show no signs of wear. Therefore, periodic checks of dwell are unnecessary; besides, the dwell cannot be altered.

There is, however, an adjusting slot on the distributor plate that is used to change the air gap between the reluctor teeth and the pole piece of the coil. Unlike breaker points, reducing the air gap will not retard the timing. Since dwell is determined by the control unit and is independent of the pickup unit, changing the air gap will not affect timing or dwell. The gap between the pickup and the reluctor should be properly set, however.

One of the main advantages of the electronic ignition system is improved starting. Removal of the breaker points eliminates the possibility of arcing across the points. However, a pickup gap that is too wide can cause starting problems. A no-start condition can exist if the gap is too wide.

If you encounter a hard starting condition, don't immediately blame the pickup gap and change the adjustment. The entire system should be left alone, except as a last resort. Make sure that the fuel system and the rest of the ignition system are performing satisfactorily. Although setting the pickup gap correctly is a must when installing a new reluctor or pickup unit, the gap does not change in service (due to wear) and should not require periodic checking or adjustment. The main reason that the minimum air gap specification exists is to make sure that the reluctor does not contact the pole piece as the vacuum plate moves.

➥ When checking the pickup gap, use a non-magnetic feeler gauge. This is because a feeler blade that is attracted to the magnetism of the pole piece will give a false feel or drag. If non-magnetic feeler blades are not available, use brass shim stock of the proper thickness.

> ### ✷✷ WARNING
>
> When working on a truck with electronic ignition, be careful not to touch the round transistor located in the control unit heat sink when the ignition is ON. It can give out a very large shock.

1984 V8 ENGINES WITH DUAL PICKUP DISTRIBUTORS AND VACUUM ADVANCE

♦ See Figures 27 thru 39

➥ To properly test the Electronic Ignition System, special testers should be used. In the event they are not available, the system may be tested using a voltmeter with a 20,000 ohm/volt rating and an ohmmeter which uses a 9 volt battery for its operation. Both meters should be properly calibrated.

1. Visually inspect all secondary cables at the coil, distributor and spark plugs for cracks and wear. Check for tight connections.
2. Check the primary wire at the coil and ballast resistor for a clean, tight connection.

> ### ✷✷ WARNING
>
> When removing or installing the wiring harness connector to the control unit, the ignition switch must be in the OFF position.

3. Using a voltmeter, measure the voltage at the battery, in order to assure that enough current is available to operate the starting and ignition systems.
4. Remove the coil secondary wire from the distributor cap.
5. With the key in the **ON** position, use a jumper wire to momentarily touch the negative terminal of the coil to ground while holding the coil secondary wire approximately ¼ (6mm) from a good engine ground. A spark should be observed.
6. If no spark is observed, turn the ignition key to the **OFF** position, then disconnect the four-wire harness going to the Electronic Control Unit (ECU).
7. With the ignition key in the **ON** position, again use the jumper wire and

ENGINE PERFORMANCE AND TUNE-UP

Fig. 26 The electronic control unit can give you a dangerous shock if touched while the ignition is ON

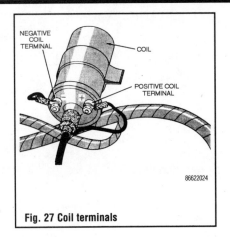

Fig. 27 Coil terminals

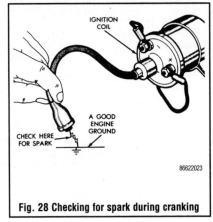

Fig. 28 Checking for spark during cranking

ground the negative terminal of the coil while holding the coil secondary wire approximately ¼ in. (6mm) from a good engine ground. If a spark is observed, replace the ECU.

8. If no spark is observed, measure the voltage at the coil positive terminal. The voltage should be within one volt of battery voltage.

9. If battery voltage is not present, check the wiring between the battery positive terminal and coil. Replace the starter relay if the wiring is correct.

10. If the current is not continuous between the battery and the coil positive terminal, replace the ignition resistor and repeat the test.

11. Check the battery voltage at the coil negative terminal. It should be within one volt of battery voltage.

12. If battery voltage is present at the negative coil terminal, but no spark is obtained when shorting the terminal with a jumper wire, replace the ignition coil.

13. If spark is obtained, but the engine will not start, turn the ignition switch to the **OFF** position and pull the ECU harness connector off, then turn the ignition switch to the **ON** position and check for battery voltage at cavity No. 2 of the ECU harness connector. The voltage should be within one volt of battery voltage.

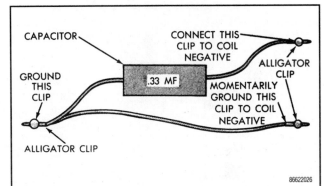

Fig. 29 Use a special jumper to ground the coil negative terminal on 1972–83 systems

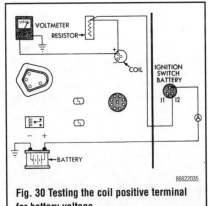

Fig. 30 Testing the coil positive terminal for battery voltage

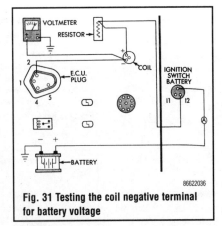

Fig. 31 Testing the coil negative terminal for battery voltage

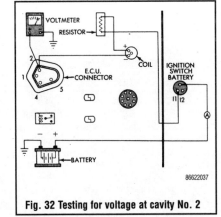

Fig. 32 Testing for voltage at cavity No. 2

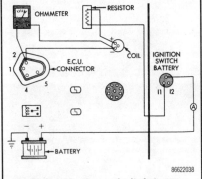

Fig. 33 Checking for continuity between cavity No. 2 and the coil negative terminal

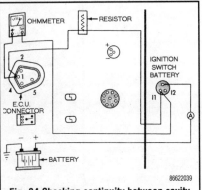

Fig. 34 Checking continuity between cavity No. 1 and the ignition switch

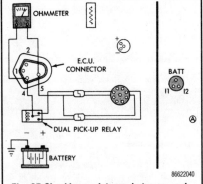

Fig. 35 Checking resistance between cavities No. 4 and 5

2-14 ENGINE PERFORMANCE AND TUNE-UP

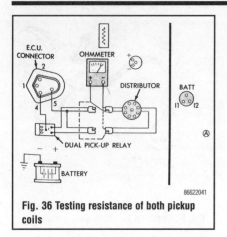

Fig. 36 Testing resistance of both pickup coils

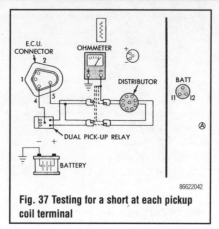

Fig. 37 Testing for a short at each pickup coil terminal

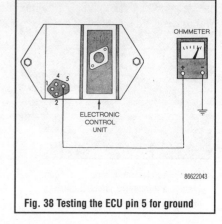

Fig. 38 Testing the ECU pin 5 for ground

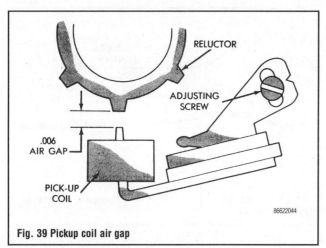

Fig. 39 Pickup coil air gap

14. If no battery voltage is present, turn the ignition switch to the **OFF** position and check for continuity between cavity No. 2 and the coil negative terminal. If no continuity is obtained, find the wiring fault, repair it and retest.
15. Check for continuity between cavity No. 1 of the ECU connector and the ignition switch. If none exists, find the fault, repair it and retest.
16. If voltage is obtained at cavity No. 2 of the ECU connector, turn the ignition switch to the **OFF** position and, with an ohmmeter, check the resistance between cavities No. 4 and No. 5 of the ECU connector. The reading should range between 150 and 900 ohms.
17. If the resistance is not between 150 and 900 ohms, disconnect the distributor pickup leads. Measure the resistance at the pickup leads. The resistance should be between 150 and 900 ohms. If the resistance is not within the accepted range, the pickup coils are bad and must be replaced.
18. If the resistance at the pickup leads is within specifications, this indicates that wiring between cavities No. 4 and No. 5 is open or shorted, or the dual pickup start/run relay is defective. Repair and retest as required.
19. Check pin No. 5 of the ECU for ground. If no ground is obtained, check the ECU for poor or dirty connections and tight mounting screws.
20. Reinstall all connections and check for spark. If no spark occurs, replace the ECU.

Dual Pickup Start/Run Relay

1. Remove the two-way connector from pins No. 4 and No. 5 of the dual pickup start/run relay.
2. Using an ohmmeter, touch pins No. 4 and No. 5. The meter should read 20–30 ohms. If not, replace the relay.

Centrifugal Advance

1. Connect a timing light according to the manufacturer's instructions.
2. Operate the engine at idle and remove the vacuum hose from the vacuum controller.
3. Slowly accelerate the engine to check for advance.
4. Excessive advance indicates a damaged governor spring (a broken spring will result in abrupt advance).
5. Insufficient advance is usually caused by a broken governor weight or a malfunction in the cam operation. Correct as necessary.

Vacuum Advance

▶ See Figure 40

1. Connect a timing light and adjust the engine speed to 2500 rpm.
2. Check for advance by disconnecting, then reconnecting the vacuum hose at the distributor, and watching the advance or retard at the crankshaft indicator.
3. For a more accurate determination of whether the vacuum advance mechanism is operating properly, remove the vacuum hose from the distributor and connect a hand vacuum pump.
4. Run the engine at idle and slowly apply vacuum pressure to check for advance.
5. If excessive advance is noted, look for a deteriorated vacuum controller spring.
6. If insufficient advance or no advance is noted, this could be caused by linkage problems or a ruptured vacuum diaphragm. Correct as necessary.

➡The electronic ignition system can be tested with either special ignition testers or a voltmeter with a 20,000 ohm/volt rating and an ohmmeter using a 9 volt battery as a power source. Since special ignition system testers have manufacturer's instructions accompanying them, be sure to refer to the procedural steps necessary to operate them. The following is based on usage of an ohm/volt combination meter.

Fig. 40 Distributor with a vacuum advance

ENGINE PERFORMANCE AND TUNE-UP   2-15

1987–88 ENGINES WITH SINGLE PICKUP DISTRIBUTORS AND NO VACUUM ADVANCE; 1984–88 ENGINES WITH DUAL PICKUP DISTRIBUTORS AND NO VACUUM ADVANCE

Secondary Circuit

1. Remove the coil wire from the distributor cap. Wrap it with cloth and hold it cautiously about ¼ in. (6mm) away from an engine ground. Use a remote starter switch or have an assistant crank the engine while checking for spark.
2. If a good spark is present, slowly move the coil wire away from the engine and check for arcing at the coil while cranking.
3. If good spark is present and it is not arcing at the coil, check the rest of the parts of the ignition system.

Ignition System Starting

1. Visually inspect all secondary cables at the coil, distributor and spark plugs for cracks. Check for tight connections.
2. Check the primary wire at the coil and ballast resistor for clean, tight connections.

> **WARNING**
>
> **When removing or installing the wiring harness connector to the control unit, the ignition switch must be in the OFF position.**

3. Use a voltmeter to measure the voltage at the battery and confirm that enough current is available to operate the starting and ignition systems.
4. Remove the coil secondary wire from the distributor cap.
5. With the key in the **ON** position, use a jumper wire and momentarily touch the negative terminal of the coil to ground while holding the coil secondary wire approximately ¼ in. (6mm) from a good engine ground. A spark should be observed.
6. Verify that spark is getting to the spark plugs. If the spark plugs are being fired, the ignition system is not responsible for the engine not starting.
7. If no spark is observed at the ignition coil wire, turn the ignition switch to the **OFF** position and detach the 10-way connector from the bottom of the Spark Control Computer. Turn the ignition switch to the **ON** position, and hold the ignition coil wire approximately ¼ in. (6mm) away from a good engine ground.
8. With battery current flowing to the coil negative terminal, intermittently short the terminal to ground. If spark now occurs, replace the Spark Control Computer.
9. If the voltage is incorrect, check the continuity of the wiring between the battery and the coil positive terminal. Repair the wiring as required and retest.
10. With the ignition key in the **ON** position, check the voltage at the coil negative terminal. If it is not within one volt of the battery's voltage, replace the ignition coil.
11. If battery voltage (within one volt) is present, but no spark is obtained when shorting the negative terminal, replace the ignition coil.
12. If spark is obtained, but the engine will still not start, turn the ignition switch to the **RUN** position and, using the positive lead of the voltmeter, measure the voltage from cavity No. 1 to the disconnected ground lead of the computer. The voltage should be within 1 volt of the battery voltage noted earlier.
13. If battery voltage is not present, check the wire for an open circuit and repair. Retest as required.
14. Place a thin insulator between the curb idle adjusting screw and the carburetor switch, or make sure the curb idle adjusting screw is not touching the carburetor switch.
15. Connect the negative voltmeter lead to a good engine ground. Turn the ignition switch to the **RUN** position and measure the voltage at the carburetor switch terminal. The voltage should be approximately 5 volts.
16. If the voltage is not 5 volts, turn the ignition switch to the **OFF** position and detach the 10-way connector from the bottom of the Spark Control Computer. Turn the ignition switch back to the **RUN** position and measure the voltage at terminal 2 of the connector.
17. Voltage should be within 1 volt of the battery's voltage. If the correct voltage is not present, check the wiring between terminal 2 of the connector and the ignition switch for an open or shorted circuit or a poor connections.
18. Turn the ignition switch to the **OFF** position and detach the connector from the bottom of the spark computer, if not already done. With an ohmmeter, check the continuity between terminal 7 of the connector and the carburetor switch terminal. Continuity should exist between these two points. If not, check for an open circuit poor connection.
19. Check for continuity between terminal 10 of the connector and engine ground. If continuity exists, replace the Spark Control Computer assembly. If continuity does not exist, check the wiring for open circuits or poor connections. Repeat Step 18.
20. If the engine still fails to start, turn the ignition switch to the **OFF** position and, with an ohmmeter, measure the resistance of the start pickup coil between terminal 5 and terminal 9 of the 10-way connector. The resistance should be 150–900 ohms.
21. If the resistance is not within the specified range, disconnect the start pickup coil leads from the distributor. Measure the resistance at the lead going into the distributor. If the reading is now 150–900 ohms, an open circuit or faulty connection exists between the distributor connector and terminals 5 and 9 of the 10-way connector. If the resistance is not within specifications, the pickup coil is bad. Replace it and set the air gap to specifications.
22. Connect one lead of the ohmmeter to the engine ground and, with the other lead, check for continuity at each terminal of the leads going to the distributor. There should be no continuity.
23. If there is continuity, replace the pickup coils. Adjust the air gap to specifications.
24. Attempt to start the engine. If it fails to start, repeat the tests. If the engine still fails to start, replace the Spark Control Computer.

➡ Should the engine still fail to start with the replaced Spark Control Computer, Chrysler Corporation suggests reinstalling the original Spark Control Computer and repeating the tests. However, proper testing of the circuits and pickup should result in the engine starting, unless unrelated problems exist.

Basic Timing

Correct basic timing is essential for optimum engine performance. Before any testing and service is begun in response to poor performance, the basic timing must be checked and adjusted as required. Refer to the underhood specifications label for timing adjustment specifications.

Carburetor Switch

➡ **Grounding the carburetor switch eliminates all spark advance on most systems.**

1. With the ignition key in the **OFF** position, detach the 10-way connector from the Spark Control Computer.
2. With the throttle completely closed, check the continuity between pin 7 of the 10-way connector and a good engine ground.
3. If no continuity exists, check the wires and the carburetor switch. Recheck the basic timing.
4. With the throttle open, check the continuity between pin 7 of the 10-way connector harness connector and a good engine ground. There should be no continuity.

Engine Temperature Sensor

1. Turn the ignition switch to the **OFF** position and disconnect the wire from the temperature switch.
2. Connect one lead of an ohmmeter to a good ground on the engine, or in the case of the charge temperature switch, to its ground terminal.
3. Connect the other lead of the ohmmeter to the center terminal of the coolant temperature switch.
4. Check for continuity using the following ohmmeter readings:
   a. Cold engine: continuity should be present with a resistance less than 100 ohms. If not, replace the switch. The charge temperature switch must be cooler than 60°F (15°C) in order to achieve this reading.
   b. Hot engine at normal operating temperature: the terminal reading should show no continuity. If it does, replace the coolant temperature switch or the charge temperature switch.

Coolant Sensor

1. Connect the leads of an ohmmeter to the terminals of the sensor.
2. With the engine cold and the ambient temperature less than 90°F (32°), the resistance should be between 500–1100 ohms.

2-16 ENGINE PERFORMANCE AND TUNE-UP

3. With the engine at normal operating temperature, the resistance should be greater than 1300 ohms.

→ **The sensor will continually change its resistance with a change in engine operating temperature.**

4. If the resistance is not within the specified ranges, replace the sensor.

Detonation Sensor

1. Connect a timing light to the engine, according to the manufacturer's instructions.
2. Start the engine and run it with the fast idle cam on its second highest step (at least 1200 rpm).
3. Connect an auxiliary vacuum supply to the vacuum transducer and apply 16 in. Hg (54 kPa).
4. Tap lightly on the intake manifold near the sensor with a small metal object.
5. Using the timing light, look for a decrease in the spark advance. The amount of decrease in the timing is directly proportional to the strength and frequency of the tapping. The maximum decrease in timing should be 11° for 1984 models, or 20° for 1985 and later models.
6. Turn the ignition switch to the **OFF** position. With the engine stopped, disconnect the timing light.

Electronic Exhaust Gas Recirculation (EGR) System

▶ See Figure 41

→**The Electronic EGR control is located within the electronic circuitry of the Spark Control Computer, and its testing procedure is outlined.**

1. All the engine temperature sensors must be operating properly before the tests can be performed.
2. With the engine temperature cold and the ignition switch turned to the **OFF** position, connect one voltmeter lead to the gray wire on the EGR solenoid and the other lead to a good engine ground.
3. Start the engine. The voltage should be less than one volt. It will remain at this level until the engine has reached its normal operating temperature range and the electronic EGR schedule has timed out. The solenoid will then de-energize and the voltmeter will read charging system voltage.
4. If the charging system voltage is not obtained, replace the solenoid and repeat the test.
5. If the voltmeter indicates charging system voltage before the EGR schedule is complete, replace the computer or the externally mounted timer.

→**The 318 cu. in. non-California engines with 2-bbl. carburetors have no thermal delay below 60°F (15°C) ambient temperature. They will follow the EGR time delay schedule only.**

6. If an engine is started with the temperature hot, the EGR solenoid will be energized for the length of the time delay schedule only. It will then de-energize.

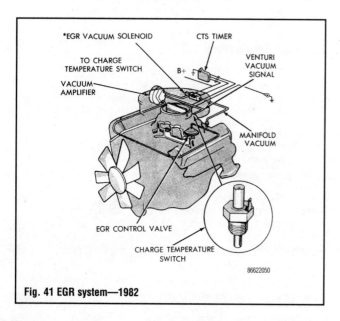

Fig. 41 EGR system—1982

Electronic Throttle Control System

Incorporated within the Spark Control Computer is the electronic throttle system. A carburetor mounted solenoid is energized when the air conditioner, electric back light or electric timers are activated. The two timers which are incorporated in the ignition electronics operate two seconds after the throttle is closed, or after an engine start condition.

1. Connect a tachometer to the engine.
2. Start the engine and run it until normal operating temperature is reached.
3. Depress the accelerator and release it. A higher than curb idle speed should be seen on the tachometer for the length of the EGR schedule.
4. On air conditioned vehicles, turning on the air conditioning or the back light and depressing the accelerator for a moment should give a higher than curb idle speed. Turning the air conditioning and back light off should produce the normal idle speed.

→**With the air conditioning system on, the air conditioning clutch will cycle on and off. This should not be mistaken as a part of the electronic control system.**

5. If the speed increases do not occur, disconnect the three-way connector at the carburetor.
6. Check the solenoid with an ohmmeter by measuring the resistance from the terminal that contains the black wire to ground. The resistance should be 15–35 ohms. If it is not within specifications, replace the solenoid.
7. Start the engine and, before the delay has timed out, measure the voltage of the three-way connector's black wire. The voltmeter should read charging system voltage. If it does not, replace the computer.
8. Turning the air conditioning or the back light on should also produce charging system voltage after the time delay has timed out. If not, check the wiring back to the instrument panel for an open circuit.

DUAL PICKUP START/RUN RELAY

1. Remove the two-way connector from pins No. 4 and No. 5 of the dual pickup start/run relay.
2. Using an ohmmeter, touch pins No. 4 and No. 5. The meter should read 20–30 ohms. If not, replace the relay.

Centrifugal Advance

1. Connect a timing light according to the manufacturer's instructions.
2. Operate the engine at idle, then remove the vacuum hose from the vacuum controller.
3. Slowly accelerate the engine to check for advance.
4. Excessive advance indicates a damaged governor spring (a broken spring will result in abrupt advance).
5. Insufficient advance is usually caused by a broken governor weight or a malfunction in cam operation. Correct as necessary.

Adjustments

1972–83 MODELS

Air Gap

SINGLE PICKUP DISTRIBUTOR

▶ See Figures 42, 43 and 44

1. Raise the hood or engine compartment lid.
2. Remove the distributor cap.
3. Align one reluctor tooth with the pole piece pickup coil. If the truck is equipped with an automatic transmission, bump the starter motor using the key. If it is equipped with a manual transmission, place the truck in 3rd or 4th gear and roll the truck until the tooth is aligned.
4. Loosen the pickup adjusting screw. On 1972–76 models, insert a 0.008 in. (0.20mm) feeler gauge. On 1977 and later models, insert a 0.006 in. (0.15mm), feeler gauge. The gauge should not fit into the gap. Do not try to force it in.
5. Apply vacuum to the vacuum unit and crank the engine. The pickup pole should not hit the reluctor teeth. If it does hit, readjust the gap. If it only hits on one side, the distributor shaft is probably bent and must be replaced.
6. Install the distributor cap.

ENGINE PERFORMANCE AND TUNE-UP

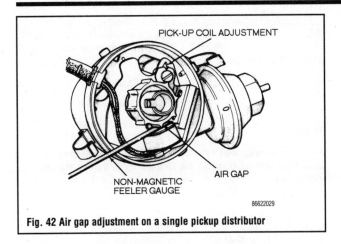

Fig. 42 Air gap adjustment on a single pickup distributor

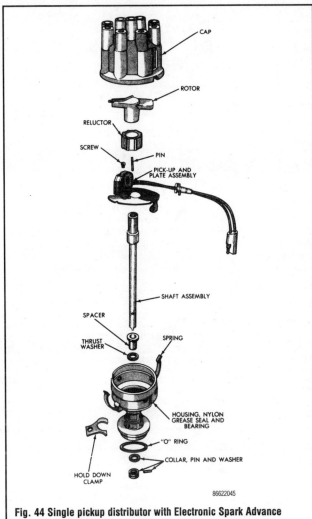

Fig. 44 Single pickup distributor with Electronic Spark Advance (ESA)—V8 engines

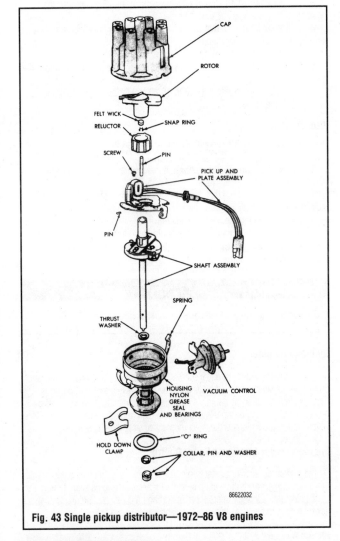

Fig. 43 Single pickup distributor—1972–86 V8 engines

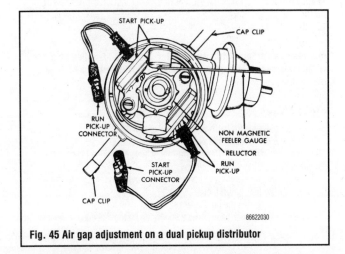

Fig. 45 Air gap adjustment on a dual pickup distributor

DUAL PICKUP DISTRIBUTOR

▶ See Figures 45 and 46

➡ In the dual pickup distributor, the start pickup is identified by a two-prong male connector. The run pickup is identified by a male and a female plug.

Start Pickup:

To adjust the air gap on the start pickup, follow the previous procedure for single pickup distributors.

Run Pickup:

1. Align one reluctor tooth with the pickup coil tooth.
2. Loosen the pickup coil hold-down screw.
3. Insert a non-magnetic feeler gauge 0.012 in. (0.30mm) between the reluctor tooth and the pickup coil tooth.
4. Adjust the air gap so that contact is made between the reluctor tooth, feeler gauge and pickup coil tooth.
5. Tighten the hold-down screw.

2-18 ENGINE PERFORMANCE AND TUNE-UP

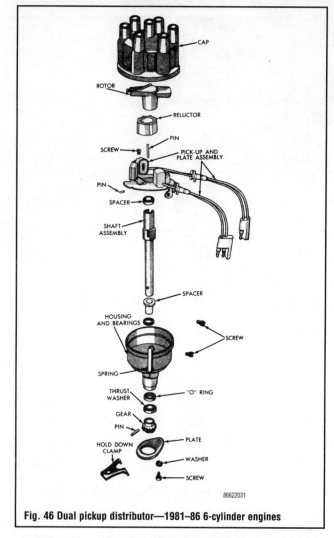

Fig. 46 Dual pickup distributor—1981–86 6-cylinder engines

1984 V8 ENGINES WITH DUAL PICKUP AND VACUUM ADVANCE

Air Gap

➡ In the dual pickup distributor, the start pickup is identified by a two-prong male connector and the run pickup is identified by a male and female plug.

START PICKUP

1. Align one reluctor tooth with the pickup coil tooth.
2. Loosen the pickup coil hold-down screw.
3. Insert a 0.006 in. (0.15mm) non-magnetic feeler gauge between the reluctor tooth and the pickup coil tooth.
4. Adjust the air gap so that contact is made between the reluctor tooth, the feeler gauge and the pickup coil tooth.
5. Carefully tighten the hold-down screw.
6. Remove the feeler gauge. There should be no force needed to remove the gauge.
7. Check the air gap with a 0.008 in. (0.20mm) feeler gauge. Do not force the gauge into the air gap.

RUN PICKUP

1. Align one reluctor tooth with the pickup coil tooth.
2. Loosen the pickup coil hold-down screw.
3. Insert a 0.012 in. (0.30mm) non-magnetic feeler gauge between the reluctor tooth and the pickup coil tooth.
4. Adjust the air gap so that contact is made between the reluctor tooth, feeler gauge and the pickup coil tooth.
5. Carefully tighten the hold-down screw.
6. Remove the feeler gauge. There should be no force required to remove it.
7. Check the air gap with a 0.014 in. (0.35mm) feeler gauge. Do not force the gauge into the air gap.

1984–88 V8 ENGINES WITH DUAL PICKUP AND NO VACUUM ADVANCE

Air Gap

➡ In the dual pickup distributor, the start pickup is identified by a two-prong male connector, and the run pickup is identified by a male and female plug.

START PICKUP

1. Align one reluctor tooth with the pickup coil tooth.
2. Loosen the pickup coil hold-down screw.
3. Insert a 0.006 in. (0.15mm) non-magnetic feeler gauge between the reluctor tooth and the pickup coil tooth.
4. Adjust the air gap so that contact is made between the reluctor tooth, the feeler gauge and the pickup coil tooth.
5. Carefully tighten the hold-down screw.
6. Remove the feeler gauge. There should be no force needed to remove the gauge.
7. Check the air gap with a 0.008 in. (0.20mm) feeler gauge. Do not force the gauge in the air gap.

RUN PICKUP

1. Align one reluctor tooth with the pickup coil tooth.
2. Loosen the pickup coil hold-down screw.
3. Insert a 0.012 in. (0.30mm) non-magnetic feeler gauge between the reluctor tooth and the pickup coil tooth.
4. Adjust the air gap so that contact is made between the reluctor tooth, feeler gauge and the pickup coil tooth.
5. Carefully tighten the hold-down screw.
6. Remove the feeler gauge. There should be no force required to remove it.
7. Check the air gap with a 0.014 in. (0.35mm) feeler gauge. Do not force the gauge into the air gap.

Components

1984–88 CARBURETED ENGINES

Ignition Computer

The computer consists of one electronic printed circuit board which simultaneously receives signals from all the sensors and, within milliseconds, analyzes them to determine how the engine is operating. The computer then advances or retards ignition timing by signaling the ignition coil to produce electrical impulses which fire the spark plugs at the exact moment when ignition is required.

Microprocessor Electronic Spark Control

The microprocessor is an electronic module located within the computer that processes signals from the engine sensors for accurate engine spark timing. Its digital electronic circuitry offers more operating precision and programming flexibility than the voltage-dependent analog system used previously.

Pickup Sensors

The start and run pickup sensors are located inside the distributor, supplying a signal to the computer to provide a fixed timing point used for starting (start pickup) and for normal engine operation (run pickup). The start pickup also has a back-up function of taking over engine timing in case the run pickup fails. Since the timing in this pickup is fixed at one point, the truck will be able to run, but not very well. The run pickup sensor also monitors engine speed and helps the computer decide when the piston is reaching the top of its compression stroke.

➡ These two sensors will not operate at the same time.

ENGINE PERFORMANCE AND TUNE-UP 2-19

Coolant Sensor

The coolant temperature sensor, located in the intake manifold, informs the computer when the coolant temperature reaches a predetermined operating level. Its signals to the computer also help to control the amount of spark advance for a cold engine.

Carburetor Switch

The carburetor switch sensor is located on the end of the idle stop solenoid and signals the computer when the engine is at idle or off-idle. With the carburetor switch grounding out at idle, the computer cancels the spark advance and the idle control of the air/fuel ratio at the carburetor.

Vacuum Transducer

♦ See Figure 47

The vacuum transducer, located on the computer, monitors the amount of intake manifold vacuum present in the engine. Engine vacuum is one of the factors that determines how the computer will advance/retard the ignition timing and, in conjunction with a feedback carburetor, change the air/fuel ratio.

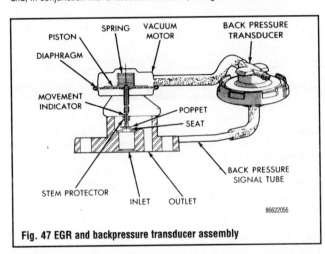

Fig. 47 EGR and backpressure transducer assembly

Detonation Sensor

The detonation sensor is mounted in the No. 2 branch of the intake manifold, and is tuned to the frequency characteristic of engine knocking. When detonation (knocking) occurs, the sensor sends a low voltage signal to the computer, which retards ignition timing in proportion to the strength and frequency of the signal. The maximum amount of retard is 11° for 1984 models, or 20° for 1985 and later models. When the detonation has ceased, the computer advances timing to the original value.

Oxygen (O₂) Sensor

The oxygen sensor is used when the engine is equipped with a feedback carburetor. The sensor is located in the exhaust manifold and, through the use of a self-produced electrical current, signals the computer as to the oxygen content within the exhaust gases flowing past it. Since the electrical output of the oxygen sensor reflects the amount of oxygen in the exhaust, the results are proportional to the rich and lean mixture of the air/fuel ratio. The computer then adjusts the air/fuel ratio to a level that maintains the operating efficiency of the three-way catalytic converter and the engine.

Charge Temperature Switch (CTS)

♦ See Figure 48

The CTS is located in the No. 6 runner of the intake manifold on 6-cylinder engines, or in the No. 8 runner of the intake manifold on 8-cylinder engines. When the intake air temperature is below approximately 60°F (15°C), the CTS is closed, allowing no EGR timer function or valve operation. The injected air is switched to the exhaust manifold (upstream). The CTS opens when the intake air temperature is above approximately 60°F (15°C), thus allowing the EGR

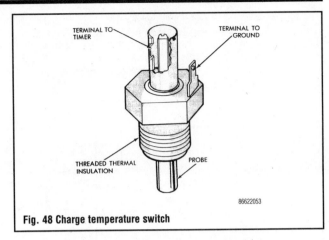

Fig. 48 Charge temperature switch

timer to time out and the EGR valve to operate, and diverts injected air to the catalytic converter (downstream).

1988 FUEL INJECTED ENGINES

Ignition Computer

The computer consists of one electronic printed circuit board which simultaneously receives signals from all the sensors and within milliseconds, analyzes them to determine how the engine is operating. The computer then advances or retards ignition timing by signaling the ignition coil to produce electrical impulses which fire the spark plugs at the exact moment when ignition is required.

Microprocessor Electronic Spark Control

The microprocessor is an electronic module located within the computer that processes the signals from the engine sensors for accurate engine spark timing. Its digital electronic circuitry offers more operating precision and programming flexibility than the voltage-dependent analog system used previously.

Coolant Sensor

♦ See Figures 49, 50 and 51

The coolant temperature sensor is a device which monitors coolant temperature. This sensor provides the data on engine operating temperature to the Single Module Engine Control (SMEC). This allows the SMEC to demand slightly richer air-fuel mixtures and higher idle speeds until normal operating temperatures are reached.

Five Port Coolant Vacuum Switch

♦ See Figure 52

The five port coolant vacuum switch combines the functions of the Coolant Controlled Engine Vacuum Switch (CCEVS) and the three port Coolant Vacuum Switch (CVS3P).

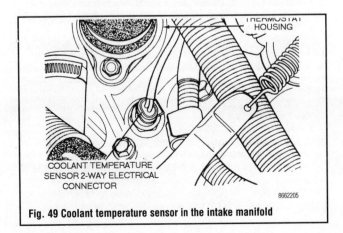

Fig. 49 Coolant temperature sensor in the intake manifold

2-20 ENGINE PERFORMANCE AND TUNE-UP

This valve can be best described as two entirely separate switches. One half of the part behaves as a two port CCEVS. The switch is normally closed up to 150°F (65°C); above this temperature the switch opens, supplying vacuum to open the EGR. Above 150°F (65°C), the other half of the part acts as a CVS3P. At idle, full distributor advance is ensured by supplying manifold vacuum to the distributor under 150°F (65°C).

Oxygen (O₂) Sensor

The sensor is located in the exhaust system and is electrically heated internally for faster switching when the engine is running. When there is a large amount of oxygen present, the sensor produces a low voltage. By monitoring the oxygen content and converting it to electrical voltage, the sensor acts as a rich/lean switch. Voltage is supplied by the SMEC computer, which then adjusts the fuel delivery accordingly.

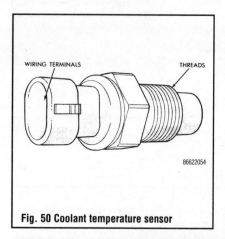

Fig. 50 Coolant temperature sensor

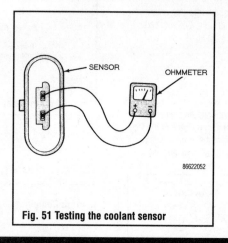

Fig. 51 Testing the coolant sensor

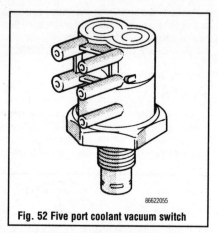

Fig. 52 Five port coolant vacuum switch

IGNITION TIMING

General Information

Ignition timing is the measurement, in degrees of crankshaft rotation, of the point at which the spark plugs fire in each of the cylinders. It is measured in degrees before or after Top Dead Center (TDC) of the compression stroke.

Ideally, the air/fuel mixture in the cylinder will be ignited by the spark plug just as the piston passes TDC of the compression stroke. If this happens, the piston will be beginning the power stroke just as the compressed and ignited air/fuel mixture starts to expand. The expansion of the air/fuel mixture then forces the piston down on the power stroke and turns the crankshaft.

Because it takes a fraction of a second for the spark plug to ignite the mixture in the cylinder, the spark plug must fire a little before the piston reaches TDC. Otherwise, the mixture will not be completely ignited as the piston passes TDC, and the full power of the explosion will not be used by the engine.

The timing measurement is given in degrees of crankshaft rotation before the piston reaches TDC (Before Top Dead Center or BTDC). If the setting for the ignition timing is 5° BTDC, each spark plug must fire 5° before each piston reaches TDC. This only holds true, however, when the engine is at idle speed.

As the engine speed increases, the piston go faster. The spark plugs have to ignite the fuel even sooner if it is to be completely ignited when the piston reaches TDC.

With both the Point Type and Electronic Ignition systems, the distributor has a means to advance the timing of the spark as the engine speed increases. In some cases, this is accomplished by centrifugal weights within the distributor and a vacuum diaphragm mounted on the side of the distributor. On distributors equipped with a vacuum diaphragm, it is necessary to disconnect the vacuum line when the ignition timing is being set.

If the ignition is set too far advanced (BTDC), the ignition and expansion of the fuel in the cylinder will occur too soon and tend to force the piston down while it is still traveling up. This causes engine ping. If the ignition spark is set too far retarded after TDC (ATDC), the piston will have already passed TDC and started on its way down when the fuel is ignited. This will cause the piston to be forced down for only a portion of its travel. This will result in poor engine performance and lack of power.

The timing is best checked with a timing light. This device is connected in series with the No. 1 spark plug. The current that fires the spark plug also causes the timing light to flash.

Setting the ignition timing is basically the same for all engines. It is best set with a timing light. The simple 12v test light should not be considered a substitute for a timing light. Test lights are generally useful, however, for finding approximate settings after the distributor has been removed and ignition timing disturbed.

Before setting the ignition timing, be sure that the dwell is set to the proper specification, since this will influence the timing. This is not possible on electronic ignitions. If so equipped, the vacuum line at the distributor should be disconnected and plugged (a golf tee is handy for doing this) and the timing set while at idle speed.

It is a good idea to paint the timing mark with day-glow or white paint to make it quickly and easily visible. Be sure that all wires, hands and arms are out of the way of the fan. Do not wear any loose clothing such as ties, when reaching anywhere near the fan.

➥**On engines with electronic ignition, your timing light may or may not work, depending on the construction of the light. Consult the manufacturer of the light if in doubt.**

Timing

INSPECTION AND ADJUSTMENT

♦ See Figures 53 and 54

1967–83 Models

1. Connect a timing light and a tachometer in accordance with the manufacturer's instructions. Never puncture the spark plug wires or boots with a probe. Always use the proper adapters.
2. Start the engine and allow it to reach normal operating temperature.
3. Run the engine at its specified idle speed.
4. Put the transmission in Neutral.
5. On models through 1980, disconnect and plug the vacuum advance line at the distributor. A golf tee or pencil usually works well for this.
6. On 1981–83 models, disconnect and plug the vacuum hoses to the EGR valve and the distributor.
7. Loosen the distributor hold-down screw just enough to permit the distributor to be turned.
8. Aim the timing light at the timing marks on the case cover. As the light flashes, you will be able to see the timing scale. Slowly turn the distributor to align the marks at the proper setting.
9. Turn the engine **OFF** and tighten the distributor hold-down bolt. Be careful not to move the distributor while tightening the bolt.
10. Start the engine and recheck the timing.
11. When the timing is correct, stop the engine, then reconnect the vacuum line.

ENGINE PERFORMANCE AND TUNE-UP

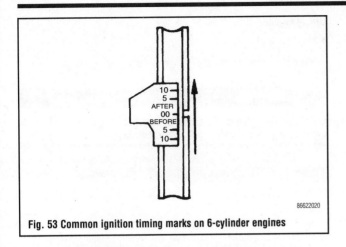

Fig. 53 Common ignition timing marks on 6-cylinder engines

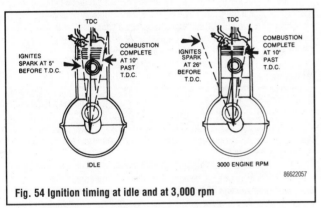

Fig. 54 Ignition timing at idle and at 3,000 rpm

12. If the engine idle speed has changed, readjust the carburetor. Do not reset the timing.
13. Remove the timing light from the engine.

1984–88 Carbureted Engines

1. Connect a power timing light to the number one cylinder, or a magnetic timing unit to the engine. Use a 10° offset when required.
2. Connect a tachometer to the engine and turn the selector to the proper cylinder position.
3. Start the engine and run it until normal operating temperature is reached.
4. On 1984–86 models, unfasten, then attach, the coolant temperature sensor connector on the thermostat housing. The loss of power lamp on the dash must come on and stay on. On 1987–88 models, detach the coolant temperature sensor connector. Engine rpm should be within emission label specifications.
5. Aim the power timing light at the timing hole in the bell housing, or read the magnetic timing unit.
6. Loosen the distributor and adjust the timing to emission label specifications, if necessary.
7. Shut the engine **OFF**. On 1987–88 models, reconnect the coolant temperature sensor. Disconnect, then reconnect the positive battery quick disconnect terminal (or erase the fault codes with sensor test #10 on 1987$FR1/2–88 models). Start the vehicle. The loss of power (check engine) lamp should be off.
8. Shut the engine off, then turn the ignition **ON**, **OFF**, **ON**, **OFF**, **ON**.

1988 Fuel Injected Engines

1. Connect a power timing light to the number one cylinder, or a magnetic timing unit to the engine. Use a 10 ° offset when required.
2. Connect a tachometer to the engine and turn the selector to the proper cylinder position.
3. Start the engine and run it until normal operating temperature is reached.
4. Detach the coolant temperature sensor connector. Engine rpm should be within emission label specifications.
5. Aim the power timing light at the timing hole in the bell housing, or read the magnetic timing unit.
6. Loosen the distributor and adjust the timing to emission label specifications if necessary.
7. Shut the engine off. Reconnect the coolant temperature sensor. Disconnect, then reconnect the positive battery quick disconnect terminal (or erase the fault codes with sensor test #10). Start the vehicle. The loss of power (check engine) lamp should be off.
8. Shut the engine off, then turn the ignition **ON**, **OFF**, **ON**, **OFF**, **ON**.

VALVE LASH

This adjustment is required only on the 6–198, 6–251 and 1967–80 6–225 engines. It need not be done at every tune-up, but should be done whenever there is excessive noise from the valve mechanism, or at least every 20,000 miles (32,186 km).

No valve lash adjustment is necessary or possible on any other Chrysler-built engine. Hydraulic valve lifters automatically maintain zero clearance. After engine reassembly, these lifters adjust themselves as soon as engine oil pressure builds up.

✷✷ WARNING

Do not set the valve lash closer than specified in an attempt to quiet the valve mechanism. This will result in burned valves.

Adjustment

GASOLINE ENGINES

6–198 and 6–225 Engines

▶ See Figure 55

The valves should be adjusted with the engine running at idle and at normal operating temperature.

1. Start the engine and allow it to warm to normal operating temperature. Make sure that the engine idles down to normal curb idle. With manual transmissions, the transmission should be in Neutral. With automatic transmissions, the transmission should be in Drive, with the parking brake set and the wheels blocked.

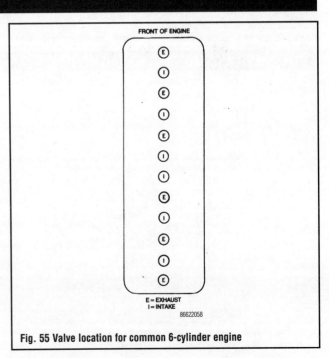

Fig. 55 Valve location for common 6-cylinder engine

2. **Carefully** remove the rocker arm cover. Remember, the rocker arms are moving!

2-22 ENGINE PERFORMANCE AND TUNE-UP

3. Using a flat feeler gauge, pass the gauge between the rocker arm and the top of the valve stem. A slight drag should be felt. See the accompanying illustration for valve identification. The valve clearances should be:

1967–75 Models
- Intake: 0.012 in. (0.30mm)
- Exhaust: 0.024 in. (0.60mm)

1976–80 Models
- Intake: 0.010 in. (0.25mm)
- Exhaust: 0.020 in. (0.50mm)

4. If clearance is not as specified, turn the adjusting screw on the end of the rocker arm to adjust it. We recommend a socket and ratchet with a long extension for this job.

5. When all valves are adjusted, shut off the engine, wipe up the mess and install the valve cover, using a new gasket coated with sealer.

6–251 Engine

♦ See Figure 55

The valves should be adjusted with the engine running at idle and at normal operating temperature.

1. Start the engine and allow it to warm to normal operating temperature. Make sure that the engine idles down to normal curb idle.
2. Remove the valve side cover.
3. Using a flat feeler gauge, pass the gauge between the tappet and the valve stem. A slight drag should be felt. See the accompanying illustration for valve identification. The valve clearances should be:
- Intake: 0.010 in. (0.25mm)
- Exhaust: 0.014 in. (0.35mm)

4. If clearance is not as specified, turn the adjusting screw on the end of the tappet to adjust it. If the engine is to be operated under abnormal conditions, such as extreme heat or continuous high speeds, an additional 0.002 in. (0.05mm) clearance is recommended for both intake and exhaust valves.

5. When all valves are adjusted, shut off the engine, wipe up the mess and install the valve cover, using a new gasket coated with sealer.

CYLINDER NO.	1	2	3	4	5	6
VALVE ARRANGEMENT	I E	I E	I E	I E	I E	I E

I = INTAKE VALVE
E = EXHAUST VALVE

Fig. 56 Diesel valve arrangement

Diesel Engine

♦ See Figure 56

Valve adjustment is required on the diesel engine every 36,000 miles (57,971 km).

** WARNING

Do not set the valve lash closer than specified in an attempt to quiet the lifters. This will only result in burned valves.

1. The engine must be cold for this adjustment. Mark the crankshaft pulley into three equal 120° sections, starting at TDC or the **0** mark.
2. Remove the valve cover.
3. Disconnect the fuel line from the injector at cylinder No. 1. Be very careful not to kink the line.
4. Using a socket and a breaker bar on the crankshaft bolt, turn the engine in the same direction as it normally runs, until the **0** mark on the crankshaft damper rear face is aligned with the pointer on the bottom of the timing gear case. As you are turning, keep an eye on the fuel line that was disconnected. Fuel will squirt out of the line a few degrees before you reach the **0** mark. If it doesn't squirt out, you've got the wrong piston at TDC. Turn the engine another 360° (one revolution) and you will have the No. 1 piston at TDC.
5. The cylinders are numbered from front to rear. Refer to the illustration for valve identification.
6. Valve lash is measured between the rocker arm and the end of the valve. To check the lash, insert a 0.012 in. (0.30mm) feeler gauge between the rocker arm and the valve. Adjust the proper clearance by loosening the locknut on the rocker arm and turning the adjusting screw. After the adjustment is made, tighten the locknut and recheck the clearance to be sure it did not change as the locknut was being tightened.
7. After both valves for the No. 1 cylinder are adjusted, turn the engine so that the pulley turns 120° in the normal direction of rotation (clockwise). The distributor rotor will turn 60°, since it turns at half engine speed.
8. Check that the rocker arms are free and adjust the valves for the next cylinder in the firing order (the firing order is 1–5–3–6–2–4). Intake and exhaust valves should have the same clearance of 0.012 in. (0.30mm).
9. Turn the engine 120° to adjust each of the remaining cylinders in the firing order. When you are done, the crankshaft will have made two complete revolutions (720°).
10. Install the rocker cover with a new gasket, then attach the fuel line to the injector. Start the engine and check for leaks.

IDLE SPEED AND MIXTURE ADJUSTMENTS

♦ See Figure 57

The only adjustments covered here are the idle speed and mixture adjustments. These are performed in the course of a normal tune-up. Other carburetor adjustments are covered in Section 5.

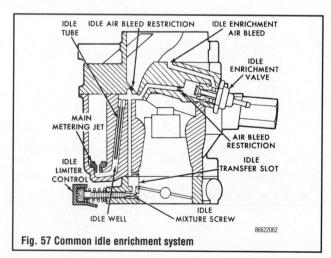

Fig. 57 Common idle enrichment system

Attempting to reset the mixture on your truck can be difficult and expensive. It is generally not recommended, except on 1967 models without the Cleaner Air Package. No special equipment is required for these models. On all other models, CO meters and propane enrichment systems must be used. These are not only difficult to obtain, but can be very expensive.

Mixture is preset at the factory when the engine is manufactured, and tampering with the mixture screws will usually produce very little change. When performing a tune-up, it is advisable to simply adjust the idle speed screw or solenoid screw, and leave the mixture alone.

Before suspecting the carburetor as the cause of poor performance or rough idle, check the ignition system thoroughly, including the distributor, timing, spark plugs and wires. Also, be sure to check the air cleaner, evaporative emission system, PCV system, EGR valve and engine compression. Check the intake manifold, vacuum hoses and other connections for leaks and cracks.

Carbureted Engines

ALL 1967 MODELS

Without Cleaner Air Package (CAP)

➡1967 CAP carburetors can be identified by a green tag on the air horn.

ENGINE PERFORMANCE AND TUNE-UP   2-23

1. Remove the air cleaner.
2. Run the engine at fast idle to stabilize the engine temperature.
3. Make sure that the choke plate is fully released.
4. Connect a tachometer to the engine following the manufacturer's instructions.
5. On models with 6-cylinder engines, turn the high beam headlights on. If equipped with air conditioning, turn the air conditioner on. The transmission should be in Neutral (manual) or Park (automatic).
6. Adjust the carburetor idle speed screw to obtain the specified idle speed.
7. Turn the idle mixture screws in or out to obtain the highest possible rpm. After obtaining the highest rpm, turn each mixture screw clockwise until the rpm start to drop. Then, turn the screws counterclockwise just enough to regain the lost rpm.
8. If the idle mixture adjustment has changed the idle speed, readjust the idle speed.
9. Remove the tachometer and install the air cleaner.
10. Remember to turn the lights off when you're finished.

ALL 1967–76 MODELS AND 1977 CALIFORNIA MODELS

With Cleaner Air Package (CAP) or Cleaner Air System (CAS)

➡CAS replaced CAP in the 1968 model year. CAP carburetors are identified by a green tag attached to the carburetor air horn.

To adjust the idle speed and mixture on these carburetors, particularly on later models, it is best to use an exhaust gas analyzer. This will insure that the proper level of emissions is maintained. However, if you do not have an exhaust gas analyzer, use the following procedure and eliminate those steps which pertain to the exhaust gas analyzer. When you have adjusted the carburetor, it would be wise to have it checked with an exhaust gas analyzer.

1. Leave the air cleaner installed.
2. Run the engine at fast idle speed to stabilize the engine temperature.
3. Make sure the choke plate is fully released.
4. Connect a tachometer to the engine, following the manufacturer's instructions.
5. Connect an exhaust gas analyzer and insert the probe as far into the tailpipe as possible. On vehicles with dual exhaust, insert the probe into the left side pipe, since this is the side with the heat riser.
6. Check the ignition timing, and set it to specification if necessary.
7. If equipped with air conditioning, turn the air conditioner off. On 6-cylinder engines, turn the high beam headlights on.
8. Put the transmission in Neutral (manual) or Park (automatic). Make sure the hot idle compensator valve is fully seated.
9. If equipped with a distributor vacuum control valve, place a clamp on the line between the valve and the intake manifold.
10. Turn the engine idle speed adjusting screw in or out to adjust the idle speed to specification. If the carburetor is equipped with an electric solenoid throttle positioner, turn the solenoid adjusting screw in or out to obtain the specified rpm.
11. Adjust the curb idle speed screw until it just touches the stop on the carburetor body. Back the curb idle speed screw out 1 full turn.
12. Turn each idle mixture adjustment screw 1/16 turn richer (counterclockwise). Wait 10 seconds and observe the reading on the exhaust gas analyzer. Continue this procedure until the meter indicates a definite increase in richness of the mixture.

➡This step is very important when using an exhaust gas analyzer. A carburetor that is set too lean will cause a false reading from the analyzer, indicating a rich mixture. Because of this, the carburetor must first be known to have a rich mixture to verify the reading on the analyzer.

13. After verifying the reading on the meter, adjust the mixture screws to obtain an air/fuel ratio of 14.2:1. Turn the mixture screws clockwise (leaner) to raise the meter reading or counterclockwise (richer) to lower the meter reading.

➡On 1975–77 models, adjust to get the air/fuel ratio and percentage of CO indicated on the engine compartment sticker.

14. If the idle speed changes as the mixture screws are adjusted, adjust the speed to specification (see Step 10), then readjust the mixture so that the specified air/fuel ratio is maintained at the specified idle speed. If the idle is rough, the screws may be adjusted independently, provided that the 14.2:1 air/fuel ratio is maintained.
15. Remove the analyzer, the tachometer and the clamp on the vacuum line.

HOLLEY 6145 CARBURETOR

◆ See Figure 58

Idle Set RPM Adjustment

1977 AND LATER MODELS

1. Disconnect and plug vacuum hose at the EGR valve and ground the carburetor switch with a jumper wire.
2. Disconnect and plug the 3/16 in. diameter hose at the canister.
3. Remove the PCV valve from the valve cover and allow it to draw underhood air.
4. Connect a tachometer to the engine, then start the engine and let the speed stabilize for two minutes.
5. Remove and plug the vacuum hose from the computer. Connect an auxiliary vacuum supply to the computer and apply 16 in. Hg (54 kPa).
6. Disconnect the engine harness connector from the O_2 sensor and ground the engine harness lead with a jumper wire.

➡Care should be exercised so that no pulling force is put on the wire attached to the O$BSB2 sensor. The bullet connector to be disconnected is approximately 4 in. (10.2cm) from the sensor. Use care in working around the sensor, as the exhaust manifold is extremely hot.

7. Let the engine run for 4 minutes to allow the effect of disconnecting the O_2 sensor to take place.
8. Turn the screw on the solenoid and adjust to the idle rpm, as specified on the Emission Label.
9. Reconnect O_2 sensor wire, hose to computer, PCV valve and canister hose.
10. Remove ground wire from carburetor switch and reconnect hose to EGR valve.

➡The idle speed with the engine in normal operating condition (everything connected) may vary from set speeds. DO NOT READJUST.

11. Turn the engine **OFF** and remove the tachometer.

Solenoid Idle Stop (SIS) RPM Adjustment

1977 AND LATER MODELS

➡This adjustment may not apply to all vehicles.

1. Disconnect and plug vacuum hose at the EGR valve.
2. Ground the carburetor switch with a jumper wire.
3. Disconnect and plug the 3/16 in. diameter hose at the canister and remove the PCV valve from the valve cover and allow it to draw underhood air.
4. Connect a tachometer to the engine, then start the engine and let the speed stabilize for two minutes.
5. Energize the solenoid by one of the following methods:
    a. Without air conditioning: Connect one end of a jumper wire to the solenoid wire and the other end to the battery positive post.

➡Use care in jumping to the correct wire on the solenoid. Applying battery voltage to the wrong wire will damage the wiring harness.

   b. With air conditioning: Press the air conditioning button on, set blower speed to low and disconnect the air conditioning compressor clutch wire.
6. Open throttle slightly to allow the solenoid plunger to extend.
7. Remove the adjusting screw and spring from the solenoid. Insert a 1/8 in. Allen wrench into the solenoid and turn to adjust to the specified S.I.S. rpm.
8. Reinstall solenoid screw and spring and de-energize solenoid.
9. Disconnect and plug the vacuum hose from the computer. Connect an auxiliary vacuum supply to the computer and apply 16 in. Hg (54 kPa).
10. Disconnect the engine harness connector from the O_2 sensor and ground the engine harness lead with a jumper wire.

➡Care should be exercised so that no pulling force is put on the wire attached to the O$BSB2 sensor. The bullet connector to be disconnected is approximately 4 in. (10.2cm) from the sensor. Use care in working around the sensor, as the exhaust manifold is extremely hot.

2-24 ENGINE PERFORMANCE AND TUNE-UP

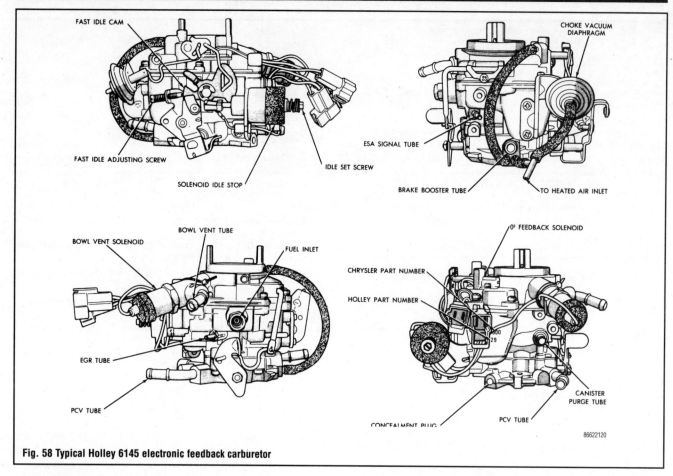

Fig. 58 Typical Holley 6145 electronic feedback carburetor

11. Let the engine run for 4 minutes to allow the effect of disconnecting the O₂ sensor to take place.
12. Turn the screw on the solenoid and adjust to the idle rpm, as specified on the Emission Label.
13. Reconnect the O₂ sensor wire, hose the computer, PCV valve and canister hose.
14. Remove ground wire from carburetor switch and reconnect hose to EGR valve.

➡ The idle rpm with the engine in normal operating condition (everything connected) may vary from set speeds. DO NOT READJUST.

15. Turn the engine **OFF** and remove the tachometer.

Propane Assisted Idle Mixture Adjustment

1977 AND LATER MODELS

➡ This procedure should only be used if an idle defect still exists after normal diagnosis has revealed no other faulty condition, such as incorrect idle speed, incorrect basic timing, faulty hose or wire connections, etc. It is also important to make sure the combustion computer systems are operating properly. Adjustment of the air-fuel mixture should also be performed after a major carburetor overhaul.

1. Disconnect and plug vacuum hose at the EGR valve.
2. Ground the carburetor switch with a jumper wire.
3. Disconnect and plug ³⁄₁₆ in. diameter hose at the canister.
4. Remove the PCV valve from the valve cover and allow it to draw underhood air.
5. Connect a tachometer to the engine, then start the engine and let the speed stabilize for two minutes.
6. Remove and plug the vacuum hose from the computer. Connect an auxiliary vacuum supply to the computer and apply 16 in. Hg (54 kPa).
7. Disconnect the engine harness connector from the O₂ sensor and ground the engine harness lead with a jumper wire.

➡ Care should be exercised so that no pulling force is put on the wire attached to the O$BSB2 sensor. The bullet connector to be disconnected is approximately 4 in. (10.2cm) from the sensor. Use care in working around the sensor, as the exhaust manifold is extremely hot.

8. Let the engine run for 4 minutes to allow the effect of disconnecting the O₂ sensor to take place.
9. Disconnect the vacuum hose from the heated air door sensor at the carburetor and install the propane supply in its place.
10. Open the propane main valve. Slowly open the propane metering valve until maximum engine rpm is reached.

➡ When too much propane is added, engine speed will decrease. Fine tune the metering valve for the highest engine rpm. Also, if the idle mixture is extremely rich, engine rpm will decrease with any amount of propane. In this case, turn the idle mixture screw in about ½ turn and repeat Step 10.

11. With the propane still flowing, adjust the idle speeds screw on the solenoid until the tachometer indicates the specified propane rpm.
12. Fine tune the metering valve for the highest engine rpm. If there has been a change in the maximum rpm, readjust the idle speed screw to the specified propane rpm.
13. Turn off the main propane valve and allow the engine speed to stabilize.
14. Remove the concealment plug as follows:
    a. Remove the air cleaner.
    b. Disconnect all hoses from front of the carburetor base.
    c. Center punch at a point ¼ in. (6mm) from the end of the mixture screw housing. The center punch mark should be indexed at about the 2 o'clock position.
    d. Drill through the outer housing at the punch mark with a ³⁄₁₆ in. drill bit.
    e. If the concealment plug does not pop out when the drill bit enters the plug cavity, use a small drift, punch or Allen wrench to pry out plug. Save concealment plug for reinstallation.

ENGINE PERFORMANCE AND TUNE-UP 2-25

➡ **Never place any tool against the mixture screw during this operation.**

15. Slowly adjust the mixture screw until the tachometer indicates the specified idle rpm. Pause between adjustments to allow the engine speed to stabilize.
16. Turn on the propane valve.
17. Fine tune the metering valve to get the highest engine rpm. If the maximum speed is more than 25 rpm different from the specified propane rpm, repeat Steps 10–13 and 15–16. If okay, proceed to Step 18.
18. Turn off both valves on the propane bottle.
19. Remove propane supply hose and reinstall the vacuum hose that goes to the heated air door sensor.
20. Remove the jumper wire from the carburetor ground switch.
21. Reinstall the PCV valve, remove the jumper wire and reconnect radiator fan plug and reconnect O2 system test connector.
22. Unplug and reconnect the vacuum hose connector to the EGR valve.

➡ **After Steps 18–21 are completed, the curb idle speed may be different than the idle set rpm. This is normal and engine speed should not be readjusted.**

23. Turn the engine **OFF** and remove tachometer. Reinstall the concealment plug.
24. Reinstall hoses and air cleaner.

HOLLEY 2280/6280 CARBURETOR

♦ See Figure 59

Idle RPM Adjustment

♦ See Figure 60

1. Turn off all lights and accessories.
2. Place the transmission in Neutral (manual) or Park (automatic) and set the parking brake.
3. Start engine and run until operating temperature is reached.

4. Ground the carburetor switch with a jumper wire.
5. Disconnect and plug computer, EGR valve and 3/16 in. diameter canister vacuum hoses.
6. Remove PCV valve from the valve cover and allow it to draw underhood air.
7. Disconnect wire from the O2 sensor and ground it with a jumper wire. Let the engine run for 4 minutes before proceeding.
8. Connect a tachometer to engine.
9. Turn the screw on the solenoid and adjust engine speed to the idle rpm, as specified on the Emission Label.
10. Remove jumper wire from O2 sensor harness connector and reconnect to O2 sensor.
11. Reinstall PCV into valve cover.
12. Reconnect all vacuum hoses.
13. Remove jumper wire from carburetor switch.

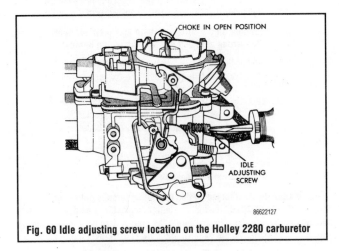

Fig. 60 Idle adjusting screw location on the Holley 2280 carburetor

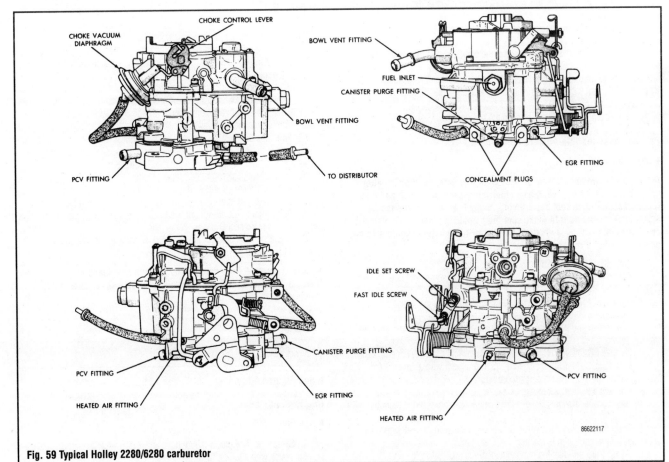

Fig. 59 Typical Holley 2280/6280 carburetor

2-26 ENGINE PERFORMANCE AND TUNE-UP

➡ The idle speed with the engine in normal operating condition (everything connected) may vary from set speeds. DO NOT READJUST.

14. Turn the engine **OFF** and remove the tachometer.

Solenoid Idle Stop (SIS) RPM Adjustment

1. Turn off all lights and accessories, place the transmission in Neutral (manual) or Park (automatic) and set the parking brake.
2. Start and run the engine until operating temperature is reached.
3. Ground the carburetor switch with a jumper wire.
4. Disconnect and plug the EGR valve and ³⁄₁₆ in. diameter canister vacuum hoses.
5. Remove PCV valve from the valve cover and allow to draw underhood air.
6. Connect a tachometer to engine.
7. Energize the solenoid by one of the following methods:
   a. Without air conditioning: Connect one end of a jumper wire to the solenoid wire and the other end to the battery positive post.

➡ Use care in jumping to the correct wire on the solenoid. Applying battery voltage to the wrong wire will damage the wiring harness.

   b. With air conditioning: Press the air conditioning button on, set blower speed to low and disconnect the air conditioning compressor clutch wire.
8. Open throttle slightly to allow the solenoid plunger to extend.
9. Remove the adjusting screw and spring from the solenoid. Insert a ⅛ in. Allen wrench into the solenoid and turn to adjust to specified SIS rpm.
10. Reinstall solenoid screw and spring until it lightly bottoms out and de-energize solenoid.
11. Remove and plug the vacuum hose from the computer.
12. Disconnect the engine harness connector from the O₂ sensor and ground the engine harness lead with a jumper wire.

➡ Care should be exercised so that no pulling force is put on the wire attached to the O₂ sensor. The bullet connector to be disconnected is approximately 4 in. (10.2cm) from the sensor. Use care in working around the sensor, as the exhaust manifold is extremely hot.

13. Let the engine run for 4 minutes to allow the effect of disconnecting the O₂ sensor to take place.
14. Turn the screw on the solenoid and adjust to the idle rpm, as specified on the Emission Label.
15. Reconnect the O₂ sensor wire, hose the computer, PCV valve and canister hose.
16. Remove ground wire from carburetor switch and reconnect hose to EGR valve. The idle rpm with the engine in normal operating condition (everything connected) may vary from set speeds. DO NOT READJUST.
17. Turn the engine **OFF** and remove the tachometer.

Propane Assisted Idle Mixture Adjustment

♦ See Figure 61

➡ This procedure should only be used if an idle defect still exists after normal diagnosis has revealed no other faulty condition, such as incorrect idle speed, incorrect basic timing, faulty hose or wire connections, etc. It is also important to make sure the combustion computer systems are operating properly. Adjustment of the air-fuel mixture should also be performed after a major carburetor overhaul.

1. Turn off all lights and accessories.
2. Place transmission in Neutral (manual) or Park (automatic) and set the parking brake.
3. Start the engine and run until operating temperature is reached.
4. Ground the carburetor switch with a jumper wire.
5. Disconnect and plug computer, EGR valve and ³⁄₁₆ in. diameter canister vacuum hoses.
6. Remove PCV valve from the valve cover and allow it to draw underhood air.
7. Disconnect wire from the O₂ sensor and ground it with a jumper wire. Let the engine run for 4 minutes before proceeding.
8. Connect a tachometer to engine.
9. Tee in propane supply hose in the vacuum line to the choke vacuum kick diaphragm.
10. Open the propane main valve. Slowly open the propane metering valve until maximum engine rpm is reached.
11. If your truck still has the concealment plugs proceed as follows:

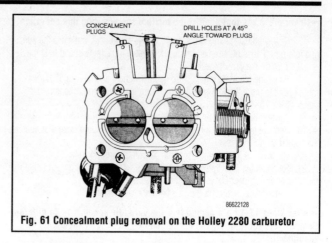

Fig. 61 Concealment plug removal on the Holley 2280 carburetor

   a. Remove the air cleaner and disconnect all hoses from front of the carburetor base.
   b. Remove the carburetor from the engine.
   c. Remove the throttle body and place in a vise, with gasket surfaces not touching the jaws of the vise.
   d. Drill a $FR5/64 in. (2mm) pilot hole at a 45° angle into the casting towards the concealment plugs.
   e. Redrill the hole to ⅛ in. (3mm). Repeat this procedure on the opposite side, as illustrated.
   f. Insert a blunt punch into the holes and drive out the plugs.
   g. Reassemble and reinstall carburetor on engine.
   h. Reinstall hoses and air cleaner.

➡ When too much propane is added, engine speed will decrease. Fine tune the metering valve for the highest engine rpm. Also, if the idle mixture is extremely rich, engine rpm will decrease with any amount of propane. In this case, turn the idle mixture screw in about ½ turn and repeat Step 12.

12. With the propane still flowing, adjust the idle speeds screw on the solenoid until the tachometer indicates the specified propane rpm.
13. Fine tune the metering valve for the highest engine rpm. If there has been a change in the maximum rpm, readjust the idle speed screw to the specified propane rpm.
14. Turn off the main propane valve and allow the engine speed to stabilize.
15. Slowly adjust the mixture screw(s) until the tachometer indicates the specified idle rpm. Pause between adjustments to allow the engine speed to stabilize.
16. Turn on the propane valve.
17. Fine tune the metering valve to get the highest engine rpm. If the maximum speed is more than 25 rpm different from the specified propane rpm, repeat Steps 12 and 14–18. If okay, proceed to Step 20.
18. Turn off both valves on the propane bottle.
19. Remove propane supply hose.
20. Remove the jumper wire from the carburetor ground switch.
21. Reinstall the PCV valve, remove the jumper wire from O₂ sensor harness connector and reconnect O₂ sensor connector.
22. Unplug and reconnect the vacuum hose connector to the computer, canister and EGR valve.

➡ After Steps 20–24 are completed, the curb idle speed may be different than the idle set rpm. This is normal and engine speed should not be readjusted.

23. Turn the engine **OFF** and remove the tachometer. Reinstall the concealment plug.

CARTER BBD CARBURETOR

♦ See Figures 62 and 63

Idle RPM Adjustment

♦ See Figure 64

1. Disconnect and plug vacuum hose at the EGR valve and ground the carburetor switch with a jumper wire.

ENGINE PERFORMANCE AND TUNE-UP 2-27

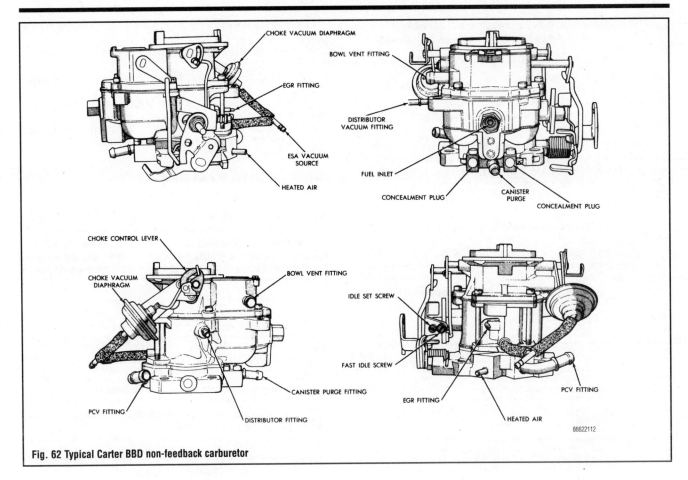

Fig. 62 Typical Carter BBD non-feedback carburetor

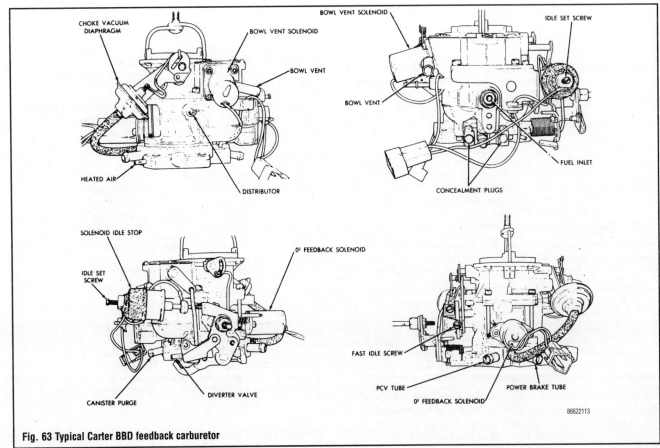

Fig. 63 Typical Carter BBD feedback carburetor

2. Disconnect and plug the 3/16 in. diameter hose at the canister.
3. Remove the PCV valve from the valve cover and allow it to draw underhood air.
4. Connect a tachometer to the engine, then start the engine and let the speed stabilize for two minutes.
5. Remove and plug the vacuum hose from the computer. Connect an auxiliary vacuum supply to the computer and apply 16 in. Hg (54 kPa).
6. Disconnect the engine harness connector from the O₂sensor and ground the engine harness lead with a jumper wire.

➥Care should be exercised so that no pulling force is put on the wire attached to the O₂ sensor. The bullet connector to be disconnected is approximately 4 in. (10.2cm) from the sensor. Use care in working around the sensor, as the exhaust manifold is extremely hot.

7. Let the engine run for 4 minutes to allow the effect of disconnecting the O₂sensor to take place.
8. Turn the screw on the solenoid and adjust to the idle rpm, as specified on the Emission Label.
9. Reconnect O₂sensor wire, hose to computer, PCV valve and canister hose.
10. Remove ground wire from carburetor switch and reconnect hose to EGR valve.
11. The idle speed with the engine in normal operating condition (everything connected) may vary from set speeds. DO NOT READJUST. Turn the engine **OFF** and remove the tachometer.

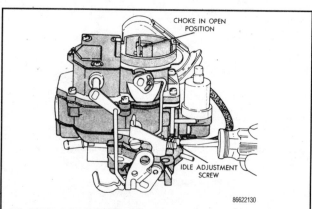

Fig. 64 Idle adjustment screw location on the Carter BBD carburetor

Solenoid Idle Stop (SIS) RPM Adjustment

1. Disconnect and plug vacuum hose at the EGR valve.
2. Ground the carburetor switch with a jumper wire.
3. Disconnect and plug the 3/16 in. diameter hose at the canister and remove the PCV valve from the valve cover and allow it to draw underhood air.
4. Connect a tachometer to the engine, then start the engine and let the speed stabilize for two minutes.
5. Energize the solenoid by one of the following methods:
   a. Without air conditioning: Connect one end of a jumper wire to the solenoid wire and the other end to the battery positive post.

➥Use care in jumping to the correct wire on the solenoid. Applying battery voltage to the wrong wire will damage the wiring harness.

   b. With air conditioning: Press the air conditioning button ON, set blower speed to low and disconnect the air conditioning compressor clutch wire.
6. Open throttle slightly to allow the solenoid plunger to extend.
7. Turn the screw on the throttle lever to adjust to specified SIS rpm.
8. De-energize solenoid.
9. Remove and plug the vacuum hose from the computer. Connect an auxiliary vacuum supply to the computer and apply 16 in. Hg (54 kPa).
10. Disconnect the engine harness connector from the O₂sensor and ground the engine harness lead with a jumper wire.

➥Care should be exercised so that no pulling force is put on the wire attached to the O₂ sensor. The bullet connector to be disconnected is approximately 4 in. (10.2cm) from the sensor. Use care in working around the sensor as the exhaust manifold is extremely hot.

11. Let the engine run for 4 minutes to allow the effect of disconnecting the O₂sensor to take place.
12. Turn the screw on the solenoid and adjust to the idle rpm, as specified on the Emission Label.
13. Reconnect the O₂sensor wire, hose to the computer, PCV valve and canister hose.
14. Remove ground wire from carburetor switch and reconnect hose to EGR valve.
15. The idle rpm with the engine in its normal operating mode (everything connected) may vary from set speeds. DO NOT READJUST. Turn the engine **OFF** and remove the tachometer.

Propane Assisted Idle Mixture Adjustment

♦ See Figure 65

➥This procedure should only be used if an idle defect still exists after normal diagnosis has revealed no other faulty condition, such as incorrect idle speed, incorrect basic timing, faulty hose or wire connections, etc. It is also important to make sure the combustion computer systems are operating properly. Adjustment of the air-fuel mixture should also be performed after a major carburetor overhaul.

1. Disconnect and plug vacuum hose at the EGR valve.
2. Ground the carburetor switch with a jumper wire.
3. Disconnect and plug 3/16 in. diameter hose at the canister.
4. Remove the PCV valve from the valve cover and allow it to draw underhood air.
5. Connect a tachometer to the engine, then start the engine and let the speed stabilize for two minutes.
6. Remove and plug the vacuum hose from the computer. Connect an auxiliary vacuum supply to the computer and apply 16 in. Hg (54 kPa).
7. Disconnect the engine harness connector from the O₂sensor and ground the engine harness lead with a jumper wire.

➥Care should be exercised so that no pulling force is put on the wire attached to the O$BSB2sensor. The bullet connector to be disconnected is approximately 4 in. (10.2cm) from the sensor. Use care in working around the sensor, as the exhaust manifold is extremely hot.

8. Let the engine run for 4 minutes to allow the effect of disconnecting the O₂sensor to take place.
9. Disconnect the vacuum hose from the heated air door sensor at the carburetor and install the propane supply in its place.
10. Open the propane main valve. Slowly open the propane metering valve until maximum engine rpm is reached.

➥When too much propane is added, engine speed will decrease. Fine tune the metering valve for the highest engine rpm. Also, if the idle mixture is extremely rich, engine rpm will decrease with any amount of propane. In this case, turn the idle mixture screw in about ½ turn and repeat Step 10.

11. With the propane still flowing, adjust the idle speeds screw on the solenoid until the tachometer indicates the specified propane rpm.

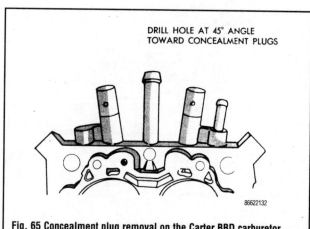

Fig. 65 Concealment plug removal on the Carter BBD carburetor

ENGINE PERFORMANCE AND TUNE-UP

12. Fine tune the metering valve for the highest engine rpm. If there has been a change in the maximum rpm, readjust the idle speed screw to the specified propane rpm.
13. Turn off the main propane valve and allow the engine speed to stabilize.
14. If your truck has not had the concealment plug removed, proceed as follows:
    a. Remove the air cleaner and disconnect all hoses from front of the carburetor base.
    b. Remove the carburetor from the engine.
    c. Remove the throttle body and place in a vise, with gasket surfaces not touching the jaws of the vise.
    d. Drill a 5/64 in. (2mm) pilot hole at a 45° angle into the casting towards the concealment plugs.
    e. Redrill the hole to 1/8 in. (3mm). Repeat this procedure on the opposite side, as illustrated.
    f. Insert a blunt punch into the holes and drive out the plugs.
    g. Reassemble, then reinstall the carburetor on the engine.
15. Reinstall hoses and air cleaner.
16. Slowly adjust the mixture screw until the tachometer indicates the specified idle rpm. Pause between adjustments to allow the engine speed to stabilize.
17. Turn on the propane valve.
18. Fine tune the metering valve to get the highest engine rpm. If the maximum speed is more than 25 rpm different from the specified propane rpm, repeat Steps 10–13 and 14–15. If okay, proceed to Step 19.
19. Turn off both valves on the propane bottle.
20. Remove propane supply and reinstall the vacuum hose that goes to the heated air door sensor.
21. Remove the jumper wire from the carburetor ground switch.
22. Reinstall the PCV valve, remove the jumper wire and reconnect radiator fan plug and reconnect O2 system test connector.
23. Unplug and reconnect the vacuum hose connector to the EGR valve.
24. After Steps 19–23 are completed, the curb idle speed may be different than the idle set rpm. This is normal and engine speed should not be readjusted. Turn the engine **OFF** and remove the tachometer. Reinstall the concealment plug.

CARTER THERMO-QUAD CARBURETOR

◆ See Figure 66

Idle RPM Adjustment

1. Disconnect and plug vacuum hose at the EGR valve and ground the carburetor switch with a jumper wire.
2. Disconnect and plug the 3/16 in. diameter hose at the canister.
3. Remove the PCV valve from the valve cover and allow it to draw underhood air.
4. Connect a tachometer to the engine, then start the engine and let the speed stabilize for two minutes.
5. Remove and plug the vacuum hose from the computer. Connect an auxiliary vacuum supply to the computer and apply 16 in. Hg (54 kPa).
6. Disconnect the engine harness connector from the O2 sensor and ground the engine harness lead with a jumper wire.

➥Care should be exercised so that no pulling force is put on the wire attached to the O2 sensor. The bullet connector to be disconnected is approximately 4 in. (10.2cm) from the sensor. Use care in working around the sensor, as the exhaust manifold is extremely hot.

7. Let the engine run for 4 minutes to allow the effect of disconnecting the O2 sensor to take place.
8. Turn the screw on the solenoid and adjust to the idle rpm, as specified on the Emission Label.
9. Reconnect O2 sensor wire, hose to computer, PCV valve and canister hose.
10. Remove ground wire from carburetor switch and reconnect hose to EGR valve.
11. The idle speed with the engine in normal operating condition (everything connected) may vary from set speeds. DO NOT READJUST. Turn the engine **OFF** and remove the tachometer.

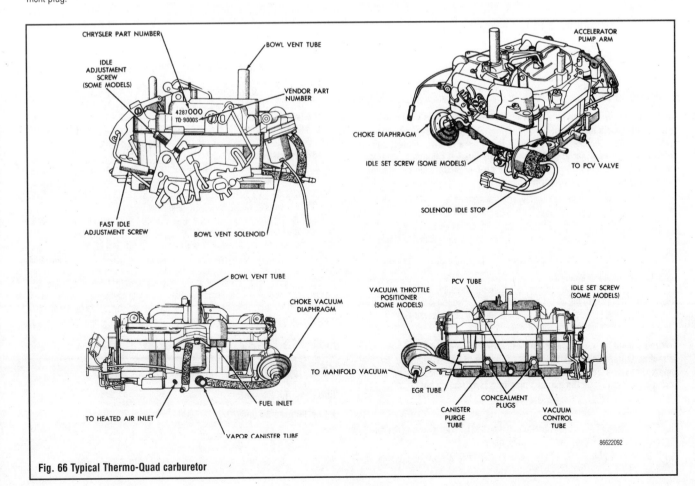

Fig. 66 Typical Thermo-Quad carburetor

2-30 ENGINE PERFORMANCE AND TUNE-UP

Solenoid Idle Stop (SIS) RPM Adjustment

1. Disconnect and plug vacuum hose at the EGR valve.
2. Ground the carburetor switch with a jumper wire.
3. Disconnect and plug the 3/16 in. diameter hose at the canister and remove the PCV valve from the valve cover and allow it to draw underhood air.
4. Connect a tachometer to the engine, then start the engine and let the speed stabilize for two minutes.
5. Energize the solenoid by one of the following methods:
   a. Without air conditioning: Connect one end of a jumper wire to the solenoid wire and the other end to the battery positive post.

➡ Use care in jumping to the correct wire on the solenoid. Applying battery voltage to the wrong wire will damage the wiring harness.

   b. With air conditioning: Press the air conditioning button on, set blower speed to low and disconnect the air conditioning compressor clutch wire.
6. Open throttle slightly to allow the solenoid plunger to extend.
7. Turn the screw on the throttle lever to adjust to specified SIS rpm.
8. De-energize the solenoid.
9. Remove and plug the vacuum hose from the computer. Connect an auxiliary vacuum supply to the computer and apply 16 in. Hg (54 kPa).
10. Disconnect the engine harness connector from the O₂ sensor and ground the engine harness lead with a jumper wire.

➡ Care should be exercised so that no pulling force is put on the wire attached to the O₂ sensor. The bullet connector to be disconnected is approximately 4 in. (10.2cm) from the sensor. Use care in working around the sensor, as the exhaust manifold is extremely hot.

11. Let the engine run for 4 minutes to allow the effect of disconnecting the O₂ sensor to take place.
12. Turn the screw on the solenoid and adjust to the idle rpm, as specified on the Emission Label.
13. Reconnect the O₂ sensor wire, hose the computer, PCV valve and canister hose.
14. Remove ground wire from carburetor switch and reconnect hose to EGR valve.
15. The idle rpm with the engine in normal operating condition (everything connected) may vary from set speeds. DO NOT READJUST. Turn the engine **OFF** and remove the tachometer.

Propane Assisted Idle Mixture

▸ See Figure 67

➡ This procedure should only be used if an idle defect still exists after normal diagnosis has revealed no other faulty condition, such as incorrect idle speed, incorrect basic timing, faulty hose or wire connections, etc. It is also important to make sure the combustion computer systems are operating properly. Adjustment of the air-fuel mixture should also be performed after a major carburetor overhaul.

1. Disconnect and plug vacuum hose at the EGR valve.
2. Ground the carburetor switch with a jumper wire.
3. Disconnect and plug 3/16 in. diameter hose at the canister.
4. Remove the PCV valve from the valve cover and allow it to draw underhood air.
5. Connect a tachometer to the engine, then start the engine and let the speed stabilize for two minutes.
6. Remove and plug the vacuum hose from the computer. Connect an auxiliary vacuum supply to the computer and apply 16 in. Hg (54 kPa).
7. Disconnect the engine harness connector from the O₂ sensor and ground the engine harness lead with a jumper wire.

➡ Care should be exercised so that no pulling force is put on the wire attached to the O₂ sensor. The bullet connector to be disconnected is approximately 4 in. (10.2cm) from the sensor. Use care in working around the sensor, as the exhaust manifold is extremely hot.

8. Let the engine run for 4 minutes to allow the effect of disconnecting the O₂ sensor to take place.
9. Disconnect the vacuum hose from the heated air door sensor at the carburetor and install the propane supply in its place.
10. Open the propane main valve. Slowly open the propane metering valve until maximum engine rpm is reached.

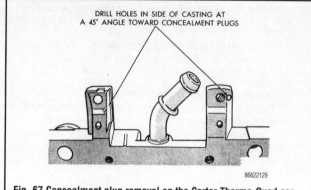

Fig. 67 Concealment plug removal on the Carter Thermo-Quad carburetor

➡ When too much propane is added, engine speed will decrease. Fine tune the metering valve for the highest engine rpm. Also, if the idle mixture is extremely rich, engine rpm will decrease with any amount of propane. In this case, turn the idle mixture screw in about ½ turn and repeat Step 10.

11. With the propane still flowing, adjust the idle speeds screw on the solenoid until the tachometer indicates the specified propane rpm.
12. Fine tune the metering valve for the highest engine rpm. If there has been a change in the maximum rpm, readjust the idle speed screw to the specified propane rpm.
13. Turn off the main propane valve and allow the engine speed to stabilize.
14. If your truck has not had the concealment plug removed, proceed as follows:
   a. Remove the air cleaner and disconnect all hoses from front of the carburetor base.
   b. Remove the carburetor from engine.
   c. Remove the throttle body and place in a vise, with gasket surfaces not touching the jaws of the vise.
   d. Drill a $FR5/64 in. (2mm) pilot hole at a 45° angle into the casting towards the concealment plugs.
   e. Redrill the hole to 1/8 in. (3mm). Repeat this procedure on the opposite side, as illustrated.
   f. Insert a blunt punch into the holes and drive out the plugs.
15. Reassemble, then reinstall the carburetor on the engine.
16. Reinstall hoses and air cleaner.
17. Slowly adjust the mixture screw until the tachometer indicates the specified idle rpm. Pause between adjustments to allow the engine speed to stabilize.
18. Turn on the propane valve.
19. Fine tune the metering valve to get the highest engine rpm. If the maximum speed is more than 25 rpm different from the specified propane rpm, repeat Steps 10–13 and 15–18. If okay, proceed to Step 20.
20. Turn off both valves on the propane bottle.
21. Remove propane supply hose and reinstall the vacuum hose that goes to the heated air door sensor.
22. Remove the jumper wire from the carburetor ground switch.
23. Reinstall the PCV valve, remove the jumper wire and reconnect radiator fan plug and reconnect O₂ system test connector.
24. Unplug and reconnect the vacuum hose connector to the EGR valve.
25. After Steps 20–24 are completed, the curb idle speed may be different than the idle set rpm. This is normal and engine speed should not be readjusted. Turn the engine **OFF** and remove the tachometer. Reinstall the concealment plug.

ROCHESTER QUADRAJET CARBURETOR

▸ See Figure 68

Idle RPM Adjustment

▸ See Figures 69 and 70

1. Disconnect and plug vacuum hose at the EGR valve.
2. Ground the carburetor switch with a jumper wire.
3. Disconnect and plug the 3/16 in. diameter hose at the canister.

ENGINE PERFORMANCE AND TUNE-UP

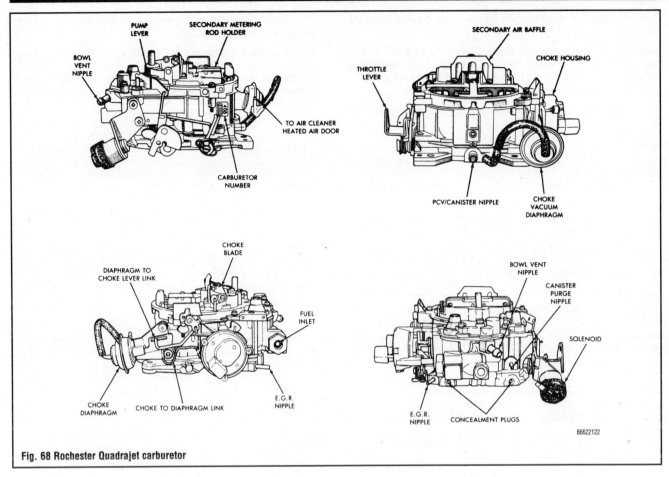

Fig. 68 Rochester Quadrajet carburetor

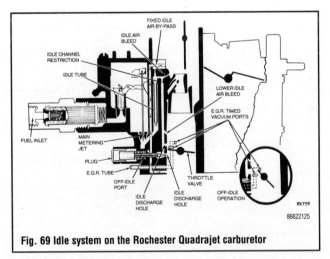

Fig. 69 Idle system on the Rochester Quadrajet carburetor

4. Remove the PCV valve from the valve cover and allow it to draw underhood air.
5. Connect a tachometer to the engine.
6. Start the engine and let the speed stabilize for two minutes.
7. Disconnect the engine harness connector from the O₂ sensor and ground the engine harness lead with a jumper wire.

➡ Care should be exercised so that no pulling force is put on the wire attached to the O₂ sensor. The bullet connector to be disconnected is approximately 4 in. (10.2cm) from the sensor. Use care in working around the sensor, as the exhaust manifold is extremely hot.

8. Let the engine run for four minutes to allow the effect of disconnecting the O₂ sensor to take place.

9. Turn the screw on the solenoid and adjust to the idle rpm, as specified on the Emission Label.
10. Reconnect O₂ sensor wire.
11. Reinstall PCV valve.
12. Reconnect canister hose.
13. Remove ground wire from carburetor switch.
14. Reconnect hose to EGR valve.
15. The idle speed with the engine in normal operating condition (everything connected) may vary from set speeds. DO NOT READJUST. Turn the engine **OFF** and remove the tachometer.

Solenoid Idle Stop (SIS) RPM Adjustment

1. Disconnect and plug vacuum hose at the EGR valve.
2. Ground the carburetor switch with a jumper wire.
3. Disconnect and plug the ³⁄₁₆ in. diameter hose at the canister.
4. Remove the PCV valve from the valve cover and allow it to draw underhood air.
5. Connect a tachometer to the engine.
6. Start the engine and let the speed stabilize for two minutes.
7. Energize the solenoid by one of the following methods:
   a. Without air conditioning: Connect one end of a jumper wire to the solenoid wire and the other end to the battery positive post.

➡ **Use care in jumping to the correct wire on the solenoid. Applying battery voltage to the wrong wire will damage the wiring harness.**

   b. With air conditioning: Press the air conditioning button on, set blower speed to low and disconnect the air conditioning compressor clutch wire.
8. Open throttle slightly to allow the solenoid plunger to extend.
9. Remove the adjusting screw and spring from the solenoid. Insert a ⅛ in. Allen wrench into the solenoid and turn to adjust to specified SIS rpm.
10. Reinstall solenoid screw and spring until it lightly bottoms out. De-energize solenoid.

2-32 ENGINE PERFORMANCE AND TUNE-UP

11. Disconnect the engine harness connector from the O_2 sensor and ground the engine harness lead with a jumper wire.

➡ Care should be exercised so that no pulling force is put on the wire attached to the O$BSB2sensor. The bullet connector to be disconnected is approximately 4 in. (10.2cm) from the sensor. Use care in working around the sensor, as the exhaust manifold is extremely hot.

12. Let the engine run for 4 minutes to allow the effect of disconnecting the O_2 sensor to take place.
13. Turn the screw on the solenoid and adjust to the idle rpm, as specified on the Emission Label.
14. Reconnect the O_2 sensor wire, hose the computer, PCV valve and canister hose.
15. Remove ground wire from carburetor switch and reconnect hose to EGR valve.

➡ The idle rpm with the engine in normal operating condition (everything connected) may vary from set speeds. DO NOT READJUST.

16. Turn the engine **OFF** and remove the tachometer.

Propane Idle Mixture Adjustment

➡ This procedure should only be used if an idle defect still exists after normal diagnosis has revealed no other faulty condition, such as incorrect idle speed, incorrect basic timing, faulty hose or wire connections, etc. It is also important to make sure the combustion computer systems are operating properly. Adjustment of the air/fuel mixture should also be performed after a major carburetor overhaul.

1. Disconnect and plug vacuum hose at the EGR valve.
2. Ground the carburetor switch with a jumper wire.
3. Disconnect and plug 3/16 in. diameter hose at the canister.
4. Remove the PCV valve from the valve cover and allow it to draw underhood air.
5. Connect a tachometer to the engine, then start the engine and let the speed stabilize for two minutes.
6. Disconnect the engine harness connector from the O_2 sensor and ground the engine harness lead with a jumper wire.

➡ Care should be exercised so that no pulling force is put on the wire attached to the O_2 sensor. The bullet connector to be disconnected is approximately 4 in. (10.2cm) from the sensor. Use care in working around the sensor, as the exhaust manifold is extremely hot.

7. Let the engine run for 4 minutes to allow the effect of disconnecting the O_2 sensor to take place.
8. Disconnect the vacuum hose from the heated air door sensor at the carburetor and install the propane supply in its place.

9. Open the propane main valve. Slowly open the propane metering valve until maximum engine rpm is reached.

➡ When too much propane is added, engine speed will decrease. Fine tune the metering valve for the highest engine rpm. Also, if the idle mixture is extremely rich, engine rpm will decrease with any amount of propane. In this case, turn the idle mixture screw in about ½ turn and repeat Step 9.

10. If your concealment plug has not been removed proceed as follows:
    a. Invert the carburetor and use a hacksaw to make two parallel cuts in the throttle body. Make cuts on each side of the locator points beneath the concealment plug. The cuts should reach down to the plug but should not extend more than 1/8 in. (3mm) beyond the locator points. The distance between the saw cuts will depend on the size of the punch to be used.
    b. Place a flat punch at a point near the ends of the saw marks in the throttle body. Hold the punch at a 45° angle and drive it into the throttle body until the casting breaks away, exposing the steel plug.
    c. Repeat the procedure for the other concealment plug.
    d. Use Tool C–4895 (BT–7610B) or equivalent, to remove idle mixture screws.
11. With the propane still flowing, adjust the idle speeds screw on the solenoid until the tachometer indicates the specified propane rpm.
12. Fine tune the metering valve for the highest engine rpm. If there has been a change in the maximum rpm, readjust the idle speed screw to the specified propane rpm.
13. Turn off the main propane valve and allow the engine speed to stabilize.
14. Slowly adjust the mixture screw until the tachometer indicates the specified idle rpm. Pause between adjustments to allow the engine speed to stabilize.
15. Turn on the propane valve.
16. Fine tune the metering valve to get the highest engine rpm. If the maximum speed is more than 25 rpm different from the specified propane rpm, repeat Steps 9 and 11–15. If okay, proceed to Step 17.
17. Turn off both valves on the propane bottle.
18. Remove propane supply hose and reinstall the vacuum hose that goes to the heated air door sensor.
19. Remove the jumper wire from the carburetor ground switch.
20. Reinstall the PCV valve, remove the jumper wire and reconnect radiator fan plug and reconnect O_2 system test connector.
21. Unplug and reconnect the vacuum hose connector to the EGR valve.
22. After Steps 17–21 are completed, the curb idle speed may be different than the idle set rpm. This is normal and engine speed should not be readjusted. Turn the engine **OFF** and remove the tachometer. Reinstall the concealment plug.

HOLLEY 2210 CARBURETOR

Idle RPM Adjustment

1. Check and adjust the timing.
2. Disconnect the vacuum hose at the EGR valve.
3. Disconnect and plug the 3/16 in. hose at the canister.
4. Remove the PCV valve from the valve cover.
5. Connect a tachometer.
6. Start the engine and run it to normal operating temperature.
7. Turn the idle speed control screw to adjust the engine rpm.

Propane Idle Mixture Adjustment

➡ This procedure should only be used if an idle defect still exists after normal diagnosis has revealed no other faulty condition, such as incorrect idle speed, incorrect basic timing, faulty hose or wire connections, etc. It is also important to make sure the combustion computer systems are operating properly. Adjustment of the air/fuel mixture should also be performed after a major carburetor overhaul.

1. Disconnect and plug vacuum hose at the EGR valve.
2. Ground the carburetor switch with a jumper wire.
3. Disconnect and plug 3/16 in. diameter hose at the canister.
4. Remove the PCV valve from the valve cover and allow it to draw underhood air.
5. Connect a tachometer to the engine, then start the engine and let the speed stabilize for two minutes.
6. Disconnect the engine harness connector from the O_2 sensor and ground the engine harness lead with a jumper wire.

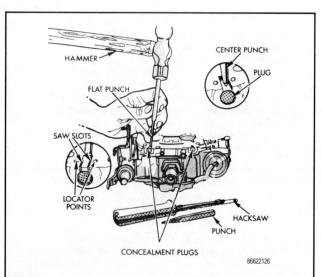

Fig. 70 Concealment plug removal on the Rochester Quadrajet carburetor

ENGINE PERFORMANCE AND TUNE-UP   2-33

➡ Care should be exercised so that no pulling force is put on the wire attached to the O_2 sensor. The bullet connector to be disconnected is approximately 4 in. (10.2cm) from the sensor. Use care in working around the sensor as the exhaust manifold is extremely hot.

    7. Let the engine run for 4 minutes to allow the effect of disconnecting the O_2 sensor to take place.

    8. Disconnect the vacuum hose from the heated air door sensor at the carburetor and install the propane supply in its place.

    9. Open the propane main valve. Slowly open the propane metering valve until maximum engine rpm is reached.

➡ When too much propane is added, engine speed will decrease. Fine tune the metering valve for the highest engine rpm. Also, if the idle mixture is extremely rich, engine rpm will decrease with any amount of propane. In this case, turn the idle mixture screw in about ½ turn and repeat Step 9.

    10. With the propane still flowing, adjust the idle speeds screw on the solenoid until the tachometer indicates the specified propane rpm.

    11. Fine tune the metering valve for the highest engine rpm. If there has been a change in the maximum rpm, readjust the idle speed screw to the specified propane rpm.

    12. Turn off the main propane valve and allow the engine speed to stabilize.

    13. If your concealment plug has not been removed proceed as follows:

      a. Invert the carburetor and use a hacksaw to make two parallel cuts in the throttle body. Make cuts on each side of the locator points beneath the concealment plug. The cuts should reach down to the plug but should not extend more than ⅛ in. (3mm) beyond the locator points. The distance between the saw cuts will depend on the size of the punch to be used.

      b. Place a flat punch at a point near the ends of the saw marks in the throttle body. Hold the punch at a 45° angle and drive it into the throttle body until the casting breaks away, exposing the steel plug.

      c. Repeat the procedure for the other concealment plug.

      d. Use Tool C–4895 (BT–7610B) or equivalent to remove the idle mixture screws.

    14. Slowly adjust the mixture screw until the tachometer indicates the specified idle rpm. Pause between adjustments to allow the engine speed to stabilize.

    15. Turn on the propane valve.

    16. Fine tune the metering valve to get the highest engine rpm. If the maximum speed is more than 25 rpm different than the specified propane rpm, repeat Steps 9–12 and 14–15. If okay, proceed to Step 17.

    17. Turn off both valves on the propane bottle.

    18. Remove propane supply hose and reinstall the vacuum hose that goes to the heated air door sensor.

    19. Remove the jumper wire from the carburetor ground switch.

    20. Reinstall the PCV valve. Remove the jumper wire, then attach the radiator fan plug and O_2 system test connector.

    21. Unplug and reconnect the vacuum hose connector to the EGR valve.

    22. After Steps 17–21 are completed, the curb idle speed may be different than the idle set rpm. This is normal and engine speed should not be readjusted. Turn the engine **OFF** and remove the tachometer. Reinstall the concealment plug.

HOLLEY 2245 CARBURETOR

◆ See Figure 71

Idle RPM Adjustment

◆ See Figure 72

    1. Check and adjust the timing.
    2. Disconnect the vacuum hose at the EGR valve.
    3. Disconnect and plug the ³⁄₁₆ in. hose at the canister.
    4. Remove the PCV valve from the valve cover.
    5. Connect a tachometer.
    6. Start the engine and run it to normal operating temperature.
    7. Turn the idle speed control screw to adjust the engine rpm.

Propane Idle Mixture Adjustment

➡ This procedure should only be used if an idle defect still exists after normal diagnosis has revealed no other faulty condition, such as incorrect idle speed, incorrect basic timing, faulty hose or wire connections, etc. It is also important to make sure the combustion computer systems are operating properly. Adjustment of the air/fuel mixture should also be performed after a major carburetor overhaul.

    1. Disconnect and plug vacuum hose at the EGR valve.
    2. Ground the carburetor switch with a jumper wire.
    3. Disconnect and plug ³⁄₁₆ in. diameter hose at the canister.
    4. Remove the PCV valve from the valve cover and allow it to draw underhood air.
    5. Connect a tachometer to the engine, then start the engine and let the speed stabilize for two minutes.
    6. Disconnect the engine harness connector from the O_2 sensor and ground the engine harness lead with a jumper wire.

➡ Care should be exercised so that no pulling force is put on the wire attached to the O_2 sensor. The bullet connector to be disconnected is approximately 4 in. (10.2cm) from the sensor. Use care in working around the sensor, as the exhaust manifold is extremely hot.

    7. Let the engine run for 4 minutes to allow the effect of disconnecting the O_2 sensor to take place.

    8. Disconnect the vacuum hose from the heated air door sensor at the carburetor and install the propane supply in its place.

    9. Open the propane main valve. Slowly open the propane metering valve until maximum engine rpm is reached.

➡ When too much propane is added, engine speed will decrease. Fine tune the metering valve for the highest engine rpm. Also, if the idle mixture is extremely rich, engine rpm will decrease with any amount of propane. In this case, turn the idle mixture screw in about ½ turn and repeat Step 9.

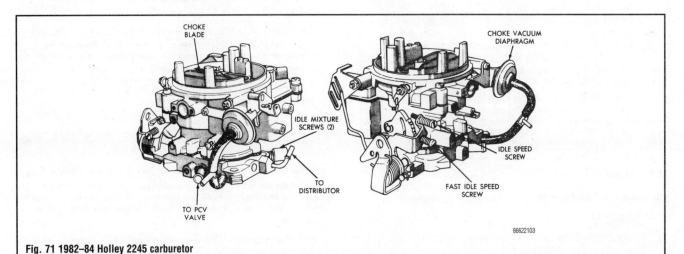

Fig. 71 1982–84 Holley 2245 carburetor

2-34 ENGINE PERFORMANCE AND TUNE-UP

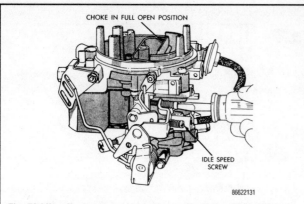

Fig. 72 Idle adjustment screw location on the Holley 2245 carburetor

10. If your concealment plug has not been removed proceed as follows:
  a. Invert the carburetor and use a hacksaw to make two parallel cuts in the throttle body. Make cuts on each side of the locator points beneath the concealment plug. The cuts should reach down to the plug but should not extend more than 1/8 in. beyond the locator points. The distance between the saw cuts will depend on the size of the punch to be used.
  b. Place a flat punch at a point near the ends of the saw marks in the throttle body. Hold the punch at a 45° angle and drive it into the throttle body until the casting breaks away, exposing the steel plug.
11. Repeat the procedure for the other concealment plug.
12. Use Tool C–4895 (BT–7610B) or equivalent, to remove idle mixture screws.
13. With the propane still flowing, adjust the idle speeds screw on the solenoid until the tachometer indicates the specified propane rpm.
14. Fine tune the metering valve for the highest engine rpm. If there has been a change in the maximum rpm, readjust the idle speed screw to the specified propane rpm.
15. Turn off the main propane valve and allow the engine speed to stabilize.
16. If your concealment plug has not been removed proceed as follows:
  a. Invert the carburetor and use a hacksaw to make two parallel cuts in the throttle body. Make cuts on each side of the locator points beneath the concealment plug. The cuts should reach down to the plug but should not extend more than 1/8 in. beyond the locator points. The distance between the saw cuts will depend on the size of the punch to be used.
  b. Place a flat punch at a point near the ends of the saw marks in the throttle body. Hold the punch at a 45° angle and drive it into the throttle body until the casting breaks away, exposing the steel plug.
17. Slowly adjust the mixture screw until the tachometer indicates the specified idle rpm. Pause between adjustments to allow the engine speed to stabilize.
18. Turn on the propane valve.
19. Fine tune the metering valve to get the highest engine rpm. If the maximum speed is more than 25 rpm different from the specified propane rpm, repeat Steps 9–14. If okay, proceed to Step 16.
20. Turn off both valves on the propane bottle.
21. Remove propane supply hose and reinstall the vacuum hose that goes to the heated air door sensor.
22. Remove the jumper wire from the carburetor ground switch.
23. Reinstall the PCV valve, remove the jumper wire and reconnect radiator fan plug and reconnect O2 system test connector.
24. Unplug and reconnect the vacuum hose connector to the EGR valve.
25. After Steps 16–20 are completed, the curb idle speed may be different than the idle set rpm. This is normal and engine speed should not be readjusted. Turn the engine **OFF** and remove the tachometer. Reinstall the concealment plug.

HOLLEY 1945 CARBURETOR

♦ See Figure 73

Solenoid Idle Stop Adjustment

♦ See Figure 74

1. Check ignition timing to ensure proper idle speed.
2. Disconnect and plug the vacuum hose at the EGR valve.

3. Disconnect and plug the 3/16 in. diameter control hose at the canister.
4. Remove the PCV valve to allow it to draw air.
5. Turn on the air conditioning and set the blower on low.
6. Disconnect the air conditioning clutch wire.
7. On trucks without A/C, connect a jumper wire between the battery positive post and the SIS lead wire.

✱✱ WARNING

Make sure to use care when jumping to the proper wire on the solenoid. Applying battery voltage to other than the correct wire will damage the wiring harness.

8. Open the throttle slightly to allow the solenoid plunger to extend.
9. Remove the adjusting screw and spring from the solenoid. Insert a 1/8 in. Allen head wrench into the solenoid and turn to set the correct idle speed.
10. Turn the A/C off and reconnect the clutch wire, or remove the jumper wire.
11. Replace the solenoid screw and spring. Proceed to the Idle RPM Adjustment.

Idle RPM Adjustment

♦ See Figure 75

1. Check and adjust the timing.
2. Disconnect the vacuum hose at the EGR valve.
3. Disconnect and plug the 3/16 in. hose at the canister.
4. Remove the PCV valve from the valve cover.
5. Ground the carburetor switch with a jumper wire.
6. Connect a tachometer.
7. Start the engine and run it to normal operating temperature.
8. Turn the idle speed control screw on the idle solenoid to adjust the engine rpm.

Propane Idle Mixture Adjustment

♦ See Figure 76

➡This procedure should only be used if an idle defect still exists after normal diagnosis has revealed no other faulty condition, such as incorrect idle speed, incorrect basic timing, faulty hose or wire connections, etc. It is also important to make sure the combustion computer systems are operating properly. Adjustment of the air/fuel mixture should also be performed after a major carburetor overhaul.

1. Disconnect and plug vacuum hose at the EGR valve.
2. Ground the carburetor switch with a jumper wire.
3. Disconnect and plug 3/16 in. diameter hose at the canister.
4. Remove the PCV valve from the valve cover and allow it to draw underhood air.
5. Connect a tachometer to the engine, then start the engine and let the speed stabilize for two minutes.
6. Disconnect the engine harness connector from the O2 sensor and ground the engine harness lead with a jumper wire.

➡Care should be exercised so that no pulling force is put on the wire attached to the O2 sensor. The bullet connector to be disconnected is approximately 4 in. (10.2cm) from the sensor. Use care in working around the sensor, as the exhaust manifold is extremely hot.

7. Let the engine run for 4 minutes to allow the effect of disconnecting the O2 sensor to take place.
8. Disconnect the vacuum hose from the heated air door sensor at the carburetor and install the propane supply in its place.
9. Open the propane main valve. Slowly open the propane metering valve until maximum engine rpm is reached.

➡When too much propane is added, engine speed will decrease. Fine tune the metering valve for the highest engine rpm. Also, if the idle mixture is extremely rich, engine rpm will decrease with any amount of propane. In this case, turn the idle mixture screw in about 1/2 turn and repeat Step 9.

10. With the propane still flowing, adjust the idle speeds screw on the solenoid until the tachometer indicates the specified propane rpm.

ENGINE PERFORMANCE AND TUNE-UP

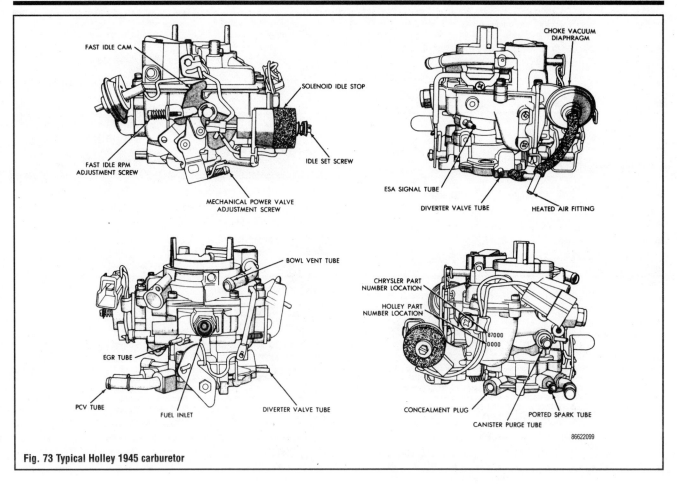

Fig. 73 Typical Holley 1945 carburetor

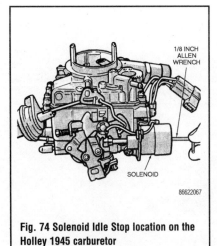

Fig. 74 Solenoid Idle Stop location on the Holley 1945 carburetor

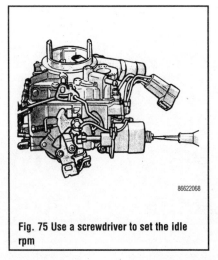

Fig. 75 Use a screwdriver to set the idle rpm

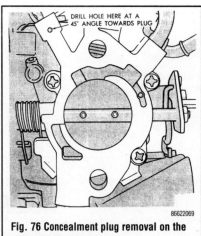

Fig. 76 Concealment plug removal on the Holley 1945 carburetor

11. Fine tune the metering valve for the highest engine rpm. If there has been a change in the maximum rpm, readjust the idle speed screw to the specified propane rpm.
12. Turn off the main propane valve and allow the engine speed to stabilize.
13. If your concealment plug has not been removed proceed as follows:
   a. Remove the carburetor from the engine.
   b. Remove the throttle body from the carburetor.
   c. Using a vise, clamp the carburetor, with gasket surfaces not touching the vise jaws.
   d. Drill a $FR5/64 in. (2mm) hole in the casting around the idle mixture screw, then redrill the hole to 1/8 in. (3mm).
   e. Insert a blunt punch into the hole and drive out the plug.
14. Install the carburetor on the engine.
15. Proceed with the Propane assisted idle procedure.
16. Slowly adjust the mixture screw until the tachometer indicates the specified idle rpm. Pause between adjustments to allow the engine speed to stabilize.
17. Turn on the propane valve.
18. Fine tune the metering valve to get the highest engine rpm. If the maximum speed is more than 25 rpm different from the specified propane rpm, repeat Steps 9–12 and 14–17. If okay, proceed to Step 19.
19. Turn off both valves on the propane bottle.
20. Remove propane supply hose and reinstall the vacuum hose that goes to the heated air door sensor.
21. Remove the jumper wire from the carburetor ground switch.
22. Reinstall the PCV valve, remove the jumper wire and reconnect radiator fan plug and reconnect O_2 system test connector.

2-36 ENGINE PERFORMANCE AND TUNE-UP

23. Unplug and reconnect the vacuum hose connector to the EGR valve.

24. After Steps 17–23 are completed, the curb idle speed may be different than the idle set rpm. This is normal and engine speed should not be readjusted. Turn the engine **OFF** and remove the tachometer. Reinstall the concealment plug.

Fuel Injected Engines

MINIMUM IDLE SPEED ADJUSTMENT

♦ See Figures 77 and 78

➥Normal idle speed is controlled by the logic module or SMEC. This adjustment is the minimum idle speed with the Automatic Idle Speed (AIS) closed.

1. Before adjusting the idle on an electronic fuel injected vehicle, the following items must be checked (and corrected, if necessary):
   - AIS motor operation
   - Engine vacuum and/or EGR leaks
   - Engine timing
   - Coolant temperature sensor operation

2. Connect a tachometer and timing light to the engine, according to the manufacturer's instructions.

3. Close the AIS by using ATM tester C–4805 or equivalent, and ATM test code #03.

4. Connect a jumper to the radiator fan, so that it will run continuously.

5. Start and run the engine for 3 minutes to allow the idle speed to stabilize.

6. Check engine rpm and compare the result with the specifications listed on the underhood emission control sticker.

7. If idle rpm is not within specifications, use tool C–4804 or equivalent to turn the idle speed adjusting screw to obtain 790–810 rpm. If the underhood emission sticker specifications are different, use those values for adjustment.

➥If idle will not adjust down check for binding linkage, speed control servo cable adjustment or throttle shaft binding.

8. Turn the engine **OFF**, then disconnect the tachometer, reattach the AIS wire, and remove the jumper wire from the fan motor.

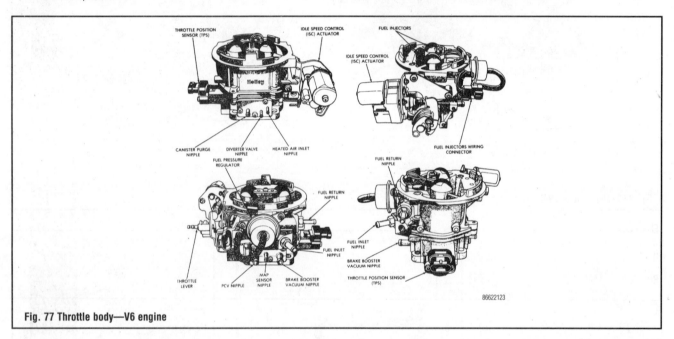

Fig. 77 Throttle body—V6 engine

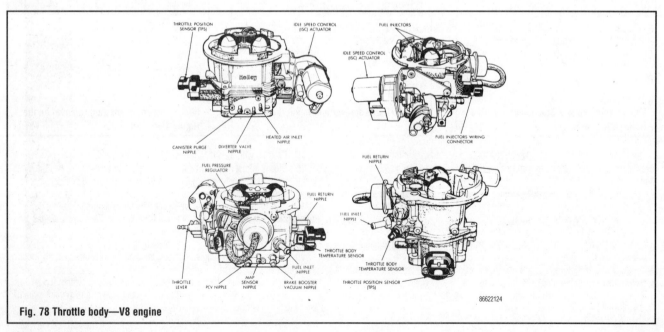

Fig. 78 Throttle body—V8 engine

ENGINE ELECTRICAL 3-2
IGNITION COIL 3-2
    REMOVAL & INSTALLATION 3-2
IGNITION MODULE 3-2
    REMOVAL & INSTALLATION 3-2
DISTRIBUTOR 3-3
    REMOVAL & INSTALLATION 3-3
    INSTALLATION IF TIMING WAS LOST 3-3
ALTERNATOR 3-3
    ALTERNATOR PRECAUTIONS 3-3
    TESTING 3-4
    REMOVAL & INSTALLATION 3-4
    BELT TENSION ADJUSTMENT 3-5
REGULATOR 3-5
    REMOVAL & INSTALLATION 3-5
    ADJUSTMENTS 3-5
BATTERY 3-6
    REMOVAL & INSTALLATION 3-6
STARTER 3-6
    TESTING 3-8
    REMOVAL & INSTALLATION 3-8
    SOLENOID & BRUSH REPLACEMENT 3-9
SENDING UNITS AND SENSORS 3-9
    REMOVAL & INSTALLATION 3-10
ENGINE MECHANICAL 3-10
DESCRIPTION 3-10
ENGINE OVERHAUL TIPS 3-10
    TOOLS 3-11
    INSPECTION TECHNIQUES 3-11
    REPAIRING DAMAGED THREADS 3-11
CHECKING ENGINE COMPRESSION 3-12
    GASOLINE ENGINES 3-12
    DIESEL ENGINES 3-12
ENGINE 3-16
    REMOVAL & INSTALLATION 3-16
ROCKER ARM (VALVE) COVER 3-19
    REMOVAL & INSTALLATION 3-19
ROCKER ARMS/SHAFTS 3-20
    REMOVAL & INSTALLATION 3-20
THERMOSTAT 3-22
    REMOVAL & INSTALLATION 3-22
    TESTING 3-23
INTAKE MANIFOLD 3-23
    REMOVAL & INSTALLATION 3-23
EXHAUST MANIFOLD 3-24
    REMOVAL & INSTALLATION 3-24
COMBINATION MANIFOLD 3-25
    REMOVAL & INSTALLATION 3-25
RADIATOR 3-26
    REMOVAL & INSTALLATION 3-26
WATER PUMP 3-27
    REMOVAL & INSTALLATION 3-27
CYLINDER HEAD 3-28
    REMOVAL & INSTALLATION 3-28
    INSPECTION 3-31
    RESURFACING 3-32
VALVE STEM SEALS 3-32
    REMOVAL & INSTALLATION 3-32
VALVES AND SPRINGS 3-32
    REMOVAL & INSTALLATION 3-32
    INSPECTION 3-35
VALVE SEATS 3-35
    REMOVAL & INSTALLATION 3-35
VALVE GUIDES 3-35
    REMOVAL & INSTALLATION 3-35
OIL PAN 3-35
    REMOVAL & INSTALLATION 3-35

OIL PUMP 3-37
    REMOVAL & INSTALLATION 3-37
FRONT COVER AND SEAL 3-38
    REMOVAL & INSTALLATION 3-38
TIMING CHAIN AND SPROCKETS 3-40
    REMOVAL & INSTALLATION 3-40
    CHECKING TIMING CHAIN SLACK 3-41
TIMING GEARS 3-42
    REMOVAL & INSTALLATION 3-42
VALVE TIMING 3-42
    ADJUSTMENT 3-42
AUXILIARY (IDLER) SHAFT 3-43
    REMOVAL & INSTALLATION 3-43
CAMSHAFT AND BEARINGS 3-43
    REMOVAL & INSTALLATION 3-43
    INSPECTION 3-45
    CAMSHAFT BEARING REPLACEMENT 3-46
PISTONS AND CONNECTING RODS 3-46
    REMOVAL & INSTALLATION 3-46
PISTON RING AND PIN REPLACEMENT 3-48
    CLEANING & INSPECTION 3-49
    SELECTING NEW PISTONS 3-49
    HONING 3-50
    ROD BEARING REPLACEMENT 3-51
    INSTALLATION 3-51
CYLINDER LINERS AND SEALS 3-52
    INSPECTION 3-52
    REMOVAL 3-52
    INSTALLATION 3-52
REAR MAIN SEAL 3-52
    REMOVAL & INSTALLATION 3-52
    CRANKSHAFT AND MAIN BEARINGS 3-53
    REMOVAL & INSTALLATION 3-54
    CLEANING & INSPECTION 3-55
    INSPECTION & REPLACEMENT 3-55
    COMPLETING THE REBUILDING PROCESS 3-57
    BREAK-IN PROCEDURE 3-57
FLYWHEEL AND RING GEAR 3-57
    REMOVAL & INSTALLATION 3-57
EXHAUST SYSTEM 3-57
GENERAL INFORMATION 3-57
SAFETY PRECAUTIONS 3-58
    COMPONENT REPLACEMENT 3-58
MUFFLER AND OUTLET PIPES 3-58
    REMOVAL & INSTALLATION 3-58
FRONT HEADER PIPES, CATALYTIC CONVERTER AND INLET PIPES 3-59
SPECIFICATIONS CHARTS
    DIRECT DRIVE STARTER DIAGNOSIS 3-7
    REDUCTION GEAR STARTER DISGNOSIS 3-7
    GENERAL ENGINE SPECIFICATIONS 3-13
    VALVE SPECIFICATIONS 3-13
    CAMSHAFT SPECIFICATIONS 3-14
    CRANKSHAFT AND CONNECTING ROD SPECIFICATIONS 3-14
    PISTON AND RING SPECIFICATIONS 3-15
    TORQUE SPECIFICATIONS 3-15
    TORQUE SPECIFICATIONS, ADDITIONAL 3-62

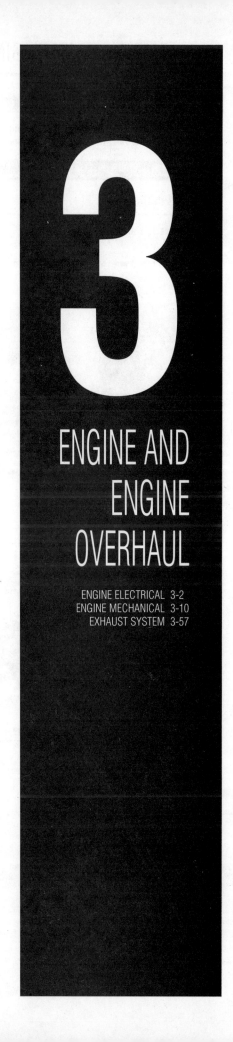

3

ENGINE AND ENGINE OVERHAUL

ENGINE ELECTRICAL 3-2
ENGINE MECHANICAL 3-10
EXHAUST SYSTEM 3-57

3-2 ENGINE AND ENGINE OVERHAUL

ENGINE ELECTRICAL

→ For information on understanding electricity and troubleshooting electrical circuits, please refer to Section 6 of this manual.

Ignition Coil

REMOVAL & INSTALLATION

▶ See Figures 1, 2 and 3 and 4

1. Disconnect the battery ground.
2. Disconnect the 3 wires from the coil. Mark them to identify for installation.
3. Disconnect the condenser suppressor connector from the coil, if equipped.
4. Unbolt and remove the coil.

To install:

5. Bolt down new coil with old bolts.
6. Connect wires to coil making sure that the proper wires are connected where they should be.
7. Connect the condenser suppressor, if equipped.
8. Connect battery ground.

Ignition Module

REMOVAL & INSTALLATION

Carbureted Engines

▶ See Figures 5 and 6

1. Disconnect the negative battery cable.
2. Check to see if your model is equipped with a small screw through the connector. If so, carefully remove it.
3. Unplug the control unit connector and remove the mounting screws.
4. Reinstall the mounting screws on the new control unit and plug in connector.
5. Connect the negative battery cable.

Fuel Injected Engines

This unit is called a, Single Module Engine Controller (SMEC).

✳✳ WARNING

Do not remove the grease from the 14-way connector or the connector terminal in the computer. The grease is used to prevent corrosion of the terminals. There should be at least a ⅛ in. (3.1mm) coating of grease on the bottom of the connector terminals. If not, apply a liberal coating of Mopar Multi-purpose grease part number 2932524 or equivalent, over the entire end of the connector plug.

1. Disconnect the negative battery cable.
2. Remove the air cleaner duct from the SMEC.
3. Remove the 3 module retaining screws.
4. Remove the 14–way and 60–way connectors from the SMEC.

To install:

5. Connect the 14–way and 60–way connectors to the SMEC.
6. Install and tighten the module retaining screws.
7. Install the air cleaner duct to the SMEC.
8. Connect the negative battery cable.

Fig. 1 Disconnect the wires from the coil

Fig. 2 Remove the bolts from the coil assembly

Fig. 3 Once all of the connections are removed, lift the coil from the engine

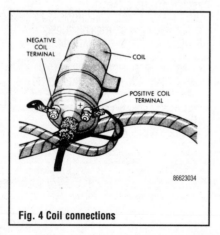

Fig. 4 Coil connections

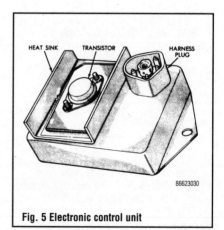

Fig. 5 Electronic control unit

ENGINE AND ENGINE OVERHAUL

Fig. 6 Electronic control unit connector

Distributor

REMOVAL & INSTALLATION

1. Remove the splash shield (if equipped). Disconnect the vacuum line(s) at the distributor, making sure you mark them accordingly.
2. Disconnect the pickup lead wire connector or connectors from the wiring harness.
3. Leaving the distributor wires connected, unfasten the clips or screws that retain the distributor cap and lift off the cap.

➡ **If insufficient clearance is obtained by removing the cap with the wires still connected, all or some of the spark plug wires should be tagged and disconnected from the cap for better access.**

4. Bump the engine around until the rotor is pointing at No. 1 cylinder firing position, with the timing marks on the front case and crank pulley are aligned. Disconnect the negative battery cable from the battery.
5. Mark the distributor body and the engine block to indicate the position of the distributor in the block. Mark the distributor body to indicate the rotor position. These marks are used as guides when installing the distributor.
6. Remove the distributor hold-down bolt and bracket. Carefully lift the distributor from the engine. The shaft may rotate slightly as the distributor is removed. Make a note of where the movement stops. That is where the rotor must point when the distributor is reinstalled into the block.
7. If the crankshaft has not been rotated while the distributor was removed from the engine, use the reference marks made before removal to correctly position the distributor in the block. The shaft may have to be rotated slightly to engage the cam gear (in-line 6 cylinder) or intermediate shaft gear (V6 and V8).

If the crankshaft was rotated or otherwise distributed (e.g. during engine rebuilding) after the distributor was removed, proceed as follows:

INSTALLATION IF TIMING WAS LOST

Inline 6 Cylinder Engines

1. Remove No. 1 spark plug. With your thumb plugging the hole, rotate the engine until the no 1 piston is up on the compression at top dead center. You'll feel the pressure of the compression stroke with your thumb and the **0** mark on the crankshaft pulley hub will be aligned with the timing pointer.
2. Turn the rotor to a position just ahead of the No. 1 distributor cap terminal.
3. Lower the distributor into the opening engaging the distributor gear with the drive gear on camshaft. With the distributor fully seated in the engine, the rotor should be under the cap No. 1 tower.
4. Install the cap, then tighten the hold-down bracket bolt. Connect the wiring and the vacuum hose. Check the timing with a timing light. Adjust if necessary.

V6 and V8 Gasoline Engines

1. Rotate the crankshaft until No. 1 cylinder is at Top Dead Center (TDC) of the compression stroke. To do this, remove the spark plug from the No. 1 cylinder and place your thumb over the hole. Slowly turn the engine by hand in the normal direction of rotation until compression is felt at the hole. The **0** mark on the crankshaft pulley should be aligned with the pointer on the timing case cover.
2. Hold the distributor over the mounting pad on the cylinder block so that the distributor body flange coincides with the mounting pad and the rotor points to the No. 1 cylinder firing position.
3. Install the distributor while holding the rotor in position, allowing it to move only enough to engage the slot in the drive gear.
4. Install pickup coil leads and distributor cap. Make sure all high tension wires are firmly snapped in cap towers. Install distributor hold-down clamp screw, and finger-tighten.
5. Connect the wiring and vacuum hose. Check the timing, then adjust if necessary.

Alternator

The alternator charging system is a negative (–) ground system which consists of an alternator, a regulator, a charge indicator, a storage battery, the wiring connecting the components, and fuse link wire.

The alternator is belt-driven from the engine. Energy is supplied from the alternator/regulator system to the rotating field through two brushes and finally two slip rings. The slip rings are mounted on the rotor shaft and are connected to the field coil. This energy supplied to the rotating field from the battery is called excitation current and is used to initially energize the field to begin the generation of electricity. Once the alternator starts to generate electricity, the excitation current comes from its own output rather than the battery.

The alternator produces power in the form of alternating voltage. The alternating current is rectified by 6 diodes into direct current. The direct current is then used to charge the battery and power the rest of the electrical system.

When the ignition key is turned **ON**, current flows from the battery, through the charging system indicator light on the instrument panel, to the voltage regulator, and to the alternator. Since the alternator is not producing any current, the alternator warning light comes on. When the engine is started, the alternator begins to produce current and turns the alternator light off. As the alternator spins and produces current, the current is divided in two ways: part to the battery to charge the battery and power the electrical components of the vehicle, and part is returned to the alternator to enable it to increase its output. In this situation, the alternator is receiving current from the battery and from itself. A voltage regulator is wired into the current supply to the alternator to prevent it from receiving too much current which would cause it to put out too much current. Conversely, if the voltage regulator does not allow the alternator to receive enough current, the battery will not be charged fully and will eventually go dead.

The battery is connected to the alternator at all times, whether or not the ignition key is turned **ON** or not. If the battery were shorted to ground, the alternator would also be shorted. This would damage the alternator. To prevent this, a fuse link is installed in the wiring between the battery and the alternator. If the battery is shorted, the fuse link is melted, protecting the alternator.

ALTERNATOR PRECAUTIONS

To prevent damage to the alternator and regulator, the following precautions should be taken when working with the electrical system.
- Never reverse the battery connections. This would cause BIG PROBLEMS!
- Booster batteries for starting must be connected properly: positive-to-positive and negative-to-ground.
- Disconnect the battery cables before using a fast charger; the charger has a tendency to force current through the diodes in the opposite direction for which they were designed. This burns out the diodes.
- Never use a fast charger as a booster for starting the vehicle.
- Never disconnect the voltage regulator while the engine is running.
- Avoid long soldering times when replacing diodes or transistors. Prolonged heat is damaging to AC generators.
- Do not use test lamps of more than 12 volts (V) for checking diode continuity.
- Do not short across or ground any of the terminals on the AC generator.
- The polarity of the battery, generator, and regulator must be matched and considered before making any electrical connections within the system.
- Never operate the alternator on an open circuit. make sure that all connections within the circuit are clean and tight.

3-4 ENGINE AND ENGINE OVERHAUL

- Disconnect the battery terminals when performing any service on the electrical system. This will eliminate the possibility of accidental reversal of polarity.

TESTING

There are many possible ways in which the charging system can malfunction. Often the source of a problem is difficult to diagnose, requiring special equipment and a good deal of experience. This is usually not the case, however, when the charging system fails completely and causes the dash board warning light to come on or the battery to become dead. To troubleshoot a complete system failure only two pieces of equipment are needed: a test light, to determine that current is reaching a certain point; and a current indicator (ammeter), to determine the direction of the current flow and its measurement in amps. This test works under three assumptions:

- The battery is known to be good and fully charged.
- The alternator belt is in good condition and adjusted to the proper tension.
- All connections in the system are clean and tight.

➥In order for the current indicator to give a valid reading, the truck must be equipped with battery cables which are of the same gauge size and quality as original equipment battery cables.

1. Turn off all electrical components on the truck. Make sure the doors of the truck are closed. If the truck is equipped with a clock, disconnect the clock by removing the lead wire from the rear of the clock. Disconnect the positive battery cable from the battery and connect the ground wire on a test light to the disconnected positive battery cable. Touch the probe end of the test light to the positive battery post. The test light should not light. If the test light does light, there is a short or open circuit on the truck.

2. Disconnect the voltage regulator wiring harness connector at the regulator. Turn the ignition key **ON**. Connect the wire on a test light to a good ground (engine bolt). Touch the probe end of a test light to the ignition wire connector into the voltage regulator wiring connector. This wire corresponds to the **I** terminal on the regulator. If the test light goes on, the charging system warning light circuit is complete. If the test light does not come on and the warning light on the instrument panel is on, either the resistor wire, which is parallel with the warning light, or the wiring to the voltage regulator, is defective. If the test light does not come on and the warning light is not on, either the bulb is defective or the power supply wire form the battery through the ignition switch to the bulb has an open circuit. Connect the wiring harness to the regulator.

3. Examine the fuse link wire in the wiring harness from the starter relay to the alternator. If the insulation on the wire is cracked or split, the fuse link may be melted. Connect a test light to the fuse link by attaching the ground wire on the test light to an engine bolt and touching the probe end of the light to the bottom of the fuse link wire where it splices into the alternator output wire. If the bulb in the test light does not light, the fuse link is melted.

4. Start the engine and place a current indicator on the positive battery cable. Turn off all electrical accessories and make sure the doors are closed. If the charging system is working properly, the gauge will show a draw of less than 5 amps. If the system is not working properly, the gauge will show a draw of more than 5 amps. A charge moves the needle toward the battery, a draw moves the needle away from the battery. Turn the engine **OFF**.

5. Disconnect the wiring harness from the voltage regulator at the regulator connector. Connect a male spade terminal (solderless connector) to each end of a jumper wire. Insert one end of the wire into the wiring harness connector which corresponds to the **A** terminal on the regulator. Insert the other end of the wire into the wiring harness connector which corresponds to the **F** terminal on the regulator. Position the connector with the jumper wire installed so that it cannot contact any metal surface under the hood. Position a current indicator gauge on the positive battery cable. Have an assistant start the engine. Observe the reading on the current indicator. Have your assistant slowly raise the speed of the engine to about 2,000 rpm or until the current indicator needle stops moving, whichever comes first. Do not run the engine for more than a short period of time in this condition. If the wiring harness connector or jumper wire becomes excessively hot during this test, turn **OFF** the engine and check for a grounded wire in the regulator wiring harness. If the current indicator shows a charge of about three amps less than the output of the alternator, the alternator is working properly. If the previous tests showed a draw, the voltage regulator is defective. If the gauge does not show the proper charging rate, the alternator is defective.

REMOVAL & INSTALLATION

▶ See Figures 7, 8, 9 and 10

Though internal alternator repairs are possible, they require specialized tools and training. Therefore, it is advisable to replace a defective alternator, or have it repaired by a qualified shop.

1. Disconnect the ground cable at the battery.
2. Disconnect and label the alternator output (BATT) and field (FLD) leads, then disconnect the ground wire.
3. You may need to spray a lubricant on the existing nuts and bolts for easy removal. Sometime it may be necessary to allow the lubricant to sit for a few minutes.
4. Loosen the alternator adjusting bolt and swing the alternator in toward the engine. Disengage the alternator drive belt.
5. Remove the alternator mounting bolts and remove the alternator from the vehicle.

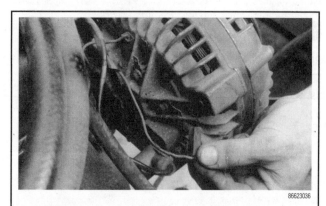

Fig. 7 Disconnect field (FLD) leads

Fig. 8 Disconnect output lead

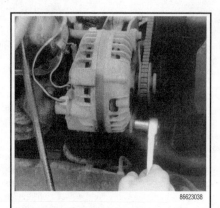

Fig. 9 Adjusting bolt removal

Fig. 10 Removal of mounting bolts

ENGINE AND ENGINE OVERHAUL

To install:

6. Install the alternator using the old bolts. Tighten the bolts, but not all the way, you still need to install the belt.

7. Install the old belt, or a replacement if worn. Always look at your belts before reinstalling an old one, you wouldn't want to do this job over again due to a junk belt.

8. Be sure to connect all ground wires and leads securely.
9. Adjust the belt tension. See belt tension adjustment.
10. Connect the battery ground cable.

BELT TENSION ADJUSTMENT

➡ On some models it may be necessary to remove the lower splash shield to gain clearance when installing a new drive belt.

Belt tension should be checked with a gauge made for the purpose. If a gauge is not available, tension can be checked with moderate thumb pressure applied to the belt at its longest span midway between pulleys. If the belt has a free span less than 12 in. (304mm), it should deflect approximately ¼ in. (6.3mm). If the span is longer than 12 in. (304mm), deflection can range between ¼ in. (6.3mm) and ⅜ in. (9.5mm). To adjust or replace belts:

1. Loosen the driven accessory's pivot and mounting bolts.
2. Move the accessory toward or away from the engine until the tension is correct. You can use a wood hammer handle as a lever, but do not use anything metallic.
3. Tighten the bolts and re-check the tension. If new belts have been installed, run the engine for a few minutes, then re-check and readjust as necessary.

➡ If the driven component has two drive belts, the belts should be replaced in pairs to maintain proper tension.

It is better to have belts too loose than too tight, because overtightened belts will lead to bearing failure in the alternator. However, loose belts place an extremely high impact load on the driven components due to the whipping action of the belt.

Regulator

REMOVAL & INSTALLATION

1967-69 Mechanical Regulator

♦ See Figure 11

1. Disconnect the negative battery cable.
2. Disconnect the wire connectors on the field "FLD" and ignition "IGN" sides of the regulator.
3. If bolts are rusty or hard to remove, use lubricant sprayed on the bolts, and allow to sit for a few minutes before attempting to remove. Loosen the hold-down bolts.
4. Remove the regulator.

To install:

5. Install the regulator and secure using the hold-down bolts. Fasten the wire connectors.
6. Connect negative battery cable.

1970-88 Electronic Regulator

♦ See Figure 12

1. Disconnect the negative battery cable.
2. Release the spring clips and pull off the regulator wiring plug.
3. See if your bolts are rusty or hard to remove, if so use lubricant and allow to sit for a few minutes before removing. Loosen the hold-down bolts.

To install:

4. Install the regulator and secure using the hold-down bolts.
5. Be sure that the spring clips engage the wiring plug.
6. Connect the battery cable.

ADJUSTMENTS

1967-69 Mechanical Regulator

♦ See Figures 13 thru 18

Normally, when the voltage regulator is suspected of being the cause of a vehicle charging system problem, the procedure is to remove the old unit and replace it with a new or reconditioned regulator. However, since these regulators are adjustable, it is advisable to perform the adjustments before removing the old unit. If the problem cannot be corrected easily by adjusting the voltage regulator, and no other possible causes of the problem can be found, the old regulator should then be replaced. In addition, adjustment procedures can be used when installing a new regulator to be sure that the voltage setting is correct.

➡ Do not remove the regulator when making voltage adjustments. Regulator removed in the preceding photos for explanatory purposes only.

1. Adjust the lower contact voltage setting as necessary by turning the adjustment screw clockwise to increase the voltage or counterclockwise to decrease the voltage. If this does not bring the voltage regulator to within specification, proceed to the next step.

If this does not bring the voltage regulator to within specifications, proceed to Step 2.

2. Remove the regulator cover and measure the upper contact point gap with a gauge. The point gap should be 0.010–0.014 in. (0.25–0.35mm). Adjust the upper contact gap as necessary by bending the armature upper contact bracket, making sure the contacts are in alignment. If the upper contact gap is correct and a difference of 0.2–0.7 volts exists between the upper and lower points, adjust the air gap as follows:

➡ If the difference is above 0.7 volts, reduce the air gap by bending down the fixed contact bracket; if the difference is below 0.2 volts, increase the air gap by bending the fixed contact bracket up.

   a. Connect a small dry cell test lamp in series with a IGN and FLD terminals of the voltage regulator.
   b. Insert a 0.032 in. (0.8mm) wire gauge between the regulator armature

Fig. 11 Though not always necessary, the cover of the mechanical voltage regulator may be removed for access to its components

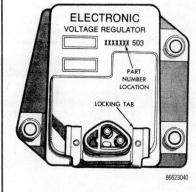

Fig. 12 1970-88 Voltage Regulator

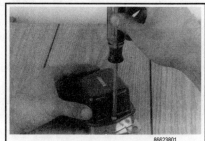

Fig. 13 If proper adjustment cannot be obtained with the cover installed, remove the cover retainers—Note; the regulator was removed for photographic purposes only

3-6 ENGINE AND ENGINE OVERHAUL

Fig. 14 Once the retainers are removed, lift the cover off for access to the internal components

Fig. 15 Use a gage to measure the gap

Fig. 16 Bend the contact to adjust the gap

Fig. 17 Wire gages are a necessity for testing many electrical devices on your truck

Fig. 18 When you are finished, make sure the rubber gasket is in position to ensure no moisture will enter the regulator

and the core of the voltage coil next to the stop on the armature. Press down on the armature until the armature contacts the wire gauge. The lower contacts should just open and the test lamp should be dim.

    c. With the air gap adjusted, a 0.042 in. (1mm) wire gauge cannot be inserted between the armature and voltage core.

3. Before installing the cover screws, make sure the rubber grommet is engaged over the voltage adjustment screw.

Battery

For additional information on battery maintenance and service, refer to Section 1 of this manual.

REMOVAL & INSTALLATION

➡For this job you should use gloves and old clothes due to possibly destroying your clothes with battery acid.

1. Disconnect the negative (ground) cable from the battery terminal, then disconnect the positive cable. Special pullers are available to remove post cable clamps, if they seem stuck.

➡To avoid sparks, always disconnect the ground cable first, and connect it last.

2. Remove the battery hold-down clamp.
3. Remove the battery, being careful not to spill the acid.

➡Spilled acid can be neutralized with a baking soda/water solution. If you somehow get acid into your eyes, flush it out with lots of water and get to a doctor.

To install:

4. Clean the battery posts thoroughly before installing a new or used battery.
5. Clean the cable clamps, using a wire brush, both inside and out.
6. Install the battery and hold-down clamp or strap. Connect the positive, and then the negative cable (see Note above). Do not hammer post cables onto the terminal posts. The complete terminals should be given a light external coating of petroleum jelly or grease to help prevent corrosion. There are felt washers available which have been impregnated with an anti-corrosion substance. These can be slipped over the battery posts before installing the cables, and are available in most auto parts stores.

✱✱ WARNING

Make absolutely sure that the battery is connected properly (positive to positive, negative to negative) before you turn the ignition key. Reversed polarity can burn out your alternator and regulator in a matter of seconds.

Starter

Almost all models are equipped with a reduction gear type starter motor. The only exception are some 1967 models with the 8–318. In 1967, a few models came equipped with a direct drive starter motor because of a higher compression ratio in some 318 V8's.

The diesel uses a reduction gear starter which differs slightly from the regular unit, having a 3.75:1 ratio as compared to a 3.5:1 ratio.

ENGINE AND ENGINE OVERHAUL 3-7

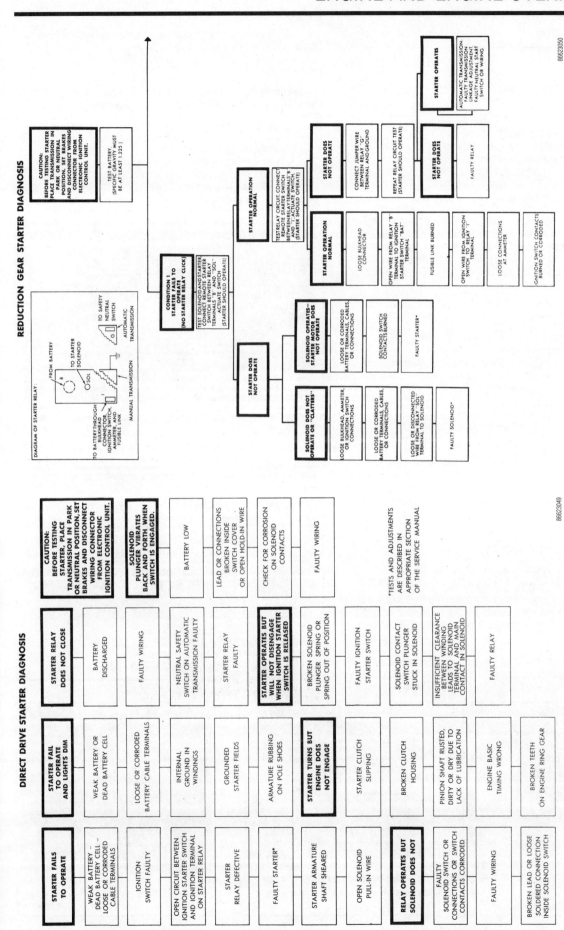

3-8 ENGINE AND ENGINE OVERHAUL

TESTING

Bench Test

GASOLINE ENGINES

1. Remove starter from vehicle.
2. Place starter in a soft jawed vise and position a fully charged, 12-volt battery so it can be connected to the starter.
3. Connect a test ammeter (100 amp scale) and a carbon pile rheostat in series with battery positive post and starter terminal.
4. Connect a voltmeter (15 volt scale) across starter from starter battery terminal to ground.
5. Rotate the carbon pile to full-resistance position.
6. Connect the battery cable from battery negative post to starter frame.
7. Adjust rheostat until battery voltage shown on voltmeter reads 11 volts.
8. With the starter engaged, check the specifications for maximum amperage draw and minimum RPM's At 11 volts, the allowable amperage draw is approximately 90 amps, while the allowable minimum RPM rate is around 3700 RPM's. If either of these specifications are not within range, the starter should be replaced or rebuilt..

DIESEL ENGINES

1. Remove starter from vehicle.
2. Place starter in a soft jawed vise and position a fully charged, 12–volt battery so it can be connected to the starter.
3. Connect a test ammeter (250 amp scale) and a carbon pile rheostat in series with battery positive post and starter terminal.
4. Connect a voltmeter (15 volt scale) across starter from starter battery terminal to ground.
5. Rotate the carbon pile to full-resistance position.
6. Connect the battery cable from battery negative post to starter frame.
7. Adjust rheostat until battery voltage shown on voltmeter reads 11 volts. Read the amperage draw on the ammeter, draw should be 180 amps or less.

REMOVAL & INSTALLATION

Gasoline Engines

▶ See Figures 19, 20, 21, 22 and 23

1. Disconnect the ground cable at the battery.
2. Remove the cable from the starter.
3. Disconnect the solenoid leads at their solenoid terminals.
4. Remove the starter attachment bolts and withdraw the starter from the engine flywheel housing. On some models with automatic transmissions, the oil cooler tube bracket will interfere with the starter removal. In this case, remove the starter attachment bolts, slide the cooler tube bracket off the stud, and then withdraw the starter.

   To install:

5. Be sure that the starter and flywheel housing mating surfaces are free of dirt and oil to make a good electrical contact.

6. Slide the starter in place, secure using the bolts and washers removed. Connect wires and battery cable end at the starter.
7. Secure the oil cooler bracket if equipped. Connect the negative battery cable on the battery.

➥When tightening the mounting bolt and nut on the starter, hold the starter away from the engine for the correct alignment.

Diesel Engines

1. Disconnect the negative battery cable.
2. Raise the truck and support it safely on jackstands.
3. Disconnect and label the wires at the starter motor.
4. Remove the attaching bolt, nut and washer, then lift the starter and solenoid assembly from the engine.

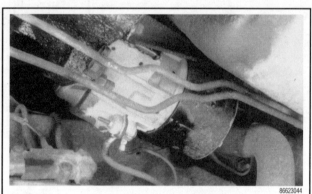

Fig. 19 The starter is usually easiest to access from under the vehicle

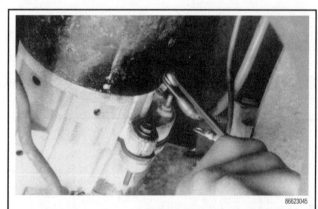

Fig. 20 Disconnect the battery cable from the solenoid terminal

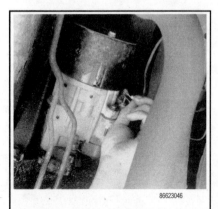

Fig. 21 Remove all solenoid wire leads

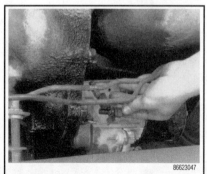

Fig. 22 On automatic transmissions you may need to unbolt the oil cooler lines or bracket

Fig. 23 Carefully remove starter, don't drop it as your head will be needed later

ENGINE AND ENGINE OVERHAUL 3-9

To install:

5. Before installing the starter motor, be sure the mounting surface on the drive end housing and the flywheel housing are clean, to ensure good electrical contact. When tightening the attaching bolt and nut, hold the starter away from the engine to ensure the proper alignment.
6. Attach the wiring at the starter.
7. Attach the negative battery cable.

SOLENOID & BRUSH REPLACEMENT

➡ You will need to purchase new brushes and a solenoid before proceeding on this job.

Reduction Gear Starter

♦ See Figure 24

1. Disconnect the ground cable at the battery.
2. Remove the cable from the starter.
3. Remove the starter from the truck and support the starter gear housing in a vise fitted with soft jaws. Do not clamp.
4. Remove the two through-bolts and the starter end assembly.
5. Carefully pull the armature up and out of the gear housing and the starter frame field assembly.
6. Carefully pull the frame and field assembly up just enough to expose the terminal screw (which connects the series field coils to one pair of motor brushes) and support it with two blocks.
7. Support the terminal by placing a finger behind it and remove the terminal screw.
8. Unwrap the shunt field coil lead from the other starter brush terminal. Unwrap the solenoid lead wire from the brush terminal.
9. Remove the steel and fiber thrust washer.
10. Remove the nut, steel washer, and insulating washer from the solenoid terminal.
11. Straighten the solenoid wire and remove the brush holder plate with the brushes and solenoid as an assembly.

✲✲ WARNING

Do not break the shunt field wire units when removing and installing the brushes.

12. Inspect the starter brushes. Brushes which are worn more than one-half the length of new brushes, or are oil-soaked, should be replaced.

➡ When resoldering the shunt field and solenoid leads, make a strong, low-resistance connection using a high-temperature solder and resin flux.

13. Assemble the brush holder plate with the brushes and solenoid.
14. Install the nut, steel washer, and insulating washer on the solenoid terminal.
15. Install the steel and fiber thrust washer.
16. Wrap the shunt field coil lead around the other starter brush terminal. Wrap the solenoid lead wire around the brush terminal.

17. Install the terminal screw which connects the series field coils to one pair of motor brushes.
18. Carefully push the armature down into the gear housing and the starter frame field assembly.
19. Install the starter end assembly and the two through-bolts.
20. Install the starter.

Direct Drive Starter

♦ See Figure 25

1. Remove the starter from the truck and support it in a vise fitted with soft jaws. Do not clamp.
2. Remove the through-bolts and tap the commutator and head from the field frame.
3. Remove the thrust washers from the armature shaft.
4. Lift the brush holder springs and remove the brushes from the holders. Remove the brush plate.
5. Disconnect the field coil leads at the solenoid connector.
6. Inspect the starter brushes. Brushes that are worn more than one-half the length of new brushes, or are oil-soaked, should be replaced. To replace the brushes, continue this procedure.
7. Remove the ground brush terminal screw and carefully remove the ground brush set to prevent breaking the shunt field lead. Remove the shunt field lead from the old brush set to ensure as much length as possible.
8. Remove the field terminal plastic covering and remove the old brushes. Use side cutters to break the weld by rolling the stranded wire off the terminal.
9. Drill a 0.174–0.184 in. (4.41–4.67mm) hole in the series coil terminal ³⁄₁₆ in. (4.7mm) from the top of the terminal to the centerline of the hole (use a number 16 drill).

✲✲ WARNING

Do not damage the field coil during the drilling operation.

10. Attach the insulated brush set to the series field terminal with a flat washer and a number 8 self-tapping screw. Attach the shunt field lead to the new ground brush set by making a loop around the terminal and soldering the lead to the terminal with resin core solder.
11. Attach the ground brush terminal to the field frame with the attachment screw. Fold the extra shunt field lead back along the brush lead and secure it with electrical tape.
12. Connect the field coil leads at the solenoid connector.
13. Install the plate and the brushes in the brush holders.
14. Install the thrust washers on the armature shaft.
15. Install the armature.
16. Install the field frame and through-bolts.
17. Install the starter.

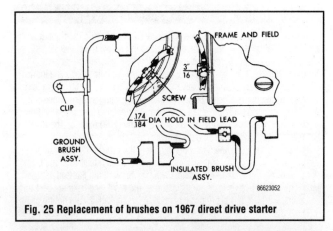

Fig. 25 Replacement of brushes on 1967 direct drive starter

Sending Units and Sensors

➡ Before proceeding with sensor removal you will need to purchase a new sensor and possibly a gasket or O-ring whichever is needed for your truck.

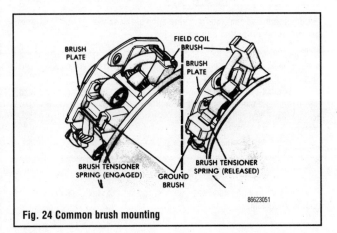

Fig. 24 Common brush mounting

3-10 ENGINE AND ENGINE OVERHAUL

REMOVAL & INSTALLATION

Oil Pressure Sensor

♦ See Figure 26

The oil pressure sending unit and oil pressure gauges are warning switches and need to be taken seriously if the light is on or gauge is low. This could mean the death of your engine if ignored for long enough; an expensive mistake.

These sensors are mounted on the engine and are controlled by the oil pressure. When the pressure is high, the switch is held in the off or open position allowing no current to flow to the oil pressure warning lamp on the instrument panel. When the oil pressure switch is in the low, on or open position, current is permitted to flow to the oil pressure switch warning lamp. This will cause the light to illuminate telling you that oil is needed immediately. You should always keep a quart of oil in your vehicle at all times in case of such an emergency.

1. Disconnect the negative battery cable.
2. Disconnect the terminal ends on the unit.
3. Spray lubricant on the unit, to ensure an easy removal.
4. With a suitable open-end wrench or a socket, unscrew the sending unit.

To install:

5. Make sure area is clean before replacing the sensor. Scrape any remaining gasket material that may be left behind. Use a wire brush or a gasket scraper.

6. Lube the threads with oil on the new sensor and place the O-ring or gasket on the end going into the engine. Carefully thread the sensor by hand, making sure the threads are even, and you are not forcing the sensor into the block. Using a tool, tighten sensor but not to tight as it could break easily.
7. Connect the wires on the sensor.
8. Connect the negative battery cable.
9. Start engine and look for any leaks in case the sensor is not tight enough.

Coolant Sensor

The coolant sensor is similar to the oil pressure switch. Except in that the temperature sending unit is controlled by the coolant not oil and it reacts to temperature not pressure. When the engine is cold the resistance of the disc in temperature sending unit is high and a low temperature will be indicated on the gauge. When your engine heats up at operating temperature the gauge will at its normal location between cold and hot. If your gauge reads **HOT**, or the temperature light comes on, this means there is a potential mechanical problem. Turn off your engine immediately. Overheating is not a pleasant thing to deal with in rush hour traffic or while on a vacation. We have all seen or at least known someone who has experienced it at one point.

➡ **If the engine has been run recently, allow time to cool down before servicing.**

1. Disconnect the negative battery cable.
2. Drain the cooling system into a suitable container. Just enough coolant should be removed to drop the system to a level below the sensor.
3. Spray lubricant on the unit, to ensure an easy removal.
4. Disconnect the coolant sensor wires from the unit.
5. Unscrew the sending unit, using a suitable open-end wrench or a socket.

To install:

6. Make sure area is clean before replacing the sensor. Remove any gasket material that may be left behind. Use a wire brush or a gasket scraper
7. Lube the threads with clean coolant on the new sensor and place the O-ring or gasket on the end going into the engine. Carefully thread the sensor by hand, making sure the threads are even, and you are not forcing the sensor into the block. Using a tool, tighten sensor but not to tight as it could break easily.
8. Connect the wires on the sensor.
9. Fill the cooling system with coolant.
10. Connect the negative battery cable.
11. Start the vehicle, and check for leaks. Also check the temperature gauge.
12. When the job is complete, make sure the vehicle has enough coolant in the radiator or expansion tank, if equipped.

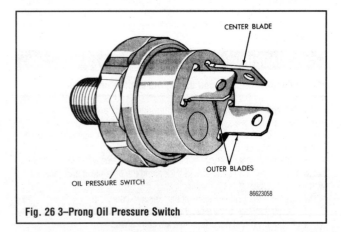

Fig. 26 3-Prong Oil Pressure Switch

ENGINE MECHANICAL

Description

The 6-198 and 6-225 slant-six engines are inclined toward the right at an angle of 30° from the vertical. The engine uses in-line overhead valves and wedge shaped combustion chambers with adjustable mechanical tappets through 1980. The 1981 and later engines employ hydraulic lifters. The lubrication system consists of an externally mounted rotor type oil pump on the lower right-hand side of the block. The semi-series flow cooling system contains an aluminum water pump body with a pressed-in ball bearing and seal assembly.

The 6-198 was used in limited numbers on early D100 models. The 6-225 was the standard engine on all other models.

The 6-251 is and in-line 6 cylinder engine of the L-head, or "flathead" design, with all the valves and valve actuating mechanism located in the block. The are no moving parts in the cylinder head, giving it a thin flathead appearance. The exhaust valve seats are replaceable. The block and head are cast iron. The camshaft rides in 4 bearings and is driven by crankshaft via a timing chain.

The diesel engine is a Mitsubishi built, in-line 6 cylinder with overhead valves. The diesel engine is entirely metric, therefore requiring the use of metric tools.

All V6 and V8 engines used are valve-in head type engines with wedge shaped combustion chambers. All are equipped with hydraulic tappets. The 318 and 360 lubrication system is a rotor type oil pump mounted on the rear main bearing cap and a full-flow, throwaway element filter located on the lower right-hand side of the block. The 400 and 440 oil pump and filter are on the outside of the block at the front of the engine.

Engine Overhaul Tips

Most engine overhaul procedures are fairly standard. In addition to specific parts replacement procedures and specifications for your individual engine, this section also is a guide to acceptable rebuilding procedures. Examples of standard rebuilding practice are shown and should be used along with specific details concerning your particular engine.

➡ **Competent and accurate machine shop services will ensure maximum performance, reliability and engine life.**

In most instances it is more profitable for the do-it-yourself mechanic to remove, clean and inspect the component, buy the necessary parts and deliver these to a shop for actual machine work.

On the other hand, much of the rebuilding work (crankshaft, block, bearings, piston rods, and other components) is well within the scope of the do-it-yourself mechanic. You will have to decide for yourself how involved you wish to become.

Aluminum has become extremely popular for use in engines, due to its low weight. Observe the following precautions when handling aluminum parts:
- Never hot tank aluminum parts (the caustic hot tank solution will eat the aluminum.
- Remove all aluminum parts (identification tag, etc.) from iron engine parts prior to the tanking.

ENGINE AND ENGINE OVERHAUL   3-11

- Always coat threads lightly with engine oil or anti-seize compounds before installation, to prevent seizure.
- Never overtorque bolts or spark plugs especially in aluminum threads.

Stripped threads in most any component can be repaired using any of several commercial repair kits (Heli-Coil®, Microdot®, Keenserts®, etc.).

When assembling the engine, any parts that will be in frictional contact must be prelubed to provide lubrication at initial start-up. Any product specifically formulated for this purpose can be used, but engine oil is not recommended as a prelube. This is especially true if the engine will be sitting unused for an extended period of time.

When semi-permanent (locked, but removable) installation of bolts or nuts is desired, threads should be cleaned and coated with Loctite® or other similar, commercial non-hardening sealant.

TOOLS

The tools required for an engine overhaul or parts replacement will depend on the depth of your involvement. With a few exceptions, they will be the tools found in a mechanic's tool kit. More in-depth work will require any or all of the following:

- A dial indicator (reading in thousandths) mounted on a universal base
- Micrometers and telescope gauges
- Jaw and screw-type pullers
- Gasket scraper
- Valve spring compressor
- Ring groove cleaner
- Piston ring expander and compressor
- Ridge reamer
- Cylinder hone or glaze breaker
- Plastigage®
- Engine stand

The use of most of these tools is illustrated in this section. Many can be rented for a one-time use from a local parts jobber or tool supply house specializing in automotive work.

Occasionally, the use of special tools is called for. See the information on the Special Tools and the Safety Notice in the front of this book before substituting another tool.

INSPECTION TECHNIQUES

Procedures and specifications are given in this section for inspecting, cleaning and assessing the wear limits of most major components. Other procedures such as Magnaflux® and Zyglo® can be used to locate material flaws and stress cracks. Magnaflux® is a magnetic process applicable only to ferrous materials. The Zyglo® process coats the material with a fluorescent dye penetrant and can be used on any material Check for suspected surface cracks can be more readily made using spot check dye. The dye is sprayed onto the suspected area, wiped off and the area sprayed with a developer. Cracks will show up brightly.

REPAIRING DAMAGED THREADS

▶ See Figures 27, 28, 29, 30 and 31

Several methods of repairing damaged threads are available. Heli-Coil® (shown here), Keenserts® and Microdot® are among the most widely used. All involve basically the same principle drilling out stripped threads, tapping the hole and installing a prewound insert making welding, plugging and oversize fasteners unnecessary.

Two types of thread repair inserts are usually supplied: a standard type for most inch coarse, inch fine, metric course and metric fine thread sizes and a spark lug type to fit most spark plug port sizes. Consult the individual manufacturer's catalog to determine exact applications. Typical thread repair kits will

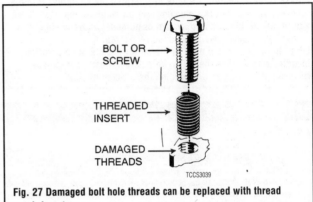

Fig. 27 Damaged bolt hole threads can be replaced with thread repair inserts

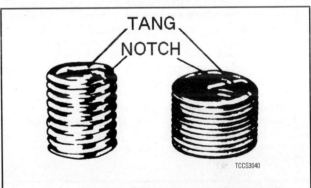

Fig. 28 Standard thread repair insert (left), and spark plug thread insert

Fig. 29 Drill out the damaged threads with the specified drill. Be sure to drill completely through the hole or to the bottom of a blind hole

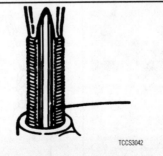

Fig. 30 Using the kit, tap the hole in order to receive the thread insert. Keep the tap well oiled and back it out frequently to avoid clogging the threads.

Fig. 31 Screw the threaded insert onto the installer tool until the tang engages the slot. Thread the insert into the hole until it is ¼ or ½ turn below the top surface, then remove the tool and break off the tang using a punch.

3-12 ENGINE AND ENGINE OVERHAUL

contain a selection of prewound threaded inserts, a tap (corresponding to the outside diameter threads of the insert) and an installation tool. Spark plug inserts usually differ because they require a tap equipped with pilot threads and a combined reamer/tap section. Most manufacturers also supply blister-packed thread repair inserts separately in addition to a master kit containing a variety of taps and inserts plus installation tools.

Before repairing to a threaded hole, remove any snapped, broken or damaged bolts or studs. Penetrating oil can be used to free frozen threads. The offending item can be removed with locking pliers or with a screw or stud extractor. After the hole is clear, the thread can be repaired, as shown in the series of accompanying illustrations.

✳✳ CAUTION

Please refer to Section 1 before discharging the compressor into a recovery station, or disconnecting any air conditioning lines. Damage to the air conditioning system or personal injury could result. Consult your local laws concerning refrigerant discharge and recycling. In many areas it may be illegal for anyone but a certified technician to service the A/C system. Always use an approved recovery station when discharging the air conditioning.

Checking Engine Compression

♦ See Figure 32

A noticeable lack of engine power, excessive oil consumption and/or poor fuel mileage measured over an extended period are all indicators of internal engine wear. Worn piston rings, scored or worn cylinder bores, blown head gaskets, sticking or burnt valves and worn valve seats are all possible culprits here. A check of each cylinder's compression will help you locate the problems.

As mentioned earlier, a screw-in type compression gauge is more accurate than the type you simply hold against the spark plug hole, although it takes slightly longer to use. It's worth it to obtain a more accurate reading. Follow the procedures below.

GASOLINE ENGINES

1. Warm up the engine to normal operating temperature.
2. Remove all the spark plugs.
3. Disconnect the high tension lead from the ignition coil.
4. Fully open the throttle either by operating the carburetor/throttle body linkage by hand or by having an assistant floor the accelerator pedal.
5. Screw the compression gauge into the No. 1 spark plug hole until the fitting is snug.

✳✳ WARNING

Be careful not to crossthread the plug hole. On aluminum cylinder heads use extra care, as the threads in these heads are easily ruined.

6. If you are not moving the linkage by hand, ask an assistant to depress the accelerator pedal fully on both carbureted and fuel injected vehicles. Then, while you read the compression gauge, ask the assistant to crank the engine two or three times in short bursts using the ignition switch.
7. Read the compression gauge at the end of each series of cranks, and record the highest of these readings. Repeat this procedure for each of the engine's cylinders. A cylinder's compression pressure is usually acceptable if it is no less than 80% of the highest cylinder's compression reading on the series of cranks.
8. If a cylinder is unusually low, pour a tablespoon of clean engine oil into the cylinder through the spark plug hole and repeat the compression test. If the compression comes up after adding the oil, it appears that the cylinder's piston rings or bore are damaged or worn. If the pressure remains low, the valves may not be seating properly (a valve job is needed), or the head gasket may be blown near that cylinder. If compression in any two adjacent cylinders is low, and if the addition of oil doesn't help the compression, there is probably leakage past the head gasket. Oil and coolant water in the combustion chamber can result from this problem. There may be evidence of water droplets on the engine dipstick when a head gasket has blown.

DIESEL ENGINES

♦ See Figure 33

Checking cylinder compression on diesel engines is basically the same procedure as on gasoline engines except for the following:

- A special compression gauge adaptor suitable for diesel engines (because these engines have much greater compression pressures) must be used.
- Remove the injector tubes and injectors from each cylinder.

✳✳ WARNING

Don't forget to remove the washer underneath each injector. Otherwise, it may get lost when the engine is cranked.

1. When fitting the compression gauge adaptor to the cylinder head, make sure the bleeder of the gauge (if equipped) is closed.
2. When reinstalling the injector assemblies, install new washers underneath each injector.

Fig. 32 A screw-in type compression gauge is more accurate and easier to use without an assistant

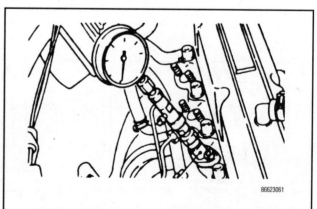

Fig. 33 Diesel engines require a special compression gauge adapter

ENGINE AND ENGINE OVERHAUL 3-13

GENERAL ENGINE SPECIFICATIONS

Engine	Engine Displacement Liters (cc)	Years	Fuel System Type	SAE net Horsepower @ rpm	SAE net Torque ft. lbs. @ rpm	Bore x Stroke (in.)	Comp. Ratio	Oil Press. (psi.) @ 2000 rpm
198	3.2	1968	1-bbl	125 @ 3900	190 @ 1600	3.400 x 3.640	8.40:1	30–70
225	3.7	1967–87	1-bbl	140 @ 3900	215 @ 1600	3.400 x 4.125	8.40:1	30–70
		1977–82	2-bbl	150 @ 3700	225 @ 1800	3.400 x 4.125	8.40:1	30–70
238	3.9	1988	EFI	N.A.	N.A.	3.910 x 3.310	9.0:1	30–80
243	4.0	1978–79	Diesel	100 @ 3700	163 @ 2200	3.620 x 3.940	20.0:1	40–45
251	4.1	1967–68	1-bbl	110 @ 3200	175 @ 1800	3.437 x 4.500	7.0:1	35–45
318	5.2	1967–87	2-bbl	120 @ 4200	250 @ 1600	3.910 x 3.310	8.6:1	30–80
		1979–84	4-bbl	150 @ 3900	245 @ 1800	3.910 x 3.310	8.5:1	30–80
		1988	EFI	135 @ 4000	240 @ 1800	3.910 x 3.310	9.0:1	30–80
360	5.9	1972–84	2-bbl	130 @ 3200	255 @ 2000	4.000 x 3.580	8.5:1	30–80
		1972–88	4-bbl	170 @ 3300	275 @ 2000	4.000 x 3.580	8.5:1	30–80
383	6.3	1967–71	2-bbl	258 @ 4400	375 @ 2800	4.250 x 3.375	7.5:1	45–65
400	6.6	1972–78	2-bbl	180 @ 3600	315 @ 2400	4.340 x 3.380	8.2:1	45–65
413	6.8	1967–68	2-bbl	217 @ 3600	373 @ 2000	4.188 x 3.750	7.5:1	45–65
		1967–68	4-bbl	220 @ 3600	407 @ 2000	4.188 x 3.750	7.5:1	45–65
440	7.2	1974–78	4-bbl	225 @ 4400	360 @ 3200	4.320 x 3.750	8.2:1	30–80

N.A.: Not Available

VALVE SPECIFICATIONS

Engine	Engine Displacement Liters (cc)	Years	Seat Angle (deg.)	Face Angle (deg.)	Spring Test Pressure (lbs. @ in.)	Spring Installed Height (in.)	Stem-to-Guide Clearance (in.) Intake	Stem-to-Guide Clearance (in.) Exhaust	Stem Diameter (in.) Intake	Stem Diameter (in.) Exhaust
198	3.2	1968	45	①	137–150 @ 1.3125	1.6875	0.0010–0.0030	0.0020–0.0040	0.3720–0.3730	0.3710–0.3720
225	3.7	1967–87	45	①	137–150 @ 1.3125	1.6875	0.0010–0.0030	0.0020–0.0040	0.3720–0.3730	0.3710–0.3720
238	3.9	1988	45	45	⑪	⑪	0.0010–0.0030	0.0020–0.0040	0.3720–0.3730	0.3710–0.3720
243	4.0	1978–79	45	45	②	⑨	0.0020–0.0030	0.0030–0.0040	0.3150	0.3150
251	4.1	1967–68	45	45	②	③	0.0010–0.0030	0.0020–0.0040	0.3405–0.3415	0.3395–0.3405
318	5.2	1967–68	45	④	170–184 @ 1.3125	1.6875	0.0010–0.0030	0.0020–0.0040	0.3720–0.3730	0.3710–0.3720
		1969–74	45	⑧	170–184 @ 1.3125	1.6875	0.0010–0.0030	0.0020–0.0040	0.3720–0.3730	0.3710–0.3720
		1975–76	45	45	⑦	1.65625	0.0010–0.0030	0.0020–0.0040	0.3720–0.3730	0.3710–0.3720
		1979	45	①	⑨	⑫	0.0010–0.0030	0.0020–0.0040	0.3720–0.3730	0.3710–0.3720
		1980–88	45	45	⑨	⑨	0.0010–0.0030	0.0020–0.0040	0.3720–0.3730	0.3710–0.3720
360	5.9	1972–76	45	①	170–184 @ 1.3125	1.6875	0.0010–0.0030	0.0020–0.0040	0.3720–0.3730	0.3710–0.3720
		1979	45	①	⑨	⑨	0.0010–0.0030	0.0020–0.0040	0.3720–0.3730	0.3710–0.3720
		1980–88	45	45	⑨	⑨	0.0010–0.0030	0.0020–0.0040	0.3720–0.3730	0.3710–0.3720
383	6.3	1967–68	45	45	⑤	1.85938	0.0010–0.0030	0.0020–0.0040	0.3720–0.3730	0.3710–0.3720
		1969–71	45	45	⑥	1.85938	0.0010–0.0030	0.0020–0.0040	0.3720–0.3730	0.3710–0.3720
400	6.6	1972–78	45	45	192–208 @ 1.4375	1.85938	0.0010–0.0030	0.0010–0.0040	0.3720–0.3730	0.3710–0.3720
413	6.8	1967–71	45	45	⑥	⑦	0.0010–0.0027	0.0010–0.0027	0.3720–0.3730	0.3723–0.3730
440	7.2	1974–78	45	45	236–256 @ 1.35938	1.85938	0.0010–0.0030	0.0030–0.0050	0.3718–0.3725	0.4330–0.4340
							0.0015–0.0032	0.0015–0.0032		

① Intake: 45
　Exhaust: 43
② Intake: 110–120 @ 1.3875
　Exhaust: 100–110 @ 1.21875
③ Exhaust: 1.59375
④ Intake: 45
　Exhaust: 47
⑤ Intake: 192–208 @ 1.46875
　Exhaust: 187–203 @ 1.46875
⑥ Intake: 173–187 @ 1.46875
　Exhaust: 110–120 @ 1.3875
⑦ Intake: 1.859375
　Exhaust: 1.734375
⑧ Intake: 45
　Exhaust: 43
⑨ Intake: 192–208 @ 1.46875
　Exhaust: 192–208 @ 1.46875
⑩ Intake: 170–184 @ 1.3125
　Exhaust: 180–194 @ 1.0625
⑪ Intake: 1.6875
　Exhaust: 1.203125
⑫ Intake: 1.6875
　Exhaust: 1.484375
⑬ Intake: 170–184 @ 1.3125
　Exhaust: 183–199 @ 1.0625
⑭ Intake: 45
　Exhaust: 43
⑮ Intake: 177–192 @ 1.250
　Exhaust: 184–199 @ 1.28125
⑯ Outer: 35.5–39.02 @ 1.772
　Inner: 15.21–16.53 @ 1.530
⑰ Outer: 1.772
　Inner: 1.530

3-14 ENGINE AND ENGINE OVERHAUL

CAMSHAFT SPECIFICATIONS
(All specifications in inches)

Engine	Engine Displacement Liters (cc)	Journal Diameter 1	2	3	4	5	Bearing Clearance	Elevation Int.	Elevation Exh.	End Play
198	3.2	2.0015	1.9845	1.9695	1.9535	—	0.0010–0.0030	0.397	0.392	0
225	3.7	1.9980–1.9990	1.9820–1.9830	1.9670–1.9680	1.9510–1.9520	—	0.0010–0.0030	②	②	0
238	3.7	1.9980–1.9990	1.9670–1.9680	1.9510–1.9520	1.5605–1.5615	—	0.0010–0.0030	0.373	0.400	0.006
243	4.0	2.1450–2.1460	2.1450–2.1460	2.1250–2.1260	2.0864–2.0865	—	0.0016–0.0035	0.419	0.419	0
251	4.1	1.9990–2.0010	1.9590–1.9610	1.9290–1.9310	1.2490–1.2510	—	0.0020–0.0040	0.379	0.379	0.004
318	5.2	⑤	⑤	⑤	⑥	—	0.0010–0.0030	①	①	③
360	5.9	1.9980–1.9990	1.9820–1.9830	1.9670–1.9680	1.9510–1.9520	1.5605–1.5615	0.0010–0.0030	0.410	0.435	0.004
383	6.3	1.9990–2.0010	1.9830–1.9950	1.9680–1.9700	1.9520–1.9540	1.7490–1.7510	0.0010–0.0030	0.425	0.435	0.004
400	6.6	1.9980–1.9990	1.9820–1.9830	1.9670–1.9680	1.9510–1.9520	1.7480–1.7500	0.0010–0.0030	0.434	0.430	0.004
413	6.8	1.9980–1.9990	1.9820–1.9830	1.9680–1.9700	1.9520–1.9540	1.7490–1.7510	0.0010–0.0030	0.360	0.360	0.004
440	7.2	1.9980–1.9990	1.9820–1.9830	1.9670–1.9680	1.9510–1.9520	1.7480–1.7500	0.0010–0.0030	④	④	0.004

① 1967–68:
  Intake—0.390
  Exhaust—0.391
1969–88:
  Intake—0.372
  Exhaust—0.400
② 1967–73:
  Intake—0.397
  Exhaust—0.392
1974–80:
  Intake—0.406
  Exhaust—0.414
1981–87:
  Intake—0.378
  Exhaust—0.378
③ 1967–74: 0.004
1975–88: 0.006
④ 1972–74:
  Intake—0.464
  Exhaust—0.464
1975–76:
  Intake—0.425
  Exhaust—0.435
1977:
  Intake—0.434
  Exhaust—0.430
⑤ 1967–76:
  No. 1—1.9980–1.9990
  No. 2—1.9820–1.9830
  No. 3—1.9670–1.9680
  No. 4—1.9510–1.9520
  No. 5—1.5605–1.5615
1977–80:
  No. 1—1.9970–1.9990
  No. 2—1.9830–1.9910
  No. 3—1.9680–1.9960
  No. 4—1.9500–1.9520
  No. 5—1.5595–1.5615
1981–88:
  No. 1—1.9980–1.9990
  No. 2—1.9820–1.9830
  No. 3—1.9670–1.9680
  No. 4—1.9510–1.9520
  No. 5—1.5605–1.5615
⑥ 1972–76: 0.400
1977–78: 0.410

CRANKSHAFT AND CONNECTING ROD SPECIFICATIONS
(All specifications in inches)

Engine	Engine Displacement Liters (cc)	Years	Main Brg. Journal Dia.	Crankshaft Main Brg. Oil Clearance	Shaft End-play	Thrust on No.	Journal Diameter	Connecting Rod Oil Clearance	Side Clearance
198	3.2	1968	2.4995–2.7505	0.0005–0.0015	0.0035–0.0085	3	2.1865–2.1875	0.0005–0.0015	0.006–0.012
225	3.7	1967–76	2.7495–2.7505	0.0005–0.0015	③	3	2.1865–2.1875	0.0005–0.0015	0.006–0.012
		1977–78	2.7495–2.7505	0.0005–0.0020	0.0020–0.0090	3	2.1865–2.1875	0.0005–0.0025	0.006–0.025
		1979–80	2.7495–2.7505	0.0002–0.0022	0.0020–0.0090	3	2.1865–2.1875	0.0002–0.0022	0.006–0.025
		1981–87	2.7495–2.7505	0.0010–0.0025	0.0035–0.0090	3	2.1865–2.1875	0.0010–0.0022	0.007–0.013
238	3.9	1988	2.4995–2.5005	②	0.0020–0.0070	3	2.1240–2.1250	0.0005–0.0022	0.006–0.014
243	4.0	1978–79	2.7539–2.7547	0.0012–0.0035	0.0039–0.0098	7	2.2813–2.2821	0.0015–0.0044	0.005–0.018
251	4.1	1967–68	2.4985–2.4995	0.0005–0.0015	0.0030–0.0070	3	2.1195–2.1205	0.0005–0.0015	0.006–0.011
318	5.2	1967–72	2.4995–2.5005	0.0005–0.0015	0.0020–0.0070	3	2.1240–2.1250	0.0005–0.0015	0.006–0.014
		1973–74	2.4995–2.5005	0.0005–0.0020	0.0020–0.0090	3	2.1240–2.1250	0.0005–0.0020	0.006–0.014
		1975–76	2.4995–2.5005	0.0005–0.0015	0.0020–0.0090	3	2.1240–2.1250	0.0005–0.0015	0.006–0.014
		1977–79	2.4995–2.5005	0.0005–0.0020	④	3	2.1240–2.1250	0.0005–0.0022	0.006–0.014
		1980–88	2.4995–2.5005	①	0.0020–0.0070	3	2.1240–2.1250	0.0005–0.0025	0.006–0.014
360	5.9	1972–74	2.8095–2.8105	0.0005–0.0020	0.0020–0.0090	3	2.1240–2.1250	0.0005–0.0020	0.006–0.014
		1975–79	2.8095–2.8105	0.0005–0.0020	0.0020–0.0090	3	2.1240–2.1250	0.0005–0.0025	0.006–0.014
		1980–88	2.8095–2.8105	①	0.0020–0.0070	3	2.1240–2.1250	0.0005–0.0022	0.006–0.014
383	6.3	1967–72	2.6245–2.6255	0.0005–0.0015	0.0020–0.0090	3	2.3740–2.3750	0.0005–0.0015	0.009–0.017
400	6.6	1974–78	2.6245–2.6255	0.0005–0.0020	⑥	3	2.3750–2.3760	⑤	0.009–0.017
413	6.8	1967–72	2.7495–2.7505	0.0015–0.0025	0.0020–0.0070	3	2.3740–2.3750	0.0010–0.0020	0.009–0.017
440	7.2	1974	2.7495–2.7505	0.0005–0.0020	0.0020–0.0070	3	2.3740–2.3750	0.0010–0.0025	0.009–0.017
		1975–76	2.7495–2.7505	0.0002–0.0022	0.0020–0.0070	3	2.3740–2.3750	0.0005–0.0015	0.009–0.017
		1977–78	2.7495–2.7505	0.0005–0.0020	0.0020–0.0090	3	2.3750–2.3760	0.0005–0.0030	0.009–0.017

① No. 1: 0.005–0.0015
Nos. 2, 3, 4, 5: 0.0005–0.0020
② No. 1: 0.005–0.0015
Nos. 2, 3, 4: 0.0005–0.0020
③ 1967–74: 0.0035–0.0085
1975–76: 0.0020–0.0090
1977–78: 0.0020–0.0090
1979: 0.0020–0.0070
④ 2-bbl: 0.0005–0.0025
4-bbl: 0.0005–0.0030
⑤ 1974: 0.0020–0.0070
1975–78: 0.0020–0.0090

ENGINE AND ENGINE OVERHAUL 3-15

TORQUE SPECIFICATIONS
All readings in ft. lbs.

Engine	Engine Displacement Liters (cc)	Year	Cylinder Head Bolts	Main Bearing Bolts	Rod Bearing Bolts	Crankshaft Damper Bolts	Flywheel Bolts	Manifold Intake	Manifold Exhaust
198	3.2	1968	65	85	45	—	55	③	10
225	3.7	1975–87	70	85	45	—	55	②	10
		1967–74	65	85	45	—	55	③	10
238	3.9	1988	105	85	45	135	55	45	—
243	4.0	1978–79	90	80	58	289	65	—	—
251	4.1	1967–68	65	85	45	135	60	25	20
318	5.2	1986–88	105	85	45	100	55	45	①
		1985	105	85	45	100	55	40	①
		1981–84	95	85	45	100	55	40	①
		1978–80	105	85	45	100	55	40	①
		1977	95	85	45	100	55	45	20
		1972–76	95	85	45	100	55	35	25
		1967–71	85	85	45	135	55	35	①
360	5.9	1986–88	105	85	45	100	55	45	①
		1984–85	105	85	45	100	55	40	①
		1981–83	95	85	45	100	55	40	①
		1978–80	105	85	45	100	55	40	①
		1977	95	85	45	100	55	45	20
		1972–76	95	85	45	100	55	35	20
383	6.3	1967–71	70	85	45	135	55	50	30
400	6.6	1975–78	70	85	45	135	55	45	30
		1973–74	70	85	45	135	55	40	30
413	6.8	1967–68	70	85	45	135	55	50	30
440	7.2	1975–78	70	85	45	135	55	45	30
		1973–74	70	85	45	135	55	40	30

① Screw: 20
  Nut: 15
② 1978–87:
  Intake-to-exhaust manifold stud: 25
  Intake-to-exhaust manifold bolt: 22
  1975–77:
  Intake-to-exhaust manifold stud: 20
  Intake-to-exhaust manifold bolt: 16
③ 1967–74:
  Intake-to-exhaust manifold nut: 30
  Intake-to-exhaust manifold screw: 20

PISTON AND RING SPECIFICATIONS
All measurements are given in inches.

Engine	Engine Displacement Liters (cc)	Years	Piston Clearance	Ring Gap Top Compression	Ring Gap Bottom Compression	Ring Gap Oil Control	Ring Side Clearance Top Compression	Ring Side Clearance Bottom Compression	Ring Side Clearance Oil Control
198	3.2	1968	0.0005–0.0015	0.010–0.020	0.010–0.020	0.015–0.025	0.0015–0.0030	0.0015–0.0030	0.0010–0.0030
225	3.7	1967–72	0.0005–0.0015	0.010–0.020	0.010–0.020	0.015–0.025	0.0015–0.0030	0.0015–0.0030	0.0010–0.0030
		1973–76	0.0005–0.0015	0.010–0.020	0.010–0.020	0.015–0.055	0.0015–0.0030	0.0015–0.0030	0.0010–0.0030
		1977–87	0.0005–0.0015	0.010–0.020	0.010–0.020	0.015–0.055	0.0015–0.0030	0.0015–0.0030	0.0002–0.0050
238	3.9	1988	0.0005–0.0015	0.010–0.020	0.010–0.020	0.015–0.055	0.0015–0.0030	0.0015–0.0030	0.0002–0.0050
243	4.0	1978–79	0.0060–0.0080	0.012–0.020	0.012–0.020	0.012–0.020	0.0010–0.0020	0.0010–0.0020	0.0010–0.0020
251	4.1	1967–68	0.0002–0.0012	0.010–0.020	0.010–0.020	0.010–0.020	0.0020–0.0035	0.0020–0.0035	0.0015–0.0030
318	5.2	1967–72	0.0005–0.0015	0.010–0.020	0.010–0.020	0.015–0.055	0.0015–0.0030	0.0015–0.0030	0.0010–0.0050
		1973–74	0.0005–0.0015	0.010–0.020	0.010–0.020	0.015–0.055	0.0015–0.0030	0.0015–0.0030	0.0020–0.0050
		1975–76	0.0005–0.0015	0.010–0.020	0.010–0.020	0.015–0.055	0.0015–0.0030	0.0015–0.0030	0.0005–0.0050
		1977–88	0.0005–0.0015	0.010–0.020	0.010–0.020	0.015–0.055	0.0015–0.0030	0.0015–0.0030	0.0002–0.0050
360	5.9	1972–74	0.0005–0.0015	0.010–0.020	0.010–0.020	0.015–0.055	0.0015–0.0030	0.0015–0.0030	0.0020–0.0050
		1975–76	0.0005–0.0015	0.010–0.020	0.010–0.020	0.015–0.055	0.0015–0.0030	0.0015–0.0030	0.0005–0.0050
		1977–88	0.0005–0.0015	0.010–0.020	0.010–0.020	0.015–0.055	0.0015–0.0030	0.0015–0.0030	0.0002–0.0050
383	6.3	1967–72	0.0005–0.0015	0.013–0.025	0.013–0.025	0.013–0.025	0.0015–0.0030	0.0015–0.0030	0.0002–0.0050
400	6.6	1972–76	0.0003–0.0013	0.010–0.020	0.010–0.020	0.015–0.055	0.0015–0.0030	0.0015–0.0030	0.0020–0.0050
		1977–78	0.0003–0.0013	0.013–0.023	0.013–0.023	0.015–0.055	0.0015–0.0030	0.0015–0.0030	0.0002–0.0050
413	6.8	1967–72	0.0005–0.0015	0.013–0.025	0.013–0.025	0.013–0.025	0.0025–0.0040	0.0025–0.0040	0.0010–0.0030
440	7.2	1972–74	0.0003–0.0013	0.010–0.020	0.010–0.020	0.015–0.055	0.0015–0.0040	0.0015–0.0040	0.0020–0.0050
		1975–76	0.0003–0.0013	0.010–0.020	0.010–0.020	0.015–0.055	0.0015–0.0030	0.0015–0.0030	0.0010–0.0030
		1977–78	0.0003–0.0013	0.013–0.023	0.013–0.023	0.015–0.055	0.0015–0.0030	0.0015–0.0030	0.0002–0.0050

3-16 ENGINE AND ENGINE OVERHAUL

Engine

REMOVAL & INSTALLATION

▶ See Figures 34 thru 46

➡It is always advisable to purchase new tune-up parts, filters, and fluids before you start this project. If you are going to all the trouble to replace an engine, you should make sure it is tuned-up and has fresh fluids.

Carbureted Engines

2-WHEEL DRIVE

1. Scribe matchmarks on the hood hinges and remove the hood from the truck, this makes it easier to work.
2. Disconnect and remove the battery.
3. Drain the coolant from the radiator and engine block.
4. Disconnect both radiator hoses, then remove with radiator and support brace as a unit. Set the fan shroud aside.

✱✱ CAUTION

When draining the coolant, keep in mind that cats and dogs are attracted to ethylene glycol antifreeze, and are quite likely to drink any that is left in an uncovered container or in puddles on the ground. This will prove fatal in sufficient quantity. Always drain the coolant into a sealable container. Coolant should be reused unless it is contaminated or several years old.

5. Drain the engine oil. On V8s, remove the oil filter.

✱✱ CAUTION

The EPA warns that prolonged contact with used engine oil may cause a number of skin disorders, including cancer! You should make every effort to minimize your exposure to used engine oil. Protective gloves should be worn when changing the oil. Wash your hands and any other exposed skin areas as soon as possible after exposure to used engine oil. Soap and water, or waterless hand cleaner should be used.

6. Remove the air cleaner.
7. Remove the starter.
8. On some models, it may be helpful to remove the front bumper, grille, support brace and radiator. This will allow more access to the front of the engine, as well as requiring less lifting of the engine out of the vehicle. Although this procedure is not totally necessary, many individuals find it a time saver.
9. Discharge the air-conditioning if so equipped, and remove the condenser.
10. Remove the power steering and air pumps with the hoses attached, make sure you plug the lines.
11. Disconnect the throttle linkage, heater and vacuum hoses and all electri-

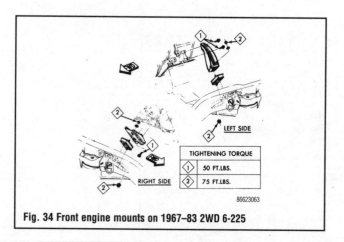
Fig. 34 Front engine mounts on 1967–83 2WD 6-225

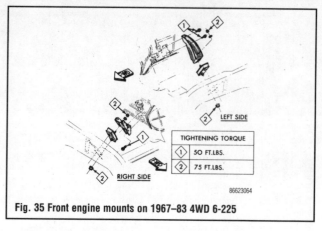
Fig. 35 Front engine mounts on 1967–83 4WD 6-225

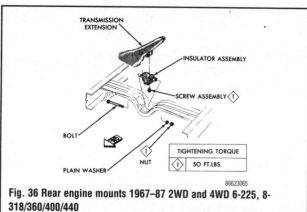
Fig. 36 Rear engine mounts 1967–87 2WD and 4WD 6-225, 8-318/360/400/440

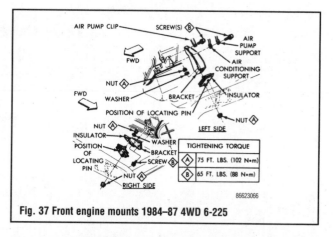
Fig. 37 Front engine mounts 1984–87 4WD 6-225

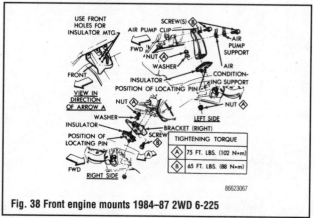
Fig. 38 Front engine mounts 1984–87 2WD 6-225

ENGINE AND ENGINE OVERHAUL   3-17

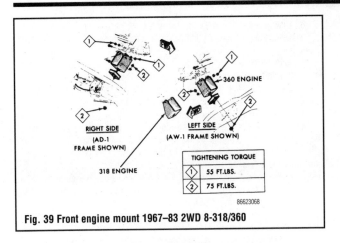

Fig. 39 Front engine mount 1967–83 2WD 8-318/360

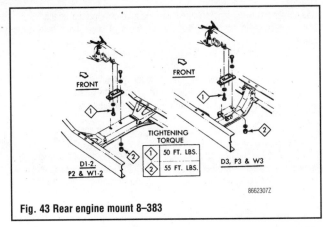

Fig. 43 Rear engine mount 8-383

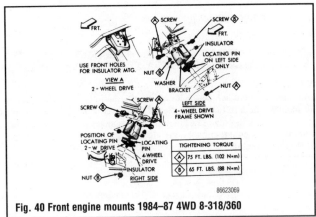

Fig. 40 Front engine mounts 1984–87 4WD 8-318/360

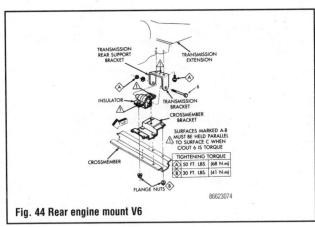

Fig. 44 Rear engine mount V6

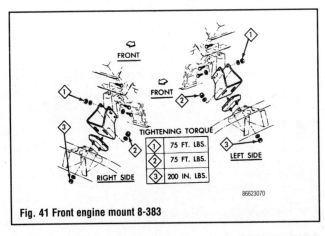

Fig. 41 Front engine mount 8-383

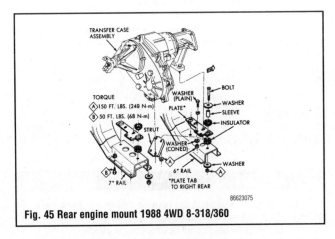

Fig. 45 Rear engine mount 1988 4WD 8-318/360

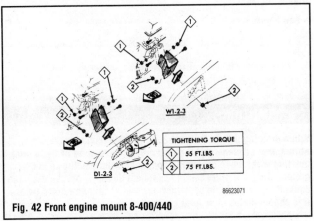

Fig. 42 Front engine mount 8-400/440

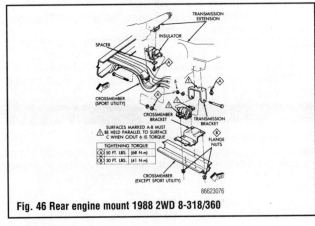

Fig. 46 Rear engine mount 1988 2WD 8-318/360

3-18 ENGINE AND ENGINE OVERHAUL

cal connections to the ignition, alternator, and all other electrical connections. Make sure you mark any wiring that you are unsure of where it may belong on replacement.

12. Remove the alternator, fan, pulley and drive belts.
13. Remove the heater blower motor.
14. Remove and plug the inlet line to the fuel pump.
15. Remove the oil dipstick tube. On V8s, remove the intake manifold and left exhaust manifold. If equipped with air conditioning, remove the right side valve cover.
16. To provide clearance on some models, the oil pan and transmission must be removed.
17. Raise the engine slightly in preparation for removal. Support it with an engine lifting fixture. This tool can be fabricated from galvanized pipe fittings obtained locally. Use only galvanized parts with an inside diameter of 1½ in. (38mm) or larger. Be sure they are firmly threaded together to assure maximum strength.
18. Raise the vehicle and support it on jackstands. Remove the starter and distributor.
19. Remove the driveshaft and engine rear support. Remove the rear support by removing the rear mount through bolt and the U-shaped bracket from the crossmember. Remove the insulator from the bottom face of the transmission housing.
20. If equipped with an automatic transmission, remove the transmission intact with the filler tube and the torque converter separated from the drive plate.
21. Raise the rear of the engine approximately 2 in. (50mm), then remove the clutch or drive plate and the flywheel.
22. On some models equipped with V8 engines, the oil pan should be removed to provide added clearance. In order to gain the necessary clearance for pan removal, position the cut-out in the crankshaft flange at 3 o'clock. Remove the oil pan screws and lower the oil pan far enough to reach inside and turn the oil pump pick-up tube slightly to the right to clear the pan. Remove the oil pan.
23. Lower the vehicle.
24. Using a suitable hoist attached to the engine with the shortest hook-up possible, take up all tension and support the engine. If you are using a hoist without removing the bumper and other portions of the front of the vehicle, lift the engine up and out of the engine compartment. Make sure you have cleared the front support as well as the fenders before backing up and lowering the engine to the floor. If you have removed the radiator and the front of the vehicle, raise the engine enough to clear any frame members, then back out the hoist from the engine compartment. The advantage with this method is that the engine does not have to be raised nearly as high as the previous method, which is safer for most individuals.
25. Remove the engine front mounts and insulator.
26. Carefully remove the engine from the vehicle.
27. Installation is the reverse of removal.

4-WHEEL DRIVE—EXCEPT WM-300

1. Drain the coolant from the radiator and cylinder block.

> **※※ CAUTION**
>
> When draining the coolant, keep in mind that cats and dogs are attracted to ethylene glycol antifreeze, and are quite likely to drink any that is left in an uncovered container or in puddles on the ground. This will prove fatal in sufficient quantity. Always drain the coolant into a sealable container. Coolant should be reused unless it is contaminated or several years old.

2. Disconnect the battery ground cable. Remove the battery.
3. Scribe the outline on the hood hinges and remove the hood.
4. If equipped with air conditioning, remove the compressor with lines attached and lay it aside.

> **※※ CAUTION**
>
> Do not disconnect any refrigerant lines!

5. Engage the electrical connections at the alternator, ignition coil, temperature and oil pressure sending units, starter-to-solenoid and engine/body ground.
6. Remove the air cleaner and carburetor. Install an engine lifting fixture.
7. Remove the distributor cap and rotor.

8. Disconnect and plug the fuel pump line.
9. Disconnect the radiator and heater hoses. Disconnect and plug the oil cooler lines.
10. Remove the fan, spacer, fluid drive, and radiator. Do not store the fan drive unit with the shaft pointing downward. Fluid will leak out.
11. Raise the truck and support the rear of the engine.
12. Disconnect the exhaust pipes at the manifolds.
13. Remove the starter on V8 models.
14. Remove the automatic transmission dust cover and attach a C-clamp to the front bottom of the torque converter housing to prevent the converter from falling out. Remove the drive plate bolts from the torque converter. On manual transmission models, remove the rear crossmember, transmission, transfer case and adapter. You can leave the transfer case in place on six-cylinder models.
15. Support the transmission and remove the transmission attaching bolts.
16. Lower the truck and attach a hoist to the engine.
17. Remove the bolts, nuts and washers from the front motor mounts.
18. Carefully remove the engine.
19. Installation is the reverse of removal.

4-WHEEL DRIVE—WM-300

1. Drain the cooling system.

> **※※ CAUTION**
>
> When draining the coolant, keep in mind that cats and dogs are attracted by the ethylene glycol antifreeze, and are quite likely to drink any that is left in an uncovered container or in puddles on the ground. This will prove fatal in sufficient quantity. Always drain the coolant into a sealable container. Coolant should be reused unless it is contaminated or several years old.

2. Remove the battery.
3. Disconnect the fuel line at the pump.
4. Disconnect the headlight wiring.
5. Remove the upper and lower radiator hoses.
6. Remove the front sheet metal and radiator as a unit.
7. Remove the floor mat and remove the floor pan cover.
8. Remove the transmission and transfer case. See Section 7.
9. Disconnect the clutch yoke by removing the cotter key and pin.
10. Disconnect the exhaust pipe at the manifold.
11. Disconnect the throttle and choke control cables.
12. Disconnect the temperature sending unit wire.
13. Disconnect the oil pressure tube.
14. Disconnect the starter wires, ignition wires and the alternator wiring.
15. Disconnect the brake booster hose.
16. Remove the air cleaner.
17. Remove the crankcase ventilation hoses.
18. Remove the carburetor.
19. Remove the ignition coil.
20. Attach a lifting bracket and shop crane and take up the weight of the engine.
21. Remove the front and rear engine mount bolts and lift the engine from the truck.
22. Installation is the reverse of removal.

Diesel Engines

▶ See Figure 47

1. Scribe matchmarks on the hood hinges and remove the hood, this makes the job much easier.
2. Disconnect the battery cables and remove the battery.
3. Remove the air cleaner.
4. Drain the cooling system.

> **※※ CAUTION**
>
> When draining the coolant, keep in mind that cats and dogs are attracted to ethylene glycol antifreeze, and are quite likely to drink any that is left in an uncovered container or in puddles on the ground. This will prove fatal in sufficient quantity. Always drain the coolant into a sealable container. Coolant should be reused unless it is contaminated or several years old.

ENGINE AND ENGINE OVERHAUL   3-19

5. Remove the upper and lower radiator hoses.
6. Remove the coolant reserve tank.
7. Raise the truck and safely support on jackstands. Disconnect and remove the transmission oil cooler lines from the radiator. Remove the lower radiator and fan shroud mounting screws.
8. Lower the truck, then remove the upper radiator and fan shroud mounting screws. Remove the radiator and fan shroud.
9. Disconnect the heater hoses from the engine and push them aside.
10. Disconnect the speedometer cable housing from the engine.
11. Disengage the electrical connections at the alternator, temperature sending unit, starter relay-to-solenoid wires, the oil gauge sending unit and the injection pump control motor.
12. Make sure you mark any wiring that you are unsure of where it may belong on reassembly. Set the wiring harnesses aside.
13. Remove and plug the fuel line at the transfer pump inlet. Disconnect and cap the return line at the injector lines bleed-back connection.
14. Disconnect and remove the injection pump linkage. Disconnect and remove the accelerator and throttle cable linkage.
15. Disconnect the starter motor wire from the solenoid. Remove the starter motor.
16. Remove the battery ground cable from the engine block.
17. Disconnect and plug the power steering hoses at the power steering gear.
18. Raise the truck and disconnect the exhaust pipe from the exhaust manifold.
19. Drain the engine oil and remove the dipstick tube from the oil pan. Remove the transmission cooler line and road draft tube bracket from the oil pan.

✳✳ CAUTION

The EPA warns that prolonged contact with used engine oil may cause a number of skin disorders, including cancer! You should make every effort to minimize your exposure to used engine oil. Protective gloves should be worn when changing the oil. Wash your hands and any other exposed skin areas as soon as possible after exposure to used engine oil. Soap and water, or waterless hand cleaner should be used.

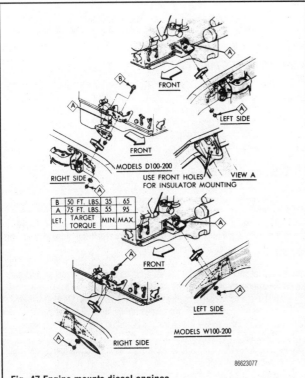

Fig. 47 Engine mounts diesel engines

20. Remove the oil pan bolts. Unfasten the transmission inspection plate. Use a new gasket upon installation.
21. Remove the four flex plate-to-torque converter cover bolts.
22. Remove the exhaust pipe bracket and the lower housing bolts.
23. Remove any other brackets that can interfere with removal.
24. Support the transmission with a floor jack.
25. Remove the cylinder head (valve) cover and the gasket.
26. Attach a boom hoist to the engine, wrapping the chain as tight and close as possible.
27. Remove the four bolts and six nuts from the engine mounts.
28. Remove the two upper bell housing bolts.
29. Roll the boom hoist back, removing the engine from the truck.
30. Installation is the reverse of removal.

Fuel Injected Engines

The mounting of the engine for a manual transmission is different from an automatic transmission. The procedure will varies slightly depending on which you may have.
1. Scribe the hood hinges and remove the hood.
2. Drain the cooling system, and engine oil, remove the battery and air cleaner.
3. Disconnect and remove the radiator hoses, fan shroud and radiator, along with heater hoses.
4. If equipped, discharge the air conditioning system.
5. Tag all vacuum lines and remove them. Tag the wiring to the distributor cap, remove as an assembly.
6. Disconnect throttle body linkage and remove the throttle body. Disconnect starter and oil pressure wires. Mark and remove any other wiring harnesses that may need to be removed and lay aside.
7. Remove all air conditioning and power steering hoses (if equipped).
8. Remove the starter, alternator, charcoal canister and horns.
9. Remove the exhaust pipe at the manifold.
10. On automatics, remove the bell housing bolts and inspection plate. Attach a C-clamp on the bottom front of converter housing to prevent the converter from coming out. Mark the converter and drive plate, then remove the drive plate bolts. Support the transmission in place for ease of replacement. Disconnect the engine from the torque converter drive plate.
11. Install an engine lifting device, attach a chain hoist to the device eyebolts.
12. Remove the engine front mounting bolts. Remove the engine from the engine compartment and insert on an engine repair stand.
13. Inspect, and replace if needed the engine mounts.
14. Installation is the reverse of removal.

Rocker Arm (Valve) Cover

REMOVAL & INSTALLATION

♦ See Figures 48, 49 and 50

➥It is always advisable to purchase new parts before proceeding with a job. You will need a new valve cover gaskets and or RTV sealant. It is best to look at the engine to see if while you are doing a job, you may need to replace a hose or wire that is worn or damaged. Even though it may not pertain to the current procedure, it may take only a minute to fix another problem that is about to occur.

1. Disconnect the negative battery cable.
2. Disconnect all wires, cable and hoses crossing the rocker cover. Make sure you mark them accordingly if unsure of assembly.
3. Unfasten and/or remove any accessory belts or brackets necessary to remove the cover.
4. Remove the rocker cover bolts.
5. Using a soft mallet, tap loose the rocker cover.

✳✳ WARNING

Never pry the cover loose. You may damage the cover or head surface!

3-20 ENGINE AND ENGINE OVERHAUL

Fig. 48 Using a ratchet and a suitable extension, unthread and remove the valve cover bolts

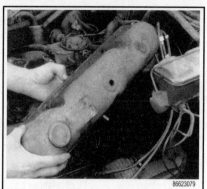

Fig. 49 Make sure all of the bolts are removed, and lift the valve cover

Fig. 50 Scrape all traces of gasket material or sealant from the head and valve cover itself

6. Lift the cover off the engine.
7. Thoroughly clean all gasket material from the mating surfaces of the head and cover. Make sure all traces of old RTV silicone sealant is removed.
8. On models using a gasket, place a new gasket on the head (coated with sealer, if recommended by the gasket manufacturer), then install the cover. Tighten the bolts to 40 inch lbs. (5 Nm) on models with a gasket.
9. On models with RTV silicone material, place a bead of sealer around the cover and place on to engine. Torque the nuts to 80 inch lbs. (9 Nm); the studs to 9 ft. lbs. (13 Nm).

Rocker Arms/Shafts

REMOVAL & INSTALLATION

▶ See Figure 51

6-198 and 6-225 Engines

ADJUSTABLE TAPPETS

➥It is always advisable to purchase new parts before proceeding with a job. You will need a new valve cover gaskets and or RTV sealant. It is best to look at the engine to see if while you are doing a job, you may need to replace a hose or wire that is worn or damaged. Even though it may not pertain to the current procedure, it may take only a minute to fix another problem that is about to occur.

The rocker arm shaft has 12 straight steel rocker arms arranged on it with hardened steel spacers fitted between each pair of arms. The shaft is secured by bolts and steel retainers which are attached to the 7 cylinder head brackets. To remove the rocker arms and shaft:
1. Remove the negative battery cable.
2. Remove the closed ventilation system.
3. Remove the evaporative control system (if so equipped).
4. Remove the valve cover and gasket.
5. Remove the rocker shaft bolts and retainers.
6. Remove the rocker arm and shaft assembly.

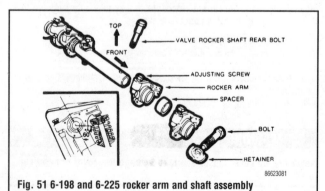

Fig. 51 6-198 and 6-225 rocker arm and shaft assembly

To install:

7. The rocker arms and shaft assembly must be installed so that the flat end of the rocker shaft is on top and points towards the front of the engine. This provides proper lubrication to the rocker arms.
8. Be sure to install the long retainer in the center position only. Install the rocker shaft retainers between the rocker arms so they seat on rocker shaft and not on the extended bushing of the rocker arms.
9. Install the rocker shaft bolts and tighten to 25 ft. lbs. (34 Nm). Also install the special bolt in the rear of engine and tighten to 23 ft. lbs. (31 Nm).
10. Temporarily set the cold valve tappet clearance to: 0.015 in. (0.38mm) on the intake valve, and 0.025 in. (0.63mm) on the exhaust valve.
11. Run the engine at 550 rpm until it is fully warmed up and adjust the valves.
12. After the engine has run for at least 15 minutes, adjust the warm valve tappets to: .010 in. (0.254mm) on the intake valve, and and 0.020 in. (0.508mm) on the exhaust valve.
13. Inspect the valve cover gasket flange for any distortion and straighten if necessary.
14. Scrape any old gasket materials from the cover and head. Place the new gasket in position along with sealant, if instructed by the gasket manufacturer, then install the valve cover. Tighten the bolts to 40 inch lbs. (5 Nm). If the valve cover is sealed using RTV sealant, place a bead of sealant around the cover, then place on engine, securing with the retaining hardware.
15. Reinstall the closed ventilation and evaporative systems.
16. Connect the negative battery cable. Start the engine and make any necessary adjustments.

NON-ADJUSTABLE TAPPETS

The rocker arm shaft has 12 straight steel rocker arms arranged on it with hardened steel spacers fitted between each pair of rocker arms. The shaft is secured by bolts and steel retainers which are attached to the 7 cylinder head brackets. To remove the rocker arm and shaft:
1. Remove the negative battery cable.
2. Remove the closed ventilation system.
3. Remove the evaporative control system (if so equipped).
4. Remove the valve cover and gasket.
5. Remove the rocker shaft bolts and retainers.
6. Remove the rocker arm and shaft assembly.

To install:

7. The rocker arms and shaft assembly must be installed so that the flat end of the rocker shaft is on top and points towards the front of the engine. This provides proper lubrication to the rocker arms.
8. Be sure to install the long retainer in the center position only. Install the rocker shaft retainers between the rocker arms so they seat on rocker shaft and not on the extending bushing of the rocker arms.
9. Install the rocker shaft bolts and tighten to 25 ft. lbs. (34 Nm).
10. Scrape any gasket or RTV materials from the head and valve cover. Inspect the valve cover gasket flange for any distortion and straighten if necessary.
11. Place the new gasket in position make sure to apply the RTV to the cylinder head itself NOT the valve cover. Install the valve cover and tighten bolts to 80 inch lbs. (9 Nm), within 10 minutes of RTV application.
12. Replace the closed ventilation and evaporative systems.
13. Connect the negative battery cable.

ENGINE AND ENGINE OVERHAUL

6-238, 8-318, 8-360, 8-400 and 8-440 Engines

♦ See Figures 52, 53, 54 and 55

The stamped steel rocker arms are arranged on one rocker arm shaft for each cylinder head. Because the angle of the pushrods tends to force the rocker arm pairs toward each other, oil spacers are fitted to absorb the side thrust at each rocker arm. The shaft is secured by bolts and steel retainers attached to the brackets on the cylinder head. To remove the arms and shaft from each cylinder head:

1. Disconnect the negative battery cable.
2. Disconnect the spark plug wires.
3. Disconnect the closed ventilation system and evaporative control system (if so equipped) from the valve cover.
4. Remove each valve cover and gasket.
5. Remove the rocker shaft bolts and retainer.
6. Remove each rocker arm and shaft assembly. Keep everything in order for installation in the original position.

To install:

✱✱ WARNING

The rocker arm shaft should be torqued down slowly, starting with the centermost bolts. Allow approximately 20 minutes of tappet bleed down time, after installation of the rocker shafts, before engine operation.

7. The notch on the end of both 318 and 360 rocker shafts should point to the engine centerline and either toward the front of the engine (on the left cylinder head), or toward the rear (on the right head). On the 400 and 440, the rocker arm lubrication holes must point down and toward the valves. Torque the rocker shaft bolts to 17 ft. lbs. (23 Nm) on the 318 and 360, and to 25 ft. lbs. (34 Nm) on the others.
8. Clean the valve cover gasket surfaces and inspect cover for any distortion. Straighten if necessary. Clean the head rail if needed.
9. Install new gasket or sealant and torque the cover bolts to 80 inch lbs. (9 Nm).

➥Whenever the valve cover gasket flange has been reworked, either by bending, refinishing or straightening, it may be necessary to install load spreading washers. Make sure the load spreader washers are positioned so they will fit free when the cover attaching bolts are tightened. If any interference is noticed between the load washer and the cover remove the bolt and washer Reposition the washer to eliminate the interference. Install the bolt and tighten as specified.

10. Install the crankcase and evaporative systems.
11. Connect the negative battery cable.

8-383 and 8-413 Engines

♦ See Figure 56

1. Disconnect the negative battery cable.
2. Remove cylinder head cover and scrape gasket materials thoroughly on the heads and covers.
3. Remove the bolts which attach the rocker arm assemblies to the head.
4. Remove rocker arms and shaft as an assembly.
5. If rocker assemblies are to be disassembled, refer to illustration for correct assembly. Note that stamped steel arms are right or left handed depending upon location of pushrod well.

To install:

6. Install the rocker shaft so that the 3/16 in. (4.7mm) shaft lubrication holes point downward into the rocker arm at an angle of 15° LOWER than centerline of the shaft mounting bolts.
7. Install the rocker arms and shaft assembly, making sure that the long stamped steel retainers are in the No. 2 and No. 4 positions. Tighten bolts to 25 ft. lbs. (34 Nm) torque.

Fig. 52 Remove the rocker arm shaft retaining bolts

Fig. 53 The lift the rocker shaft assembly from the cylinder head as one unit

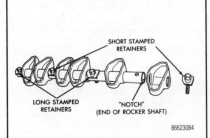

Fig. 54 6-238 Rocker shaft and arm notch location

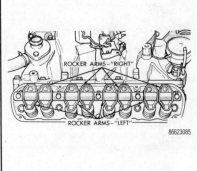

Fig. 55 V8—318 and 360 Rocker shaft and arm notch location

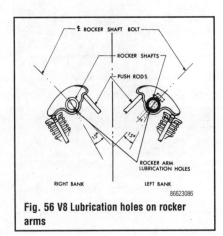

Fig. 56 V8 Lubrication holes on rocker arms

3-22 ENGINE AND ENGINE OVERHAUL

8. Install the rocker cover, using a new gasket and tighten the nuts to 3–4 ft. lbs. (4–5 Nm).
9. Connect the negative battery cable.

Diesel Engines

▶ See Figures 57 and 58

1. Disconnect the negative battery cable.
2. Remove the valve cover from the engine.
3. Remove any gasket material remaining on the valve cover or the engine block.
4. Remove the nozzle holders and the glow plugs.
5. Remove the rocker shaft retaining bolts.
6. Remove the rocker arm and shaft assembly. Keep everything in order so the rocker assembly can be installed in the original position.

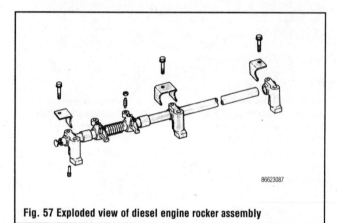

Fig. 57 Exploded view of diesel engine rocker assembly

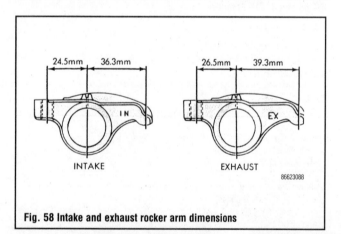

Fig. 58 Intake and exhaust rocker arm dimensions

To install:
7. Position the rocker arm and shaft assembly, such that the bracket with the oil hole, is at the front of the engine.
8. Install the rocker shaft retaining bolts and tighten to 90 ft. lbs. (123 Nm).
9. Install the nozzle holders and the glow plugs.
10. Install and tighten the injection lines. Tighten the nozzle holder retaining nuts to 36 ft. lbs. (49 Nm).
11. With the engine cold, adjust the valve clearance with each cylinder at top dead center of compression stroke. (Firing order is 1–5–3–6–2–4) Set the valve clearance at 0.012 in. (0.3mm).
12. Install valve cover and gasket.
13. Connect the negative battery cable.

Thermostat

REMOVAL & INSTALLATION

▶ See Figures 59, 60 and 61

➡It is always advisable to purchase new parts before proceeding with a job. This includes a gasket thermostat and coolant. If your truck has a plastic or metal petcock in the radiator to drain the fluid, a new O-ring or gasket may be needed. It is also advisable to look at the engine to see if while you are doing a job, you may need to replace a hose or wire that is damaged. Even though it may not pertain to the current procedure, it may take only a minute to fix another problem which is about to occur.

1. Drain the cooling system to below the level of the thermostat.

✱✱ CAUTION

When draining the coolant, keep in mind that cats and dogs are attracted to ethylene glycol antifreeze, and are quite likely to drink any that is left in an uncovered container or in puddles on the ground. This will prove fatal in sufficient quantity. Always drain the coolant into a sealable container. Coolant should be reused unless it is contaminated or several years old.

2. Remove the upper radiator hose from the thermostat housing. Note the positioning of the thermostat. It is important that the thermostat is correctly installed.
3. Withdraw the housing bolts, then remove the housing and the thermostat.
4. Clean the thermostat area thoroughly by scraping old gasket material off the housing and seating areas. It is very important to remove all traces of gasket/sealant because you do not want any coolant leaks after installation.

To install:
5. Using a new gasket and sealant, position the thermostat so that its pellet end (the part with the spring) is toward the engine block. On six cylinder engines, the vent hole must be up. Refit the thermostat housing and tighten its securing bolts to 25–30 ft. lbs. (34–41 Nm).

Fig. 59 Using a ratchet loosen the thermostat bolts

Fig. 60 Remove housing and thermostat

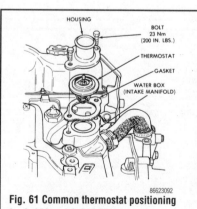

Fig. 61 Common thermostat positioning for 6–238 and 8–318/360

ENGINE AND ENGINE OVERHAUL

6. Connect the upper radiator hose.

7. Fill the cooling system with a 50/50 water to antifreeze mixture. Warm the engine then inspect the upper radiator hose and the thermostat housing for leaks.

➡ Poor heater output and slow engine warm-up is often caused by a thermostat stuck in the open position; occasionally one sticks shut causing immediate overheating. Do not attempt to correct an overheating condition by permanently removing the thermostat. Thermostat flow restriction is designed into the system; without it, localized overheating due to turbulence may occur.

TESTING

1. Check to make sure that the thermostat valve closes tightly. If the valve does not close completely due to foreign material, carefully clean the sealing edge of the valve while being careful not to damage the sealing edge. If the valve does not close tightly after it has been cleaned, a new thermostat must be installed.

2. Immerse the thermostat in a container of warm water so that its pellet is completely covered and does not touch the bottom or sides of the container.

3. Heat the water and, while stirring the water continuously (to ensure uniform temperature), check the temperature with a thermometer.

4. Continue heating the water to a temperature approximately 20°F higher than the standard thermostat opening temperature. At this point, the thermostat should be fully open. If it is not, install a new thermostat.

Intake Manifold

➡ The V6 and V8 engines use an intake manifold installed between the cylinder heads. This is in contrast with the inline 6 cylinder gasoline engines which are equipped with combination manifolds. As the name implies, these manifolds combine the intake and exhaust manifolds by securing them together with screws.

REMOVAL & INSTALLATION

➡ It is always advisable to purchase new parts before proceeding with a job. A valve cover gasket, RTV sealant if needed, and intake gasket set can be purchased separately if need be. If you are planning on doing more than this procedure, a head set, which comes with all gaskets will do just as good. It is best to look at the engine to see if while you are doing a job, you may need to replace a hose or wire that is damaged. Even though it may not pertain to the current procedure, it may only take but a minute to fix another problem which is about to occur.

V6 and V8 Gasoline Engines

♦ See Figures 62 thru 69

1. Drain the cooling system and disconnect the negative battery cable.
2. Remove the alternator, carburetor air cleaner and fuel line. Identify and tag all connections.
3. Disconnect the accelerator linkage.
4. Remove vacuum control between carburetor and distributor.
5. Remove the distributor cap and wires. Mark the individual wires.
6. Disconnect and tag the coil wires, temperature sending unit wire, heater hoses and bypass hose.
7. If necessary, disconnect the exhaust downpipe at the exhaust manifolds. Remove the nuts and washers attaching the exhaust manifold assembly to the cylinder head, then remove the manifolds.
8. Remove the bolts attaching the intake manifold to the cylinder heads.
9. Remove the ignition coil and and any remaining hoses or wires around the intake manifold. Finally, remove the intake manifold, with the carburetor intact, from the engine.
10. If replacing the carburetor, remove the hardware securing it to the intake manifold.
11. Remove all traces of intake manifold gasket material from the intake manifold as well as the cylinder heads. Inspect the manifold for cracks or any other damage in case you may need to replace it.
12. Installation is the reverse of the above procedure. Make sure you use new gaskets before installing the manifold assembly. Tighten the intake manifold to head bolts in the sequence illustrated, from center alternating out.
13. Tighten the exhaust manifold mounting nuts to the required torque which is listed in the specifications chart of this section.

➡ Refer to the Combination Manifold information found in this section for information on inline 6 cylinder manifold removal and installation

Diesel Engines

1. Drain the cooling system.
2. Disconnect the battery ground cable.
3. Remove the air cleaner.
4. Disconnect the fuel lines at the fuel filter, transfer pump and injection pump. See Section 5.
5. Drain the fuel filter and remove it from the back of the manifold. See Section 1.
6. Remove the manifold and air cleaner mounting bracket bolts.
7. Disconnect the injection lines at the injection pump and remove the nozzle holder from the cylinder head. See Section 5.
8. Remove the fuel line clamps from the manifold and push the fuel lines up and out of the way.
9. Remove the manifold and gaskets from the head.

To install:

10. Install the manifold and new gaskets on the head.
11. Install the fuel lines and clamps on the manifold.
12. Connect the injection lines at the injection pump.
13. Install the nozzle holder on the cylinder head. See Section 5.
14. Install the manifold and air cleaner mounting bracket bolts.
15. Install the fuel filter on the back of the manifold. See Section 1.
16. Connect the fuel lines at the fuel filter, transfer pump and injection pump. See Section 5.
17. Install the air cleaner.
18. Connect the battery ground cable.
19. Fill the cooling system.

Fig. 62 Once all interfering components are removed, loosen and remove the retainers from the intake manifold

Fig. 63 Remove the intake manifold as an assembly with carburetor installed

Fig. 64 Discard of the old intake gasket

3-24 ENGINE AND ENGINE OVERHAUL

Fig. 65 Remove any other gasket materials, clean and scrape area completely

Fig. 66 On a V engine, place new gaskets on the top and side portions of the cylinder head. Use sealer in accordance with gasket manufacturer recommendations

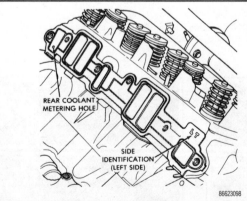

Fig. 67 Correct placement of the side intake manifold gasket. Notice the coolant metering hole, and lettering corresponding to the cylinder head side

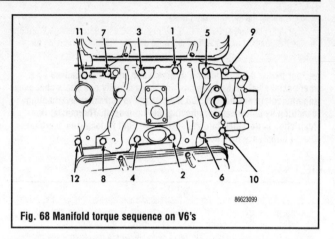

Fig. 68 Manifold torque sequence on V6's

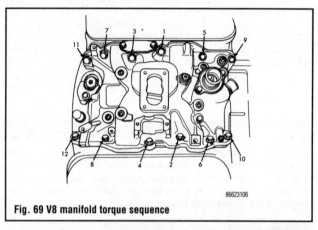

Fig. 69 V8 manifold torque sequence

Exhaust Manifold

REMOVAL & INSTALLATION

➥It is always advisable to purchase new parts before proceeding with a job. Exhaust gaskets and down pipe gaskets can be purchased separately if need be. If you are planning on doing more than this procedure, a head set, which comes with all gaskets will do just as good. It is also advisable to look at the engine to see if while you are doing a job, you may need to replace a hose or wire that could be damaged. Even though it may not pertain to the current procedure, it can't take but a minute to fix another problem about to occur.

V6 and V8 Gasoline Engines

♦ See Figures 70 and 71

1. Disconnect the negative battery cable.
2. Disconnect the exhaust manifold at the flange where it mates to the exhaust pipe.
3. If the vehicle is equipped with air injection and/or a carburetor-heated air stove, remove them.
4. Remove the exhaust manifold by removing the securing nuts, washers and screws. To reach these pieces, it may be necessary to jack the engine slightly off its front mounts. **When the exhaust manifold is removed, sometimes the securing studs will screw out with the nuts. If this occurs, the studs must be replaced with the aid of sealing compound on the coarse thread ends. If this is not done, water leaks may develop at the studs.**
5. Remove any gasket material left behind on the manifold and cylinder head.

ENGINE AND ENGINE OVERHAUL 3-25

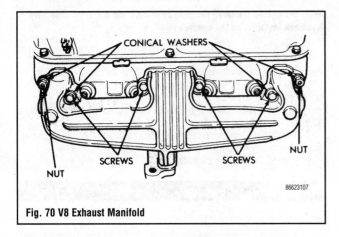

Fig. 70 V8 Exhaust Manifold

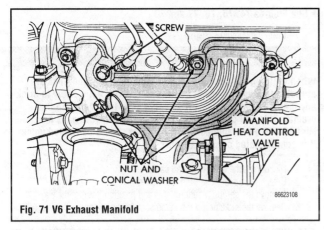

Fig. 71 V6 Exhaust Manifold

6. Inspect the manifold for cracks, flatness, or warping which can occur and cause a leak. You would need to purchase a new manifold in this case.

To install:

7. Position the arms of the manifolds on the studs of the cylinder head with a new gasket between them. Install conical washers and nuts on studs.

8. Install the two screws and conical washers at inner ends of outboard arms of manifold. Install two screws **without** washers on center arm of the manifold. Tighten the screws and nuts (starting at the center arm and working outwards) to 20 ft. lbs. (27 Nm).

9. Assemble the exhaust pipe to the manifold, and secure with bolts, nuts and washers, tightening to 25 ft. lbs. (34 Nm).

Diesel Engines

1. Disconnect the battery ground cable.
2. Remove the air cleaner.
3. Remove the exhaust manifold heat shield.
4. Disconnect the exhaust pipe from the manifold.
5. Remove the exhaust manifold bridges and manifold hold-down bolts.
6. Remove the manifold and gaskets.
7. Inspect the manifold for cracks and heat damage. The gasket surfaces must be flat within 0.008 in. (0.20mm).

To install:

8. Install the gasket and manifold. Install exhaust manifold bridges and hold-down bolts. Tighten to specifications.
9. Connect the exhaust pipe to the manifold, tighten nuts. Install the heatshield.
10. Install the air cleaner, then connect the battery cable.
11. Check for leaks.

Combination Manifold

A combination manifold is a sandwiched intake and exhaust manifold secured with screws, installed on many inline 6 cylinder gasoline engines.

Although it is called a combination manifold, with the assembly sandwiching hardware unfastened, the combination manifold can be separated to reveal both an intake portion as well as an exhaust manifold section.

REMOVAL & INSTALLATION

◆ See Figure 72

Inline 6 Cylinder Gasoline Engines

EXCEPT 251

1. Disconnect the negative battery cable.
2. Disconnect the air cleaner vacuum line from the carburetor, then the flexible connector between the air cleaner and carburetor air heater.
3. Disconnect the crankcase inlet air cleaner to air cleaner hose and remove the air cleaner assembly and set aside.
4. Tag then disconnect the distributor vacuum line, crankcase ventilator valve hose and carburetor bowl vent line. (If equipped).
5. Remove the carburetor air heater. Tag and disconnect the fuel line, throttle linkage, and automatic choke rod from the carburetor. Remove the carburetor.
6. Disconnect the exhaust manifold at the flange where it mates to the exhaust downpipe.
7. Detach the exhaust manifold by removing the nuts and washers at the cylinder head.

  Remove the three bolts securing the intake manifold portion to the exhaust manifold section, then carefully separate the manifolds. Slowly remove the exhaust manifold from the engine compartment.

8. If the intake portion needs to be removed, unfasten the retaining hardware securing the manifold to the engine. remove the assembly, with carburetor, from the engine compartment.
9. Remove any gasket material left behind on the manifold surface and cylinder head. Clean the manifolds in solvent and dry with compressed air.
10. Inspect the manifold for cracks and flatness; warping can occur and cause a leak. You would need to purchase a new manifold in this case.

To install:

11. Install a new gasket between the exhaust and intake manifolds, coat both sides of the gasket with sealer, if recommended by the gasket manufacturer. Install the long screws holding the manifolds together.

❈❈ CAUTION

When installing the manifolds on the cylinder head of the engine, it is very important the procedure is followed correctly to permit the exhaust manifold to expand and contract with the heating and cooling cycles of normal engine operation, otherwise manifold breakage will occur.

12. Install the manifold, then washers in place. Washers spanning intake and exhaust flanges must be flat, replace any washers that are distorted.
13. Install the steel conical washer with the cup side facing the nut. Install the brass washer with flat side facing the manifold. Install the nuts with cone side facing the washers.

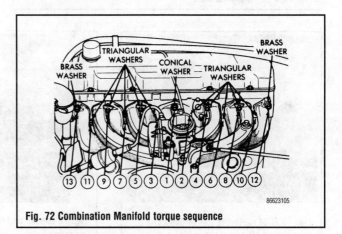

Fig. 72 Combination Manifold torque sequence

3-26 ENGINE AND ENGINE OVERHAUL

14. Carefully snug all **intake-to-exhaust manifold** bolts and manifold-to-cylinder headnuts. Snug all nuts and bolts to 10 inch lbs. (1 Nm). **DO NOT OVERTIGHTEN.**
15. Tighten **inboard** intake-to-exhaust manifold bolts to 20–23 ft. lbs. (27–31 Nm).
16. Tighten **outboard** intake-to-exhaust manifold bolts to 20–23 ft. lbs. (27–31 Nm).
17. Repeat the tightening procedures 14 through 16 until all two/three manifold bolts are at specified torque.
18. Tighten the manifold-to-cylinder head nuts to 120 inch lbs. (14 Nm), in tightening sequence shown. **DO NOT OVERTIGHTEN.**
19. Attach the exhaust pipe-to-manifold flange, with new gasket, tighten all stud nuts to 35 ft. lbs. (47 Nm).
20. Install the carburetor air heater.
21. Install air injection tube with gasket and tighten to 17 ft. lbs. (23 Nm). Install carburetor, all fuel lines, automatic choke rod, and throttle linkage.
22. Install air cleaner and connect the crankcase inlet air cleaner to air cleaner hose. Install any lines carb and air system left.
23. Connect the negative battery cable.

251 ENGINE

◆ See Figure 73

1. Disconnect the negative battery cable.
2. Remove the air cleaner, followed by all the lines and tubes from the carburetor.
3. Disconnect all the linkages to the carburetor and remove the carburetor from the manifold assembly.
4. Disconnect the exhaust pipe from the manifold, remove the manifold attaching washers and retaining nuts, then remove the manifold from the cylinder head.
5. Separate the exhaust manifold from the intake manifold, if necessary, and install a new gasket between the two upon re-assembly. Torque the bolts to 25 ft. lbs. (34 Nm).

➥Do not tighten the three securing bolts until the manifold assembly has been installed on the cylinder head.

To install:

6. Position the manifold on the cylinder head using a new gasket, then install the conical and triangular washers, along with the retaining nuts, and torque the retaining nuts and the three securing bolts to 20 ft. lbs. (27 Nm) in a spiral sequence from the center to the ends.
7. Attach the exhaust pipe to the exhaust manifold flange. Torque the nuts to 30 ft. lbs. (41 Nm).
8. Install the carburetor then attach all the lines, tubes, and linkages. Install the air cleaner assembly.
9. Connect the negative battery terminal.

Radiator

REMOVAL & INSTALLATION

◆ See Figures 74, 75, 76, 77 and 78

1. Drain the cooling system.

✽✽ CAUTION

When draining the coolant, keep in mind that cats and dogs are attracted to ethylene glycol antifreeze, and are quite likely to drink any that is left in an uncovered container or in puddles on the ground. This will prove fatal in sufficient quantity. Always drain the coolant into a sealable container. Coolant should be reused unless it is contaminated or several years old.

2. Disconnect the battery ground cable.
3. Detach the upper hose from the radiator.
4. Remove the shroud mounting nuts and position it out of the way.
5. Remove the radiator top mounting screws. If equipped with air condi-

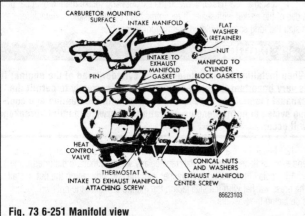

Fig. 73 6-251 Manifold view

Fig. 74 Using a ratchet, loosen and remove all mounting bolts connecting the fan shroud

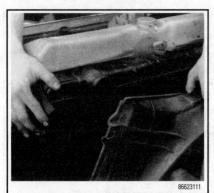

Fig. 75 After removing fan shroud bolts, take shroud off and place aside

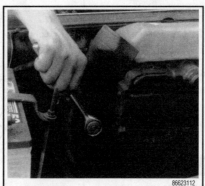

Fig. 76 Loosen and remove radiator mounting bolts

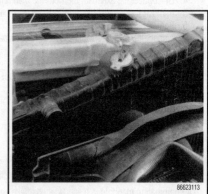

Fig. 77 Install radiator being careful not to damage fins

ENGINE AND ENGINE OVERHAUL 3-27

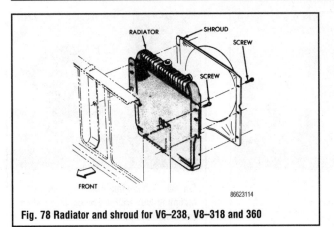

Fig. 78 Radiator and shroud for V6–238, V8–318 and 360

tioning, remove the condenser attaching screws, accessible through the grille. DO NOT disconnect any air conditioning lines.

6. Raise the vehicle and support it. Disconnect and plug the automatic transmission cooler lines and cap the openings in the cooler.
7. Hold the radiator in place and remove the lower mounting screws. Carefully lift it up and out of the truck.

To install:

8. Hold the radiator in place and install the lower mounting screws.
9. Connect the automatic transmission cooler lines.
10. Install the radiator top mounting screws. If equipped with air conditioning, install the condenser attaching screws, accessible through the grille.
11. Install the shroud mounting nuts.
12. Connect the upper hose from the radiator.
13. Connect the battery ground cable.
14. Fill the cooling system.
15. Check all fluid levels and run the engine, making sure there are no leaks.

Water Pump

REMOVAL & INSTALLATION

6-198, 6-225 and 6-251 Engines

➡ This job can sometimes be done without removing the radiator on models without air conditioning, but only if there is enough room to get at the water pump bolts.

1. Remove the negative battery terminal.
2. Remove the radiator.
3. Remove all the accessary drive belts and any brackets in the way of the water pump.
4. If necessary, remove the alternator and/or power steering pump. In most cases, these items can be loosened and slid out of the way.
5. Remove the fan, spacer, pulley, and bolts as an assembly.
6. If equipped with an air pump, remove the pump brackets with the hoses attached and tie it out of the way.
7. Disconnect the heater hose and all other hoses from the pump.
8. Remove the pump from the block.
9. Clean all mating surfaces

To install:

10. Use a new gasket coated with sealer. Mount the pump to the block.
11. Torque the bolts to 30 ft. lbs. (41 Nm). Insert all hoses. Install the air pump.
12. If removed earlier, install the alternator and/or the power steering pump.
13. Attach the fan and pulley assembly. Install all belts.
14. Install the radiator and adjoining components.
15. Connect the negative battery cable.
16. Fill the cooling system and adjust the tension of the drive belts.

8–318 and 8–360 Engines

♦ See Figures 79 thru 85

1. Disconnect the negative battery cable.
2. Drain the cooling system.
3. Remove the radiator.
4. Loosen all accessories that are belt driven and remove all the drive belts, as well as any brackets which could prevent the unit from being removed..
5. Remove the alternator bracket attaching bolts, then tie the alternator and bracket out of the way.
6. Loosen and remove the power steering pump retaining bolts. If necessary, remove the power steering pump to make the job easier, by unfastening the remaining pump bracket bolts. Place the pump out of the way, and strap down so it will not come free. The hoses attached to the pump DO NOT have to be removed.
7. On engines with air conditioning, remove the idler pulley assembly, alternator, and adjusting bracket.

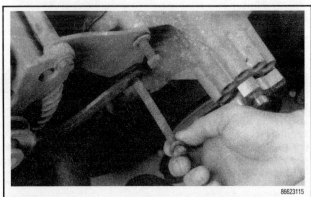

Fig. 79 Because some of the alternator bracket bolts usually thread into the water pump, the alternator will have to be unbolted and supported aside

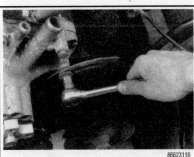

Fig. 80 Loosen and remove the power steering pump bracket, and bolt. If necessary, the pump can be repositioned after unthreading the remaining bolt(s)

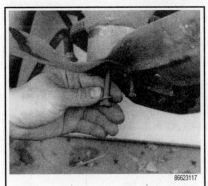

Fig. 81 To free the fan, remove the four bolts

Fig. 82 After removing the blade, slide the pulley off the water pump

3-28 ENGINE AND ENGINE OVERHAUL

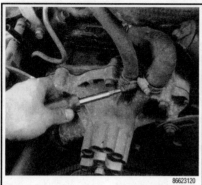

Fig. 83 Loosen the clamps and disconnect the hoses from the water pump

Fig. 84 Make sure to clean all traces of old gasket with a scraper

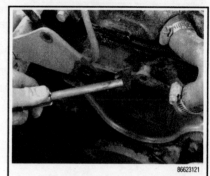

Fig. 85 It is very important to clean the mounting area well to prevent leaks when you install the pump

8. Remove the fan blade, spacer (or fluid unit), pulley, and bolts as an assembly.

➡ To prevent silicone fluid from draining into the drive bearing and ruining the lubricant, do not place the thermostatic fan drive unit with the shaft pointing downward.

9. Disconnect all hoses from the water pump.
10. Remove the air conditioning compressor front mounting bolts.
11. Remove the water pump-to-compressor front bracket bolts and the bracket.

➡ Do not disconnect any refrigerant lines from the compressor.

12. Remove the water pump. Make sure to remove all traces of gasket material from the water pump and block.
13. Installation is the reverse of removal. Use a new gasket coated with sealer. Torque the bolts to 30 ft. lbs. (41 Nm). Fill the cooling system and adjust the tension of the drive belts.

8-383, 8-400, 8-413 and 8-440 Engines

1. Disconnect the negative battery cable and drain the cooling system.

✱✱ CAUTION

When draining the coolant, keep in mind that cats and dogs are attracted to ethylene glycol antifreeze, and are quite likely to drink any that is left in an uncovered container or in puddles on the ground. This will prove fatal in sufficient quantity. Always drain the coolant into a sealable container. Coolant should be reused unless it is contaminated or several years old.

2. Loosen all of the drive belts.
3. Remove the lower crankshaft pulley.
4. Remove the fan shroud screws and set the shroud back out of the way.
5. Remove the fluid fan drive bolts and set the fan assembly aside.
6. Remove the water pump and the gasket.
7. Installation is the reverse of removal. Use a new gasket coated with sealer. Torque the bolts to 30 ft. lbs. (41 Nm). Fill the cooling system and adjust the tension of the drive belts.

Diesel Engines

1. Disconnect the negative battery cable.
2. Drain the cooling system then remove the heater hoses and the bypass hose.

✱✱ CAUTION

When draining the coolant, keep in mind that cats and dogs are attracted to ethylene glycol antifreeze, and are quite likely to drink any that is left in an uncovered container or in puddles on the ground. This will prove fatal in sufficient quantity. Always drain the coolant into a sealable container. Coolant should be reused unless it is contaminated or several years old.

3. Loosen the alternator mounting bolts and remove the belt.
4. Remove the cooling fan, the spacer and the drive pulley.
5. Remove the water pump mounting bolts and remove the pump.
6. Install the pump, use a new gasket coated with sealer. Torque the bolts to 30 ft. lbs. (41 Nm).
7. Install the cooling fan system.
8. Insert the alternator belt and retighten the bolts.
9. Connect the negative battery cable.
10. Fill the cooling system and adjust the tension of the drive belts.

Cylinder Head

REMOVAL & INSTALLATION

6-198 and 6-225 Engines

▶ See Figures 86 and 87

1. Disconnect the negative battery cable.
2. Drain the cooling system.
3. Remove the air cleaner and the fuel line from the carburetor.
4. Disconnect the accelerator linkage.
5. Remove the vacuum advance line from between the carburetor and the distributor.
6. Disconnect the cables from the spark plugs, then remove the plugs.
7. Disconnect the heater hose and the clamp which secures the by-pass hose.
8. Disconnect the water temperature sending unit.
9. Disconnect the exhaust pipe at the exhaust manifold flange. Disconnect the diverter valve line (if equipped) from the intake manifold and remove the air tube assembly from the cylinder head.
10. Remove the intake and exhaust manifolds along with the carburetor as an assembly.

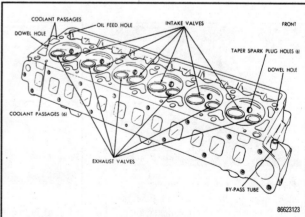

Fig. 86 L6-225 cylinder head assembly

ENGINE AND ENGINE OVERHAUL   3-29

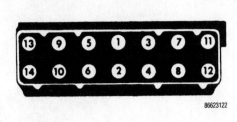

Fig. 87 6-198, 6-225 cylinder head torque sequence

11. Remove the closed ventilation systems, the evaporative control system (if so equipped), and the valve cover.
12. Remove the rocker arm and shaft assembly.
13. Remove the pushrods and keep them in order to ensure installation in their original locations.
14. Remove the head bolts then remove the cylinder head.

To install:
15. Clean all of the gasket surfaces of the engine block and the cylinder head, then install the spark plugs.

➡If your truck hasn't had a tune-up in a while this is now a good opportunity to do one.

16. Inspect all surfaces with a straightedge. If warpage is indicated, measure the amount. This amount must not exceed 0.00075 times the span length in any direction. For example, if a 12 inch span is 0.004 in. (0.10mm) warped, the maximum allowable is 12 x 0.00075 in. (0.019mm) = 0.009 in. (0.22mm). In this case, the head is within limits. If warpage exceeds the specified limits, either replace the head or lightly machine the head gasket surface.

To install:
17. Coat a new cylinder head gasket with sealer, install the gasket and cylinder head.
18. Install the cylinder head bolts. Torque the cylinder head bolts to 35 ft. lbs. (47 Nm) in the sequence indicated in the illustration. Repeat this sequence to re-torque all the head bolts to 70 ft. lbs. (95 Nm).
19. Install the pushrods in their original locations.
20. Install the rocker arm and shaft assembly.
21. Install valve cover, the closed ventilation systems, and the evaporative control system.
22. Install the intake and exhaust manifolds along with the carburetor as an assembly.

➡When installing the intake and exhaust manifold assembly, loosen the 3 bolts which secure the intake manifold to the exhaust manifold to maintain proper alignment. After installation, torque the 3 bolts in this sequence: inner bolt, then outer bolts. Refer to the manifold section, later in this section, for the proper tightening sequence. Check the valve adjustment.

23. Connect the exhaust pipe at the exhaust manifold flange. Connect the diverter valve line (if equipped) at the intake manifold and install the air tube assembly from the cylinder head.
24. Connect the water temperature sending unit.
25. Connect the heater hose and the clamp which secures the by-pass hose.
26. Connect the cables at the spark plugs.
27. Install the vacuum advance line between the carburetor and the distributor.
28. Connect the accelerator linkage.
29. Install the air cleaner and the fuel line at the carburetor.
30. Fill the cooling system and connect the battery cable.

6-251 Engine

◆ See Figure 88

1. Disconnect the negative battery cable.
2. Drain the cooling system.

※※ CAUTION

When draining the coolant, keep in mind that cats and dogs are attracted to ethylene glycol antifreeze, and are quite likely to drink any that is left in an uncovered container or in puddles on the ground. This will prove fatal in sufficient quantity. Always drain the coolant into a sealable container. Coolant should be reused unless it is contaminated or several years old.

3. Remove the carburetor.
4. Disconnect any hoses, lines and wires attached to the head.
5. Remove the spark plugs.
6. Remove the bolts in reverse of the tightening sequence. See the illustration.
7. Lift off the head.
8. Inspect the head for signs of damage.
9. Clean the head thoroughly and check it for warpage. Lay a good straightedge across the head, diagonally and lengthwise. If the head is off by more than 0.024 in. (0.60mm) lengthwise or 0.006 in. (0.15mm) crosswise, it must be machined. Maximum material removal is 0.20 in. (5mm).

➡If your truck hasn't had a tune-up in a while this is now a good opportunity to do one.

10. When installing the head, always use a new gasket coated on both sides with sealer. Following the tightening sequence shown when tightening the head bolts. Torque the bolts to 70 ft. lbs. (95 Nm). Run the engine to normal operating temperature and retorque the bolts with the engine hot to 70 ft. lbs. (95 Nm). After 20 hours or 500 miles of operation, whichever comes first, retorque the bolts to 70 ft. lbs. (95 Nm).

V6 and V8 Gasoline Engines

◆ See Figures 89 thru 97

1. Drain the cooling system and disconnect the battery ground cable.
2. Remove the alternator, air cleaner, and fuel line.

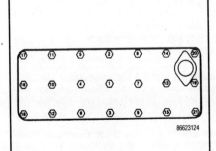

Fig. 88 6-251 cylinder head torque sequence

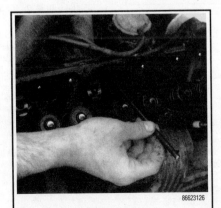

Fig. 89 Remove all the pushrods

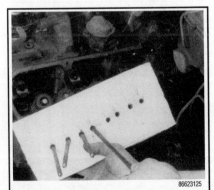

Fig. 90 V8—Make sure you keep the pushrods in order for installation purposes

3-30 ENGINE AND ENGINE OVERHAUL

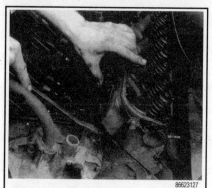
Fig. 91 Carefully pry the cylinder head up to loosen and remove.

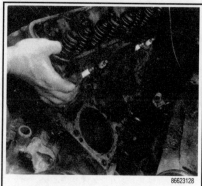
Fig. 92 Remove the cylinder head; careful, its heavy

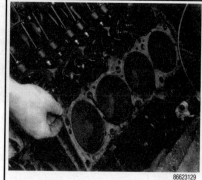
Fig. 93 Discard the old cylinder head gasket

Fig. 94 Scrape all gasket material from the cylinder head surface before installing a new gasket—note you should place a clean rag in each of the cylinders to keep debris out

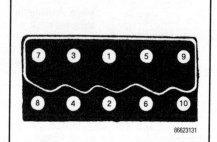
Fig. 95 8–318, 360 cylinder head bolt torque sequence

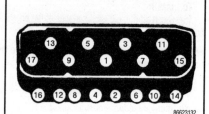
Fig. 96 8–383, 400, 413 and 440 cylinder head bolt torque sequence

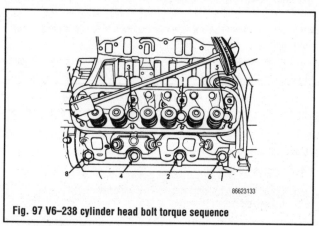
Fig. 97 V6–238 cylinder head bolt torque sequence

3. Disconnect the accelerator linkage.
4. Remove the vacuum advance line from between the carburetor and the distributor. On trucks with the 360 cu. in. engine, remove the battery.
5. Remove the distributor cap and wires as an assembly.
6. Disconnect the coil wires, water temperature sending unit, heater hoses, and bypass hose. On the 360 and 413, remove the distributor and governor.
7. Remove the closed ventilation system, the evaporative control system (if so equipped), and the valve covers.
8. Remove the intake manifold, ignition coil, and carburetor as an assembly.
9. Remove the exhaust manifolds. On 360 and 413, tag the center bolts.
10. Remove the tappet chamber cover. Remove the rocker and shaft assemblies.
11. Remove the pushrods and keep them in order to ensure installation in their original locations. On the 360 and 413, remove the water pump-to-heads bolts.
12. Remove the head bolts from each cylinder head and remove the cylinder heads.
13. Clean all the gasket surfaces of the engine block and the cylinder heads.
14. Inspect all surfaces with a straightedge. If warpage is indicated, measure the amount. This measurement must not exceed 0.00075 times the span length in any direction. For example, if a 12 in. span is 0.004 in. (0.10mm) warped, the maximum allowable difference is 12 x 0.00075 (0.019mm) = 0.009 in. (0.22mm) In this case, the head is within limits. If the warpage exceeds the specified limits, either replace the head or lightly machine the head gasket surface.
15. Coat new cylinder head gaskets with sealer, install the gaskets and install the cylinder heads.

➡ The number and size of the cooling passages in the 318 heads were changed during the 1976 model year. The new type gasket can be used with the old heads, but the old type gasket can't be used with the new heads.

16. Install the cylinder head bolts. Torque the cylinder head bolts to 50 ft. lbs. (68 Nm) in the sequence indicated. Repeat this sequence to re-torque all the cylinder head bolts to specifications.
17. Install the pushrods.
18. On the 360 and 413, install the water pump-to-heads bolts.
19. Install the rocker and shaft assemblies. Install the tappet chamber cover.
20. Install the exhaust manifolds.
21. Install the intake manifold, ignition coil, and carburetor as an assembly.
22. Install the closed ventilation system, the evaporative control system (if so equipped), and the valve covers.
23. Connect the coil wires, water temperature sending unit, heater hoses, and bypass hose. On the 360 and 413, install the distributor and governor.

➡ If your truck hasn't had a tune-up in a while this is a good opportunity to do one.

24. Install the distributor cap and wires as an assembly.
25. Install the vacuum advance line between the carburetor and the distributor. On trucks with the 360 cu. in. engine, install the battery.

ENGINE AND ENGINE OVERHAUL   3-31

26. Connect the accelerator linkage.
27. Install the alternator, air cleaner, and fuel line.
28. Fill the cooling system and connect the battery ground cable.

Diesel Engines

1. Remove the negative battery cable.
2. Drain the cooling system.

❄️ CAUTION

When draining the coolant, keep in mind that cats and dogs are attracted to ethylene glycol antifreeze, and are quite likely to drink any that is left in an uncovered container or in puddles on the ground. This will prove fatal in sufficient quantity. Always drain the coolant into a sealable container. Coolant should be reused unless it is contaminated or several years old.

3. Disconnect the negative battery cable.
4. Remove the air cleaner.
5. Disconnect the hoses from the fuel filter at the transfer pump and the injection pump. Drain the filter and remove it from the manifold.
6. Remove the manifold nuts and air cleaner mounting bracket attaching nuts.
7. Disconnect the injection lines for cylinders 3 and 6 from the injection pump.
8. Remove the intake manifold and gaskets from the head.
9. Push the exhaust manifold shield to one side.
10. Remove the heater hose and the bypass hose.
11. Remove the thermostat housing and the upper radiator hose from the water manifold. Remove the spray gasket.
12. Disconnect the temperature sending unit wire.
13. Disconnect the fuel line mounting brackets from the cylinder head and push the fuel lines aside.
14. Remove the three exhaust manifold bridges.
15. Remove the water manifold and gasket from the cylinder head.
16. Raise the truck and support it with jackstands.
17. Disconnect the exhaust pipe from the exhaust manifold.
18. Lower the truck. Remove the exhaust manifold, heat shield and gasket.
19. Disconnect and remove the wire from each glow plug.
20. Remove the injection lines from the injection pump.
21. Disconnect the fuel injection line from the head. Remove the bracket and the ground strap.
22. Disconnect the alternator bracket and the engine lifting fixture. Push them aside.
23. Remove the cylinder head cover and the gasket.
24. Loosen and remove the cylinder head bolts in the sequence illustrated.
25. Lift out the rocker arm and shaft assembly.
26. Remove the pushrods, keeping them in order. The pushrods MUST be installed in their original locations.
27. Disconnect and remove the glow plug buss bar.
28. Remove the six glow plugs from the cylinder head.
29. Remove the cylinder head. Check the head for cracks, damage or evidence of water leaks. Clean all the oil, grease, scale, sealant and carbon from the head. Thoroughly clean the gasket surfaces. Also check each combustion chamber jet for cracks or melting. If a jet is cracked or melted, remove it with a pushrod inserted through a glow plug bore.

To install:

30. Inspect all cylinder head surfaces with a straightedge. Out-of-flatness must not exceed 0.010 in. (0.25mm). If it does, a surface grinder must be used to bring the head to an out-of-flatness of less than 0.006 in. (0.15mm).
31. Install the glow plugs in the head. Tighten them firmly.
32. Install the injectors, injector tubes and the injector holders in the head. Tighten the nozzle holder attaching nuts to 37 ft. lbs. (50 Nm).
33. Coat the new gasket lightly with sealer. Place the gasket on the block and place the cylinder head over the dowels.
34. Install the cylinder head bolts and tighten them in the sequence to 90 ft. lbs. (122 Nm). Do not install the head bolts which retain the rocker shaft assembly.
35. Install the pushrods in their original locations.
36. Install the rocker arm and shaft assembly. Tighten the mounting bolts to 90 ft. lbs. (122 Nm).
37. Adjust the valve clearance to 0.012 in. (0.30mm) at top dead center of each cylinder compression stroke.
38. Install the cylinder head cover and gasket.
39. Install the alternator bracket and the engine lifting fixture.
40. Connect the fuel lines to the injection pump (except nos. 3 and 6). Install the bracket and the group strap.
41. Install the fuel line to the transfer pump.
42. Install the exhaust manifold and the heat shield assembly, using a new gasket.
43. Raise the truck and support it safely. Attach the exhaust pipe to the exhaust manifold.
44. Lower the truck and install the water manifold on the head using a new gasket.
45. Install the three exhaust manifold bridges.
46. Install the fuel lines in the bracket.
47. Connect the temperature sending unit wire.
48. Using a new gasket, install the thermostat housing. Attach the upper radiator hose to the thermostat housing.
49. Install the bypass and heater hoses.
50. Install the exhaust manifold heat shield and the exhaust manifold.
51. Using a new gasket and spray shield, install the air intake manifold.
52. Connect the injection lines from cylinders 3 and 6 to the injection pump.
53. Install the fuel filter to the back of the manifold.
54. Connect the fuel hoses.
55. Install the air cleaner bracket and install the air cleaner.
56. Connect the negative battery cable, and finally, fill the cooling system.

INSPECTION

▶ See Figures 98, 99 and 100

1. With the valves installed to protect the valve seats, remove deposits from the combustion chambers and valve heads with a scraper and a wire brush. Be careful not to damage the cylinder head gasket surface. After the valves are

Fig. 98 With the valves removed, a wire wheel may be used to clean the combustion chambers of carbon deposits

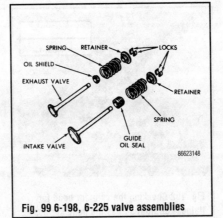

Fig. 99 6-198, 6-225 valve assemblies

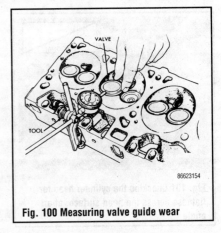

Fig. 100 Measuring valve guide wear

3-32 ENGINE AND ENGINE OVERHAUL

removed, clean the valve guide bores with a guide cleaning tool. Use cleaning solvent to remove the dirt, grease and other deposits. Clean all the retaining bolt holes, and make sure all the oil passages are clear.

2. Remove all deposits from the valves with a fine wire brush or buffing wheel.
3. Inspect the cylinder heads for cracks or excessively burned areas in the exhaust outlet ports.
4. Check the cylinder head for cracks and inspect the gasket surface for burrs and nicks. Replace the head if it is cracked.
5. On cylinder heads that incorporate valve seat inserts, check the inserts for excessive wear, cracks, or looseness.

RESURFACING

Cylinder Head Flatness

♦ See Figures 101 and 102

When the cylinder head is removed, check the flatness of the cylinder head gasket surfaces.

1. Place a straightedge across the gasket surface of the cylinder head. Using feeler gauges, determine the clearance at the center of the straightedge.
2. If warpage exceeds 0.003 in. (0.07mm) in a 6 in. (152mm) span, or 0.006 in. (0.15mm) for gasoline trucks, and 0.008 in. (0.20mm) for the diesel trucks, over the total length, the cylinder head must be resurfaced.
3. If necessary to refinish the cylinder head gasket surface, do not plane or grind off more than 0.010 in. (0.25mm) for gasoline vehicles, 0.002 in. 0.05mm, for the diesel trucks, from the original gasket surface.

➡ When milling the cylinder heads of V6 and V8 engines, the intake manifold mounting position is altered, and must be corrected by milling the manifold flange a proportionate amount. Consult an experienced machinist about this.

Valve Stem Seals

REMOVAL & INSTALLATION

Cylinder Head Installed

➡ For this procedure, you will need an air compressor, a spark plug adaptor and a dummy shaft.

If valve stem oil seals are found to be the cause of excessive oil consumption, the seal can be replaced without removing the cylinder head.

➡ The procedure below applies to both gasoline and diesel engines.

1. Remove the air cleaner.
2. Remove rocker arm covers, spark plugs, (if gasoline, or injectors (if diesel).
3. Unplug the coil wire from the distributor, if gasoline.
4. Turn the engine so that No. 1 cylinder is at Top Dead Center on the compression stroke. Both valves for No. 1 cylinder should be fully closed and the crankshaft damper timing mark is at TDC. The distributor rotor will point at the No. 1 spark plug wire location in the cap, (if gasoline). On diesel engines, use a timing gauge to align to TDC.
5. Remove the rocker shaft and install a dummy shaft.
6. Apply 90–100 psi air pressure to No. 1 cylinder, using a spark plug hole air hose adaptor.
7. Use a valve spring compressor to compress each No. 1 cylinder valve spring then remove the retainer locks and the spring. Remove the old seals.

To install:

8. Install a cup shield on the exhaust valve stem, as well as the intake valve stem. Position it down against the valve guide. Push the valve stem seal firmly and squarely over the valve guide. Do not bottom the seal on the guide, leave 0.06 in. (1.6mm) gap.
9. Compress the valve spring only enough to install the lock.
10. Repeat the operation on each successive cylinder in the respective firing order, making sure that the crankshaft is exactly on TDC for each cylinder.
11. Remove the dummy shaft, and install the original rocker shaft.
12. Replace the rocker arms, covers, spark plugs, coil wire, (if gasoline), injectors (if diesel).

Cylinder Head Removed

1. Remove the cylinder head as outlined. Place head on flat clean surface.
2. Turn the camshaft so that both valves for No. 1 cylinder should be fully closed.
3. Remove the rocker shaft and install a dummy shaft.
4. Use a valve spring compressor to compress No. 1 cylinder valve spring, then remove the retainer locks and the spring. Allow the valve to fall out. Mark valve as to which cylinder it belongs to, and whether it is an intake or an exhaust valve.
5. Remove the old seal with a suitable tool, making sure you do not score the sides of the hole.

To install:

6. Install a cup shield on the exhaust valve stem, as well as the intake valve stem. Position it down against the valve guide. Push the valve stem seal firmly and squarely over the valve guide. Do not bottom the seal on the guide, leave 0.06 in. (1.6mm) gap.
7. Install the valve and spring, then compress the valve spring only enough to install the lock.
8. Repeat the operation on each successive cylinder in the respective firing order, making sure that the crankshaft is exactly on TDC for each cylinder.
9. Remove the dummy shaft, and install the original rocker shaft.
10. Replace the cylinder head to the engine block.

Valves and Springs

REMOVAL & INSTALLATION

Except 6-251 Engine

♦ See Figures 103 thru 119

1. Remove the cylinder head from the vehicle.
2. Block the head on its side, or install a pair of head-holding brackets made especially for valve removal.

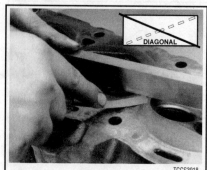

Fig. 101 Checking the cylinder head for flatness across the head surface, at an angle

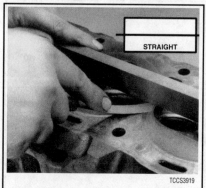

Fig. 102 Checking the cylinder head for flatness straight across the head surface

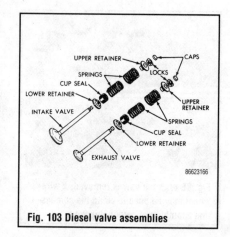

Fig. 103 Diesel valve assemblies

ENGINE AND ENGINE OVERHAUL   3-33

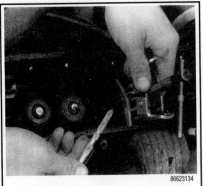
Fig. 104 V8—A magnetic pencil is helpful for keeper removal

Fig. 105 Use a valve spring compressor to remove the spring assembly

Fig. 106 Make sure you remove and discard each valve seal after removing the spring

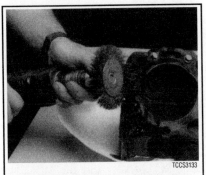
Fig. 107 An electric drill equipped with a wire wheel will expedite complete gasket removal

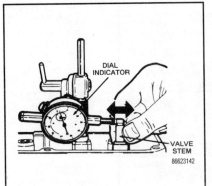
Fig. 108 Check the valve stem-to-guide clearance

Fig. 109 Checking valve seat concentricity with a dial gauge

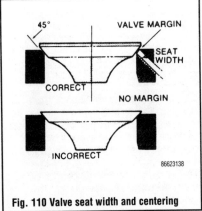
Fig. 110 Valve seat width and centering

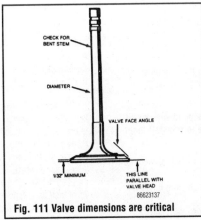
Fig. 111 Valve dimensions are critical

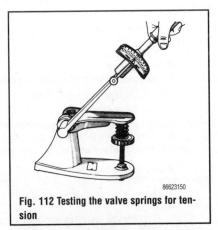
Fig. 112 Testing the valve springs for tension

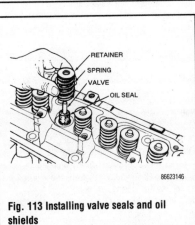
Fig. 113 Installing valve seals and oil shields

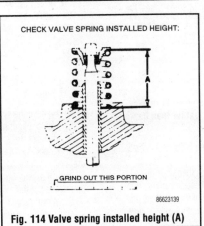
Fig. 114 Valve spring installed height (A)

Fig. 115 Be careful not to lose the valve keys

3-34 ENGINE AND ENGINE OVERHAUL

Fig. 116 Use a caliper gauge to check the valve spring free-length

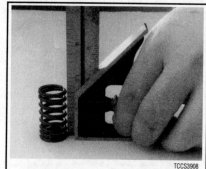

Fig. 117 Check the valve spring for squareness on a flat service, a carpenters square can be used

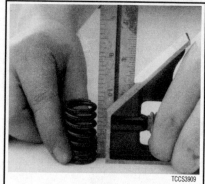

Fig. 118 The valve spring should be straight up and down when placed like this

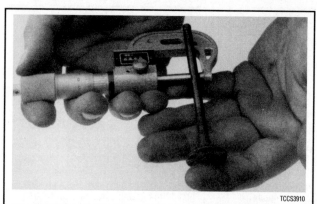

Fig. 119 Use a micrometer to check the valve stem diameter

3. Use a socket slightly larger than the valve stem and keepers, place the socket over the valve stem and gently hit the socket with a soft faced hammer to break loose any varnish buildup.

4. Remove the valve keepers, retainer, spring shield and valve spring using a valve spring compressor.

5. Remove the valves from the cylinder head and place them, in order, through numbered holes punched in a stiff piece of cardboard or wood valve holding stick.

➡ The exhaust valve stems, on some engines, are equipped with small metal caps. Take care not to lose the caps. Make sure to reinstall them at assembly time. Replace any caps that are worn.

6. Put the parts in a container numbered for the cylinder being worked on; do not mix them with other parts removed.

7. Remove and discard the valve stem oil seals. A new seal will be used at assembly time.

8. Use an electric drill and rotary wire brush to clean the intake and exhaust valve ports, combustion chamber and valve seats. In some cases, the carbon will need to be chipped away. Use a blunt pointed drift for carbon chipping. Be careful around the valve seat areas.

9. Use a wire valve guide cleaning brush and safe solvent to clean the valve guides.

10. Clean the valves with a revolving wire brush. Heavy carbon deposits may be removed with the blunt drift.

➡ When using a wire brush to clean carbon on the valve ports, valves etc., be sure that the deposits are actually removed, rather than burnished.

11. Wash and clean all valve springs, keepers, retaining caps etc., in safe solvent.

12. Clean the head with a brush and some safe solvent, then wipe dry.

13. Check the head for cracks. Cracks in the cylinder head usually start around an exhaust valve seat because it is the hottest part of the combustion chamber. If a crack is suspected but cannot be detected visually have the area checked with dye penetrant or other method by a machine shop.

14. After all cylinder head parts are reasonably clean, check the valve stem-to-guide clearance. If a dial indicator is not on hand, a visual inspection can give you a fairly good idea if the guide, valve stem or both are worn. Use a dial indicator to be sure.

15. Insert the valve into the guide, slightly away from the valve seat. Wiggle the valve sideways. A small amount of wobble is normal, excessive wobble means a worn guide or valve stem. If a dial indicator is on hand, mount the indicator so that the stem of the valve is at 90° to the valve stem, as close to the valve guide as possible. Move the valve off the seat, and measure the valve guide-to-stem clearance by rocking the stem back and forth to actuate the dial indicator. Measure the valve stem using a micrometer and compare to specifications to determine whether stem or guide wear is causing excessive clearance.

16. The valve guide, if worn, must be repaired before the valve seats can be resurfaced. Chrysler supplies valves with oversize stems to fit valve guides that are reamed to oversize for repair. A machine shop will be able to handle the guide reaming for you. In some cases, if the guide is not too badly worn, knurling may be all that is required.

17. The valve seats should be a true 45° angle. Remove only enough metal to clean up the valve face or to correct runout. If the edge of a valve head, after machining, is 1/32 in. (0.8mm) or less replace the valve. The tip of the valve stem should also be dressed on the valve grinding machine, however, do not remove more than 0.010 in. (0.254mm). If necessary, have a machine shop resurface the valves and seats. Remove only enough material to clean up any pits or grooves. Be sure the valve seat is not too wide or narrow.

18. After the valves are refaced by machine, they may have to be hand lapped. Check with your machine shop. If so, hand lap them with grinding compound. Clean the grinding compound off and check the position of face-to-seat contact. Contact should be close to the center of the valve face. If contact is close to the top edge of the valve, narrow the seat; if too close to the bottom edge, raise the seat.

19. After all valve and valve seats have been machined, check the remaining valve train parts (springs, retainers, keepers, etc.) for wear. Check the valve springs for straightness and tension.

20. Install the valves in the cylinder head and metal caps.

21. Install new valve stem oil seals.

22. Install the valve keepers, retainer, spring shield and valve spring using a valve spring compressor.

23. Check the valve spring installed height, and shim or replace as necessary.

6-251 Engine

1. Remove the cylinder head.
2. Using a spring compressor, remove the valve locks.
3. Remove the valves, keeping them in order for installation.
4. Check each valve for damage or burning. Check the valve stems at several points with a micrometer. Valves with stems worn more than 0.002 in. (0.05mm) or with burned or cracked faces should be replaced. The valves may be refaced but the margin can't be less than 1/32 in. (0.79mm).
5. When installing the valves, make certain that the locks are in place and secure after the spring compressor is removed.

ENGINE AND ENGINE OVERHAUL

INSPECTION

Place the valve spring on a flat surface next to a carpenter's square. Measure the height of the spring, and rotate the spring against the edge of the square to measure distortion. If the spring height varies (by comparison) by more than 1/16 in. (1.6mm) or if the distortion exceeds 1/16 in. (1.6mm), replace the spring.

Have the valve springs tested for spring pressure at the installed and compressed (installed height minus valve lift) height using a valve spring tester. Springs should be within one pound, plus or minus each other. Replace springs as necessary.

After installing the valve spring, measure the distance between the spring mounting pad and the lower edge of the spring retainer. Compare the measurement to specifications. If the installed height is incorrect, add shim washers between the spring mounting pad and the spring. Use only washers designed for valve springs, available at most parts houses.

Valve Seats

REMOVAL & INSTALLATION

Except the 6-251 Gasoline and 6-243 Diesel Engines

If the valve seat is damaged or burnt and cannot be serviced by refacing, it may be possible to have the seat machined and an insert installed. Consult an automotive machine shop for their advice.

6-251 Gasoline and 6-243 Diesel

♦ See Figure 120

Valve seats are replaceable. Special tools are required to remove and install the seats. Considerable care must be exercised when installing the seat inserts. The inserts are installed with a 0.002–0.004 in. (0.05–0.10mm) press fit and must be started in place, true with the counterbore in the block. To install the inserts:

➡Valve seats are an interference component. This procedure should be done by a reputable machine shop because of the extreme care involved.

1. You will need to place the inserts in a cool place; one way is the use of dry ice. Approximately 10 minutes would do fine. If this is not available, you may place them in a freezer at least overnight.
2. Make certain that the block and counterbore are absolutely clean.
3. Place the chilled inserts in the counterbore and, using a seat driver, press the insert in until it bottoms.

➡If the standard insert is too loose, 0.010 in. (0.25mm) oversize are available. If this is necessary, counterbore the block 0.0035 in. (0.088mm) smaller than the insert to be installed. Run the boring tool down until it bottoms out.

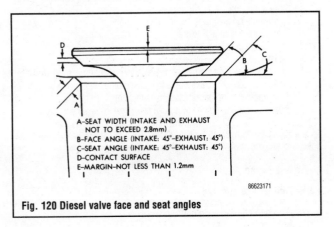

Fig. 120 Diesel valve face and seat angles

Valve Guides

REMOVAL & INSTALLATION

Except the 6-251 Gasoline and 6-243 Diesel

Worn valve guides can, in most cases, be reamed to accept a valve with an oversized stem. Valve guides that are not excessively worn or distorted may, in some cases, be knurled rather than reamed. However, if the valve stem is worn reaming for an oversized valve stem is the answer since a new valve would be required.

Knurling is a process in which metal is displaced and raised, thereby reducing clearance. Knurling also produces excellent oil control. The possibility of knurling instead of reaming the valve guides should be discussed with a machinist.

6-251 Engine

These guides are replaceable. Special tools are required.
1. Drive the guides down into the tappet chamber using a guide driver. Drivers should be 7/16 in. (11.1mm) and 11/32 in. (8.7mm).
2. If the guides don't clear the chamber, break off the lower end with a hammer and drift then drive out the remaining piece.
3. Lubricate the new guides, insert them into position from above and drive them into place. Intake valve guides are installed with the counterbore down; exhausts with the counterbore up. Top of guide-to-block height must be 0.875 in. (22.2mm).

6-243 Diesel

♦ See Figure 121

These guides are replaceable.
1. Press out the old guide using tool #31691–10500 or equivalent.
2. Press the new guide into the head using tool #31691–00800 or equivalent. Installed height, above the head, should be 0.69–0.72 in. (17.7–18.3mm).

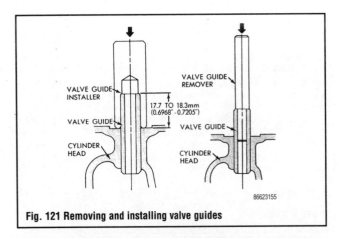

Fig. 121 Removing and installing valve guides

Oil Pan

REMOVAL & INSTALLATION

6-198 and 6-225 Engines

♦ See Figure 122

1. Disconnect the battery ground cable.
2. Drain the engine oil by removing the oil drain plug, located on the bottom of the pan.

3-36 ENGINE AND ENGINE OVERHAUL

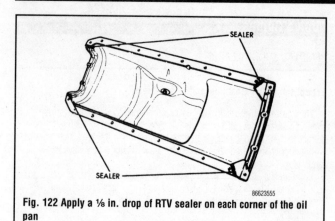

Fig. 122 Apply a ⅛ in. drop of RTV sealer on each corner of the oil pan

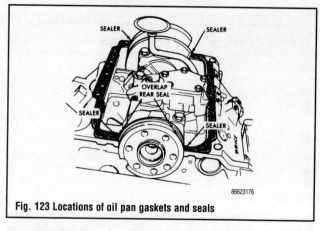

Fig. 123 Locations of oil pan gaskets and seals

✱✱ CAUTION

The EPA warns that prolonged contact with used engine oil may cause a number of skin disorders, including cancer! You should make every effort to minimize your exposure to used engine oil. Protective gloves should be worn when changing the oil. Wash your hands and any other exposed skin areas as soon as possible after exposure to used engine oil. Soap and water, or waterless hand cleaner, should be used.

3. Clean the drain plug and pan plug area thoroughly of old gasket material.
4. Remove the dipstick.
5. On models with automatic transmission, remove the torque converter inspection cover.
6. Raise and support the front end on jackstands placed under the frame. This should drop the driving axle on 4 wheel drive models far enough to clear the pan.
7. Remove the crossmember if it interferes, and the left bell housing brace.
8. Remove the pan bolts and, if necessary, tap the pan loose with a soft mallet. Never pry the pan loose!

To install:

9. Thoroughly clean all gasket material from the pan and block. On engines using RTV silicone sealer in place of a gasket, remove all traces of the material. Install the new plug gasket, and insert the plug.
10. When installing the pan, coat the block and pan mating surfaces with sealer and place a new gasket on the pan. Place new rubber end seals in the pan. Put a ⅛ in. drop of silicone sealer at the 4 points where the seals and gaskets meet. On models using RTV silicone material instead of a gasket, apply a ⅛ in. diameter bead of seal on the pan, around the bolt holes. On models with a gasket, position the pan and install the bolts. Tighten the bolts to 75 inch lbs. (8 Nm), then, retighten the bolts to 16 ft. lbs. (22 Nm). On models with RTV silicone sealant in place of a gasket, torque the bolts to 16 ft. lbs. (22 Nm).

6-251 Engine

▶ See Figure 123

1. Disconnect the battery ground cable.
2. Drain the engine oil and remove the pan bolts.
3. Carefully break the seal between the pan and engine, and remove the pan from the truck.

To install:

4. Use a tool to scrape the gasket mating surfaces, thoroughly clean. This should be done on the pan, drain plug and pan and plug mating areas.
5. Install the new plug gasket, and insert the plug.
6. Always use new gaskets coated with sealer when installing the pan.
7. When installing the pan, don't cut the ends off the new gasket. They must protrude ⅛–¼ in. (3–6mm) above the pan.
8. Torque the bolts to 15 ft. lbs. (20 Nm).

6-243 Diesel

1. Disconnect the battery ground.
2. Remove the oil dipstick.

3. Raise and support the front end on jackstands enough such that you can work comfortably under the truck, BUT also access the engine compartment from above.
4. Drain the engine oil by removing the oil drain plug, located on the bottom of the pan.
5. Remove the dipstick tube from the pan.
6. With automatic transmission equipped, disconnect the oil cooler lines.
7. Remove the road draft tube.
8. Remove the oil pan bolts and begin lowering the pan.
9. Remove the nuts from the engine mounts.
10. Remove the transmission inspection plate.
11. Complete the oil pan removal, and discard the gasket.

To install:

12. Use a tool to scrape the gasket mating surfaces, thoroughly clean. This should be done on the pan, the drain plug and pan and plug mating areas.
13. Install the new plug gasket, and insert the plug.
14. Position the oil pan using a new gasket coated with sealer.
15. Install the transmission inspection plate.
16. Install the oil pan bolts and torque them to 15 ft. lbs. (20 Nm).
17. Install the road draft tube.
18. With automatic transmission, connect the oil cooler lines.
19. Install the dipstick tube on the pan.
20. Install the nuts on the engine mounts.
21. Install the oil dipstick.
22. Fill the crankcase.
23. Lower the truck to the ground.
24. Connect the battery ground.

6-238 Engine

1. Disconnect the battery ground cable.
2. Remove the oil dipstick.
3. Raise and support the front end on jackstands.
4. Drain the engine oil.
5. Remove the exhaust cross-over pipe.
6. Remove the left engine-to-transmission strut.
7. Remove the bolts and lower the oil pan.

To install:

8. Use a tool to scrape the gasket mating surfaces, thoroughly clean. This should be done on the pan, drain plug and pan and plug mating areas.
9. Install the new plug gasket, and insert the plug.
10. When installing the pan, always use new gaskets coated with sealer. Apply a drop of RTV silicone sealer where the cork and rubber gaskets meet. Torque the oil pan bolts to 15 ft. lbs. (20 Nm). Tighten the cross-over pipe to 24 ft. lbs. (33 Nm).

8-318 and 8-360 Engine

▶ See Figures 124 and 125

1. Disconnect the battery ground cable.
2. Remove the oil dipstick.
3. Raise and support the front end on jackstands.
4. Drain the engine oil.

ENGINE AND ENGINE OVERHAUL 3-37

Fig. 124 Remove the plug and drain the pan of oil

Fig. 125 Use caution when removing the oil pan, there is always a little oil left behind in the pan

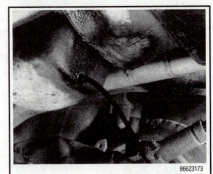

Fig. 126 Make sure you place a drain pan under the flow of the oil, it can get very messy

5. Remove the exhaust cross-over pipe.
6. On 1979 and later trucks, remove the left engine-to-transmission strut.
7. Remove the bolts and lower the oil pan.

To install:

8. Use a tool to scrape the gasket mating surfaces, thoroughly clean. This should be done on the pan, drain plug and pan and plug mating areas.
9. Install the new plug gasket, and insert the plug.
10. When installing the pan, always use new gaskets coated with sealer. Apply a drop of RTV silicone sealer where the cork and rubber gaskets meet. On the 8-360, make sure the gasket notches are positioned as shown. On trucks through 1977, the oil strainer must be parallel with the bottom of the pan and must touch the pan with a 1/16–1/8 in. (1.5–3.1mm) interference fit. Torque the oil pan bolts to 15 ft. lbs. (20 Nm). Tighten the cross-over pipe to 24 ft. lbs. (33 Nm).

8-383 Engine

▶ See Figure 126

1. Disconnect the battery ground cable.
2. Remove the oil dipstick.
3. On models with automatic transmission, remove the torque converter inspection cover.
4. Raise and support the front end on jackstands placed under the frame. This will drop the driving axle far enough to clear the pan.
5. Remove the crossmember if it interferes, and the left bell housing brace.
6. Drain the engine oil.
7. Remove the pan bolts and, if necessary, tap the pan loose with a soft mallet. Never pry the pan loose!

To install:

8. Use a tool to scrape the gasket mating surfaces, thoroughly clean. This should be done on the pan, drain plug and pan and plug mating areas.
9. Install the new plug gasket, and insert the plug.
10. When installing the pan, coat the block and pan mating surfaces with sealer, then place a new gasket on the pan. Place new rubber end seals in the pan. Put a 1/8 in. (3.1mm) drop of silicone sealer at the 4 points where the seals and gaskets meet. Tighten the bolts to 75 inch lbs. (8 Nm), then, retighten the bolts to 16 ft. lbs. (22 Nm).

8-413 Engine

1. Disconnect the battery ground cable.
2. Remove the oil dipstick.
3. On models with automatic transmission, remove the torque converter inspection cover.
4. Raise and support the front end on jackstands placed under the frame. This should drop the driving axle on 4 wheel drive trucks far enough to clear the pan.
5. Remove the crossmember if it interferes, and the left bell housing brace.
6. Drain the engine oil.
7. Remove the pan bolts and, if necessary, tap the pan loose with a soft mallet. Never pry the pan loose!

To install:

8. Use a tool to scrape the gasket mating surfaces, thoroughly clean. This should be done on the pan, drain plug and pan and plug mating areas.

9. Install the new plug gasket, and insert the plug.
10. When installing the pan, coat the block and pan mating surfaces with sealer then place a new gasket on the pan. Place new rubber end seals in the pan. Put a 1/8 in. (3.1mm) drop of silicone sealer at the 4 points where the seals and gaskets meet.
11. Position the pan and install the bolts. Tighten the bolts to 75 inch lbs. (8 Nm), then, retighten the bolts to 16 ft. lbs. (22 Nm).

8-400 and 8-440 Engines

1. Disconnect the battery ground cable.
2. Remove the oil dipstick.
3. Raise and support the front end on jackstands.
4. Drain the oil.
5. Remove the bolts and lower the oil pan.

To install:

6. Use a tool to scrape the gasket mating surfaces, thoroughly clean. This should be done on the pan, drain plug and the pan and plug mating areas.
7. Install the new plug gasket, and insert the plug.
8. When installing the pan, always use new gaskets coated with sealer. Apply a drop of RTV silicone sealer where the cork and rubber gaskets meet. The oil strainer must be parallel with the bottom of the pan and must touch the pan with a 1/16–1/8 in. (1.6–3.2mm) interference fit. Torque the oil pan bolts to 15 ft. lbs. (20 Nm). Tighten the cross-over pipe to 24 ft. lbs. (33 Nm).

Oil Pump

REMOVAL & INSTALLATION

❈❈ CAUTION

The EPA warns that prolonged contact with used engine oil may cause a number of skin disorders, including cancer! You should make every effort to minimize your exposure to used engine oil. Protective gloves should be worn when changing the oil. Wash your hands and any other exposed skin areas as soon as possible after exposure to used engine oil. Soap and water, or waterless hand cleaner should be used.

6-198 and 6-225 Engines

The rotor type of pump is externally mounted on the rear right-hand (camshaft) side of the engine and is gear driven (helical) from the camshaft. The oil filter screws into the pump body.

1. Remove the outer cover and catch the rotor, as it will fall. Remove the oil pump mounting bolts then remove the pump and filter assembly from engine.
2. Install the oil pump to engine block using a new gasket and tightening mounting bolts to 16 ft. lbs. (22 Nm).
3. Install new oil seal rings between the cover and body, tightening cover attaching bolts to 95 inch lbs. (11 Nm).

3-38 ENGINE AND ENGINE OVERHAUL

6-251 Engine

1. Remove the distributor cap and rotate the crankshaft until the rotor is pointing to the No. 1 cylinder firing position.
2. Remove the pump mounting bolts and remove the pump from the engine.
3. Install the oil pump without the outer rotor and cover, using a new gasket. Tighten to 16 ft. lbs. (23 Nm).
4. Install the outer rotor, seal and pump cover. Torque the pump cover bolts to 130 inch lbs. (15 Nm).

6-243 Diesel Engines

♦ See Figure 127

1. Remove the oil pan.
2. Remove the oil pickup tube, strainer and all old gaskets.
3. Remove the oil pump joint bolt.
4. Remove the filter assembly-to-oil pump tube.
5. Remove the joint bolt then remove the oil pump and gasket.
6. Clean all gasket material from the mating surfaces, then replace with a new gaskets.
7. Install the oil pump and gasket.
8. Install the filter assembly-to-oil pump tube.
9. Install the oil pump joint bolt. Torque the bolt to 39 ft. lbs. (53 Nm).
10. Install the oil pickup tube and strainer.
11. Install the oil pan.

6-238, 8-318 and 8-360 Engines

♦ See Figure 128

➡It is necessary to remove the oil pan, and to remove the oil pump from the rear main bearing cap to service the pump.

1. Drain the engine oil and remove the oil pan.
2. Remove the oil pump mounting bolts and remove the oil pump from the rear main bearing cap.
3. Install the oil pump.
4. Tighten the cover bolts to 95 inch lbs. (11 Nm).
5. Prime the oil pump before installation by filling the rotor cavity with engine oil. Install the oil pump on the engine.

➡During installation slowly rotate the pump body to ensure driveshaft-to-pump rotor shaft engagement and that pump is fully seated before installing fasteners.

6. Tighten the pump attaching bolts to 30 ft. lbs. (41 Nm).
7. Install the oil pan.
8. Fill the engine with the proper grade motor oil. Start the engine and check for leaks.

8-383, 8-400, 8-413 and 8-440 Engines

The rotor type oil pump is externally mounted and gear driven from the camshaft. The oil filters screws into the pump body.

1. Drain engine oil.
2. Remove oil pump and filter assembly.

3. Install oil pump on engine using new gasket and tightening bolts to 30 ft. lbs. (41 Nm). The distributor drive gear slot should parallel the crankshaft with No. 1 cylinder on TDC.
4. Install oil filter and fill crankcase with oil.

Front Cover and Seal

REMOVAL & INSTALLATION

➡If replacing only a cover seal, the cover does not have to be removed. With the balancer removed, the seal can be replaced.

Inline 6 Cylinder Gasoline Engines

♦ See Figure 129

1. Drain the cooling system and disconnect the battery cable.

✳✳ CAUTION

When draining the coolant, keep in mind that cats and dogs are attracted by the ethylene glycol antifreeze, and are quite likely to drink any that is left in an uncovered container or in puddles on the ground. This will prove fatal in sufficient quantity. Always drain the coolant into a sealable container. Coolant should be reused unless it is contaminated or several years old.

2. Remove the radiator and fan.
3. With a puller, remove the vibration damper.
4. Loosen the oil pan bolts to allow clearance, then remove the timing case cover and gasket.
5. Clean all gasket surfaces thoroughly.
6. Install a new seal in the case.
7. Install the timing case cover with a new gasket and torque the bolts to 17 ft. lbs. (23 Nm). Re-tighten the engine oil pan to 17 ft. lbs. (23 Nm). Always use a centering tool to ensure that the seal will not be damaged and that it is properly aligned.
8. On the 6-198 and 6-225, press the vibration damper back on. On the 6-251, install the damper and torque the bolt to 135 ft. lbs. (182 Nm)
9. Replace the radiator and hoses.
10. Connect the battery cable.
11. Refill the cooling system.

V6 and V8 Gasoline Engines

EXCEPT 8-413

♦ See Figures 130 thru 137

1. Disconnect the battery and drain the cooling system. Remove the radiator.
2. Remove the water pump.
3. Remove the power steering pump.

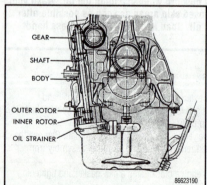

Fig. 127 Cross-sectional view of the oil pump mounting

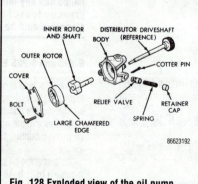

Fig. 128 Exploded view of the oil pump assembly

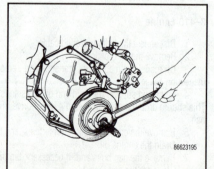

Fig. 129 The damper nut may be run on with an open-end wrench, but a torque wrench is necessary for proper tightening

ENGNE AND ENGINE OVERHAUL 3-39

Fig. 130 Remove the crankshaft pulley for access to the damper

Fig. 131 To ease assembly, always align the TDC mark on the pulley to the 0° timing mark on the front cover

Fig. 132 Loosen and remove the crankshaft bolt

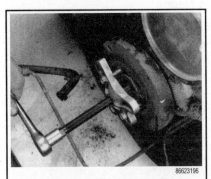
Fig. 133 Always use a threaded puller to remove the damper—jawed pullers would damage dampers with bonded hubs

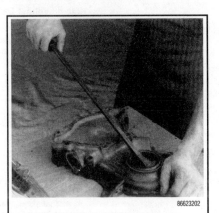
Fig. 134 Carefully pry the oil seal out

Fig. 135 Use a socket and hammer to install the new oil seal

Fig. 136 Position the new gasket and coat with a bead of sealer

Fig. 137 Be sure to use a thin bead of RTV sealant at the oil pan gasket mating surface

4. Remove the crankshaft pulley by using a large socket and another wrench to hold the small bolts.
5. Mark the vibration damper with white paint at the Top Dead Center (TDC) timing mark.
6. Loosen the crankshaft bolt with a wrench and put aside.
7. Remove the vibration damper with a puller. On 318 and 360 engines, remove the fuel lines and fuel pump, then loosen the oil pan bolts and remove the front bolt on each side.

➡When the upper bolt is removed, fluid may come out.

8. Remove the timing gear cover and the crankshaft oil slinger.
9. Remove the seal with a suitable prytool, place the tool behind the lip of the seal and pry upwards. Do this carefully making sure not to damage the crankshaft seal surface of the cover.

➡A seal remover and installer tool is required to prevent seal damage.

10. Clean all gasket surfaces thoroughly.

To install:

11. Install a new seal in the cover. Use a socket placed evenly over the seal and apply blows with a hammer.
12. Insert the seal into the opening with the springs towards the inside of the engine. Make sure to lube the seal first before installing.
13. Install the timing case cover with a new gasket. A 1/8 in. (25.5mm) bead of RTV sealer is recommended on the oil pan gasket. Torque the cover bolts to 30 ft. lbs. (41 Nm). Retighten the engine oil pan to 17 ft. lbs. (23 Nm). Always use a centering tool to ensure that the seal will not be damaged and that it is properly aligned.
14. Lubricate the seal lip with lithium white grease and slide the damper back into position. Using tool C–3688, press the damper onto the shaft. When reinstalling the bolt, use a sealant on the bolt surface. Torque the bolt to 135 ft. lbs. (182 Nm).
15. On the 318 and 360 engines install the fuel pump and lines.
16. Install the water pump, using new gaskets and tighten to 30 ft. lbs. (41 Nm).

17. Install the power steering pump.
18. Replace the radiator and hoses.
19. Tighten all drive belts.
20. Connect the battery cable.
21. Fill the cooling system.

8-413 ENGINE

1. Remove the cover as outlined in the previous procedure.
2. Position remover screw of Tool C–3506 through case cover, inside of case cover up.
3. Position remover blocks directly opposite each other, and force angular lip between neoprene and flange of seal retainer.
4. Place washer and nut on remover screw.
5. Tighten nut as tightly as possible by hand, forcing blocks into gap to a point of distorting the seal retainer lip. Remove blocks and screw are then in proper position.
6. Place sleeve over retainer and place removing and installing plate into sleeve. Place flat washer and nut on remover screw. Hold center screw and tighten lock nut to remove seal.
7. Insert remover screw through removing and installing plate so that thin shoulder will be facing up.

To install:

8. Insert remover screw with plate through seal opening (inside of gear case cover facing up.) Place seal in cover opening, with neoprene down.
9. Place seal installing plate into new seal, with protective recess toward lip off seal retainer.
10. Install flat washer and nut on remover screw, hold screw and tighten the nut. The seal is properly installed when neoprene is tight against face of cover.
11. Try to insert a 0.0015 in. (0.038mm) feeler gauge between neoprene and cover. If seal is installed properly, feeler gauge cannot be inserted. It is normal to find particles of neoprene collected between seal retainer and crankshaft oil slinger after seal has been in operation.
12. Be sure mating surfaces of gear case cover and cylinder block are clean and free from burrs.
13. Lubricate oil seal with Lubriplate® using a new gasket, slide gear cover over locating dowels and tighten upper four 5/16 (25.7mm) bolts to 15 ft. lbs. (20 Nm). Install front engine mount using lower four holes. Be sure to use special hardened bolts with beveled washers. Tighten to 40 ft. lbs. (54 Nm).

6-243 Diesel Engines

1. Disconnect the battery ground cable.
2. Drain the cooling system.
3. Disconnect and remove the upper and lower hoses.
4. Unhook the overflow tank.
5. Remove the automatic transmission oil cooler lines and bracket.
6. Loosen the radiator mount bolts.
7. Remove the fan.
8. Take out the rubber shield from between the radiator and grille.
9. Remove the radiator and fan shroud.
10. Remove all drive belts.
11. Loosen and remove the crankshaft pulley nut.
12. Turn the crankshaft until the keyway is at the 12 o'clock position.
13. Mark the vibration damper with white paint TDC, 0° timing mark for correct installation.
14. Remove the crankshaft pulley and damper assembly with tool MH–061101.
15. Remove the timing gear case and gasket.
16. Remove the front oil seal from the case.

➡ A seal remover and installer tool is required to prevent seal damage.

17. Coat a new timing case gasket with sealer and position it over the dowels on the block.

To install:

18. Install the timing gear case Torque the bolts to 84 inch lb. (9 Nm).
19. Install the crankshaft pulley and damper assembly. Be careful to avoid damage to the seal.
20. Install the crankshaft pulley cone and nut. Torque the nut to 290 ft. lbs. (392 Nm).
21. Install all drive belts.

22. Install the radiator and fan shroud. Tighten the lower radiator mounting nuts finger-tight.
23. Install the rubber shield between the radiator and grille.
24. Install the fan.
25. Align the radiator and tighten the radiator mount bolts.
26. Install the automatic transmission oil cooler lines and bracket.
27. Connect the overflow tank.
28. Install and tighten the upper and lower radiator hoses.
29. Connect the battery cable.
30. Fill the cooling system.
31. Check for leaks.

Timing Chain and Sprockets

REMOVAL & INSTALLATION

Inline 6 Cylinder Gasoline Engines

▶ See Figure 138

1. Remove the front cover.
2. Slide the crankshaft oil slinger off the front of the crankshaft.

➡ It is a good practice to mark the timing marks with white paint before proceeding.

3. Remove the camshaft sprocket bolt.
4. Remove the timing chain with the camshaft sprocket.

To install:

5. Turn the crankshaft to line up the timing mark on the crankshaft sprocket with the centerline of the camshaft (without the chain).
6. Install the camshaft sprocket and chain. Align the timing marks which were painted earlier.
7. Torque the camshaft sprocket bolt to 35 ft. lbs. (47 Nm) for the 6-198 and 6-225; 20 ft. lbs. (27 Nm) for the 6-251.
8. Replace the oil slinger.
9. Install the timing case cover.

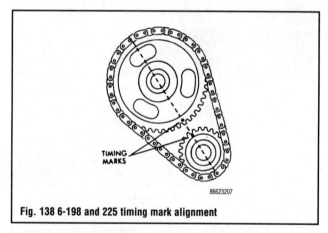

Fig. 138 6-198 and 225 timing mark alignment

V6 and V8 Gasoline Engines

▶ See Figures 139 thru 144

1. Remove the front cover.
2. On 238, 318, 383, and 360 engines, remove the camshaft sprocket lock bolt, securing cup washer, and fuel pump eccentric. Remove the timing chain with both sprockets. On 400 and 440 engines, remove the camshaft sprocket lockbolt, then remove the timing chain with the camshaft and crankshaft sprockets.
3. Place the camshaft and crankshaft sprockets on a flat surface with the timing indicators on an imaginary centerline through both sprocket boxes.

To install:

4. Place the timing chain around both sprockets. Be sure that the timing marks are in alignment.

ENGINE AND ENGINE OVERHAUL 3-41

Fig. 139 Before loosening and removing the camshaft sprocket bolt, align the timing marks

Fig. 140 Slide the securing cup washer off after removing the camshaft sprocket bolt

Fig. 141 When removing and installing the chain make sure the timing marks are in alignment

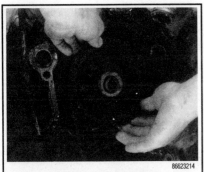
Fig. 142 Remove the sprocket/chain assembly by hand; DO NOT use a pry tool as this may damage the sprockets

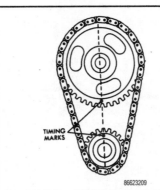
Fig. 143 V–6 and V–8 timing mark alignment

Fig. 144 ALWAYS double check timing mark alignment before installing the timing cover

✽✽ CAUTION

When installing the timing chain, have an assistant support the camshaft with a suitable tool to prevent it from contacting the plug in the rear of the engine block. Remove the distributor and the oil pump/distributor drive gear. Position the suitable tool against the rear side of the cam gear and be careful not to damage the cam lobes.

5. Turn the crankshaft and camshaft to align them with the keyway location in the crankshaft sprocket and the keyway or dowel hole in the camshaft sprocket.

6. Lift the sprockets and timing chain while keeping the sprockets tight against the chain in the correct position. Slide both sprockets evenly onto their respective shafts.

7. Use a straightedge to measure the alignment of the sprocket timing marks. They must be perfectly aligned.

8. On 238, 318 and 360 engines, install the fuel pump eccentric, cup washer, and camshaft sprocket lockbolt and torque to 35 ft. lbs. (47 Nm) If camshaft end-play exceeds 0.010 in. (0.25mm), install a new thrust plate. It should be 0.002–0.006 in. (0.05–0.15mm) with the new plate.

9. On 400 and 440 engines, install the washer and camshaft sprocket lockbolt(s) and then torque the lockbolt to 35–40 ft. lbs. (47–54 Nm). Check to make sure that the rear face of the camshaft sprocket is flush with the camshaft end.

CHECKING TIMING CHAIN SLACK

▶ See Figures 145 and 146

1. Position a scale (ruler or straightedge) next to the timing chain to detect any movement in the chain.

2. Place a torque wrench and socket on the camshaft sprocket attaching bolt. Apply either 30 ft. lbs. (41 Nm), if the cylinder heads are installed on the engine, or 15 ft. lbs. (20 Nm), cylinder heads removed, of force to the bolt and

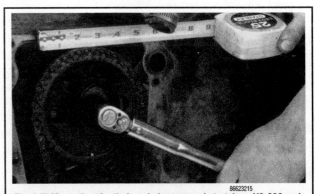
Fig. 145 Measuring the timing chain wear and stretch on V6-238 and V8-318/360—If wear exceeds ⅛ in. (3.175mm) install a new chain.

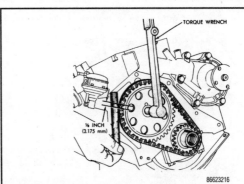
Fig. 146 Measuring the timing chain wear and stretch on L6-198 and L6-225—If wear exceeds ⅛ in. (3.175mm) install a new chain.

3-42 ENGINE AND ENGINE OVERHAUL

rotate the bolt in the direction of crankshaft rotation in order to remove all slack from the chain.

3. While applying torque to the camshaft sprocket bolt, the crankshaft should not be allowed to rotate. It may be necessary to block the crankshaft to prevent rotation.

4. Position the scale over the edge of a timing chain link and apply an equal amount of torque in the opposite direction. If the movement of the chain exceeds 1/8 in. (25.5mm), replace the chain.

Timing Gears

REMOVAL & INSTALLATION

Diesel Engines

▶ See Figures 147 and 148

To remove:
1. Remove the timing gear cover, the gasket and the front seal.
2. Remove the idler pulley bracket.
3. Align the timing marks.
4. Using a puller, remove the camshaft drive gear.
5. Turn the injection pump to allow the notch in the drive gear to pass by the idler gear teeth.
6. Loosen the idler gear mounting bolt. Remove the thrust plate and remove the idler gear.
7. Disconnect the injection lines at the pump.
8. Disconnect the fuel line at the transfer pump and cap all openings.
9. Disconnect the transfer pump-to-filter hose.
10. Disconnect the filter-to-injection pump hose.
11. Loosen the stay bolt on the back of the injection pump. Remove the pump, automatic timing gear and the flange, by pulling toward the back of the engine.

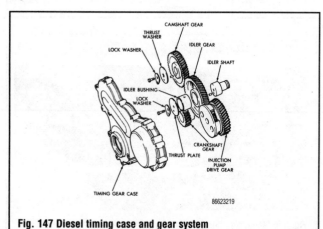

Fig. 147 Diesel timing case and gear system

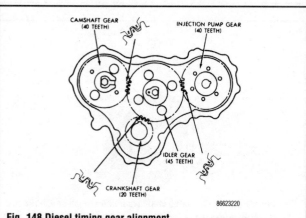

Fig. 148 Diesel timing gear alignment

To inspect:
12. Inspect all parts for wear or damage. Replace any suspect parts.
13. Put the camshaft gear back on the shaft and check for shaft end-play with a dial indicator. End-play should be 0.001–0.008 in. (0.05–0.22mm). If end-play exceeds the limit of 0.01 in. (0.30mm), replace the thrust plate.
14. Check the idler gear and shaft to make sure that the oil passage is open.
15. Measure the inside diameter of the idler bushing and the outside diameter of the idler shaft. ID should be 1.574–1.575 in. (40.000–40.025mm). OD should be 1.572–1.573 in. (39.950–39.975mm). Idler shaft-to-bushing clearance should be 0.0009–0.0029 in. (0.025–0.075mm). If the clearance exceeds 0.003 in. (0.100mm), replace the bushing. Use bushing replacer tool MH–061228.

To install:
16. Be sure that the crankshaft is set with No. 1 cylinder at TDC.
17. Install the idler gear on the shaft so the marks on the camshaft drive gear match up with the marks on the idler gear.
18. Install the thrust plate and the hold-down bolt. Torque the bolt to 25 ft. lbs. (34 Nm).
19. Install the camshaft gear and the thrust plate on the camshaft. Be sure all the marks line up with the marks on the idler gear. Tighten the hold-down bolt to 12 ft. lbs. (16 Nm).
20. Put the injection pump in position and mesh the pump drive gear with the idler gear so the marks on the drive gear match up properly with the marks on the idler gear. Be sure the pump mounting flange scale is set at the proper injection point.
21. Install the mounting nuts on the timing gear case and tighten them.
22. Connect the fuel feed line and the filter hoses to the pump.
23. Operate the primer pump to bleed the air from the fuel system.
24. Connect the injector pipes.
25. Check the idler gear for end-play using a feeler gauge between the gear and the thrust plate. It should be 0.001–0.005 in. (0.05–0.15mm). If it exceeds 0.013 in. (0.35mm), replace the thrust plate.
26. Check the gears for backlash by mounting a dial indicator so that lash is measured from the gear tooth profile at right angles to the gear shaft. When checking lash between the idler gear and injection pump drive gear, be sure that the stay bolt at the back of the pump is tight. Backlash should be 0.004–0.009 in. (0.11–0.24mm). If backlash exceeds 0.30mm, replace the gear.
27. Install a new front seal (using a new gasket), the timing gear cover and the crankshaft drive pulley.
28. Check the oil seal and cone surfaces. Runout should not exceed 0.01 in. (0.5mm). If it does, or if any contact surface is damaged, replace the pulley.

Valve Timing

ADJUSTMENT

6-198 and 6-225 Engines

1. Rotate the crankshaft until No. 6 exhaust valve is closing and No. 6 intake valve is opening.
2. Install a dial indicator so that the indicator pointer contact the valve spring retainer on the No. 1 intake valve parallel to the axis of the valve stem.
3. Turn No. 1 intake adjusting screw in one complete turn to remove the lash. Adjust the dial indicator to zero.
4. Rotate the crankshaft clockwise normal running direction until the valve has lifted 0.029 in. (0.73mm).
5. The timing of the crankshaft pulley should now read from 12° BTDC to TDC. Re-adjust lash.

➥If the reading is not within specified limits, inspect the sprocket index marks, inspect the timing chain for wear, and inspect the accuracy of the "TDC" mark on the timing indicator.

6-251 Engine

1. Rotate the crankshaft until No. 1 exhaust valve is closing and No. 1 intake valve is opening.
2. Check the accuracy of the **TDC** mark by bring No. 6 piston up to TDC using a dial indicator placed in the opening provided in the cylinder head.
3. Set the valve lash on No. 6 intake to 0.027 in. (0.68mm).

ENGINE AND ENGINE OVERHAUL   3-43

4. Rotate the crankshaft clockwise until No. 6 intake tappet just contacts the valve stem.
5. The timing mark on the chain cover should read from 10° BTC to TDC; piston height should be read at 0.045 in. (1.1mm) BTC to 0°.
6. Reset the valve lash.

6-243 Diesel

Valve timing is accomplished by aligning all gear timing marks.

V6 and V8 Gasoline Engines

EXCEPT 8-413 ENGINE

1. Turn the crankshaft until the No. 6 exhaust valve is closing and the intake valve is opening.
2. Insert a ¼ in. (25mm) spacer between the rocker arm pad and stem tip of No. 1 intake valve. Allow the spring load to bleed the tappet down.
3. Install a dial indicator so that the plunger contacts the valve spring retainer and nearly perpendicular as possible. Zero the indicator.
4. Rotate the crankshaft clockwise until the valve has lifted 0.010 in. (0.25mm) on the 8–318; 0.034 in. (0.86mm) on the 8–360; 0.025 in. (0.63mm) on the 8–383, 8–400 and 8–440.

※※ WARNING

Do not rotate the crankshaft any further, as serious damage will result!

5. The ignition timing marks should now read anywhere from 10° BTDC to 2° ATDC.
6. If the reading is not within specifications, check for timing mark alignment, timing chain wear and the accuracy of the ignition timing indicator.

8-413 ENGINE

1. Check the accuracy of the TDC mark on the indicator plate by bringing the number one piston to TDC by means of an indicator placed in the spark plug openings.
2. Rotate the crankshaft clockwise (normal running direction) until No. 1 intake is fully open. Install a dial indicator No. 1 exhaust valve so that the indicator pointer contacts the spring retainer as near to 90° angle as possible.
3. Insert a ¼ in. (25.6mm) spacer between rocker arm and stem of No. 1 exhaust valve. Allow spring load to bleed tappet down giving, in effect, a solid tappet.
4. Reset the dial indicator to zero. Rotate crankshaft counter-clockwise (opposite to normal running direction) until exhaust valve has lifted 0.090 in. (0.22mm).
5. The timing marks should now read from 12° BTDC to TDC. If the reading is over the specified limits, check timing gear marks and timing chain wear.
6. After timing has been checked, turn crankshaft clockwise (normal running direction) until tappet is back down to valve closed position. Remove spacer from between rocker arm and valve stem.

Auxiliary (Idler) Shaft

REMOVAL & INSTALLATION

6-243 Diesel

1. Remove the timing gear cover, the gasket and the front seal. Remove the idler pulley bracket.
2. Align the timing marks.
3. Using a puller, remove the camshaft drive gear.
4. Turn the injection pump to allow the notch in the drive gear to pass by the idler gear teeth.
5. Loosen the idler gear mounting bolt. Remove the thrust plate and remove the idler gear.
6. Using puller MH–061077, remove the idler shaft from the block.
To install:
7. Use a brass drift and soft hammer, to install the idler gear on the shaft so that the timing marks are aligned.
8. Install the thrust plate and torque the bolt to 25 ft. lbs. (34 Nm).

9. Check the idler gear end-play at the thrust plate. End-play can be measured with a flat feeler gauge. End-play should be 0.001–0.005 in. (0.05–0.15mm). If the end-play exceeds 0.01 in. (0.35mm), you must replace the thrust plate.
10. Check the idler gear backlash at the injection pump gear. Backlash should be 0.004–0.009 in. (0.101–0.228mm). If the backlash exceeds 0.01 in. (0.30mm), replace the idler gear.

Camshaft and Bearings

REMOVAL & INSTALLATION

6-198 and 6-225 Engines

♦ See Figures 149 and 150

1. Remove the cylinder head, timing gear cover, camshaft sprocket, and timing chain.
2. Remove the valve tappets, keeping them in order to ensure installation in their original locations.
3. Remove the camshaft sprocket.
4. Remove the distributor and oil pump.
5. Remove the fuel pump.
6. Install a long bolt into the front of the camshaft to facilitate its removal.
7. Remove the camshaft, being careful not to damage the cam bearings with the cam lobes.
To install:
8. Prior to installation, lubricate the camshaft lobes and bearing journals. It is recommended that 1 pt. of crankcase conditioner be added to the initial crankcase oil fill.

➡If replacing the camshaft, all of the tappet faces must be inspected for crown using a straightedge. If any negative crown (dishing) is observed, tappet must be replaced. The tappet must have a defined crown.

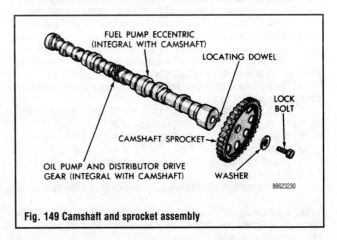

Fig. 149 Camshaft and sprocket assembly

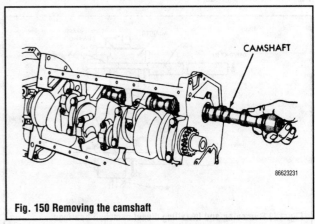

Fig. 150 Removing the camshaft

ENGINE AND ENGINE OVERHAUL

9. Install the camshaft in the engine block.
10. Reinstall the long bolt into the front of the camshaft.
11. Install the fuel pump making sure you use a new gasket.
12. Install the distributor and oil pump.
13. Install the timing sprocket.
14. Install the valve tappets, in their original locations. If installing a new camshaft, install new tappets.
15. Install the cylinder head, using new gaskets, timing chain, and timing gear cover.

6-243 Diesel

♦ See Figure 151

1. Remove the timing gear cover, the gasket and the front seal.
2. Remove the idler pulley bracket.
3. Align the timing marks.
4. Using a puller, remove the camshaft drive gear.
5. Remove the camshaft thrust plate.
6. Remove the cylinder head.
7. Using a magnet, remove the tappets, keeping them in order.
8. Drain the cooling system and remove the radiator.

✵ CAUTION

When draining the coolant, keep in mind that cats and dogs are attracted to ethylene glycol antifreeze, and are quite likely to drink any that is left in an uncovered container or in puddles on the ground. This will prove fatal in sufficient quantity. Always drain the coolant into a sealable container. Coolant should be reused unless it is contaminated or several years old.

9. If equipped with air conditioning, remove the condenser. See Section 1.
10. Carefully slide the camshaft from the block.
11. Check the runout with a dial indicator. Support journals 1 and 4 on V-blocks and set the dial indicator on 2 and 3. Runout should be less than 0.07 in. (0.0177mm). If runout exceeds 0.001 in. (0.05mm), replace the camshaft.
12. Check the cam profile by measuring the cam long and short diameters with a micrometer. Inspect the cam profile for wear or damage. The long diameter should measure 1.816 in. (46.615mm); the short diameter should measure 1.552 in. (39.426mm). If the cam profile is worn or damaged, or the diameters differ from standard by 0.01 in. (0.5mm) or more, replace the camshaft.
13. Check the camshaft journals for damage and wear. If excessively worn or damaged, the camshaft must be replaced.
14. Check the journal ODs as given in the chart. Check the bearing IDs and figure the clearances. Clearances are given in the chart.
15. Bearings are removed and installed with tool MH–061070.

To install:

16. Be sure that the crankshaft is set with No. 1 cylinder at TDC. Torque the bolt to 25 ft. lbs. (34 Nm).
17. Coat the camshaft with engine oil and carefully slide it into place. Don't damage the bearings.
18. Install the tappets in their original order, if using original camshaft. If the camshaft was replaced, new tappets should be installed. When complete, assemble the cylinder head.

19. Install the camshaft gear and the thrust plate on the camshaft. Be sure all the marks line up with the marks on the idler gear. Tighten the hold-down bolt to 12 ft. lbs. (16 Nm).
20. Put the injection pump in position and mesh the pump drive gear with the idler gear so the marks on the drive gear match up properly with the marks on the idler gear. Be sure the pump mounting flange scale is set at the proper injection point.
21. Install the mounting nuts on the timing gear case and tighten them.
22. Connect the fuel feed line and the filter hoses to the pump.
23. Operate the primer pump to bleed the air from the fuel system.
24. Connect the injector pipes.
25. Check the idler gear for end-play using a feeler gauge between the gear and the thrust plate. It should be 0.001–0.005 in. (0.05–0.15mm). If it exceeds 0.01 in. (0.35mm), replace the thrust plate.
26. Check the gears for backlash by mounting a dial indicator so that lash is measured from the gear tooth profile at right angles to the gear shaft. When checking lash between the idler gear and injection pump drive gear, be sure that the stay bolt at the back of the pump is tight. Backlash should be 0.004–0.009 in. (0.11–0.24mm). If backlash exceeds 0.011 in. (0.30mm), replace the gear.
27. Install a new front seal (using a new gasket), the timing gear cover and the crankshaft drive pulley.
28. Check the oil seal and cone surfaces. Runout should not exceed 0.001 in. (0.5mm). If it does, or if any contact surface is damaged, replace the pulley.
29. Install the radiator and condenser.
30. Fill the cooling system and crankcase.

6-251 Engine

1. Drain the cooling system.
2. Remove the radiator.
3. Remove the fan.
4. Remove the timing chain cover.
5. Rotate the crankshaft until the timing marks are aligned.
6. Remove the camshaft sprocket bolt.
7. Remove the valve covers.
8. Lift the tappets out by hand and hold them in position using spring-type clothes pins and blocks.
9. At this point, measure the camshaft end-play. If end-play exceeds 0.006 in. (0.15 mm), replace the thrust plate.
10. Slide the sprocket and chain off of the camshaft.
11. Slide the camshaft from the block.

To install:

12. Coat the new camshaft with clean engine oil and carefully slide it into place without nicking the bearings.
13. Align the timing marks, then install the camshaft sprocket and timing chain.
14. Torque the sprocket bolt to 20 ft. lbs. (27 Nm). If a new thrust plate is being installed, torque the bolts to 35 ft. lbs. (47 Nm).
15. Install the timing chain cover, fan and radiator.
16. Fill the cooling system.

V6 and V8 Gasoline Engines

EXCEPT 8-413

♦ See Figures 152 thru 158

1. Remove the intake manifold, cylinder head covers, rocker arm assemblies, pushrods, and valve tappets, keeping them in order to insure the installation in their original locations.
2. Remove the timing gear cover, the camshaft and the crankshaft sprockets, along with the timing chain.
3. Remove the distributor, then lift out the oil pump and distributor driveshaft. On 400 and 440 cu. in. engines, remove the fuel pump to allow the pushrod to drop away from the cam eccentric.
4. Remove the camshaft thrust plate (on the 238, 318 and 360). Note the location of the oil tab.
5. Install a long bolt into the front of the camshaft and remove the camshaft, being careful not to damage the cam bearings with the cam lobes.

To install:

6. Prior to installation, lubricate the camshaft lobes and bearings journals. It is recommended that 1 pt. of Crankcase Conditioner be added to the initial

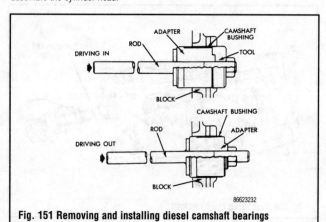

Fig. 151 Removing and installing diesel camshaft bearings

ENGINE AND ENGINE OVERHAUL 3-45

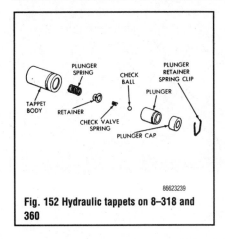
Fig. 152 Hydraulic tappets on 8–318 and 360

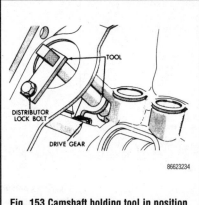
Fig. 153 Camshaft holding tool in position

Fig. 154 Camshaft and dual sprocket 6–238

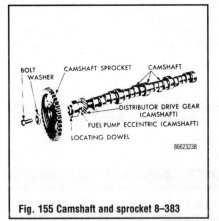
Fig. 155 Camshaft and sprocket 8–383

Fig. 156 Thrust plate location

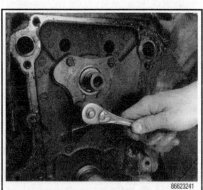
Fig. 157 Loosen the oil tab retaining bolts using a ratchet

Fig. 158 Once the bolts are removed, the oil tab may be separated from the engine

crankcase oil fill. Insert the camshaft into the engine block within 2 in. (50.8mm) of its final position in the block.

7. Have an assistant support the camshaft with a suitable tool to prevent the camshaft from contacting the welch plug in the rear of the engine block. Position the suitable tool against the rear side of the cam gear and be careful not to damage the cam lobes.

➡ This tool should remain intact until the camshaft and crankshaft sprockets and timing chain have been installed.

8. Replace the camshaft thrust plate. If camshaft end-play exceeds 0.010 in. (0.25mm), install a new thrust plate. It should be 0.002–0.006 in. (0.05–0.15mm) with the new plate.
9. Install the timing chain and sprockets, timing gear cover, and pulley.
10. Install the tappets, pushrods, rocker arms, and cylinder head covers. Install fuel pump, if removed.
11. Install the oil pump driveshaft, followed by the distributor.
12. After starting the engine, adjust the ignition timing.

8-413 ENGINE

The camshaft has an integral oil pump, distributor drive gear and fuel pump eccentric.

Rearward camshaft thrust is taken by rear face of the cast iron camshaft gear hub, bearing directly on the front of the cylinder block, eliminating the need for a thrust plate. The helical oil pump and distributor drive gear and the camshaft lobe taper both tend to produce only a rearward thrust.

1. With tappets and timing gears removed, withdraw the distributor and governor assembly.
2. Lift out oil pump distributor driveshaft.
3. Remove fuel pump to allow pushrod to drop away from cam eccentric.
4. Remove camshaft, being careful not to damage cam bearings with cam lobes.

To install:

5. Lubricate camshaft lobes and camshaft bearing journals.
6. Insert camshaft to within 2 in. (51mm) of its final position in cylinder block.
7. Modify Tool C–3509 by grinding off index lug holding upper arm on tool and rotate arm 180°.
8. Install Tool C–3509 in place of distributor drive gear and shaft.
9. Hold tool in position with distributor lock plate screw. This tool will restrict camshaft from being pushed in too far and prevent knocking out the welch plug in rear of the cylinder block. The tool should remain installed until camshaft and crankshaft gear have been installed.

INSPECTION

Camshaft Lobe Lift

Check the lift of each lobe in consecutive order and make a note of the reading.

3-46 ENGINE AND ENGINE OVERHAUL

1. Remove the fresh air inlet tube and the air cleaner. Remove the heater hose and crankcase ventilation hoses. Remove valve rocker arm cover(s).
2. Remove the rocker arm stud nut or fulcrum bolts, fulcrum seat and rocker arm.
3. Make sure the pushrod is in the valve tappet socket. Install a dial indicator so that the actuating point of the indicator is in the pushrod socket (or the indicator ball socket adaptor is on the end of the pushrod) and in the same plane as the pushrod movement.
4. Disconnect the I (ignition) terminal, and the S (starter) terminal at the starter relay. Install an auxiliary starter switch between the battery and S terminals of the start relay. Crank the engine with the ignition switch **OFF**. Turn the crankshaft over until the tappet is on the base circle of the camshaft lobe. At this position, the pushrod will be in its lowest position.
5. Zero the dial indicator. Continue to rotate the crankshaft slowly until the pushrod is in the fully raised position.
6. Compare the total lift recorded on the dial indicator with the specification shown on the Camshaft Specification chart.

➡ To check the accuracy of the original indicator reading, continue to rotate the crankshaft until the indicator reads zero. If the lift on any lobe is below specified wear limits listed, the camshaft and the valve tappets must be replaced.

7. Install the dial indicator and auxiliary starter switch.
8. Install the rocker arm, fulcrum seat and stud nut or fulcrum bolts. Check the valve clearance. Adjust if required (refer to procedure in this section).
9. Install the valve rocker arm cover(s) and the air cleaner.

Camshaft End-play

➡ On all gasoline V8 engines, prying against the aluminum-nylon camshaft sprocket, with the valve train load on the camshaft, can break or damage the sprocket. Therefore, the rocker arm adjusting nuts must be backed off, or the rocker arm and shaft assembly must be loosened sufficiently to free the camshaft. After checking the camshaft end-play, check the valve clearance. Adjust if required.

1. Push the camshaft toward the rear of the engine. Install a dial indicator so that the indicator point is on the camshaft sprocket attaching screw.
2. Zero the dial indicator. Position a pry tool between the camshaft gear and the block. Pull the camshaft forward and release it. Compare the dial indicator reading with the specifications.
3. If the end-play is excessive, check the spacer for correct installation before it is removed. If the spacer is correctly installed, replace the thrust plate.
4. Remove the dial indicator.

CAMSHAFT BEARING REPLACEMENT

▶ See Figure 159

1. Remove the engine following the procedures in this section and install it on a work stand.
2. Remove the camshaft, flywheel and crankshaft, following the appropriate procedures. Push the pistons to the top of the cylinder.
3. Remove the camshaft rear bearing bore plug. Remove the camshaft bearings with a bearing removal tool.
4. Select the proper size expanding collect and back-up nut, then assemble on the mandrel. With the expanding collect collapsed, install the collect assembly in the camshaft bearing and tighten the back-up nut on the expanding mandrel until the collect fits the camshaft bearing.
5. Convoke the puller screw and extension (if necessary) and install on the expanding mandrel. Wrap a cloth around the threads of the puller screw to protect the front bearing or journal. Tighten the pulling nut against the thrust bearing and pulling plate to remove the camshaft bearing. Be sure to hold a wrench on the end of the puller screw to prevent it from turning.
6. To remove the front bearing, install the puller from the rear of the cylinder block.

To install:

7. Position the new bearings at the bearing bores, and press them in place. Be sure to center the pulling plate and puller screw to avoid damage to the bearing. Failure to use the correct expanding collect can cause severe bearing dam-

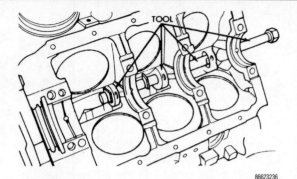

Fig. 159 Camshaft bearings are removed or installed using a special tool—V6 shown

age. Align the oil holes in the bearings with the oil holes in the cylinder block before pressing bearings into place.

8. Install the camshaft rear bearing bore plug.
9. Install the camshaft, crankshaft, flywheel and related parts, following the appropriate procedures.
10. Install the engine in the truck, following procedures described earlier in this section.

Pistons and Connecting Rods

REMOVAL & INSTALLATION

✱✱ CAUTION

When draining the coolant, keep in mind that cats and dogs are attracted to ethylene glycol antifreeze, and are quite likely to drink any that is left in an uncovered container or in puddles on the ground. This will prove fatal in sufficient quantity. Always drain the coolant into a sealable container. Coolant should be reused unless it is contaminated or several years old.

All Gasoline Engines

▶ See Figures 160 thru 164

On all but the 6-251, the notch on the top of each piston must face the front of the engine.

On the 6-251, the slot in the piston should be on the side away from the valves.

✱✱ CAUTION

The EPA warns that prolonged contact with used engine oil may cause a number of skin disorders, including cancer! You should make every effort to minimize your exposure to used engine oil. Protective gloves should be worn when changing the oil. Wash your hands and any other exposed skin areas as soon as possible after exposure to used engine oil. Soap and water, or waterless hand cleaner should be used.

To position the connecting rod correctly, the oil squirt hole should point to the right side on all six-cylinder engines. On all V8 engines, the larger chamfer of the lower connecting rod bore must face to the rear on the right bank and to the front on the left bank.

1. Disconnect the battery ground cable.
2. Drain the engine oil and cooling system.
3. Disconnect and remove parts for removal of the cylinder head.
4. Remove the cylinder head.
5. Remove the timing chain/gears.
6. Remove the oil pan.

ENGINE AND ENGINE OVERHAUL   3-47

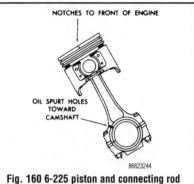

Fig. 160 6-225 piston and connecting rod assembly with oil squirt holes and notch location

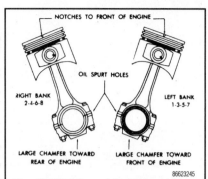

Fig. 161 V8 piston and connecting rod assembly with oil squirt holes and notch location

Fig. 162 Clean the piston grooves using a ring groove cleaner

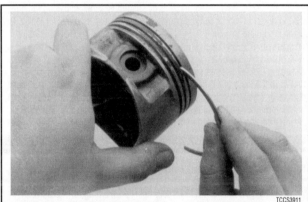

Fig. 163 You can use a piece of an old ring to clean the ring grooves, BUT be careful the ring is sharp

Fig. 164 Place lengths of rubber hose over the connecting rod studs in order to protect the crankshaft and cylinders from damage

7. Pistons should be removed following the firing order of the engine. Turn the crankshaft until the piston to be removed is at the bottom of its stroke.

8. Place a cloth on the head of the piston to be removed and, using a ridge reamer, remove the deposits from the upper end of the cylinder bore.

✲✲ WARNING

Never remove more than 1/32 in. (25.4mm) from the ring travel area when removing the ridges!

9. Mark all connecting rod bearing caps so that they may be returned to their original locations in the engine. The connecting rod caps are usually marked. The marks must be matched when re-assembling the engine. Mark all pistons so they can be returned to their original cylinders.

➡ After removing the connecting rod cap and bearing, place a short length of rubber hose over the rod bolts to prevent cylinder wall and crank journal scoring when removing or installing the piston and rod assembly.

10. Using an internal micrometer, measure the bores across the thrust faces of the cylinder and parallel to the axis of the crankshaft at a minimum of four equally spaced locations. The bore must not be out-of-round by more than 0.005 in. (0.12mm) and it must not taper more than 0.010 in. (0.25mm). Taper is the difference in wear between two bore measurements in any one cylinder.

11. If the cylinder bore is in satisfactory condition, place each ring in the bore in turn and square it in the bore with the head of the piston. Measure the ring gap. If the ring gap is greater than the limit, get a new ring. If the ring gap is less than the limit, file the end of the ring to obtain the correct gap.

12. Check the ring side clearance by installing rings on the piston, and inserting a feeler gauge of the correct dimension between the ring and the lower land. The gauge should slide freely around the ring circumference without binding. Any wear will form a step on the lower land. Replace any pistons having high steps. Before checking the ring side clearance, be sure that the ring grooves are clean and free of carbon, sludge, or grit.

13. Piston rings should be installed so that their ends are at three equal spacings. Avoid installing rings with their ends in line with the piston pin bosses and the thrust direction.

14. Install the pistons in their original bores, if you are reusing the same pistons. Install short lengths of rubber hose over the connecting rod bolts to prevent damage to the cylinder walls or rod journal.

15. Install a ring compressor over the rings on the piston. Lower the piston and rod assembly into the bore until the ring compressor contacts the block. Using a wooden hammer handle, push the rod into the bore while guiding the rod onto the journal.

Diesel Engines

▶ See Figures 165, 166 and 167

1. Disconnect the battery ground.
2. Drain the cooling system.
3. Remove the dipstick and tube.
4. Disconnect and remove the road draft tube from the oil pan.
5. Remove the automatic transmission cooling lines and bracket.
6. Remove the oil pan.
7. Remove the oil pick-up tube and gasket.
8. Turn the crankshaft until the connecting rod journal of the piston to be removed is at bottom center. Remove the connecting rod cap nuts. Install short pieces of hose on the studs to prevent journal damage. Mark the rod cap to ensure proper identification. Remove the cap and bearing inserts.
9. Push the connecting rod and piston assembly up and out of the way and measure the rod journal OD with a micrometer. It should be 2.281–2.282 in. (57.945–57.965mm). The crankpin repair limit is 0.006 in. (0.15mm). If the crankpin OD measures 0.035 in. (0.9mm) or more, the crankshaft must be replaced.
10. Remove the cylinder head.
11. Remove the ridge from the top of the sleeve with a ridge reamer.

3-48 ENGINE AND ENGINE OVERHAUL

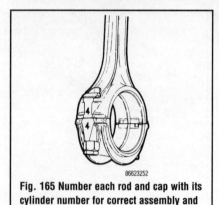
Fig. 165 Number each rod and cap with its cylinder number for correct assembly and installation

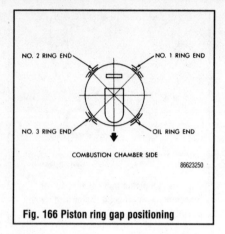
Fig. 166 Piston ring gap positioning

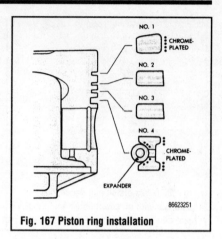
Fig. 167 Piston ring installation

12. Using a hardwood block, drive the piston up and out of the block.

13. Using an internal micrometer, measure the bores across the thrust faces of the cylinder and parallel to the axis of the crankshaft at a minimum of four equally spaced locations. The bore must not be out-of-round by more than 0.005 in. (0.12mm) and it must not taper more than 0.010 in. (0.25mm). Taper is the difference in wear between two bore measurements in any one cylinder.

14. If the cylinder bore is in satisfactory condition, place each ring in the bore in turn and square it in the bore with the head of the piston. Measure the ring gap. If the ring gap is greater than the limit, get a new ring. If the ring gap is less than the limit, file the end of the ring to obtain the correct gap.

15. Check the ring side clearance by installing rings on the piston, and inserting a feeler gauge of the correct dimension between the ring and the lower land. The gauge should slide freely around the ring circumference without binding. Any wear will form a step on the lower land. Replace any pistons having high steps. Before checking the ring side clearance, be sure that the ring grooves are clean and free of carbon, sludge, or grit.

16. Piston rings should be installed so that their ends are at three equal spacings. Avoid installing rings with their ends in line with the piston pin bosses and the thrust direction.

17. Install the pistons in their original bores, if you are reusing the same pistons. Install short lengths of rubber hose over the connecting rod bolts to prevent damage to the cylinder walls or rod journal.

18. Install a ring compressor over the rings on the piston. Lower the piston and rod assembly into the bore until the ring compressor contacts the block. Using a wooden hammer handle, push the rod into the bore while guiding the rod onto the journal.

Piston Ring and Pin Replacement

♦ See Figures 168, 169 and 170

All of the gasoline engines covered in this guide, except the 6-251, utilize pressed-in wrist pins, which can only be removed by an arbor press. The diesel piston pins are removed in the same way, only the pistons are heated before the wrist pins are pressed out.

On the 6-251, the pins are retained by snaprings. When installing the pins, the pin fit in the connecting rod should be thumb pressure at 70°F (21°C). Test fit the pin before installing it. Pin fit in the piston should be DOUBLE thumb pressure at 70°F (21°C).

A piston ring expander is necessary for removing the piston rings without damaging them; any other method (screwdriver blades, pliers, etc.) usually results in the rings being bent, scratched or distorted, or the piston itself being damaged. When the rings are removed, clean the ring grooves using an appropriate ring groove cleaning tool, using care not to cut too deeply. Thoroughly clean all carbon and varnish from the piston with solvent.

✻✻✻ WARNING

Do not use a wire brush or caustic solvent (acids, etc.) on pistons.

Inspect the pistons for scuffing, scoring, cracks, pitting, or excessive ring groove wear. If these are evident, the piston must be replaced.

The piston should also be checked in relation to the cylinder diameter. Using a telescoping gauge and micrometer, or a dial gauge, measure the cylinder bore diameter perpendicular (90°) to the piston pin, 2½ in. (64mm) below the cylinder block deck (surface where the block mates with the heads). Then, with the micrometer, measure the piston, perpendicular to its wrist pin on the skirt. the difference between the two measurements is the piston clearance. If the clearance is within specifications or slightly below, (after the cylinders have been bored or honed), finish honing is all that is necessary. If the clearance is excessive, try to obtain a slightly larger piston to bring clearance to within specifications. If this is not possible, obtain the first oversize piston and hone (or if necessary, bore) the cylinder to size. Generally, if the cylinder bore is tapered 0.005 in. (0.127mm) or more or is out-of-round 0.003 in. (0.076mm) or more, it is advisable to rebore for the smallest possible oversize piston and rings.

After measuring, mark pistons with a felt tip pen for reference and for assembly.

➡ **Cylinder honing and/or boring should be performed by a reputable, professional mechanic with the proper equipment. In some cases, clean-up honing can be done with the cylinder block in the truck, but most excessive honing and all cylinder boring must be done with the**

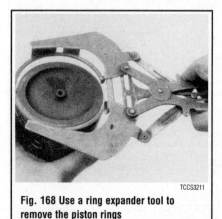
Fig. 168 Use a ring expander tool to remove the piston rings

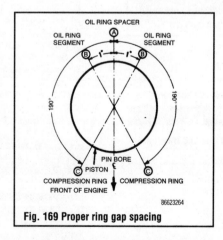
Fig. 169 Proper ring gap spacing

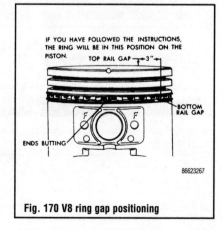
Fig. 170 V8 ring gap positioning

ENGINE AND ENGINE OVERHAUL 3-49

block stripped and removed from the truck. Before honing the diesel cylinders, the piston oil cooling jets must be removed. this procedure should be handled by a diesel specialist, as special tools are needed. Jets cannot be reused; new jets should be fitted.

Piston ring end-gap should be checked while the rings are removed from the pistons. Incorrect end-gap indicates that the wrong size rings are being used; ring breakage could occur.

Compress the piston rings to be used in a cylinder, one at a time, into that cylinder. Squirt clean oil into the cylinder, so that the rings and the top 2 in. (51mm) of cylinder wall are coated. Using an inverted piston, press the rings approximately 1 in. (25mm) below the deck of the block (on diesels, measure ring gap clearance with the ring positioned at the bottom of ring travel in the bore). Measure the ring end-gap with the feeler gauge, and compare to the Ring specifications chart in this section. Carefully pull the ring out of the cylinder and file the ends squarely with a fine file to obtain the proper clearance.

Check the pistons to see that the ring grooves and oil return holes have been properly cleaned. Slide a piston ring into its groove, and check the side clearance with a feeler gauge. On gasoline engines, make sure you insert the gauge between the ring and its lower land (lower edge of the groove), because any wear that occurs forms a step at the inner portion of the lower land. On diesels, insert the gauge between the ring and the upper land. If the piston grooves have worn to the extent that relatively high steps exist on the lower land, the piston should be replaced, because these will interfere with the operation of the new rings and ring clearance will be excessive. Piston rings are not furnished in oversize widths to compensate for ring groove wear.

Install the rings on the piston, lowest ring first, using a piston ring expander. There is a high risk of breaking or distorting the rings, or scratching the piston, if the rings are installed by hand or other means.

Position the rings on the piston, spacing of the various piston ring gaps is crucial to proper oil retention and even cylinder wear. When installing new rings, refer to the installation diagram furnished with the new parts.

CLEANING & INSPECTION

▶ See Figures 171 thru 181

Check the piston-to-cylinder bore clearance as follows:
1. Measure the cylinder bore diameter with a telescope gauge.
2. Measure the piston diameter. When measuring the pistons for size or taper, measurements must be made with the piston pin removed.

➡ **Piston and cylinder bores should be measured at normal room temperature, 70°F (21°C).**

3. Subtract the piston diameter from the cylinder bore diameter to determine piston-to-bore clearance.
4. Compare the piston-to-bore clearances obtained with those clearances recommended. Determine if the piston-to-bore clearance is in the acceptable range.
5. When measuring taper, the largest reading must be at the bottom of the skirt.

SELECTING NEW PISTONS

1. If the used piston is not acceptable, check the service piston size and determine if a new piston can be selected. Service pistons are available in standard, high limit and standard oversize.
2. If the cylinder bore must be reconditioned, measure the new piston diameter, then hone the cylinder bore to obtain the preferred clearance.
3. Select a new piston and mark the piston to identify the cylinder for which it was fitted. On some vehicles, oversize pistons may be found. These pistons will be 0.010 in. (0.254mm) oversize.

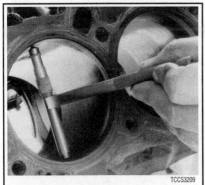
Fig. 171 A telescoping gauge may be used to measure the cylinder bore diameter

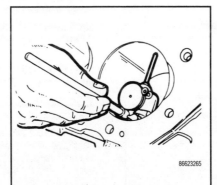
Fig. 172 A dial gauge can be used to measure the cylinder bore diameter

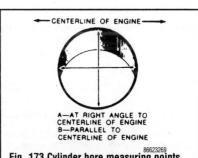
Fig. 173 Cylinder bore measuring points. Take the top measurement ½ in. (13mm) below the top, and the bottom measurement ½ in. (13mm) above the top of the piston at BDC

Fig. 174 Measure the piston's outer diameter using a micrometer

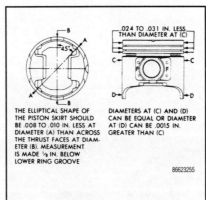
Fig. 175 Measurements on 6-225 piston

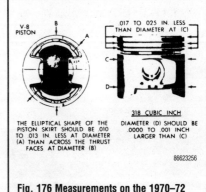
Fig. 176 Measurements on the 1970-72 V8 pistons

3-50 ENGINE AND ENGINE OVERHAUL

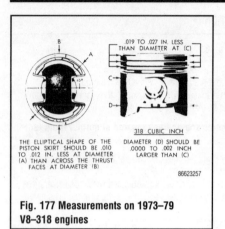

Fig. 177 Measurements on 1973–79 V8–318 engines

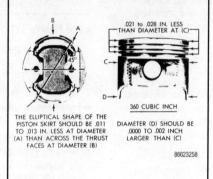

Fig. 178 Piston measurements on 1973–79 V8–360 engines

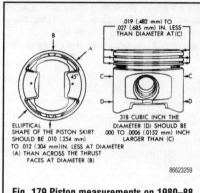

Fig. 179 Piston measurements on 1980–88 V8–318 engines

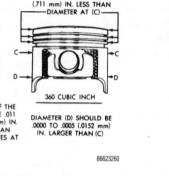

Fig. 180 Piston measurements on 1980–88 V8–360 engines

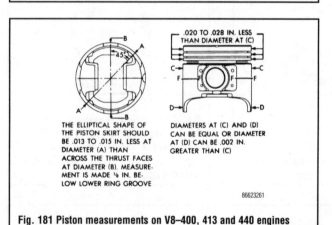

Fig. 181 Piston measurements on V8–400, 413 and 440 engines

HONING

♦ See Figures 182, 183 and 184

➡ When cylinders are being honed, follow the tool manufacturer's recommendations for the use of the hone.

Occasionally, during the honing operation, the cylinder bore should be thoroughly cleaned and the selected piston checked for correct fit.

When finish-honing a cylinder bore, the hone should be moved up and down at a sufficient speed to obtain a very fine uniform surface finish in a cross-hatch pattern of approximately 45–65° included angle. The finish marks should be clean but not sharp, free from imbedded particles and torn or folded metal.

Permanently mark the piston for the cylinder to which it has been fitted and proceed to hone the remaining cylinders.

✻✻ WARNING

Handle the pistons with care. Do not attempt to force the pistons through the cylinders until the cylinders have been honed to the correct size. Pistons can be distorted through careless handling.

Thoroughly clean the bores with hot water and detergent. Scrub well with a stiff bristle brush and rinse thoroughly with hot water. It is extremely essential that a good cleaning operation be performed. If any of the abrasive material is allowed to remain in the cylinder bores, it will rapidly wear the new rings and cylinder bores. The bores should be swabbed several times with light engine oil and a clean cloth and then wiped with a clean dry cloth. CYLINDERS SHOULD NOT BE CLEANED WITH KEROSENE OR GASOLINE! Clean the remainder of the cylinder block to remove the excess material spread during the honing operation.

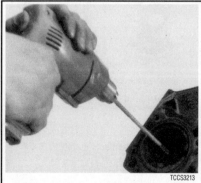

Fig. 182 Removing cylinder glazing using a flexible hone

Fig. 183 A properly cross-hatched cylinder bore

Fig. 184 Using a ball type cylinder hone is an easy way to hone the cylinder bore

ENGINE AND ENGINE OVERHAUL 3-51

ROD BEARING REPLACEMENT

▶ See Figure 185

Connecting rod bearings for the engines covered in this guide consist of two halves or shells which are interchangeable in the rod and cap. when the shells are placed in position, the ends extend slightly beyond the rod and cap surfaces so that when the rod bolts are torqued the shells will be clamped tightly in place to insure positive seating and to prevent turning. A tang holds the shells in place.

➡ The ends of the bearing shells must never be filed flush with the mating surfaces of the rod and cap.

If a rod bearing becomes noisy or is worn so that its clearance on the crank journal is sloppy, a new bearing of the correct undersize must be selected and installed since there is no provision for adjustment.

✱✱ WARNING

Under no circumstances should the rod end or cap be filed to adjust the bearing clearance, nor should shims of any kind be used.

Inspect the rod bearings while the rod assemblies are out of the engine. If the shells are scored or show flaking, they should be replaced. If they are in good shape, check for proper clearance on the crank journal (see the following). Any scoring or ridges on the crank journal means the crankshaft must be reground and fitted with undersized bearings, or replaced.

➡ Make sure connecting rods and their caps are kept together, and that the caps are installed in the proper direction.

Replacement bearings are available in standard size, and in undersizes for reground crankshaft. Connecting rod-to-crankshaft bearing clearance is checked using Plastigage® or an equivalent gauging material at either the top or bottom of each crank journal. the Plastigage® has a range of 0 to 0.003 in. (0.076mm).

1. Remove the rod cap with the bearing shell. Completely clean the bearing shell and the crank journal, and blow any oil from the oil hole in the crankshaft.

➡ The journal surfaces and bearing shells must be completely free of oil, because Plastigage® is soluble in oil.

2. Place a strip of Plastigage® lengthwise along the bottom center of the lower bearing shell, then install the cap with shell and torque the bolt or nuts to specification. DO NOT TURN the crankshaft with the Plastigage® installed in the bearing.
3. Remove the bearing cap with the shell. The flattened Plastigage® will be found sticking to either the bearing shell or crank journal. Do not remove it yet.
4. Use the printed scale on the Plastigage® envelope to measure the flattened material at its widest point. The number within the scale which most closely corresponds to the width of the Plastigage® indicated bearing clearance in thousandths of an inch.
5. Check the specifications chart in this section for the desired clearance. It is advisable to install a new bearing if clearance exceeds 0.003 in. (0.076mm); however, if the bearing is in good condition and is not being checked because of bearing noise, bearing replacement is not necessary.
6. If you are installing new bearings, try a standard size, then each undersize in order until one is found that is within the specified limits when checked for clearance with Plastigage®. Each under size has its size stamped on it.
7. When the proper size shell is found, clean off the Plastigage® material from the shell, oil the bearing thoroughly, reinstall the cap with its shell and torque the rod bolt nuts to specification.

➡ With the proper bearing selected and the nuts torqued, it should be possible to move the connecting rod back and forth freely on the crank journal as allowed by the specified connecting rod end clearance. If the rod cannot be moved, either the rod bearing is too far undersize or the rod is misaligned.

INSTALLATION

▶ See Figures 186, 187 and 188

Install the connecting rod to the piston making sure piston installation notches and any marks on the rod are in proper relation to one another. Lubricate the wrist pin with clean engine oil and install the pin into the rod and piston assembly by using an arbor press as required. Install the wrist pin snaprings if equipped, and rotate them in their grooves to make sure they are seated.

1. Make sure the connecting rod big bearings (including end cap) are of the correct size and properly installed.
2. Fit rubber hoses over the connecting rod bolt to protect the crankshaft

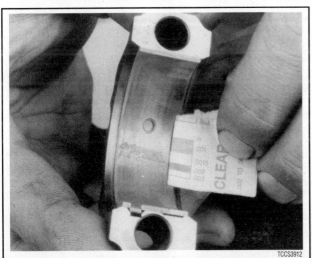

Fig. 185 After the bearing cap has been removed, use the gauge supplied with the gauge material to check bearing clearances

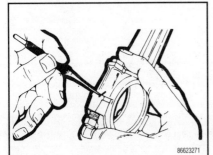

Fig. 186 Match the connecting rods with there end caps with a scribe mark for reassembly

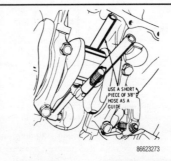

Fig. 187 Make connecting bolt guides out of rubber tubing; these also protect the cylinder walls and crank journal from scratches

Fig. 188 Use a ring compressor to install a piston

3-52 ENGINE AND ENGINE OVERHAUL

journals, as in the Piston Removal procedure. Coat the rod bearings with clean oil.

3. Using the proper ring compressor, insert the piston assembly into the cylinder so that the notch in the top of the piston faces the front of the engine (this assumes that the dimple or other markings on the connecting rods are in correct relation to the piston notch).

4. From beneath the engine, coat each crank journal with clean oil. Pull the connecting rod, with the bearing shell in place, into position against the crank journal.

5. Remove the rubber hoses. Install the bearing cap and cap nuts and torque to specification.

➡ When more than one rod and piston assembly is being installed, the connecting rod cap attaching nuts should only be tightened enough to keep each rod in position until all have been installed. This will ease the installation of the remaining piston assemblies.

6. Check the clearance between the sides of the connecting rods and the crankshaft using a feeler gauge. Spread the rods slightly with a screwdriver to insert the gauge. If clearance is below the minimum tolerance, the rod may be machined to provide adequate clearance. If clearance is excessive, substitute an unworn rod, and recheck. If clearance is still outside specifications, the crankshaft must be welded and reground, or replaced.

7. Replace the oil pump if removed, and the oil pan.
8. Install the cylinder head(s) and intake manifold.

Cylinder Liners and Seals

INSPECTION

1. Check the front plate mounting surface and flywheel housing for distortion.
2. Using a straightedge, check the cylinder block mating surface. The mating surface must be flat within 0.003 in. (0.076mm). If distortion exceeds 0.008 in. (0.2mm), the block surface may be reground.

➡ Do not grind more than necessary to make specifications.

3. Measure the ID of the sleeve at three points: top (where stepped wear usually occurs), middle and bottom with an inside micrometer or a telescope gauge. Measurements should be both parallel to, and at right angles with, the crankshaft centerline at each point.

4. The sleeve ID should be 3.6200–3.6213 in. (92.000–92.035mm). Allowable out-of-round is 0.003 in. (0.076mm) or less, and allowable taper is 0.002 in. (0.05mm) or less. If the ID deviates by more than the standard diameter of 0.047 in. (1.20mm), the sleeve must be replaced. If ID deviation is 0.009 in.–0.047 in. (0.25mm–1.20mm), the sleeve may be bored to an oversize of 0.009 in.–0.039 in. (0.25mm–1.00mm), in increments of 0.009 in. (0.25mm). Rebored sleeves must be honed to within 0.001 in. (0.035mm). Oversized pistons and rings must be used. If the ID deviates from the standard dimension by less than 0.009 in. (0.25mm), hone out the sleeve and replace the rings. If the sleeve wear is uneven, the amount of oversize is determined by maximum wear. If maximum uneven wear is 0.016 in. (0.4mm), the sleeve must be rebored to 0.039 in. (1.00mm) to ensure compliance with taper and out-of-round.

➡ If one sleeve is rebored to a given oversize, all other sleeves must be rebored to the same oversize.

REMOVAL

1. Mount a portable boring bar on the top of the block.
2. Align a boring bar with the center of the sleeve at the bottom where the eccentric wear is minimum.
3. Bore the sleeve wall out to a thickness of 0.02 in. (0.5mm).
4. Pull the sleeve with a puller.

✱✱ WARNING

Take great pains to avoid damage to the block!

5. Check the bottom hole condition after the sleeve has been pulled. If damage or any defect is noted, the bottom hole must be rebored.

INSTALLATION

Bottom Hole Not Rebored

1. Measure the inside diameter of the bottom hole and the outside diameter of the sleeve. Sleeve-to-bottom hole interference must be 0.003–0.006 in. (0.08–0.145mm) after installation.
2. Press the sleeve into the block with a hydraulic press and sleeve installer. The sleeve is pressed in flush with the block surface.
3. After installation, bore the sleeve and finish it to an ID of 3.620–3.623 in. (92.000–92.035mm) by honing.

Bottom Hole Rebored

1. The standard bottom hole dimension is 3.738–3.739 in. (94.955–94.990mm). Select an oversize sleeve with an OD 0.02 in. (0.5mm) larger.
2. Bore the bottom hole to 3.738–3.739 in. (95.455–95.490mm). This will ensure an interference fit of 0.003–0.006 in. (0.08–0.145mm).
3. Press the sleeve in as described above.
4. After the sleeves are installed, bore the sleeves and finish hone to an ID of 3.620–3.623 in. (92.000–92.035mm).

Rear Main Seal

REMOVAL & INSTALLATION

One-Piece Seal

♦ See Figure 189

1. Remove the transmission, clutch assembly or converter and flywheel.
2. Lower the oil pan if necessary for working room.
3. On gasoline engines, use an awl to punch two small holes on opposite sides of the seal just above the split between the main bearing cap and engine block. Install a sheet metal screw in each hole. Use two small prybars and pry evenly on both screws using two small blocks of wood as a fulcrum point for the prybars. Use caution throughout to avoid scratching or damaging the oil seal mounting surfaces.
4. On diesel engines, remove the bolts that secure the oil seal retaining plate. Grasp and pull the oil seal assembly from the crankshaft.
5. When the seal has been removed, clean the mounting recess.
6. Coat the seal and block mounting surfaces with oil. Apply white lube to the contact surface of the seal and crankshaft. Start the seal into the mounting recess and install with a seal driver. After inserting the seal on diesel engines, install the oil seal retaining plate, then tighten the bolts to 2.2 ft. lbs. (3 Nm).
7. Install the remaining components in the reverse of removal.

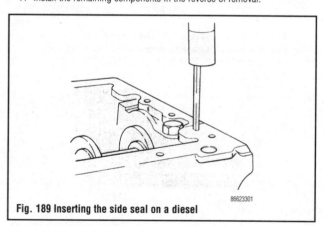

Fig. 189 Inserting the side seal on a diesel

Two-Piece Seal

♦ See Figures 190 thru 195

1. Remove the oil pan and the oil pump (if required).
2. Loosen all the main bearing cap bolts, thereby lowering the crankshaft slightly but not to exceed 1/32 in. (0.8mm).

ENGINE AND ENGINE OVERHAUL   3-53

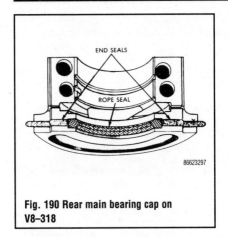

Fig. 190 Rear main bearing cap on V8–318

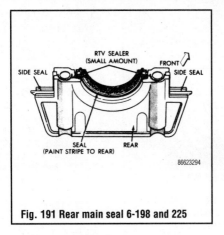

Fig. 191 Rear main seal 6-198 and 225

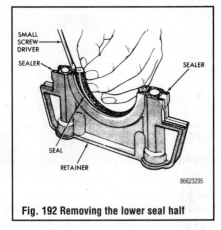

Fig. 192 Removing the lower seal half

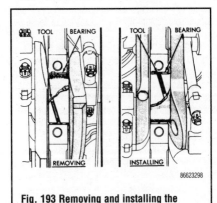

Fig. 193 Removing and installing the upper main bearing

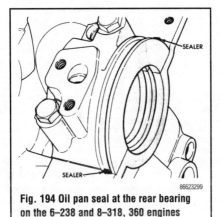

Fig. 194 Oil pan seal at the rear bearing on the 6–238 and 8–318, 360 engines

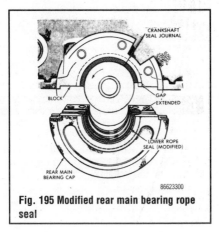

Fig. 195 Modified rear main bearing rope seal

3. Remove the rear main bearing cap, then remove the oil seal from the bearing cap and cylinder block. On the block half of the seal use a seal removal tool, or install a small metal screw in one end of the seal, and pull on the screw to remove the seal. Exercise caution to prevent scratching or damaging the crankshaft seal surfaces.

4. Remove the oil seal retaining pin from the bearing cap if so equipped. The pin is not used with the split-lip seal.

5. Carefully clean the seal groove in the cap and block with a brush and solvent such as lacquer thinner, trichloroethylene, or equivalent. Clean the area thoroughly, so that no solvent touches the seal.

To install:

6. Dip the split lip-type seal halves in clean engine oil.

7. Carefully install the upper seal (cylinder block) into its groove with undercut side of the seal toward the FRONT of the engine, by rotating it on the seal journal of the crankshaft until approximately 3/8 in. (9.5mm) protrudes below the parting surface.

Be sure no rubber has been shaved from the outside diameter of the seal by the bottom edge of the groove. Do not allow oil to get on the sealer area.

8. Tighten the remaining bearing cap bolts to the specifications listed in the Torque chart in this section.

9. Install the lower seal in the rear main bearing cap, with the undercut side of seal toward the FRONT of the engine, allow the seal to protrude approximately 3/8 in. (9.5mm) above the parting surface to mate with the upper seal when the cap is installed.

10. Apply an even 1/16 in. (1.6mm) bead of RTV silicone rubber sealer to the rope seal section. Do not apply any to the side section. Refer to the diagram given earlier in this section.

➡This sealer sets up in about 15 minutes.

11. Install the rear main bearing cap. Tighten the cap bolts to specifications.

12. Install the oil pump and oil pan. Fill the crankcase with the proper amount and type of oil.

13. Operate the engine and check for oil leaks.

Crankshaft and Main Bearings

6-198 and 6-225 Engines

➡**The maximum allowable bearing clearance is 0.001 in. (0.02mm)**

No. 1, No. 2 and No. 4 lower inserts are interchangeable. No. 1 upper insert has a chamfer on the tab side for timing chain oiling and is identified by the red mark on the edge of the bearing. Finally, No. 3 upper and lower inserts are flanged.

Bearing caps are not interchangeable and are numbered for correct installation. Maximum end-play is 0.0085 in. (0.21mm). Replace No. 3 (thrust) bearing if end-play exceeds that amount. Undersized bearings are available in the following sizes: 0.001 in. (0.21mm), 0.002 in. (0.05mm), 0.003 in. (0.07mm), 0.010 in. (0.25mm), 0.012 in. (0.30mm). Never install an undersize bearing that will reduce the clearance to below specification.

6-251 Engine

Crankshaft end-play is checked with a dial indicator between the end of the rear main bearing and the thrust shoulder. Maximum bearing taper and out-of-round is 0.001 in. (0.21mm) Undersized bearings are available in the following sizes: 0.001 in. (0.21mm), 0.002 in. (0.05mm), 0.003 in. (0.07mm), 0.010 in. (0.25mm), 0.020 in. (0.50mm), 0.030 in. (0.76mm), 0.040 in. (1.0mm).

V6 and V8 Gasoline Engines

▶ See Figure 196

A Maltese Cross stamped on the engine (except on the 238, 318 and 360) numbering pad indicates that the engine is equipped with a crankshaft which has one or more connecting rods and/or main bearing journals finished 0.001 in. (0.025mm) undersize. The position of the underside journal(s) is stamped on a machine surface of the No. 3 counterweight. On the 238, marks are stamped

3-54 ENGINE AND ENGINE OVERHAUL

Fig. 196 The main bearings found in these engines are of the replaceable inserts type which are installed in the block and bearing cap

near the notch of the No. 6 crankshaft counterweight. The letter R or M signifies whether the undersize journal is a rod or main, and the number following the letter indicates which one it is. A Maltese Cross with an X indicates that all those journals are 0.010 in. (0.25mm) undersize. On the 318 and 360 engines, 0.001 in. (0.02mm) undersize journals are indicated by marks on the No. 8 crankshaft counterweight. If the R or M is followed by an X, all those journals are 0.010 in. (0.25mm) undersize.

Upper and lower bearing inserts are not interchangeable on any of the V8 engines due to the oil hole and V-groove in the uppers. On the 238 cu.in. engine, the lower main bearing halves of No 1, and 3 are interchangeable, while the upper and lower No. 2 are flanged and not interchangeable. On the 318 and 360 cu.in. engine, the lower and upper bearing halves of No. 1, No. 2 and No. 4 are interchangeable, while the No. 3 bearing is the thrust bearing, and No. 5 is the wider rear main bearing.

On 400 and 440 cu.in. engines, the No. 1, No. 2, No. 4 and No. 5 lower bearing halves are interchangeable. No. 2, No. 4 and No. 5 upper bearing halves are interchangeable, while No. 1 upper insert has a chamfer on the tab side for timing chain oiling and is identified by the red marking on the edge of the piece. No. 3 bearing is a thrust bearing and should be replaced if end-play exceeds 0.007 in. (0.17mm).

Remove the main bearing caps one at a time and check the clearance. Check cap number for proper location when installing.

On the 400 and 440 cu. in. engines, the rear main bearing lower seal is held in place by a seal retainer. On the 318 and 360 cu. in. engine, the rear main bearing lower seal is held in place by the rear main bearing cap. Note that the oil pump is mounted on this cap and that there is a hollow dowel which must be in place when the cap is installed.

REMOVAL & INSTALLATION

Gasoline Engines

♦ See Figures 197, 198 and 199

1. With the engine removed from the vehicle and placed in a work stand, disconnect the spark plug wires from the spark plugs and remove the wires and bracket assembly from the attaching stud on the valve rocker arm cover(s) if so equipped. Disconnect the coil to distributor high tension lead at the coil. Remove the distributor cap and spark plug wires as an assembly. Remove the spark plugs to allow easy rotation of the crankshaft.
2. Remove the fuel pump and oil filter. Slide the water pump by-pass hose clamp (if so equipped) toward the water pump. Remove the alternator and mounting brackets.
3. Remove the crankshaft pulley from the crankshaft vibration damper. Remove the capscrew and washer from the end of the crankshaft. Install a universal puller on the crankshaft vibration damper and remove the damper.
4. Remove the cylinder front cover and crankshaft gear, refer to the earlier procedure on removing the front cover, in this section.
5. Invert the engine on the work stand. Remove the clutch pressure plate and disc (manual shift transmission). Remove the flywheel and engine rear cover plate. Remove the oil pan and gasket. Remove the oil pump.
6. Make sure all bearing caps (main and connecting rod) are marked so that they can be installed in their original locations. Turn the crankshaft until the connecting rod from which the cap is being removed is down, and remove the bearing cap. Push the connecting rod and piston assembly up into the cylinder. Repeat this procedure until all the connecting rod bearing caps are removed.
7. Remove the main bearings caps.
8. Carefully lift the crankshaft out of the block so that the thrust bearing surfaces are not damaged. Handle the crankshaft with care to avoid possible fracture to the finished surfaces.
9. Remove the rear journal seal from the block and rear main bearing cap.
10. Remove the main bearing inserts from the block and bearing caps.
11. Remove the connecting rod bearing inserts from the connecting rods and caps.
12. If the crankshaft main bearing journals have been refinished to a definite undersize, install the correct undersize bearings. Be sure the bearing inserts and bearing bores are clean. Foreign material under the inserts will distort the bearing and cause a failure.
13. Place the upper main bearing inserts in position in the bores with the tang fitting in the slot. Be sure the oil holes in the bearing inserts are aligned with the oil holes in the cylinder block.
14. Install the lower main bearing inserts in the bearing caps.
15. Clean the rear journal oil seal groove and the mating surfaces of the block and rear main bearing cap.
16. Dip the lip-type seal halves in clean engine oil. Install the seals in the bearing cap and block with the undercut side of the seal toward the front of the engine.

➥This procedure applies only to engines with two piece rear main bearing oil seals. those having one piece seals will be installed after the crankshaft is in place.

17. Carefully lower the crankshaft into place. Be careful not to damage the bearing surfaces.

Diesel Engines

1. With the engine secured on a workstand, with the cylinder head unfastened and placed aside, start by removing the top ridge from cylinder sleeve with a Ridge Reamer, tool C–3012.

Fig. 197 Carefully loosen and remove the main bearing cap retainers

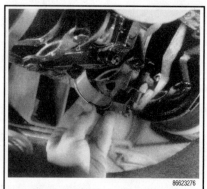

Fig. 198 Installing the main bearing inserts

Fig. 199 ALWAYS use a torque wrench to assure proper tightening of the main bearing cap retainers

ENGINE AND ENGINE OVERHAUL   3-55

➡ Keep tops of pistons covered during this procedure.

   2. As each piston and rod assembly is pushed out of bore, match the cap and rod assemblies. Also, identify the pistons and rods by cylinder.

   3. Rotate the crankshaft to center each one of the connecting rods in the bore. Remove cap.

   4. Turn the block sideways to remove the pistons and rod assemblies through the top of the block. Use bolt covers to protect journal surfaces. Push on upper bearing inserts with a hardwood blocks to remove assemblies.

   5. Remove the main bearing caps from Nos. 1 and 7 bearings using puller C–3752-D and adapters. Remove the lower bearing inserts. Make sure to mark them as to cap number.

   6. Remove the caps from Nos. 2 through 6 main bearings using the puller and adapters. Remove the lower bearing inserts. Make sure to mark them as to cap number.

   7. Lift out the crankshaft.

   8. Remove the upper bearing inserts. Identify the upper main bearings inserts, mate with corresponding lower main bearing inserts. Identify bearing pairs as to cap number.

   9. Remove the thrust plates from No. 7 main bearing journal.

CLEANING & INSPECTION

Crankshaft

➡ Handle the crankshaft carefully to avoid damage to the finish surfaces.

   1. Clean the crankshaft with solvent, and blow out all oil passages with compressed air.

   2. Use crocus cloth to remove any sharp edges, burrs or other imperfections which might damage the oil seal during installation or cause premature seal wear.

➡ Do not use crocus cloth to polish the seal surfaces. A finely polished surface may produce poor sealing or cause premature seal wear.

   3. Inspect the main and connecting rod journals for cracks, scratches, grooves or scores.

   4. Measure the diameter of each journal in at least four places to determine the out-of-round, taper or undersize condition.

   5. On an engine with a manual transmission, check the fit of the clutch pilot bearing in the bore of the crankshaft. A needle roller bearing and adapter assembly is used as a clutch pilot bearing. It is inserted directly into the engine crankshaft. The bearing and adapter assembly cannot be serviced separately.

   6. Inspect the pilot bearing, when used, for roughness, evidence of overheating or loss of lubricant. Replace if any of these conditions are found.

Main Bearings

   1. Clean the bearing inserts and caps thoroughly in solvent, and dry them with compressed air.

➡ Do not scrape varnish or gum deposits from the bearing shells.

   2. Inspect each bearing carefully. Bearings that have a scored, chipped, or worn surface should be replaced.

   3. The copper-lead bearing base may be visible through the bearing overlay in small localized areas. This may not mean that the bearing is excessively worn. It is not necessary to replace the bearing if the bearing clearance is within recommended specifications.

   4. Check the clearance of bearings that appear to be satisfactory with Plastigage® or its equivalent. Fit the new bearings following the procedure Crankshaft and Main Bearings removal and installation, they should be reground to size for the next undersize bearing.

   5. Regrind the journals to give the proper clearance with the next undersize bearing. If the journal will not clean up to maximum undersize bearing available, replace the crankshaft.

   6. Always reproduce the same journal shoulder radius that existed originally. Too small a radius will result in fatigue failure of the crankshaft. Too large a radius will result in bearing failure due to radius ride of the bearing.

   7. After regrinding the journals, chamfer the oil holes, then polish the journals with a #320 grit polishing cloth and engine oil. Crocus cloth may also be used as a polishing agent.

INSPECTION & REPLACEMENT

Gasoline Engines

▸ See Figures 200, 201 and 202

   1. Check the clearance of each main bearing by using the following procedure:

     a. Place a piece of Plastigage® or its equivalent, on bearing surface across full width of bearing cap and about ¼ in. (6mm) off center.

     b. Install cap and tighten bolts to specifications. Do not turn crankshaft while Plastigage® is in place.

     c. Remove the cap. Using Plastigage® scale, check width of Plastigage® at widest point to get the minimum clearance. Check at narrowest point to get maximum clearance. Difference between readings is taper of journal.

     d. If clearance exceeds specified limits, try a 0.001 in. (0.0254mm) or 0.002 in. (0.051mm) undersize bearing in combination with the standard bearing. Bearing clearance must be within specified limits. If standard and 0.002 in. (0.051mm) undersize bearing does not bring clearance within desired limits, refinish crankshaft journal, then install undersize bearings.

➡ Refer to Rear Main Oil Seal removal and installation, for special instructions in applying RTV sealer to rear main bearing cup.

   2. Install all the bearing caps except the thrust bearing cap. Be sure the main bearing caps are installed in their original locations. Tighten the bearing cap bolts to specifications.

   3. Install the thrust bearing cap with the bolts finger-tight.

   4. Pry the crankshaft forward against the thrust surface of the upper half of the bearing.

   5. Hold the crankshaft forward and pry the thrust bearing cap to the rear. This will align the thrust surfaces of both halves of the bearing.

   6. Retain the forward pressure on the crankshaft. Tighten the cap bolts to specifications.

   7. Check the crankshaft end-play using the following procedures:

     a. Force the crankshaft toward the rear of the engine.

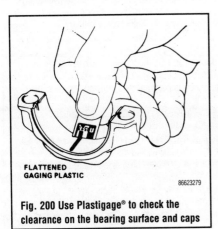

Fig. 200 Use Plastigage® to check the clearance on the bearing surface and caps

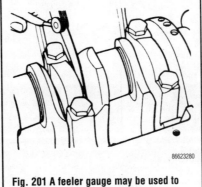

Fig. 201 A feeler gauge may be used to check end-play in a crankshaft

Fig. 202 If a dial gauge is available, it may also be used to check crankshaft end-play

ENGINE AND ENGINE OVERHAUL

    b. Install a dial indicator so that the contact point rests against the crankshaft flange and the indicator axis is parallel to the crankshaft axis.

    c. Zero the dial indicator. Push the crankshaft forward and note the reading on the dial.

    d. If the end-play exceeds the wear limit listed in the Crankshaft and Connecting Rod Specifications chart, replace the thrust bearing. If the end-play is less than the minimum limit, inspect the thrust bearing faces for scratches, burrs, nicks, or dirt. If the thrust faces are not damaged or dirty, then they probably were not aligned properly. Lubricate and install the new thrust bearing and align the faces following the procedure outlined earlier.

  8. On engines with one piece rear main bearing oil seal, coat a new crankshaft rear oil seal with oil and install using a seal driver. Inspect the seal to be sure it was not damaged during installation.

  9. Install new bearing inserts in the connecting rods and caps. Check the clearance of each bearing, following the procedure (1a through 1d).

  10. After the connecting rod bearings have been fitted, apply a light coat of engine oil to the journals and bearings.

  11. Turn the crankshaft throw to the bottom of its stroke. Push the piston all the way down until the rod bearing seats on the crankshaft journal.

  12. Install the connecting rod cap. Tighten the nuts to specification.

  13. After the piston and connecting rod assemblies have been installed, check the side clearance with a feeler gauge between the connecting rods on each crankshaft journal. Refer to Crankshaft and Connecting Rod specifications chart in this section.

  14. Install the timing chain, sprockets or gears, cylinder front cover and crankshaft pulley and adapter. Following the steps under Front Cover and Timing Chain Installation in this section.

Diesel Engines

◆ See Figures 203, 204 and 205

  1. Support the crankshaft on V-blocks under Nos. 1 and 7 journals.

  2. Mount a dial indicator contacting the center main bearing journal.

  3. Rotate the crankshaft and note the reading. This is the crankshaft runout. One half of the runout is known as "bend". Bend should be 0.0011 in. (0.03mm) or less. If bend exceeds 0.0027 in. (0.07mm), replace the crankshaft.

  4. Inspect all journals for wear, damage or overheating (blue color).

  5. Check the clearance of each main bearing by using the following procedure:

    a. Place a piece of Plastigage® or its equivalent, on bearing surface across full width of bearing cap and about ¼ in. (6mm) off center.

    b. Install cap and tighten bolts to specifications. Do not turn crankshaft while Plastigage® is in place.

    c. Remove the cap. Using Plastigage® scale, check width of Plastigage® at widest point to get the minimum clearance. Check at narrowest point to get maximum clearance. Difference between readings is taper of journal.

    d. If clearance exceeds specified limits, try a 0.001 in. (0.0254mm) or 0.002 in. (0.051mm) undersize bearing in combination with the standard bearing. Bearing clearance must be within specified limits. If standard and 0.002 in. (0.051mm) undersize bearing does not bring clearance within desired limits, refinish crankshaft journal, then install undersize bearings.

Fig. 203 A dial gauge must be used to check crankshaft runout

Fig. 204 Mounting a dial gauge to read crankshaft runout

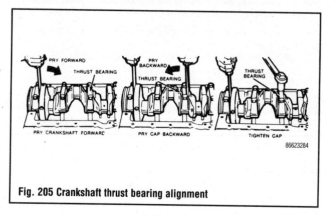

Fig. 205 Crankshaft thrust bearing alignment

➥Refer to Rear Main Oil Seal removal and installation, for special instructions in applying RTV sealer to rear main bearing cup.

  6. Install all the bearing caps except the thrust bearing cap. Be sure the main bearing caps are installed in their original locations. Tighten the bearing cap bolts to specifications.

  7. Install the thrust bearing cap with the bolts finger-tight.

  8. Pry the crankshaft forward against the thrust surface of the upper half of the bearing.

  9. Hold the crankshaft forward and pry the thrust bearing cap to the rear. This will align the thrust surfaces of both halves of the bearing.

  10. Retain the forward pressure on the crankshaft. Tighten the cap bolts to specifications.

  11. Check the crankshaft end-play using the following procedures:

    a. Force the crankshaft toward the rear of the engine.

    b. Install a dial indicator so that the contact point rests against the crankshaft flange and the indicator axis is parallel to the crankshaft axis.

    c. Zero the dial indicator. Push the crankshaft forward and note the reading on the dial.

    d. If the end-play exceeds the wear limit listed in the Crankshaft and Connecting Rod Specifications chart, replace the thrust bearing. If the end-play is less than the minimum limit, inspect the thrust bearing faces for

ENGINE AND ENGINE OVERHAUL

scratches, burrs, nicks, or dirt. If the thrust faces are not damaged or dirty, then they probably were not aligned properly. Lubricate and install the new thrust bearing and align the faces following procedures above.

12. On engines with one piece rear main bearing oil seal, coat a new crankshaft rear oil seal with oil and install using a seal driver. Inspect the seal to be sure it was not damaged during installation.

13. Install new bearing inserts in the connecting rods and caps. Check the clearance of each bearing, following the procedure.

14. After the connecting rod bearings have been fitted, apply a light coat of engine oil to the journals and bearings.

15. Turn the crankshaft throw to the bottom of its stroke. Push the piston all the way down until the rod bearing seats on the crankshaft journal.

16. Install the connecting rod cap. Tighten the nuts to specification.

17. After the piston and connecting rod assemblies have been installed, check the side clearance with a feeler gauge between the connecting rods on each connecting rod crankshaft journal. Refer to Crankshaft and Connecting Rod specifications chart in this section.

18. Install the timing chain and sprockets or gears, cylinder front cover and crankshaft pulley and adapter, following steps under Front Cover and Timing Chain Installation in this section.

COMPLETING THE REBUILDING PROCESS

Fill the oil pump with oil, to prevent cavitating (sucking air) on initial engine start up. Install the oil pump and the pickup tube on the engine. Coat the oil pan gasket as necessary, and install the gasket and the oil pan. Mount the flywheel and the crankshaft vibration damper or pulley on the crankshaft.

➥Always use new bolts when installing the flywheel. Inspect the clutch shaft pilot bushing in the crankshaft. If the bushing is excessively worn, remove it with an expanding puller and a slide hammer, and tap a new bushing into place.

Position the engine, cylinder head side up. Lubricate the lifters, and install them into their bores. Install the cylinder head, and torque it as specified. Insert the pushrods (where applicable), and install the rocker shaft(s), if so equipped or position the rockers.

Install the intake and exhaust manifolds, the carburetor(s), the distributor and spark plugs. Mount all accessories and install the engine in the truck. Fill the radiator with coolant, and the crankcase with high quality engine oil.

BREAK-IN PROCEDURE

Start the engine, and allow it to run at low speed for a few minutes, while checking for leaks. Stop the engine, check the oil level, and fill as necessary. Restart the engine, and fill the cooling system to capacity. Check and adjust the ignition timing. Run the engine at low to medium speed (800–2,500 rpm) for approximately ½ hour, and retorque the cylinder head bolts. Road test the truck, and check again for leaks.

➥Some gasket manufacturers recommend not retorquing the cylinder head(s) due to the composition of the head gasket. Follow the directions in the gasket set.

Flywheel and Ring Gear

REMOVAL & INSTALLATION

▶ See Figure 206

1. Remove the transmission and transfer case.
2. Remove the clutch, if equipped, or torque converter from the flywheel. The flywheel bolts should be loosened a little at a time in a cross pattern to avoid warping the flywheel. On trucks with manual transmissions, replace the pilot bearing in the end of the crankshaft if removing the flywheel.
3. The flywheel should be checked for cracks and glazing. It can be resurfaced by a machine shop.
4. If the ring gear is to be replaced, drill a hole in the gear between two teeth, being careful not to contact the flywheel surface. Using a drift or a cold chisel, tap downward on the ring gear near welded areas to break any weld material. Tap around the ring gear until it comes off.

To install:

5. Polish the inner surface of the new ring gear and heat it in an oven to about 200°F (93°C), allow to stay there for 15 to 20 minutes. Quickly place the ring gear on the flywheel/torque converter and tap it into place, making sure that it is fully seated.

✱✱ WARNING

Never heat the ring gear past 800°F (426°C), or the tempering will be destroyed.

6. Reweld the ring gear, being careful to place, as near as possible, the same amount of weld in the exact same places that were used in the original weld.
7. Position the assembly on the end of the crankshaft. Torque the bolts a little at a time, in a cross pattern, to the torque figure shown in the Torque Specifications Chart.
8. Install the clutch or torque converter.
9. Install the transmission and transfer case.

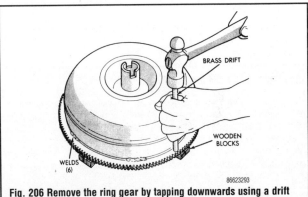

Fig. 206 Remove the ring gear by tapping downwards using a drift or chisel

EXHAUST SYSTEM

General Information

➥Safety glasses should be worn at all times when working on or near the exhaust system. Older exhaust systems will almost always be covered with loose rust particles which will shower you when disturbed. These particles are more than a nuisance and could injure your eye.

Whenever working on the exhaust system always keep the following in mind:
• Check the complete exhaust system for open seams, holes loose connections, or other deterioration which could permit exhaust fumes to seep into the passenger compartment.
• The exhaust system is usually supported by free-hanging rubber mountings which permit some movement of the exhaust system, but does not permit transfer of noise and vibration into the passenger compartment. Do not replace the rubber mounts with solid ones.
• Before removing any component of the exhaust system, ALWAYS squirt a liquid rust dissolving agent onto the fasteners for ease of removal. A lot of knuckle skin will be saved by following this rule. It may even be wise to spray the fasteners and allow them to sit overnight.

✱✱ CAUTION

Because many rust dissolving liquids are flammable, Never use them on a hot exhaust system, or near an open flame.

• Annoying rattles and noise vibrations in the exhaust system are usually caused by misalignment of the parts. When aligning the system, leave all bolts and nuts loose until all parts are properly aligned, then tighten, working from front to rear.
• When installing exhaust system parts, make sure there is enough clear-

3-58 ENGINE AND ENGINE OVERHAUL

ance between the hot exhaust parts and pipes and hoses that would be adversely affected by excessive heat. Also make sure there is adequate clearance from the floor pan to avoid possible overheating of the floor.

Safety Precautions

For a number of reasons, exhaust system work can be among the most dangerous type of work you can do on your truck. Always observe the following precautions:

- Support the truck extra securely. Not only will you often be working directly under it, but you'll frequently be using a lot of force, say, heavy hammer blows, to dislodge rusted parts. This can cause a truck that's improperly supported to shift and possibly fall.
- Wear goggles. Exhaust system parts are always rusty. Metal chips can be dislodged, even when you're only turning rusted bolts. Attempting to pry pipes apart with a chisel makes the chips fly even more frequently.
- If you're using a cutting torch, keep it a great distance from either the fuel tank or lines. Stop what you're doing and feel the temperature of the fuel bearing pipes on the tank frequently. Even slight heat can expand and/or vaporize fuel, resulting in accumulated vapor, or even a liquid leak, near your torch.
- Watch where your hammer blows fall and make sure you hit squarely. You could easily tap a brake or fuel line when you hit an exhaust system part with a glancing blow. Inspect all lines and hoses in the area where you've been working.

✱✱ CAUTION

Be very careful when working on or near the catalytic converter. External temperatures can reach 1,500°F (816°C) and more, causing severe burns. Removal or installation should be performed only on a cold exhaust system.

A number of special exhaust system tools can be rented from auto supply houses or local stores that rent special equipment. A common one is a tail pipe expander, designed to enable you to join pipes of identical diameter.

It may also be quite helpful to use solvents designed to loosen rusted bolts or flanges. Soaking rusted parts the night before you do the job can speed the work of freeing rusted parts considerably. Remember that these solvents are often flammable. Apply only to parts after they are cool!

COMPONENT REPLACEMENT

♦ See Figures 207 and 208

System components may be welded or clamped together. The system consists of a head pipe, catalytic converter, intermediate pipe, muffler and tail pipe, in that order from the engine to the back of the truck.

The head pipe is bolted to the exhaust manifold, on one end, and the catalytic converter on the other. Various hangers suspend the system from the floor pan. When assembling exhaust system parts, the relative clearances around all system parts is extremely critical. See the accompanying illustration and observe all clearances during assembly. In the event that the system is welded, the various parts will have to be cut apart for removal. In these cases, the cut parts may not be reused. To cut the parts, a hacksaw is the best choice. An oxyacetylene cutting torch may be faster but the sparks are DANGEROUS near the fuel tank and, at the very least, accidents could happen, resulting in damage to other under-truck parts, not to mention yourself!

The following replacement steps relate to clamped parts:

1. Raise and support the truck on jackstands. It's much easier on you if you can get the truck up on 4 jackstands. Some pipes need lots of clearance for removal and installation. If the system has been in the truck for a long time, spray the clamped joints with a rust dissolving solutions such as WD-40® or Liquid Wrench®, and let it set according to the instructions on the can.
2. Remove the nuts from the U-bolts; don't be surprised if the U-bolts break while removing the nuts. Age and rust account for this. Besides, you shouldn't reuse old U-bolts. When unbolting the headpipe from the exhaust manifold, make sure that the bolts are free before trying to remove them. If you snap a stud in the exhaust manifold, the stud will have to be removed with a bolt extractor, which often necessitates the removal of the manifold itself.
3. After the clamps are removed from the joints, first twist the parts at the joints to break loose rust and scale, then pull the components apart with a twisting motion. If the parts twist freely but won't pull apart, check the joint. The clamp may have been installed so tightly that it has caused a slight crushing of the joint. In this event, the best thing to do is secure a chisel designed for the purpose and, using the chisel and a hammer, peel back the female pipe end until the parts are freed.
4. Once the parts are freed, check the condition of the pipes which you had intended keeping. If their condition is at all in doubt, replace them too. You went to a lot of work to get one or more components out. You don't want to have to go through that again in the near future. If you are retaining a pipe, check the pipe end. If it was crushed by a clamp, it can be restored to its original diameter using a pipe expander, which can be rented at many good auto parts stores. Check, also, the condition of the exhaust system hangers. If ANY deterioration is noted, replace them. Oh, and one note about parts: use only parts designed for your truck. Don't use fits-all parts or flex pipes. The fits-all parts rarely fit like originals and the flex pipes don't last very long.
5. When installing the new parts, coat the pipe ends with exhaust system lubricant. It makes fitting the parts much easier. It's also a good idea to assemble all the parts in position before clamping them. This will ensure a good fit, detect any problems and allow you to check all clearances between the parts and surrounding frame and floor members.
6. When you are satisfied with all fits and clearances, install the clamps. The headpipe-to-manifold nuts should be torqued to 20 ft. lbs. (27 Nm). If the studs were rusty, wire-brush them clean and spray them with WD-40® or Liquid Wrench®. This will ensure a proper torque reading. Position the clamps on the slip points as illustrated. The slits in the female pipe ends should be under the U-bolts, not under the clamp end. Tighten the U-bolt nuts securely, without crushing the pipe. The pipe fit should be tight, so that you can't swivel the pipe by hand. Don't forget: always use new clamps. When the system is tight, recheck all clearances. Start the engine and check the joints for leaks. A leak can be felt by hand.

✱✱ CAUTION

MAKE CERTAIN THAT THE TRUCK IS SECURE BEFORE GETTING UNDER IT WITH THE ENGINE RUNNING!!

7. If any leaks are detected, tighten the clamp until the leak stops. If the pipe starts to deform before the leak stops, reposition the clamp and tighten it. If that still doesn't stop the leak, it may be that you don't have enough overlap on the pipe fit. Shut off the engine and try pushing the pipe together further. Be careful; the pipe gets hot quickly.
8. When everything is tight and secure, lower the truck and take it for a road test. Make sure there are no unusual sounds or vibration. Most new pipes are coated with a preservative, so the system will be pretty smelly for a day or two while the coating burns off.

Muffler and Outlet Pipes

REMOVAL & INSTALLATION

♦ See Figures 209, 210 and 211

➡**The following applies to exhaust systems using clamped joints. Some models, use welded joints at the muffler. These joints will have to be cut. Always use new gaskets during installation. It is also wise to purchase new clamps or hangers**

1. Raise and support the truck on jackstands.
2. Remove the U-clamps securing the muffler and outlet pipe.
3. Disconnect the muffler and outlet pipe bracket and insulator assemblies.
4. Remove the muffler and outlet pipe assembly. It may be necessary to heat the joints to get the parts to come off. Special tools are available to aid in breaking loose the joints. Discard any old exhaust pipes, or mufflers, along with any clamps or rusty nuts and bolts that are not usable again.
5. On Crew Cab models, remove the extension pipe.

➡**For rod and insulator type hangers, apply a soap solution to the insulator surface and rod ends to allow easier removal of the insulator from the rod end. Don't use oil-based or silicone-based solutions since they will allow the insulator to slip back off once it's installed.**

ENGINE AND ENGINE OVERHAUL 3-59

To install:

6. Assemble the muffler and rear exhaust pipes together, along with supports and clamps before installing.

7. Install the components making sure that all the components in the system are properly aligned before tightening any fasteners. Make sure all tabs are indexed and all parts are clear of surrounding body panels.

Front Header Pipes, Catalytic Converter and Inlet Pipes

➡ The following applies to exhaust systems using clamped joints. Some models, use welded joints at the muffler. These joints will have to be cut. Always use new gaskets during installation. It is also wise to purchase new clamps or hangers.

1. Raise and support the truck on jackstands.
2. Disconnect the front exhaust pipe flange or flanges for V engines, nuts and bolts connected to the exhaust manifold.
3. Loosen and remove any bolts to the catalytic converter (if equipped), or the flange prior to the muffler. If your system has no flanges all the way to the end of the exhaust, you will either have to cut the exhaust where you are replacing the piece, or replace the unit as an assembly.
4. Most aftermarket parts suppliers have your exhaust in cut sections, (unlike your original exhaust). It is wise to look at your exhaust before cutting any pipe if you are not purchasing your exhaust parts from the dealer.
5. Remove the pipe assembly. It may be necessary to heat the joints to separate the parts. Special tools are available to aid in breaking loose the joints. Discard any old pipes, and any clamps or rusty nuts and bolts.

➡ For rod and insulator type hangers, apply a soap solution to the insulator surface and rod ends to allow easier removal of the insulator from the rod end. Don't use oil-based or silicone-based solutions since they will allow the insulator to slip back off once it's installed.

To install:

6. Install the front header pipe with new exhaust nuts and gaskets. Attach the catalytic converter (if equipped) at the flange of the header pipe and tighten. Install any rear exhaust pipes together, along with supports and clamps.

7. Make sure that all the system components are properly aligned before tightening fasteners. Make sure all tabs are indexed and all parts are clear of surrounding body panels.

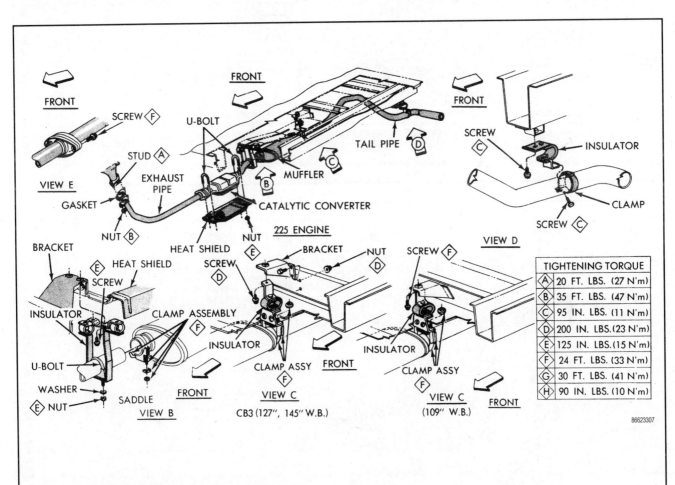

Fig. 207 Common system with catalytic converter on 6-225 engine

3-60 ENGINE AND ENGINE OVERHAUL

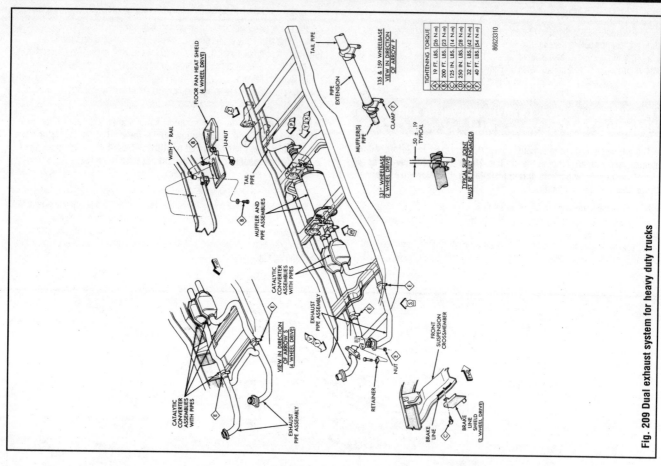

Fig. 209 Dual exhaust system for heavy duty trucks

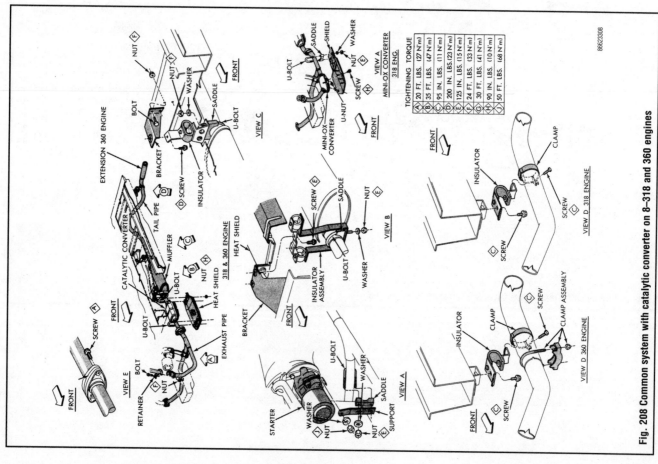

Fig. 208 Common system with catalytic converter on 8-318 and 360 engines

ENGINE AND ENGINE OVERHAUL 3-61

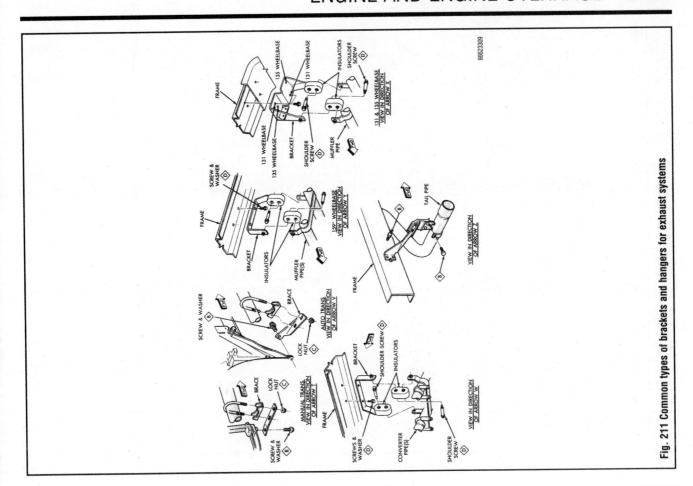

Fig. 211 Common types of brackets and hangers for exhaust systems

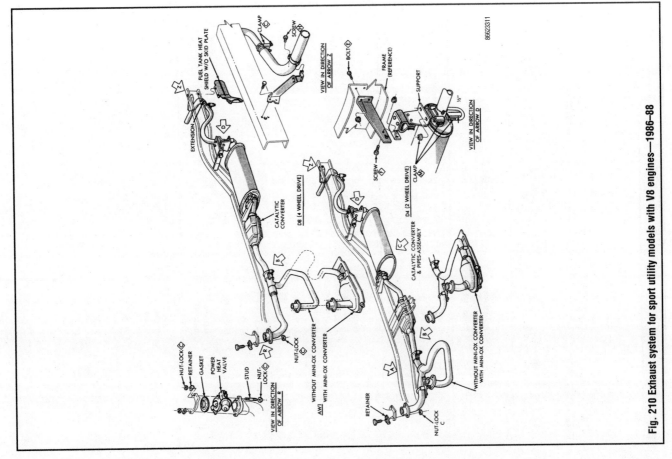

Fig. 210 Exhaust system for sport utility models with V8 engines—1986-88

3-62 ENGINE AND ENGINE OVERHAUL

TORQUE SPECIFICATIONS

Component			US	Metric
Camshaft				
Sprocket bolt	198-225 cu. in.		35 ft. lbs.	47 Nm
	251 cu. in.		20 ft. lbs.	27 Nm
	V6 & V8		35 ft. lbs.	47 Nm
	400, 440 cu. in.		35-40 ft. lbs.	47-54 Nm
Crankshaft Damper				
	238, 251 cu. in.		135 ft. lbs.	183 Nm
	243 cu. in.		289 ft. lbs.	392 Nm
	318, 360 cu. in.		100 ft. lbs.	135 Nm
	383, 400, 413, 440 cu. in.		135 ft. lbs.	183 Nm
Combination Manifold				
251 cu. in.	Intake-to-exhaust		25 ft. lbs.	34 Nm
	Manifold-to-head		20 ft. lbs.	27 Nm
	Exhaust pipe-to-manifold		30 ft. lbs.	41 Nm
Cylinder Head				
198, 225 cu. in.			35 ft. lbs.	47 Nm
	retorqued		70 ft. lbs.	95 Nm
251 cu. in.			70 ft. lbs.	95 Nm
V6 & V8			50 ft. lbs.	68 Nm
243 cu. in.			90 ft. lbs.	122 Nm
Exhaust Manifold				
V6	Inboard/Outboard arms		20 ft. lbs.	27 Nm
	Exhaust manifold-to-head		120 inch lbs.	14 Nm
	Intake manifold-to-head		35 ft. lbs.	47 Nm
	Air injection tube		120 inch lbs.	14 Nm
238, 318, 360 cu. in.			200 inch lbs.	23 Nm
	Inboard/Outboard arms		20 ft. lbs.	27 Nm
	Exhaust pipe-to-manifold		25 ft. lbs.	34 Nm
	Intake manifold-to-head		35 ft. lbs.	47 Nm
	Air injection tube		200 inch lbs.	23 Nm
400, 413, 440 cu. in.	Exhaust manifold-to-head		30 ft. lbs.	41 Nm
	Exhaust pipe-to-manifold 413 cu. in.		24 ft. lbs.	33 Nm
	Exhaust manifold-to-head		50 ft. lbs.	68 Nm
	Intake manifold-to-head		30 ft. lbs.	41 Nm
			40 ft. lbs.	54 Nm
Oil Pan				
198, 225, 383, 413 cu. in.			75 inch lbs.	8 Nm
	with gasket		200 inch lbs.	23 Nm
	retighten		200 inch lbs.	23 Nm
	with RTV		15 ft. lbs.	20 Nm
238, 251, 243, 318, 360, 400, 440 cu. in.				

TORQUE SPECIFICATIONS

Component			US	Metric
Oil Pump				
	198, 225 cu. in.	Pump	200 inch lbs.	23 Nm
		Cover	95 inch lbs.	11 Nm
	251 cu. in.	Pump	200 inch lbs.	23 Nm
		Cover	130 inch lbs.	15 Nm
	243 cu. in.	Pump	39 ft. lbs.	53 Nm
	238, 318, 360 cu. in.	Pump	30 ft. lbs.	41 Nm
		Cover	95 inch lbs.	11 Nm
	383, 400, 413, 440 cu. in.	Pump	30 ft. lbs.	41 Nm
Rocker Arms				
	198, 225 cu. in.	Adjustable tappets shaft bolts	25 ft. lbs.	34 Nm
		rear engine bolt	200 ft. lbs.	271 Nm
	238, 318, 360, 413 cu. in.	shaft bolts	25 ft. lbs.	34 Nm
	400, 440 cu. in.	shaft bolts	17 ft. lbs.	23 Nm
	243 cu. in.	shaft bolts	90 ft. lbs.	123 Nm
Timing Cover				
	198, 225, 251 cu. in.		17 ft. lbs.	23 Nm
	243 cu. in.		84 inch lbs.	9 Nm
	V6 & V8		30 ft. lbs.	41 Nm
	413 cu. in.		15 ft. lbs.	20 Nm
Timing Thrust Plate				
	243 cu. in.		25 ft. lbs.	34 Nm
	251 cu. in.		35 ft. lbs.	47 Nm
Valve Cover		nuts	40-80 inch lbs.	4.4-9 Nm
Waterpump			30 ft. lbs.	41 Nm
		fan attaching bolts	200 inch lbs.	23 Nm
		petcock	150 inch lbs.	17 Nm
		radiator mounting	95 inch lbs.	11 Nm

EMISSION CONTROLS 4-2
CRANKCASE VENTILATION SYSTEM 4-2
    OPERATION 4-2
    COMPONENT TESTING 4-3
    REMOVAL & INSTALLATION 4-3
EVAPORATIVE EMISSION
  CONTROLS 4-3
    OPERATION 4-3
    COMPONENT TESTING 4-4
AIR INJECTION SYSTEM 4-4
    OPERATION 4-4
    COMPONENT TESTING 4-5
    REMOVAL & INSTALLATION 4-5
EXHAUST GAS RECIRCULATION
  SYSTEM 4-7
    OPERATION 4-7
    COMPONENT TESTING 4-8
EMISSIONS MAINTENANCE REMINDER
  LIGHT 4-8
    RESETTING 4-8
OXYGEN SENSOR 4-8
    OPERATION 4-8
    REMOVAL & INSTALLATION 4-8
ELECTRONIC ENGINE
  CONTROLS 4-8
ELECTRONIC CARBURETOR
  SYSTEM 4-8
    GENERAL INFORMATION 4-8
FUEL INJECTION 4-9
    GENERAL INFORMATION 4-9
VACUUM DIAGRAMS 4-12

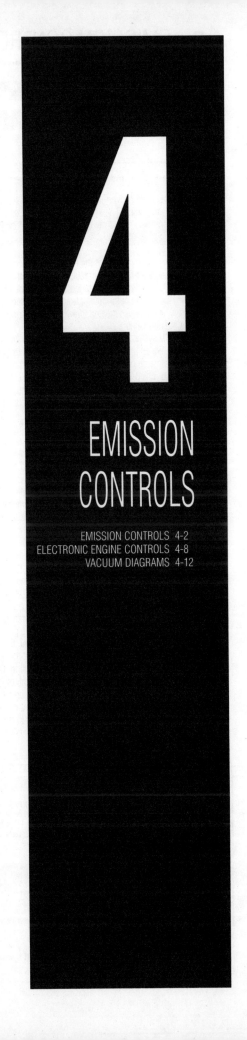

4
EMISSION CONTROLS

EMISSION CONTROLS 4-2
ELECTRONIC ENGINE CONTROLS 4-8
VACUUM DIAGRAMS 4-12

4-2 EMISSION CONTROLS

EMISSION CONTROLS

Crankcase Ventilation System

OPERATION

♦ See Figures 1, 2, 3 and 4

The Positive Crankcase Ventilation (PCV) system is used in two forms, the standard and closed types. The standard type is used on all applications except 1967 California models, while the closed type is used exclusively on 1967 California models.

Blowby gasses or crankcase vapors must be removed from the crankcase to prevent oil dilution and to prevent the formation of sludge. Traditionally, this was accomplished with a road draft tube. Air entered the rocker arm cover through an open oil filler cap and flowed down past the pushrods, mixing with the blow-by gases in the crankcase. It was finally routed into the road draft tube where a partial vacuum was created, drawing the mixture into the road draft tube and out into the atmosphere.

The open PCV system replaced the road draft tube and engine manifold vacuum was used instead of the action of a moving vehicle to create a low pressure area. Air flowed into an open oil filler cap, which is characteristic of an open PCV system, and mixed with the crankcase fumes. These vapors were then drawn into the intake manifold and burned in the combustion chamber. Under heavy acceleration, however, manifold vacuum would decrease and crankcase pressure would build up. When this happened, a portion of the crankcase vapors were forced back out of the oil filter cap, creating a system which was only about 75% efficient.

The closed PCV system operates in a similar manner as the open system, except that a sealed oil filler cap and dipstick are used in place of a vented oil filler cap. In addition, an air intake hose is installed between the carburetor air filter and crankcase opening in the valve cover. A separate PCV air filter is used when the air intake hose is connected to the "dirty" side of the carburetor air cleaner. This filter is located where the intake air line connects to the valve cover.

Under normal engine operation, the closed PCV system operates the way an open system does, except that air enters through the intake hose via the air filter. Under heavy acceleration, any excess vapors back up through the air intake hose. They are forced to mix with incoming air from the carburetor and are burned in the combustion chamber. Back-up fumes cannot escape into the atmosphere, thereby creating a closed system.

he PCV valve is used to control the rate at which crankcase vapors are returned to the intake manifold. The action of the valve plunger is controlled by intake manifold vacuum and the spring. During deceleration and idle (when manifold vacuum is high), it overcomes the tension of the valve spring and the plunger bottoms in the manifold end of the valve housing. Because of the valve construction, it reduces (but does not stop) the passage of vapors to the intake manifold. When the engine is lightly accelerated or operated at constant speed, spring tension matches intake manifold vacuum pull, and the plunger takes a mid-position in the valve body, allowing more vapors to flow into the manifold.

An inoperative PCV system will cause rough idling, sludge and oil dilution.

In the event of erratic idle, never attempt to compensate by disconnecting the PCV system. Disconnecting the PCV system will adversely shorten engine life through the buildup of sludge.

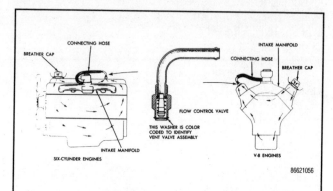

Fig. 2 Typical partially closed crankcase ventilation system on 6-225, 8-318 and 8-383 engines

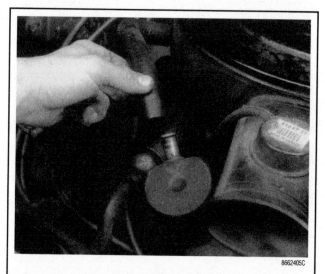

Fig. 3 Remove the crankcase intake air filter hose . . .

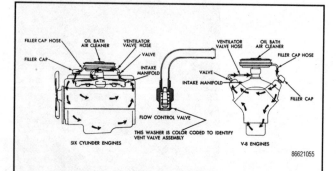

Fig. 1 Typical fully closed crankcase ventilation system on 6-225 and 8-318 engines

Fig. 4 . . . then pull the filter from the retaining grommet

EMISSION CONTROLS 4-3

COMPONENT TESTING

◆ See Figure 5

1. With the engne idling, remove the PCV valve from the rocker arm cover. If the valve is not plugged, a hissing sound will be heard. A strong vacuum should be felt when you place your finger over the valve.
2. Reinstall the PCV valve and allow about a minute for pressure to drop.
3. Remove the crankcase intake air cleaner. Cover the opening in the rocker arm cover with a piece of stiff paper. The paper should be sucked against the opening with noticeable force.
4. With the engine stopped, remove the PCV valve and shake it. A rattle or clicking should be heard to indicate that the valve is unobstructed.
5. Install the new PCV valve into the grommet.
6. With a new PCV valve installed, if the paper is not sucked against the crankcase air intake opening, it will be necessary to clean the PCV valve hose and the passage in the lower part of the carburetor. If the hose is cracked, oil soaked, or in otherwise poor condition, replace the hose with a new one.

➥**If necessary, clean the hose with Combustion Chamber Conditioner or similar solvent, then allow it to dry. Do not leave the hose in solvent for more than ½ hour.**

7. If the carburetor passage is blocked, remove the carburetor, as described in Section 5. **Hand turn** a ¼ in. drill through the passage to dislodge solid particles, then blow clean.

➥**It is necessary to disassemble the carburetor for this operation. If necessary, use a smaller drill, so that no metal is removed.**

8. Remove the crankcase intake air cleaner and wash it thoroughly in kerosene or similar solvent. Lubricate the filter by inverting it and filling with SAE 30 engine oil. Position the filter to allow excess oil to drain thoroughly through the vent nipple.

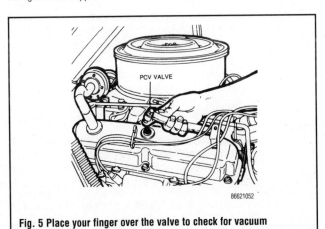

Fig. 5 Place your finger over the valve to check for vacuum

REMOVAL & INSTALLATION

◆ See Figure 6

1. With the engine **OFF**, remove the PCV valve by disconnecting the vacuum hose attached to it.

➥**Do not attempt to clean a clogged PCV valve.**

2. Inspect the PCV valve's rubber grommet and hoses for any excessive wear or cracks, and replace them if necessary. Be careful when replacing the grommet that you do not drop any pieces of rubber into the rocker arm cover. You can use needlenose pliers to remove the grommet.

To install:

3. Apply lubricant on the outside of the grommet (if a new one is to be installed) to ease installation.
4. Install the new PCV valve into the grommet, then connect the vacuum hose.

➥**After checking and/or servicing the Crankcase Ventilation System, any components that do not allow passage of air to the intake manifold should be replaced.**

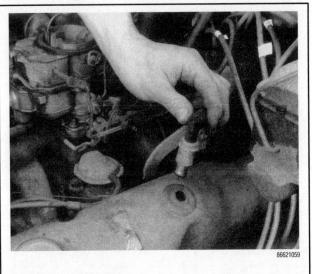

Fig. 6 Common PCV location

Evaporative Emission Controls

OPERATION

◆ See Figures 7 and 8

Changes in atmospheric temperature cause fuel tanks to breathe; that is, the air within the tank expands and contracts with outside temperature changes. As the temperature rises, air escapes through the tank vent tube or the vent in the tank cap. The air which escapes contains gasoline vapors. In a similar manner on carbureted engines, the gasoline which fills the carburetor float bowl expands when the engine is stopped. Engine heat causes this expansion. The vapors escape through the air cleaner.

The Evaporative Emission Control System (ECS) provides a sealed fuel system with the capability to store and condense fuel vapors. The system has three parts: 1) a fill control vent system, 2) a vapor vent and storage system, and 3) a pressure and vacuum relief system (special fill cap).

The fill control vent system is a modification to the fuel tank. It uses a dome air space within the tank which is 10–12% of the tank's volume. The air space is sufficient to provide for the thermal expansion of the fuel. The space also serves as part of the in-tank vapor vent system.

The in-tank vent system consists of the domed air space previously described and a vapor separator assembly. The separator assembly is mounted to the top of the fuel tank and is secured by a cam lockring, similar to the one which secures the fuel sending unit. Foam material fills the vapor separator

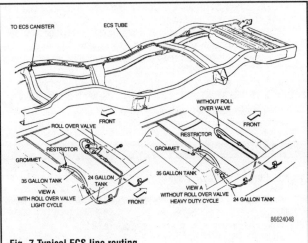

Fig. 7 Typical ECS line routing

4-4 EMISSION CONTROLS

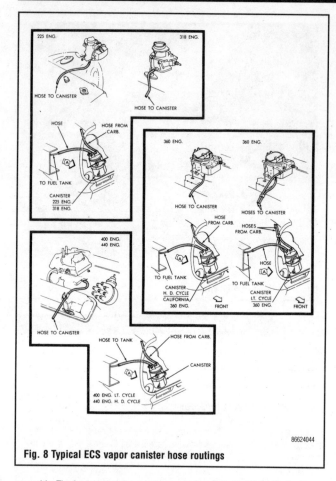

Fig. 8 Typical ECS vapor canister hose routings

assembly. The foam material separates raw fuel and vapors, thus retarding the entrance of fuel into the vapor line

The vapor separator is an orifice valve located in the dome of the tank. The restricted size of the orifice, 0.050 in. (1.27mm) tends to allow only vapor to pass out of the tank. The orifice valve is connected to the vent line which runs forward to the carbon filled canister in the engine compartment.

The sealed filler cap has a pressure-vacuum relief valve. Under normal operating conditions, the filler cap operates as a check valve, allowing air to enter the tank to replace the fuel consumed. At the same time, it prevents vapors from escaping through the cap. In case of excessive pressure within the tank, the filler cap valve opens to relieve the pressure.

Because the filler cap is sealed, fuel vapors have only one place through which they may escape: the vapor separator assembly at the top of the fuel tank. The vapors pass through the foam material and continue through a single vapor line which leads to a canister in the engine compartment. The canister is filled with activated charcoal.

Another vapor line runs from the top of the carburetor float chamber or the intake manifold, or the throttle body, to the charcoal canister.

As the fuel vapors (hydrocarbons) enter the charcoal canister, they are absorbed by the charcoal. The air is dispelled through the open bottom of the charcoal canister, leaving the hydrocarbons trapped within the charcoal. When the engine is started, vacuum causes fresh air to be drawn into the canister from its open bottom. The fresh air passes through the charcoal, picking up the hydrocarbons which are trapped there, and feeding them into the engine for burning with the fuel mixture.

COMPONENT TESTING

Canister Purge Regulator Valve

1. Disconnect the hoses at the purge regulator valve. Disconnect the electrical lead.
2. Connect a vacuum pump to the vacuum source port.
3. Apply 5 in. Hg (17 kPa) to the port. The valve should hold the vacuum. If not, replace it.

Canister Purge Valve

1. Apply vacuum to port **A**. The valve should hold vacuum. If not, replace it.
2. Apply vacuum to port **B**. All valves should hold vacuum. If the valve doesn't operate properly, replace it.
3. Apply 16 in. Hg (54 kPa) to port **A** and apply vacuum to port **B**. Air should pass.

➡ Never apply vacuum to port C. Doing so will damage the valve.

4. If the valve fails to perform properly in any of these tests, replace it.

Air Injection System

♦ See Figure 9

OPERATION

The air injection emission control system makes use of a belt driven air pump to inject fresh air into the hot exhaust stream through the engine exhaust ports. The result is the extended burning of those fumes which were not completely ignited in the combustion chamber, and the subsequent reduction of some of the hydrocarbon and carbon monoxide content of the exhaust emissions into harmless carbon dioxide and water.

The air injection system is composed of the following components:
- Air supply pump (belt driven)
- Air bypass valve
- Check valves
- Air manifolds (internal or external)
- Air supply tubes (on external manifolds only)

Air for the air injection system is cleaned by means of a centrifugal filter fan mounted on the air pump driveshaft. The air filter does not require a replaceable element.

To prevent excessive pressure, the air pump is equipped with a pressure relief valve which uses a replaceable plastic plug to control the pressure setting.

The air injection air pump has sealed bearings which are lubricated for the life of the unit, and preset rotor vane and bearing clearances, which do not require any periodic adjustments.

The air supply from the pump is controlled by the air bypass valve, sometimes called a dump valve. During deceleration, the air bypass valve opens, momentarily diverting the air supply through a silencer and into the atmosphere, thus preventing backfires within the exhaust system during sudden deceleration.

A check valve is incorporated in the air inlet side of the air manifolds. Its purpose is to prevent exhaust gases from backing up into the air injection system. This valve is especially important in the event of drive belt failure, and during deceleration, when the air bypass valve is dumping the air supply.

The air manifolds and air supply tubes channel the air from the air injection air pump into the exhaust ports of each cylinder, thus completing the cycle of the air injection system.

Orifice Spark Advance Control (OSAC)

♦ See Figure 10

The OSAC system is used on light duty trucks to aid in control of nitrous oxide (NOx) emissions. The system controls the vacuum signal to the distributor vacuum advance unit.

A tiny orifice is incorporated in the OSAC valve which delays the change in ported vacuum to the distributor by 17 to 27 seconds, depending on the engine and truck model, when going from idle to part throttle.

When going from part throttle to idle, the change in ported vacuum is instantaneous.

Catalytic Converters

The catalytic converter, mounted in the truck's exhaust system, is a muffler-shaped device containing a ceramic honeycomb-shaped material that is coated with alumina and impregnated with catalytically active precious metals such as platinum, palladium and rhodium.

The catalyst's job is to reduce air pollutants by oxidizing hydrocarbons (HC) and carbon monoxide (CO). Catalysts containing palladium and rhodium also oxidize nitrous oxides (NOx).

EMISSION CONTROLS 4-5

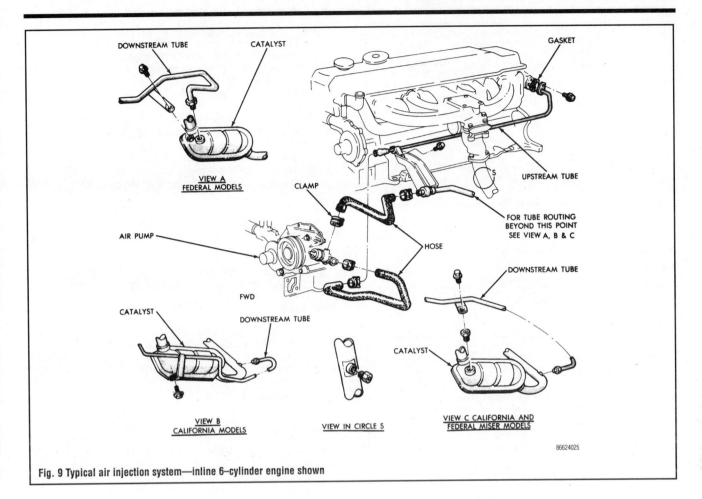

Fig. 9 Typical air injection system—inline 6–cylinder engine shown

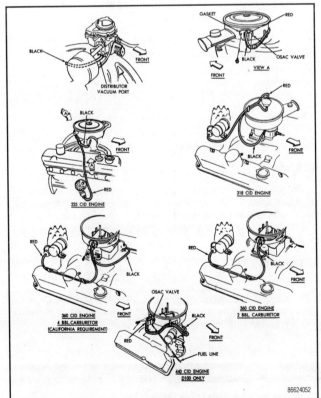

Fig. 10 Common OSAC valve vacuum hose routing for D100/W100 vehicles

On some trucks, the catalyst is also fed by the secondary air system, via a small supply tube in the side of the catalyst.

No maintenance is possible on the converter, other than keeping the heat shield clear of flammable debris, such as leaves and twigs.

Other than external damage, the only significant damage possible to a converter is through the use of leaded gasoline, or by way of a too rich fuel/air mixture. Both of these problems will ruin the converter through contamination of the catalyst and will eventually plug the converter, causing loss of power and engine performance.

When this occurs, the catalyst must be replaced. For catalyst replacement, see the Exhaust System portion of Section 3.

COMPONENT TESTING

Air Pump

1. Check and, if necessary, adjust the belt tension. Press at the mid-point of the belt's longest straight run. You should be able to depress the belt about ½ in. (13mm) maximum.
2. Run the engine to normal operating temperature and let it idle.
3. Disconnect the air supply hose from the bypass control valve. If the pump is operating properly, airflow should be felt at the pump outlet. The flow should increase as you increase the engine speed. The pump is not serviceable and should be replaced if it is not functioning properly.

REMOVAL & INSTALLATION

Air Bypass Valve

♦ See Figure 11

1. Disconnect the air and vacuum hoses at the air bypass valve body.
2. Position the air bypass valve and connect the respective hoses.

4-6 EMISSION CONTROLS

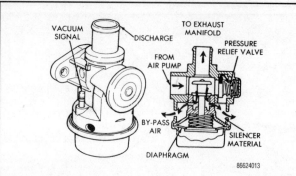

Fig. 11 An air bypass valve prevents backfire during sudden deceleration

Aspirator Valve and Tube Assembly

♦ See Figures 12 and 13

This system utilizes exhaust pressure pulsation to draw clean air from inside the air cleaner into the exhaust system. The system's function is to reduce hydrocarbon (HC) emissions.

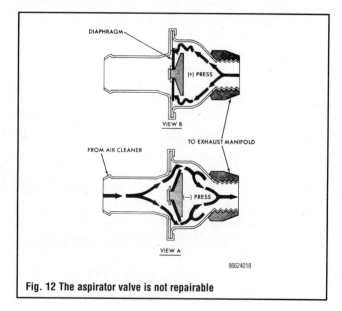

Fig. 12 The aspirator valve is not repairable

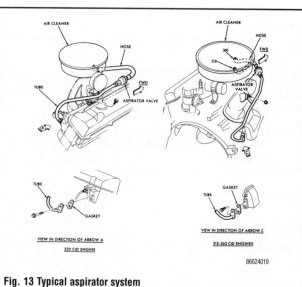

Fig. 13 Typical aspirator system

1. Disconnect the air supply hose at the check valve, position the hose out of the way and remove the valve.
2. Disconnect the air hose from the aspirator valve inlet.
3. Unscrew the valve from the tube assembly; you will need a hexagonal wrench at the threaded joint.
4. Remove the screws securing the aspirator tube to the exhaust manifold and engine.
5. Remove the aspirator tube assembly from the engine; also remove any gasket material from the exhaust manifold and aspirator tube flange.

To install:

6. Install a new gasket on the exhaust manifold flange and position the aspirator tube assembly to the valve.
7. Attach the aspirator valve to the tube assembly using a hexagonal wrench. Tighten to 25 ft. lbs. (34 Nm).
8. Fasten the tube flange's mounting screw to 150 inch lbs. (17 Nm).
9. Tighten the aspirator tube bracket hold-down screws to the following torque specifications:
   - 6–225 engine: 40 ft. lbs. (54 Nm)
   - 8–318 engine: 115 inch lbs. (13 Nm)
   - 8–360 engine: 115 inch lbs. (13 Nm)
10. Connect the air hose to the aspirator valve inlet and air cleaner nipple.

Check Valve

1. Disconnect the air supply hose at the valve. Use a 1¼ in. crow's foot wrench. The valve has a standard, right-hand pipe thread.
2. Clean the threads on the air manifold adapter (air supply tube on the V8 engines) with a wire brush. Do not blow compressed air through the check valve in either direction.
3. Install the check valve and tighten.
4. Connect the air supply hose.

Air Supply Tube

1. Disconnect the air supply hose at the check valve and position the hose out of the way.
2. Remove the check valve.
3. Remove the air supply tube bolt and seal washer.
4. Carefully remove the air supply tube and seal washer from the cylinder head. Inspect the air supply tube for evidence of leaking threads or seal surfaces. Examine the attaching bolt head, seal washers, and supply tube surface for leaks. Inspect the attaching bolt and cylinder head threads for damage. Clean the air supply tube, seal washers, and bolt with kerosene. Do not dry the parts with compressed air.

To install:

5. Install the seal washer and air supply tube on the cylinder head. Be sure that it is positioned in the same manner as before removal.
6. Install the seal washer and mounting bolt. Tighten the bolt.
7. Install the check valve and tighten it.
8. Connect the air supply hose to the check valve.

Air Nozzle

Normally, air nozzles should be replaced during cylinder head reconditioning. A nozzle may be replaced, however, without removing the cylinder head, by removing the air manifold and using a hooked tool.

Clean the nozzle with kerosene and a stiff brush. Inspect the air nozzles for eroded tips.

Air Pump Filter Fan

1. Loosen the air pump attaching bolts.
2. Remove the drive pulley attaching bolts and pull the pulley off the air pump shaft.
3. Pry the outer disc loose, then remove the centrifugal filter fan. Care must be used to prevent foreign matter from entering the air intake hole, especially if the fan breaks during removal. Do not attempt to remove the metal drive hub.

✲✲✲ WARNING

Do not use a screwdriver to pry between the filter and the pump. It is seldom possible to remove the fan without destroying it. Do not attempt to remove the metal drive tab.

EMISSION CONTROLS 4-7

4. Install the new filter fan by drawing it into position with the pulley bolts. Make sure the fan slips into the housing. Do not attempt to install the fan by hammering or pressing it on. After the fan is installed, it may squeal for a short while until the sealing lip is fully seated (approximately 20–30 miles or 32–48 km of driving).

➡ Some 1967 air pumps have air filters with replaceable, non-cleanable elements.

Air Pump

♦ See Figure 14

1. Disconnect the air outlet hose at the air pump.
2. Loosen the pump belt tension adjuster.
3. Disengage the drive belt.
4. Remove the mounting bolt and air pump.

To install:

5. Position the air pump on the mounting bracket and install the mounting bolt.
6. Place the drive belt in the pulley and attach the adjusting arm to the air pump.
7. Adjust the drive belt tension, then tighten the adjusting arm and mounting bolts.
8. Connect the air outlet hose to the air pump.

Relief Valve

♦ See Figure 15

➡ Do not disassemble the air pump on the truck to replace the relief valve; first remove the pump from the engine.

1. Disconnect the relief valve air hose.
2. Unfasten the two mounting screws and release the valve.
3. Remove the gasket from the mounting surface and the valve, then discard it.

To install:

4. Position a new gasket on the mounting surface, making sure the holes line up.
5. Position the relief valve on the mounting surface and secure with the screws. Tighten them to 125 inch lbs. (14 Nm).
6. Install the air and vacuum hoses to the switch relief valve.

Relief Valve Pressure Setting Plug

1. Compress the locking tabs inward (together) and remove the plastic pressure setting plug.
2. Before installing the new plug, be sure that the plug is the correct one. The plugs are color coded.
3. Insert the plug in the relief valve hole and push in until it snaps into place.

Exhaust Gas Recirculation System

OPERATION

Ported EGR

♦ See Figures 16, 17 and 18

The ported EGR valve is operated by engine vacuum. A vacuum signal from the carburetor or throttle body activates the EGR valve diaphragm. As the vacuum signal increases, it gradually opens the valve pintle allowing exhaust gases to flow. The amount of flow is directly proportional to the pintle position.

Heated Air Intake

♦ See Figure 19

The system is used to inject fresh air into the exhaust manifolds or catalytic converters via an air control valve. Under some operating conditions, the air can be returned to the atmosphere via an air bypass valve. On some applications, the two valves are combined into one unit. The bypass valve can be either the normally-closed type (if the 2 valves are separate) or the normally-open type (if the valves are combined).

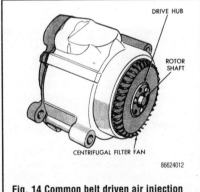

Fig. 14 Common belt driven air injection pump

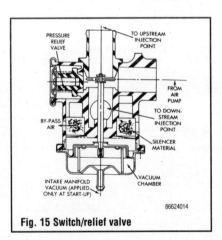

Fig. 15 Switch/relief valve

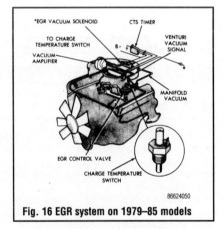

Fig. 16 EGR system on 1979–85 models

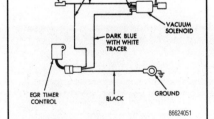

Fig. 17 EGR time delay system

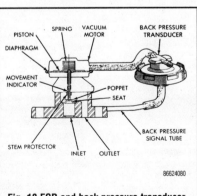

Fig. 18 EGR and back pressure transducer assembly

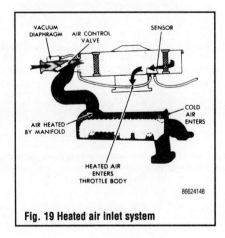

Fig. 19 Heated air inlet system

4-8 EMISSION CONTROLS

COMPONENT TESTING

EGR System

1. The engine should be warmed up, at normal operating temperature, with the parking brake set.
2. Allow the engine to idle in Neutral with the throttle closed, then quickly accelerate to approximately 2000 rpm, watching the groove carefully on the EGR valve stem.
3. You should notice movement of the valve stem during the acceleration period, and there should be a change in the location of the groove on the stem. If movement is noticed this means that the control system is functioning properly and the EGR flow test can be performed.
4. If no movement is noticed, you may have to replace the valve or another component in the system.

EGR Gas Flow

1. Connect a tachometer to the engine.
2. Remove the vacuum hose from the EGR valve and connect a hand vacuum pump to the valve vacuum motor nipple.
3. Start the engine and slowly apply vacuum to the motor.
4. The engine rpm should drop as the vacuum reaches 3–5 in. Hg (10–17 kPa), and continue to drop as more vacuum is applied. Your engine may even stall out during this test (meaning that EGR gases are flowing through the system).
5. If this and system tests are good, your EGR system is fully functioning.
6. If the rpm does not drop, the valve may be plugged or defective. If so, remove the valve and inspect it, along with the intake manifold passages for any deposits. Clean if necessary.

Emissions Maintenance Reminder Light

RESETTING

The light uses a time measuring module which relies upon ignition on-time as a basis to calculate maintenance intervals. When the interval has elapsed, the light will come illuminate until the module is reset. To do this press the reset switch by inserting a small rod into the hole in the module. The module is located behind the far right side of the instrument panel, next to the glove box.

Oxygen Sensor

OPERATION

The oxygen sensor produces an electrical voltage when exposed to the oxygen present in the exhaust gases. The sensor is usually mounted in the exhaust manifold. On some applications, the sensor is heated internally (with an electric element) for faster/more reliable performance. When there is a large amount of oxygen present (lean mixture), the sensor produces a low voltage. When there is less oxygen present (rich mixture) it produces a higher voltage. By monitoring the oxygen content and converting it to electrical voltage, the sensor acts as a rich-lean switch. The voltage is transmitted to the SMEC, which then signals the power module to trigger the fuel injector. The injector controls fuel mixture.

REMOVAL & INSTALLATION

1. Disconnect the engine harness wire from the sensor.
2. Remove the sensor using tool C-4589 or equivalent.

❊❊ CAUTION

Do NOT pull on the sensor wire. Be careful when working around the sensor, as the exhaust manifold is HOT and can cause severe burns.

3. Always clean the threads of the exhaust manifold before replacing the sensor. Use an anti-seize compound to lubricate the threads of the new sensor before installation. New sensors are usually packaged with the compound already in place; if this is the case, you not need to apply additional compound.
4. Torque the sensor to 20 ft. lbs. (27 Nm).

ELECTRONIC ENGINE CONTROLS

Electronic Carburetor System

GENERAL INFORMATION

The Chrysler Electronic Feedback Carburetor (EFC) system incorporates an oxygen sensor, a three-way catalytic converter, an oxidizing catalytic converter, a feedback carburetor, a solenoid-operated vacuum regulator valve, and a Combustion Computer. Also incorporated into the system is Chrysler's Electronic Spark Control computer.

In Chrysler's system, "Combustion Computer" is a collective term for the Feedback Carburetor Controller and the Electronic Spark Control computer, which are housed together in a case located on the air cleaner on rear wheel drive models, and in the left front engine compartment on most front wheel drive models. The feedback carburetor controller is the information processing component of the system, monitoring oxygen sensor voltage (low voltage/lean mixture, high voltage/rich mixture), engine coolant temperature, manifold vacuum, engine speed, and engine operating mode (starting or running). The controller examines the incoming information, then sends a signal to the solenoid-operated vacuum regulator valve (also located in the Combustion Computer housing), which sends the proper rich or lean signal to the carburetor.

Electronic Feedback Control (EFC) System

The EFC system is essentially an emissions control system which utilizes an electronic signal, generated by an exhaust gas oxygen sensor to precisely control the air/fuel mixture ratio in the carburetor. This, in turn, allows the engine to produce exhaust gases of the proper composition to permit the use of a three-way catalyst. The three-way catalyst is designed to convert the three pollutants (1) hydrocarbons (HC), (2) carbon monoxide (CO), and (3) oxides of Nitrogen (NOx) into harmless substances.

There are two operating modes in the EFC system:
1. Open Loop air/fuel ratio is controlled by information programmed into the computer at manufacture.
2. Closed Loop air/fuel ratio is varied by the computer based on information supplied by the oxygen sensor.

When the engine is cold, the system will be operating in the open loop mode. During that time, the air/fuel ratio will be fixed at a richer level. This will allow proper engine warm-up. Also, during this period, air injection (from the air injection pump) will be injected upstream in the exhaust manifold.

Both closed loop and open loop operation are possible in the EFC system. Open loop operation occurs under any one of the following conditions: coolant temperature under 150°F (66°C); oxygen sensor temperature under 660°F (349°C); low manifold vacuum (less than 4.5 in. Hg/15 kPa with a cold engine, or less than 3.0 in. Hg/10 kPa with a hot engine); oxygen sensor failure; or hot engine starting. Closed loop operation begins when engine temperature reaches 150°F (66°C).

Oxygen (O_2) Sensor

The oxygen sensor is a device which produces electrical voltage. The sensor is usually mounted in the exhaust manifold and must be heated by the exhaust gas before producing a voltage. When there is a large amount of oxygen present (lean mixture) the sensor produces a low voltage. When there is a lesser amount present, it produces a higher voltage. By monitoring the oxygen content and converting it to electrical voltage, the sensor acts as a rich/lean switch. The voltage is transmitted to the Spark Control Computer. The computer sends a signal to the Oxygen Feedback Solenoid mounted on the carburetor to change the air/fuel ratio back to stoichiometric.

EMISSION CONTROLS 4-9

Charge Temperature Switch (CTS)

▶ See Figure 20

The CTS is located in the No. 6 runner of the intake manifold on 6-cylinder engines, or in the No. 8 runner of the intake manifold on 8-cylinder engines. When the intake air temperature is below approximately 60°F, (15°C) the CTS will be closed, allowing no EGR timer function or valve operation. The injected air is switched to the exhaust manifold (upstream). The CTS opens when the intake air temperature is above approximately 60°F (15°C), thus allowing the EGR timer to time out and the EGR valve to operate, and diverts injected air to the catalytic converter (downstream).

Coolant Vacuum Switch

▶ See Figures 21 and 22

➡A variety of coolant vacuum switches were used over the years, including three and five port designs.

Some vehicles are equipped with a three port Coolant Vacuum Switch Cold Closed (CVSCC) mounted in the radiator. When engine coolant temperature reaches 108–125°F (42–52°C), the CVSCC mounted in the thermostat housing will open; vacuum is then applied to open the EGR control valve, thereby allowing exhaust gas to recirculate.

Other vehicles utilize a five port coolant switch, which combines the functions of the Coolant Controlled Engine Vacuum Switch (CCEVS) and the three port Coolant Vacuum Switch (CVS3P). This valve can be best described as two entirely separate switches. One half of the part behaves as a two port CCEVS. The switch is normally closed up to 150°F (66°C); above this temperature the switch opens, supplying vacuum to open the EGR. Above 150°F (66°C), the other half of the part acts as a CVS3P. In idle, full distributor advance is ensured by supplying manifold vacuum to the distributor under 150°F (66°C).

Electric Choke

▶ See Figure 23

An electric heater and switch assembly is sealed within the choke housing. Electrical current is supplied through the oil pressure switch. A minimum of 4 psi (13.5 kPa) oil pressure is necessary to close the contacts in the oil pressure switch and feed current to the automatic choke system. Electricity must be present when the engine is running to open the choke and keep it open.

The heater can be tested with a direct B+ connection. The choke valve should reach the open position within five minutes.

✱✱ WARNING

Operation of any type, including idling, should be avoided if there is any loss of choke power. Under this condition, any loss of power to the choke will cause the choke to remain fully on during the operation of the vehicle. This will produce a very rich fuel mixture and result in abnormally high exhaust system temperatures, which may cause damage to the catalyst or to the vehicle's underbody. It is recommended that the electric choke power not be disconnected to troubleshoot cold start problems.

Fuel Injection

GENERAL INFORMATION

The Electronic Fuel Injection System is a computer regulated single point fuel injection system that provides precise air/fuel ratio for all driving conditions. At the center of this system is a Single Module Engine Controller (SMEC) that regulates ignition timing, air/fuel ratio, emission control devices and idle speed, as well as the cooling fan and charging system. The SMEC has the ability to update and revise its programming to meet changing operating conditions.

Various sensors provide the input necessary for the SMEC to correctly regulate the fuel flow at the fuel injectors. These include manifold absolute pressure, throttle position, oxygen, coolant temperature, vehicle speed (distance) and throttle body temperature sensors. In addition to the sensors, various switches also provide important information. These include the neutral-safety, heated rear window, air conditioning, air conditioning clutch and electronic idle switches.

All inputs to the SMEC are converted into signals sent to the power module. These signals cause the power module to change either the fuel flow at the injector, the ignition timing, or both.

The SMEC tests many of its own input and output circuits. If a fault is found in a major system, this information is stored in the SMEC. Information on this fault can be displayed by means of the instrument panel power loss (check engine) lamp, or by connecting a diagnostic readout tool and reading a numbered display code which directly relates to a specific fault.

Power Module

The power module contains the circuits necessary to power the ignition coil and the fuel injector. These are high current devices and their power supply has been isolated to minimize any "electrical noise" reaching the SMEC. The power module energizes the Automatic Shut Down (ASD) relay, which activates the fuel pump, ignition coil, and the power module itself. The module also receives a signal from the distributor and sends this signal to the logic module. In the event of no distributor signal, the ASD relay is not activated and power is shut off from the fuel pump and ignition coil. The power module contains a voltage converter which reduces battery voltage to a regulated 8.0 volt output. This 8.0 volt output powers the distributor and also powers the SMEC.

Single Module Engine Controller (SMEC)

▶ See Figure 24

The SMEC contains the circuits necessary to drive the ignition coil, fuel injector, and the alternator field. These are high current devices and have been isolated to minimize any electrical noise in the passenger compartment.

The Automatic Shut Down (ASD) relay is mounted externally, but is turned on and off by the SMEC. Distributor pick-up signal goes to the SMEC. In the event of no distributor signal, the ASD relay is not activated and power is shut off from the fuel injector and ignition coil. The SMEC contains a voltage converter which converts battery voltage to a regulated 8.0 volt output. This 8.0 volt output powers the distributor pick-up. The internal 5 volt supply powers the MAP sensor and TPS.

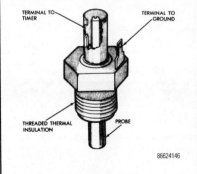

Fig. 20 Charge temperature switch found on 1986–87 models

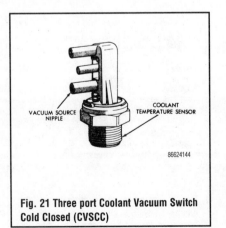

Fig. 21 Three port Coolant Vacuum Switch Cold Closed (CVSCC)

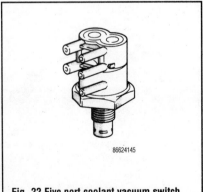

Fig. 22 Five port coolant vacuum switch found on 1988 models

4-10 EMISSION CONTROLS

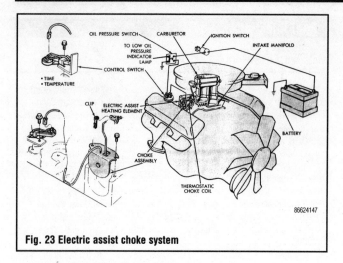

Fig. 23 Electric assist choke system

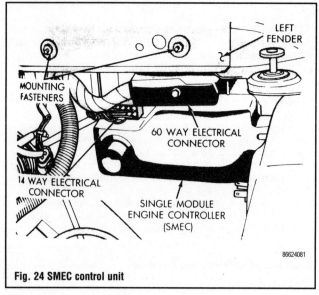

Fig. 24 SMEC control unit

The SMEC is a digital computer containing a microprocessor. The module receives input signals from various switches and sensors. It then computes the fuel injector pulse width, spark advance, ignition coil dwell, idle speed, purge, cooling fan turn-on, and alternator charge rate.

The SMEC tests many of its own input and output circuits. If a fault is found in a major system, this information is stored in the SMEC. Information on this fault can be displayed by means of the instrument panel check engine lamp or by connecting diagnostic readout tool C–4805 (or equivalent) and reading a numbered display code which directly relates to a general fault.

TESTING

1. Set the ignition timing, as described in Section 2.
2. Warm the engine to operating temperature.

➡ The temperature sensor must be working correctly for an accurate test.

3. Raise the idle to 2,000 rpm, wait one minute, then check the specifications.

✱✱ WARNING

While doing this test, you must use a metal exhaust tube. The use of a rubber hose may result in a fire because of high temperatures and a long testing period.

4. If the SMEC fails to obtain the settings, replace the unit.

Manifold Absolute Pressure (MAP) Sensor

The manifold absolute pressure (MAP) sensor is a device which monitors manifold vacuum. It is connected to a vacuum nipple on the throttle body and electrically to the logic module or SMEC. The sensor transmits information on manifold vacuum conditions and barometric pressure to the logic module or SMEC. The MAP sensor data on engine load is used with data from other sensors to determine the correct air/fuel mixture.

Oxygen Sensor

♦ See Figures 25, 26, 27 and 28

The oxygen sensor is a device which produces an electrical voltage when exposed to the oxygen present in the exhaust gases. The sensor is usually mounted in the exhaust manifold. The oxygen sensor is electrically heated internally for faster switching when the engine is running. When there is a large amount of oxygen present (lean mixture), the sensor produces a low voltage. When there is a lesser amount present (rich mixture) it produces a higher voltage. By monitoring the oxygen content and converting it to electrical voltage, the sensor acts as a rich-lean switch. The voltage is transmitted to the SMEC. The SMEC signals the power module to trigger the fuel injector. The injector changes the mixture.

Coolant Temperature Sensor

♦ See Figures 29 and 30

The coolant temperature sensor is a device that monitors coolant temperature (which is the same as engine operating temperature). It is mounted in the intake manifold, near the thermostat housing. This sensor provides data on engine operating temperature to the SMEC. This allows the SMEC to demand slightly richer air/fuel mixtures and higher idle speeds until normal operating temperatures are reached. This sensor is also used for cooling fan control.

1. With the key in the **OFF** position, detach the wire connector from the coolant sensor.
2. Connect one lead of an ohmmeter to one terminal on the sensor, and the other lead to the sensor's remaining connector. The ohmmeter should read 700–1,000 ohms at 200°F (93°C), and 7,000–13,000 ohms at 70°F (21°C).

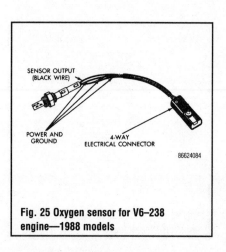

Fig. 25 Oxygen sensor for V6–238 engine—1988 models

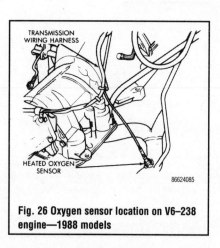

Fig. 26 Oxygen sensor location on V6–238 engine—1988 models

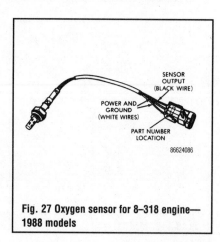

Fig. 27 Oxygen sensor for 8–318 engine—1988 models

EMISSION CONTROLS 4-11

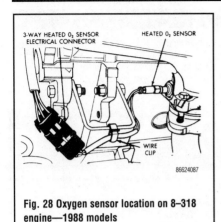

Fig. 28 Oxygen sensor location on 8–318 engine—1988 models

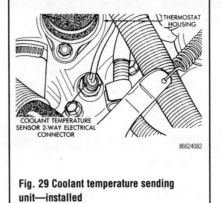

Fig. 29 Coolant temperature sending unit—installed

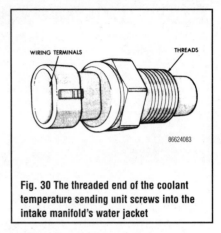

Fig. 30 The threaded end of the coolant temperature sending unit screws into the intake manifold's water jacket

Power Loss/Limited (Check Engine) Lamp

The power loss (check engine) lamp comes on each time the ignition key is turned **ON** and stays on for a few seconds as a bulb test. If the SMEC receives an incorrect signal or no signal from either the coolant temperature sensor, manifold absolute pressure sensor, or the throttle position sensor, the lamp on the instrument panel is illuminated. This is a warning that the SMEC has gone into limp-in mode in an attempt to keep the system operational.

The lamp can also be used to display fault codes. Cycle the ignition switch **ON, OFF, ON, OFF, ON,** within five seconds and any fault code stored in the memory will be displayed.

Coolant Control Exhaust Gas Recirculation (CCEGR) Valve

The CCEGR valve is operated by the SMEC. When engine temperature is 108°–125°F (42°–52°C), the CCEGR valve mounted in the thermostat housing will open, so vacuum is applied to open the EGR valve allowing the gases to recirculate. Some vehicles have these CCEGR valves in the radiator, there opening temperature is 59°F (15°C).

1. To test, remove the valve and place it in an ice bath, below 40°F (5°C), so that the threaded portion is covered.
2. Attach a vacuum pump and gauge tool C–4207, or equivalent, to the CCEGR valve nipple corresponding to the blue stripe hose.
3. Apply more than 10 inches (34 kPa) of vacuum to the valve; there should be no more than a 1 inch (3.4 kPa) drop in vacuum in one minute, according to the gauge.
4. If the CCEGR valve fails this test, replace it.

Air Conditioning Cutout Relay

The air conditioning cutout relay is connected, in series, electrically with the A/C damped pressure switch, the A/C switch and, on some models, the A/C fan relay. This relay is in the energized, closed (on) position during engine operation. When the module senses low idle speeds and wide open throttle through the throttle position sensor, it will de-energize the relay, open its contacts and prevent air conditioning clutch engagement.

Throttle Body

The throttle body assembly replaces a conventional carburetor and is mounted on top of the intake manifold. The throttle body houses the fuel injector, pressure regulator, throttle position sensor, automatic idle speed motor and throttle body temperature sensor. Air flow through the throttle body is controlled by a cable operated throttle blade located in the base of the throttle body. The throttle body itself provides the chamber for metering, atomizing and distributing fuel throughout the air entering the engine.

Fuel Injector

The fuel injector is an electric solenoid driven by the power module, but controlled by the SMEC. The SMEC, based on ambient, mechanical, and sensor input, determines when and how long the power module should operate the injector. When an electric current is supplied to the injector, a spring loaded ball is lifted from its seat. This allows fuel to flow through six spray orifices and deflects off the sharp edge of the injector nozzle. This action causes the fuel to form a 45° cone shaped spray pattern before entering the air stream in the throttle body.

Fuel Pressure Regulator

The pressure regulator is a mechanical device located downstream of the fuel injector on the throttle body. Its function is to maintain a constant 14.5 psi (100 kPa) across the fuel injector tip. The regulator uses a spring loaded rubber diaphragm to uncover a fuel return port. When the fuel pump becomes operational, fuel flows past the injector into the regulator, and is restricted from flowing any further by the blocked return port. When fuel pressure reaches the predetermined setting, it pushes on the diaphragm, compressing the spring, and uncovers the fuel return port. The diaphragm and spring will constantly move from an open to closed position to keep the fuel pressure constant.

Throttle Position Sensor (TPS)

The throttle position sensor (TPS) is an electric resistor which is activated by the movement of the throttle shaft. It is mounted on the throttle body and senses the angle of the throttle blade opening. The voltage that the sensor produces increases or decreases according to the throttle blade opening. This voltage is transmitted to the SMEC, where it is used along with data from other sensors to adjust the air/fuel ratio to varying conditions and during acceleration, deceleration, idle, and wide open throttle operations.

Automatic Idle Speed (AIS) Motor

The automatic idle speed motor (AIS) is operated by the SMEC. Data from the throttle position sensor, speed sensor, coolant temperature sensor, and various switch operations, (heated rear window, air conditioning, safety/neutral, brake) are used by the module to adjust engine idle to an optimum during all idle conditions. The AIS adjusts the air portion of the air/fuel mixture through an air bypass on the back of the throttle body. Basic (no load) idle is determined by the minimum air flow through the throttle body. The AIS opens or closes off the air bypass as an increase or decrease is needed due to engine loads or ambient conditions. The module senses an air/fuel change and increases or decreases fuel proportionally to change engine idle. Deceleration die out is also prevented by increasing engine idle when the throttle is closed quickly after a driving (speed) condition.

Throttle Body Temperature Sensor

The throttle body temperature sensor is a device that monitors throttle body temperature (which is the same as fuel temperature). It is mounted in the throttle body. This sensor provides information on fuel temperature, which allows the SMEC to provide the correct air fuel mixture for a hot restart condition.

4-12 EMISSION CONTROLS

VACUUM DIAGRAMS

Following is a listing of vacuum diagrams for most of the engine and emissions package combinations covered by this manual. Because vacuum circuits will vary based on various engine and vehicle options, always refer first to the vehicle emission control information label, if present. Should the label be missing, or should the vehicle be equipped with an engine other than the original, refer to the following diagrams for the same or similar configuration.

If you wish to obtain a replacement emissions label, most manufacturers make the labels available for purchase. The labels can usually be ordered from a local dealer.

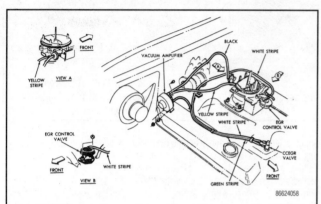

Fig. 31 EGR vacuum hose routings for 6-225 engines—1974 California D100/W100 models

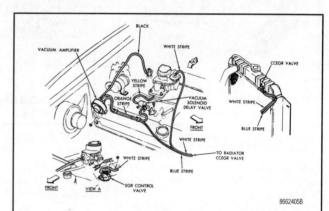

Fig. 33 EGR vacuum hose routings for 8-318 engines—1974 California D100 models

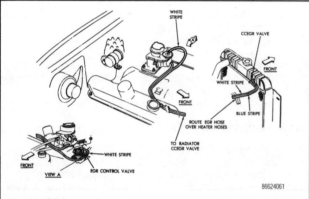

Fig. 32 EGR vacuum hose routings for 8-318 engines with a ported system—1974 non-California D100/W100 models

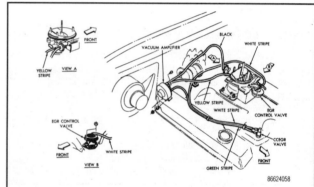

Fig. 34 EGR vacuum hose routings for 8-360 engines—1974 non-California D100/W100 models

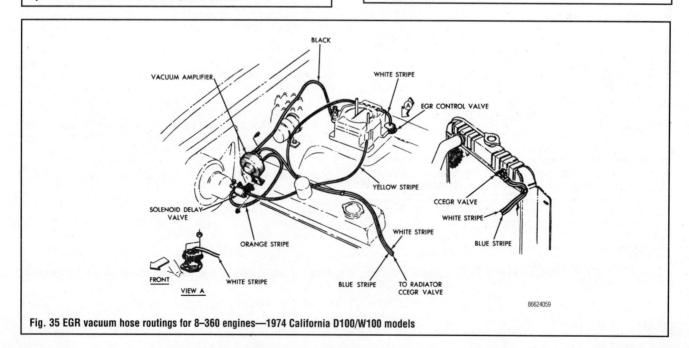

Fig. 35 EGR vacuum hose routings for 8-360 engines—1974 California D100/W100 models

EMISSION CONTROLS 4-13

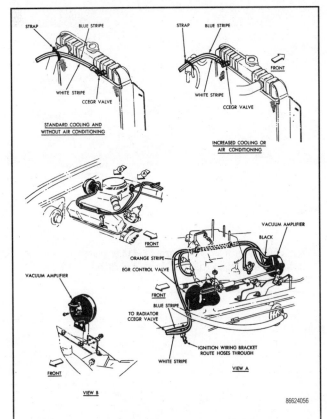

Fig. 36 EGR vacuum hose routings for 8–400 and 440 engines—1974 non-California D100 models

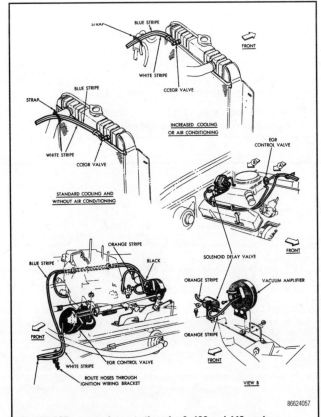

Fig. 37 EGR vacuum hose routings for 8–400 and 440 engines—1974 California D100 models

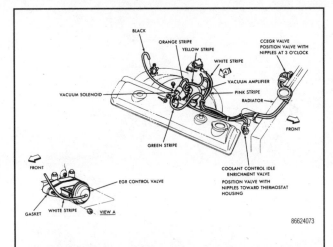

Fig. 38 EGR and idle enrichment vacuum hose routings for 6–225 engines equipped with an automatic transmission—1975–76 D100 models

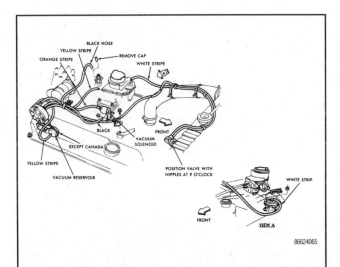

Fig. 39 EGR vacuum hose routings for 8–318 engines equipped with a manual transmission—1975–76 D100 and W100 models

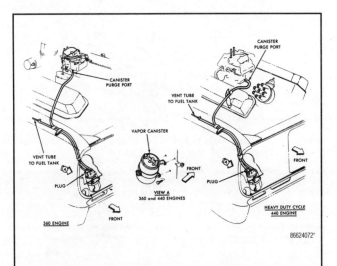

Fig. 40 EGR vacuum hose routings for 6–225 engines equipped with a manual transmission—1975–76 light duty models

4-14 EMISSION CONTROLS

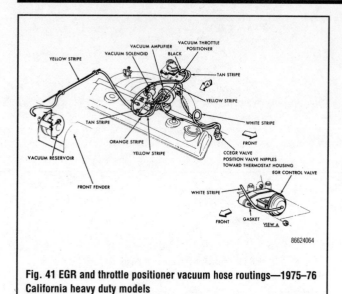

Fig. 41 EGR and throttle positioner vacuum hose routings—1975-76 California heavy duty models

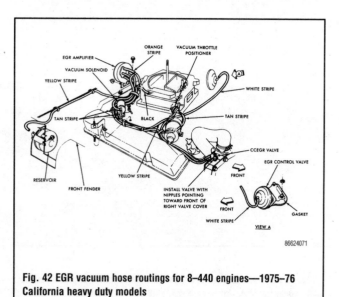

Fig. 42 EGR vacuum hose routings for 8-440 engines—1975-76 California heavy duty models

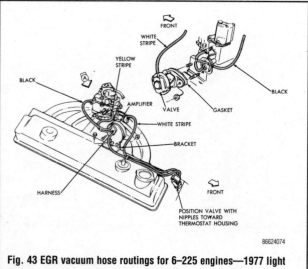

Fig. 43 EGR vacuum hose routings for 6-225 engines—1977 light duty Ramcharger and Trail Duster models

Fig. 44 EGR vacuum hose routings for 8-318 engines equipped with a manual transmission—1977 light duty Ramcharger and Trail Duster models

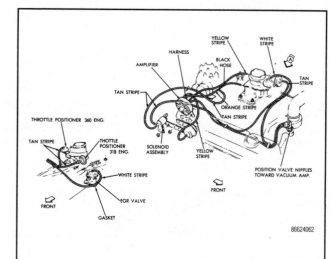

Fig. 45 EGR vacuum hose routings for 8-318 and 360 engines—1977 California heavy duty Ramcharger and Trail Duster models

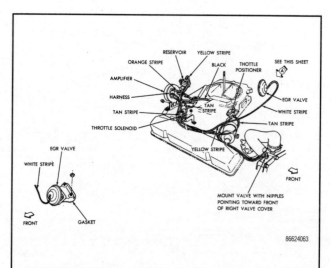

Fig. 46 EGR vacuum hose routings for 8-440 engines—1977 California heavy duty Ramcharger and Trail Duster models

EMISSION CONTROLS 4-15

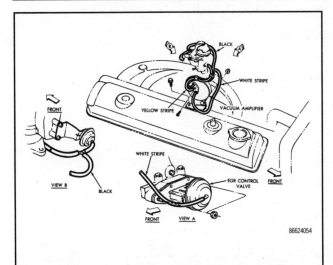

Fig. 47 EGR vacuum hose routings for 6-225 engines—all 1979 models

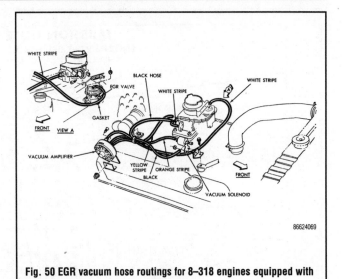

Fig. 50 EGR vacuum hose routings for 8-318 engines equipped with a manual transmission—all 1980 models

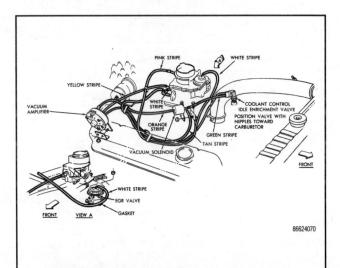

Fig. 48 EGR vacuum hose routings for 8-318 engines equipped with a manual transmission—all 1979 models

Fig. 51 EGR vacuum hose routings for 8-318 and 360 engines equipped with an automatic transmission—1980 light duty models

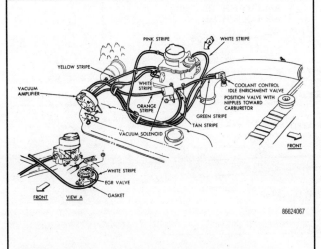

Fig. 49 EGR vacuum hose routings for 8-318 and 360 engines equipped with an automatic transmission—1979 light duty models

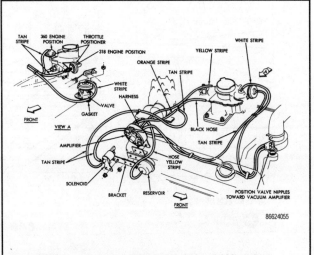

Fig. 52 EGR vacuum hose routings for 8-318 and 360 engines—1980 California heavy duty models

4-16 EMISSION CONTROLS

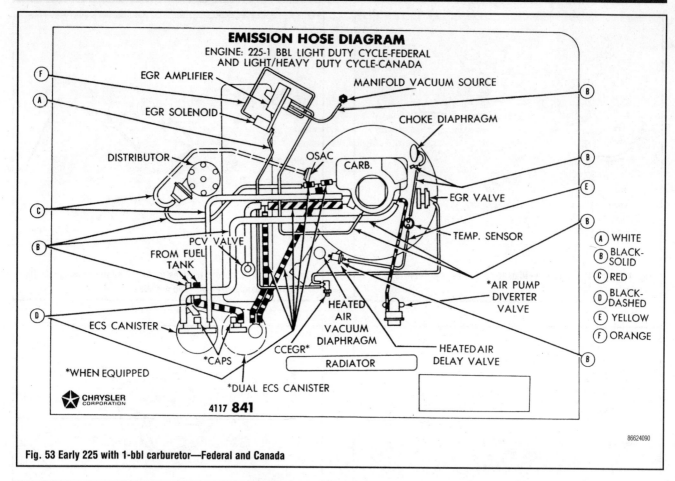

Fig. 53 Early 225 with 1-bbl carburetor—Federal and Canada

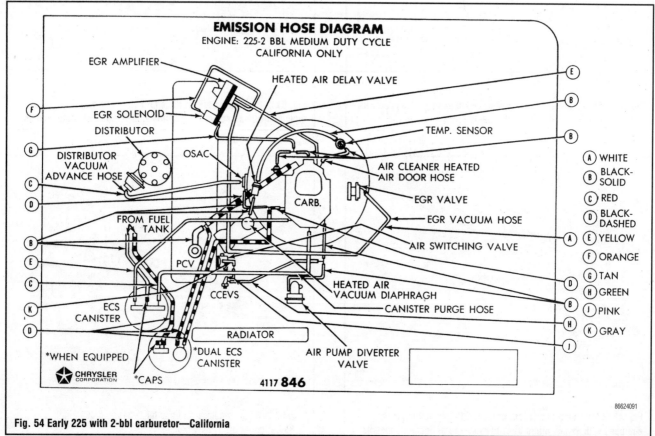

Fig. 54 Early 225 with 2-bbl carburetor—California

EMISSION CONTROLS 4-17

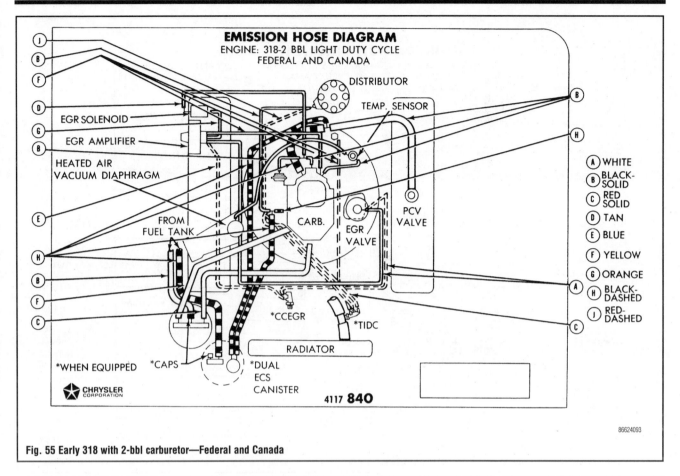

Fig. 55 Early 318 with 2-bbl carburetor—Federal and Canada

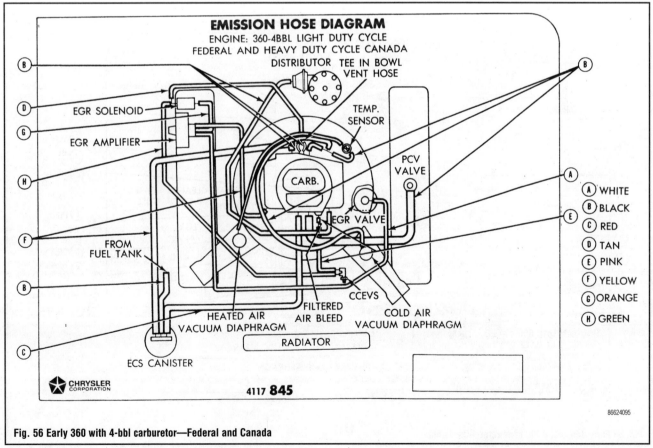

Fig. 56 Early 360 with 4-bbl carburetor—Federal and Canada

4-18 EMISSION CONTROLS

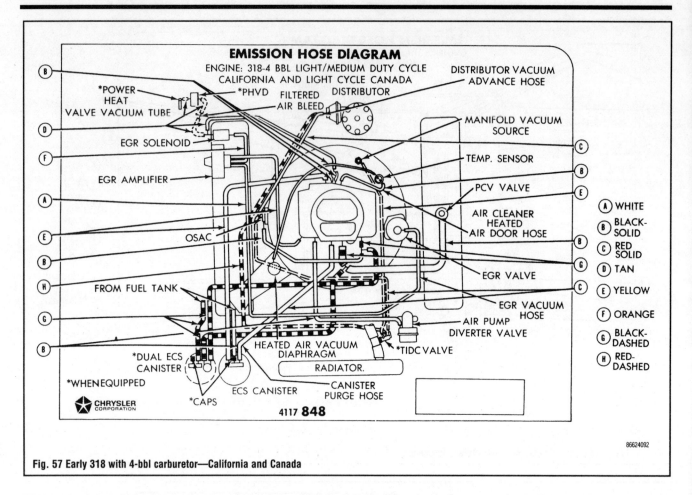

Fig. 57 Early 318 with 4-bbl carburetor—California and Canada

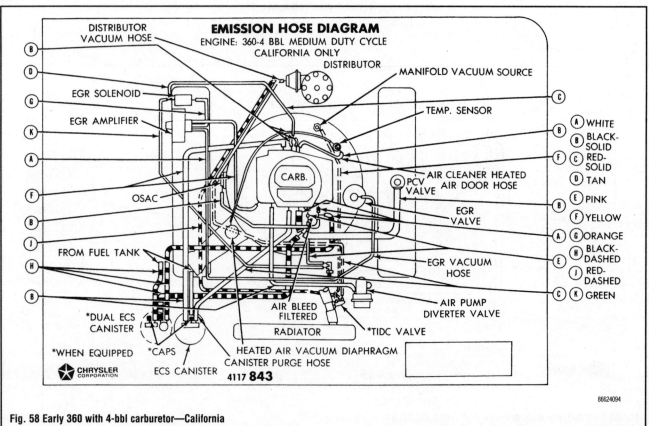

Fig. 58 Early 360 with 4-bbl carburetor—California

EMISSION CONTROLS 4-19

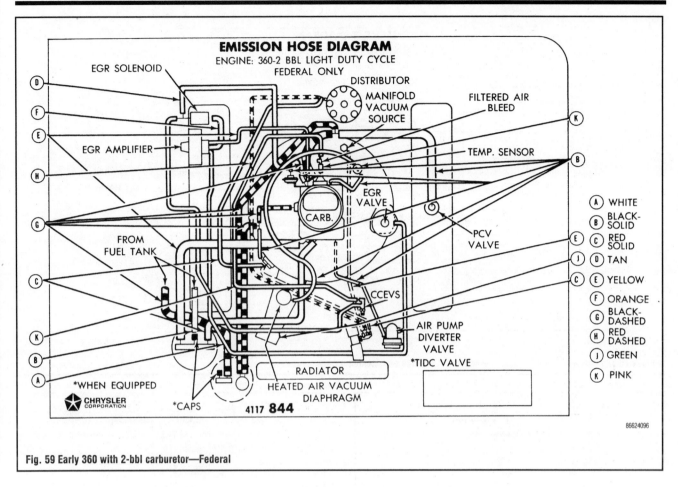

Fig. 59 Early 360 with 2-bbl carburetor—Federal

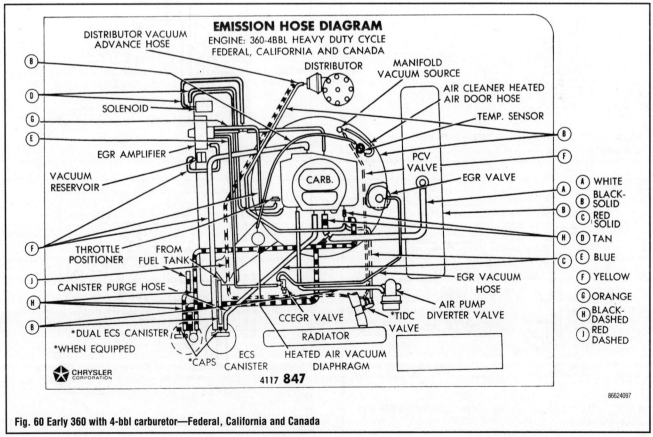

Fig. 60 Early 360 with 4-bbl carburetor—Federal, California and Canada

4-20 EMISSION CONTROLS

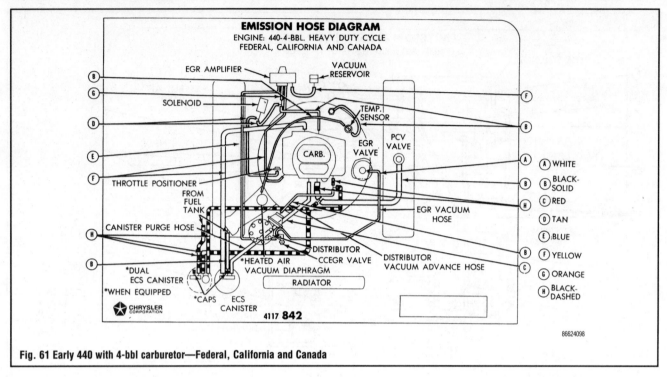

Fig. 61 Early 440 with 4-bbl carburetor—Federal, California and Canada

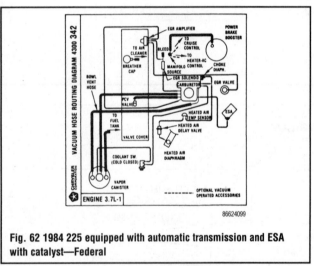

Fig. 62 1984 225 equipped with automatic transmission and ESA with catalyst—Federal

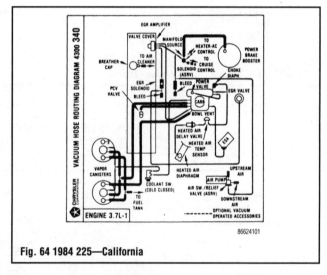

Fig. 64 1984 225—California

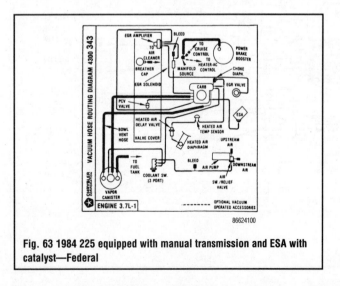

Fig. 63 1984 225 equipped with manual transmission and ESA with catalyst—Federal

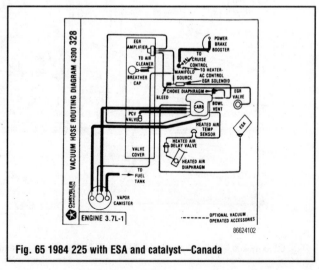

Fig. 65 1984 225 with ESA and catalyst—Canada

EMISSION CONTROLS 4-21

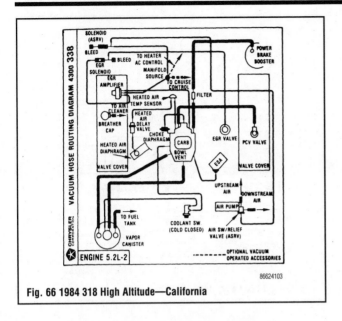

Fig. 66 1984 318 High Altitude—California

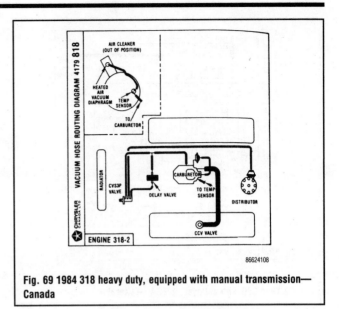

Fig. 69 1984 318 heavy duty, equipped with manual transmission—Canada

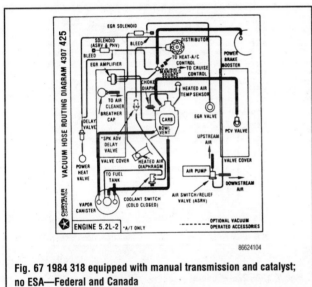

Fig. 67 1984 318 equipped with manual transmission and catalyst; no ESA—Federal and Canada

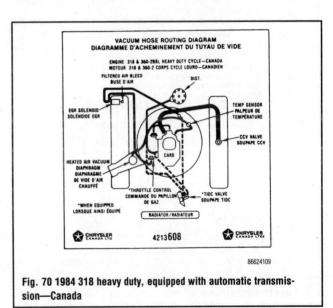

Fig. 70 1984 318 heavy duty, equipped with automatic transmission—Canada

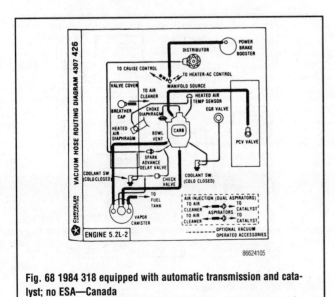

Fig. 68 1984 318 equipped with automatic transmission and catalyst; no ESA—Canada

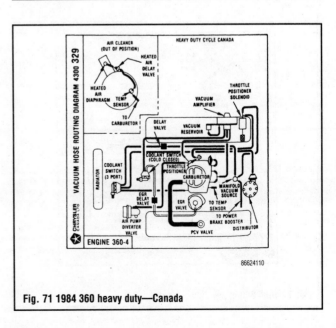

Fig. 71 1984 360 heavy duty—Canada

4-22 EMISSION CONTROLS

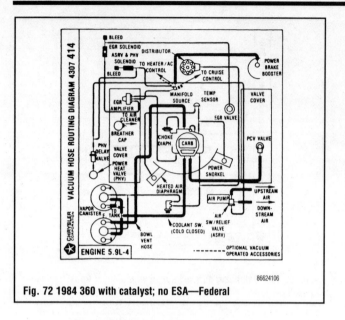

Fig. 72 1984 360 with catalyst; no ESA—Federal

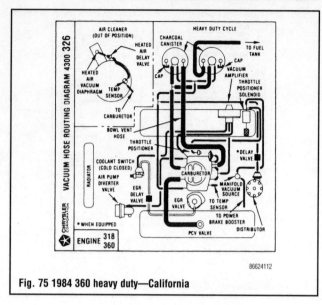

Fig. 75 1984 360 heavy duty—California

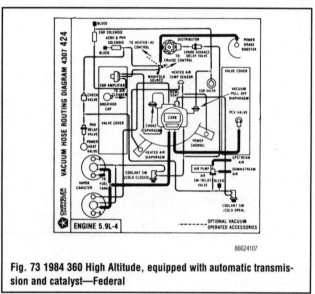

Fig. 73 1984 360 High Altitude, equipped with automatic transmission and catalyst—Federal

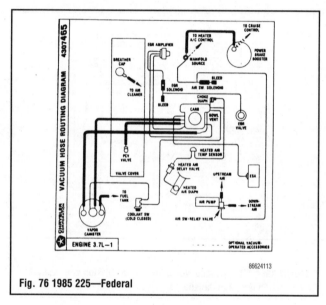

Fig. 76 1985 225—Federal

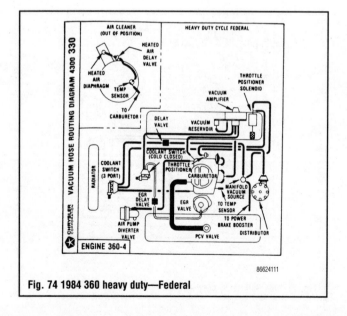

Fig. 74 1984 360 heavy duty—Federal

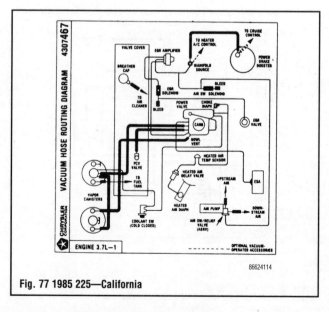

Fig. 77 1985 225—California

EMISSION CONTROLS 4-23

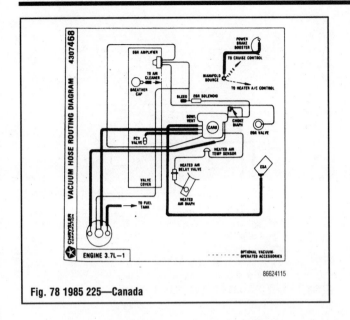

Fig. 78 1985 225—Canada

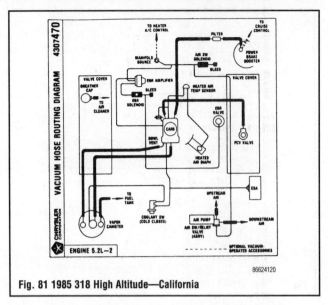

Fig. 81 1985 318 High Altitude—California

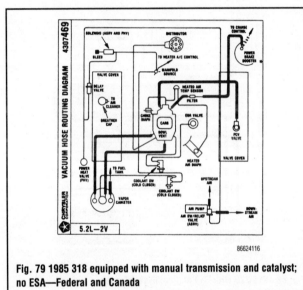

Fig. 79 1985 318 equipped with manual transmission and catalyst; no ESA—Federal and Canada

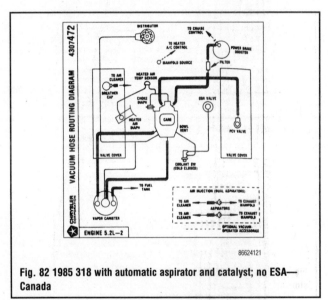

Fig. 82 1985 318 with automatic aspirator and catalyst; no ESA—Canada

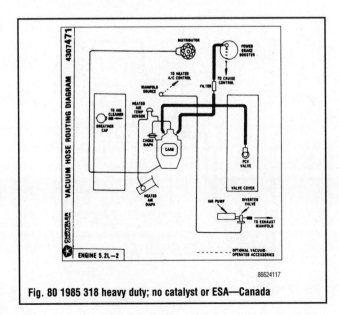

Fig. 80 1985 318 heavy duty; no catalyst or ESA—Canada

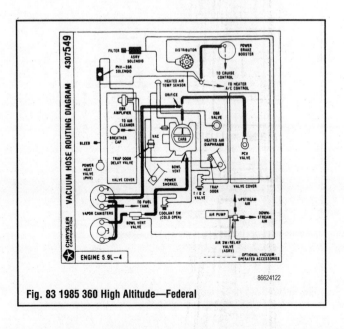

Fig. 83 1985 360 High Altitude—Federal

4-24 EMISSION CONTROLS

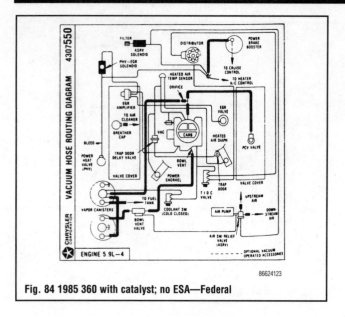

Fig. 84 1985 360 with catalyst; no ESA—Federal

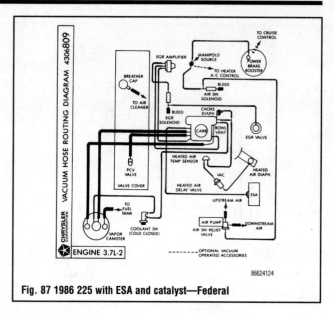

Fig. 87 1986 225 with ESA and catalyst—Federal

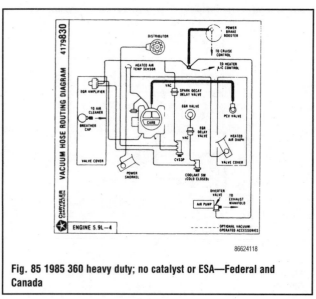

Fig. 85 1985 360 heavy duty; no catalyst or ESA—Federal and Canada

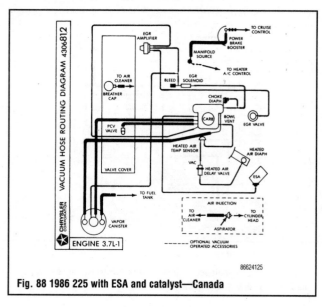

Fig. 88 1986 225 with ESA and catalyst—Canada

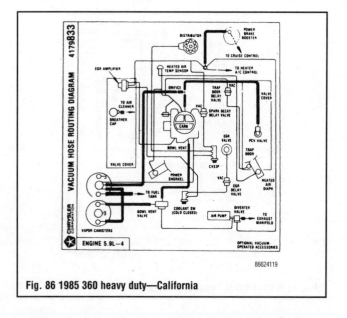

Fig. 86 1985 360 heavy duty—California

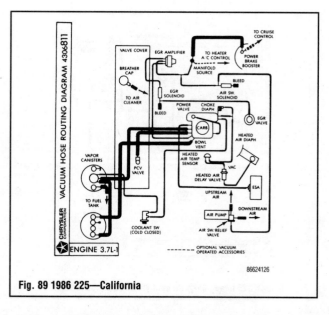

Fig. 89 1986 225—California

EMISSION CONTROLS 4-25

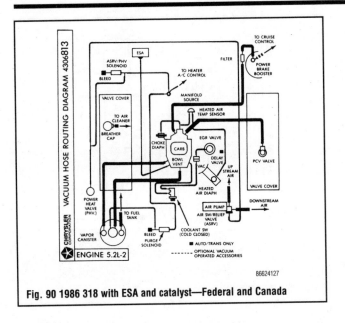

Fig. 90 1986 318 with ESA and catalyst—Federal and Canada

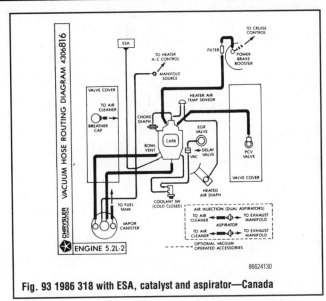

Fig. 93 1986 318 with ESA, catalyst and aspirator—Canada

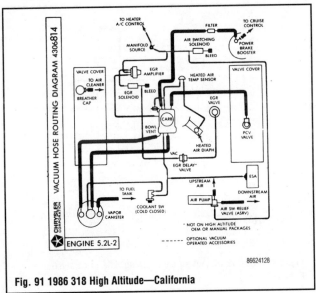

Fig. 91 1986 318 High Altitude—California

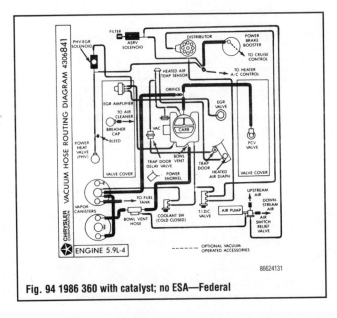

Fig. 94 1986 360 with catalyst; no ESA—Federal

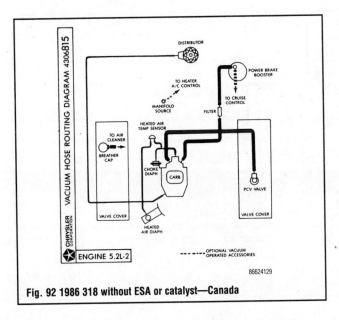

Fig. 92 1986 318 without ESA or catalyst—Canada

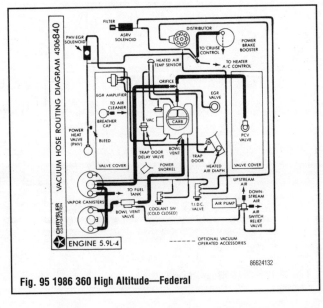

Fig. 95 1986 360 High Altitude—Federal

4-26 EMISSION CONTROLS

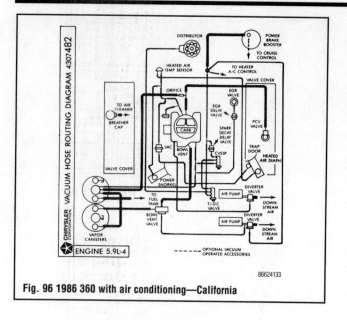

Fig. 96 1986 360 with air conditioning—California

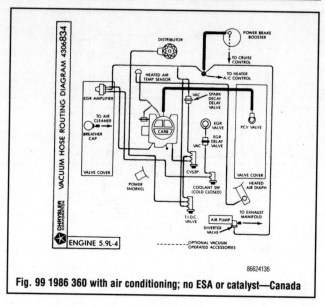

Fig. 99 1986 360 with air conditioning; no ESA or catalyst—Canada

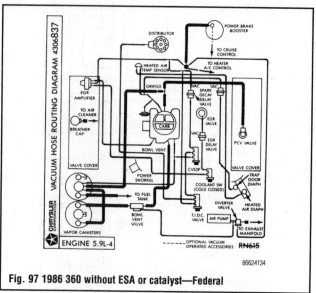

Fig. 97 1986 360 without ESA or catalyst—Federal

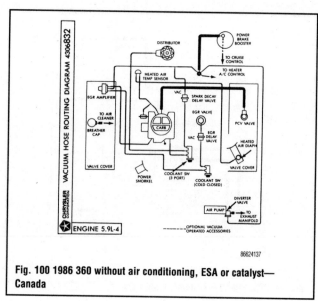

Fig. 100 1986 360 without air conditioning, ESA or catalyst—Canada

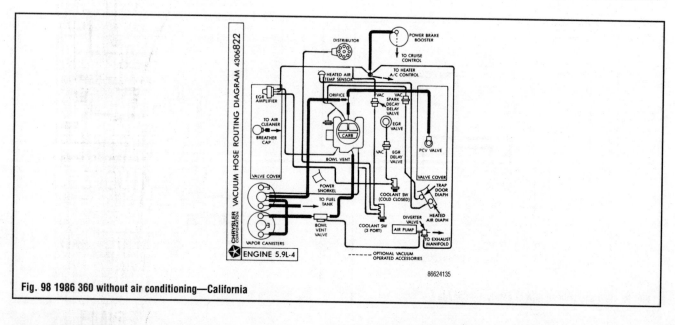

Fig. 98 1986 360 without air conditioning—California

EMISSION CONTROLS 4-27

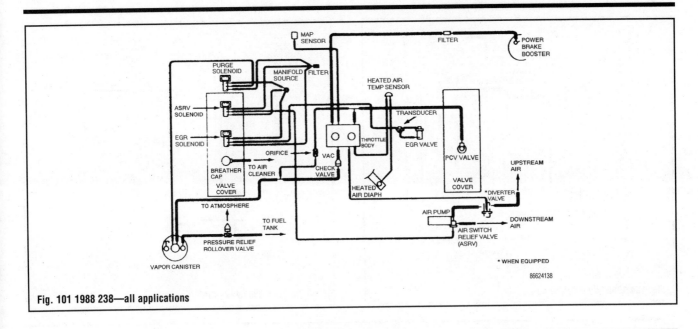

Fig. 101 1988 238—all applications

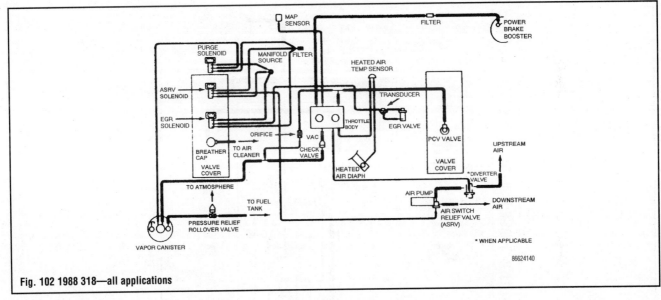

Fig. 102 1988 318—all applications

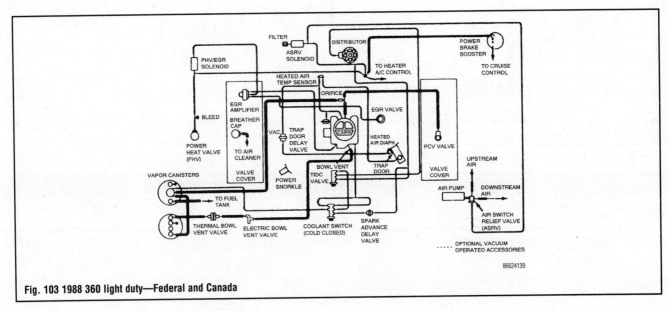

Fig. 103 1988 360 light duty—Federal and Canada

4-28 EMISSION CONTROLS

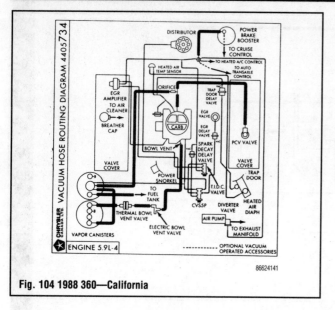

Fig. 104 1988 360—California

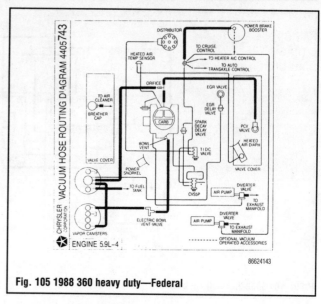

Fig. 105 1988 360 heavy duty—Federal

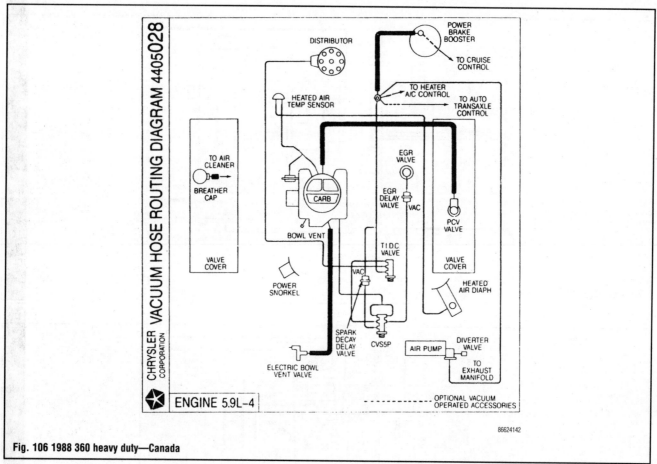

Fig. 106 1988 360 heavy duty—Canada

**BASIC FUEL SYSTEM
DIAGNOSIS 5-2
CARBURETED FUEL SYSTEM 5-2**
CARBURETOR APPLICATION: 5-2
    1967 MODELS 5-2
    1968 MODELS 5-2
    1969–72 MODELS 5-2
    1973–74 MODELS 5-2
    1975–77 MODELS 5-2
    1978–79 MODELS 5-2
    1980–81 MODELS 5-2
    1982 MODELS 5-2
    1983 MODELS 5-3
    1984 MODELS 5-3
    1985–87 MODELS 5-3
    1988 MODELS 5-3
MECHANICAL FUEL PUMP 5-3
    REMOVAL & INSTALLATION 5-3
    TESTING 5-3
CARBURETOR 5-4
    ADJUSTMENTS FOR CARTER AFB 5-4
    ADJUSTMENTS FOR CARTER BBS 5-5
    ADJUSTMENTS FOR CARTER BBD 5-6
    ADJUSTMENTS FOR CARTER THERMO–QUAD 5-8
    ADJUSTMENTS FOR HOLLEY 1945 5-12
    ADJUSTMENTS FOR HOLLEY 2210 5-13
    ADJUSTMENTS FOR HOLLEY 2300G 5-14
    ADJUSTMENTS FOR HOLLEY 2245 5-14
    ADJUSTMENTS FOR HOLLEY 2280 5-16
    ADJUSTMENTS FOR HOLLEY 4150G 5-18
    ADJUSTMENTS FOR HOLLEY 6145 5-18
    ADJUSTMENTS FOR HOLLEY 6280 5-20
    ADJUSTMENTS FOR ROCHESTER QUADRAJET 5-22
    ADJUSTMENTS FOR STROMBERG WW3 5-25
    REMOVAL & INSTALLATION 5-26
**CARBURETOR SPECIFICATIONS
CHARTS 5-27
THROTTLE BODY FUEL INJECTION
SYSTEM 5-36**
SYSTEM DESCRIPTION 5-36
SERVICE PRECAUTIONS 5-36
MINIMUM IDLE SPEED ADJUSTMENT 5-36
RELIEVING FUEL SYSTEM PRESSURE 5-36
FUEL SYSTEM PRESSURE TESTING 5-36
ELECTRIC FUEL PUMP 5-36
    REMOVAL & INSTALLATION 5-36
THROTTLE BODY 5-38
    REMOVAL & INSTALLATION 5-38
FUEL FITTINGS 5-38
    REMOVAL & INSTALLATION 5-38
FUEL PRESSURE REGULATOR 5-39
    REMOVAL & INSTALLATION 5-39
FUEL INJECTORS 5-39
    REMOVAL & INSTALLATION 5-39
THROTTLE POSITION SENSOR 5-40
    REMOVAL & INSTALLATION 5-40
THROTTLE BODY TEMPERATURE SENSOR 5-40
    REMOVAL & INSTALLATION 5-40
AUTOMATIC IDLE SPEED (AIS) MOTOR 5-40
    REMOVAL & INSTALLATION 5-40
DIESEL FUEL SYSTEM 5-41
INJECTION PUMP 5-41
    TESTING 5-41
    REMOVAL & INSTALLATION 5-41
    INJECTION TIMING 5-42
INJECTORS 5-42
    REMOVAL & INSTALLATION 5-42
    TESTING 5-43
FUEL TANK 5-43
TANK ASSEMBLY 5-43
    REMOVAL & INSTALLATION 5-43
    SENDING UNIT 5-44

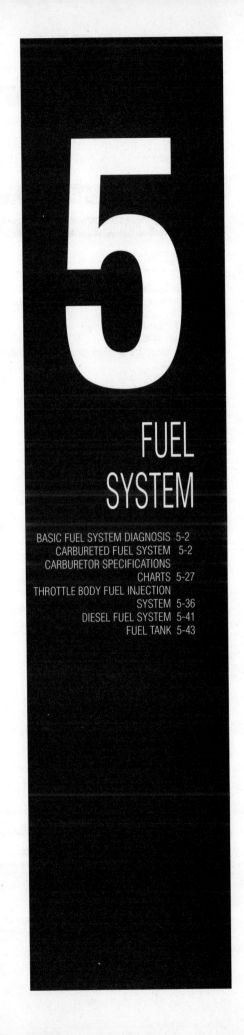

5

FUEL SYSTEM

BASIC FUEL SYSTEM DIAGNOSIS 5-2
CARBURETED FUEL SYSTEM 5-2
CARBURETOR SPECIFICATIONS CHARTS 5-27
THROTTLE BODY FUEL INJECTION SYSTEM 5-36
DIESEL FUEL SYSTEM 5-41
FUEL TANK 5-43

5-2 FUEL SYSTEM

BASIC FUEL SYSTEM DIAGNOSIS

When there is a problem starting or driving a vehicle, two of the most important checks involve the ignition and the fuel systems. The questions most mechanics attempt to answer first, "is there spark?" and "is there fuel?" will often lead to solving most basic problems. For ignition system diagnosis and testing, please refer to Section 2 of this manual. If the ignition system checks out (there is spark), then you must determine if fuel system is operating properly (is there fuel?).

CARBURETED FUEL SYSTEM

Carburetor Application:

1967 MODELS

Carter BBS 1-bbl:
- 6–198 and 6–225 manual transmission (manual choke) and automatic transmission automatic choke
- 6–251 manual choke

Stromberg WW3 2-bbl:
- 8–318 manual transmission manual choke and automatic transmission automatic choke
- 8–361 manual choke

Carter BBD 2-bbl:
- 8–383 automatic choke
- 8–361 manual choke
- 8–413 manual choke

Carter AFB 4-bbl:
- 8–413 automatic choke

1968 MODELS

Carter BBS 1-bbl:
- 6–198 and 6–225 manual and automatic choke

Carter BBD 2-bbl:
- 8–318 manual and automatic choke
- 8–383 automatic choke
- 8–361 manual choke

Holley 4150 4-bbl:
- 8–413 automatic choke

Holley 2300G 2-bbl:
- 8–361 manual choke
- 8–413 automatic choke

1969–72 MODELS

Carter BBS 1-bbl:
- 6–225 manual choke, automatic choke

Stromberg WW3 2-bbl:
- 8–361 manual choke
- 8–318 manual choke, automatic choke

Carter BBD 2-bbl:
- 8–383 automatic choke

Holley 2300G 2-bbl:
- 8–361 and 8–413 manual choke

Holley 4150G 4-bbl:
- 8–413 manual choke

1973–74 MODELS

Holley 1945 1-bbl:
- 6–225

Carter BBS 1-bbl:
- 6–225

Carter BBD 2-bbl:
- 8–318
- 8–361 manual choke

Holley 2245 2-bbl:
- 8–360
- 8–400

Holley 2210 2-bbl:
- 8–360
- 8–400

Holley 2300G 2-bbl:
- 8–361 manual choke
- 8–413 manual choke

Carter Thermo-Quad 4-bbl:
- 8–360
- 8–440

1975–77 MODELS

Holley 1945 1-bbl:
- 6–225

Carter BBD 2-bbl:
- 8–318

Holley 2210 2-bbl:
- 8–360

Holley 2245 2-bbl:
- 8–360

Holley 2300G 2-bbl:
- 8–361 manual choke

Holley 4150G 4-bbl:
- 8–413 manual choke

Carter Thermo-Quad 4-bbl:
- 8–440

1978–79 MODELS

Holley 1945 1-bbl:
- 6–225 49 state and Canada

Carter BBD 2-bbl:
- 6–225 California
- 8–318 49 state
- 8–360 49 state

Carter Thermo-Quad 4-bbl:
- 8–318 Calif. and Canada
- 8–360 US and Canada

1980–81 MODELS

Holley 1945 1-bbl:
- 6–225 US and Canada

Holley 2280 2-bbl:
- 8–318 US and Canada

Carter BBD 2-bbl:
- 8–318 Canada

Holley 2245 2-bbl:
- 8–360 Canada

Carter Thermo-Quad 4-bbl:
- 8–318 US
- 8–360 US and Canada

1982 MODELS

Holley 1945 1-bbl:
- 6–225 US and Canada

Holley 2280 2-bbl:
- 8–318 US and Canada

Carter BBD 2-bbl:

FUEL SYSTEM   5-3

- 6–225 US
- 8–318 US and Canada

Holley 2245 2–bbl:
- 8–360 Canada

Carter Thermo-Quad 4–bbl:
- 8–318 US and Canada
- 8–360 California

1983 MODELS

Holley 1945 1–bbl:
- 6–225 US and Canada

Holley 6145 1–bbl:
- 6–225 California

Holley 2280 2–bbl:
- 8–318 US

Holley 2245 2–bbl:
- 8–360 Canada

Carter BBD 2–bbl:
- 6–225 US
- 8–318 US and Canada

Carter Thermo-Quad 4–bbl:
- 8–318 US
- 8–360 US and Canada

1984 MODELS

Holley 1945 1–bbl:
- 6–225 49 state and Canada

Holley 6145 1–bbl:
- 6–225 California

Holley 2280 2–bbl:
- 8–318 US and Canada

Carter BBD 2–bbl:
- 8–318 US and Canada

Carter Thermo-Quad 4–bbl:
- 8–360 US and Canada

1985–87 MODELS

Holley 1945 1–bbl:
- 6–225 49 state and Canada

Holley 6145 1–bbl:
- 6–225 California

Holley 2280 2–bbl:
- 8–318 49 state and Canada

Holley 6280 2–bbl:
- 8–318 US

Rochester Quadrajet 4–bbl:
- 8–360 US and Canada

1988 MODELS

Rochester Quadrajet 4–bbl:
- 8–360 US and Canada

Mechanical Fuel Pump

REMOVAL & INSTALLATION

♦ See Figures 1 thru 7

※※ CAUTION

Never smoke when working around gasoline! Avoid all sources of sparks or ignition. Gasoline vapors are EXTREMELY volatile!

1. Disconnect the negative battery cable.
2. Disconnect the fuel lines from the inlet and outlet sides of the fuel pump.
3. Plug these lines to prevent gasoline from leaking out.
4. Unscrew the retaining bolts from the fuel pump and remove the fuel pump from the engine.
5. Remove the old gasket from the engine and/or fuel pump.
6. Clean all mounting surfaces.
7. Using a new gasket, install the fuel pump in the reverse of the removal procedure.

TESTING

♦ See Figures 4, 5, 6 and 7

Pressure Test

♦ See Figure 8

➡Before proceeding with this test, verify there is no leakage. If leakage is found, repair or replace components as necessary.

If leakage is not apparent, the following pressure test should be performed.
1. Insert a "T" fitting into the fuel line at the carburetor.
2. Connect a 6 in. (152mm) piece of hose between the "Tee" fitting and a pressure gauge.
3. Drain the fuel line leading to the carburetor in order to allow the pump to operate at maximum capacity.
4. Connect a tachometer and start the engine. Allow the engine to run at idle speed. The fuel pump pressure should be 3.5–5.0 psi (24–34 kPa) for 6–cylinder engines or 5.0–7.0 psi (34–48 kPa) for V8 engines. When the engine is stopped, the pressure should return to zero very slowly. If it rapidly or instantly drops to zero, a leaky outlet valve is indicated.

Volume Test

1. Disconnect the fuel line from the carburetor. Place the end of the line in a container holding at least 1 quart.

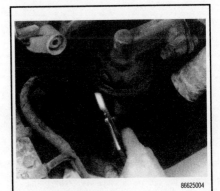

Fig. 1 Disconnect the fuel lines at the pump assembly

Fig. 2 After you have unthreaded the mounting bolts, remove the pump from the engine

Fig. 3 Before installation, cleaning all traces of the old gasket, then position a new one on the pump

5-4 FUEL SYSTEM

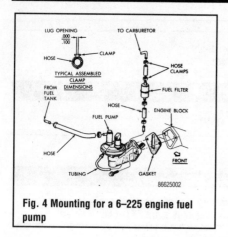

Fig. 4 Mounting for a 6–225 engine fuel pump

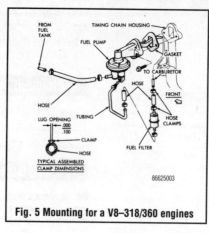

Fig. 5 Mounting for a V8–318/360 engines

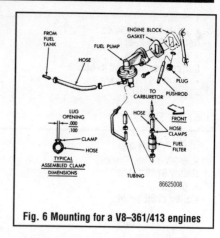

Fig. 6 Mounting for a V8–361/413 engines

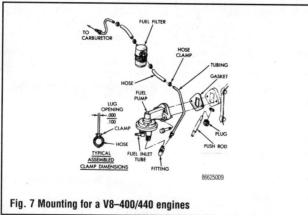

Fig. 7 Mounting for a V8–400/440 engines

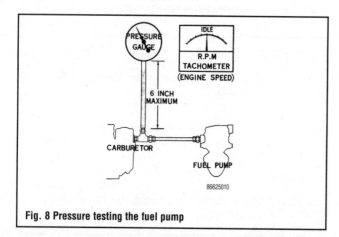

Fig. 8 Pressure testing the fuel pump

2. If the sides are not in alignment, bend the float lever by applying pressure to the end of the float shell while supporting the float lever with your thumb.
3. After aligning the floats, remove as much clearance as possible between the arms of the float lever and the lugs on the air horn. To do this, bend the float lever.

Float Level Setting

1. Invert the air horn with the gasket in place and the float needles seated.
2. Measure between the top of the float at the outer end and the air horn gasket. The gap should be 7/32 in. (5.5mm).
3. Check the other float in the same way.
4. If the setting needs adjustment, bend the float arm to obtain proper adjustment.

Float Drop Setting

1. Hold the air horn in an upright position. Measure the gap between the top of the floats at the outer ends and the air horn gasket. The gap should be 3/4 in. (19mm).
2. If an adjustment is necessary, bend the stop tabs on the float levers.

Accelerator Pump

➡This procedure is performed with the air horn installed.

1. Back off the idle speed adjusting screw until the throttle valves are completely closed.
2. Measure the distance from the top of the air horn to the top of the plunger shaft using a T-scale. The distance should be 7/16 in. (11mm).
3. If an adjustment is necessary, bend the pump rod at the lower angle with a needle–nosed pliers.
4. Re–adjust the curb idle.

Secondary Throttle Lever

1. Remove the carburetor from the engine.

➡Position the carburetor on clean rags to catch any remaining fuel.

2. Invert the carburetor and slowly open the primary throttle valves until there is a gap of 23/64 – 3/8 in. (9.2–9.5mm) between the lower edge of the primary valve and the bore opposite the idle port. At this point the secondary throttle valves should just start to open. The stop lugs on both primary and secondary throttle levers should contact the bosses on the flange at the same time.
3. If an adjustment is necessary, bend the secondary throttle operating rod at the angle with a needle–nosed pliers. At wide-open throttle, both primary and secondary throttle valves should be vertical.
4. With the primary and secondary throttle valves closed, it should be possible to insert wire gauge tool No. T-109-29 or equivalent, between the positive closing shoes on the primary and secondary levers.
5. If an adjustment is necessary, bend the shoe on the primary lever until the correct clearance is reached.

2. The fuel pump output should be 1 quart in 1 minute or less at 500 rpm.
3. If the pump doesn't operate as specified, replace the fuel filter and check for a pinched and/or blocked fuel line. If the pump output is still insufficient, replace the pump.

Carburetor

ADJUSTMENTS FOR CARTER AFB

➡Most of these adjustments require that measurements be gauged in thousandths of an inch. Drill bits are ideal for this purpose.

Float Alignment

1. Sight down each side of the float shell to determine if the side of the float is parallel to the outer edge of the air horn casting.

ADJUSTMENTS FOR CARTER BBS

➡ Most of these adjustments require that measurements be gauged in thousandths of an inch. Drill bits are ideal for this purpose.

Accelerator Pump And Bowl Vent

1. Back off the idle speed screw and open the choke valve so that when the throttle valves are closed the fast idle adjustment screw does not contact the fast idle cam.
2. Be sure that the pump operating rod is in the medium stroke hole (long hole for the BBS–4340S and BBS–4341S) in the throttle lever and that the bowl vent clip on the pump stem is in the center notch (lower notch on the BBS–4340S and BBS–4341S).
3. Close the throttle valves tightly. It should just be possible to insert a 1/16 in. (1.5mm) gauge between the bowl vent and the air horn 27/32 in. (21.4mm) on the BBS–3277S accelerator pump plunger travel).
4. If an adjustment is necessary, bend the pump operating rod at the lower angle.

Fast Idle Cam Position Automatic Choke

1. Adjust the fast idle speed as described later.
2. Place the fast idle screw on the second highest step of the fast idle cam.
3. Move the choke valve towards the closed position using light pressure on the choke shaft lever.
4. Insert a 5/64 in. (2mm) wire gauge between the choke valve and the wall of the air horn. If an adjustment is necessary, bend the fast idle rod at the upper angle.

Vacuum Kick

1. If the adjustment is to be made on the engine (with the engine running at curb idle), back off the fast idle screw until the choke can be closed to the kick position. Note the number of screw turns required so that the fast idle can be returned to the original adjustment.
2. If the adjustment is to be made off the engine, open the throttle valve and move the choke to its closed position. Release the throttle first and then release the choke. Disconnect the vacuum hose from the carburetor body and apply a vacuum of at least 10 in. Hg (34 kPa) for trucks through 1975 or to 15 in. Hg (51 kPa) for 1976 and later trucks.
3. Insert a 7/64 in. (2.8mm) gauge between the choke valve and the wall of the air horn.
4. Apply sufficient closing pressure to the choke lever to provide a minimum valve opening without distorting the diaphragm link (which connects the choke lever to the vacuum diaphragm). Note that the cylindrical stem of the diaphragm will extend as its internal spring is compressed. This spring must be fully compressed for the proper measurement of the vacuum kick adjustment.
5. Remove the gauge. If a slight drag is not felt as the gauge is removed, an adjustment of the diaphragm link is necessary to obtain the proper clearance. Shorten or lengthen the diaphragm link by carefully closing or opening the U–bend in the link until the correct adjustment is obtained.

✷✷ WARNING

When adjusting the link, be careful not to bend or twist the diaphragm.

6. Connect the vacuum hose to the carburetor body (if it had been removed) and return the fast idle screw to its original location.
7. With no vacuum applied to the diaphragm, the choke valve should move freely between its open and closed positions. If it does not move freely, examine the linkage for misalignment or interference which may have been caused by the bending operation. If necessary, repeat the adjustment to provide the proper link operation.

Choke Unloader

The choke unloader adjustment is a mechanical device that partially opens the choke valve at wide-open throttle. It should be adjusted as follows:
1. Hold the throttle valve in the wide-open position.
2. Insert a 3/16 in. (4.7mm) gauge between the upper edge of the choke valve and the wall of the air horn.
3. While pressing lightly against the choke lever, a slight drag should be felt as the gauge is being withdrawn.
4. If adjustment is necessary, bend the unloader tang on the throttle lever until the correct opening is obtained.

Fast Idle Speed

1. Run the engine until it reaches normal operating temperature.
2. With the engine off and the transmission in Park or Neutral, open the throttle slightly.
3. On models without the Clean Air Package, close the choke plate about 20°, then allow the throttle plates to close. The fast idle screw should now rest on the slowest speed step of the cam. On models with the Clean Air Package, close the choke plate until the fast idle screw can be positioned on the second highest speed step of the cam.
4. Start the engine.
5. Turn the fast idle speed screw in or out until the specified speed is obtained.
6. Stopping the engine between adjustments is not necessary. However, be sure the fast idle speed screw is positioning on the cam after each speed adjustment.

Spring Staged Choke

1. Push on the choke hub lever with your finger, at the closed position. A small opening should exist between the shaft and hub levers.
2. Using a gauge bit, measure the opening. The opening should be 0.010–0.040 in. (0.25–1.00mm).
3. If not, bend the hub lever tang until the correct opening is reached.

Dashpot

➡ This procedure is performed on manual transmissions only.

1. With the idle speed and mixture properly set, position the throttle lever so that the actuating tab on the lever contacts the stem of the dashpot, but does not depress it.
2. The engine speed should be 1,000 rpm. To adjust the setting, loosen the locknut, then screw the dashpot in or out as required. When the correct setting has been obtained, tighten the locknut against the bracket.

Float

➡ This procedure can be performed without removing the carburetor from the engine.

1. Remove the accelerator pump operating rod.
2. Remove 2 of the long air horn screws and 2 of the short screws. Install the 2 short screws in place of the long screws. This will hold the main body to the throttle body. Tighten the screws securely.
3. Remove the remaining air horn screws.
4. Tilt the air horn far enough to disengage the fast idle cam link from the fast idle cam. Remove the air horn and gasket.
5. Seat the float fulcrum pin by pressing on the fulcrum pin retainer. There should be enough fuel in the bowl to raise the float so that the lip bears firmly against the needle. Additional fuel may be entered by slightly depressing the float. If there is not enough pressure in the line to enter more fuel, you'll have to add some from a clean container.

✷✷ CAUTION

Never smoke when working around gasoline! Avoid all sources of sparks or ignition. Gasoline vapors are EXTREMELY volatile!

6. With the fuel level holding the tip of the float against the inlet needle, check the gap between the gasket surface of the bowl (gasket removed) and the center crown of the floats. The gap should be 1/4 in. (6mm) on BBS models 4177S, 4342S and 4341S; 7/32 in. (5.5mm) on models 4340S and 3277S.
7. If adjustment is necessary, hold the float on the bottom of the bowl and bend the float tip toward or away from the needle as required. Recheck the gap.

5-6 FUEL SYSTEM

> ※ **WARNING**
>
> Do not allow the float lip to depress the needle, as this will give you a false reading. When correctly set, the float lip should be perpendicular to the needle within 10°.

8. Assemble the air horn.
9. Check the idle speed.

ADJUSTMENTS FOR CARTER BBD

➡ Most of these adjustments require that measurements be gauged in thousandths of an inch. Drill bits are ideal for this purpose.

Accelerator Pump

1967–72

1. Back off the idle speed screw.
2. Make sure that the pump connector rod is in the center hole of the throttle lever.
3. Close the throttle valves tightly. On all models, except those with 8–383 engine, it should just be possible to insert a 1/64 in. (0.39mm) gauge between the top of the air horn and the end of the plunger shaft. On the 8–383 without the Clean Air Package, the gap should be 29/32 in. (23mm); or 1 in. (25mm) on Clean Air Package models.
4. If an adjustment is necessary, bend the pump operating rod at the lower angle.
5. Reset the idle.

1973–84

♦ See Figure 9

1. Remove the cover plate.
2. Back off the idle speed screw to completely close the throttle plate.
3. Open the choke plate so that the fast idle cam allows the throttle plates to seat in their bores.
4. Turn the curb idle adjusting screw clockwise until it just contacts the stop, then, turn it 2 full turns further.
5. Make sure that the accelerator pump S–link is in the outer hole of the pump arm.
6. Measure the distance between the surface of the air horn and the top of the accelerator pump shaft. The gap should be 1/2 in. (12mm).
7. To adjust the pump travel, loosen the pump arm adjusting lockscrew and rotate the sleeve until the proper gap is reached. Then tighten the lockscrew.

➡ If the accelerator pump stroke adjustment is changed, the bowl vent valve adjustment must be reset.

Fast Idle Cam-Automatic Choke

♦ See Figure 10

1. Adjust the fast idle speed (as described later in this section).
2. Place the fast idle screw on the second highest step of the fast idle cam.

3. Move the choke valve towards the closed position using light pressure on the choke shaft lever.
4. Insert a 5/64 in. (2mm) gauge between the choke valve and the wall of the air horn on models through 1972. On 1973–84 models use a 0.110 in. (2.7mm) gauge on carburetor. models 8147S; an 0.070 in. (1.7mm) gauge on all other models. If an adjustment is necessary, bend the fast idle rod at the upper angle.

Vacuum Kick

♦ See Figure 11

1. If the adjustment is to be made on the engine (with the engine running at curb idle), back off the fast idle screw until the choke can be closed to the kick position. Note the number of screw turns required so that the fast idle can be returned to the original adjustment.
2. If the adjustment is to be made off the engine, open the throttle valve and move the choke to its closed position. Release the throttle first and then release the choke. Disconnect the vacuum hose from the carburetor body and apply a vacuum of at least 10 in. Hg (34 kPa) for trucks through 1975 or to 15 in. Hg (51 kPa) for 1976 and later trucks.
3. Insert the specified gauge between the choke valve and the wall of the air horn:
   - Models through 1972— 0.109 in. (2.7mm)
   - Models 1973 though 1979— 0.110 in. (2.7mm)
   - Models 1980 through 1984— 0.070 in. (1.7mm)
   - Model 8146S— 0.150 in. (3.8mm)
   - Model 8147S— 0.130 in. (3.3mm)
4. Apply sufficient closing pressure to the choke lever to provide a minimum valve opening without distorting the diaphragm link (which connects the choke lever to the vacuum diaphragm). Note that the cylindrical stem of the diaphragm will extend as its internal spring is compressed. This spring must be fully compressed for the proper measurement of the vacuum kick adjustment.
5. Remove the gauge bit. If a slight drag is not felt as the gauge is removed, an adjustment of the diaphragm link is necessary to obtain the proper clearance. Shorten or lengthen the diaphragm link by carefully closing or opening the U–bend in the link until the correct adjustment is obtained.

> ※ **WARNING**
>
> When adjusting the link, be careful not to bend or twist the diaphragm.

6. Connect the vacuum hose to the carburetor body (if it had been removed) and return the fast idle screw to its original location.
7. With no vacuum applied to the diaphragm, the choke valve should move freely between its open and closed positions. If it does not move freely, examine the linkage for misalignment or interference which may have been caused by the bending operation. If necessary, repeat the adjustment to provide the proper link operation.

Choke Unloader

♦ See Figure 12

The choke unloader adjustment is a mechanical device that partially opens the choke valve at wide-open throttle. It should be adjusted as follows:

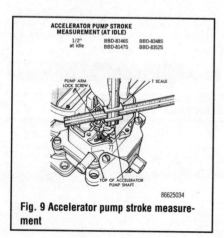

Fig. 9 Accelerator pump stroke measurement

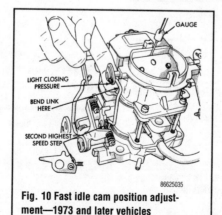

Fig. 10 Fast idle cam position adjustment—1973 and later vehicles

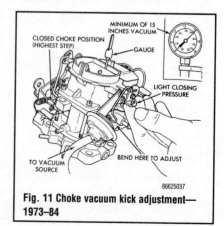

Fig. 11 Choke vacuum kick adjustment—1973–84

FUEL SYSTEM

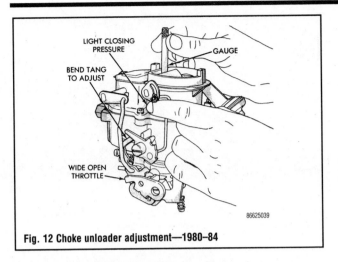

Fig. 12 Choke unloader adjustment—1980–84

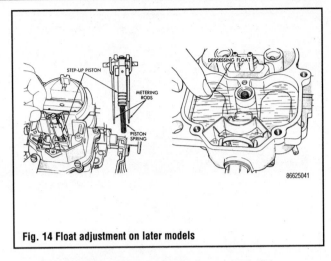

Fig. 14 Float adjustment on later models

1. Hold the throttle valve in the wide-open position.
2. Insert a gauge between the upper edge of the choke valve and the wall of the air horn:
   - Models through 1972— 0.16 in. (4.0mm)
   - Models 1973 through 79— 0.28 in. (7.1mm)
   - Models 1980 through 81— 0.31 in. (7.8mm)
   - Models 1982 through 84— 0.31 in. (7.8mm)
3. While pressing lightly against the choke lever, a slight drag should be felt as the gauge is being withdrawn.
4. If adjustment is necessary, bend the unloader tang on the throttle lever until the correct opening is obtained.

Bowl Vent Valve

♦ See Figure 13

1. Remove the vent valve cover.
2. Hold the throttle plates closed. It should be possible to insert a 0.060 in. (1.5mm) gauge between the bowl vent valve and the air horn on models though 1979; or a 0.080 in. (2.0mm) gauge on 1980–84 models.
3. If adjustment is necessary, bend the short tang on the vent operating lever until the proper clearance is reached.

Float

♦ See Figures 14, 15 and 16

This procedure is performed with the carburetor on the engine.
1. Remove the clips, then disengage the accelerator pump operating rod from the throttle lever and the pump rocker arm.

2. Remove the fast idle cam retaining clip, then remove the link.
3. Remove the step-up piston cover plate and gasket from the air horn top.
4. Remove the metering rod lifter lockscrew, then lift the step-up piston and metering rod assembly straight up and out of the air horn.
5. Remove the air horn retaining screws and lift the air horn straight up and away from the main body.
6. Remove the float baffle.
7. Seat the float fulcrum pin by pressing on the fulcrum pin retainer. There should be enough fuel in the bowl to raise the float so that the lip bears firmly against the needle. Additional fuel may be entered by slightly depressing the float. If there is not enough pressure in the line to enter more fuel, you'll have to add some from a clean container.

※※ CAUTION

Never smoke when working around gasoline! Avoid all sources of sparks or ignition. Gasoline vapors are EXTREMELY volatile!

8. With the fuel level holding the tip of the float against the inlet needle, check the gap between the gasket surface of the bowl (gasket removed) and the center crown of the floats. On models through 1972, the gap should be 15/64 in. (5.9mm) on models with a manual choke; 5/16 in. (7.9mm) on models with an automatic choke. On later models, the gap should be 1/4 in. (6.3mm).
9. If adjustment is necessary, hold the float on the bottom of the bowl and bend the float tip toward or away from the needle as required. Recheck the gap.

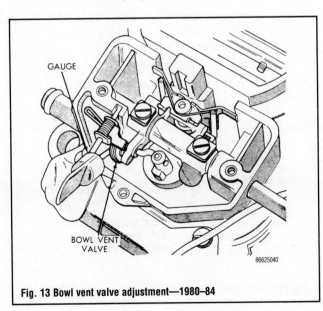

Fig. 13 Bowl vent valve adjustment—1980–84

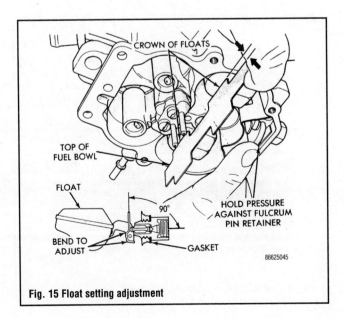

Fig. 15 Float setting adjustment

5-8 FUEL SYSTEM

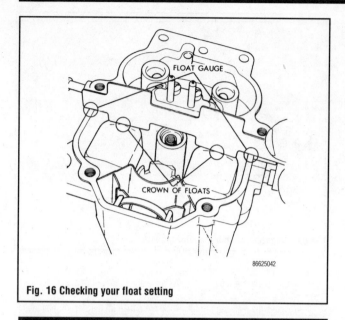

Fig. 16 Checking your float setting

⁂ WARNING

Do not allow the float lip to depress the needle, as this will give you a false reading.

When correctly set, the float lip should be perpendicular to the needle within 10°.
10. Assemble the air horn.
11. Check the idle speed.

Fast Idle Speed

♦ See Figure 17

1. Run the engine until it reaches normal operating temperature.
2. With the engine off and the transmission in Park or Neutral, open the throttle slightly.
3. On models without the Clean Air Package, close the choke plate about 20°, then allow the throttle plates to close. The fast idle screw should now rest on the slowest speed step of the cam. On models with the Clean Air Package, close the choke plate until the fast idle screw can be positioned on the second highest speed step of the cam.
4. Start the engine.
5. On trucks through 1972, turn the fast idle speed screw in or out until

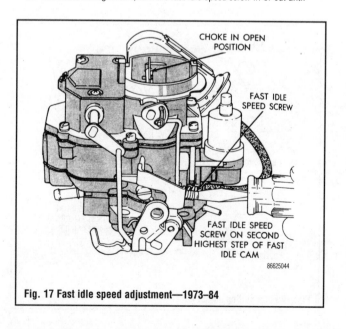

Fig. 17 Fast idle speed adjustment—1973–84

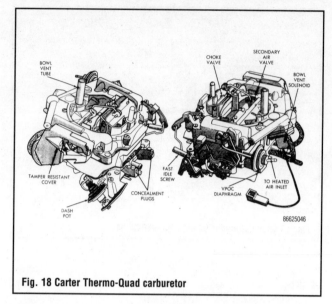

Fig. 18 Carter Thermo-Quad carburetor

1,700 rpm is obtained for carburetor model 6536S; 1,500 rpm for all other models. On 1973–84 models, check your underhood sticker for the proper speed.
6. Stopping the engine between adjustments is not necessary. However, be sure the fast idle speed screw is positioned on the cam after each speed adjustment.

ADJUSTMENTS FOR CARTER THERMO–QUAD

➥ Most of these adjustments require that measurements be gauged in thousandths of an inch. Drill bits are ideal for this purpose.

♦ See Figure 18

Float Setting

♦ See Figure 19

1. Remove the bowl cover and invert it.
2. Place the gasket on the cover and, with the floats resting on the needle, check the distance from the gasket surface to the float bottom (currently the top side) on each float. The distance should be $^{29}/_{32}$ in. plus or minus$FR1/32 in.
3. If not, bend the float lever arm.

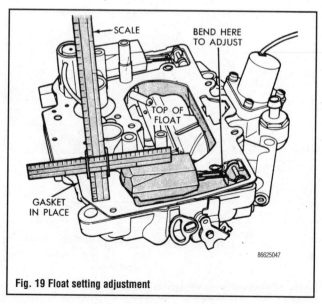

Fig. 19 Float setting adjustment

FUEL SYSTEM 5-9

✱✱ WARNING

Never allow the float lever to depress the needle when measuring or adjusting!

Secondary Throttle Linkage

▶ See Figure 20

1. Remove the carburetor.

➡ Position the carburetor on clean rags to catch any remaining fuel.

2. Hold the fast idle lever in the curb idle position and invert the carburetor.
3. Slowly open the primary throttle plates to the wide-open position. The primary and secondary levers should both contact the stops at the same time.
4. If an adjustment is necessary, bend the secondary throttle operating rod at the angle.

Secondary Air Valve Opening

▶ See Figure 21

1. With the air valve in the wide-open position, the gap between the air valve (at the short side) and the air horn should be set to the specifications for

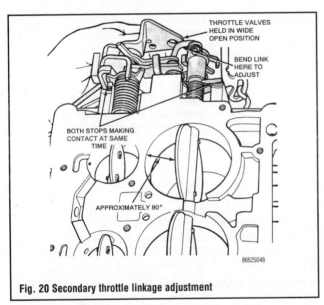

Fig. 20 Secondary throttle linkage adjustment

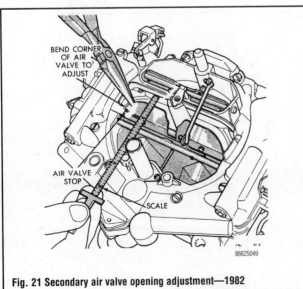

Fig. 21 Secondary air valve opening adjustment—1982

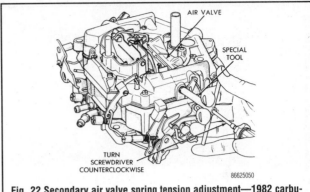

Fig. 22 Secondary air valve spring tension adjustment—1982 carburetor

your carburetor. Please refer to the carburetor specifications charts found later in this section.

2. If not, the corner of the air valve is notched for adjustment. Bend the corner with a needle–nosed pliers for proper adjustment.

Secondary Air Valve Spring Tension

▶ See Figure 22

✱✱ WARNING

Hold the air valve adjustment plug with a screwdriver while loosening the lock plug to avoid the spring's snapping out of position. If the spring snaps out, you'll have to disassemble the carburetor!

1. Loosen the air valve lock plug and allow the valve to go to the wide-open position.
2. Using a long screwdriver and tool C–4152 on the plug, turn the plug counterclockwise until the air valve contacts its stop lightly, then rotate the plug any additional turns as necessary for specification. Please refer to the carburetor specifications charts found later in this section.
3. Hold the adjustment plug securely and tighten the lock plug with tool C–4152, make sure the adjustment does not move.
4. Check the air valve for freedom of movement.

Accelerator Pump Stroke

FIRST STAGE

▶ See Figures 23 and 24

1. Be sure that the throttle connector rod is in the center hole of the pump arm, or the inner hole on 2–hole arms.
2. Measure the height of the accelerator pump plunger link at curb idle. On trucks with a solenoid idle stop, the ignition switch should be in the **ON** position.

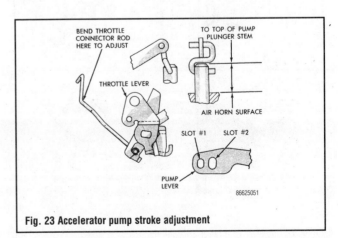

Fig. 23 Accelerator pump stroke adjustment

5-10 FUEL SYSTEM

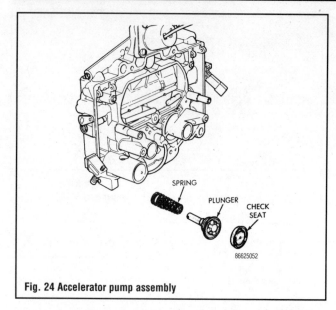

Fig. 24 Accelerator pump assembly

3. The height should be adjusted to specifications. If not, bend the throttle connector rod at the second angle from the top.

SECOND STAGE

1. Open the choke, then open the throttle until the secondary lockout latch is just applied. Downward travel of the plunger stops at this point.
2. Measure the height of the pump plunger link. The height should be 5/16 in. (7.9mm). If not, bend the tang at the bottom of the throttle lever.

Choke Control Lever

▶ See Figure 25

1. Remove the carburetor.

➡ Use rags to catch any remaining fuel.

2. Place the carburetor on a clean, flat surface. The surface must be flush with the bottom of the flange and extend out under the choke control lever.
3. Close the choke by pushing the lever with the throttle partially open.
4. Measure the vertical distance from the top of the rod hole in the control lever, down to the flat surface on which the carburetor is resting. The distance should be 3 3/8 in. (85mm).
5. If not, bend the link connecting the two choke shafts at the upper angle.

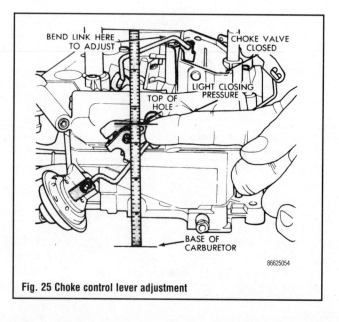

Fig. 25 Choke control lever adjustment

➡ If you change this adjustment, you'll have to reset the vacuum kick, fast idle cam and choke unloader adjustments.

Choke Diaphragm Connector Rod

▶ See Figure 26

1. Fully depress the diaphragm stem, either using a vacuum source, or by hand.
2. With light opening pressure on the air valve connector rod, check the gap between the air valve and its stop. The gap should be 0.040 in. (1.0mm).
3. If not, bend the diaphragm control rod at its angle.

➡ If you change this setting, you'll have to adjust the vacuum kick.

Choke Vacuum Kick

▶ See Figure 27

1. Remove the carburetor.

➡ Position the carburetor on clean rags to catch any remaining fuel.

2. Using a vacuum source, or by hand, fully depress the vacuum diaphragm plunger.
3. Using a 0.16 in. (4.mm) gauge for 49 states and Canada, or 0.10 in. (2.5mm) for California, measure between the lower edge of the choke plate and the air horn wall at a point close to the outboard end.

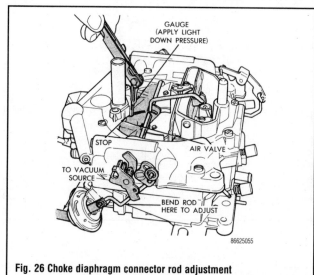

Fig. 26 Choke diaphragm connector rod adjustment

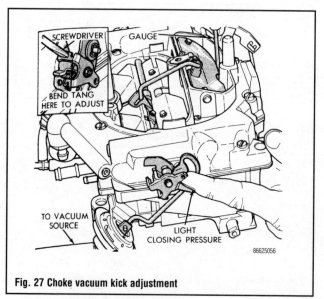

Fig. 27 Choke vacuum kick adjustment

FUEL SYSTEM 5-11

✽✽ CAUTION

Do not change position of choke with the gauge during measurement.

4. Adjust by twisting a screwdriver into the tang slot. **DO not adjust diaphragm rod.**
5. Check for free movement between open and adjust positions. Correct any misalignment or interference and repeat the adjustment if needed.

Fast Idle Cam Position

▶ See Figure 28

1. Position the fast idle speed adjusting screw so that it contacts the second highest step of the cam. Move the choke valve toward the closed position using light pressure on the choke linkage.
2. Measure by inserting a 0.310 in. (7.8mm) gauge between the bottom of the choke valve and air horn wall at the throttle lever side.
3. If adjustment is necessary, bend the fast idle link at the angle until the correct valve opening has been obtained.

➡ When this adjustment is made, the choke unloader adjustment and secondary throttle lockout adjustment must be reset.

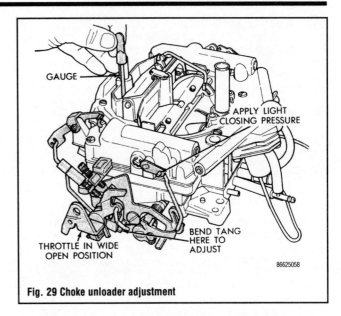

Fig. 29 Choke unloader adjustment

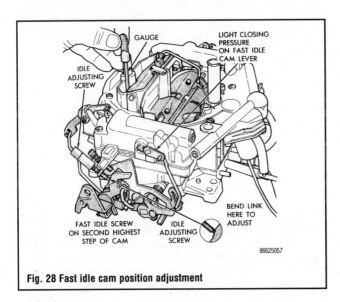

Fig. 28 Fast idle cam position adjustment

Choke Unloader

▶ See Figure 29

1. Hold the throttle valves in the wide-open position.
2. Press lightly against the choke lever while measuring by inserting the specified gauge between the bottom of the choke valve and air horn wall (at the throttle lever side).
3. If adjustment is necessary, bend the unloader tang on the throttle lever until the correct opening is obtained.

Secondary Throttle Lockout

▶ See Figure 30

1. Move the fast idle control lever to the open choke position.
2. Measure the clearance between the lockout lever and the stop. The gap should be 0.06–0.09 in. (1.5–2.2mm).
3. If not, bend the tang on the fast idle control lever.

Fast Idle Speed

▶ See Figure 31

1. Run the engine to normal operating temperature.
2. With the engine off and the transmission in Park or Neutral, open the throttle slightly. Remove the air cleaner and disconnect the vacuum lines to the

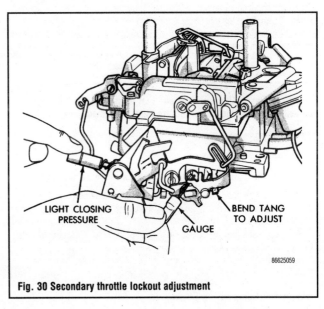

Fig. 30 Secondary throttle lockout adjustment

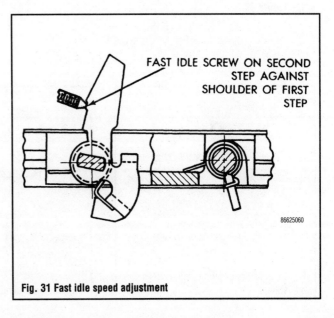

Fig. 31 Fast idle speed adjustment

5-12 FUEL SYSTEM

heated air control and the Orifice Spark Advance Control (OSAC) valve. If not equipped with an OSAC valve, disconnect the distributor vacuum advance line. Disconnect the EGR hose. Cap all carburetor vacuum fittings.

3. Start the engine. Adjust the idle speed and mixture, if necessary.
4. Close the throttle plates until the fast idle screw is positioned on the second highest speed step of the cam.
5. Turn the fast idle speed screw in or out to obtain the correct speed, adjustment procedures are located on the emissions label.
6. Stopping the engine between adjustments is not necessary. However, be sure the fast idle speed screw is positioned on the cam after each speed adjustment.

Vacuum Throttle Positioner

1. Run the engine to normal operating temperature.
2. With the transmission in Neutral and the brakes applied, accelerate the engine to above 2,000 rpm. Check that the vacuum positioner unit operates and can withstand a hand-applied load in the operating position. If not, replace the positioner.
3. Accelerate the engine, by hand–moving the linkage, to 2,500 rpm.
4. Loosen the positioner adjustment locknut, then rotate the positioner assembly until it just contacts the throttle lever.
5. Release the throttle lever and slowly adjust the positioner to decrease the engine speed until a sudden drop in engine speed occurs, above 1,000 rpm. At this point, continue turning the positioner, in the decreasing direction, an additional ¼ turn. Hold the positioner and tighten the locknut.
6. Accelerate the engine, by hand, to 2,500 rpm and release the throttle. The engine should return to normal idle.

ADJUSTMENTS FOR HOLLEY 1945

➡ **Most of these adjustments require that measurements be gauged in thousandths of an inch. Drill bits are ideal for this purpose.**

Float Setting

1. Remove the carburetor.

➡ **Position the carburetor on clean rags to catch any remaining fuel.**

2. Remove the float bowl cover. Drain all fuel from the bowl.
3. Place the gasket on the float bowl, then invert the bowl. Hold the retaining spring in place.
4. Place a straightedge across the surface of the bowl. It should just touch the floats. A tolerance of $\frac{1}{32}$ in. (0.8mm) is allowable.
5. If adjustment is necessary, bend the float tang to obtain the correct adjustment.

Accelerator Pump Piston Stroke

▶ See Figure 32

1. Place the throttle linkage in the curb idle position
2. Place the pump operating link in the middle slot on carburetor model R–7847–A, or in the left slot on all others.

3. With a T-scale, measure the length of the pump operating link. On models through 1972, the link should be $2\frac{7}{32}$ in. (2.21mm) on R–7847–A models; $2\frac{21}{64}$ in. (2.32mm) on all other models. On 1973–79 models, the link should be $2\frac{7}{32}$ in. (2.21mm) for trucks with manual transmission, or $2\frac{11}{32}$ in. (2.34mm) for trucks with automatic transmission. On 1980 and later trucks, the link should be $1\frac{5}{8}$ in. (1.62mm).
4. To adjust, bend the link at the angle.

Fast Idle Cam Position

1. Position the fast idle speed adjusting screw so that it contacts the second highest step of the cam. Move the choke valve toward the closed position using light pressure on the choke linkage.
2. Insert a 0.08 in. (2mm) gauge between the upper edge of the choke plate and the wall of the air horn.
3. If adjustment is necessary, bend the fast idle link at the angle until the gauge fits between the choke plate and the wall of the air horn.

Choke Unloader

▶ See Figure 33

1. Hold the throttle valve in the wide-open position.
2. With a light closing pressure against the choke lever, a slight drag should be felt as the gauge is being withdrawn.
3. Measure by inserting a 0.250 in. (6.3mm) gauge between the top of the choke valve and air horn wall at the throttle lever side.
4. Adjust by bending the tang on the throttle lever.

Choke Vacuum Kick

▶ See Figure 34

1. If the adjustment is to be made on the engine (with the engine running at curb idle), back off the fast idle screw until the choke can be closed to the kick position. Note the number of screw turns required so that the fast idle can be returned to the original adjustment.
2. If the adjustment is to be made off the engine, open the throttle valve and move the choke to its closed position. Release the throttle first and then release the choke. Disconnect the vacuum hose from the carburetor body and apply a vacuum of at least 15 in. Hg (51 kPa).
3. On models through 1972, insert a 0.11 in. (2.7mm) gauge between the choke valve and the wall of the air horn. On 1973–77 models, use a 0.14 in. (3.5mm) gauge for manual transmission trucks or 0.09 in. (2.2mm) for automatic transmission trucks. On 1978–79 models, use a 0.10 in. (2.5mm) gauge bit. On 1980 and later models, use a 0.13 in. (3.3mm) gauge bit.
4. Apply sufficient closing pressure to the choke lever to provide a minimum valve opening without distorting the diaphragm link (which connects the choke lever to the vacuum diaphragm). Note that the cylindrical stem of the diaphragm will extend as its internal spring is compressed. This spring must be fully compressed for the proper measurement of the vacuum kick adjustment.
5. Remove the gauge bit. If a slight drag is not felt as the gauge or gauge is removed, an adjustment of the diaphragm link is necessary to obtain the proper clearance. Shorten or lengthen the diaphragm link by carefully closing or opening the U–bend in the link until the correct adjustment is obtained.

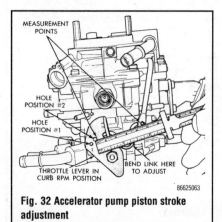

Fig. 32 Accelerator pump piston stroke adjustment

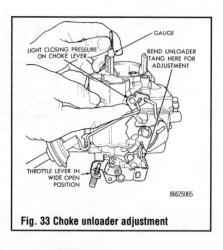

Fig. 33 Choke unloader adjustment

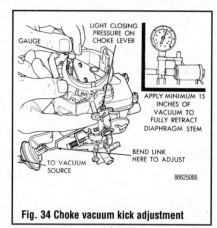

Fig. 34 Choke vacuum kick adjustment

WARNING

When adjusting the link, be careful not to bend or twist the diaphragm.

6. Connect the vacuum hose to the carburetor body (if it had been removed) and return the fast idle screw to its original location.
7. With no vacuum applied to the diaphragm, the choke valve should move freely between its open and closed positions. If it does not move freely, examine the linkage for misalignment or interference which may have been caused by the bending operation. If necessary, repeat the adjustment to provide the proper link operation.

Fast Idle Speed

1. Run the engine to normal operating temperature.
2. With the engine off and the transmission in Park or Neutral, open the throttle slightly. Remove the air cleaner and disconnect the vacuum lines to the heated air control and the Orifice Spark Advance Control (OSAC) valve. If not equipped with an OSAC valve, disconnect the distributor vacuum advance line. Disconnect the EGR hose. Cap all carburetor vacuum fittings.
3. Close the choke plate until the fast idle screw can be positioned on the second highest speed step of the cam.
4. Start the engine and determine the idle speed.
5. Turn the fast idle speed screw in or out until the speed shown on your truck's underhood sticker is obtained.
6. Stopping the engine between adjustments is not necessary. However, be sure the fast idle speed screw is positioned on the cam after each speed adjustment.

Dashpot

▶ See Figure 35

This procedure is for manual transmissions only.
1. Set the curb idle and mixture.
2. Start the engine and position the throttle lever so that the actuating tab on the lever is contacting the stem of the dashpot without depressing it.
3. Allow about 30 seconds for the engine speed to stabilize. The engine speed should be 2,500 rpm.
4. If not, loosen the locknut and turn the dashpot in or out as necessary.
5. Hold the dashpot and tighten the locknut.

ADJUSTMENTS FOR HOLLEY 2210

Fast Idle Cam Position

1. Position the fast idle speed adjusting screw so that it contacts the second highest step of the cam. Move the choke valve toward the closed position using light pressure on the choke linkage.

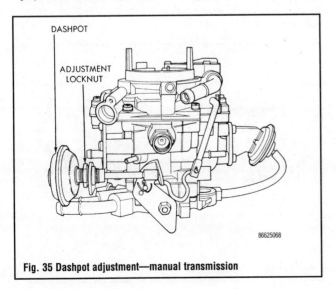

Fig. 35 Dashpot adjustment—manual transmission

2. Insert a 0.11 in. (2.7mm) gauge between the upper edge of the choke plate and the wall of the air horn.
3. If adjustment is necessary, bend the fast idle link at the angle until the specified gauge fits between the choke plate and the wall of the air horn.

Vacuum Kick

1. If the adjustment is to be made on the engine (with the engine running at curb idle), back off the fast idle screw until the choke can be closed to the kick position. Note the number of screw turns required so that the fast idle can be returned to the original adjustment.
2. If the adjustment is to be made off the engine, open the throttle valve and move the choke to its closed position. Release the throttle first and then release the choke. Disconnect the vacuum hose from the carburetor body and apply a vacuum of at least 15 in. Hg (51 kPa).
3. Insert a 0.15 in. (3.8mm) gauge between the choke valve and the wall of the air horn.
4. Apply sufficient closing pressure to the choke lever to provide a minimum valve opening without distorting the diaphragm link (which connects the choke lever to the vacuum diaphragm). Note that the cylindrical stem of the diaphragm will extend as its internal spring is compressed. This spring must be fully compressed for the proper measurement of the vacuum kick adjustment.
5. Remove the gauge bit. If a slight drag is not felt as the gauge or gauge is removed, an adjustment of the diaphragm link is necessary to obtain the proper clearance. Shorten or lengthen the diaphragm link by carefully closing or opening the U-bend in the link until the correct adjustment is obtained.

WARNING

When adjusting the link, be careful not to bend or twist the diaphragm.

6. Connect the vacuum hose to the carburetor body (if it had been removed) and return the fast idle screw to its original location.
7. With no vacuum applied to the diaphragm, the choke valve should move freely between its open and closed positions. If it does not move freely, examine the linkage for misalignment or interference which may have been caused by the bending operation. If necessary, repeat the adjustment to provide the proper link operation.

Choke Unloader

1. Hold the throttle valve in the wide-open position.
2. With light closing pressure against the choke lever, a slight drag should be felt as the gauge is being withdrawn.
3. Measure by inverting a 0.170 in. (4.3mm) gauge between the top of the choke valve and air horn wall at the throttle lever side.
4. If adjustment is necessary, bend the unloader tang on the throttle lever until the correct opening is obtained.

Accelerator Pump Stroke

1. Make sure that the pump connector rod is in the first slot (closest to the retaining nut) of the pump arm.
2. Measure the travel (drop) of the accelerator pump plunger between curb idle, or closed throttle, and wide-open throttle. Closed idle is obtained by backing off the curb idle screw and moving the fast idle cam to open chock position. To adjust pump travel, bend the pump operating rod in the proper area until the correct setting has been obtained.
3. Travel should be 0.26 in. (6.6mm) for curb idle through wide-open throttle, or 0.31 in. (7.8mm) for closed throttle through wide-open throttle.
4. If not, bend the pump operating rod at the angle.

Fast Idle Speed

1. Run the engine until it reaches normal operating temperature.
2. With the engine off and the transmission in Park or Neutral, open the throttle slightly. Remove the air cleaner and disconnect the vacuum lines to the heated air control and the Orifice Spark Advance Control (OSAC) valve. If not equipped with an OSAC valve, disconnect the distributor vacuum advance line. Disconnect the EGR hose. Cap all carburetor vacuum fittings.

5-14 FUEL SYSTEM

3. Close the choke plate until the fast idle screw can be positioned on the second highest speed step of the cam.
4. Start the engine.
5. Turn the fast idle speed screw in or out until the a speed of 1,700 rpm for manual transmissions or 1,800 rpm for automatic transmissions is reached.
6. Stopping the engine between adjustments is not necessary. However, be sure the fast idle speed screw is positioned on the cam after each speed adjustment.

Vacuum Throttle Positioner

1. Run the engine to normal operating temperature.
2. With the transmission in Neutral and the brakes applied, accelerate the engine to above 2,000 rpm. Check that the vacuum positioner unit operates and can withstand a hand–applied load in the operating position. If not, replace the positioner.
3. Accelerate the engine, by hand–moving the linkage, to 2,500 rpm.
4. Loosen the positioner adjustment locknut, then rotate the positioner assembly until it just contacts the throttle lever.
5. Release the throttle lever and slowly adjust the positioner to decrease the engine speed until a sudden drop in engine speed occurs, above 1,000 rpm. At this point, continue turning the positioner, in the decreasing direction, an additional ¼ turn. Hold the positioner and tighten the locknut.
6. Accelerate the engine, by hand, to 2,500 rpm and release the throttle. The engine should return to normal idle.

Float Setting

1. Invert the air horn so that the weight of the float alone is forcing the needle against the seat.
2. Measure the clearance between the top of the float and the float stop. The clearance should be 0.08 in. (2mm).
3. If an adjustment is necessary, bend the flat tab toward or away from the needle using a narrow blade prytool.
4. Check the float drop by holding the air horn in an upright position. The bottom edge of the float should be even with and parallel to the underside surface of the air horn. If necessary, bend the tang on the float arm to make an adjustment.

ADJUSTMENTS FOR HOLLEY 2300G

Fast Idle Cam

1. Adjust the curb idle and mixture.
2. Place the choke in the wide-open position.
3. Adjust the clearance between the fast idle cam and the screw to 0.035 in. (0.8mm).

Fuel Level

1. Place a shop towel under the sight plug to catch any spilled fuel.
2. Start the engine.
3. Remove the sight plug from the fuel bowl.
4. Loosen the lockscrew, then turn the adjusting nut until the fuel just seeps from the sight hole.

➥The truck should be on a level floor.

5. Tighten the lockscrew while holding the adjusting nut.
6. Install the sight plug.

Accelerator Pump Lever Clearance

1. Hold the throttle plates wide-open while holding the pump lever down. At this point it should be just possible to insert a 0.015 in. (3.8mm) gauge between the adjusting nut and the lever.
2. If not, turn the pump override screw until the correct clearance has been reached.

➥There should be no free movement of the pump lever when the throttle is at curb idle.

Loading The Positive Throttle Return Spring

✱✱✱ CAUTION

Whenever the throttle return spring is disconnected at either end, the throttle lever at the carburetor will snap to the closed position with considerable force. This could cause personal injury if your hands are in the way!

To prevent personal injury, perform the following in the order given, and keep your hands clear of the throttle linkage when disconnecting or connecting the return spring.

➥If the throttle return spring has been disconnected or removed, the throttle linkage will be in the "unloaded" position. The truck can be driven this way, however an increased throttle effort will be noted.

To load the linkage:
1. With the engine off, have an assistant fully depress the accelerator pedal. This will rotate the throttle assembly to the wide-open position.
2. Connect the return spring between the trip lever and the anchor bracket. Make sure that the tab is engaged in the notch.
3. Move your hands away and have your assistant let up on the pedal **slowly**.
4. The linkage is now loaded and normal pedal should be felt.

ADJUSTMENTS FOR HOLLEY 2245

▶ See Figure 36

Fast Idle Cam Position

1. Position the fast idle speed adjusting screw so that it contacts the second highest step of the cam. Move the choke valve toward the closed position using light pressure on the choke linkage.
2. Insert a 0.110 in. (2.7mm) gauge between the top of the choke valve and wall of the air horn.
3. If a slight drag is not felt, it will be necessary to make an adjustment.
4. If adjustment is necessary, bend the fast idle link at the angle until the specified gauge fits between the choke plate and the wall of the air horn.

Vacuum Kick

▶ See Figure 37

1. If the adjustment is to be made on the engine (with the engine running at curb idle), back off the fast idle screw until the choke can be closed to the kick position. Note the number of screw turns required so that the fast idle can be returned to the original adjustment.
2. If the adjustment is to be made off the engine, open the throttle valve and move the choke to its closed position. Release the throttle first and then release the choke. Disconnect the vacuum hose from the carburetor body and apply a vacuum of at least 15 in. Hg (51 kPa)

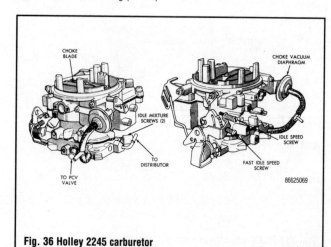

Fig. 36 Holley 2245 carburetor

FUEL SYSTEM 5-15

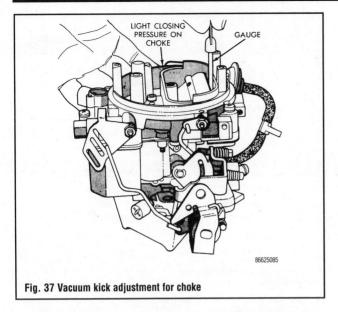
Fig. 37 Vacuum kick adjustment for choke

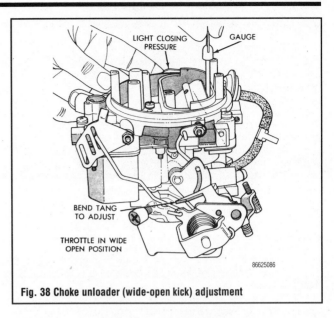
Fig. 38 Choke unloader (wide-open kick) adjustment

3. For models through 1977, insert a 0.15 in. (3.8mm) gauge between the choke valve and the wall of the air horn. On 1978 and later models, use a 0.11 in. (2.7mm) gauge.

4. Apply sufficient closing pressure to the choke lever to provide a minimum valve opening without distorting the diaphragm link (which connects the choke lever to the vacuum diaphragm). Note that the cylindrical stem of the diaphragm will extend as its internal spring is compressed. This spring must be fully compressed for the proper measurement of the vacuum kick adjustment.

5. Remove the gauge. If a slight drag is not felt as the gauge is removed, an adjustment of the diaphragm link is necessary to obtain the proper clearance. Shorten or lengthen the diaphragm link by carefully closing or opening the U-bend in the link until the correct adjustment is obtained.

✲✲ WARNING

When adjusting the link, be careful not to bend or twist the diaphragm.

6. Connect the vacuum hose to the carburetor body (if it had been removed) and return the fast idle screw to its original location.

7. With no vacuum applied to the diaphragm, the choke valve should move freely between its open and closed positions. If it does not move freely, examine the linkage for misalignment or interference which may have been caused by the bending operation. If necessary, repeat the adjustment to provide the proper link operation.

8. Reinstall vacuum hoses on the correct carburetor fittings.

Choke Unloader

♦ See Figure 38

1. Hold the throttle valve in the wide-open position.
2. Insert a 0.17 in. (4.3mm) gauge between the upper edge of the choke valve and the wall of the air horn.
3. While pressing lightly against the choke lever, a slight drag should be felt as the gauge is being withdrawn.
4. If adjustment is necessary, bend the unloader tang on the throttle lever until the correct opening is obtained.

Accelerator Pump Stroke

1. Make sure that the pump connector rod is in the first slot (closest to the retaining nut) of the pump arm.
2. Measure the travel (drop) of the accelerator pump plunger between curb idle, or closed throttle, and wide-open throttle. Closed idle is obtained by backing off the curb idle screw and moving the fast idle cam to open chock position. To adjust pump travel, bend the pump operating rod in the proper area until the correct setting has been obtained.

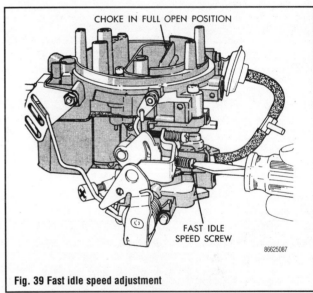
Fig. 39 Fast idle speed adjustment

3. Travel should be 0.26 in. (6.6mm) for curb idle through wide-open throttle, or 0.31 in. (7.8mm) for closed throttle through wide-open throttle.
4. If not, bend the pump operating rod at the angle.

Fast Idle Speed

♦ See Figure 39

1. Run the engine until it reaches normal operating temperature.
2. With the engine off and the transmission in Park or Neutral, open the throttle slightly. Remove the air cleaner and disconnect the vacuum lines to the heated air control and the Orifice Spark Advance Control (OSAC) valve. If not equipped with an OSAC valve, disconnect the distributor vacuum advance line. Disconnect the EGR hose. Cap all carburetor vacuum fittings.
3. Close the choke plate until the fast idle screw can be positioned on the second highest speed step of the cam.
4. Start the engine.
5. Turn the fast idle speed screw in or out until the a speed of 1,700 rpm for manual transmissions or 1,800 rpm for automatic transmissions is reached on models through 1977; 1,600 rpm on 1978 and later models.
6. Stopping the engine between adjustments is not necessary. However, be sure the fast idle speed screw is positioned on the cam after each speed adjustment.

FUEL SYSTEM

Vacuum Throttle Positioner

1. Run the engine to normal operating temperature.
2. With the transmission in Neutral and the brakes applied, accelerate the engine to above 2,000 rpm. Check that the vacuum positioner unit operates and can withstand a hand-applied load in the operating position. If not, replace the positioner.
3. Accelerate the engine, by hand-moving the linkage, to 2,500 rpm.
4. Loosen the positioner adjustment locknut, then rotate the positioner assembly until it just contacts the throttle lever.
5. Release the throttle lever and slowly adjust the positioner to decrease the engine speed until a sudden drop in engine speed occurs, above 1,000 rpm. At this point, continue turning the positioner, in the decreasing direction, an additional ¼ turn. Hold the positioner and tighten the locknut.
6. Accelerate the engine, by hand, to 2,500 rpm, then release the throttle. The engine should return to normal idle.

Float Setting

1. Remove the air horn.
2. Invert the air horn so that the weight of the float alone is forcing the needle against the seat.
3. Measure the clearance between the top of the float and the float stop. The clearance should be 0.08 in. (2mm) on models through 1977; 0.20 in. (5mm) on 1978 and later models.
4. If an adjustment is necessary, bend the flat tab toward or away from the needle using a narrow blade prytool.
5. Check the float drop by holding the air horn in an upright position. The bottom edge of the float should be even with and parallel to the underside surface of the air horn. If necessary, bend the tang on the float arm to make an adjustment.

Float Drop

1978 AND LATER

1. Remove the air horn.
2. Allow the float to hang. The bottom of the float should be parallel with the air horn gasket surface.
3. Bend the tang on the float arm to correct the float drop.

ADJUSTMENTS FOR HOLLEY 2280

Fast Idle Cam Position

♦ See Figure 40

1. Position the fast idle speed adjusting screw so that it contacts the second highest step of the cam. Move the choke valve toward the closed position using light pressure on the choke linkage.
2. Insert a 0.07 in. (1.7mm) gauge between the upper edge of the choke plate and the wall of the air horn. On carburetor No. 40172-A, use a 0.052 in. (1.3mm) gauge.
3. If adjustment is necessary, bend the fast idle link at the angle until the specified gauge fits between the choke plate and the wall of the air horn.

Vacuum Kick

♦ See Figure 41

1. If the adjustment is to be made on the engine (with the engine running at curb idle), back off the fast idle screw until the choke can be closed to the kick position. Note the number of screw turns required so that the fast idle can be returned to the original adjustment.
2. If the adjustment is to be made off the engine, open the throttle valve and move the choke to its closed position. Release the throttle first and then release the choke. Disconnect the vacuum hose from the carburetor body and apply a vacuum of at least 15 in. Hg. (51 kPa).
3. For models R-8999A and R-9000A, insert a 0.13 in. (3.3mm) gauge between the choke valve and the wall of the air horn. On all other models, use a 0.15 in. gauge.
4. Apply sufficient closing pressure to the choke lever to provide a minimum valve opening without distorting the diaphragm link (which connects the choke lever to the vacuum diaphragm). Note that the cylindrical stem of the

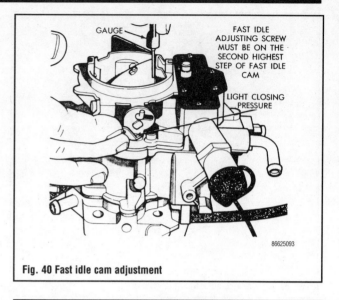

Fig. 40 Fast idle cam adjustment

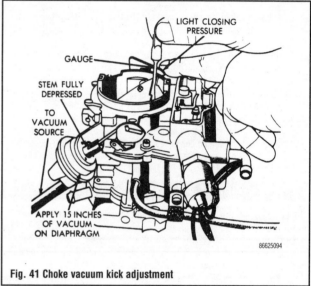

Fig. 41 Choke vacuum kick adjustment

diaphragm will extend as its internal spring is compressed. This spring must be fully compressed for the proper measurement of the vacuum kick adjustment.

5. Remove the gauge. If a slight drag is not felt as the gauge is removed, an adjustment of the diaphragm link is necessary to obtain the proper clearance. Shorten or lengthen the diaphragm link by carefully closing or opening the U-bend in the link until the correct adjustment is obtained.

✱✱ WARNING

When adjusting the link, be careful not to bend or twist the diaphragm.

6. Connect the vacuum hose to the carburetor body (if it had been removed) and return the fast idle screw to its original location.
7. With no vacuum applied to the diaphragm, the choke valve should move freely between its open and closed positions. If it does not move freely, examine the linkage for misalignment or interference which may have been caused by the bending operation. If necessary, repeat the adjustment to provide the proper link operation.

Choke Unloader

♦ See Figure 42

1. Hold the throttle valve in the wide-open position.
2. On 1980-81 trucks, insert a 0.31 in. (7.8mm) gauge between the upper

FUEL SYSTEM   5-17

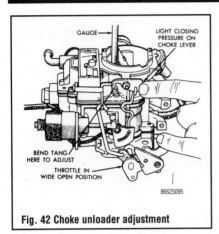

Fig. 42 Choke unloader adjustment

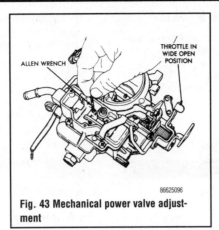

Fig. 43 Mechanical power valve adjustment

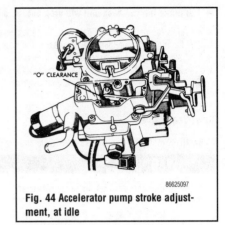

Fig. 44 Accelerator pump stroke adjustment, at idle

edge of the choke valve and the wall of the air horn. On 1982–84 models, use a 0.20 in. (5mm) gauge. On 1985–87 models, the gauge is 0.15 in. (3.8mm) for all except carburetor No. 40172–A; which is 0.20 in. (5mm).

3. While pressing lightly against the choke lever, a slight drag should be felt as the gauge is being withdrawn.

4. If adjustment is necessary, bend the unloader tang on the throttle lever until the correct opening is obtained.

Mechanical Power Valve

♦ See Figure 43

1. Remove the bowl vent cover plate, vent valve lever spring and retainer. Remove the vent valve lever and pivot pin.
2. Hold the throttle in the wide-open position.
3. Insert a 5/64 in. (1.9mm) Allen wrench in the power valve adjustment screw.
4. Push the screw down, then release it to determine if any clearance exists. Turn the screw clockwise until clearance is zero.
5. Turn the screw 1 turn counterclockwise.
6. Install the bowl vent gasket and cover plate.

Accelerator Pump Stroke

♦ See Figure 44

1. Remove the bowl vent cover plate and vent valve lever spring. Be careful not to dislodge or lose the vent valve retainer.
2. Make sure that the pump connector rod is in the inner slot of the pump arm.
3. Position the throttle at curb idle; the choke must be open and the fast idle cam must be engaged.
4. Place a straightedge on the bowl vent cover surface of the air horn over the accelerator pump connector rod in the center of the bowl.
5. Bend the accelerator pump connector rod until the lever surface is flush with the air horn surface on models through 1985. On 1986–87 models, 0.210 in. (5.3mm) gap.
6. Install the vent valve lever spring and bowl vent cover plate.

➡ If this adjustment is changed, both the bowl vent and the mechanical power valve adjustment must be reset.

Fast Idle Speed

♦ See Figure 45

1. Run the engine to normal operating temperature.
2. Remove the air cleaner, then disconnect and plug the EGR vacuum line and distributor advance vacuum line. If the engine has Electronic Spark Control, remove only the top of the air cleaner housing and lift the air cleaner to access the carburetor. Do not disconnect the vacuum line to the spark control computer. Instead, use a jumper wire to ground the idle stop switch.
3. Set the parking brake and place the transmission in Neutral. With the engine off, open the throttle and close the choke, then close the throttle.
4. Rotate the fast idle cam until the fast idle screw can be positioned on the second highest speed step of the cam.

5. Start the engine. Let the engine speed stabilize. If the engine speed continues to rise, the idle switch has not been properly grounded.
6. Turn the fast idle speed screw in or out until the engine speed listed on your truck's underhood sticker is reached.
7. Reposition the screw on the cam after each adjustment in order to allow the idle to properly stabilize.
8. Remove the jumper wire, reconnect the vacuum hoses and install the air cleaner.

Float Setting

♦ See Figure 46

1. Remove the carburetor.

➡ Position the carburetor on clean rags to catch any remaining fuel.

2. Remove the air horn.
3. Invert the carburetor body.

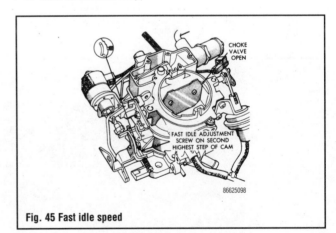

Fig. 45 Fast idle speed

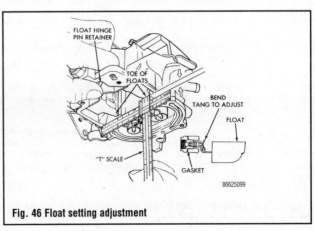

Fig. 46 Float setting adjustment

5-18 FUEL SYSTEM

➡ **The pump intake check ball will drop out. Be sure to catch it!**

4. Allow the weight of the floats to rest on the needle valve. Hold your finger against the hinge pin retainer to fully seat it in the float pin cradle.
5. Using a T-scale, measure the gap between the surface of the float bowl and the toe of each float. The gap should be $FR1/4–5/16 in. (6.35–7.94mm).
6. If adjustment is necessary, bend the float tang. Bend either float arm to equalize the individual float positions.

Bowl Vent Valve

1. Remove the bowl vent valve cover plate and the vent lever spring.

※ WARNING

Don't dislodge the vent valve lever retainer/pivot pin.

2. With the throttle in the curb idle position (choke open and the fast idle cam disengaged), press down firmly on the vent valve lever where the spring seats. Simultaneously, press down on the vent valve tang until the vent valve is lightly seated.

➡ **If this adjustment is being performed with the carburetor off-engine, the carburetor must be on a raised flat surface so that the curb idle throttle plate position is not changed.**

3. While holding the lever and tang down, measure the gap between the contact surfaces of the vent valve lever and the vent valve tang. The gap should be 0.03 in. (0.7mm).
4. If not, adjust by bending the end of the vent valve lever.
5. Install the lever spring and cover.

➡ **If this adjustment is changed, the accelerator pump adjustment must be reset.**

ADJUSTMENTS FOR HOLLEY 4150G

Fast Idle

1. Set the curb idle speed to the specifications listed on the emissions label.
2. Place the choke plate in the fully open position.
3. Place the throttle plates in the curb idle position.
4. Adjust the fast idle stud to give a clearance of 0.035 in. (0.88mm) between the stud and the fast idle cam.

Fuel Level

1. Place a shop towel under the sight plug to catch any spilled fuel.
2. Start the engine.
3. Remove the sight plug from the fuel bowl.
4. Loosen the lockscrew, then turn the adjusting nut until the fuel just seeps from the sight hole.

➡ **The truck should be on a level floor.**

5. Tighten the lockscrew while holding the adjusting nut.
6. Install the sight plug and tighten securely.

Accelerator Pump Lever Clearance

1. Hold the throttle plates wide-open while holding the pump lever down. At this point it should be just possible to insert a 0.015 in. (0.38mm) gauge between the adjusting nut and the lever.
2. If not, turn the pump override screw until the correct clearance has been reached.

➡ **There should be no free movement of the pump lever when the throttle is at curb idle.**

ADJUSTMENTS FOR HOLLEY 6145

◆ See Figure 47

Fast Idle Cam

◆ See Figure 48

1. Position the fast idle speed adjusting screw so that it contacts the second highest step of the cam. Move the choke valve toward the closed position using light pressure on the choke linkage.
2. Insert a 0.07 in. (1.7mm) gauge between the upper edge of the choke plate and the wall of the air horn on trucks with automatic transmission; 0.06 in. (1.5mm) on trucks with manual transmission.

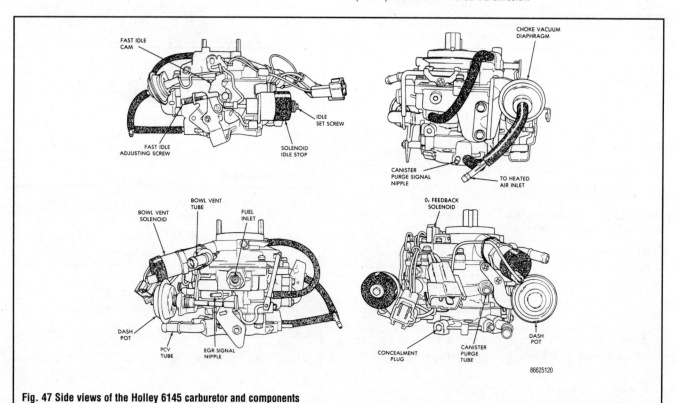

Fig. 47 Side views of the Holley 6145 carburetor and components

FUEL SYSTEM 5-19

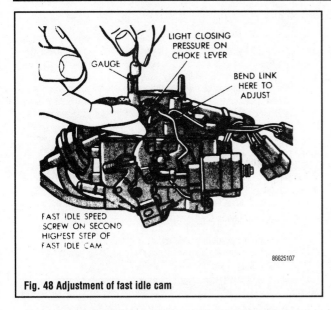

Fig. 48 Adjustment of fast idle cam

3. If adjustment is necessary, bend the fast idle link at the angle until the specified gauge fits between the choke plate and the wall of the air horn.

Vacuum Kick

◆ See Figure 49

1. If the adjustment is to be made on the engine (with the engine running at curb idle), back off the fast idle screw until the choke can be closed to the kick position. Note the number of screw turns required so that the fast idle can be returned to the original adjustment.
2. If the adjustment is to be made off the engine, open the throttle valve and move the choke to its closed position. Release the throttle first and then release the choke. Disconnect the vacuum hose from the carburetor body and apply a vacuum of at least 15 in. Hg (51 kPa).
3. Apply sufficient closing pressure to the choke lever to provide a minimum valve opening without distorting the diaphragm link (which connects the choke lever to the vacuum diaphragm). Note that the cylindrical stem of the diaphragm will extend as its internal spring is compressed. This spring must be fully compressed for the proper measurement of the vacuum kick adjustment.
4. Using a 5/64 in. (1.9mm) Allen wrench in the diaphragm adjuster, adjust the clearance so that a 0.15 in. (3.8mm) gauge can fit between the choke valve and the wall of the air horn.
5. Remove the gauge.

6. Connect the vacuum hose to the carburetor body (if it had been removed) and return the fast idle screw to its original location.
7. With no vacuum applied to the diaphragm, the choke valve should move freely between its open and closed positions. If it does not move freely, examine the linkage for misalignment or interference which may have been caused by the bending operation. If necessary, repeat the adjustment to provide the proper link operation.

Choke Unloader

1. Hold the throttle valve in the wide-open position.
2. Insert a 1/4 in. (6mm) gauge between the upper edge of the choke valve and the wall of the air horn.
3. While pressing lightly against the choke lever, a slight drag should be felt as the gauge is being withdrawn.
4. If adjustment is necessary, bend the unloader tang on the throttle lever until the correct opening is obtained.

Accelerator Pump Stroke

◆ See Figure 50

1. Place the throttle in the curb idle position with the accelerator pump operating link in the #2 (upper) hole in the throttle lever.
2. Measure the length of the operating link. The length should be 1.61 in. (40.8mm) on 1983–84 models; 1.75 in. (44.4mm) on 1985–87 models. If not, bend it at the U-bend.

Fast Idle Speed

1. Run the engine to normal operating temperature.
2. Remove the air cleaner, then disconnect and plug the EGR vacuum line. Disconnect the vacuum hose at the heated air temperature sensor. Plug the hose. Disconnect and plug the 3/16 in. (4.7mm) hose at the charcoal canister. Remove the PCV valve from the rocker cover and allow it to draw fresh air.
3. Disconnect and plug the vacuum advance hose at the distributor. Disconnect the engine harness lead at the oxygen sensor. Ground the harness lead. Allow the engine to run for at least 2 minutes after disconnecting the O_2 sensor.

➡ Don't put any stress on the oxygen sensor lead!

4. Open the throttle slightly and place the fast idle screw on the second highest speed step of the cam.
5. With the choke fully open, turn the fast idle speed screw in or out until the engine speed listed on your truck's underhood sticker is reached.
6. Reposition the screw on the cam after each adjustment in order to allow the idle to properly stabilize.
7. Remove the jumper wire, reconnect the vacuum hoses and install the air cleaner.

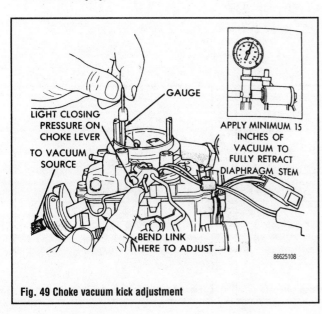

Fig. 49 Choke vacuum kick adjustment

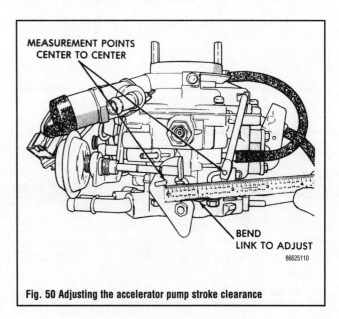

Fig. 50 Adjusting the accelerator pump stroke clearance

FUEL SYSTEM

Float Setting

♦ See Figure 51

1. Remove the carburetor.

➡ Position the carburetor on clean rags to catch any remaining fuel.

2. Remove the air horn.
3. Drain the float bowl of fuel.
4. Invert the carburetor body.

➡ The pump intake check ball will drop out. be sure to catch it!

5. Allow the weight of the floats to rest on the needle valve. Hold your finger against the hinge pin retainer to fully seat it in the float pin cradle.
6. Using a straightedge, the floats should just touch the straightedge at the point on the floats farthest from the fuel inlet.
7. If adjustment is necessary, bend the float tang. Bend either float arm to equalize the individual float positions.

Idle Stop Solenoid

♦ See Figure 52

1. Run the engine to normal operating temperature.
2. Disconnect and plug the EGR vacuum line. Connect a jumper wire between the carburetor switch and a good ground. Disconnect and plug the 3/16 in. (4.7mm) hose at the charcoal canister. The air cleaner must not be removed, but should be propped up to gain access to the carburetor. Remove the PCV valve from the rocker cover and allow it to draw fresh air.
3. Turn on the air conditioning and set the blower to **Low**.
4. Disconnect the compressor clutch wire.
5. On models without air conditioning, connect a jumper wire between the battery positive pole and the solenoid idle stop lead wire.
6. Open the throttle slightly and allow the plunger to extend.
7. Remove the adjusting screw and spring from the solenoid.
8. Insert a 1/8 in. (3mm) Allen wrench into the solenoid and adjust the engine speed to 850 rpm.
9. Turn off the air conditioning and reconnect all wires and hoses.

ADJUSTMENTS FOR HOLLEY 6280

Fast Idle Cam Position

♦ See Figure 53

1. Position the fast idle speed adjusting screw so that it contacts the second highest step of the cam. Move the choke valve toward the closed position using light pressure on the choke linkage.
2. Insert a 0.07 in. (1.7mm) gauge between the upper edge of the choke plate and the wall.
3. If adjustment is necessary, bend the fast idle link at the angle until the specified gauge fits between the choke plate and the wall of the air horn.

Vacuum Kick

1. If the adjustment is to be made on the engine (with the engine running at curb idle), back off the fast idle screw until the choke can be closed to the kick position. Note the number of screw turns required so that the fast idle can be returned to the original adjustment.
2. If the adjustment is to be made off the engine, open the throttle valve and move the choke to its closed position. Release the throttle first and then release the choke. Disconnect the vacuum hose from the carburetor body and apply a vacuum of at least 15 in. Hg (51 kPa).
3. Apply sufficient closing pressure to the choke lever to provide a minimum valve opening without distorting the diaphragm link (which connects the choke lever to the vacuum diaphragm). Note that the cylindrical stem of the diaphragm will extend as its internal spring is compressed. This spring must be fully compressed for the proper measurement of the vacuum kick adjustment.
4. Insert a 0.13 in. (3.3mm) gauge between the choke valve and the wall of the air horn.
5. Remove the gauge. If a slight drag is not felt as the gauge is removed, an adjustment of the diaphragm link is necessary to obtain the proper clearance. Shorten or lengthen the diaphragm link by carefully closing or opening the U–bend in the link until the correct adjustment is obtained.

✷✷ WARNING

When adjusting the link, be careful not to bend or twist the diaphragm.

6. Connect the vacuum hose to the carburetor body (if it had been removed) and return the fast idle screw to its original location.
7. With no vacuum applied to the diaphragm, the choke valve should move freely between its open and closed positions. If it does not move freely, examine the linkage for misalignment or interference which may have been caused by the bending operation. If necessary, repeat the adjustment to provide the proper link operation.

Choke Unloader

♦ See Figure 54

1. Hold the throttle valve in the wide-open position.
2. Insert a 0.25 in. (6.3mm) gauge between the upper edge of the choke valve and the wall of the air horn for carburetor model R–40132; or a 0.15 in. (3.8mm) gauge for all other carburetors.
3. While pressing lightly against the choke lever, a slight drag should be felt as the gauge is being withdrawn.
4. If adjustment is necessary, bend the unloader tang on the throttle lever until the correct opening is obtained.

Accelerator Pump Stroke

♦ See Figure 55

1. Remove the bowl vent cover plate and vent valve lever spring. Be careful not to dislodge or lose the vent valve retainer.
2. Make sure that the pump connector rod is in the inner slot of the pump arm.

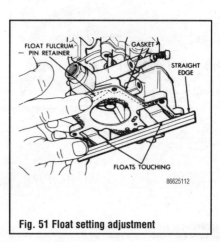

Fig. 51 Float setting adjustment

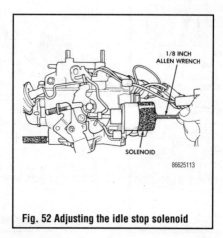

Fig. 52 Adjusting the idle stop solenoid

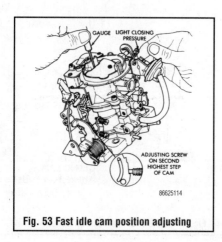

Fig. 53 Fast idle cam position adjusting

FUEL SYSTEM 5-21

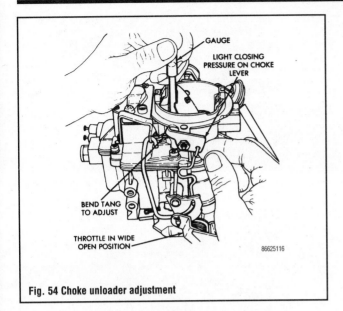

Fig. 54 Choke unloader adjustment

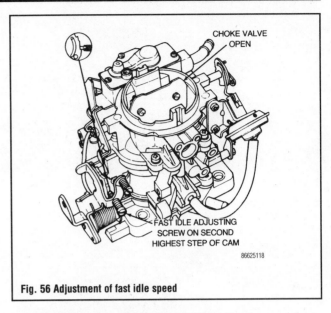

Fig. 56 Adjustment of fast idle speed

5. Start the engine. Let the engine speed stabilize.
6. Turn the fast idle speed screw in or out until the engine speed listed on the underhood sticker is reached.
7. Reposition the screw on the cam after each adjustment in order to allow the idle to properly stabilize.
8. Reconnect the vacuum hoses and install the air cleaner.

Float Setting

▶ See Figure 57

1. Remove the carburetor.

➡ Position the carburetor on clean rags to catch any remaining fuel.

2. Remove the air horn.
3. Drain the float bowl of fuel.
4. Invert the carburetor body.

➡ The pump intake check ball will drop out. Be sure to catch it!

5. Allow the weight of the floats to rest on the needle valve. Hold your finger against the hinge pin retainer to fully seat it in the float pin cradle.
6. Using a T-scale, measure the gap between the surface of the float bowl and the toe of each float. The gap should be 9/32 in. plus or minus 1/32 in.

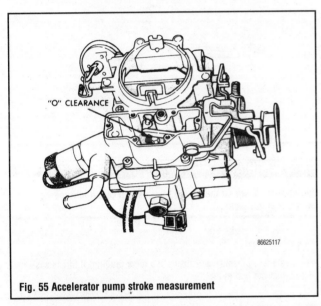

Fig. 55 Accelerator pump stroke measurement

3. Position the throttle at curb idle, you can obtain the idle speed from the emissions label located in the engine compartment.
4. Place a straightedge on the bowl vent cover surface of the air horn over the accelerator pump connector rod in the center of the bowl.
5. On 1985 models, bend the accelerator pump connector rod until the lever surface is flush with the air horn surface. On 1986–87 models, the lever surface should be 0.135 in. (3.4mm) above the casting.
6. Install the vent valve lever spring and bowl vent cover plate.

➡ If this adjustment is changed, both the bowl vent and the mechanical power valve adjustment must be reset.

Fast Idle Speed

▶ See Figure 56

1. Run the engine to normal operating temperature.
2. Disconnect and plug the EGR vacuum line and distributor advance vacuum line. Disconnect and plug the carburetor vacuum line at the heated air temperature sensor. Remove the air cleaner and plug the 3/16 in. (4.7mm) vacuum line at the charcoal canister. Remove the PCV valve from the rocker cover and allow it to draw fresh air.
3. Set the parking brake and place the transmission in Neutral.
4. With the engine off, open the throttle and place the fast idle adjusting screw on the second highest speed step of the cam.

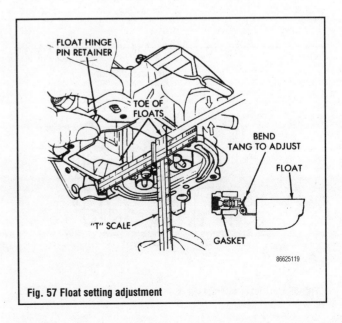

Fig. 57 Float setting adjustment

5-22 FUEL SYSTEM

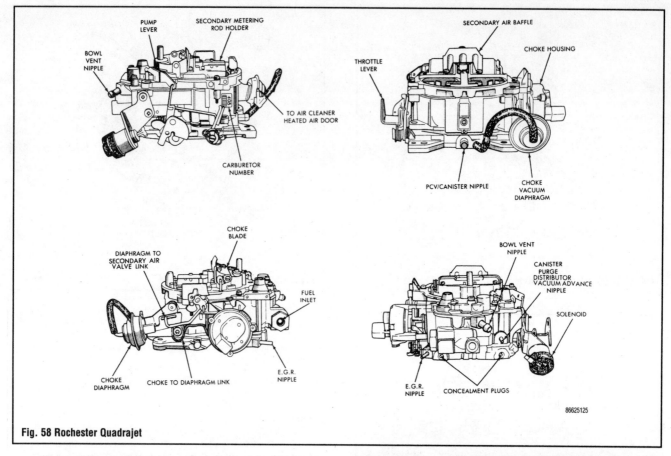

Fig. 58 Rochester Quadrajet

7. If adjustment is necessary, bend the float tang. Bend either float arm to equalize the individual float positions.

ADJUSTMENTS FOR ROCHESTER QUADRAJET

♦ See Figure 58

Float Level External Check

♦ See Figure 59

1. With the engine idling at normal operating temperature and the choke wide-open, insert float gauge C–4900 in the vent hole. Allow the gauge to float freely.

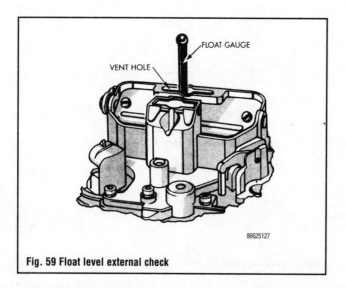

Fig. 59 Float level external check

✺✺ WARNING

Do not press down on the gauge, as this will result in flooding and/or float damage!

2. Look at the mark on the gauge that lines up with the top of the casting. The reading should be $FR13/32 in. plus or minus 1/16 in.

➡ Incorrect fuel pressure will result in a false reading. If this is suspected, test the fuel pump.

3. If not, remove the air horn and set the float as described under Float Setting, later in this section.

Float Setting

♦ See Figure 60

1. Remove the air horn, gasket, power piston, and the plastic float bowl insert.
2. Hold the float bowl retainer firmly in place.
3. Push the float down lightly against the needle.
4. Measure the float height from the top of the casting to the top of the float at a point 3/16 in. from the end of the float. The height should be 13/32 in. plus or minus 2/32 in.
5. If the float level is too high, hold the retainer in place and push down on the center of the float pontoon to get the correct setting.
6. If the float level is too low, bend the float upward to get the correct setting.
7. Recheck the float level.
8. Install the bowl insert, power piston and gasket, and air horn.

Air Valve Spring

♦ See Figure 61

1. Using a 3/32 in. (2.3mm) wrench, loosen the air valve spring lockscrew.

FUEL SYSTEM 5-23

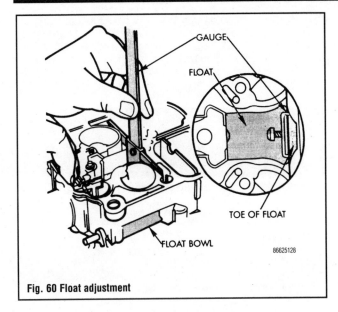

Fig. 60 Float adjustment

3. Push up on the choke coil lever to close the choke plate.
4. Insert a 0.12 in. (3mm) plug gauge in the hole just below the choke coil lever. The lower edge of the lever just contact the gauge.
5. If not, bend the choke rod at the upper angle.

Fast Idle Cam

♦ See Figure 63

1. Attach a rubber band to the green tang of the intermediate choke shaft.
2. Open the throttle to allow the choke valve to close.
3. Place the cam follower on the second step of the cam. If the cam follower won't touch the cam, turn the fast idle speed screw in until it does.
4. Apply a slight opening pressure on the choke blade and insert a 0.125 in. (3.1mm) plug gauge between the top of the choke blade and air horn casting.
5. If adjustment is needed, bend the tang of the fast idle cam until a slight drag is felt when the gauge is removed.

Choke Vacuum Kick

♦ See Figures 64 and 65

1. Attach a rubber band to the green tang of the intermediate choke shaft.
2. Open the throttle to allow the choke valve to close.

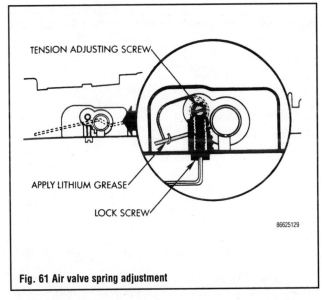

Fig. 61 Air valve spring adjustment

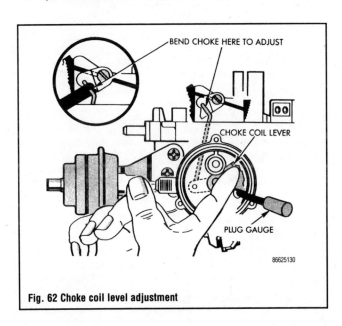

Fig. 62 Choke coil level adjustment

2. Turn the tension adjusting screw counterclockwise until the air valve opens part way.
3. Turn the screw clockwise until the just closes.
4. Turn the screw clockwise for the following vender numbers, measured in turns:

- 17085408—½ turn
- 17085409—⅝ turn
- 17085415—½ turn
- 17085417—¾ turn
- 17086425—½ turn
- 17087245—⅝ turn
- 17087176—¾ turn
- 17087175—¾ turn
- 17087177—1 turn
- 17085431—½ turn

5. Hold the adjusting screw and tighten the locknut.
6. Apply a light film of lithium based grease to the contact area.

Choke Coil Lever

♦ See Figure 62

1. Remove the choke cover.
2. Place the fast idle cam follower on the highest step of the cam.

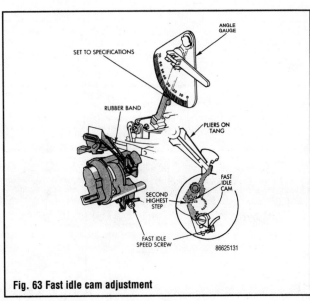

Fig. 63 Fast idle cam adjustment

5-24 FUEL SYSTEM

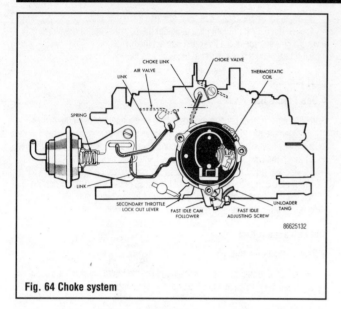

Fig. 64 Choke system

Fig. 65 Choke vacuum kick adjustment

choke plate and insert a 0.214 in. (5.4mm) gauge between the top of the choke plate and the air horn casting on all 1985 models, or a 0.17 in. (4.3mm) gauge on all 1986 models. On 1987–88 models, the gauge should be 0.150 in. (3.8mm) for 49 state models, 0.17 in. (4.3mm) for high altitude models, or 0.14 in. (3.5mm) for California and Canada models. A slight drag should be felt.

5. If adjustment is necessary, bend the link at the upper angle.

Air Valve Rod

▶ See Figure 66

1. Using a vacuum pump, apply at least 18 in. Hg (61 kPa) to the vacuum nipple on the choke vacuum diaphragm.
2. Close the air valve.
3. Insert a 0.025 in. (0.6mm) gauge between the rod and the end of the slot. The gauge should just fit.
4. To adjust, bend the rod at the lower left angle.

Choke Unloader

▶ See Figure 67

1. Attach a rubber band to the green tang of the intermediate choke shaft.
2. Open the throttle to allow the choke plate to close.
3. Hold the secondary lockout lever away from the pin.
4. Hold the throttle lever in the wide-open position.
5. Apply a slight opening pressure on the choke plate and insert a 0.345 in. (8.7mm) gauge between the top of the choke plate and the air horn wall for all 1985 models, or a 0.26 in. (6.6mm) gauge for all 1986 models. For 1987–88 models, use a 0.20 in. (5.0mm) gauge for 49 states models, 0.22 in. (5.5mm) for high altitude models; or a 0.209 in. (7.3mm) for California and Canada models. A slight drag should be felt.
6. If adjustment is required, bend the tang of the fast idle lever.

Secondary Lockout

LOCKOUT LEVER

▶ See Figure 68

1. Close the choke plate.
2. Close the throttle plates.
3. Insert a 0.015 in. (0.38mm) plug gauge between the lockout lever and the secondary throttle plate actuating pin. The gauge should just fit. If not, bend the pin.

LOCKOUT OPENING CLEARANCE

1. Hold the choke plate wide-open by pushing down on the tail of the fast idle cam.
2. Insert a 0.015 in. plug gauge between the end of the lockout lever and the end of the secondary throttle actuating pin. The gauge should just fit. If not, file the end of the pin.

Fast Idle Speed

1. Run the engine to normal operating temperature.
2. Disconnect and plug the EGR vacuum line and distributor advance vac-

3. Using a vacuum pump, apply at least 18 in. Hg (61 kPa) to the nipple on the choke diaphragm. The air valve rod must not restrict the plunger from fully retracting. If necessary, bend the rod to permit full plunger travel. The final rod clearance must be set after the vacuum kick setting has been made.

4. With the vacuum still applied, apply a slight opening pressure on the

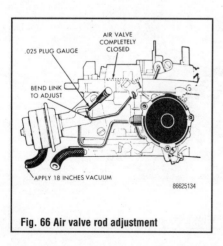

Fig. 66 Air valve rod adjustment

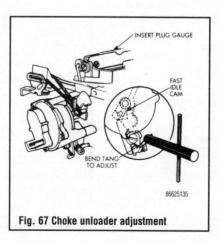

Fig. 67 Choke unloader adjustment

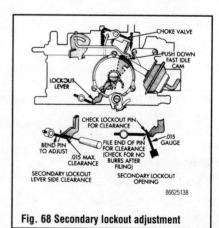

Fig. 68 Secondary lockout adjustment

uum line. Disconnect and plug the 3/16 in. vacuum hose at the charcoal canister. Remove the PCV valve from the rocker cover and allow it to draw fresh air.

3. Set the parking brake and place the transmission in Neutral.
4. With the engine off, open the throttle and place the fast idle adjusting screw on the second highest speed step of the cam.
5. Start the engine. Let the engine speed stabilize.
6. Turn the fast idle speed screw in or out until the engine speed listed on the underhood sticker is reached.
7. Reposition the screw on the cam after each adjustment in order to allow the idle to properly stabilize.
8. Reconnect the vacuum hoses and install the air cleaner.

ADJUSTMENTS FOR STROMBERG WW3

Float Height

▶ See Figure 69

1. Remove the carburetor.

➡ Position the carburetor on clean rags to catch any remaining fuel.

2. Remove the air horn.
3. Drain the float bowl of fuel.
4. Invert the main body and let the weight of the float rest on the needle and seat.
5. Using a T-scale, check the distance between the gasket surface of the fuel bowl (gasket removed) and the top of the float at the center. The gap should be 7/32 in. (5.5mm).
6. If adjustment is necessary, hold the float against the bottom of the float bowl and bend the lip towards or away from the needle.

※※ WARNING

When bending, don't allow the float lip to push against the needle. The tip of the needle will compress and give a false reading.

7. Recheck your adjustment a couple of times. It is very important that the float lip be perpendicular to the needle within 10° after the adjustment!
8. Assemble and install the carburetor.

Fast Idle Cam

1. Position the fast idle speed adjusting screw so that it contacts the second highest step of the cam. Move the choke valve toward the closed position using light pressure on the choke linkage.
2. Insert a 0.08 in. (2.25mm) gauge between the upper edge of the choke plate and the wall of the air horn on all engines except the 8-318 with the Clean Air Package. On these engines, use a 0.16 in. (4.1mm) gauge bit. A slight drag should be felt.

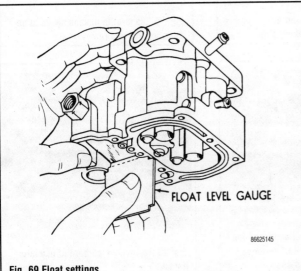

Fig. 69 Float settings

3. If adjustment is necessary, bend the fast idle link at the upper angle until the specified gauge fits between the choke plate and the wall of the air horn.

Vacuum Kick

1. If the adjustment is to be made on the engine (with the engine running at curb idle), back off the fast idle screw until the choke can be closed to the kick position. Note the number of screw turns required so that the fast idle can be returned to the original adjustment.
2. If the adjustment is to be made off the engine, open the throttle valve and move the choke to its closed position. Release the throttle first and then release the choke. Disconnect the vacuum hose from the carburetor body and apply a vacuum of at least 10 in. Hg (34 kPa).
3. Insert a 0.21 in. (5.4mm) gauge between the choke valve and the wall of the air horn.
4. Apply sufficient closing pressure to the choke lever to provide a minimum valve opening without distorting the diaphragm link (which connects the choke lever to the vacuum diaphragm). Note that the cylindrical stem of the diaphragm will extend as its internal spring is compressed. This spring must be fully compressed for the proper measurement of the vacuum kick adjustment.
5. Remove the gauge bit. If a slight drag is not felt as the gauge is removed, an adjustment of the diaphragm link is necessary to obtain the proper clearance. Shorten or lengthen the diaphragm link by carefully closing or opening the U-bend in the link until the correct adjustment is obtained.

※※ WARNING

When adjusting the link, be careful not to bend or twist the diaphragm.

6. Connect the vacuum hose to the carburetor body (if it had been removed) and return the fast idle screw to its original location.
7. With no vacuum applied to the diaphragm, the choke valve should move freely between its open and closed positions. If it does not move freely, examine the linkage for misalignment or interference which may have been caused by the bending operation. If necessary, repeat the adjustment to provide the proper link operation.

Choke Unloader

1. Hold the throttle valve in the wide-open position.
2. Insert a 5/16 in. (7.9mm) gauge between the upper edge of the choke valve and the wall of the air horn.
3. While pressing lightly against the choke lever, a slight drag should be felt as the gauge is being withdrawn.
4. If adjustment is necessary, bend the unloader tang on the throttle lever until the correct opening is obtained.

Accelerator Pump and Bowl Vent

1. Back off the idle speed adjusting screw.
2. Open the choke plate so that, with the throttle plates closed, the fast idle adjusting screw will not contact the fast idle cam.
3. Make sure that the pump rod is in the medium stroke hole in the throttle lever and the bowl vent clip on the pump stem is in the center notch.
4. Close the throttle plates tightly. It should be just possible to insert a 0.06 in. (0.15mm) gauge between the bowl vent and the vent seal. Engine equipped with the Clean Air Package use a 0.05 in. (1.2mm) gauge.
5. If adjustment is necessary, bend the pump rod at the lower angle with needle-nosed pliers.

Fast Idle Speed

1. Run the engine until it reaches normal operating temperature.
2. With the engine off and the transmission in Park or Neutral, open the throttle slightly.
3. On models without the Clean Air Package, close the choke plate about 20°, then allow the throttle plates to close. The fast idle screw should now rest on the slowest speed step of the cam. On models with the Clean Air Package, close the choke plate until the fast idle screw can be positioned on the second highest speed step of the cam.
4. Start the engine.
5. Turn the fast idle speed screw in or out until 700 rpm is obtained.

5-26 FUEL SYSTEM

6. Stopping the engine between adjustments is not necessary. However, be sure the fast idle speed screw is positioned on the cam after each speed adjustment.

REMOVAL & INSTALLATION

▶ See Figures 70 thru 78

✽✽ CAUTION

Do not attempt to remove a carburetor from a vehicle that has just been road tested. The truck MUST BE completely cooled down before working on it. The possibility of fuel igniting and severe personal injury exists. ALWAYS observe "no smoking/no open flame" precautions.

The following is general removal procedure for all carburetors.
1. Disconnect the battery ground cable.
2. Remove the air cleaner.
3. Remove the fuel tank filler cap. The tank could be under a small amount of pressure.
4. Tag all lines to the carburetor before removing them, this is important, so there is no confusion.
5. Disconnect and plug the fuel lines. Use two wrenches to avoid twisting the fuel line. A container is also useful to catch any fuel which spills from the lines.
6. Disconnect the throttle and choke linkage along with any springs.
7. Disconnect any vacuum lines.
8. Remove the mounting bolts.
9. Make sure all connections are disconnected. Carefully remove the carburetor from the engine and carry it in a level position to a clean work place.

➡ Position the carburetor on clean rags to catch any remaining fuel.

Fig. 70 The air cleaner must be removed for access to the carburetor

Fig. 71 Note the positions and routing of all carburetor linkage

Fig. 72 Vacuum lines need to be inspected and replaced if bad on installation

Fig. 73 Tag all lines before disconnecting them from the carburetor

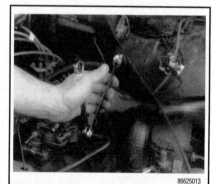
Fig. 74 Use two wrenches on fuel fittings to avoid twisting and breaking a line

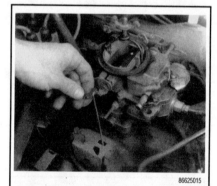
Fig. 75 The throttle linkage needs to be disconnected and removed

Fig. 76 Remove the springs and inspect them for wear or damage

Fig. 77 Make sure all components are disengaged, then remove the carburetor and place it on a clean work surface

Fig. 78 Remove the carburetor insulator assembly

FUEL SYSTEM 5-27

10. Remove the gasket and or insulator assembly. Clean the surface of the intake manifold and bottom of the carburetor. Always install the carburetor with a new insulator and gasket to prevent leaks.

➡ While the carburetor is removed, cover the openings in the intake manifold to prevent the entrance of dirt or foreign matter.

To install:
11. Place a new gasket on the manifold.
12. Carefully place the carburetor on the manifold without trapping the choke rod under carburetor linkage.
13. Install the carburetor mounting nuts and or bolts making sure to tighten alternately, a little at a time. This will compress the gasket evenly, and help prevent vacuum leakage between the carburetor and the manifold.
14. Connect the throttle linkage and the fuel inlet line.
15. Check for worn or loose vacuum hose connections. Look at your vacuum diagram label under the hood of your truck for correct placement.
16. Make sure the choke plate opens and closes completely when operated. Also check to see if throttle travel is not hindered.
17. Install the air cleaner. It is always a good idea to clean and inspect it before installation.
18. Connect the battery cable.
19. Check the idle mixture and speed adjustments.

✴✴ CAUTION

The practice of priming an engine by pouring gasoline into the carburetor air horn, should be strictly avoided. Cranking the engine, then priming by depressing the accelerator peel several times, should be adequate.

CARBURETOR SPECIFICATIONS CHARTS

CARTER THERMO-QUAD CARBURETORS

Carter Model Number	TQ-9208S	TQ-9209S	TQ-9210S	TQ-9211S	TQ-9212S	TQ-9247S	TQ-9248S
Requirement	Cal.	Fed./Can.	Cal.	Fed./Can.	Cal.	Fed./Can.	Cal.
Engine Displacement (Cu. In.)	360-1	360-3	360-3	440-1,3	440-1,3	440-1,3	440-1,3
Transmission	Man.	Auto.	Auto.	Auto.	Auto.	Auto.	Auto.
Bore							
Primary	1-3/8"	1-3/8"	1-3/8"	1-1/2"	1-1/2"	1-1/2"	1-1/2"
Secondary	2-1/4"	2-1/4"	2-1/4"	2-1/4"	2-1/4"	2-1/4"	2-1/4"
Main Venturi							
Primary	1-1/16"	1-1/16"	1-1/16"	1-3/16"	1-3/16"	1-3/16"	1-3/16"
Secondary	2-1/4"	2-1/4"	2-1/4"	2-1/4"	2-1/4"	2-1/4"	2-1/4"
Adjustments							
Float Setting (± 1/32")	29/32"	29/32"	29/32"	29/32"	29/32"	29/32"	29/32"
Secondary Throttle Linkage	Adjust Links so that Primary and Secondary Stops both contact at the same time.						
Secondary Air Valve Opening	7/16"	7/16"	7/16"	1/2"	1/2"	7/16"	7/16"
Secondary Air Valve Spring Tension (From Contact)	2 Turns	2 Turns	2 Turns	1-1/2 Turns	1-1/2 Turns	1-1/2 Turns	1-1/2 Turns
Accelerator Pump Stroke (Top of pump plunger stem to top of bowl cover @ curb idle) (Stage 1)	31/64"	31/64"	31/64"	31/64"	31/64"	31/64"	31/64"
At Secondary Pick Up (Stage 2)	23/64"	23/64"	23/64"	23/64"	23/64"	23/64"	23/64"
Choke Control Lever Adjustment Off Vehicle	3.30"	3.30"	3.30"	3.30"	3.30"	3.30"	3.30"
Choke Diaphragm Connector Rod (Clearance between Air Valve and Stop)	.040"	.040"	.040"	.040"	.040"	.040"	.040"
Vacuum Kick**	.150"	.150"	.150"	.100"	.100"	.100"	.100"
Fast Idle Cam Position**	.100"	.100"	.100"	.100"	.100"	.100"	.100"
Choke Unloader (Wide Open Kick)**	.310"	.310"	.310"	.500"	.500"	.500"	.500"
Secondary Throttle Lockout	.060"-.090"	.060"-.090"	.060"-.090"	.060"-.090"	.060"-.090"	.060"-.090"	.060"-.090"
Timing	4°BTDC	4°BTDC	4°BTDC	8°BTDC	8°BTDC	8°BTDC	8°BTDC
Propane rpm	800	820	820	790	790	790	790
Idle set rpm	700	700	700	700	700	700	700
Fast idle rpm	1600	1600	1600	1400	1400	1400	1400
Carbon monoxide (co)	*	-	*	-	*	-	*

*Refer To Emissions Label.
**Thermo-Quad Choke Adjustments are measured at the lowest edge of the choke plate.

Fig. 79 1979 Carter Thermo-Quad

5-28 FUEL SYSTEM

HOLLEY MODEL 1945 SINGLE VENTURI CARBURETORS

Holley Carburetor Number	R-8593A	R-8594A	R-8799A	R-8800A
Requirement	Federal	Federal	Canada	Canada
Engine Displacement (Cu. Inch)	225	225	225	225
Transmission	Manual	Automatic	Manual	Automatic
Bore	1-9/16"	1-9/16"	1-9/16"	1-9/16"
Venturi	1-5/16"	1-5/16"	1-5/16"	1-5/16"
Main Metering Jet				
Adjustments				
Accelerator Pump	2-7/32"	2-21/64"	2-7/32"	2-21/64"
Dry Float Setting ± (1/32)	Position-1	Position-2	Position-1	Position-2
Bowl Vent	FLUSH WITH TOP OF BOWL COVER GASKET			
Vacuum Kick	1/16"	1/16"	1/16"	1/16"
Fast Idle Cam Position	.100"	.100"	.100"	.100"
Choke Unloader	.080"	.080"	.080"	.080"
	.250"	.250"	.250"	.250"
Timing	12°BTDC	12°BTDC	12°BTDC	12°BTDC
Propane rpm	875	875	875	875
Idle set rpm	675	675	675	675
Fast idle rpm	1600	1600	1600	1600

CARTER MODEL BBD CARBURETOR

Carter Model Number	BBD-8214S	BBD-8215S	BBD-8249S	BBD-8232S	BBD-8210S	BBD-8211S
Requirement	Calif.	Calif.	Fed.	Fed.	Fed.	Fed.
Engine Displacement (Cu. In.)	225-1	225-1	318-1	318-1	318-1	318-1
Transmission	Man.	Auto.	Man.	Auto.	Man.	Auto.
Bore	1-7/16"	1-7/16"	1-7/16"	1-7/16"	1-7/16"	1-7/16"
Venturi	1-1/16"	1-1/16"	1-1/16"	1-1/16"	1-3/16"	1-1/16"
Main Metering Jets						
Standard	.086"	.086"	.086"	.086"	.086"	.086"
Metering Rods (Standard)	75-2264	75-2264	75-2216	75-2231	75-2229	75-2229
Adjustments						
Float Setting (At Center of Floats ± 1/32")	1/4"	1/4"	1/4"	1/4"	1/4"	1/4"
Accelerator Pump Setting (At Curb Idle)	.500"	.500"	.500"	.500"	.500"	.500"
Choke Unloader	.280"	.280"	.280"	.280"	.280"	.280"
Vacuum Kick	.110"	.110"	.110"	.110"	.110"	.110"
Fast Idle Cam Position	.070"	.070"	.070"	.070"	.070"	.070"
Timing	8°BTDC	8°BTDC	12°BTDC	12°BTDC	12°BTDC	12°BTDC
Propane rpm	975	975	820	820	820	820
Idle set rpm	800	800	680	680	680	680
Fast idle rpm	1400	1600	1400	1500	1400	1500
Carbon monoxide (co)	*	*	—	—	—	—

*Refer To Emissions Label For Carbon Monoxide Percentage.

Fig. 81 1979 Holley 1945 and Carter BBD

HOLLEY MODEL 2245 DUAL VENTURI CARBURETORS

Holley Model Number	R-8597A	R-8598A	R-8925A
Requirement	Fed.	Fed.	Fed.
Engine Displacement (Cu. In.)	360-1	360-1	360-1
Transmission	Man.	Auto.	Auto.
Bore	1-9/16"	1-9/16"	1-9/16"
Venturi	1-5/16"	1-5/16"	1-5/16"
Main Metering Jet	632	641	651
Adjustments			
Accelerator Pump Setting (From Curb Idle)	.290"	.290"	.290"
Accelerator Pump Setting (From Closed Throttle)	#1 Slot	#1 Slot	#1 Slot
	.290"	.290"	.290"
*Dry Float Setting Between Toe of Float and Float Stop (± 1/32")	.200"	.200"	.200"
Bowl Vent	.025"	.025"	.025"
Vacuum Kick	.110"	.110"	.110"
Fast Idle Cam Position	.110"	.110"	.110"
Choke Unloader	.170"	.170"	.170"
Timing	10°BTDC	10°BTDC	10°BTDC
Propane rpm	1000	975	975
Idle set rpm	750	750	750
Fast idle rpm	1600	1600	1600

CARTER THERMO-QUAD CARBURETORS

Carter Model Number	TQ-9228S	TQ-9229S	TQ-9223S	TQ-9227S	TQ-9224S	TQ-9225S	TQ-9207S
Requirement	Cal.	Cal.	Cal.	Can.	Cal.	Cal.	Fed./Can.
Engine Displacement (Cu. in.)	318-1	318-1	318-1	318-1	360-1	360-1	360-1
Transmission	Man.	Auto.	Auto.	Auto.	Man.	Auto.	Man.
Bore							
Primary	1-3/8"	1-3/8"	1-3/8"	1-3/8"	1-3/8"	1-3/8"	1-3/8"
Secondary	2-1/4"	2-1/4"	2-1/4"	2-1/4"	2-1/4"	2-1/4"	2-1/4"
Main Venturi							
Primary	1-1/16"	1-1/16"	1-1/16"	1-1/16"	1-1/16"	1-1/16"	1-1/16"
Secondary	2-1/4"	2-1/4"	2-1/4"	2-1/4"	2-1/4"	2-1/4"	2-1/4"
Adjustments							
Float Setting (±1/32")	29/32"	29/32"	29/32"	29/32"	29/32"	29/32"	29/32"
Secondary Throttle Linkage. Adjust Links so that Primary and Secondary Stops both contact at the same time.							
Secondary Air Valve Opening	1/2"	1/2"	1/2"	1/2"	1/2"	1/2"	7/16"
Secondary Air Valve Spring Tension (From Contact)	3 Turns	3 Turns	3 Turns	3 Turns	3 Turns	3 Turns	2 Turns
Accelerator Pump Stroke (Top of pump plunger stem to top of bowl cover @ curb idle) (Stage 1)	11/32"	11/32"	11/32"	11/32"	5/16"	5/16"	31/64"
At Secondary Pick Up (Stage 2)	3/16"	3/16"	9/64"	9/64"	3/16"	3/16"	23/64"
Choke Control Lever Adjustment Off Vehicle	3.30"	3.30"	3.30"	3.30"	3.30"	3.30"	3.30"
Choke Diaphragm Connector Rod (Clearance between Air Valve and Stop)	.040"	.040"	.040"	.040"	.040"	.040"	.040"
Vacuum Kick**	.100"	.100"	.100"	.100"	.100"	.100"	.150"
Fast Idle Cam Position**	.100"	.100"	.100"	.100"	.100"	.100"	.100"
Choke Unloader (Wide Open Kick)**	.500"	.500"	.500"	.500"	.500"	.500"	.310"
Secondary Throttle Lockout	.060"-.090"	.060"-.090"	.060"-.090"	.060"-.090"	.060"-.090"	.060"-.090"	.060"-.090"
Timing	6°BTDC	6°BTDC	6°BTDC	8°BTDC	6°BTDC	10°BTDC	4°BTDC
Propane rpm	865	860	860	880	980	960	800
Idle set rpm	750	750	750	750	750	750	700
Fast idle rpm	1600	1600	1600	1600	1600	1600	1600
Carbon monoxide (co)	*	*	*	*	*	*	*

*Refer To Emissions Label.
**Thermo-Quad Choke Adjustments are measured at the lowest edge of the choke plate.

Fig. 80 1979 Holley 2245 and Carter Thermo-Quad

FUEL SYSTEM 5-29

CARTER THERMO-QUAD CARBURETORS

Chrysler Number	4287013	4241752	4287016	4241753
Carter Model Number	TQ-9342S	TQ-9375S	TQ-9379S	TQ-9376S
Requirement	Fed./Cal.	Fed./Cal.	Fed./CAN.	Cal.
Engine Displacement (Cu. In.)	318/5.2	318/5.2	360/5.9	360/5.9
Transmission	Both	Auto	Both	Both
Bore				
Primary	1-3/8"	1-3/8"	1-3/8"	1-3/8"
Secondary	2-1/4"	2-1/4"	2-1/4"	2-1/4"
Main Venturi				
Primary	1-1/16"	1-1/16"	1-1/16"	1-1/16"
Secondary	AIR VALVE			
Adjustments				
Float Setting (± 1/32")	29/32"	29/32"	29/32"	29/32"
Secondary Throttle Linkage	Adjust links so that primary and secondary stops both contact at the same time			
Secondary Air Valve Opening	27/64"	27/64"	27/64"	27/64"
Secondary Air Valve Spring Tension (From Contact)	2-1/2 Turns	2 Turns	2 Turns	2 Turns
Accelerator Pump Stroke (Top of pump plunger stem to top of bowl cover @ curb idle) (Stage 1)	.340"	.340"	.340"	.340"
At Secondary Pick Up (Stage 2)	.190"	.190"	None	.190"
Choke Diaphragm Connector Rod (Clearance between Air Valve and Stop)	.040"	.040"	.040"	.040"
Vacuum Kick**	.130"	.130"	.130"	.130"
Fast Idle Cam Position**	.100"	.130"	.130"	.130"
Choke Unloader (Wide Open Kick)**	.310"	.310"	.310"	.310"
Secondary Throttle Lockout	.060"-.090"	.060"-.090"	.060"-.090"	.060"-.090"
Timing	8°BTDC	16°BTDC	4°BTDC	10°BTDC
Propane rpm	840	810	800	800
Idle set rpm	750	750	700	750
Fast idle rpm	1600	1800	1500	1700

*Refer To Emissions Label.
**Thermo-Quad Choke Adjustments are measured at the lowest edge of the choke plate.

Fig. 82 1982 Carter Thermo-Quad

CARTER MODEL BBD CARBURETORS

Chrysler Number	4041580	4041583	4041756	4287010
Carter Model Number	BBD-8146S	BBD-8147S	BBD-8352S	BBD-8348S
Requirement	Can.	Can.	Fed.	Fed.
Engine Displacement (Cu. In.)	318/5.2	318/5.2	225/3.7	318/5.2
Transmission	Auto.	Man.	Man.	Auto.
Bore	1-7/16"	1-7/16"	1-7/16"	1-7/16"
Venturi	1-1/16"	1-1/16"	1-1/16"	1-1/16"
Main Metering Jets				
Standard	.086"	.086"	.086"	.086"
Metering Rods (Standard)	75-2288	75-2092	75-2374	75-2216
Adjustments				
Float Setting (At Center of Floats ± 1/32")	1/4"	1/4"	1/4"	1/4"
Accelerator Pump Setting (At Curb Idle)	.500"	.500"	.500"	.500"
Choke Unloader	.31"	.31"	.31"	.31"
Vacuum Kick	.070"	.150"	.130"	.130"
Fast Idle Cam Position	.070"	.110"	.070"	.070"
Timing	2°ATDC	2°ATDC	12°BTDC	12°BTDC
Propane rpm	800	800	750	830
Idle set rpm	750	750	700	750
Fast idle rpm	1500	1500	1600	1600
Carbon monoxide (co)	*	*		

* Refer To Emissions Label For Carbon Monoxide Percentage.

HOLLEY MODEL 2245 DUAL VENTURI CARBURETORS

Chrysler Number	4241755
Holley Model Number	R-9816A
Requirement	Can.
Engine Displacement (Cu. In.)	360/5.9
Transmission	Automatic
Bore	1-9/16"
Venturi	1-5/16"
Main Metering Jet	632
Adjustments	
Accelerator Pump Setting (From Closed Throttle)	#1 Slot—17/64"
*Dry Float Setting Between Toe of Float and Float Stop (± 1/32")	3/16"
Vacuum Kick	.150"
Fast Idle Cam Position	.110"
Choke Unloader	.170"
Timing	4°BTDC
Propane rpm	810
Idle set rpm	750
Fast idle rpm	1700

Fig. 83 1982 Carter BBD and Holley 2245

5-30 FUEL SYSTEM

HOLLEY MODEL 1945 SINGLE VENTURI CARBURETORS

Chrysler Number	4287014	4287015	4213711	4213712	4213721	4213722	4213771
Holley Carburetor Number	R-9765A	R-9762A	R-9153A	R-9132A	R-9152A	R-9399A	R-9134A
Requirement	Fed.	Fed.	Cal.	Cal.	Can.	Can.	Can.
Engine (Cubic Inch)	225	225	225	225	225	225	225
Transmission	Man	Auto	Man	Auto	Auto	Man	Auto
Bore	1-11/16"	1-11/16"	1-11/16"	1-11/16"	1-11/16"	1-11/16"	1-11/16"
Venturi	1-9/32"	1-9/32"	1-9/32"	1-9/32"	1-9/32"	1-9/32"	1-9/32"
Adjustments							
Accelerator Pump	1.70"	1.61"	1.70"	1.61"	1.70"	1.70"	1.61"
Dry Float Setting ± (1/32)	FLUSH WITH TOP OF BOWL COVER GASKET						
Vacuum Kick	.130"	.130"	.130"	.130"	.130"	.130"	.130"
Fast Idle Cam Position	.080"	.090"	.080"	.090"	.080"	.080"	.090"
Choke Unloader	.250"	.250"	.250"	.250"	.250"	.250"	.250"
Timing	12°BTDC	16°BTDC	12°BTDC	16°BTDC	12°BTDC	12°BTDC	16°BTDC
Propane rpm	675	675	825	850	900	900	900
Idle set rpm	600	600	800	800	725	725	750
ETC rpm	800	800	—	—	—	—	—
Fast idle rpm	1800	1600	1800	1600	1800	1800	1600

HOLLEY MODEL 2280 CARBURETORS

Chrysler Number	4241719	4287011
Holley Carburetor Number	R-9493A	R-9491A
Requirement	Fed.	Fed.-Asp.
Engine (Cu. In.)	318	318
Transmission	Man/Auto	Man/Auto
Bore	1-7/16"	1-7/16"
Venturi	1-1/16"	1-1/16"
Adjustments		
Dry Float Setting (At End of Floats Furthest From Pivot ± 1/32")	9/32"	9/32"
Accelerator Pump Setting At (Idle)	Flush With Top of Bowl Vent Casting	
Bowl Vent	Non/Adj.	Non/Adj.
Vacuum Kick	.140"	.140"
Fast Idle Cam Position	.052"	.052"
Choke Unloader	.200"	.200"
Timing	12°BTDC	12°BTDC
Propane RPM	850	880
Idle Set RPM	750	750
Fast Idle Speed	1500	1500

Fig. 84 1982 Holley 1945 and Holley 2280

HOLLEY MODEL 2280 CARBURETORS

Chrysler Number	4287026	4287028
Holley Carburetor Number	R-9949A	R-9951A
Requirement	Fed.	Fed.-Asp.
Engine (Cu. In.)	318	318
Transmission	Auto	Man/Auto
Bore	1-7/16"	1-7/16"
Venturi	1-1/16"	1-1/16"
Adjustments		
Dry Float Setting (At End of Floats Furthest From Pivot ± 1/32)	9/32"	9/32"
Accelerator Pump Setting At (Idle)	Flush With Top of Bowl Vent Casting	
Bowl Vent	Non/Adj.	Non/Adj.
Vacuum Kick	.140"	.140"
Fast Idle Cam Position	.052"	.052"
Choke Unloader	.200"	.200"
Propane RPM	880	850
Idle Set RPM	750	750
Fast Idle Speed	1500	1500

HOLLEY MODEL 2245 DUAL VENTURI CARBURETORS

Chrysler Number	4241755
Holley Model Number	R-9816A
Requirement	Can.
Engine Displacement (Cu. In.)	360/5.9
Transmission	Automatic
Bore	1-9/16"
Venturi	1-5/16"
Main Metering Jet	632
Adjustments	
Accelerator Pump Setting (From Closed Throttle)	#1 Slot—17/64"
Dry Float Setting Between Toe of Float and Float Stop (± 1/32")	3/16"
Vacuum Kick	.150"
Fast Idle Cam Position	.110"
Choke Unloader	.170"
Propane rpm	810
Idle set rpm	750
Fast idle rpm	1700

Fig. 85 1983 Holley 2280 and Holley 2245

FUEL SYSTEM 5-31

CARTER MODEL BBD CARBURETORS

Chrysler Number	4041580	4041583	4287129	4287055	4287018	4287017
Carter Model Number	BBD-8146S	BBD-8147S	BBD-8371S	BBD-8374S	BBD-8359S	BBD-8358S
Requirement	Can.	Can.	Fed.	Fed.-Hi-Alt.	Cal.	Cal.
Engine Displacement (Cu. In.)	318/5.2	318/5.2	225/3.7	318/5.2	318/5.2	318/5.2
Transmission	Auto.	Man.	Man.	Man./Auto	Auto.	Man.
Bore	1-7/16"	1-7/16"	1-7/16"	1-7/16"	1-7/16"	1-7/16"
Venturi	1-1/16"	1-1/16"	1-1/16"	1-1/16"	1-1/16"	1-1/16"
Adjustments						
Float Setting (At Center of Floats ± (1/32")	1/4"	1/4"	1/4"	1/4"	1/4"	1/4"
Accelerator Pump Setting (At Curb Idle)	.470"	.470"	.470"	.470"	.470"	.470"
Choke Unloader	.31"	.31"	.28"	.28"	.28"	.28"
Vacuum Kick	.70"	.150"	.130"	.130"	.130"	.130"
Fast Idle Cam Position	.070"	.110"	.070"	.070"	.070"	.070"
Propane rpm	820	800	750	800	760	825
Idle set rpm	750	750	700	800	700	740
Fast idle rpm	1500	1500	1600	1400	1400	1400
Solenoid Idle Stop	—	—	—	850	850	850

CARTER THERMO-QUAD CARBURETORS

Chrysler Number	4287013	4241752	4287016	4241753
Carter Model Number	TQ-9342S	TQ-9375S	TQ-9379S	TQ-9376S
Requirement	Fed.	Fed./Cal.	Fed./Can.	Cal.
Engine Displacement (Cu. In.)	318/5.2	318/5.2	360/5.9	360/5.9
Transmission	Both	Both	Both	Both
Bore				
Primary	1-3/8"	1-3/8"	1-3/8"	1-1/2"
Secondary	2-1/4"	2-1/4"	2-1/4"	2-1/4"
Main Venturi				
Primary	1-1/16"	1-1/16"	1-1/16"	1-3/8"
Secondary	AIR VALVE			
Adjustments				
Float Setting (± 1/32")	29/32"	29/32"	29/32"	29/32"
Secondary Throttle Linkage	Adjust links so that primary and secondary stops both contact at the same time			
Secondary Air Valve Opening	27/64"	3/8"	7/16"	3/8"
Secondary Air Valve Spring Tension (From Contact)	2-1/2 Turns	2-1/2 Turns	2 Turns	2 Turns
Accelerator Pump Stroke (Top of pump plunger stem to top of bowl cover @ curb idle) (Stage 1)	.340"	.340"	.340"	.340"
At Secondary Pick Up (Stage 2)	.190"	.190"	None	.190"
Choke Diaphragm Connector Rod (Clearance between Air Valve and Stop)	.040"	.040"	.040"	.040"
Vacuum Kick**	.130"	.130"	.130"	.180"
Fast Idle Cam Position**	.100"	.130"	.130"	.100"
Choke Unloader (Wide Open Kick)**	.310"	.310"	.310"	.310"
Secondary Throttle Lockout	.060"-.090"	.060"-.090"	.060"-.090"	.060"-.090"
Propane rpm	840	810	800	800
Idle set rpm	750	750	700	750
Fast idle rpm	1600	1800	1500	1700

*Refer To Emissions Label.
**Thermo-Quad Choke Adjustments are measured at the lowest edge of the choke plate.

Fig. 87 1983 Carter BBD and Carter Thermo-Quad

HOLLEY MODEL 1945 SINGLE VENTURI CARBURETORS

Chrysler Number	4287032	4287033	4287049	4287048
Holley Carburetor Number	R-40055A	R-40056A	R-9399-1A	R-9134-1A
Requirement	Fed.	Fed.	Can.	Can.
Engine (Cubic Inch)	225	225	225	225
Transmission	Man	Auto	Man	Auto
Bore	1-11/16"	1-11/16"	1-11/16"	1-11/16"
Venturi	1-9/32"	1-9/32"	1-9/32"	1-9/32"
Adjustments				
Accelerator Pump	1.70"	1.61"	1.70"	1.61"
Dry Float Setting ± (1/32")	FLUSH WITH TOP OF BOWL COVER GASKET			
Vacuum Kick	.130"	.130"	.130"	.130"
Fast Idle Cam Position	.080"	.090"	.080"	.090"
Choke Unloader	.250"	.250"	.250"	.250"
Propane rpm	675	725	725	850
Idle set rpm	600	650	725	750
ETC rpm	800	800	825	—
Fast idle rpm	1600	1600	1800	1600

HOLLEY MODEL 6145 SINGLE VENTURI CARBURETORS

Chrysler Number	4287019	4287020
Holley Carburetor Number	R-40029A	R-40030A
Requirement	Cal.	Cal.
Engine (Cu. In.)	225	225
Transmission	Man.	Auto
Bore	1-11/16"	1-11/16"
Venturi	1-9/32"	1-9/32"
Adjustments		
Accelerator Pump	1.70"	1.61"
Dry Float Setting	Flush with top of main body casting to .050" above	
Vacuum Kick	.150"	.150"
Fast Idle Cam Position	.090"	.090"
Choke Unloader	.250"	.250"
Propane rpm	850	750
Idle Set RPM	750	750
Solenoid Idle Stop	850	850
Fast Idle Speed	1600	1600

Fig. 86 1983 Holley 1945 and Holley 6145

5-32 FUEL SYSTEM

ROCHESTER QUADRAJET CARBURETORS

Chrysler Number	4306417	4306408	4306409	4306431
Vendor Number	17085417	17085408	17085409	17085431
Requirement	Fed.	Fed.	Fed./Alt.	Cal./Can.
Engine	360/5.9L	360/5.9L	360/5.9L	360/5.9L
Transmission	Manual	Automatic	Automatic	Both
Adjustments				
Float	13/32 ± 2/32			
Air Valve Springs	3/4 Turn	1/2 Turn	5/8 Turn	1/2 Turn
Choke Coil Lever	.120"	.120"	.120"	.120"
Choke Rod Fast Idle Cam				
Angle Gauge Method	20°	20°	20°	20°
Plug Gauge Method	.125"	.125"	.125"	.125"
Choke Vacuum Kick				
Angle Gauge Method	27°	27°	27°	27°
Plug Gauge Method	.170"	.170"	.170"	.170"
Air Valve Rod	.025"	.025"	.025"	.025"
Choke Unloader				
Angle Gauge Method	38°	38°	38°	38°
Plug Gauge Method	.260"	.260"	.260"	.260"
Secondary Lockout	.015"	.015"	.015"	.015"
Solenoid Idle rpm		900	850	
Idle rpm				Refer to VECI Label
Fast Idle rpm				
Propane rpm				

Chrysler Number	4306425	4306434
Vendor Number	17085425	17085434
Requirement	Fed.	Fed.
Engine	360/5.9L	360/5.9L
Transmission	Both	Both
Adjustments		
Float	13/32 ± 2/32	
Air Valve Springs	1/2 Turn	1/2 Turn
Choke Coil Lever	.120"	.120"
Choke Rod Fast Idle Cam		
Angle Gauge Method	20°	20°
Plug Gauge Method	.125"	.125"
Choke Vacuum Kick		
Angle Gauge Method	23°	24°
Plug Gauge Method	.140"	.150"
Air Valve Rod	.025"	.025"
Choke Unloader		
Angle Gauge Method	38°	38°
Plug Gauge Method	.260"	.260"
Secondary Lockout	.015"	.015"
Solenoid Idle rpm	800	950
Idle rpm		Refer to VECI Label
Fast Idle rpm		
Propane rpm		

Fig. 88 1986 Rochester Quadrajet

HOLLEY MODEL 1945 SINGLE VENTURI CARBURETORS

Chrysler Number	4306459	4306460	4287076	4300046
Holley Carburetor Number	R-40159	R-40160	R-40102A	R-40244A
Requirement	Fed.	Fed.	Can.	Can.
Engine (Cubic Inch) Liters	225/3.7L	225/3.7L	225/3.7L	225/3.7L
Transmission	Manual	Automatic	Manual	Automatic
Bore	1-11/16"	1-11/16"	1-11/16"	1-11/16"
Venturi	1-9/32"	1-9/32"	1-9/32"	1-9/32"
Adjustments				
Accelerator Pump and Position	1.61" (2)	1.61" (2)	1.70" (1)	1.61" (2)
Dry Float Setting ± (1/32)	FLUSH WITH TOP OF BOWL COVER GASKET			
Vacuum Kick	.130"	.150"	.130"	.130"
Fast Idle Cam Position	.080"	.080"	.080"	.090"
Choke Unloader	.250"	.250"	.250"	.250"
Propane rpm				
Idle rpm		Refer to VECI Label		
Fast Idle rpm	825	850	—	850
Solenoid Idle Stop rpm				

HOLLEY MODEL 6145 SINGLE VENTURI CARBURETORS

Chrysler Number	4306461	4306462
Holley Carburetor Number	R-40161	R-40162
Requirement	Cal.	Cal.
Engine (Cu. In.) Liters	225/3.7L	225/3.7L
Transmission	Manual	Automatic
Bore	1-11/16"	1-11/16"
Venturi	1-9/32"	1-9/32"
Adjustments		
Accelerator Pump and Position	1.75" (2)	1.75" (2)
Dry Float Setting	FLUSH WITH TOP OF BOWL COVER GASKET	
Vacuum Kick	.150"	.150"
Fast Idle Cam Position	.060"	.070"
Choke Unloader	.250"	.250"
Propane rpm		
Idle Set rpm		Refer to VECI Label
Fast Idle rpm	850	850
Solenoid Idle Stop rpm		

Fig. 89 1986 Holley 1945 and Holley 6145

FUEL SYSTEM 5-33

HOLLEY 4150G SERIES 4-BARREL CARBURETOR

	R-6771-A Fed/Can 413-3 Man/Auto	R-7138-A Fed/Can 413-3 Man/Auto
Holley Carburetor Number		
Requirement		
Engine Displacement (Cu. In.)		
Transmission		
Throttle Bore		
Primary	1-9/16"	1-9/16"
Secondary	1-9/16"	1-9/16"
Main Venturi		
Primary	1-3/16"	1-3/16"
Secondary	1-3/16"	1-3/16"
Main Metering Jet		
Primary	#582-#612 Primary	#582-#612 Throt Side
Secondary	#74 Secondary	#74 Secondary
Standard	#5	#5
Power Valve (stamped)		
Adjustments		
Curb Idle Speed RPM	700	700
Fast Idle Speed RPM	.035	.035
Float Setting (Dry)	Float Lever Parallel with Floor of Bowl	
Primary and Secondary (± 1/32")		
Float Setting (Wet)	Fuel Level with Bottom of Sight Plug Hole	
Primary and Secondary		
Accelerator Pump	.015 Minimum	.015 Minimum
Override Adjustment (wide open throttle)		
Pump Position	#1 Hole	#1 Hole
Ignition Timing	5 BTC	5 BTC
Carbon Monoxide (CO) (enriched or speed rise)	750-M	750-M
	770-A	770-A

CARTER THERMO-QUAD CARBURETOR

	TQ-6545S Fed/Can 440-1 Auto	TQ-9096S Calif 440-1 Auto
Carter Model Number		
Requirement		
Engine Displacement (Cu. In.)		
Transmission		
Bore		
Primary	1-1/2"	1-1/2"
Secondary	2-1/4"	2-1/4"
Main Venturi		
Primary	1-3/16"	1-3/16"
Secondary	2-1/4"	2-1/4"
Metering Rods	2024	2110
Adjustments		
Float Setting (± 1/32")	27/32"	27/32"
Secondary Throttle Linkage	Adjust link so that primary and secondary stops both contact at the same time.	
Secondary Air Valve Opening	1/2	1/2
Secondary Air Valve Spring Tension (From Contact)	1-1/4 turn	1-1/4 turn
Accelerator Pump Stroke (Top of plunger to top of bowl cover @ curb idle)	1/2"	1/2"
At Secondary Pick Up	5/16"	5/16"
Choke Control Lever Adjustment Off Vehicle	3-3/8"	3-3/8"
Choke Diaphragm Connector Rod (Clearance between air valve and stop)	.040	.040
Vacuum Kick**	.160	.100
Fast Idle Cam Position**	.100	.100
Choke Unloader (Wide Open Kick)**	.310	.310
Secondary Throttle Lockout	.060-.090	.060-.090
Fast Idle Speed (RPM—after 500 miles)	1700	1700
Curb Idle Speed RPM	700	700
Ignition Timing	8 BTC	8 BTC
*Carbon Monoxide (enriched or speed rise)	760	760

**Thermo-Quad Choke Adjustments are measured at the lowest edge of the choke plate.
*T = @ Tailpipe

Fig. 91 1988 Holley 4150G and Carter Thermo-Quad

HOLLEY MODEL 2280 CARBURETORS

Chrysler Number	4324629	4324631
Holley Carburetor Number	R-40214A	R-40216A
Requirement	Fed./Can.	Canada
Engine (Cu. In.) Liters	318/5.2L	318/5.2L
Transmission	Both	Automatic
Bore	1-7/16"	1-7/16"
Venturi	1-1/16"	1-1/16"
Adjustments		
Dry Float Setting (At End of Floats Furthest From Pivot (±1/32")	9/32"	9/32"
Accelerator Pump Setting (At Idle)	.210"	.210"
Vacuum Kick	.140"	.140"
Fast Idle Cam Position	.070"	.070"
Choke Unloader	.250"	.250"
Bowl Vent	.035"	.035"
Propane rpm		
Idle rpm	Refer to VECI Label	Refer to VECI Label
Fast Idle rpm		
Solenoid rpm	875	875

HOLLEY MODEL 6280 CARBURETORS

Chrysler Number	4324632	4324633
Holley Carburetor Number	R-40221A	R-40222A
Requirement	Federal, Altitude	California
Engine (Cu. In.) Liters	318/5.2L	318/5.2L
Transmission	Both	Both
Bore	1-7/16"	1-7/16"
Venturi	1-1/16"	1-1/16"
Adjustments		
Dry Float Setting (At End of Floats Furthest From Pivot (±1/32")	9/32"	9/32"
Accelerator Pump Setting (At Idle)	.210"	.210"
Vacuum Kick	.130"	.130"
Fast Idle Cam Position	.070"	.070"
Choke Unloader	.150"	.150"
Propane rpm	780	
Idle rpm		Refer to VECI Label
Fast Idle rpm	850* 800	
Solenoid rpm		

* Manual Transmission

Fig. 90 1986 Holley 2280 and Holley 6280

5-34 FUEL SYSTEM

HOLLEY DUAL VENTURI CARBURETORS

MODEL 2210

	R-6764A Fed/Can	R-7870A Fed/Can	R-6886A Fed/Can	R-7697A Calif.	R-7103A Fed/Can
Holley Carburetor Number					
Requirement					
Engine Displacement (Cu. In.)	360-1	360-1	400	360-1	360-3
Transmission	Man	Auto	Man/Auto	Auto	Man
Bore	1-9/16"	1-9/16"	1-9/16"	1-9/16"	1-9/16"
Venturi	1-3/8"	1-3/8"	1-3/8"	1-3/8"	1-3/8"
Main Metering Jet	642	642	653	643	642
Adjustments—Rod in Slot Number	2	1	1	1	2
Accelerator Pump Setting (From Curb Idle)	.260	.260	.260	.260	.260
Accelerator Pump Setting (From Closed Throttle)	.310	.310	.310	.310	.310
*Dry Float Setting Between Toe of Float and Float Stop (± 1/32")	.180	.180	.180	.180	.180
Vacuum Kick	.150	.90	.150	.150	.150
Fast Idle Cam Position	.110	.110	.110	.110	.110
Choke Unloader	.170	.170	.170	.170	.170
Curb Idle Speed (RPM)	750	750	700	750	750
Fast Idle Speed (RPM after 500 Miles)	1700	1800	1600	1600	1600
Ignition Timing	TDC	TDC	2BTDC	TDC	TDC
*Carbon Monoxide (enriched or speed rise)	790	810	740-M 760-A	1.0%T	810

MODEL 2245

	R-7088A Fed/Can	R-7698A Calif	R-7871A Fed/Can	R-7091A Fed/Can	R-7092A Fed/Can
Holley Carburetor Number					
Requirement					
Engine Displacement (Cu. In.)	360-3	360-3	360-1	360-3	360-3
Transmission	Auto	Man/Auto	Man/Auto	Man	Auto
Bore	1-9/16"	1-9/16"	1-9/16"	1-9/16"	1-9/16"
Venturi	1-3/8"	1-3/8"	1-3/8"	1-3/8"	1-3/8"
Main Metering Jet	642	642	642	642	642
Adjustments—Rod in Slot Number	1	1	1	1	1
Accelerator Pump Setting (From Curb Idle)	.260	.260	.260	.260	.260
Accelerator Pump Setting (From Closed Throttle)	.310	.310	.310	.310	.310
*Dry Float Setting Between Toe of Float and Float Stop (± 1/32")	.180	.180	.180	.180	.180
Vacuum Kick	.150	.150	.130	.150	.150
Fast Idle Cam Position	.110	.110	.110	.110	.110
Choke Unloader	.170	.170	.170	.170	.170
Curb Idle Speed (RPM)	750	750	750	750	750
Fast Idle Speed (RPM after 500 Miles)	1600	1600	1600	1600	1600
Ignition Timing	TDC	TDC	4BTDC	TDC	TDC
*Carbon Monoxide (enriched or speed rise)	810	1.0%T		790	810

HOLLEY MODEL 2300G DUAL VENTURI CARBURETOR

	R-6769-1A Fed/Can	R-7137-A Fed/Can
Holley Carburetor Number		
Requirement		
Engine Displacement (Cu. In.)	361-4	361-4
Transmission	Man/Auto	Man/Auto
Bore	1-9/16"	1-9/16"
Venturi	1-1/4"	1-1/4"
Main Metering Jet	#622	#622
Power Valve	#7	#7
Adjustments		
Accelerator Pump Setting (Wide Open Throttle)	#1 Position	#1 Position
Curb Idle Speed	.015	.015
Fast Idle Speed	700	700
Float Setting (Dry) (± 1/32")	.035	.035
Float Setting (Wet on Vehicle)	Float Parting Line Parallel with Floor of Bowl	Fuel Level with Bottom of Sight Plug Hole
Ignition Timing	2-1/2 BTC	2-1/2 BTC
Carbon Monoxide (CO) (enriched or speed rise)	750-M 770-A	750-M 770-A

Fig. 93 1988 holley 2210, 2245 and Holley 2300G

CARTER MODEL BBD CARBURETOR

	BBD-8065S Fed/Can	BBD-8115S Fed/Can	BBD-8081S Fed/Can/Calif	BBD-8082S Calif	BBD-8108S Fed/Calif	BBD-8146S Fed/Can
Carter Model Number						
Requirement						
Engine Displacement (Cu. In.)	318-1	318-1	318-1	318-1	318-1	318-1
Transmission	Man	Man/4 Sp.	Auto	Man	Auto	Man
Bore	1-7/16"	1-7/16"	1-7/16"	1-7/16"	1-7/16"	1-7/16"
Venturi	1-3/16"	1-3/16"	1-3/16"	1-3/16"	1-3/16"	1-3/16"
Main Metering Jets Standard	120-392	120-389	120-392	120-392	120-392	120-392
Metering Rods (Standard)	2105	2083	2158	2104	2158	2092
Adjustments						
Step-Up Piston Gap	.035	.035	.035	.035	.035	.035
Float Setting (At Center of Floats (± 1/32")	.250	.250	.250	.250	.250	.250
Accelerator Pump Setting	.500	.500	.500	.500	.500	.500
Choke Unloader	.280	.280	.280	.280	.280	.280
Idle Speed RPM (Curb idle)	750	750	750	750	750	750
Vacuum Kick	.130	.130	.150	.130	.150	.150
Fast Idle Cam Position	.070	.070	.070	.070	.070	.070
Fast Idle Speed (RPM after 500 Miles)	1500	1500	1500	1500	1500	1600
Ignition Timing	2B	2B	2B(TDC-Calif.)	2BTDC	Cal. TDC	2 ATC
*Carbon Monoxide (enriched or speed rise)	.5%-(850)	.3%-(850)	.5%-(920)	.3%	.3%	800

	BBD-8147S BBD-8121S Fed/Can	BBD-8113S Calif	BBD-8112S Fed. Altitude	BBD-6585S Fed/Can	BBD-6586S Fed/Can
Carter Model Number					
Requirement					
Engine Displacement (Cu. In.)	318-1	318-1	318-1	318-3	318-3
Transmission	Auto	Man/Auto	Auto	Man	Auto
Bore	1-7/16"	1-7/16"	1-7/16"	1-7/16"	1-7/16"
Venturi	1-3/16"	1-3/16"	1-3/16"	1-3/16"	1-3/16"
Main Metering Jets Standard	120-386	120-392	120-392	120-392	120-392
Metering Rods (Standard)	2092	2170	2112	2023	2203
Adjustments					
Step-Up Piston Gap	.035"	.035"	.035"	.035"	.035"
Float Setting (At Center of Floats (± 1/32")	1/4"	1/4"	1/4"	1/4"	1/4"
Accelerator Pump Setting (At idle)	.500"	.500"	.500"	.500"	.500"
Choke Unloader	.310	.310	—	—	—
Idle Speed RPM (Curb idle)	750	700	700	700	700
Vacuum Kick	.130	.130	—	—	.095
Fast Idle Cam Position	.070	.070	—	—	.070
Fast Idle Speed (RPM after 500 Miles)	1500	1500	1500	1900	1500
Ignition Timing	2 ATC	TDC	6BTDC	TDC	TDC
*Carbon Monoxide (enriched or speed rise)	820	.5%T	885	750	750-M 770-Auto.

*P = @ Front of Catalyst T = @ Tailpipe

Fig. 92 1988 Carter BBD

FUEL SYSTEM 5-35

HOLLEY MODEL 1945 SINGLE VENTURI CARBURETOR

	R-7849A	R-7815A	R-7816A	R-7847A	R-7848A
Holley Carburetor Number	Fed/Can	Calif	Calif	Fed/Can	Fed/Can
Requirement	225-1	225-1	225-1	225-1	225-1
Engine Displacement (Cu. In.)	4 Sp/OD	Man	Auto	Man	Auto
Transmission	1-11/16"	1-11/16"	1-11/16"	1-11/16"	1-11/16"
Bore	1-9/32"	1-9/32"	1-9/32"	1-9/32"	1-9/32"
Venturi	#623	#631	#623	#623	#623
Main Metering Jet					
Adjustments					
Accelerator Pump (± 1/32")	2-21/64"	2-7/32"	2-21/64"	2-7/32"	2-21/64"
Dry Float Setting	3/64"	3/64"	3/64"	3/64"	3/64"
Vacuum Kick	.110	.110	.110	.110	.110
Fast Idle Cam Position	.080	.080	.080	.080	.080
Choke Unloader	.250	.250	.250	.250	.250
Curb Idle Speed (RPM)	750	800	750	750	750
Fast Idle Speed (RPM after 500 miles)	1600	1600	1700	1600	1700
Ignition Timing	2BTDC	TDC	2ATDC	2BTDC	2BTDC
*Carbon Monoxide (CO) (enriched or speed rise)	825	.3%P	.3%P	825	825

*P = @ Front of Catalyst
T = @ Tailpipe

Fig. 94 1988 Holley 1945

ROCHESTER QUADRAJET CARBURETORS

	4306420 17087176	4306419 17087175	4306424 17087177	4306431 17085431
Chrysler Number / Vendor Number				
Requirement	Fed.	Fed.	Fed./Alt.	Can./Can.
Engine	360/5.9L	360/5.9L	360/5.9L	360/5.9L
Transmission	Manual	Automatic	Manual	Both
Adjustments				
Float	3/4 Turn	3/4 Turn	1 Turn	1/2 Turn
Air Valve Springs	.120"	.120"	.120"	.120"
Chock Coil Lever				
Choke Rod Fast Idle Cam	20°	20°	20°	20°
Angle Gauge Method	.125"	.125"	.125"	.125"
Plug Gauge Method				
Choke Vacuum Kick	.26°	.26°	.27°	.23°
Angle Gauge Method	.150"	.150"	.170"	.140"
Plug Gauge Method	.025"	.025"	.025"	.025"
Air Valve Rod				
Choke Unloader	30°	30°	33°	32°
Angle Gauge Method	.200"	.200"	.220"	.209"
Plug Gauge Method	.015"	.015"	.015"	.015"
Secondary Lockout				
Solenoid Idle rpm	800	850	850	
Idle rpm				
Fast Idle rpm	Refer to EAR Label			
Propane rpm				

	4306425 17086425	4306437 17087245
Chrysler Number / Vendor Number		
Requirement	Can/Fed.	Can/Fed.
Engine	360/5.9L	360/5.9L
Transmission	Both	Both
Adjustments		
Float	1/2 Turn	5/8 Turn
Air Valve Springs	.120"	.120"
Choke Coil Lever		
Choke Rod Fast Idle Cam	20°	20°
Angle Gauge Method	.125"	.125"
Plug Gauge Method		
Choke Vacuum Kick	.23°	.23°
Angle Gauge Method	.140	.140
Plug Gauge Method	.025"	.025"
Air Valve Rod		
Choke Unloader	38°	32°
Angle Gauge Method	.260"	.209"
Plug Gauge Method	.015"	.015"
Secondary Lockout		
Solenoid Idle rpm	950	950
Idle rpm	13/32±2/32	13/32±2/32
Fast Idle rpm	Refer to EAR Label	Refer to EAR Label
Propane rpm		

Fig. 95 1988 Rochester Quadrajet

5-36 FUEL SYSTEM

THROTTLE BODY FUEL INJECTION SYSTEM

System Description

The Throttle Body Injection (TBI) system is used on 1988 V6–238 and V8–318 engines. The system is controlled by a pre-programmed digital computer known as the Single Module Engine Controller (SMEC). The SMEC controls ignition timing, air/fuel ratio, emission control devices, charging system and idle speed. The SMEC constantly varies all settings to meet changing operating conditions.

Various sensors provide the input necessary for the SMEC to correctly regulate the fuel flow at the fuel injector. These include the manifold absolute pressure, throttle position, oxygen sensor, coolant temperature, charge temperature, vehicle speed (distance) sensors and throttle body temperature. In addition to the sensors, various switches also provide important information. These include the neutral–safety, heated backlite, air conditioning, air conditioning clutch switches, and an electronic idle switch.

All inputs to the SMEC are converted into signals sent to the power module. These signals cause the power module to change either the fuel flow at the injector or ignition timing or both.

The SMEC tests many of its own input and output circuits. If a fault is found in a major system, this information is stored in the SMEC. Information on this fault can be displayed to a technician by means of the instrument panel power loss (check engine) lamp, or by connecting a diagnostic read out tool and reading a numbered display code which directly relates to a specific fault.

Service Precautions

1. When working around any part of the fuel system, take precautionary steps to prevent possible fire and/or explosion:
   a. Disconnect the negative battery terminal, except when testing with battery voltage is required.
   b. Whenever possible, use a flashlight instead of a drop light to inspect fuel system components or connections.
   c. Keep all open flames and smoking material out of the area and make sure there is adequate ventilation to remove fuel vapors.
   d. Use a clean shop cloth to catch fuel when opening a fuel system. Dispose of gasoline–soaked rags properly.
   e. Relieve the fuel system pressure before any service procedures are attempted that require disconnecting a fuel line.
   f. Use eye protection.
   g. Always keep a dry chemical (class B) fire extinguisher near the area.

Minimum Idle Speed Adjustment

➡ Normal idle speed is controlled by the SMEC. This adjustment is the minimum idle speed with the Automatic Idle Speed (AIS) closed.

1. Before adjusting the idle on an electronic fuel injected vehicle the following items must be checked.
   a. AIS motor has been checked for operation.
   b. Engine has been checked for vacuum or EGR leaks.
   c. Engine timing has been checked and set to specifications.
   d. Coolant temperature sensor has been checked for operation.
2. Connect a tachometer and timing light to engine.
3. Close the AIS by using ATM tester C–4805 or equivalent. Enter ATM test code #03.
4. Connect a jumper to radiator fan so that it will run continuously.
5. Start and run the engine for 3 minutes to allow the idle speed to stabilize.
6. Check the engine rpm and compare the result with the specifications listed on the underhood emission control sticker.
7. If idle rpm is not within specifications, use tool C–4804 or equivalent to turn the idle speed adjusting screw to obtain 790–810 rpms. If the underhood emission sticker specifications are different, use those values for adjustment.

➡ If idle will not adjust downward, check for binding linkage/throttle shaft or improper speed control servo cable adjustment.

8. Turn off the engine, then disconnect the tachometer and timing light. Remove the jumper wire from the fan motor. Remove the ATM tester.

Relieving Fuel System Pressure

✻✻ CAUTION

The fuel injection system is under a constant pressure of approximately 14.5 psi (100 kPa). Before servicing any part of the fuel injection system, the system pressure must be released. Use a clean shop towel to catch any fuel spray and take precautions to avoid the risk of fire.

1. Disconnect the negative battery cable.
2. Loosen the gas cap to release tank pressure.
3. Remove the wiring harness connector from the injector.
4. Ground one terminal of the injector.
5. Connect a jumper wire to the second terminal and touch the battery positive post for no longer than ten seconds. This releases system pressure.
6. Remove the jumper wire and continue fuel system service.

Fuel System Pressure Testing

✻✻ CAUTION

Fuel system pressure must be released as previously described each time a fuel hose is to be disconnected. Take precautions to avoid the risk of fire.

1. Remove the fuel intake hose from the throttle body and connect fuel system pressure testers C–3292, and C–4749, or equivalent, between the fuel filter hose and the throttle body.
2. Start the engine and read the gauge. Pressure should be 14.5 psi (100 kPa).

➡ ATM tester C–4805 or equivalent can be used. With the ignition in RUN, depress the ATM button. This activates the fuel pump and pressurizes the system

3. If the fuel pressure is below specifications:
   a. Install the tester between the fuel filter hose and the fuel line.
   b. Start the engine. If the pressure is now correct, replace the fuel filter. If no change is observed, gently squeeze the return hose. If the pressure increases, replace the pressure regulator. If no change is observed, the problem is either a plugged pump filter sock or a defective fuel pump.
4. If the pressure is above specifications:
   a. Remove the fuel return hose from the throttle body. Connect a substitute hose and place the other end of the hose in a clean container.
   b. Start the engine. If the pressure is now correct, check for a restricted fuel return line. If no change is observed, replace the fuel regulator.

Electric Fuel Pump

♦ See Figure 96

The TBI system uses an electric fuel pump mounted in the fuel tank. The fuel pump used in this system is a positive displacement, roller vane immersible pump with a permanent magnet electric motor. The fuel is drawn in through a filter sock and pushed through the electric motor to the outlet. The pump contains two check valves. One valve is used to relieve internal fuel pump pressure and regulate maximum pump output. The other check valve, located near the pump outlet, restricts fuel movement in either direction when the pump is not operational. Voltage to operate the pump is supplied through the Auto Shutdown Relay (ASD).

REMOVAL & INSTALLATION

♦ See Figures 97 thru 103

✻✻ CAUTION

Perform the fuel pressure release procedure described previously in this section.

FUEL SYSTEM 5-37

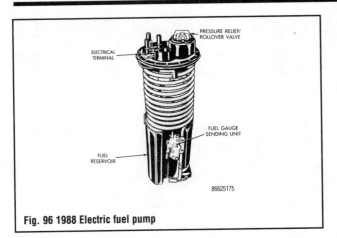

Fig. 96 1988 Electric fuel pump

9. Remove the pump mounting bracket and rubber collar from the hose. Cut the hose clamp on the supply line and discard the clamp. Remove the pump/filter assembly. Pry the filter from the pump.

To install:

10. Press a new filter onto the pump.
11. Using a new clamp, attach the supply hose.
12. Position the pump mounting bracket and rubber collar on the supply hose between the bulge in the hose and the pump.
13. Position the pump in the reservoir so that the filter aligns with the cavity in the reservoir.
14. Snap the pump bracket into the reservoir.
15. Position the coil tube on the reservoir so that the drain tube aligns with the mounting lugs on the reservoir.
16. Snap the lower-most coil into the mounting lugs on top of the reservoir.
17. Snap the drain tube into the lugs on the bottom of the reservoir.
18. Connect the wires to the sending unit.

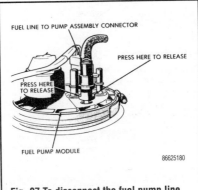

Fig. 97 To disconnect the fuel pump line, press in designated areas

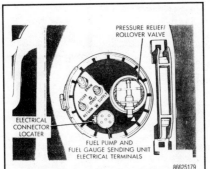

Fig. 98 After removing the fuel tank and fuel pump module, tag the lines going into the pump

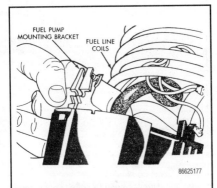

Fig. 99 Unfasten the sending unit screws, then remove the bracket

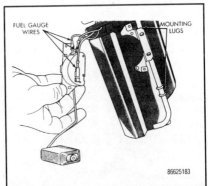

Fig. 100 Before removing the sender, disconnect the wires leading to sending unit

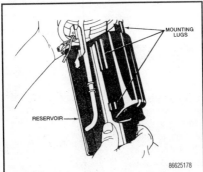

Fig. 101 After removing the sending unit, the drain tube must be removed from the mounting lugs

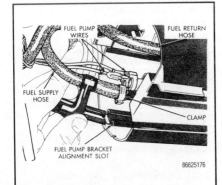

Fig. 102 The pump bracket should slide from the slot

1. Properly relieve the fuel system pressure and disconnect the negative battery cable.
2. Remove the fuel tank from the truck.
3. Remove the locking ring, then lift out the fuel pump module. Tag any lines for replacement.
4. Remove the sending unit attaching screws from the mounting bracket located on the drain tube.
5. Disconnect the wires from the sending unit, then remove the sending unit.
6. Remove the drain tube from the mounting lug at the bottom of the reservoir.
7. Remove the lower-most coil of the drain tube from the mounting lugs on top of the reservoir. Be careful to avoid unsnapping the return line check valve cover from the bottom of the reservoir.
8. Release the pump mounting bracket from the reservoir. Press the bracket with both thumbs toward the center of the reservoir.

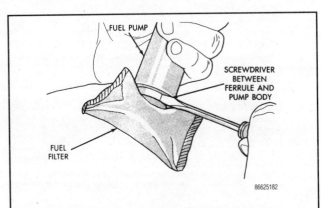

Fig. 103 Pry the filter off, and replace with a new one

5-38 FUEL SYSTEM

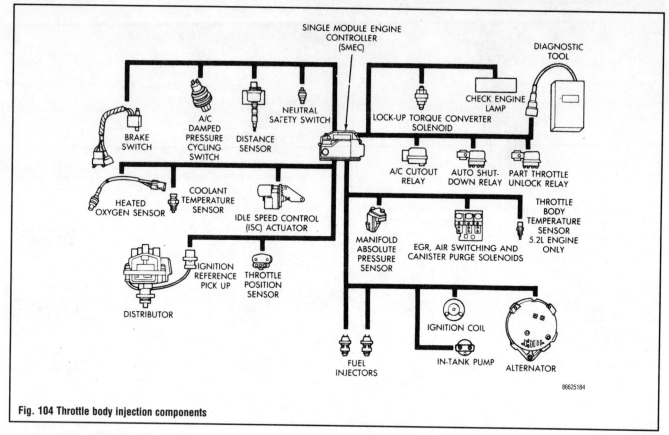

Fig. 104 Throttle body injection components

19. Align the index tab on the level unit with the index hole in the mounting bracket.
20. Install the level unit screws.
21. Install the assembly in the tank.

Throttle Body

▶ See Figures 104 and 105

The throttle body assembly replaces a conventional carburetor and is mounted on top of the intake manifold. The throttle body houses the fuel injectors, pressure regulator, throttle position sensor, automatic idle speed motor and throttle body temperature sensor. Air flow through the throttle body is controlled by cable operated throttle blades located in the base of the throttle body. The throttle body itself provides the chamber for metering, atomizing and distributing the fuel and air entering the engine.

REMOVAL & INSTALLATION

1. Remove the air cleaner.
2. Perform the fuel system pressure release.
3. Disconnect the negative battery cable.
4. Disconnect the vacuum hoses and unplug the electrical connectors.
5. Remove the throttle cable and, if so equipped, speed control and kickdown cables.
6. Remove the return spring.
7. Remove the fuel inlet and return hoses.
8. Remove the throttle body mounting screws, then lift the throttle body from the engine.

   To install:
9. Make sure the mounting surfaces are clean. When installing the throttle body, use a new gasket, then position the throttle body and torque the mounting screws to 14 ft. lbs. (1.6 Nm).
10. Install the fuel inlet and return hoses using new original equipment-type clamps.
11. Install the return spring.

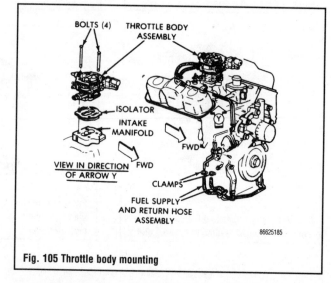

Fig. 105 Throttle body mounting

12. Install the throttle cable and bracket. If so equipped, install the kickdown and speed control cables.
13. Engage the wiring connectors and vacuum hoses.
14. Install the air cleaner.
15. Reconnect the negative battery cable.

Fuel Fittings

REMOVAL & INSTALLATION

▶ See Figure 106

1. Remove the air cleaner assembly.
2. Perform the fuel system pressure release.

FUEL SYSTEM 5-39

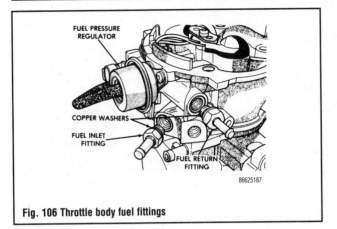

Fig. 106 Throttle body fuel fittings

3. Disconnect the negative battery cable.
4. Loosen the fuel inlet and return hose clamps. Wrap a shop towel around each hose, twist and pull off each hose.
5. Remove each fitting and note the inlet diameter. Remove the copper washers.

To install:
6. Install the fuel fittings in the proper ports using new copper washers and torque to 14 ft. lbs. (1.5 Nm).
7. Using new original equipment type hose clamps, install the fuel return and supply hoses.
8. Reconnect the negative battery cable.
9. Test for leaks using ATM tester C–4805 or equivalent. With the ignition in the **RUN** position depress the ATM button. This will activate the pump and pressurize the system. Check for leaks.
10. Reinstall the air cleaner assembly.

Fuel Pressure Regulator

The pressure regulator is a mechanical device located downstream of the fuel injector on the throttle body. Its function is to maintain a constant 14.5 psi (100 kPa) across the fuel injector tip. The regulator uses a spring loaded rubber diaphragm to uncover a fuel return port. When the fuel pump becomes operational, fuel flows past the injector into the regulator, and is restricted from flowing any further by the blocked return port. When fuel pressure reaches the predetermined setting, it pushes on the diaphragm, compressing the spring, and uncovers the fuel return port. The diaphragm and spring will constantly move from an open to closed position to keep the fuel pressure constant.

REMOVAL & INSTALLATION

♦ See Figure 107

1. Remove the air cleaner assembly.
2. Perform the fuel system pressure release.
3. Disconnect the negative battery cable.
4. Remove the screws (usually 3) attaching the pressure regulator to the throttle body. Place a shop towel around the inlet chamber to contain any fuel remaining in the system.
5. Pull the pressure regulator from the throttle body.
6. Carefully remove the O-ring from the pressure regulator and remove the gasket.

To install:
7. Place a new gasket on the pressure regulator and carefully install a new O-ring.
8. Position the pressure regulator on the throttle body press it into place.
9. Install the screws and torque them to 40 inch lbs. (4.4 Nm).
10. Connect the negative battery cable.
11. Test for leaks using ATM tester C–4805 or equivalent. With the ignition in the **RUN** position depress ATM button. This will activate the pump and pressurize the system. Check for leaks.
12. Reinstall the air cleaner assembly.

Fuel Injectors

The fuel injector is an electric solenoid driven by the power module, but controlled by the SMEC. The SMEC determines when and how long the power module should operate the injector based on various sensor input. When an electric current is supplied to the injector, a spring loaded ball is lifted from its seat. This allows fuel to flow through six spray orifices and deflects off the sharp edge of the injector nozzle. This action causes the fuel to form a 45° cone shaped spray pattern before entering the air stream in the throttle body.

REMOVAL & INSTALLATION

♦ See Figures 108, 109 and 110

1. Remove the air cleaner assembly.
2. Perform the fuel system pressure release.
3. Disconnect the negative battery cable.
4. Remove the fuel pressure regulator.
5. Remove the Torx® screw securing the injector cap.
6. With two small prytools, lift the cap off the injector using the slots provided.
7. Using a small prytool placed in the hole in the front of the electrical connector, gently pry the injector from pod.
8. Make sure the injector lower O-ring has been removed from the pod.

To install:
9. Place a new lower O-ring on the injector and a new O-ring on the injector cap. The injector should have the upper O-ring already installed.
10. Put the cap on the injector. (Injector and cap are keyed). The cap should sit on the injector without interference. Apply a light coating of castor oil or petroleum jelly on the O-rings. Place the assembly in the pod.
11. Rotate the cap and injector to line up the attachment hole.
12. Push down on the cap until it contacts the injector pod.
13. Install the Torx® screw and torque it to 35–45 inch lbs. (3.9–5.0 Nm).
14. Install the fuel pressure regulator.
15. Connect the negative battery cable.
16. Test for leaks using ATM tester C–4805 or equivalent. With the ignition

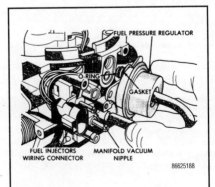

Fig. 107 Replacement of fuel pressure regulator

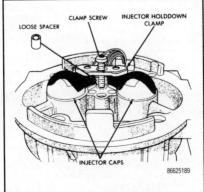

Fig. 108 Injector cap hold-down removal

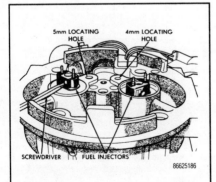

Fig. 109 Carefully pry upward to free the fuel injector

5-40 FUEL SYSTEM

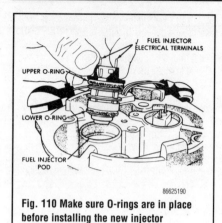

Fig. 110 Make sure O-rings are in place before installing the new injector

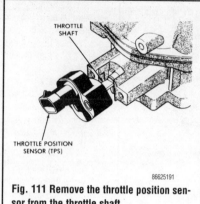

Fig. 111 Remove the throttle position sensor from the throttle shaft

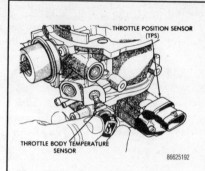

Fig. 112 After loosening it, the throttle body temperature sensor can be unthreaded by hand

in the **RUN** position depress the ATM button. This will activate the pump and pressurize the system. Check for leaks.

17. Reinstall the air cleaner assembly.

Throttle Position Sensor

The Throttle Position Sensor (TPS) is an electronic resistor which is activated by the movement of the throttle shaft. It is mounted on the throttle body and senses the angle of the throttle blade opening. The voltage increases or decreases according to the throttle blade opening. This voltage is transmitted to the SMEC, where it is used along with data from other sensors to adjust the air/fuel ratio to varying conditions.

REMOVAL & INSTALLATION

♦ See Figure 111

1. Disconnect the negative battery cable.
2. Remove the air cleaner.
3. Unplug the three way connector at the throttle position sensor.
4. Remove the two screws mounting the throttle position sensor to the throttle body.
5. Lift the throttle position sensor off the throttle shaft.

To install:

6. Install the throttle position sensor on the throttle body. Position the connector toward the rear of vehicle.
7. Torque sensor to 27 inch lbs. (3 Nm).
8. Engage the three way connector to the throttle position sensor.
9. Install the air cleaner.
10. Connect the negative battery cable.

Throttle Body Temperature Sensor

The throttle body temperature sensor is a device which monitors temperature of the throttle body. This is useful as the reading is normally very close to the fuel temperature. The sensor is mounted in the throttle body. Information provided by the sensor helps allow the SMEC to provide the correct air/fuel mixture for a hot restart condition.

REMOVAL & INSTALLATION

♦ See Figure 112

1. Disconnect the negative battery cable.
2. Remove the air cleaner.
3. Disconnect the throttle cables from the throttle body linkage.
4. Remove the screws (usually 2) from the throttle cable bracket, then position the bracket aside.
5. Disengage the wiring connector.
6. Unscrew the sensor.

To install:

7. Apply heat transfer compound (provided with the part at the dealer when the new sensor is purchased) to the tip portion of the new sensor.

8. Install the sensor and torque it to 80–120 inch lbs. (9–13 Nm).
9. Engage the wiring connector.
10. Install the throttle cable bracket with the screws.
11. Connect the throttle cables to the throttle body linkage, then install the clips.
12. Install the air cleaner.

Automatic Idle Speed (AIS) Motor

♦ See Figure 113

The Automatic Idle Speed (AIS) motor assembly is operated by the SMEC. Data from the throttle position sensor, speed sensor, coolant temperature sensor, and various switch operations, (electric backlite, air conditioning, safety/neutral and brake) are used by the module to adjust the engine to an optimum idle during all conditions. The AIS adjusts the air portion of the air/fuel mixture through an air bypass on the back of the throttle body. Basic (no load) idle is determined by the minimum air flow through the throttle body. The AIS opens or closes off the air bypass as an increase or decrease is needed due to engine loads or ambient conditions. Deceleration die out is also prevented by increasing engine idle when the throttle is closed quickly after a driving (speed) condition.

REMOVAL & INSTALLATION

1. Remove the air cleaner.
2. Disconnect the negative battery cable.
3. Unplug the four pin connector on the AIS.
4. Remove the temperature sensor from the throttle body housing.
5. Remove the Torx® head screws (usually 2).
6. Remove the AIS from the throttle body housing, making sure that the O-ring is with the AIS.

To install:

7. Install new a O-ring on the AIS.
8. Install the AIS into the housing making sure the O-ring is still in place.
9. Install the Torx® head screws.
10. Engage the four pin connector to the AIS.
11. Install the temperature sending unit into the throttle body housing.
12. Connect the negative battery cable.

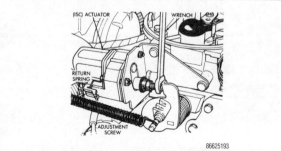

Fig. 113 Adjust the idle speed control actuator

FUEL SYSTEM 5-41

DIESEL FUEL SYSTEM

♦ See Figure 114

Injection Pump

TESTING

1. With the engine running, loosen the cap on the fuel injection line at the injection pump outlet. This will relieve pressure and prevent fuel to be injected into the cylinder.
2. If a cylinder is misfiring, uneven combustion will stop when the fuel is cut off.
3. Proceed from cylinder to cylinder until the faulty cylinder is located.
4. Perform a compression test on the cylinder in question. If the cylinder in question meets the compression specifications, replace the injection pump.

♦ See Figure 115

REMOVAL & INSTALLATION

♦ See Figures 116 and 117

1. Disconnect the batteries.
2. Disconnect the fuel shut off rod at the stop lever. The rod end snaps over a ball stud on the stop lever.

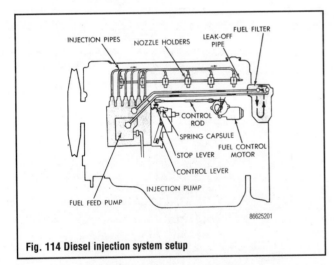

Fig. 114 Diesel injection system setup

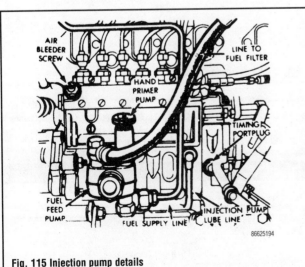

Fig. 115 Injection pump details

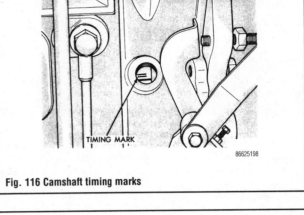

Fig. 116 Camshaft timing marks

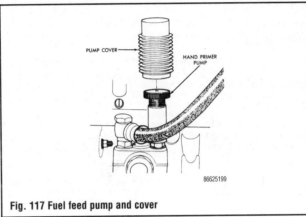

Fig. 117 Fuel feed pump and cover

3. Remove the power steering pump and the mounting bracket from the engine, then set it aside.
4. Thoroughly clean the area around the hose fittings and the injection pipes.
5. Drain the engine oil, then remove the dipstick and the dipstick tube.
6. Disconnect the throttle cable and the linkage from the injection pump control lever.
7. Remove the throttle control bracket assembly from the crankcase, injection pump and the control bracket, then set it aside.
8. Disconnect the fuel supply line to the fuel feed pump and set it aside. Loosen the anchoring clamps as necessary.
9. Disconnect the fuel hoses leading to the filter from the feed pump and the injection pump. Reinstall the screws and seals to prevent dirt from getting into the pump.
10. Rotate the engine so piston No. 1 is approximately 7° before top dead center on the compression stroke.
11. Disconnect the injection pipes from the delivery valves, then set them aside. Cap the ends of the valves to prevent the entry of dirt.
12. Disconnect the injection pump lube lines.
13. Remove the fasteners (usually 5 screws and 1 bolt) attaching the pump.
14. Pull the pump to the rear, then disengage it from the front plate and timing gear case. Rotate the pump toward the crankcase and continue pulling it to the rear until the automatic timer is free of the case.

To install:

15. Loosen the nuts attaching the pump to the mounting flange plate and align the center timing mark on the pump flange with the pointer on the plate. Tighten the four nuts.
16. Be sure that the O-ring is in place on the forward face of the pump mounting flange.
17. Remove the threaded timing port plug on the governor housing behind the control lever to expose the camshaft bushing timing mark. Rotate the pump drive gear to align the timing mark on the camshaft bushing with the pointer on

5-42 FUEL SYSTEM

the governor. The guide plate notch will be at approximately the 8 o'clock position as viewed from the front. Be sure the engine is positioned as described in Step 10 of the removal procedure.

18. Insert the automatic timer into the timing gear case and with the injection pump rotated against the crankshaft, rotate the pump driver gear to mesh with the drive and idler gears. Do not force the pump into position.

19. Push the pump forward into the case. Rotate it away from the crankcase to align the attachment holes.

20. Attach the pump to the timing gear case.

21. Rotate the engine crankshaft in the opposite direction of normal operation until the crankshaft reaches the 18° before TDC mark on the crankshaft pulley. The governor pointer and the injection pump camshaft bushing timing marks should now be aligned. If they are not aligned, the pump has been installed incorrectly and must be removed and reinstalled.

22. Install the governor housing timing port plug and proceed with the pump installation by reversing the remainder of the removal procedure. Do not connect the No. 1 injecting pipe, fuel control rod or the batteries.

23. Bleed the air from the fuel filter and the injection pump by removing the air bleeder screws.

24. Time the injection pump.

INJECTION TIMING

▶ See Figures 118 and 119

1. Disconnect the batteries and the fuel shut off rod at the stop lever.
2. Rotate the crankshaft in the direction of normal operation until the No. 1 cylinder reaches top dead center of the compression stroke. This is done by aligning the lines on the crankshaft pulley rear face with the pointer on the bottom of the case.
3. Remove the forward oil filler cap on the rocker cover and check the No. 1 cylinder valve rockers for looseness. If they are loose, you are at TDC.
4. Rotate the crankshaft in the normal direction of engine operation 1¾ turns.
5. Disconnect the No. 1 injection pipe from the delivery valve holder.
6. Turn the crankshaft in the normal direction of engine operation in small steps. Stop when fuel begins to flow from the delivery valve holder. Injection begins at this point. The control lever must be in the idle position.
7. Read the injection timing point from the scale on the back of the crankshaft damper. If the timing is correct, the timing mark should be at the value shown on the Vehicle Emission Control Information label on the rocker cover.
8. If the timing point determined differs from the standard value, more than 2 degrees, loosen the four pump-to-flange plate nuts and rotate the pump (toward the crankcase to advance the timing, away from the crankcase to retard

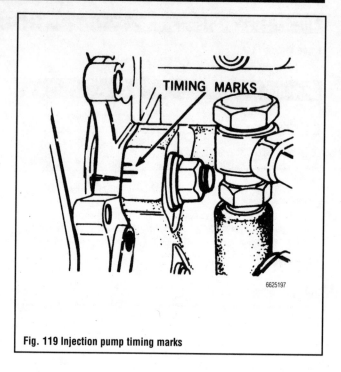

Fig. 119 Injection pump timing marks

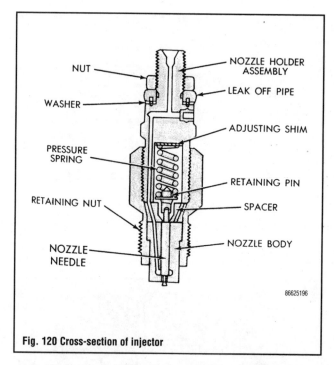

Fig. 120 Cross-section of injector

it) to correct the difference. Each mark on the injection pump timing scale represents 6 degrees. Tighten the flange plate nuts and repeat the timing procedure to be sure the timing is correct.

9. Install or connect any remaining components.

Injectors

REMOVAL & INSTALLATION

▶ See Figure 120

1. Remove the injection line at the nozzle holder.
2. Unscrew the nozzle holder.

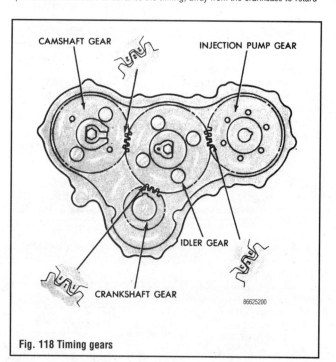

Fig. 118 Timing gears

FUEL SYSTEM 5-43

3. Place the nozzle holder in a vise bearing on the nut.
4. Remove the nozzle body from the nut. Lift the pressure adjusting shim, spring, retaining pin, spacer and nozzle tip from the nozzle holder body.
5. Clean all parts in clean diesel fuel. Replace any part which shows signs of wear or damage.
6. Assemble all parts and install the assembly in the engine. Torque the assembly to 45–55 ft. lbs. (61–74 Nm). Connect the injection line.

TESTING

♦ See Figure 121

1. Install the injector nozzle (adjusted to the specified injection pressure) on a nozzle tester.
2. Slowly and steadily increase the pressure with the tester lever to 1429 psi (9853 kPa).
3. Hold the pressure and inspect the nozzle assembly to ensure that there are no fuel leaks. If there are leaks present, replace the nozzle tip.

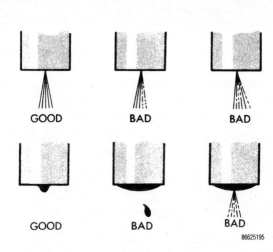

Fig. 121 Injector spray patterns (top)—The injectors should not leak during testing (bottom)

FUEL TANK

Tank Assembly

REMOVAL & INSTALLATION

Pick-Ups

1. Disconnect the battery ground cable.
2. Remove the fuel tank filler cap.
3. Pump all fuel from the tank into an approved container, then raise and safely support the vehicle.
4. Disconnect the fuel line(s) and wire leads to the gauge unit. Remove the ground strap.
5. Remove the vent hose shield and the hose clamps from the hoses running to the vapor vent tube.
6. Remove the filler tube hose clamps and disconnect the hose from the tank.
7. Place a padded transmission jack under the center of the tank and apply sufficient pressure to **just** support the tank.
8. Disconnect the two J–bolts and remove the retaining straps at the rear of the tank. Lower the tank from the vehicle. Feed the vent tube hoses (usually 2) and filler tube vent hose through the grommets in the frame as the tank is being lowered. Remove the gas tank sending unit.

To install:

9. Inspect the fuel filter, and if it is clogged or damaged, replace it.
10. Insert a new gasket in the recess of the fuel sending unit and slide the sending unit into the tank. Align the positioning tangs on the sender with those on the tank. Install the lockring and tighten securely.
11. Position the tank on a transmission jack and raise it into place, feeding the vent hoses through the grommets on the way up.
12. Connect the J-bolts and retaining straps, then tighten to 40 inch lbs. (4.5 Nm). Remove the jack.
13. Connect the filler tube and all vent hoses.
14. Connect the fuel line(s), ground strap, and sending unit wire leads.
15. Lower the vehicle.
16. Refill the tank and inspect it for leaks. Connect the battery ground cable.

Ramcharger and Trail Duster

1. Disconnect the battery ground cable.
2. If there is a tank skid plate, remove it.
3. Remove the tank filler cap.
4. Pump or siphon the contents of the tank into a safe container.

❋❋❋ CAUTION

Siphoning should not be started by mouth! Only fuel–safe pumps should be used.

5. Raise and safely support the vehicle.
6. Disconnect the fuel line(s) and tank sending unit wire(s). Remove the ground strap or wire.
7. Remove the hose clamps from the vent dome hose.
8. Remove the filler tube hose clamps. Detach the hoses from the tank.
9. Support the tank with a padded transmission jack.
10. Disconnect the two J-bolts and remove the straps at the rear of the tank.
11. Remove the tank sending unit.

To install:

12. Use a new tank sending unit gasket. Check the filter on the end of the fuel suction tube.
13. Use a new or undamaged tank-to-frame insulator. Raise the tank into position.
14. Connect the J-bolts and retaining straps. Tighten the bolts until about 1 in. (25mm) of threads protrude.
15. Connect the filler tube and all hoses. Tighten the clamps.
16. Connect the fuel line(s), ground strap or wire(s), and tank sending unit wire. Make sure that all fuel line heat shields are in place.
17. Install the skid plate.
18. Lower the vehicle, then connect the negative battery cable.

SENDING UNIT

Except Fuel Injection

1. Disconnect the negative battery cable.
2. Raise and support the vehicle.
3. Remove the fuel tank from the vehicle.
4. Unfasten the sending unit with the proper tool (either spanner wrench or screwdriver), then remove.

To install:

5. Insert a new gasket in the recess of the fuel sending unit and slide the sending unit into the tank. Align the positioning tangs on the sender with those on the tank. Install the lockring or screws and tighten securely.
6. Install the fuel tank on the vehicle.
7. Lower the vehicle, then connect the negative battery cable.

Fuel Injection

To remove the sending unit on a fuel injected vehicle, refer to the fuel pump procedure earlier in this section.

UNDERSTANDING AND
TROUBLESHOOTING ELECTRICAL
SYSTEMS 6-2
BASIC ELECTRICAL THEORY 6-2
   HOW DOES ELECTRICITY WORK: THE
    WATER ANALOGY 6-2
   OHM'S LAW 6-2
ELECTRICAL COMPONENTS 6-2
   POWER SOURCE 6-2
   GROUND 6-3
   PROTECTIVE DEVICES 6-3
   SWITCHES & RELAYS 6-3
   LOAD 6-4
   WIRING & HARNESSES 6-4
   CONNECTORS 6-4
TEST EQUIPMENT 6-5
   JUMPER WIRES 6-5
   TEST LIGHTS 6-5
   MULTIMETERS 6-5
TROUBLESHOOTING ELECTRICAL
 SYSTEMS 6-6
TESTING 6-6
   OPEN CIRCUITS 6-6
   SHORT CIRCUITS 6-6
   VOLTAGE 6-6
   VOLTAGE DROP 6-7
   RESISTANCE 6-7
WIRE AND CONNECTOR REPAIR 6-8
HEATER AND AIR CONDITIONER 6-8
BLOWER MOTOR 6-8
   REMOVAL & INSTALLATION 6-8
HEATER CORE 6-9
   REMOVAL & INSTALLATION 6-9
CONTROL CABLES 6-13
   REMOVAL & INSTALLATION 6-13
AIR CONDITIONING COMPONENTS 6-14
   REMOVAL & INSTALLATION 6-14
CONTROL UNIT 6-14
   REMOVAL & INSTALLATION 6-14
RADIO 6-15
RADIO UNIT 6-15
   REMOVAL & INSTALLATION 6-15
   ANTENNA LEAD CONNECTIONS 6-15
   TRIMMER ADJUSTMENT 6-16
ANTENNA MAST 6-16
   REMOVAL & INSTALLATION 6-16
**WINDSHIELD WIPERS AND
 WASHERS 6-16**
WIPER ARM 6-16
   REMOVAL & INSTALLATION 6-16
WIPER MOTOR 6-16
   REMOVAL & INSTALLATION 6-16
WIPER LINKAGE 6-17
   REMOVAL & INSTALLATION 6-17
**INSTRUMENTS AND
 SWITCHES 6-18**
INSTRUMENT CLUSTER 6-18
   REMOVAL & INSTALLATION 6-18
CLUSTER MASK AND LENS 6-20
   REMOVAL & INSTALLATION 6-20
SPEEDOMETER 6-20
   REMOVAL & INSTALLATION 6-20
SPEEDOMETER CABLE 6-20
WINDSHIELD WIPER SWITCH 6-20
   REMOVAL & INSTALLATION 6-20
CLOCK 6-20
   REMOVAL & INSTALLATION 6-20
FOUR WHEEL DRIVE INDICATOR 6-20
   REMOVAL & INSTALLATION 6-20
SNOW PLOW TOGGLE SWITCH 6-20
   REMOVAL & INSTALLATION 6-20
HEADLIGHT SWITCH 6-21
   REMOVAL & INSTALLATION 6-21
LIGHTING 6-21
HEADLIGHTS 6-21
   REMOVAL & INSTALLATION 6-21
   AIMING RECOMMENDATIONS 6-21
   ADJUSTING & AIMING 6-21
SIGNAL AND MARKER LIGHTS 6-22
   REMOVAL & INSTALLATION 6-22
TRAILER WIRING 6-24
CIRCUIT PROTECTION 6-24
FUSES 6-24
   REPLACEMENT 6-24
CIRCUIT BREAKERS 6-26
   RESETTING AND/OR
    REPLACEMENT 6-26
TURN SIGNAL AND HAZARD FLASHER
 LOCATIONS 6-26
FUSE LINK 6-27
WIRING DIAGRAMS 6-28

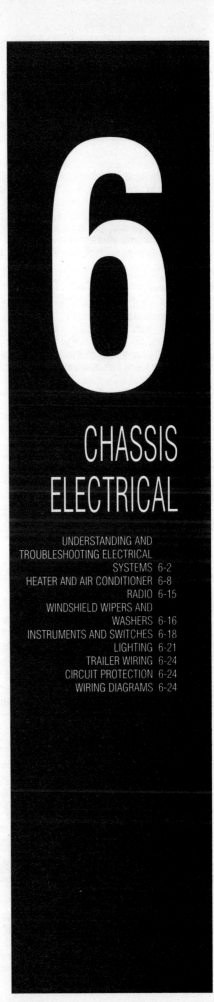

6

CHASSIS ELECTRICAL

UNDERSTANDING AND
TROUBLESHOOTING ELECTRICAL
SYSTEMS 6-2
HEATER AND AIR CONDITIONER 6-8
RADIO 6-15
WINDSHIELD WIPERS AND
WASHERS 6-16
INSTRUMENTS AND SWITCHES 6-18
LIGHTING 6-21
TRAILER WIRING 6-24
CIRCUIT PROTECTION 6-24
WIRING DIAGRAMS 6-24

6-2 CHASSIS ELECTRICAL

UNDERSTANDING AND TROUBLESHOOTING ELECTRICAL SYSTEMS

Basic Electrical Theory

♦ See Figure 1

For any 12 volt, negative ground, electrical system to operate, the electricity must travel in a complete circuit. This simply means that current (power) from the positive (+) terminal of the battery must eventually return to the negative (−) terminal of the battery. Along the way, this current will travel through wires, fuses, switches and components. If, for any reason, the flow of current through the circuit is interrupted, the component fed by that circuit will cease to function properly.

Perhaps the easiest way to visualize a circuit is to think of connecting a light bulb (with two wires attached to it) to the battery—one wire attached to the negative (−) terminal of the battery and the other wire to the positive (+) terminal. With the two wires touching the battery terminals, the circuit would be complete and the light bulb would illuminate. Electricity would follow a path from the battery to the bulb and back to the battery. It's easy to see that with longer wires on our light bulb, it could be mounted anywhere. Further, one wire could be fitted with a switch so that the light could be turned on and off.

The normal automotive circuit differs from this simple example in two ways. First, instead of having a return wire from the bulb to the battery, the current travels through the frame of the vehicle. Since the negative (−) battery cable is attached to the frame (made of electrically conductive metal), the frame of the vehicle can serve as a ground wire to complete the circuit. Secondly, most automotive circuits contain multiple components which receive power from a single circuit. This lessens the amount of wire needed to power components on the vehicle.

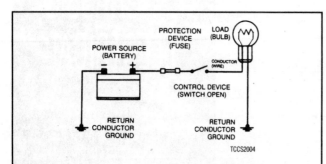

Fig. 1 This example illustrates a simple circuit. When the switch is closed, power from the positive (+) battery terminal flows through the fuse and the switch, and then to the light bulb. The light illuminates and the circuit is completed through the ground wire back to the negative (−) battery terminal. In reality, the two ground points shown in the illustration are attached to the metal frame of the vehicle, which completes the circuit back to the battery

HOW DOES ELECTRICITY WORK: THE WATER ANALOGY

Electricity is the flow of electrons—the subatomic particles that constitute the outer shell of an atom. Electrons spin in an orbit around the center core of an atom. The center core is comprised of protons (positive charge) and neutrons (neutral charge). Electrons have a negative charge and balance out the positive charge of the protons. When an outside force causes the number of electrons to unbalance the charge of the protons, the electrons will split off the atom and look for another atom to balance out. If this imbalance is kept up, electrons will continue to move and an electrical flow will exist.

Many people have been taught electrical theory using an analogy with water. In a comparison with water flowing through a pipe, the electrons would be the water and the wire is the pipe.

The flow of electricity can be measured much like the flow of water through a pipe. The unit of measurement used is amperes, frequently abbreviated as amps (a). You can compare amperage to the volume of water flowing through a pipe. When connected to a circuit, an ammeter will measure the actual amount of current flowing through the circuit. When relatively few electrons flow through a circuit, the amperage is low. When many electrons flow, the amperage is high.

Water pressure is measured in units such as pounds per square inch (psi);

The electrical pressure is measured in units called volts (v). When a voltmeter is connected to a circuit, it is measuring the electrical pressure.

The actual flow of electricity depends not only on voltage and amperage, but also on the resistance of the circuit. The higher the resistance, the higher the force necessary to push the current through the circuit. The standard unit for measuring resistance is an ohm. Resistance in a circuit varies depending on the amount and type of components used in the circuit. The main factors which determine resistance are:

• Material—some materials have more resistance than others. Those with high resistance are said to be insulators. Rubber materials (or rubber-like plastics) are some of the most common insulators used in vehicles as they have a very high resistance to electricity. Very low resistance materials are said to be conductors. Copper wire is among the best conductors. Silver is actually a superior conductor to copper and is used in some relay contacts, but its high cost prohibits its use as common wiring. Most automotive wiring is made of copper.

• Size—the larger the wire size being used, the less resistance the wire will have. This is why components which use large amounts of electricity usually have large wires supplying current to them.

• Length—for a given thickness of wire, the longer the wire, the greater the resistance. The shorter the wire, the less the resistance. When determining the proper wire for a circuit, both size and length must be considered to design a circuit that can handle the current needs of the component.

• Temperature—with many materials, the higher the temperature, the greater the resistance (positive temperature coefficient). Some materials exhibit the opposite trait of lower resistance with higher temperatures (negative temperature coefficient). These principles are used in many of the sensors on the engine.

OHM'S LAW

There is a direct relationship between current, voltage and resistance. The relationship between current, voltage and resistance can be summed up by a statement known as Ohm's law.

Voltage (E) is equal to amperage (I) times resistance (R): $E = I \times R$
Other forms of the formula are $R = E/I$ and $I = E/R$

In each of these formulas, E is the voltage in volts, I is the current in amps and R is the resistance in ohms. The basic point to remember is that as the resistance of a circuit goes up, the amount of current that flows in the circuit will go down, if voltage remains the same.

The amount of work that the electricity can perform is expressed as power. The unit of power is the watt (w). The relationship between power, voltage and current is expressed as:

Power (w) is equal to amperage (I) times voltage (E): $W = I \times E$

This is only true for direct current (DC) circuits; The alternating current formula is a tad different, but since the electrical circuits in most vehicles are DC type, we need not get into AC circuit theory.

Electrical Components

POWER SOURCE

Power is supplied to the vehicle by two devices: The battery and the alternator. The battery supplies electrical power during starting or during periods when the current demand of the vehicle's electrical system exceeds the output capacity of the alternator. The alternator supplies electrical current when the engine is running. Just not does the alternator supply the current needs of the vehicle, but it recharges the battery.

The Battery

In most modern vehicles, the battery is a lead/acid electrochemical device consisting of six 2 volt subsections (cells) connected in series, so that the unit is capable of producing approximately 12 volts of electrical pressure. Each subsection consists of a series of positive and negative plates held a short distance apart in a solution of sulfuric acid and water.

The two types of plates are of dissimilar metals. This sets up a chemical reaction, and it is this reaction which produces current flow from the battery when its positive and negative terminals are connected to an electrical load.

The power removed from the battery is replaced by the alternator, restoring the battery to its original chemical state.

The Alternator

On some vehicles there isn't an alternator, but a generator. The difference is that an alternator supplies alternating current which is then changed to direct current for use on the vehicle, while a generator produces direct current. Alternators tend to be more efficient and that is why they are used.

Alternators and generators are devices that consist of coils of wires wound together making big electromagnets. One group of coils spins within another set and the interaction of the magnetic fields causes a current to flow. This current is then drawn off the coils and fed into the vehicles electrical system.

GROUND

Two types of grounds are used in automotive electric circuits. Direct ground components are grounded to the frame through their mounting points. All other components use some sort of ground wire which is attached to the frame or chassis of the vehicle. The electrical current runs through the chassis of the vehicle and returns to the battery through the ground (-) cable; if you look, you'll see that the battery ground cable connects between the battery and the frame or chassis of the vehicle.

➡ It should be noted that a good percentage of electrical problems can be traced to bad grounds.

PROTECTIVE DEVICES

♦ See Figure 2

It is possible for large surges of current to pass through the electrical system of your vehicle. If this surge of current were to reach the load in the circuit, the surge could burn it out or severely damage it. It can also overload the wiring, causing the harness to get hot and melt the insulation. To prevent this, fuses, circuit breakers and/or fusible links are connected into the supply wires of the electrical system. These items are nothing more than a built-in weak spot in the system. When an abnormal amount of current flows through the system, these protective devices work as follows to protect the circuit:

• Fuse—when an excessive electrical current passes through a fuse, the fuse "blows" (the conductor melts) and opens the circuit, preventing the passage of current.

• Circuit Breaker—a circuit breaker is basically a self-repairing fuse. It will open the circuit in the same fashion as a fuse, but when the surge subsides, the circuit breaker can be reset and does not need replacement.

• Fusible Link—a fusible link (fuse link or main link) is a short length of special, high temperature insulated wire that acts as a fuse. When an excessive electrical current passes through a fusible link, the thin gauge wire inside the link melts, creating an intentional open to protect the circuit. To repair the circuit, the link must be replaced. Some newer type fusible links are housed in plug-in modules, which are simply replaced like a fuse, while older type fusible links must be cut and spliced if they melt. Since this link is very early in the electrical path, it's the first place to look if nothing on the vehicle works, yet the battery seems to be charged and is properly connected.

✳✳ CAUTION

Always replace fuses, circuit breakers and fusible links with identically rated components. Under no circumstances should a component of higher or lower amperage rating be substituted.

SWITCHES & RELAYS

♦ See Figures 3 and 4

Switches are used in electrical circuits to control the passage of current. The most common use is to open and close circuits between the battery and the various electric devices in the system. Switches are rated according to the amount of amperage they can handle. If a sufficient amperage rated switch is not used in a circuit, the switch could overload and cause damage.

Some electrical components which require a large amount of current to operate use a special switch called a relay. Since these circuits carry a large amount of current, the thickness of the wire in the circuit is also greater. If this large wire were connected from the load to the control switch, the switch would have to carry the high amperage load and the fairing or dash would be twice as large to accommodate the increased size of the wiring harness. To prevent these problems, a relay is used.

Relays are composed of a coil and a set of contacts. When the coil has a current passed though it, a magnetic field is formed and this field causes the contacts to move together, completing the circuit. Most relays are normally open, prevent-

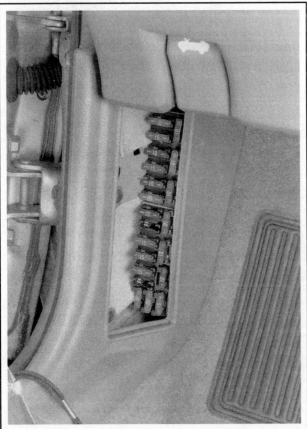

Fig. 2 Most vehicles use one or more fuse panels. This one is located on the driver's side kick panel

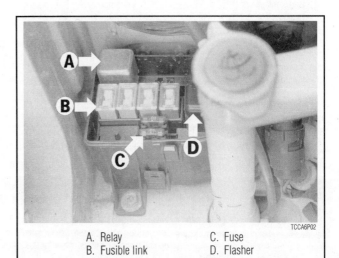

A. Relay C. Fuse
B. Fusible link D. Flasher

Fig. 3 The underhood fuse and relay panel usually contains fuses, relays, flashers and fusible links

6-4 CHASSIS ELECTRICAL

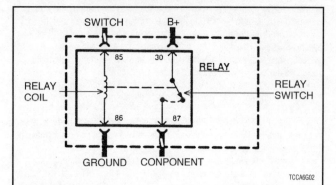

Fig. 4 Relays are composed of a coil and a switch. These two components are linked together so that when one operates, the other operates at the same time. The large wires in the circuit are connected from the battery to one side of the relay switch (B+) and from the opposite side of the relay switch to the load (component). Smaller wires are connected from the relay coil to the control switch for the circuit and from the opposite side of the relay coil to ground

ing current from passing through the circuit, but they can take any electrical form depending on the job they are intended to do. Relays can be considered "remote control switches." They allow a smaller current to operate devices that require higher amperages. When a small current operates the coil, a larger current is allowed to pass by the contacts. Some common circuits which may use relays are the horn, headlights, starter, electric fuel pump and other high draw circuits.

LOAD

Every electrical circuit must include a "load" (something to use the electricity coming from the source). Without this load, the battery would attempt to deliver its entire power supply from one pole to another. This is called a "short circuit." All this electricity would take a short cut to ground and cause a great amount of damage to other components in the circuit by developing a tremendous amount of heat. This condition could develop sufficient heat to melt the insulation on all the surrounding wires and reduce a multiple wire cable to a lump of plastic and copper.

WIRING & HARNESSES

The average vehicle contains meters and meters of wiring, with hundreds of individual connections. To protect the many wires from damage and to keep them from becoming a confusing tangle, they are organized into bundles, enclosed in plastic or taped together and called wiring harnesses. Different harnesses serve different parts of the vehicle. Individual wires are color coded to help trace them through a harness where sections are hidden from view.

Automotive wiring or circuit conductors can be either single strand wire, multi-strand wire or printed circuitry. Single strand wire has a solid metal core and is usually used inside such components as alternators, motors, relays and other devices. Multi-strand wire has a core made of many small strands of wire twisted together into a single conductor. Most of the wiring in an automotive electrical system is made up of multi-strand wire, either as a single conductor or grouped together in a harness. All wiring is color coded on the insulator, either as a solid color or as a colored wire with an identification stripe. A printed circuit is a thin film of copper or other conductor that is printed on an insulator backing. Occasionally, a printed circuit is sandwiched between two sheets of plastic for more protection and flexibility. A complete printed circuit, consisting of conductors, insulating material and connectors for lamps or other components is called a printed circuit board. Printed circuitry is used in place of individual wires or harnesses in places where space is limited, such as behind instrument panels.

Since automotive electrical systems are very sensitive to changes in resistance, the selection of properly sized wires is critical when systems are repaired. A loose or corroded connection or a replacement wire that is too small for the circuit will add extra resistance and an additional voltage drop to the circuit.

The wire gauge number is an expression of the cross-section area of the conductor. Vehicles from countries that use the metric system will typically describe the wire size as its cross-sectional area in square millimeters. In this method, the larger the wire, the greater the number. Another common system for expressing wire size is the American Wire Gauge (AWG) system. As gauge number increases, area decreases and the wire becomes smaller. An 18 gauge wire is smaller than a 4 gauge wire. A wire with a higher gauge number will carry less current than a wire with a lower gauge number. Gauge wire size refers to the size of the strands of the conductor, not the size of the complete wire with insulator. It is possible, therefore, to have two wires of the same gauge with different diameters because one may have thicker insulation than the other.

It is essential to understand how a circuit works before trying to figure out why it doesn't. An electrical schematic shows the electrical current paths when a circuit is operating properly. Schematics break the entire electrical system down into individual circuits. In a schematic, usually no attempt is made to represent wiring and components as they physically appear on the vehicle; switches and other components are shown as simply as possible. Face views of harness connectors show the cavity or terminal locations in all multi-pin connectors to help locate test points.

CONNECTORS

◆ See Figures 5 and 6

Three types of connectors are commonly used in automotive applications—weatherproof, molded and hard shell.

• Weatherproof—these connectors are most commonly used where the connector is exposed to the elements. Terminals are protected against moisture and dirt by sealing rings which provide a weathertight seal. All repairs require the use of a special terminal and the tool required to service it. Unlike standard blade type terminals, these weatherproof terminals cannot be straightened once they are bent. Make certain that the connectors are properly seated and all of the sealing rings are in place when connecting leads.

Fig. 5 Hard shell (left) and weatherproof (right) connectors have replaceable terminals

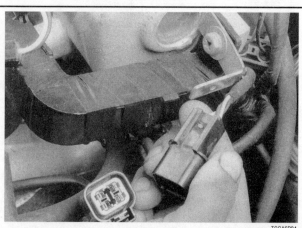

Fig. 6 Weatherproof connectors are most commonly used in the engine compartment or where the connector is exposed to the elements

- Molded—these connectors require complete replacement of the connector if found to be defective. This means splicing a new connector assembly into the harness. All splices should be soldered to insure proper contact. Use care when probing the connections or replacing terminals in them, as it is possible to create a short circuit between opposite terminals. If this happens to the wrong terminal pair, it is possible to damage certain components. Always use jumper wires between connectors for circuit checking and NEVER probe through weatherproof seals.
- Hard Shell—unlike molded connectors, the terminal contacts in hard-shell connectors can be replaced. Replacement usually involves the use of a special terminal removal tool that depresses the locking tangs (barbs) on the connector terminal and allows the connector to be removed from the rear of the shell. The connector shell should be replaced if it shows any evidence of burning, melting, cracks, or breaks. Replace individual terminals that are burnt, corroded, distorted or loose.

Test Equipment

Pinpointing the exact cause of trouble in an electrical circuit is most times accomplished by the use of special test equipment. The following describes different types of commonly used test equipment and briefly explains how to use them in diagnosis. In addition to the information covered below, the tool manufacturer's instructions booklet (provided with the tester) should be read and clearly understood before attempting any test procedures.

JUMPER WIRES

✻✻ CAUTION

Never use jumper wires made from a thinner gauge wire than the circuit being tested. If the jumper wire is of too small a gauge, it may overheat and possibly melt. Never use jumpers to bypass high resistance loads in a circuit. Bypassing resistances, in effect, creates a short circuit. This may, in turn, cause damage and fire. Jumper wires should only be used to bypass lengths of wire or to simulate switches.

Jumper wires are simple, yet extremely valuable, pieces of test equipment. They are basically test wires which are used to bypass sections of a circuit. Although jumper wires can be purchased, they are usually fabricated from lengths of standard automotive wire and whatever type of connector (alligator clip, spade connector or pin connector) that is required for the particular application being tested. In cramped, hard-to-reach areas, it is advisable to have insulated boots over the jumper wire terminals in order to prevent accidental grounding. It is also advisable to include a standard automotive fuse in any jumper wire. This is commonly referred to as a "fused jumper". By inserting an in-line fuse holder between a set of test leads, a fused jumper wire can be used for bypassing open circuits. Use a 5 amp fuse to provide protection against voltage spikes.

Jumper wires are used primarily to locate open electrical circuits, on either the ground (-) side of the circuit or on the power (+) side. If an electrical component fails to operate, connect the jumper wire between the component and a good ground. If the component operates only with the jumper installed, the ground circuit is open. If the ground circuit is good, but the component does not operate, the circuit between the power feed and component may be open. By moving the jumper wire successively back from the component toward the power source, you can isolate the area of the circuit where the open is located. When the component stops functioning, or the power is cut off, the open is in the segment of wire between the jumper and the point previously tested.

You can sometimes connect the jumper wire directly from the battery to the "hot" terminal of the component, but first make sure the component uses 12 volts in operation. Some electrical components, such as fuel injectors or sensors, are designed to operate on about 4 to 5 volts, and running 12 volts directly to these components will cause damage.

TEST LIGHTS

♦ See Figure 7

The test light is used to check circuits and components while electrical current is flowing through them. It is used for voltage and ground tests. To use a 12 volt test light, connect the ground clip to a good ground and probe wherever

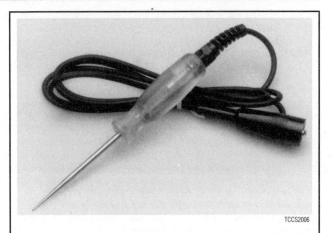

Fig. 7 A 12 volt test light is used to detect the presence of voltage in a circuit

necessary with the pick. The test light will illuminate when voltage is detected. This does not necessarily mean that 12 volts (or any particular amount of voltage) is present; it only means that some voltage is present. It is advisable before using the test light to touch its ground clip and probe across the battery posts or terminals to make sure the light is operating properly.

✻✻ WARNING

Do not use a test light to probe electronic ignition, spark plug or coil wires. Never use a pick-type test light to probe wiring on computer controlled systems unless specifically instructed to do so. Any wire insulation that is pierced by the test light probe should be taped and sealed with silicone after testing.

Like the jumper wire, the 12 volt test light is used to isolate opens in circuits. But, whereas the jumper wire is used to bypass the open to operate the load, the 12 volt test light is used to locate the presence of voltage in a circuit. If the test light illuminates, there is power up to that point in the circuit; if the test light does not illuminate, there is an open circuit (no power). Move the test light in successive steps back toward the power source until the light in the handle illuminates. The open is between the probe and a point which was previously probed.

The self-powered test light is similar in design to the 12 volt test light, but contains a 1.5 volt penlight battery in the handle. It is most often used in place of a multimeter to check for open or short circuits when power is isolated from the circuit (continuity test).

The battery in a self-powered test light does not provide much current. A weak battery may not provide enough power to illuminate the test light even when a complete circuit is made (especially if there is high resistance in the circuit). Always make sure that the test battery is strong. To check the battery, briefly touch the ground clip to the probe; if the light glows brightly, the battery is strong enough for testing.

➡**A self-powered test light should not be used on any computer controlled system or component. The small amount of electricity transmitted by the test light is enough to damage many electronic automotive components.**

MULTIMETERS

Multimeters are an extremely useful tool for troubleshooting electrical problems. They can be purchased in either analog or digital form and have a price range to suit any budget. A multimeter is a voltmeter, ammeter and ohmmeter (along with other features) combined into one instrument. It is often used when testing solid state circuits because of its high input impedance (usually 10 megaohms or more). A brief description of the multimeter main test functions follows:

- Voltmeter—the voltmeter is used to measure voltage at any point in a circuit, or to measure the voltage drop across any part of a circuit. Voltmeters usually have various scales and a selector switch to allow the reading of different

6-6 CHASSIS ELECTRICAL

voltage ranges. The voltmeter has a positive and a negative lead. To avoid damage to the meter, always connect the negative lead to the negative (-) side of the circuit (to ground or nearest the ground side of the circuit) and connect the positive lead to the positive (+) side of the circuit (to the power source or the nearest power source). Note that the negative voltmeter lead will always be black and that the positive voltmeter will always be some color other than black (usually red).

• Ohmmeter—the ohmmeter is designed to read resistance (measured in ohms) in a circuit or component. Most ohmmeters will have a selector switch which permits the measurement of different ranges of resistance (usually the selector switch allows the multiplication of the meter reading by 10, 100, 1,000 and 10,000). Some ohmmeters are "auto-ranging" which means the meter itself will determine which scale to use. Since the meters are powered by an internal battery, the ohmmeter can be used like a self-powered test light. When the ohmmeter is connected, current from the ohmmeter flows through the circuit or component being tested. Since the ohmmeter's internal resistance and voltage are known values, the amount of current flow through the meter depends on the resistance of the circuit or component being tested. The ohmmeter can also be used to perform a continuity test for suspected open circuits. In using the meter for making continuity checks, do not be concerned with the actual resistance readings. Zero resistance, or any ohm reading, indicates continuity in the circuit. Infinite resistance indicates an opening in the circuit. A high resistance reading where there should be none indicates a problem in the circuit. Checks for short circuits are made in the same manner as checks for open circuits, except that the circuit must be isolated from both power and normal ground. Infinite resistance indicates no continuity, while zero resistance indicates a dead short.

※※ WARNING

Never use an ohmmeter to check the resistance of a component or wire while there is voltage applied to the circuit.

• Ammeter—an ammeter measures the amount of current flowing through a circuit in units called amperes or amps. At normal operating voltage, most circuits have a characteristic amount of amperes, called "current draw" which can be measured using an ammeter. By referring to a specified current draw rating, then measuring the amperes and comparing the two values, one can determine what is happening within the circuit to aid in diagnosis. An open circuit, for example, will not allow any current to flow, so the ammeter reading will be zero. A damaged component or circuit will have an increased current draw, so the reading will be high. The ammeter is always connected in series with the circuit being tested. All of the current that normally flows through the circuit must also flow through the ammeter; if there is any other path for the current to follow, the ammeter reading will not be accurate. The ammeter itself has very little resistance to current flow and, therefore, will not affect the circuit, but it will measure current draw only when the circuit is closed and electricity is flowing. Excessive current draw can blow fuses and drain the battery, while a reduced current draw can cause motors to run slowly, lights to dim and other components to not operate properly.

Troubleshooting Electrical Systems

When diagnosing a specific problem, organized troubleshooting is a must. The complexity of a modern automotive vehicle demands that you approach any problem in a logical, organized manner. There are certain troubleshooting techniques, however, which are standard:

• Establish when the problem occurs. Does the problem appear only under certain conditions? Were there any noises, odors or other unusual symptoms? Isolate the problem area. To do this, make some simple tests and observations, then eliminate the systems that are working properly. Check for obvious problems, such as broken wires and loose or dirty connections. Always check the obvious before assuming something complicated is the cause.

• Test for problems systematically to determine the cause once the problem area is isolated. Are all the components functioning properly? Is there power going to electrical switches and motors? Performing careful, systematic checks will often turn up most causes on the first inspection, without wasting time checking components that have little or no relationship to the problem.

• Test all repairs after the work is done to make sure that the problem is fixed. Some causes can be traced to more than one component, so a careful verification of repair work is important in order to pick up additional malfunctions that may cause a problem to reappear or a different problem to arise. A blown fuse, for example, is a simple problem that may require more than another fuse to repair. If you don't look for a problem that caused a fuse to blow, a shorted wire (for example) may go undetected.

Experience has shown that most problems tend to be the result of a fairly simple and obvious cause, such as loose or corroded connectors, bad grounds or damaged wire insulation which causes a short. This makes careful visual inspection of components during testing essential to quick and accurate troubleshooting.

Testing

OPEN CIRCUITS

♦ See Figure 8

This test already assumes the existence of an open in the circuit and it is used to help locate the open portion.

1. Isolate the circuit from power and ground.
2. Connect the self-powered test light or ohmmeter ground clip to the ground side of the circuit and probe sections of the circuit sequentially.
3. If the light is out or there is infinite resistance, the open is between the probe and the circuit ground.
4. If the light is on or the meter shows continuity, the open is between the probe and the end of the circuit toward the power source.

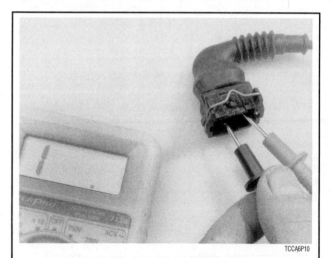

Fig. 8 The infinite reading on this multimeter indicates that the circuit is open

SHORT CIRCUITS

➡**Never use a self-powered test light to perform checks for opens or shorts when power is applied to the circuit under test. The test light can be damaged by outside power.**

1. Isolate the circuit from power and ground.
2. Connect the self-powered test light or ohmmeter ground clip to a good ground and probe any easy-to-reach point in the circuit.
3. If the light comes on or there is continuity, there is a short somewhere in the circuit.
4. To isolate the short, probe a test point at either end of the isolated circuit (the light should be on or the meter should indicate continuity).
5. Leave the test light probe engaged and sequentially open connectors or switches, remove parts, etc. until the light goes out or continuity is broken.
6. When the light goes out, the short is between the last two circuit components which were opened.

VOLTAGE

This test determines voltage available from the battery and should be the first step in any electrical troubleshooting procedure after visual inspection. Many electrical problems, especially on computer controlled systems, can be caused by a low state of charge in the battery. Excessive corrosion at the battery cable

CHASSIS ELECTRICAL 6-7

terminals can cause poor contact that will prevent proper charging and full battery current flow.

1. Set the voltmeter selector switch to the 20V position.
2. Connect the multimeter negative lead to the battery's negative (-) post or terminal and the positive lead to the battery's positive (+) post or terminal.
3. Turn the ignition switch **ON** to provide a load.
4. A well charged battery should register over 12 volts. If the meter reads below 11.5 volts, the battery power may be insufficient to operate the electrical system properly.

VOLTAGE DROP

♦ See Figure 9

When current flows through a load, the voltage beyond the load drops. This voltage drop is due to the resistance created by the load and also by small resistances created by corrosion at the connectors and damaged insulation on the wires. The maximum allowable voltage drop under load is critical, especially if there is more than one load in the circuit, since all voltage drops are cumulative.

1. Set the voltmeter selector switch to the 20 volt position.
2. Connect the multimeter negative lead to a good ground.
3. Operate the circuit and check the voltage prior to the first component (load).
4. There should be little or no voltage drop in the circuit prior to the first component. If a voltage drop exists, the wire or connectors in the circuit are suspect.
5. While operating the first component in the circuit, probe the ground side of the component with the positive meter lead and observe the voltage readings. A small voltage drop should be noticed. This voltage drop is caused by the resistance of the component.
6. Repeat the test for each component (load) down the circuit.
7. If a large voltage drop is noticed, the preceding component, wire or connector is suspect.

3. Where necessary, also isolate at least one side of the circuit to be checked, in order to avoid reading parallel resistances. Parallel circuit resistances will always give a lower reading than the actual resistance of either of the branches.
4. Connect the meter leads to both sides of the circuit (wire or component) and read the actual measured ohms on the meter scale. Make sure the selector switch is set to the proper ohm scale for the circuit being tested, to avoid misreading the ohmmeter test value.

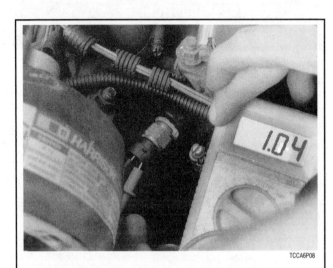

Fig. 10 Checking the resistance of a coolant temperature sensor with an ohmmeter. Reading is 1.04 kilohms

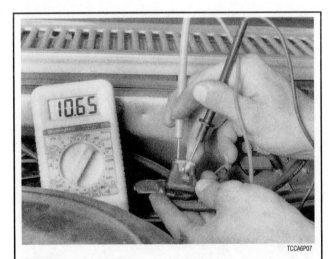

Fig. 9 This voltage drop test revealed high resistance (low voltage) in the circuit

RESISTANCE

♦ See Figures 10 and 11

※※ **WARNING**

Never use an ohmmeter with power applied to the circuit. The ohmmeter is designed to operate on its own power supply. The normal 12 volt electrical system voltage could damage the meter!

1. Isolate the circuit from the vehicle's power source.
2. Ensure that the ignition key is **OFF** when disconnecting any components or the battery.

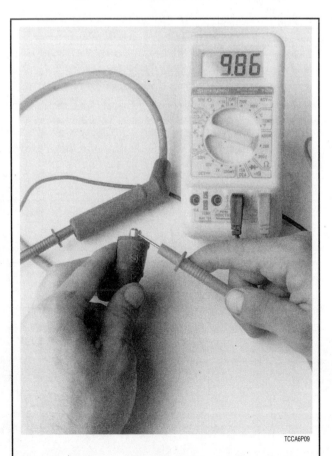

Fig. 11 Spark plug wires can be checked for excessive resistance using an ohmmeter

6-8 CHASSIS ELECTRICAL

Wire and Connector Repair

Almost anyone can replace damaged wires, as long as the proper tools and parts are available. Wire and terminals are available to fit almost any need. Even the specialized weatherproof, molded and hard shell connectors are now available from aftermarket suppliers.

Be sure the ends of all the wires are fitted with the proper terminal hardware and connectors. Wrapping a wire around a stud is never a permanent solution and will only cause trouble later. Replace wires one at a time to avoid confusion. Always route wires exactly the same as the factory.

➡ If connector repair is necessary, only attempt it if you have the proper tools. Weatherproof and hard shell connectors require special tools to release the pins inside the connector. Attempting to repair these connectors with conventional hand tools will damage them.

HEATER AND AIR CONDITIONER

Blower Motor

REMOVAL & INSTALLATION

1967 Models

♦ See Figure 12

1. Disconnect battery ground cable.
2. Drain the radiator.
3. Disconnect the blower motor resistor and ground wires from the heater.
4. Disconnect and plug the heater core hoses.

➡ Make sure you have an ample supply of rags, in case of coolant spills in the truck.

5. Disconnect the control cables and underdash braces.
6. From the engine compartment, remove the 3 heater mounting nuts or bolts.
7. Lower the heater assembly to the floor of the truck and remove the defroster hoses and air intake duct.
8. Remove the heater from the truck.
9. Remove the retaining nuts and lift the blower motor out of the housing.
10. Installation is the reverse of removal.

1968–72 Models Without Air Conditioning

1. Disconnect battery ground cable.
2. Drain the radiator.
3. Disconnect the blower motor resistor and ground wires from the heater.
4. Disconnect and plug the heater core hoses.

➡ Make sure you have an ample supply of rags, in case of coolant spills in the truck.

5. Disconnect the control cables and underdash braces.
6. From the engine compartment, remove the 3 heater mounting nuts or bolts.
7. Lower the heater assembly to the floor of the truck and remove the defroster hoses and air intake duct.
8. Remove the heater from the truck.
9. Remove the retaining screws and lift the blower motor from the heater case.
10. Installation is the reverse of removal.

1968–72 Models With Air Conditioning

1. Disconnect the battery ground cable.
2. Remove the glove box.
3. Disconnect the wiring at the blower resistor.
4. Disconnect the vacuum hoses from the fresh air door actuator.
5. Remove the support bracket attached to the face of the blower motor housing and the back of the instrument panel.
6. Separate the blower motor housing from the evaporator housing by removing the 6 sheet metal screws.
7. Remove the windshield wiper arms.
8. Remove the air inlet grille from in front of the windshield.
9. Remove the 2 support bracket bolts and lower the blower motor and housing out from under the instrument panel.
10. Disconnect the air tube and ground wire.
11. Remove the 3 screws and remove the blower motor from the housing.

To install:

12. Install the blower motor in the housing. Install the 3 screws.
13. Connect the air tube and ground wire.
14. Position the blower motor and housing under the instrument panel. Install the 2 support bracket bolts.
15. Install the air inlet grille.
16. Install the windshield wiper arms.
17. Attach the blower motor housing to the evaporator housing by installing the 6 sheet metal screws.
18. Install the support bracket attached to the face of the blower motor housing and the back of the instrument panel.
19. Connect the vacuum hoses to the fresh air door actuator.
20. Connect the wiring at the blower resistor.
21. Install the glove box.
22. Connect the battery ground cable.

1973–88 Models

♦ See Figures 13, 14 and 15

1. Disconnect the battery ground cable.
2. Disconnect the wiring.

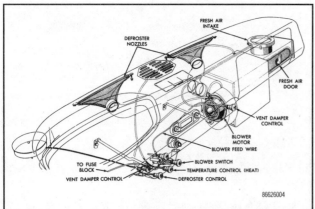

Fig. 12 Heater assembly underdash components—1967 models

Fig. 13 Disconnect and remove the hose leading to the motor

CHASSIS ELECTRICAL   6-9

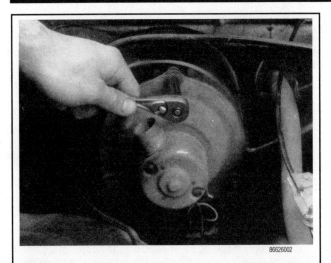

Fig. 14 Loosen and remove the mounting screws before lifting out the motor

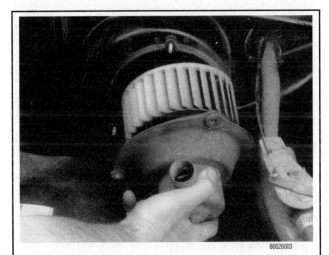

Fig. 15 Remove the motor being careful not to drop the fan cage, as it breaks easily

3. Disconnect the ground wire and cooling tube from the blower motor in the engine compartment.
4. Remove the screws and lift out the motor.
5. Drain the cooling system.
6. Disconnect the heater hoses at the core tubes. Plug the core tubes.

➡ Make sure you have an ample supply of rags, in case of coolant spills in the truck.

7. Disconnect the control cables.
8. Disconnect the defroster ducts.
9. Remove the bracket from the right side of the instrument panel and pull the panel rearward.
10. Remove the 7 mounting nuts from the engine side of the firewall, and one from the inside at the right kick panel.
11. Pull the heater assembly out.
12. Installation is the reverse of removal. Be sure to replace the sealing material.
13. Connect the battery ground cable, then refill the cooling system.

Heater Core

In order to prevent heater core freeze-up during A/C operation, it is necessary to maintain permanent type antifreeze protection of to 15°F (-9°C), or lower. A reading of -15°F (-26°C) is ideal since this protection also supplies sufficient corrosion inhibitors for the protection of the engine cooling system.

➡ The same antifreeze should not be used longer than the manufacturer specifies.

REMOVAL & INSTALLATION

✱✱ CAUTION

When draining the coolant, keep in mind that cats and dogs are attracted to ethylene glycol antifreeze, and are quite likely to drink any that is left in an uncovered container or in puddles on the ground. This will prove fatal in sufficient quantity. Always drain the coolant into a sealable container. Coolant should be reused unless it is contaminated or several years old.

1967–72 Models

WITHOUT AIR CONDITIONING

♦ See Figures 16 and 17

1. Disconnect battery ground cable.
2. Drain the radiator.
3. Disconnect the blower motor resistor and ground wires from the heater.
4. Disconnect and plug the heater core hoses.

➡ Make sure you have an ample supply of rags for any accidental

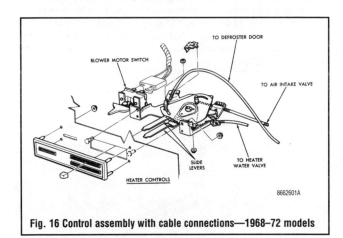

Fig. 16 Control assembly with cable connections—1968–72 models

Fig. 17 Heater unit assembly overview

6-10 CHASSIS ELECTRICAL

coolant spills. Keep them within reach while removing and installing the heater core.

5. Disconnect the control cables and underdash braces.
6. From the engine compartment, remove the 3 heater mounting nuts or bolts.
7. Lower the heater assembly to the floor of the truck, then remove the defroster hoses and air intake duct.
8. Remove the heater from the truck.
9. Remove the retaining nuts and lift the blower assembly out of the housing.
10. Remove the cover retaining nuts and lift the cover off the housing.
11. Remove the core retaining screws and lift the core out of the housing.
12. Installation is the reverse of removal.
13. Connect the battery ground cable, then fill the cooling system.
14. Let the engine warm up with the heater on, then check the coolant level.

WITH AIR CONDITIONING

▶ See Figure 18

1. Using an approved R-12 recovery/recycling station, follow the manufacturer's instructions to discharge the refrigerant. See Section 1.

➡ Be sure to consult the laws in your area before servicing the air conditioning system. In some states, it is ILLEGAL to perform repairs involving refrigerant unless the work is done by a certified technician.

2. Disconnect the battery ground cable.
3. Drain the cooling system.

✸✸ CAUTION

When draining the coolant, keep in mind that cats and dogs are attracted to ethylene glycol antifreeze, and are quite likely to drink any that is left in an uncovered container or in puddles on the ground. This will prove fatal in sufficient quantity. Always drain the coolant into a sealable container. Coolant should be reused unless it is contaminated or several years old.

4. Disconnect the heater hoses at the core tubes. Plug the tubes.

➡ Make sure you have an ample supply of rags for any accidental coolant spills. Keep them within reach while removing and installing the heater core.

5. Disconnect the refrigerant lines at the evaporator. Use a back-up wrench on each fitting. Cap all openings.
6. Disconnect the vacuum hoses, one from the intake manifold and two from the water valve. Push the hoses into the passenger compartment.
7. Remove the nuts from the mounting studs on the face of the firewall.
8. From inside, remove the glove box and disconnect the actuator vacuum hose cluster from the back of the control switch.
9. Disconnect the control cables.
10. Detach all the electrical connectors.
11. Remove the ashtray, left cooler duct and defroster ducts at the left side of the housing.
12. Disconnect the support bracket from the left side of the housing.
13. Remove the 3 retaining screws from the face of the housing and remove the appearance shield. Collapse the distribution duct towards the back of the instrument panel.
14. Remove both windshield wiper arms.
15. Remove the 7 sheet metal screws and lift off the air intake grille from in front of the windshield.
16. Remove the 2 bolts from the support bracket at the back of the blower motor housing.
17. Pull the unit towards the rear of the cab until all studs are clear of the dash panel, then move the unit to the right and tilt it down and out from under the instrument panel.
18. Place the assembly on a clean work surface and remove the front cover.
19. Carefully pull the sensing tube out from the left side of the evaporator.
20. Remove the 11 retaining screws from the top of the housing and lift the cover plate off the housing.
21. Remove one retaining screw under the foam insulator at the core tubes and carefully lift the evaporator out of the housing.
22. Lift out the heater core.

To install:

23. Replace all sealing material.
24. Install the heater core.
25. Carefully lower the evaporator into the housing. Install one retaining screw under the foam insulator at the core tubes.
26. Install the cover plate and 11 retaining screws from the top of the housing.
27. Carefully install the sensing tube in the left side of the evaporator.
28. Install the front cover.
29. Position in the cab and on the studs.
30. Install the 2 bolts on the support bracket at the back of the blower motor housing.
31. Install the air intake grille from in front of the windshield. Install the 7 sheet metal screws
32. Install both windshield wiper arms.
33. Install the distribution duct. Install the appearance shield.
34. Connect the support bracket at the left side of the housing.
35. Install the ashtray and left cooler duct and the defroster ducts at the left side of the housing.
36. Connect all electrical connectors.
37. Connect the control cables.
38. From inside, connect the actuator vacuum hose cluster from the back of the control switch and install the glove box.
39. Install the nuts on the mounting studs on the face of the firewall.
40. Connect the vacuum hoses, one at the intake manifold and two at the water valve.
41. Connect the refrigerant lines at the evaporator. Use a back-up wrench on each fitting.
42. Connect the heater hoses at the core tubes.
43. Connect the battery ground cable.
44. Fill the cooling system.
45. Using an approved R-12 recovery/recycling station, follow the manufacturer's instructions to charge the refrigerant system. See section 1.

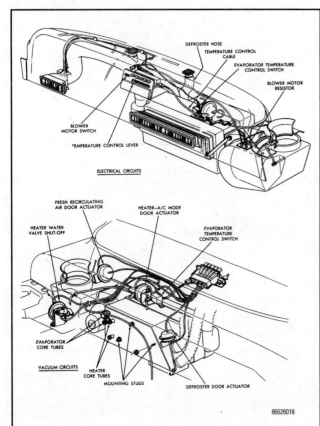

Fig. 18 These common air conditioning vacuum and electrical circuits are concealed behind the dashboard

1973–80 Models

WITHOUT AIR CONDITIONING

♦ See Figure 19

1. Disconnect the battery ground cable.
2. Drain the cooling system.
3. Disconnect the heater hoses at the core tubes. Plug the core tubes.

➡ Make sure you have an ample supply of rags for any accidental coolant spills. Keep them within reach while removing and installing the heater core.

4. Disconnect the wiring.
5. Disconnect the control cables.
6. Disconnect the defroster ducts.
7. Disconnect the ground wire and cooling tube from the blower motor in the engine compartment.
8. Remove the bracket from the right side of the instrument panel and pull the panel rearward.
9. Remove the 7 mounting nuts from the engine side of the firewall and one from the inside at the right kick panel.
10. Pull the heater assembly out of the vehicle.
11. Remove the heater core cover.
12. Unfasten and remove the screws fastening the heater core to the bottom of the heater housing.
13. Lift out the heater core.

To install:

14. Place the core in the housing and fasten.
15. Position the blend air door and right vent door in the housing, then fasten the heater core cover to the heater housing.
16. Install the heater assembly as described in reverse order. Be sure to adjust the cables.
17. Connect the battery ground cable, then fill the cooling system.

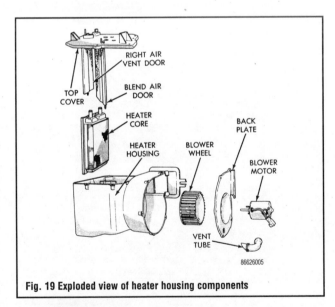

Fig. 19 Exploded view of heater housing components

WITH AIR CONDITIONING

♦ See Figure 20

1. Disconnect the battery ground cable.
2. Drain the cooling system.
3. Disconnect the heater hoses at the firewall.
4. Remove the glove box and ashtray.
5. Remove the right and left air conditioning ducts.
6. Remove the distribution duct.
7. Remove the center air outlet and duct.
8. Disconnect the wiring harness from the resistor.
9. Disconnect the vacuum lines from the rear housing.
10. Remove the 22 screws from the rear housing.

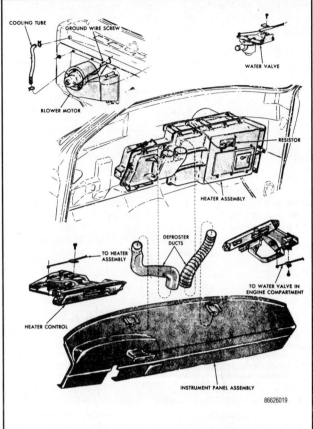

Fig. 20 Heater assembly and related components—1973–80 models

11. Remove the 2 plugs and, using a long extension, remove the 2 screws from inside the housing.
12. While holding the defroster door in the HEAT position, separate the unit.
13. Remove 1 screw from the engine side of the firewall and 2 screws from each end of the core, then slide out the core.

➡ Make sure you have an ample supply of rags for any accidental coolant spills. Keep them within reach while removing and installing the heater core.

To install:

14. Slide the core into place, then install one screw in the engine side of the firewall and two screws in each end of the core.
15. While holding the defroster door in the HEAT position, secure the unit.
16. Using a long extension, install the 2 screws inside the housing. Install the 2 plugs.
17. Install the 22 screws in the rear housing.
18. Connect the vacuum lines at the rear housing.
19. Connect the wiring harness at the resistor.
20. Install the center air outlet and duct.
21. Install the distribution duct.
22. Install the right and left air conditioning ducts.
23. Install the glove box and ashtray.
24. Connect the heater hoses at the firewall.
25. Connect the battery ground cable.
26. Fill the cooling system.

1981–88 Models

WITH STANDARD HEATER AND NO AIR CONDITIONING

1. Disconnect the battery ground cable.
2. Drain the cooling system.
3. Disconnect the heater hoses at the core tubes. Plug the tubes.

6-12 CHASSIS ELECTRICAL

➡ Make sure you have an ample supply of rags for any accidental coolant spills. Keep them within reach while removing and installing the heater core.

4. Remove the right cowl side trim panel, if equipped.
5. Remove the glove box by removing the 4 screws at the base and swinging out from the bottom to avoid catch and stops.
6. Working through the glove box opening, remove the support brace.
7. Remove the 8 screws from the right side of the instrument panel lower reinforcement. Disconnect the ground strap.
8. Disconnect the control cables.
9. Disconnect the blower motor wires.
10. Disconnect the wiring at the resistor block.
11. Remove the heater unit retaining screw from the cowl side sheet metal.
12. Remove the 6 mounting nuts from the engine side of the firewall.
13. Take out the heater unit, then remove its cover and lift out the core.

To install:
14. Insert the core and install the cover, then position the heater unit.
15. Install the 6 mounting nuts on the engine side of the firewall.
16. Install the heater unit retaining screw at the cowl side sheet metal.
17. Connect the wiring at the resistor block.
18. Connect the blower motor wires.
19. Connect the control cables.
20. Install the 8 screws at the right side of the instrument panel lower reinforcement. Connect the ground strap.
21. Working through the glove box opening, install the support brace.
22. Install the glove box.
23. Install the right cowl side trim panel, if equipped.
24. Connect the heater hoses at the core tubes.
25. Connect the battery ground cable.
26. Fill the cooling system.

WITH BI-LEVEL HEATER AND NO AIR CONDITIONING

1. Disconnect the battery ground cable.
2. Drain the cooling system.
3. Disconnect the heater hoses at the core tubes. Plug the tubes.

➡ Make sure you have an ample supply of rags for any accidental coolant spills. Keep them within reach while removing and installing the heater core.

4. Remove the drain tube.
5. Position the gearshift and transfer case levers away from the instrument panel.
6. Remove the glove box.
7. Working through the glove box opening, remove the support brace.
8. Remove the ashtray.
9. Remove the 8 screws from the right side of the instrument panel lower reinforcement. Disconnect the ground strap.
10. Remove the center distribution duct.
11. Disconnect the control cables.
12. Disconnect the vacuum lines.
13. Disconnect the blower motor wires.
14. Disconnect the wiring at the resistor block.
15. Pull the carpet back and make sure that the grommet is free from the firewall.
16. Remove the heater unit retaining screw from the cowl side sheet metal.
17. Remove the 7 mounting nuts from the engine side of the firewall.
18. Remove the heater unit. You may have to slightly bend the plastic instrument panel trim for clearance.
19. Remove the 10 screws and 3 door cranks, then separate the cover from the housing.
20. Carefully slide out the core.

To install:
21. Install the core, then assemble its housing.
22. Install the 7 mounting nuts on the engine side of the firewall.
23. Install the heater unit retaining screw at the cowl side sheet metal.
24. Install and align the carpet.
25. Connect the vacuum lines on engine side, and make sure the grommet is seated in dash panel.
26. Connect the wiring at the resistor block.
27. Connect the blower motor wires.
28. Connect the control cables.

29. Install the 8 screws at the right side of the instrument panel lower reinforcement. Connect the ground strap.
30. Working through the glove box opening, install the support brace.
31. Install the center distribution duct.
32. Install the glove box.
33. Install the ashtray.
34. Connect the heater hoses at the core tubes.
35. Connect the battery ground cable.
36. Fill the cooling system.

WITH AIR CONDITIONING

▶ See Figures 21 and 22

1. Using an approved R-12 recovery/recycling station, follow the manufacturer's instructions to discharge the refrigerant system. See Section 1.
2. Disconnect the battery ground cable.
3. Drain the cooling system.
4. Disconnect the refrigerant lines at the evaporator and the heater hoses at the core tubes. Always use a back-up wrench on the A/C fittings. Plug the all openings at once!.
5. Remove the drain tube.
6. Position the gearshift and transfer case levers away from the instrument panel.
7. Remove the glove box.
8. Working through the glove box opening, remove the support brace.
9. Remove the ashtray.
10. Remove the 8 screws from the right side of the instrument panel lower reinforcement. Disconnect the ground strap.
11. Remove the center distribution duct.
12. Disconnect the control cables.
13. Detach the vacuum lines.
14. Disconnect the blower motor wires.
15. Detach the wiring at the resistor block.
16. Pull the carpet back and make sure the grommet is free from the firewall.

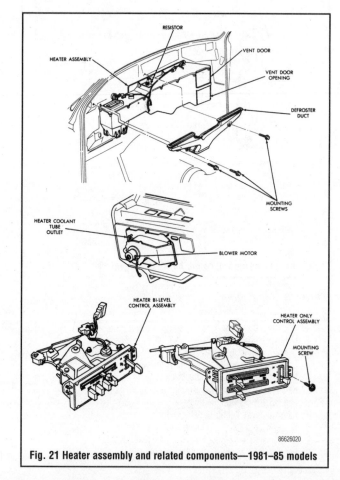

Fig. 21 Heater assembly and related components—1981–85 models

CHASSIS ELECTRICAL 6-13

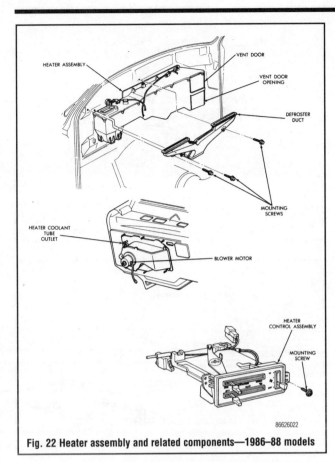

Fig. 22 Heater assembly and related components—1986–88 models

17. Remove the heater unit retaining screw from the cowl side sheet metal.
18. Remove the 7 mounting nuts from the engine side of the firewall.
19. Remove the heater unit. You may have to slightly bend the plastic instrument panel trim for clearance.
20. Remove the 10 screws and 3 door cranks, then separate the cover from the housing.
21. Carefully slide out the core.

To install:
22. Insert the heater core, then assemble its housing.
23. Properly position the heater unit to the vehicle.
24. Install the 7 mounting nuts on the engine side of the firewall.
25. Install the heater unit retaining screw at the cowl side sheet metal.
26. Connect the wiring at the resistor block.
27. Attach the blower motor wires.
28. Connect the control cables.
29. Install the 8 screws at the right side of the instrument panel lower reinforcement. Connect the ground strap.
30. Working through the glove box opening, install the support brace.
31. Install the center distribution duct.
32. Install the glove box.
33. Install the ashtray.
34. Connect the refrigerant hoses at the evaporator. Always use new O-rings coated with clean refrigerant oil. Always use a back-up wrench on the fittings. Attach the heater hoses at the core tubes.
35. Connect the battery ground cable.
36. Fill the cooling system.
37. Using an approved R-12 recovery/recycling station, follow the manufacturer's instructions to evacuate and charge the refrigerant system.

Control Cables

REMOVAL & INSTALLATION

♦ See Figures 23, 24, 25 and 26

The following is a basic type of removal/installation procedure; your truck may vary a little, depending on its year.

1. Inside the engine compartment, disconnect the control cable from the heater assembly and blend air door crank. It may be necessary to first remove an access cover.
2. Place a ¼ in. (7mm) tube over the clip and pry the self-adjust clip off the core wire.
3. Remove the glove box and cover.
4. Carefully pull the cable through the dash panel into the passengers' compartment.
5. Depress the tab on the flag, and pull the mode control cable out of the receiver on the distributor duct.
6. Remove the heater control.
7. Depress the tab on the flag, and pull the temperature cable out of the receiver on the heater control.
8. Remove the control cable.

To install:
9. Route the control cable through its original passage.
10. Position the wire loop over the temperature control lever pin, then snap the flag into its receiver on the heater control.
11. Install the heater control.
12. Snap the mode control cable flag into the receiver on distribution duct.
13. Position the self-adjusting clip on the core wire 2 in. (50mm) from the loop at the heater assembly end. With a ¼ in. (7mm) tube, pry the clip into the locked position.
14. Place the self-adjusting clip over the blend air door crank arm, then snap the cable into its retaining clip so that the locating tape is next to the side of the clip farthest from the crank. If applicable, reinstall the control cable access cover.

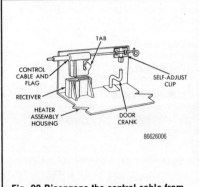

Fig. 23 Disengage the control cable from the door crank

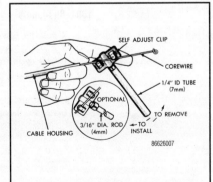

Fig. 24 Pry off the self-adjusting clip with a tube

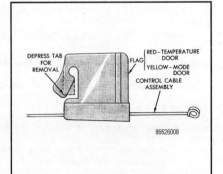

Fig. 25 Depress the flag tab to remove the cable

6-14 CHASSIS ELECTRICAL

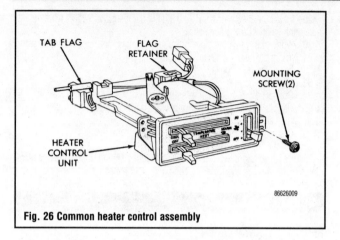

Fig. 26 Common heater control assembly

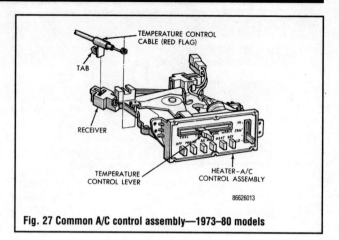

Fig. 27 Common A/C control assembly—1973–80 models

15. Adjust the cable by moving the temperature control lever to the right (WARM) position.
16. Install the glove box and cover.

Air Conditioning Components

REMOVAL & INSTALLATION

Repair or service of air conditioning components is not covered by this manual, because of the risk of personal injury or death, and because of the legal ramifications of servicing these components without the proper EPA certification and experience. Cost, personal injury or death, environmental damage, and legal considerations (such as the fact that it is a federal crime to vent refrigerant into the atmosphere), dictate that the A/C components on your vehicle should be serviced only by a Motor Vehicle Air Conditioning (MVAC) trained, and EPA certified automotive technician.

➡If your vehicle's A/C system uses R-12 refrigerant and is in need of recharging, the A/C system can be converted over to R-134a refrigerant (less environmentally harmful and expensive). Refer to Section 1 for additional information on R-12 to R-134a conversions, and for additional considerations dealing with your vehicle's A/C system.

Control Unit

REMOVAL & INSTALLATION

➡1967 models have no control unit. Instead, they have individual push/pull knobs for each control function.

1968–72 Models

1. Pull the knobs straight off the control levers.
2. Reach behind the panel and remove the retaining nuts from the face plate studs.
3. Lower the control unit and disconnect the cables and wiring.
4. Connect the control cables and wiring.
5. Replace the face plate and install mounting nuts.
6. Replace the pull knobs.
7. Adjust the cables.

1973–80 Models

◆ See Figures 27 and 28

1. Disconnect the fusible link in the engine compartment.
2. On trucks with air conditioning, remove the left duct.

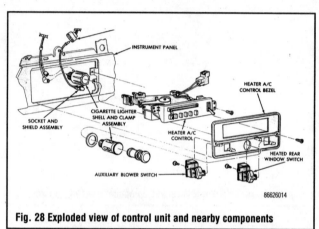

Fig. 28 Exploded view of control unit and nearby components

3. From under the instrument panel, remove the control unit-to-bracket screw.
4. Remove the control unit mounting screws from the front of the panel.
5. Carefully lower the control unit just far enough to disconnect the cables, vacuum hoses and wiring.

To install:
6. Reconnect the control unit and connect the cables, vacuum hoses and wiring.
7. Replace the control unit mounting screws from the front of the panel.
8. From under the instrument panel, replace the control unit-to-bracket screw.
9. For trucks with air conditioning, install the left duct.
10. Connect the fusible link in the engine compartment.
11. Adjust the cables.

1981–88 Models

1. Remove the face plate.
2. Remove the 2 control attaching screws.
3. Pull the control rearward.
4. On models with air conditioning, disconnect:
   a. Disconnect the blower switch wiring.
   b. Disconnect the push-button switch wiring.
5. Disconnect the panel light.
6. On models with air conditioning, disconnect the vacuum harness.
7. Disconnect the control cable(s).
8. Remove the unit.
9. Installation is the reverse of removal. Adjust the cables.

CHASSIS ELECTRICAL 6-15

RADIO

Radio Unit

REMOVAL & INSTALLATION

1967–72 Models

♦ See Figures 29 and 30

1. Disconnect the battery ground cable.
2. Disconnect all wiring and the antenna lead from the radio.
3. Remove the control knobs, bezel mounting screws, bezel, and radio mounting nuts.
4. Remove the radio mounting bracket and remove the radio.
5. Installation is the reverse of removal.

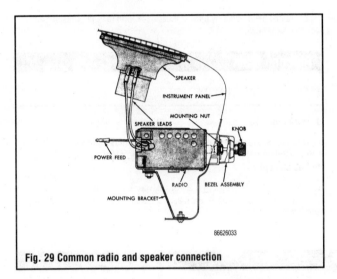
Fig. 29 Common radio and speaker connection

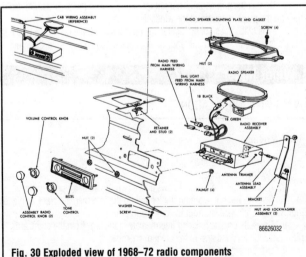
Fig. 30 Exploded view of 1968–72 radio components

1973–88 Models

♦ See Figures 31, 32 and 33

1. Disconnect the fusible link in the engine compartment.
2. Remove the instrument cluster bezel.
3. On trucks with air conditioning, remove the left air conditioner duct.
4. Remove the radio-to-cluster mounting screws.
5. Remove the ground strap screw.
6. Disconnect all wiring and the antenna lead from the radio.

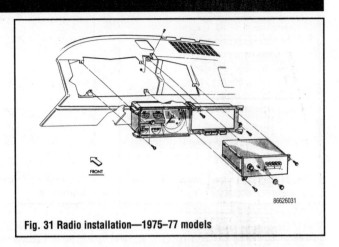
Fig. 31 Radio installation—1975–77 models

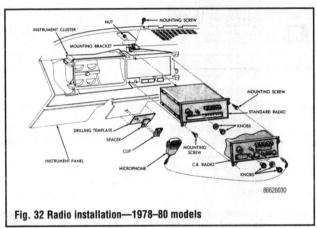
Fig. 32 Radio installation—1978–80 models

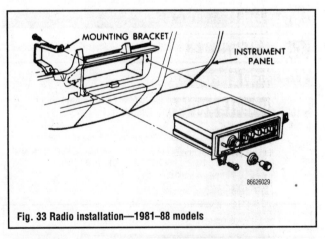
Fig. 33 Radio installation—1981–88 models

7. Push the radio away from the cluster and carefully lower it from the panel.

To install:

8. Connect the wiring and antenna lead.
9. Position the radio in place, install the mounting screws.
10. Install the ground strap screw.
11. Install the cluster bezel.
12. Connect the fusible link.

ANTENNA LEAD CONNECTIONS

♦ See Figure 34

Antenna leads are connected in one spot of the truck, depending on how many antennas you have on your truck. The end, of course, has to go to the

6-16 CHASSIS ELECTRICAL

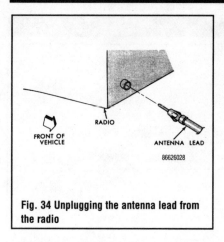

Fig. 34 Unplugging the antenna lead from the radio

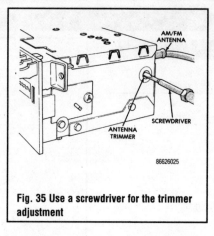

Fig. 35 Use a screwdriver for the trimmer adjustment

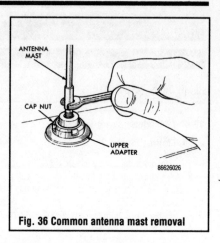

Fig. 36 Common antenna mast removal

back of the radio, CB radio, phone, etc. It is a quite simple procedure to remove and install the antenna lead cable. Locate the lead wire input on the back of your unit. Carefully pull outward on the lead to remove it from the radio, CB, etc. To install, push the lead back into the opening, making sure it is snug.

TRIMMER ADJUSTMENT

▶ See Figure 35

All radios are trimmed at the factory and should require no further trimmer adjustment, unless the radio is being installed after repair, or if trimmer adjustment is desired because of poor performance.
1. Extend the antenna to full length for best FM reception.
2. Tune the radio to a weak signal between 1400 and 1600 kilocycles on the AM band.
3. Increase the radio volume and set the tone control to maximum treble.
4. The trimmer screw on most radios is located at the lower rear right-hand corner of the radio, and can be reached by inserting a tool into the recess hole.

5. Adjust the trimmer by turning it back and forth until peak response in volume is obtained.

Antenna Mast

REMOVAL & INSTALLATION

▶ See Figure 36

➡This procedure applies only to the antenna mast. For information on removal/installation of the antenna assembly, please refer to Section 10 in this manual.

The antenna mast is usually a screw-on type. The only tool you will need for removal is a wrench to loosen the mast. To install, simply insert the new mast and tighten it securely.

WINDSHIELD WIPERS AND WASHERS

Wiper Arm

REMOVAL & INSTALLATION

▶ See Figure 37

1. Lift the wiper arm, then loosen and remove the hold-down nut.
2. Remove the wiper arm with a rocking motion.

To install:

3. Place the arm in position and install the nut, but do not tighten it yet.
4. Adjust the arm so that the heel of the blade is approximately 2.5–3.0 in. (64–76mm) above the windshield weatherstrip on the driver's side, or 1.25–1.75 in. (32–44mm) on the passenger's side.

5. Tighten the arm slightly, but not too loosely. Turn the wipers on to see if they hit the outside margin of the windshield.
6. If the blade does not hit, tighten the hold-down nut the rest of the way. If the blades do hit, adjust again until they do not hit, then tighten the hold-down nut.

Wiper Motor

REMOVAL & INSTALLATION

1967 Models

1. Disconnect the battery ground cable.
2. Remove both wiper arms.
3. Remove the 7 retaining screws and lift off the fresh air cowl grille.
4. Remove the nut retaining the left link to the intermediate crank arm and remove the 2 felt washers from the crank arm pin.
5. Carefully pry the link and intermediate crank arm from the crank arm pin. Leave the link and arm in the plenum chamber.
6. Disconnect the motor wiring.
7. Remove the left defroster hose from the heater outlet.
8. Remove the 3 nuts from the motor mounting plate studs under the instrument panel and lift out the motor.

To install:

9. Work the crank arm through the mounting plate shaft opening so that the motor rests in the recess in the plate. Install the mounting screws.

➡**Make sure that the ground strap is making good contact with the mounting screw!**

10. Position the gasket on the studs under the instrument panel and install the motor and plate assembly so that the gear box faces the left side of the truck. Install the retaining nuts.

Fig. 37 Adjusting the wiper arms so they do not hit

CHASSIS ELECTRICAL 6-17

11. Assemble the crank arm and intermediate arm. Make sure that the flats are properly indexed. Install the washers and nut.
12. Connect the wiring and defroster hose.
13. Connect the battery ground cable.

1968–72 Models

1. Disconnect the battery ground cable.
2. Remove both wiper arms.
3. Remove the 7 retaining screws and lift off the fresh air cowl grille.
4. Remove the nut retaining the left link to the intermediate crank arm and remove the 2 felt washers from the crank arm pin.
5. Carefully pry the link and intermediate crank arm from the crank arm pin. Leave the link and arm in the plenum chamber.
6. Disconnect the motor wiring.
7. Remove the left defroster hose from the heater outlet.
8. Remove the 3 nuts from the motor mounting plate studs under the instrument panel and lift out the motor.
9. Installation is the reverse of removal. Make sure that the flats on the left link and intermediate crank arm are properly indexed.

1973–88 Models

♦ See Figures 38, 39 and 40

1. Disconnect the battery ground cable.
2. Disconnect the wires at the motor.
3. Remove the motor mounting bolts.
4. Lower the motor just enough to get at the crank arm.

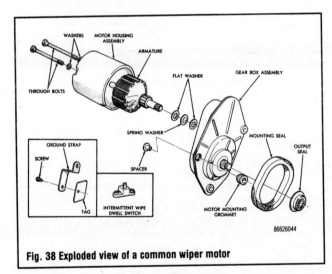

Fig. 38 Exploded view of a common wiper motor

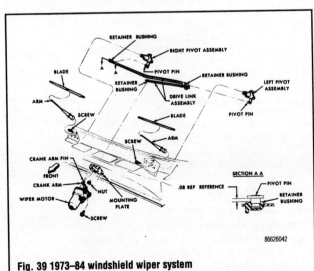

Fig. 39 1973–84 windshield wiper system

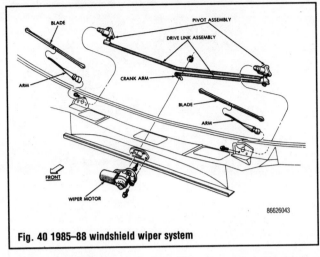

Fig. 40 1985–88 windshield wiper system

5. Pry the retainer bushing from the crank arm pin and remove the crank arm from the drive link.
6. Remove the motor.
7. If the crank arm is removed, replace it and torque the nut to 95 inch lbs. (11 Nm).
8. Position the motor and connect the crank arm and drive link. Snap the bushing into place.
9. Install the motor mounting bolts and torque them to 55 inch lbs. (6 Nm).
10. Connect the wiring to the wiper motor.
11. Connect the battery cable.

Wiper Linkage

REMOVAL & INSTALLATION

1967–72 Models

1. Remove the wiper arms.
2. Remove the 7 screws and lift the grille off the cowl.
3. Remove the clip retaining the right link to the intermediate crank arm pin, then lift the washer and link from the pin.
4. Remove the nut retaining the left link to the intermediate arm, then carefully pry the arm and link from the pin.
5. Remove the pivot retaining screws from each pivot, then push the pivots into the plenum chamber. Lift the link and pivot assembly out through the grille opening.
6. Remove the retainer clip, washer and link from the pivot arm.

To install:
7. Install the retainer clip, washer and link to the pivot arm.
8. Install the pivot retaining screws for each pivot, then push the pivot into the plenum chamber. Install the link and pivot assembly through the grille opening.
9. Fasten the nut that retains the left link to the intermediate arm, then carefully attach the pin to the arm and link.
10. Install the clip that retains the right link to the intermediate crank arm pin, along with the washer and link to the pin.
11. Position the grille on the cowl, and fasten the 7 screws.
12. Reinstall the wiper arms.

1973–88 Models

LEFT PIVOT AND DRIVE LINK

♦ See Figure 41

1. Remove the wiper arms.
2. Remove the cowl assembly.
3. Reach through the access hole and remove the drive link from the right pivot by prying the retaining bushing from the pivot pin.
4. Remove the crank arm from the drive link by prying the retaining bushing from the crank arm pin.

6-18 CHASSIS ELECTRICAL

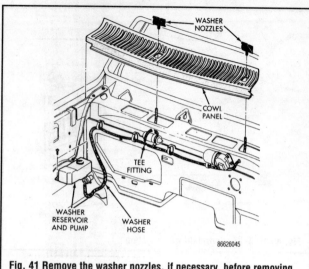

Fig. 41 Remove the washer nozzles, if necessary, before removing the cowl panel

5. Remove the left pivot mounting screws and let the pivot hang loosely.
6. Remove the drive link and left pivot through the access holes.
7. Remove the drive link from the left pivot by prying the retaining bushing from the pivot pin.

To install:

8. Install the left pivot pin in the drive link retainer bushing by snapping them together with channel lock pliers.

9. Maneuver the drive links and pivot assemblies through the access hole into their proper positions.
10. Install and tighten the pivot mounting screws to 95 inch lbs. (10.6 Nm).
11. Install the crank arm pin in the drive link retainer bushing by snapping them together with channel lock pliers.
12. Install the right pivot pin in the drive link retainer bushing by snapping them together with channel lock pliers.
13. Position the cowl cover, then install the mounting bolts and tighten securely.
14. Install the wiper arms and adjust.
15. Check the washer aim.

RIGHT PIVOT

♦ See Figure 41

1. Remove the wiper arms.
2. Remove the cowl assembly.
3. Reach through the access hole and remove the drive link from the right pivot by prying the retaining bushing from the pivot pin.
4. Remove the right pivot mounting screws.
5. Remove the pivot through the access hole.

To install:

6. Position the pivot into place, then install the mounting screws and tighten them to 95 inch lbs. (10.6 Nm).
7. Install the pivot pin in the drive link retainer bushing by snapping them together with channel lock pliers.
8. Replace the cowl cover and install mounting bolts and tighten securely.
9. Install the wiper arms and adjust.
10. Check the washer aim.

INSTRUMENTS AND SWITCHES

Instrument Cluster

REMOVAL & INSTALLATION

1967–72 Models

♦ See Figure 42

1. Tape or cover the steering wheel before you proceed with this job to prevent paint damage.
2. Disconnect the battery ground cable.
3. Remove the 6 screws attaching the cluster to the instrument panel.
4. Disconnect the speedometer cable and tachometer at the back of the cluster.
5. Disconnect all wiring at the back of the cluster.

To install:

6. Position the cluster in the panel.
7. Connect all the wiring at the back of the cluster.
8. Reconnect the speedometer cable and tachometer at the back of the cluster.
9. Replace the 6 screws that attach the cluster to the instrument panel.
10. Connect the battery cable.

1973–80 Models

♦ See Figures 43, 44 and 45

1. Tape or cover the steering wheel before you proceed with this job to prevent paint damage.
2. Disconnect the battery ground cable.
3. Disconnect the fusible link located under the hood.
4. Remove the 3 lower and 4 upper bezel retaining screws.
5. Remove the 8 mounting screws from the face of the bezel.
6. On trucks with optional gauges, pull the bezel out just far enough to disconnect any electrical or mechanical leads or controls.
7. Remove the bezel.
8. Remove the radio.
9. Remove the left air conditioner duct.
10. Disconnect the speedometer cable at the speedometer.
11. Remove the cluster mounting screws from the face of the cluster.
12. Carefully pull the cluster towards you just far enough to disconnect all wires from the back.
13. Remove the cluster assembly.

To install:

14. Position the cluster in the panel and connect the speedometer cable at the speedometer.
15. Connect all wires at the back of the cluster.
16. Install the cluster mounting screws in the face of the cluster.
17. Install the left air conditioner duct.
18. Install the radio.
19. Install the bezel.
20. On trucks with optional gauges, pull the bezel out just far enough to connect any electrical or mechanical leads or controls.
21. Install the 8 mounting screws in the face of the bezel.
22. Install the 3 lower and 4 upper bezel retaining screws.
23. Connect the battery ground cable.

Fig. 42 Instrument panel assembly—1967–72 vehicles

CHASSIS ELECTRICAL   6-19

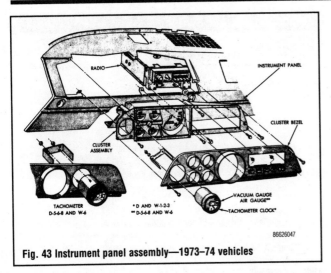

Fig. 43 Instrument panel assembly—1973–74 vehicles

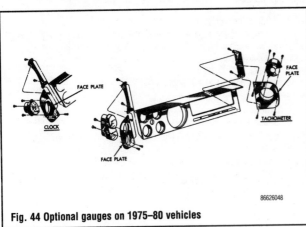

Fig. 44 Optional gauges on 1975–80 vehicles

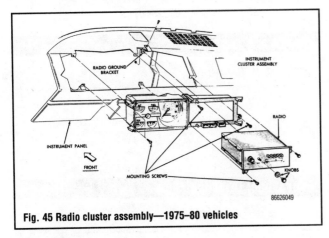

Fig. 45 Radio cluster assembly—1975–80 vehicles

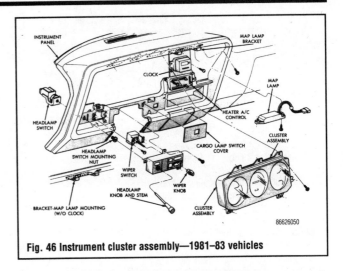

Fig. 46 Instrument cluster assembly—1981–83 vehicles

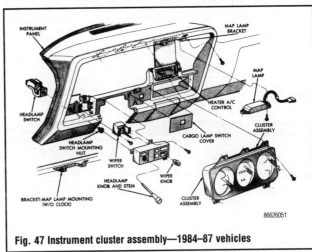

Fig. 47 Instrument cluster assembly—1984–87 vehicles

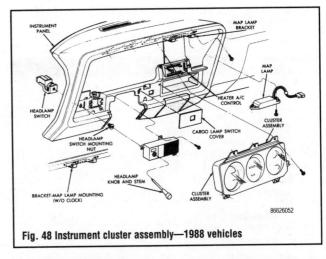

Fig. 48 Instrument cluster assembly—1988 vehicles

1981–88 Models

♦ See Figures 46, 47 and 48

1. Tape or cover the steering wheel before you proceed with this job to prevent paint damage.
2. Unfasten the 2 screws and remove the map lamp.
3. Remove the 6 cluster face plate-to-base panel screws. One of the screws is located below the A/C-Heater control unit.
4. Place the column shift lever in position **1**.
5. Remove the face plate by pulling the top edge rearward and disengaging the clips around the bottom of the face plate.

➥ **If the truck is a 4X4 model, disconnect the indicator wires as you remove the face plate.**

6. Remove the 8 cluster mask and lens screws or, on 1981–86 models, the push-pins.
7. Unscrew the odometer reset knob.
8. Remove the 4 steering column lower cover screws.
9. Spread the upper cover out of the locking tangs and slide it downward.
10. Disconnect the automatic transmission indicator actuator cable from the column.
11. Loosen the A/C-Heater control unit and pull it rearward just enough to clear the cluster housing mount.

12. Remove the 6 cluster retaining screws and pull the cluster rearward.
13. Unfasten the 2 large and 1 small connectors near the speedometer cable.
14. Disconnect the speedometer cable.
15. Remove the Emissions Maintenance Reminder (EMR) and/or gate open lamp sockets.
16. Remove the cluster.

To install:
17. Position the cluster in the panel.
18. Install the EMR and/or gate open lamp sockets.
19. Connect the speedometer cable.
20. Fasten the 2 large and 1 small connectors near the speedometer cable.
21. Install the 6 cluster retaining screws.
22. Tighten the A/C-Heater control unit.
23. Connect the automatic transmission indicator actuator cable at the column.
24. Snap the upper cover into the locking tangs.
25. Install the 4 steering column lower cover screws.
26. Install the odometer reset knob.
27. Install the 8 cluster mask and lens screws or push-pins.

➡ If the truck is a 4X4 model, connect the indicator wires as you install the face plate.

28. Install the face, engaging the clips around the bottom of the face plate.
29. Place the column shift lever in position **1**.
30. Install the 6 cluster face plate-to-base panel screws.
31. Install the map lamp.

Cluster Mask and Lens

REMOVAL & INSTALLATION

1. Remove the faceplate.
2. Remove the 8 push pins.
3. Unscrew the odometer reset knob, if so equipped.
4. Remove the mask and lens.

To install:
5. Position the mask and lens for replacement.
6. Install the odometer reset knob.
7. Install the 8 push pins.
8. Install the faceplate.

Speedometer

REMOVAL & INSTALLATION

1. Remove the faceplate.
2. Remove the instrument cluster assembly and the cluster mask lens.
3. Remove the mounting screws retaining the speedometer to the housing.
4. Remove the speedometer.

To install:
5. Position the speedometer into the cluster housing and install the mounting screws.
6. Replace the mask lens.
7. Install the cluster assembly.
8. Install the faceplate.

Speedometer Cable

The cable core may be removed from either end by disconnecting the end and pulling the core out. In the case of a broken core, the cable assembly must be removed.

To disconnect it at the upper end, remove the instrument cluster and disconnect the cable at the back of the speedometer.

To disconnect the lower end, disconnect the cable at the (depending on year, model and equipment) transmission, transfer case, distance sensor, lower cable or speed control servo.

Windshield Wiper Switch

REMOVAL & INSTALLATION

1967–80 Models

1. Disconnect the battery ground cable.
2. Remove the ashtray housing.
3. Loosen the setscrew and remove the wiper switch knob.
4. Remove the nut retaining the switch to the dash panel.
5. Reach through the ashtray housing opening and lower the switch just far enough to disconnect the wiring, and remove the lighting bracket.

To install:
6. Install the switch and connect the wiring making sure you install lighting bracket.
7. Install the nut to retain the switch to the dash panel.
8. Replace the wiper switch knob and tighten the setscrew.
9. Connect the battery ground cable.

1981–87 Models

1. Remove the instrument cluster face plate.
2. Reach under the panel and depress the release button located on the bottom of the switch while pulling out on the knob. This will allow removal of the knob and stem.
3. Remove the bezel.
4. Remove the 4 switch attaching screws.
5. Disconnect the wiring and remove the switch.

To install:
6. Connect the wiring to the switch.
7. Position the switch to the panel and install the 4 mounting screws.
8. Install the bezel.
9. Install the wiper switch knob.
10. Install the knob and stem into switch assembly.
11. Install the cluster faceplate. Check the operation of the wiper switch.

1988 Models

The wiper/washer switch is incorporated in the turn signal switch. Follow the REMOVAL & INSTALLATION procedures found in Section 8.

Clock

REMOVAL & INSTALLATION

1. Remove the faceplate.
2. Remove the 3 screws that hold the clock in place, and remove the clock.

To install:
3. Install the clock with three screws.
4. Install faceplate.

Four Wheel Drive Indicator

REMOVAL & INSTALLATION

1. Remove the faceplate.
2. Remove the 2 screws that hold the indicator on the faceplate.

To install:
3. Install the indicator with two screws.
4. Install faceplate.

Snow Plow Toggle Switch

REMOVAL & INSTALLATION

1. Remove the four screws holding the bezel to the housing.
2. Pull rearwards, disconnect the wire from the toggle switch.

CHASSIS ELECTRICAL 6-21

3. Remove the toggle switch by unscrewing the nut from the front of the bezel.

To install:
4. Position the toggle switch into the bezel and install the nut.
5. Connect the wires to the switch.
6. Install the bezel to the instrument panel and install the four mounting screws.

Headlight Switch

REMOVAL & INSTALLATION

1967–72 Models

1. Disconnect the battery ground cable.
2. Loosen the setscrew and remove the wiper switch knob.
3. Remove the nut retaining the switch to the dash panel.
4. Reach through the ashtray housing opening and lower the switch just far enough to disconnect the wiring, and remove the lighting bracket.

To install:
5. Reach through the ashtray housing, install the switch, connect the wiring, and install the lighting bracket.

6. Replace the nut that retains the switch to the dash panel.
7. Tighten the setscrew and replace the wiper switch knob.
8. Connect the battery ground cable.

1973–88 Models

1. Disconnect the battery ground cable, and fusible link under the hood.
2. Remove the left side air conditioner duct and outlet.
3. Reach under the panel and depress the release button located on the bottom of the switch while pulling out on the knob. This will allow removal of the knob and stem.
4. Remove the nut retaining the switch to the panel.
5. Lower the switch just far enough to disconnect the wires and remove the switch.

To install:
6. Connect the wiring to the headlight switch.
7. Position the switch in place in the panel and install the mounting nut. Tighten the nut securely.
8. Install the switch bezel.
9. Install the instrument and hood and bezel assembly.
10. Install the knob and stem into the switch, make sure that it locks into place.
11. Install the air-conditioning duct and air outlet assembly.
12. Connect the fusible link.

LIGHTING

Headlights

REMOVAL & INSTALLATION

▶ See Figures 49, 50, 51 and 52

1. Remove the headlight bezel attaching screws and remove the bezel. On some models it may not be necessary to remove the bezel, depending on whether the headlight retaining ring is accessible.
2. Remove the headlight ring attaching screws, then remove the ring. Do not touch the headlight aiming screws.
3. Pull the sealed beam out slightly and unplug the connector.

To install:
4. Fasten the electrical connector, then position the sealed beam in place.
5. Install the retaining ring and the headlamp bezel, if removed.

➥As long as the adjusting screws were not moved, the headlight will be held in proper adjustment by the retaining ring.

AIMING RECOMMENDATIONS

▶ See Figure 53

➥Before making any headlight adjustments, perform the following preparatory steps:

1. Check the operation of the dimmer switch; is it working properly?
2. Check for badly rusted items on the headlamp assembly; it would be advisable to replace any parts that are severely rusted.
3. Make sure your truck is on LEVEL ground.
4. Make sure all tires are properly inflated.
5. Take into consideration any faulty wheel alignment or improper rear axle tracking.
6. Make sure there is no load in the truck other than the driver.
7. Make sure all lenses are clean.

Each headlight is adjusted by means of two screws located at the 12 o'clock and 9 o'clock positions on the headlight underneath the trim ring. Always bring each beam into final position by turning the adjusting screws clockwise so that the headlight will be held against the tension springs when the operation is completed.

ADJUSTING & AIMING

➥Check with your local authorities before performing this procedure. Most areas have standards for proper adjustment. We recommend, for safety, that the adjustment always be checked by a reputable shop.

The use of SAE approved equipment is preferred to achieve exact adjustment of the headlamps, although a fairly accurate method of adjustment is as follows:

1. Position the vehicle approximately 25 ft. (7.6m) from a screen or wall, and ensure that the vehicle is facing the wall straight.

Fig. 49 Remove the retaining ring from around the bulb

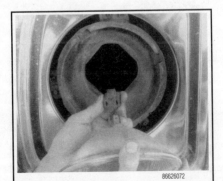

Fig. 50 Pull the bulb out slightly to disconnect it from the wiring

Fig. 51 After installing a new bulb, position the retaining ring and tighten the screws

6-22 CHASSIS ELECTRICAL

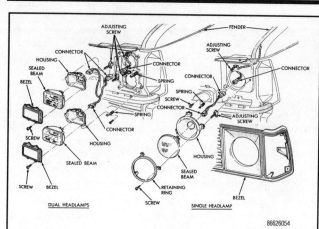

Fig. 52 Headlamps are designed as either single or dual lamp assemblies, and may be round or rectangular

Fig. 53 Headlamps can be aimed by turning the adjusting screws; however, you should have the proper aiming equipment to do the job correctly

7. Now check the horizontal aim. If properly adjusted, the left-side beams should be 4 in. (102mm) to the right of the center mark previously made, while the right-side beams should be 4 in. (102mm) to the left of the center mark.
8. Turn the horizontal (side) adjuster screw as needed to obtain the correct setting.
9. After completing an adjustment, recheck the previous adjustment, since the headlamp's aim will change slightly (up or down) when turning the opposite adjuster.

Signal and Marker Lights

REMOVAL & INSTALLATION

Rear Tail/Stop/Turn Signal/Back-Up/Clearance Lamps

▶ See Figures 54, 55 and 56

1. Unfasten the lens retaining screws, then remove the lens.
2. Carefully grasp the bulb, then lightly push in while turning the bulb counterclockwise until its locking pins disengage from the socket.
3. Withdraw the bulb from the socket.

To install:

4. Line up the locking pins on the new bulb with the socket, then lightly push and twist the bulb clockwise to lock it in place.
5. Mount the lens and reattach with its screws.

Front Parking/Turn Signal/Side Marker Lamps

▶ See Figures 57 thru 62

1. If accessible, twist and remove the socket from the rear of the lamp assembly (with the bulb intact).

➡ On some models, the socket cannot be removed from the rear of the lamp/lens assembly. In order to access the bulb in this type of assembly, first remove the lens (which is retained by screws in its outer surface).

2. If the bulb has a metal base, remove the bulb by carefully depressing and twisting it about 1/8 turn counterclockwise (to release the locking pins). Then, withdraw the bulb from its socket.

➡ Some small bulbs (such as No. 194 side marker lamps) do not have a base. These bulbs are simply pulled straight out from their sockets.

To install:

3. Insert the bulb into its socket. If the bulb has locking pins on its base, line up the pins correctly, then depress the bulb and twist clockwise until it locks in place.
4. If applicable, reinstall and twist the socket/bulb assembly into the rear of the lamp housing.
5. If applicable, reinstall the lens.

2. Measure the height from the ground to the center of the each headlamp, and note these figures.
3. Measure the same distances from the ground (as recorded in Step 2) and mark the appropriate spots on the screen or wall with chalk. Ensure that the marks are straight ahead of each headlamp.
4. Turn the headlamps on and compare their beams with the marks previously made.
5. If properly adjusted, the beams should shine from approximately 2 in. (51mm) above to 2.5 in. (63.5mm) below the center chalk marks.
6. Turn each vertical (top) adjusting screw as needed to correct the adjustment. The best overall setting is 1/2–1 in. (13–25mm) down for low beams, and 0–1/2 in. (0–13mm) down for high beams.

Fig. 54 To remove a lamp lens, unfasten the mounting screws and set them aside

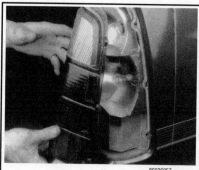

Fig. 55 The lens should come off easily after removing the screws

Fig. 56 Lightly depress and twist the bulb about one-eighth turn, then pull it out of the socket

CHASSIS ELECTRICAL 6-23

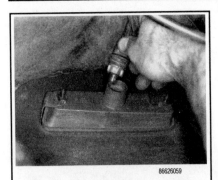
Fig. 57 Twist the socket/bulb assembly about one-eighth turn, until it can be withdrawn from the rear of the lamp housing

Fig. 58 On some models, you must unfasten the screws to remove the lamp assembly and/or lens

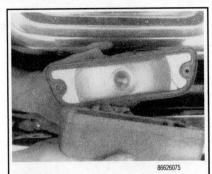
Fig. 59 After removing the retaining screws, pull the lamp assembly away from the body

Fig. 60 If the entire lamp assembly must be removed, disconnect its wire lead

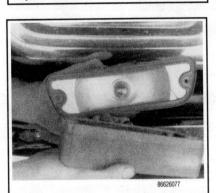
Fig. 61 Remove the lens from the socket assembly to access the bulb

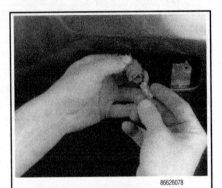
Fig. 62 Remove this type of bulb by pulling it straight out from its socket

License Plate Lens

♦ See Figures 63, 64, 65 and 66

1. Carefully pry the housing of the license plate lamp assembly away from the bumper.
2. Pull the assembly out far enough to remove the lens from the housing.
3. Remove the lens cover.
4. Depress and twist the bulb about 1/8 turn counterclockwise (to release the locking pins). Then, withdraw the bulb from its socket.

To install:

5. Correctly line up the locking pins of the replacement bulb with the socket, then depress the bulb and twist clockwise until it locks in place.
6. Install the lens cover on the lamp, then push the lamp assembly into the bumper.

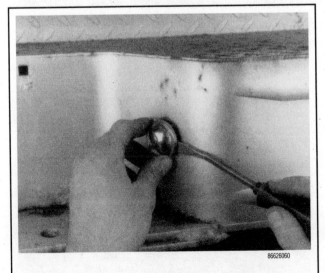
Fig. 63 Pry the license lamp assembly from the bumper

Fig. 64 Carefully withdraw the assembly enough to remove the lens cover

6-24 CHASSIS ELECTRICAL

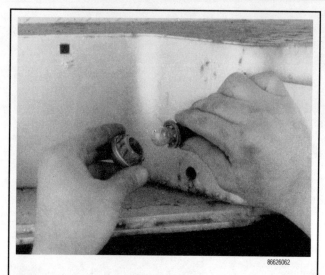

Fig. 65 Twist and pull the lens off the lamp

Fig. 66 Insert and twist the bulb into the socket assembly

TRAILER WIRING

➡ For more information on towing a trailer, please refer to Section 1 of this manual.

Wiring the truck for towing is fairly easy. There are a number of good wiring kits available and these should be used, rather than trying to design your own. All trailers will need brake lights and turn signals as well as tail lights and side marker lights. Most states require extra marker lights for overly wide trailers. Also, most states have recently required back-up lights for trailers, and most trailer manufacturers have been building trailers with back-up lights for several years. Additionally, some Class I, most Class II and just about all Class III trailers will have electric brakes. Add to this number an accessories wire, to operate trailer internal equipment or to charge the trailer's battery, and you can have as many as seven wires in the harness.

Determine the equipment on your trailer and buy the wiring kit necessary. The kit will contain all the necessary wires, plus a plug adapter set which includes the female plug, mounted on the bumper or hitch, and the male plug, which is wired or plugged into the trailer harness. When installing the kit, follow the manufacturer's instructions. The color coding of the wires tends to be standard throughout the industry.

One point to note: some domestic vehicles, and most imported vehicles, have separate turn signals. On most domestic vehicles, however, the brake lights and rear turn signals operate with the same bulb. For those vehicles without separate turn signals, you can purchase an isolation unit so that the brake lights won't blink whenever the turn signals are operated, or you can go to your local electronics supply house and buy four diodes to wire in series with the brake and turn signal bulbs. Diodes will isolate the brake and turn signals. The choice is yours. The isolation units are simple and quick to install, but far more expensive than the diodes. The diodes, however, require more work to install properly, since they require the cutting of each bulb's wire and soldering the diode in place.

One final point: the best kits are those with a spring loaded cover on the vehicle mounted socket. This cover prevents dirt and moisture from corroding the terminals. Never let the vehicle socket hang loosely; always mount it securely to the bumper or hitch.

CIRCUIT PROTECTION

Fuses

REPLACEMENT

✱✱ CAUTION

When replacing a blown fuse, it is important to use only a fuse of the same amperage rating. The use of a fuse with a rating other than what is recommended may result in a dangerous electrical overload. If you have a problem with the correct fuse continually blowing, this indicates a problem in the circuit that needs to be corrected.

Fuse Block

➡ The location of the fuse block may vary, depending on the year of your truck.

MODELS THROUGH 1979

♦ See Figure 67

On 1979 and earlier years, the fuse block is generally located under the glove box door.

1. Disconnect the negative battery cable.
2. The fuse panel is located on the firewall or kick panel above the driver's left foot.
3. Open the glove box door and remove the two mounting screws.

Fig. 67 Fuse block for models through 1979

CHASSIS ELECTRICAL 6-25

4. Lift out the fuse block.
5. If applicable, replace any damaged fuses.
6. Position the fuse block into the opening, then install the mounting screws.
7. Close the glove box door.
8. Connect the negative battery cable.

1980 AND LATER MODELS

On 1980 and later years, the fuse block is generally located directly below the steering column.

1. Disconnect the negative battery cable.
2. Push the fuse block locking tab on the column cover downward, and lower the fusebox.
3. If applicable, replace any damaged fuses.
4. Position the fuse block to the steering cover, then push the locking tab to secure the fuse block.
5. Connect the negative battery cable.

Fuses

♦ See Figures 68 thru 74

➡ Make sure your ignition is in the OFF position when working on your fuses.

There are two different types of fuses for your truck, depending on its year: the old style glass-type fuse and the plastic, two prong push-in type. Both are very easy to remove and replace. Make sure you replace the blown fuse with one having the same amperage rating. If there is any doubt as to the correct amperage rating for a particular circuit, look at the fuse panel cover; it should be clearly marked. To check if a fuse is blown, look at it carefully. A blown glass-type fuse may be black, and the wire filament or metal strip inside will be broken.

To remove a glass-type fuse, use a special fuse puller or prytool (preferably plastic). DO NOT use a metal tool, and be careful not to break the glass. To remove a plastic plug-in type fuse, simply pull the fuse out with your fingers. Install the new fuse by simply pushing it in place.

Fuses

1967–69

Circuit	Amperage
Alternator regulator	6AGC
Cigarette lighter	15AGC
Dome light	15AGC
Emergency flasher	15AGC
Heater	20AGC
Horn	30AGC
Instruments	2AGC
Parking lights	15AGC
Radio	6AGC
Stop lights	15AGC
Taillights	15AGC
Turn signals	15AGC

Fig. 68 Fuse applications for 1967–69 vehicles

1970–77

Circuit	Fuse (amp)
A. Radio—Back-up Lts.—Horn	AGC20
B. Acc.—Aux. Heater—A.C. Clutch—Speed Control	AGC20
C. Heater—A/C	AGC20
D. Cigar Lighter—Dome Lamps	AGC20
E. Exterior Lamps	AGC20
F. Instrument Lamps	AGC 2

Fig. 69 Fuse applications for 1970–77 vehicles

1978–84

Circuit	Fuse (amp)
A. Instrument lights	5 amp
B. Back up lights, turn signal lights, A/C clutch/speed control	20 amp
C. Aux. heater, aux. A/C, horn	20 amp
D. Radio	5 amp
E. Gauges, oil pressure light, brake light, clock	20 amp
F. Tail, parking, side market and license lights	20 amp
G. Dome, stop and courtesy lights, clock feed, cigarette lighter, glove box light, ignition light	20 amp 1978–79, 25 amp 1980–82
H. Hazard flashers	20 amp
I. A/C or heater blower motor	30 amp
J. Heater rear window	25 amp

Fig. 70 Fuse applications for 1978–84 vehicles

1985

Circuit	Fuse (amp.)
A. Air conditioning or heater blower motor	30 amp
B. Illumination lamps	3 amp
C. Hazard flasher	15 amp
D. Radio	10 amp
E. Turn signal flasher, backup switch and lamps	15 amp
F. Speed control, air conditioning clutch and emission maintenance reminder lamp	20 amp
G. Trailer lamps and emission maintenance reminder memory	20 amp
H. Fuse cavity 2, cigar lighter and exterior lamps	25 amp
I. Horn relay, cargo lamp, interior lamps and stop lamps	20 amp
J. Power window lift motor and door lock solenoid	30 amp c/bkr
K. Clock, four-wheel drive indicator and liftgate ajar	3 amp
L. Seat belt buzzer and cluster warning lamps	3 amp

Fig. 71 Fuse applications for 1985 vehicles

6-26 CHASSIS ELECTRICAL

CAVITY	FUSE	CIRCUITS
1	30 Amp Lt. Green	A/C or Heater Blower Motor
2	3 Amp Violet	Cluster Illumination, Switch Title Lamps, Snow Plow Control Lt. Four-wheel Ind. Light, Radio, Clock and Radio Dimming, Ash Tray
3	20 Amp Yellow	Hazard Flasher
4	10 Amp Red	Radio & Clock Power
5	20 Amp Yellow	Turn Signals, Snow Plow Control Trans, Oil Temp Lts.
6	20 Amp Yellow	Windshield Wipers
7	20 Amp Yellow	Horn & Relay, Cig. Lighter Radio & Clock Memory, Key-In & Hdl. Buzzer
8	20 Amp Yellow	Clearance and ID Lights, Park-Tail-Side Marker-License
9	20 Amp Yellow	Dome Lt., Map & Courtesy Lts., Cargo Lt.,
10	30 Amp Circuit Breaker	Power Window Motors, Door Lock Solenoids & Relay
11	5 Amp Tan	Liftgate Ajar Lt., Speed Control 4-Wheel Ind., Power Wdo. Relay
12	5 Amp Tan	Brake Warning Lt., Seat Belt Lt. and Buzzer, Fuel Gauge, Oil Gauge, Temperature Gauge, Oil & Temp. Lamps
13	20 Amp Yellow	Back-up Lts., A/C Clutch
14-15	Empty	

Additional Circuit Protection

The headlamp and windshield wiper/washer systems have circuit breakers as part of their switch assemblies.

Fig. 72 Fuse applications for 1986 vehicles

CAVITY	FUSE	CIRCUITS
1	30 Amp Lt. Green	A/C or Heater Blower Motor
2	3 Amp Violet	Cluster Illumination, Switch Title Lamps, Snow Plow Control Lt. Four-wheel Ind. Light, Radio, Clock and Radio Dimming, Ash Tray
3	20 Amp Yellow	Hazard Flasher
4	10 Amp Red	Radio & Clock Power
5	20 Amp Yellow	Turn Signals, Snow Plow Control Trans, Oil Temp Lts.
6	20 Amp Yellow	Windshield Wipers
7	20 Amp Yellow	Horn & Relay, Cig. Lighter Radio & Clock Memory, Key-In & Hdl. Buzzer
8	20 Amp Yellow	Clearance and ID Lights, Park-Tail-Side Marker-License
9	20 Amp Yellow	Dome Lt., Map & Courtesy Lts., Cargo Lt.,
10	30 Amp Circuit Breaker	Power Window Motors, Door Lock Solenoids & Relay
11	5 Amp Tan	Liftgate Ajar Lt., Speed Control 4-Wheel Ind., Power Wdo. Relay
12	5 Amp Tan	Brake Warning Lt., Seat Belt Lt. and Buzzer, Fuel Gauge, Oil Gauge, Temperature Gauge, Oil & Temp. Lamps
13	20 Amp Yellow	Back-up Lts., A/C Clutch
14-15	Empty	

Fig. 73 Fuse applications for 1987 vehicles

CAVITY	FUSE	CIRCUITS
1	30 Amp Lt. Green	A/C or Heater Blower Motor
2	30 Amp Circuit Breaker	Power Windows
3	20 Amp Yellow	Hazard Flasher
4	10 Amp Red	Radio & Clock Power
5	20 Amp Yellow	Turn Signals, Snow Plow Control Trans, Oil Temp Lts.
6	20 Amp Yellow	Windshield Wipers
7	20 Amp Yellow	Horn & Relay, Cig. Lighter Radio & Clock Memory, Key-In & Hdl. Buzzer
8	20 Amp Yellow	Clearance and ID Lights, Park-Tail-Side Marker-License
9	20 Amp Yellow	Stop Lamps, Key-in Buzzer
10	30 Amp Circuit Breaker	Power Door Lock
11	10 Amp Red	Radio & Clock Memory, Power Mirrors, Glove Box, Dome, Courtesy, Map, Cargo Lamps
12	5 Amp Tan	Brake Warning Lt., Seat Belt Lt. and Buzzer, Fuel Gauge, Oil Gauge, Temperature Gauge, Oil & Temp. Lamps, Speed Control
13	20 Amp Yellow	Back-up Lts., A/C Clutch, Solenoid Idle Stop
14	3 Amp Violet	Inst. Panel Lights, A/C and Heater, Headlight Switch, Ash Receiver, Snow Plow, Radio, Clock Display Dimming and Four-Wheel Indicator
15	Empty	

Fig. 74 Fuse applications for 1988 vehicles

Circuit Breakers

RESETTING AND/OR REPLACEMENT

One device used to protect electrical components from burning out due to excessive current is a circuit breaker. Circuit breakers rapidly open and close the flow path for the electricity, in order to protect the circuit if current is excessive. A circuit breaker is used on components which are more likely to draw excessive current, such as a breaker often found in the light switch that protects the headlight circuit. Circuit breakers are found in the protected component, the fuse block. Circuit breakers pull out of the fuse panel just like a regular fuse. The breakers are self-resetting.

Turn Signal and Hazard Flasher Locations

♦ See Figure 75

Both the turn signal flasher and the hazard warning flasher are mounted on the fuse panel. The turn signal flasher is mounted on the front of the fuse panel, and the hazard warning flasher is mounted on the rear of the fuse panel.

CHASSIS ELECTRICAL 6-27

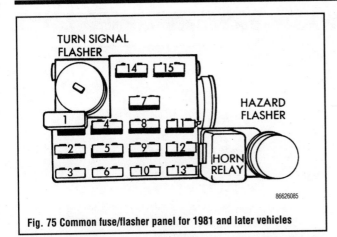

Fig. 75 Common fuse/flasher panel for 1981 and later vehicles

Fuse Link

The fuse link is a short length of special, Hypalon (high temperature) insulated wire, integral with the engine compartment wiring harness and should not be confused with standard wire. It is several wire gauges smaller than the circuit which it protects. Under no circumstances should a fuse link replacement repair be made using a length of standard wire cut from bulk stock or from another wiring harness.

To repair any blown fuse link use the following procedure:

1. Determine which circuit is damaged, its location and the cause of the open fuse link. If the damaged fuse link is one of three fed by a common No. 10 or 12 gauge feed wire, determine the specific affected circuit.
2. Disconnect the negative battery cable.
3. Cut the damaged fuse link from the wiring harness and discard it. If the fuse link is one of three circuits fed by a single feed wire, cut it out of the harness at each splice end and discard it.
4. Identify and procure the proper fuse link and butt connectors for attaching the fuse link to the harness.
5. To repair any fuse link in a 3–link group with one feed:

   a. After cutting the open link out of the harness, cut each of the remaining undamaged fuse links close to the feed wire weld.
   b. Strip approximately ½ in. (13mm) of insulation from the detached ends of the two good fuse links. Then insert two wire ends into one end of a butt connector and carefully push one stripped end of the replacement fuse link into the same end of the butt connector and crimp all three firmly together.

➡ **Care must be taken when fitting the three fuse links into the butt connector as the internal diameter is a snug it for three wires. Make sure to use a proper crimping tool. Pliers, side cutters, etc. will not apply the proper crimp to retain the wires and withstand a pull test.**

   c. After crimping the butt connector to the three fuse links, cut the weld portion from the feed wire and strip approximately ½ in. (13mm) of insulation from the cut end. Insert the stripped end into the open end of the butt connector and crimp very firm.
   d. To attach the remaining end of the replacement fuse link, strip approximately ½ in. (13mm) of insulation from the wire end of the circuit from which the blown fuse link was removed, and firmly crimp a butt connector or equivalent to the stripped wire. Then, insert the end of the replacement link into the other end of the butt connector and crimp firm.
   e. Using rosin core solder with a consistency of 60 percent tin and 40 percent lead, solder the connectors and the wires at the repairs and insulate with electrical tape.
   f. To replace any fuse link on a single circuit in a harness, cut out the damaged portion, strip approximately ½ in. (13mm) of insulation from the two wire ends and attach the appropriate replacement fuse link to the stripped wire ends with two proper size butt connectors. Solder the connectors and wires and insulate the at
   g. To repair any fuse link which has an eyelet terminal on one end such as the charging circuit, cut off the open fuse link behind the weld, strip approximately ½ in. (13mm) of insulation from the cut end and attach the appropriate new eyelet fuse link to the cut stripped wire with an appropriate size butt connector. Solder the connectors and wires at the repair and insulate with tape.
   h. Connect the negative battery cable to the battery and test the system for proper operation.

➡ **Do not mistake a resistor wire for a fuse link. The resistor wire is generally longer and has print stating, "Resistor: don't cut or splice."**

6-28 CHASSIS ELECTRICAL

WIRING DIAGRAMS

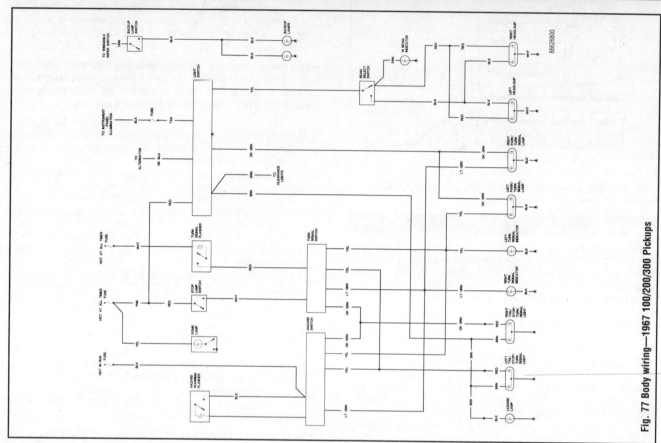

Fig. 77 Body wiring—1967 100/200/300 Pickups

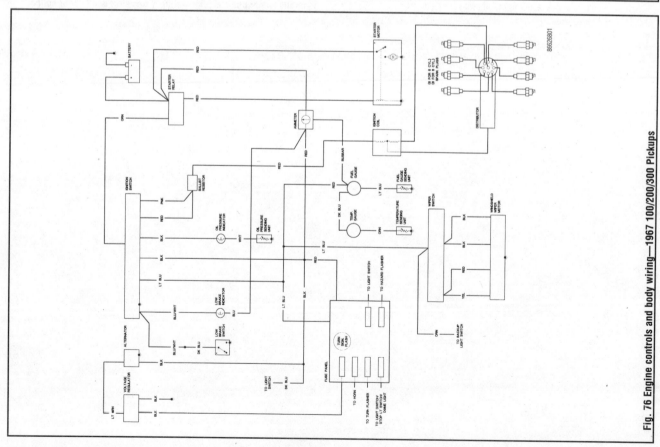

Fig. 76 Engine controls and body wiring—1967 100/200/300 Pickups

CHASSIS ELECTRICAL 6-29

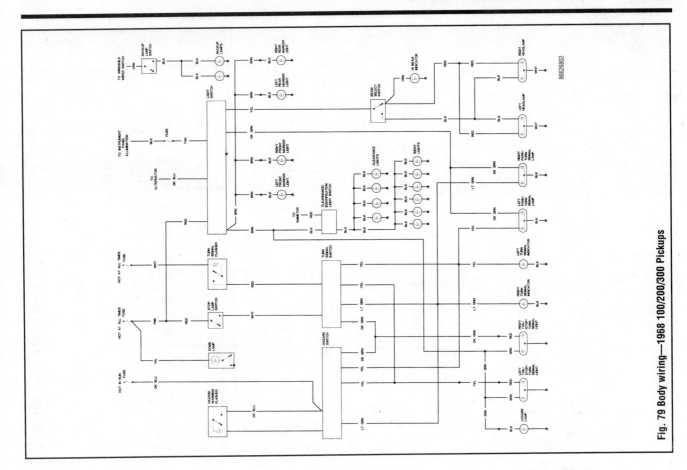

Fig. 79 Body wiring—1968 100/200/300 Pickups

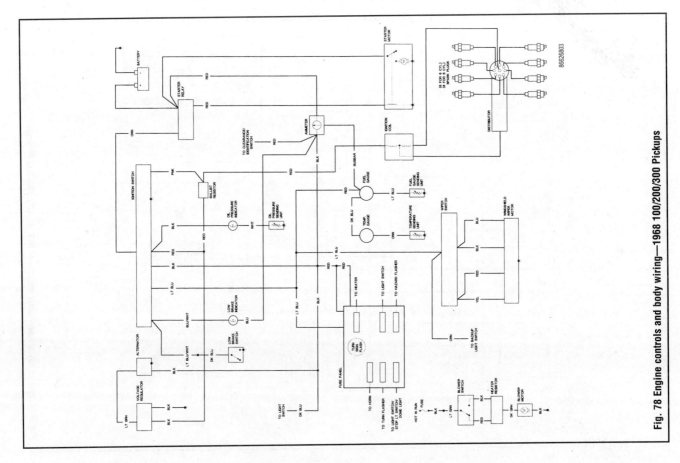

Fig. 78 Engine controls and body wiring—1968 100/200/300 Pickups

6-30 CHASSIS ELECTRICAL

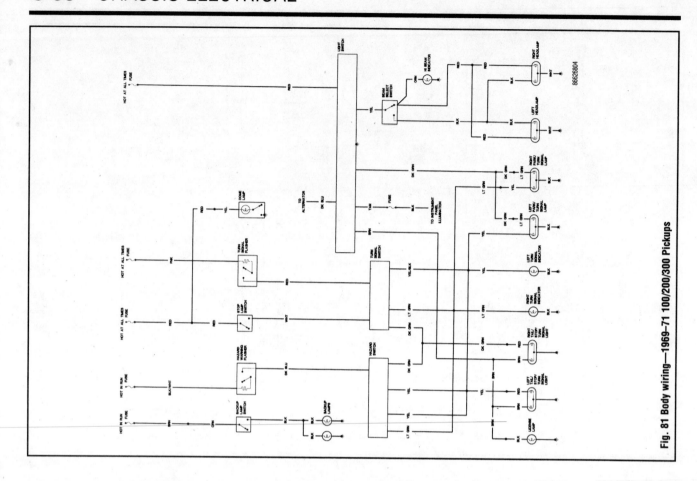

Fig. 81 Body wiring—1969-71 100/200/300 Pickups

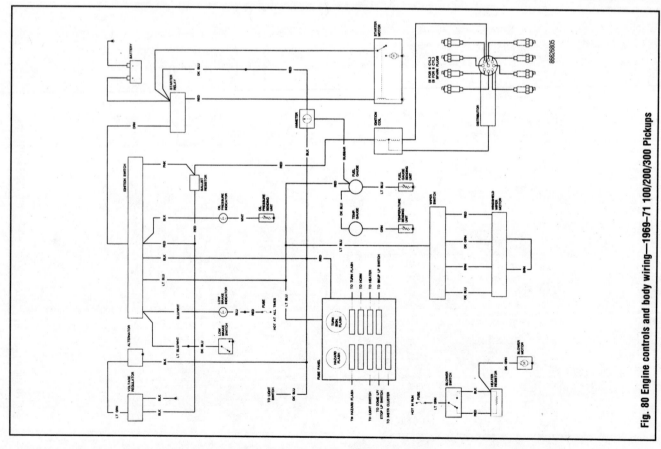

Fig. 80 Engine controls and body wiring—1969-71 100/200/300 Pickups

CHASSIS ELECTRICAL 6-31

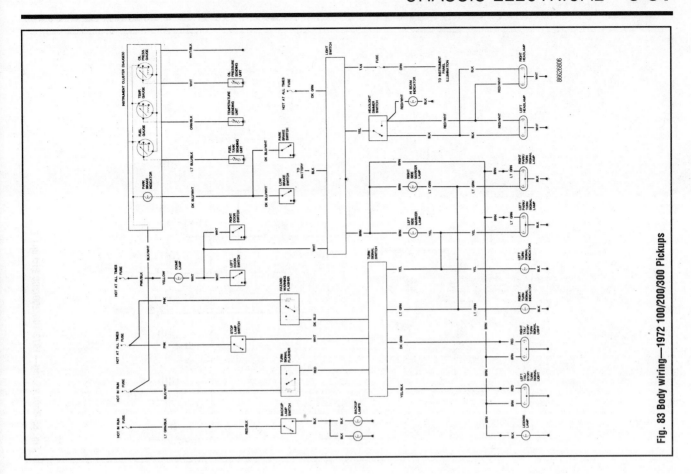

Fig. 83 Body wiring—1972 100/200/300 Pickups

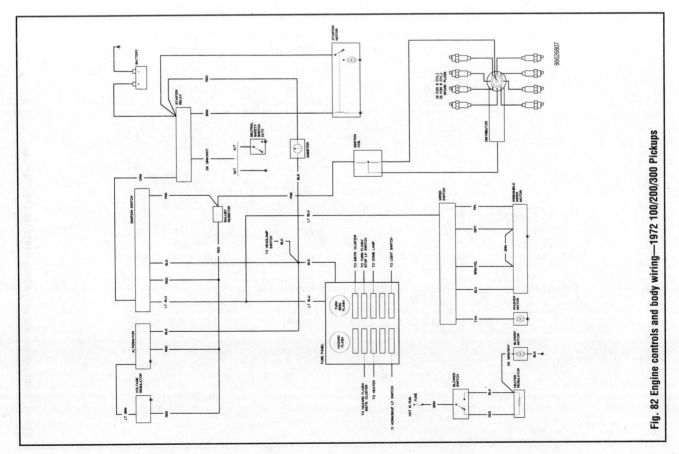

Fig. 82 Engine controls and body wiring—1972 100/200/300 Pickups

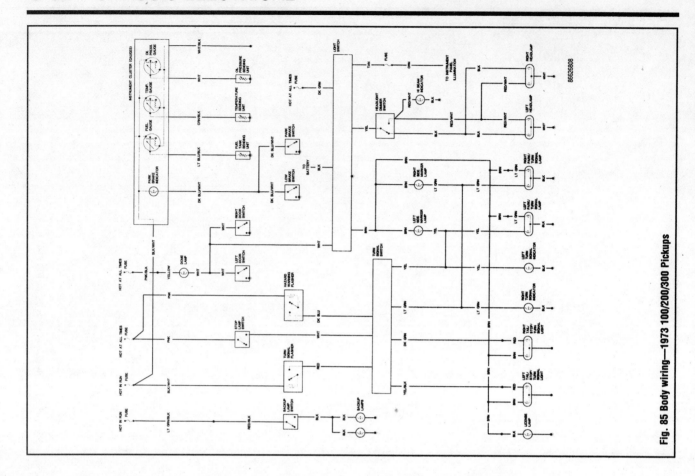

Fig. 85 Body wiring—1973 100/200/300 Pickups

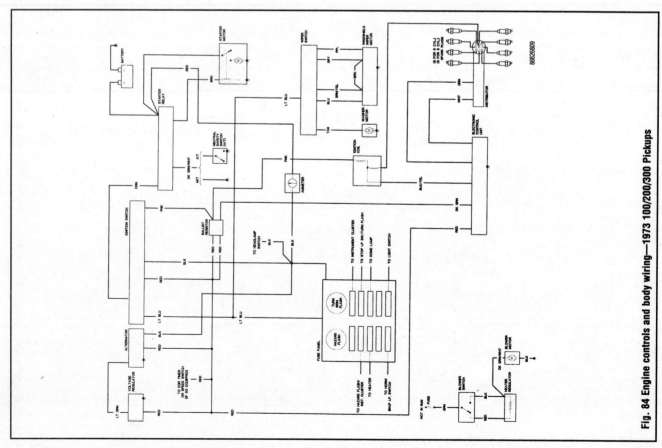

Fig. 84 Engine controls and body wiring—1973 100/200/300 Pickups

CHASSIS ELECTRICAL 6-33

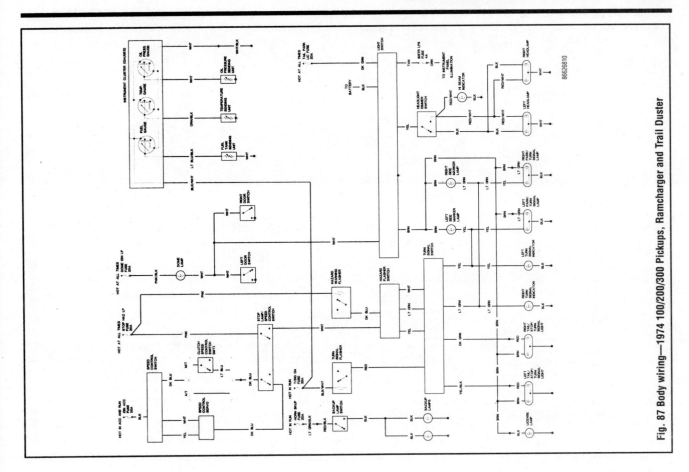

Fig. 87 Body wiring—1974 100/200/300 Pickups, Ramcharger and Trail Duster

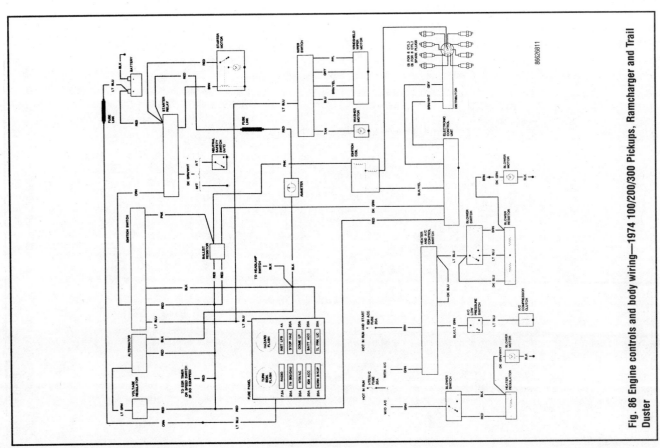

Fig. 86 Engine controls and body wiring—1974 100/200/300 Pickups, Ramcharger and Trail Duster

6-34 CHASSIS ELECTRICAL

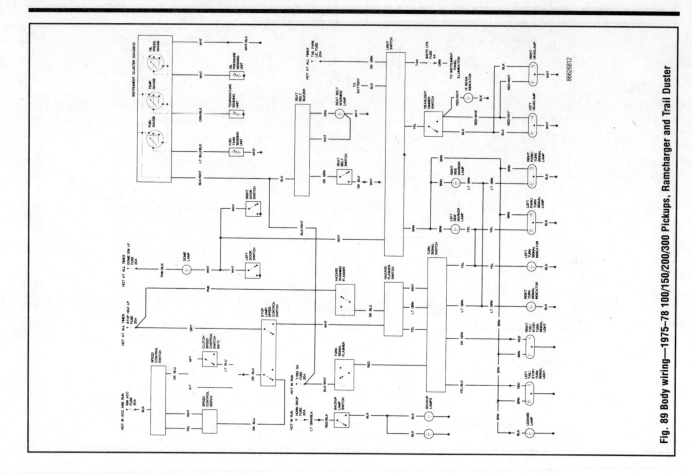

Fig. 89 Body wiring—1975-78 100/150/200/300 Pickups, Ramcharger and Trail Duster

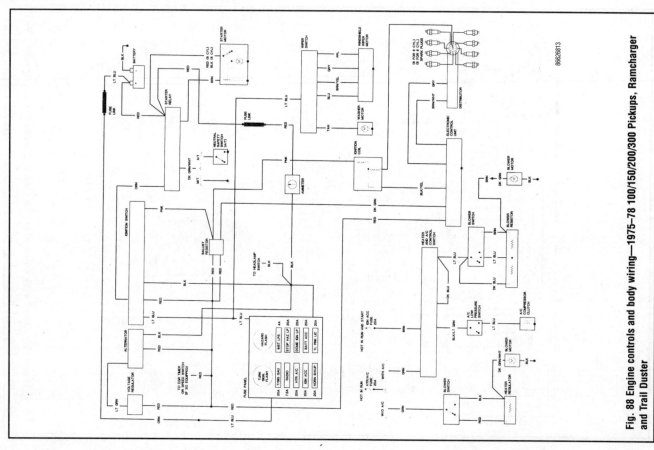

Fig. 88 Engine controls and body wiring—1975-78 100/150/200/300 Pickups, Ramcharger and Trail Duster

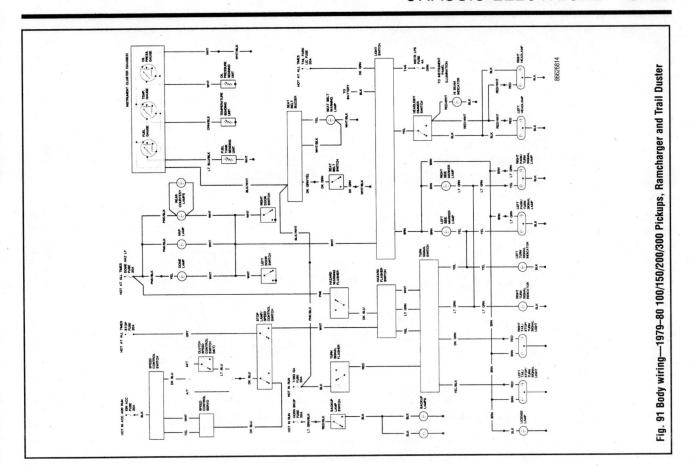

Fig. 91 Body wiring—1979-80 100/150/200/300 Pickups, Ramcharger and Trail Duster

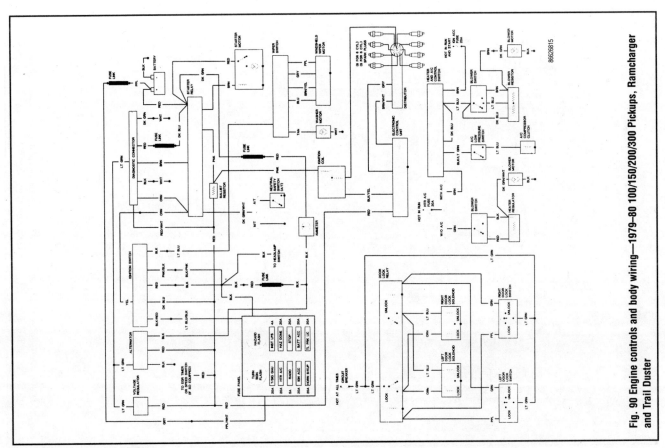

Fig. 90 Engine controls and body wiring—1979-80 100/150/200/300 Pickups, Ramcharger and Trail Duster

6-36 CHASSIS ELECTRICAL

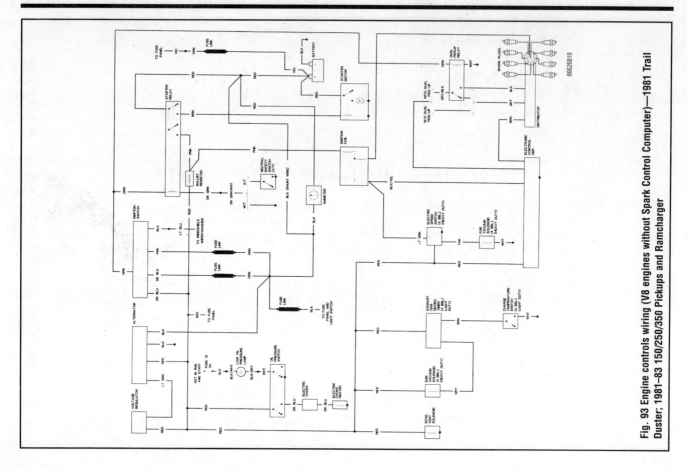

Fig. 93 Engine controls wiring (V8 engines without Spark Control Computer)—1981 Trail Duster; 1981-83 150/250/350 Pickups and Ramcharger

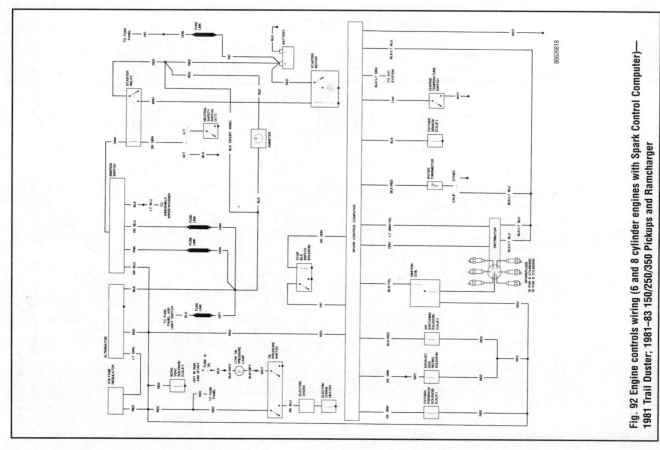

Fig. 92 Engine controls wiring (6 and 8 cylinder engines with Spark Control Computer)—1981 Trail Duster; 1981-83 150/250/350 Pickups and Ramcharger

CHASSIS ELECTRICAL 6-37

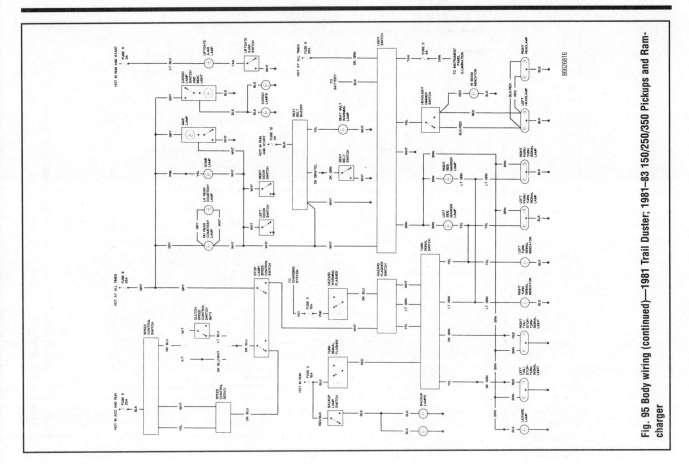

Fig. 95 Body wiring (continued)—1981 Trail Duster; 1981–83 150/250/350 Pickups and Ramcharger

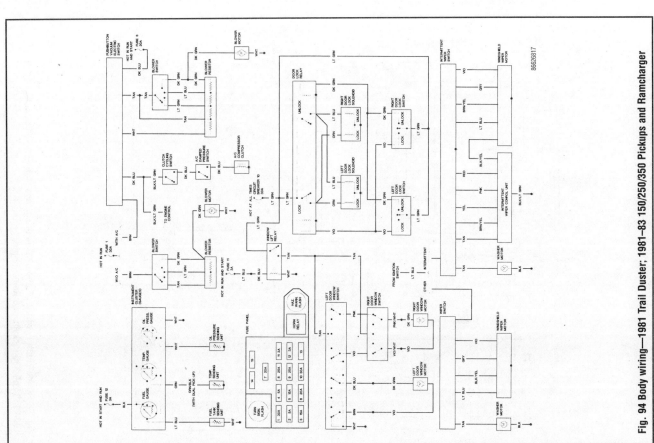

Fig. 94 Body wiring—1981 Trail Duster; 1981–83 150/250/350 Pickups and Ramcharger

6-38 CHASSIS ELECTRICAL

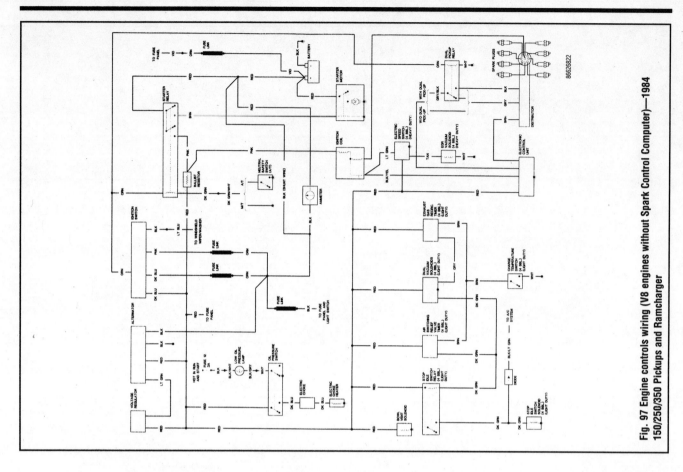

Fig. 97 Engine controls wiring (V8 engines without Spark Control Computer)—1984 150/250/350 Pickups and Ramcharger

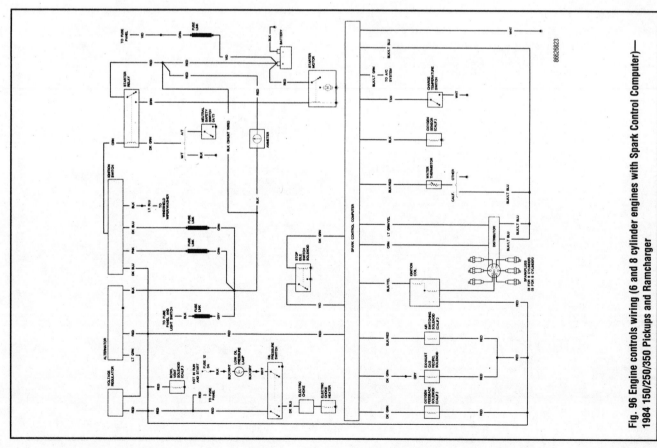

Fig. 96 Engine controls wiring (6 and 8 cylinder engines with Spark Control Computer)—1984 150/250/350 Pickups and Ramcharger

CHASSIS ELECTRICAL 6-39

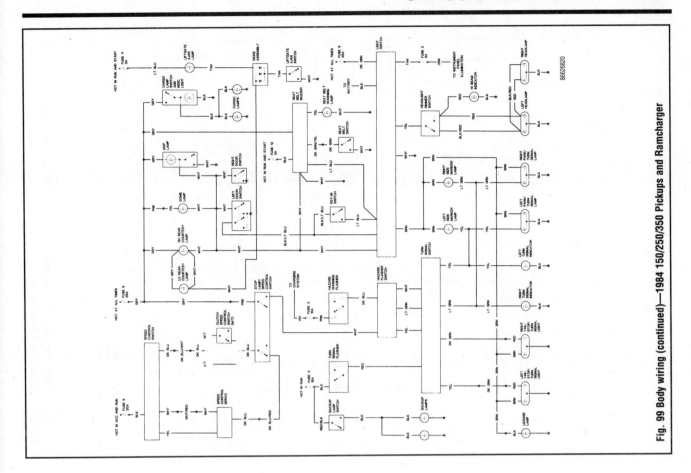

Fig. 99 Body wiring (continued)—1984 150/250/350 Pickups and Ramcharger

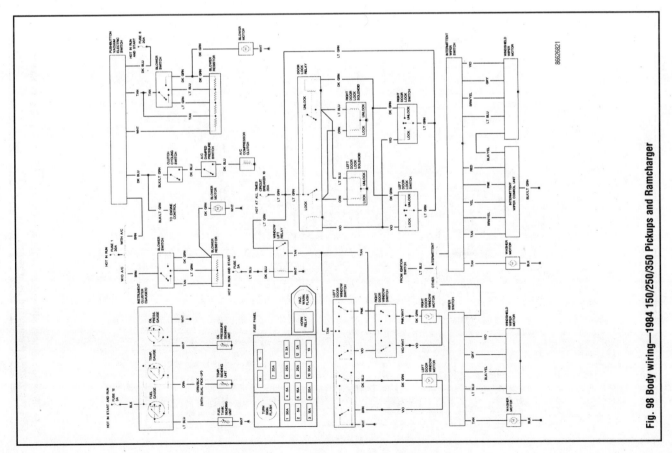

Fig. 98 Body wiring—1984 150/250/350 Pickups and Ramcharger

6-40 CHASSIS ELECTRICAL

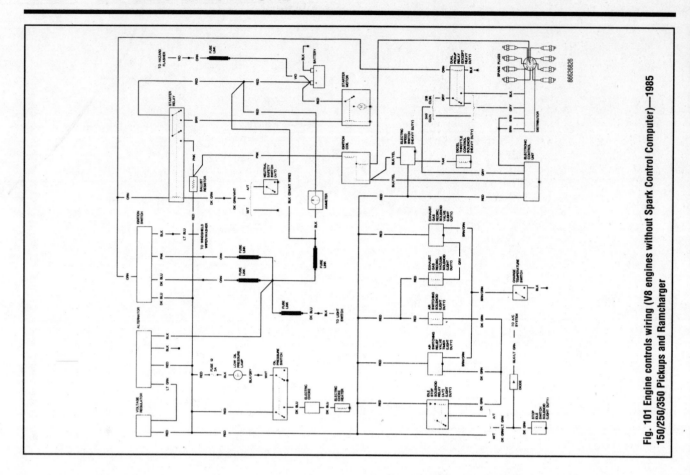

Fig. 101 Engine controls wiring (V8 engines without Spark Control Computer)—1985 150/250/350 Pickups and Ramcharger

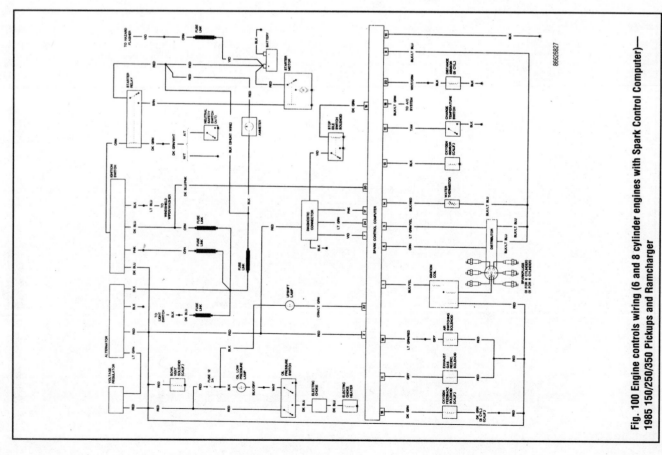

Fig. 100 Engine controls wiring (6 and 8 cylinder engines with Spark Control Computer)—1985 150/250/350 Pickups and Ramcharger

CHASSIS ELECTRICAL 6-41

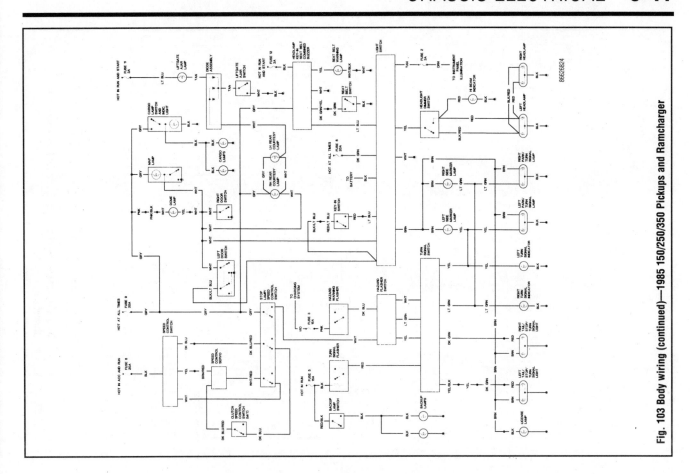

Fig. 103 Body wiring (continued)—1985 150/250/350 Pickups and Ramcharger

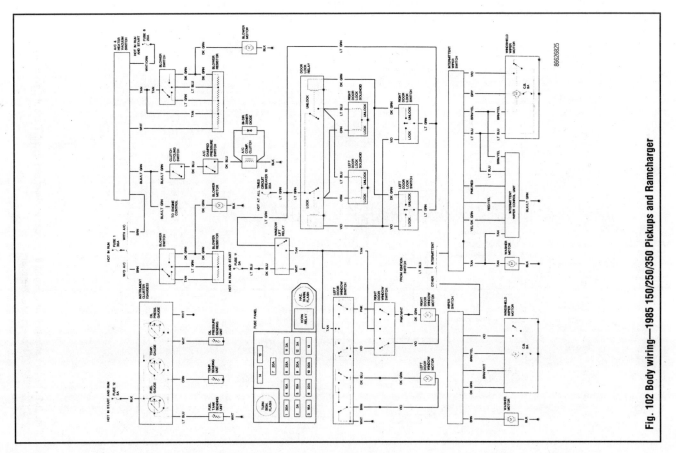

Fig. 102 Body wiring—1985 150/250/350 Pickups and Ramcharger

6-42 CHASSIS ELECTRICAL

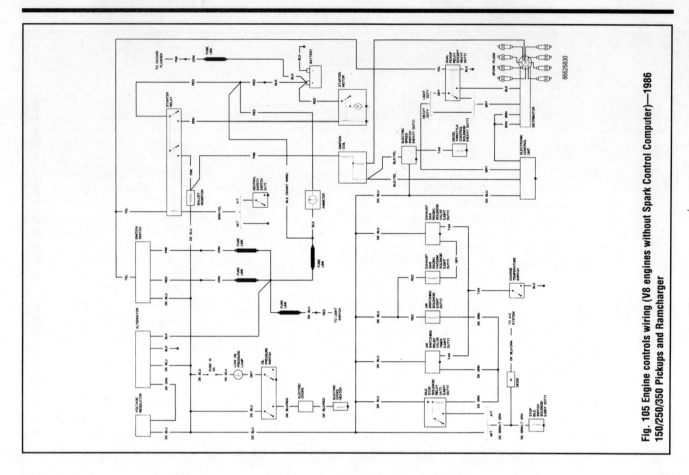

Fig. 105 Engine controls wiring (V8 engines without Spark Control Computer)—1986 150/250/350 Pickups and Ramcharger

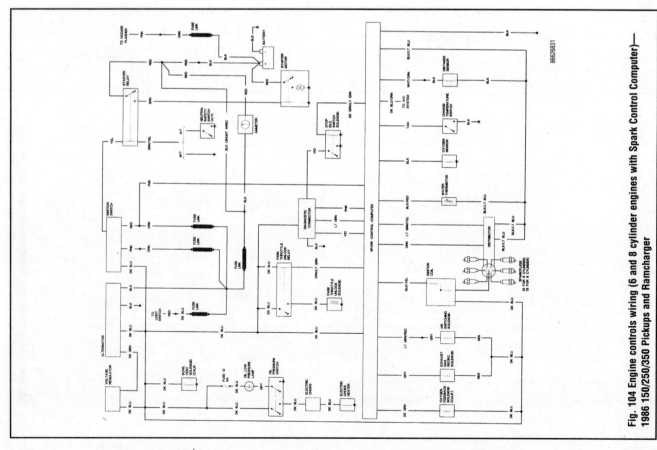

Fig. 104 Engine controls wiring (6 and 8 cylinder engines with Spark Control Computer)—1986 150/250/350 Pickups and Ramcharger

CHASSIS ELECTRICAL 6-43

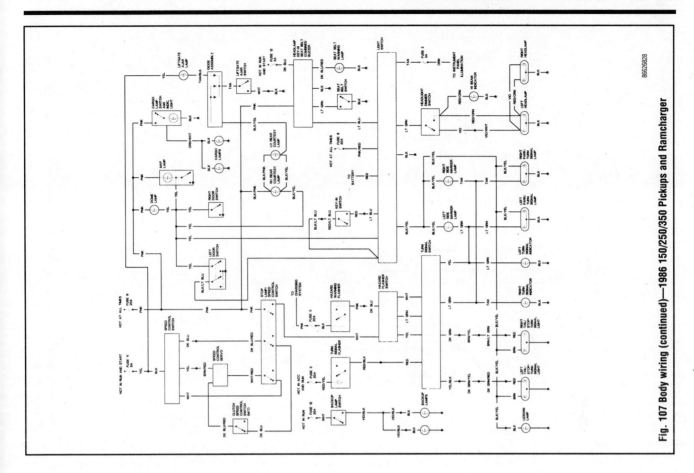

Fig. 107 Body wiring (continued)—1986 150/250/350 Pickups and Ramcharger

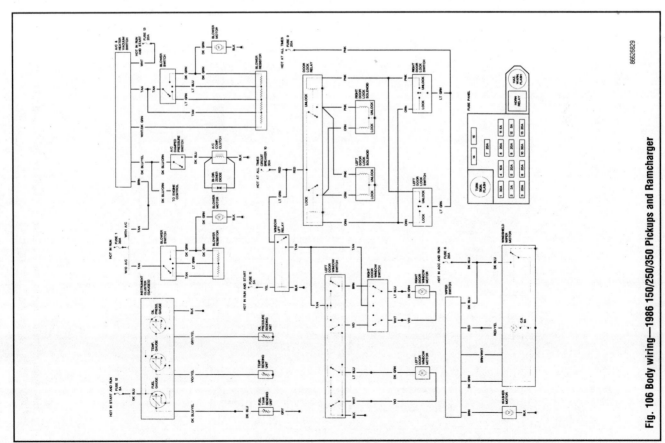

Fig. 106 Body wiring—1986 150/250/350 Pickups and Ramcharger

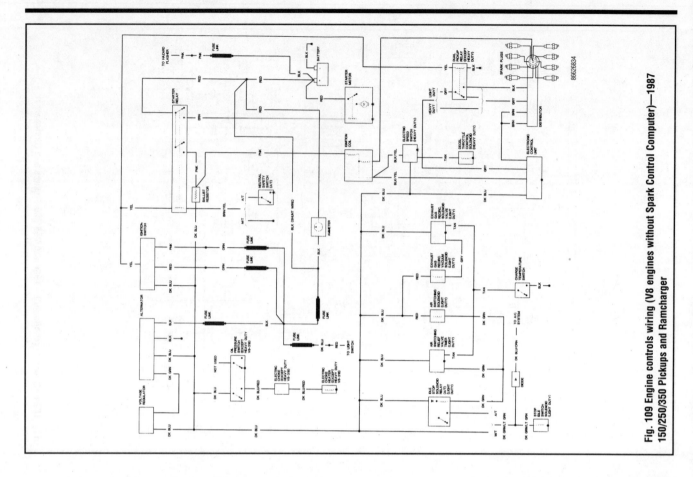

Fig. 109 Engine controls wiring (V8 engines without Spark Control Computer)—1987 150/250/350 Pickups and Ramcharger

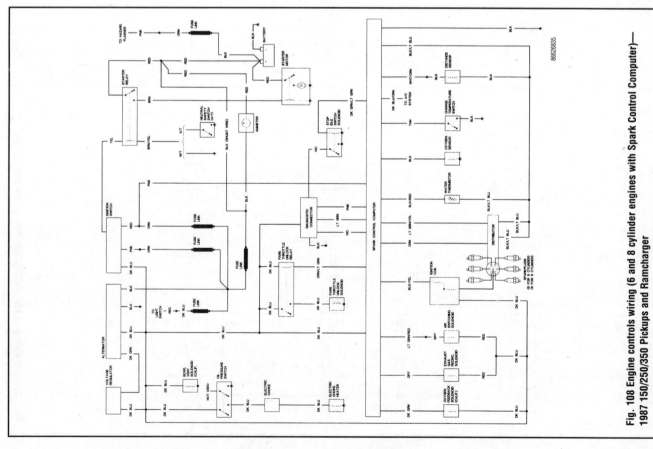

Fig. 108 Engine controls wiring (6 and 8 cylinder engines with Spark Control Computer)—1987 150/250/350 Pickups and Ramcharger

CHASSIS ELECTRICAL 6-45

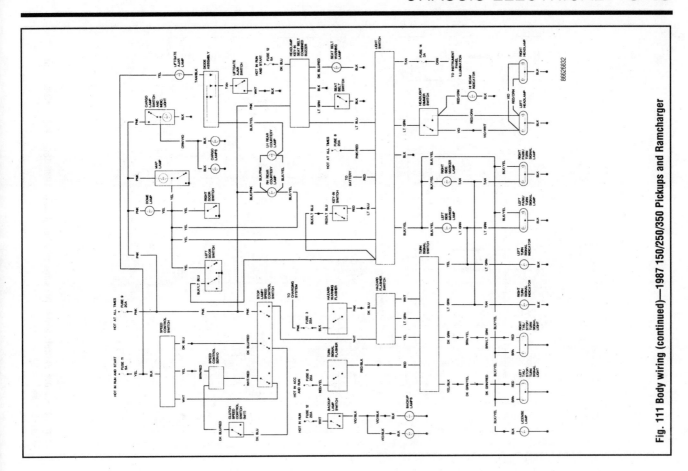

Fig. 111 Body wiring (continued)—1987 150/250/350 Pickups and Ramcharger

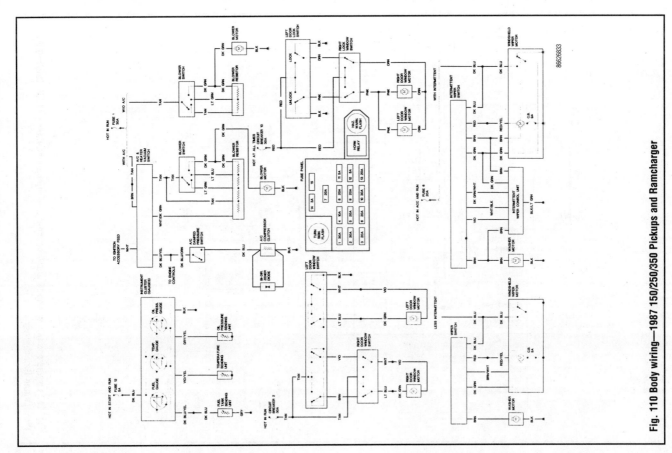

Fig. 110 Body wiring—1987 150/250/350 Pickups and Ramcharger

6-46 CHASSIS ELECTRICAL

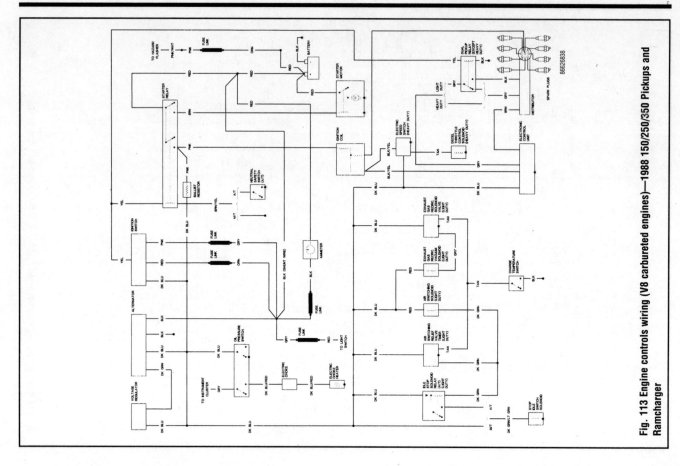

Fig. 113 Engine controls wiring (V8 carbureted engines)—1988 150/250/350 Pickups and Ramcharger

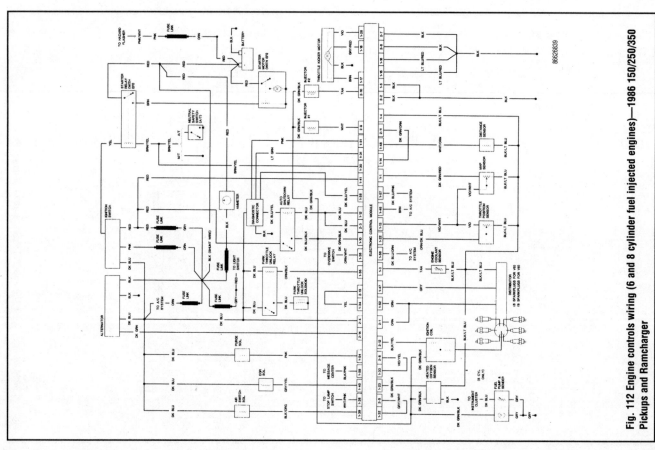

Fig. 112 Engine controls wiring (6 and 8 cylinder fuel injected engines)—1986 150/250/350 Pickups and Ramcharger

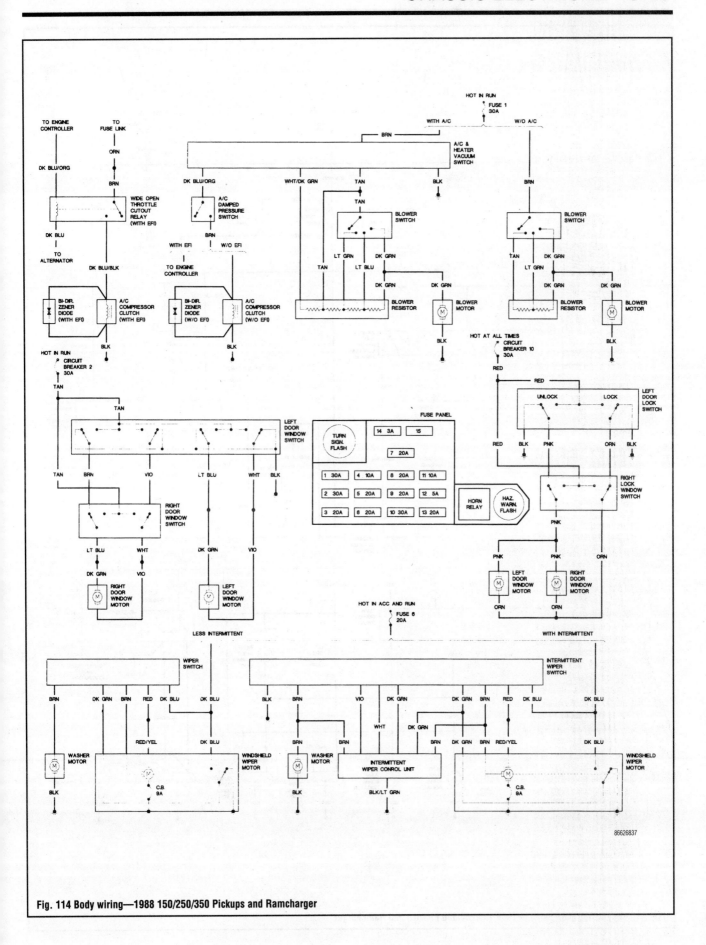

Fig. 114 Body wiring—1988 150/250/350 Pickups and Ramcharger

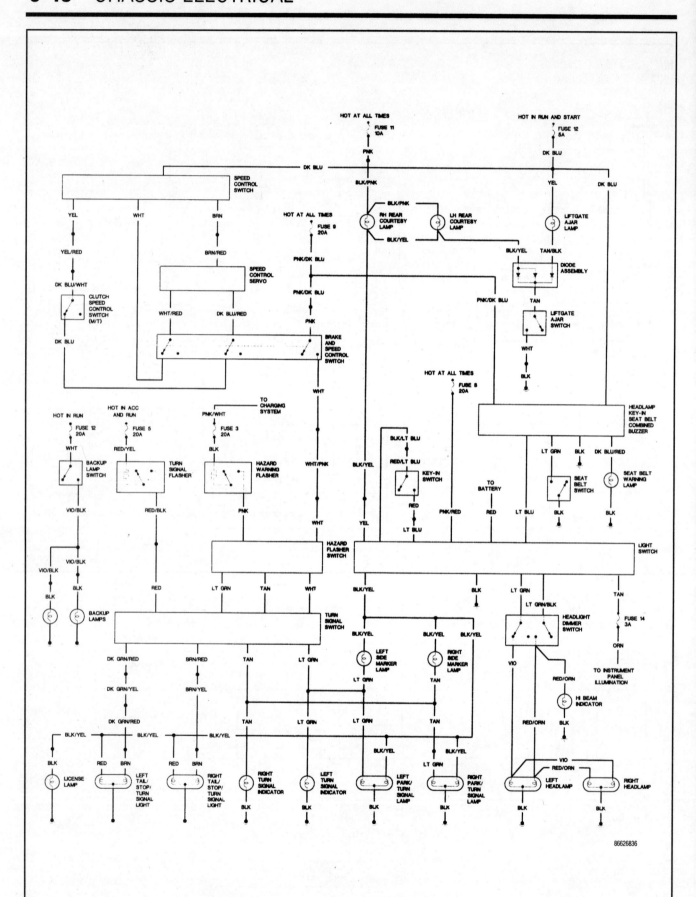

Fig. 115 Body wiring (continued)—1988 150/250/350 Pickups and Ramcharger

MANUAL TRANSMISSION 7-2
UNDERSTANDING THE MANUAL TRANS-
  MISSION 7-2
IDENTIFICATION 7-2
ADJUSTMENTS 7-2
   SHIFT LINKAGE 7-2
   CLUTCH INTERLOCK 7-4
SHIFT LINKAGE 7-4
   REMOVAL & INSTALLATION 7-4
BACK-UP LIGHT SWITCH 7-4
   REMOVAL & INSTALLATION 7-4
EXTENSION HOUSING SEAL 7-4
   REMOVAL & INSTALLATION 7-4
TRANSMISSION 7-5
   REMOVAL & INSTALLATION 7-5
CLUTCH 7-6
UNDERSTANDING THE CLUTCH 7-6
ADJUSTMENTS 7-7
   PEDAL FREE-PLAY 7-7
DRIVEN DISC AND PRESSURE
  PLATE 7-7
   REMOVAL & INSTALLATION 7-7
CLUTCH MASTER CYLINDER AND
  SLAVE CYLINDER 7-10
   REMOVAL & INSTALLATION 7-10
TRANSFER CASE 7-11
IDENTIFICATION 7-11
TRANSFER CASE ASSEMBLY 7-11
   REMOVAL & INSTALLATION 7-11
   ADJUSTMENTS 7-11
AUTOMATIC TRANSMISSION 7-13
IDENTIFICATION 7-13
UNDERSTANDING AUTOMATIC TRANS-
  MISSIONS 7-13
ADJUSTMENTS 7-13
   KICKDOWN BAND 7-13
   LOW & REVERSE BAND 7-13
   SHIFT LINKAGE 7-14
   THROTTLE KICKDOWN ROD 7-14
NEUTRAL SAFETY SWITCH 7-17
   REMOVAL & INSTALLATION 7-17
EXTENSION HOUSING SEAL 7-17
   REMOVAL & INSTALLATION 7-17
TRANSMISSION 7-17
   REMOVAL & INSTALLATION 7-17
DRIVELINE 7-18
4–WD FRONT DRIVESHAFT 7-18
   REMOVAL & INSTALLATION 7-18
REAR DRIVESHAFTS AND
  U-JOINTS 7-19
   REMOVAL & INSTALLATION 7-19
   U-JOINT OVERHAUL 7-19
CENTER SUPPORT BEARING 7-21
   REMOVAL & INSTALLATION 7-21
FRONT DRIVE AXLE 7-21
MANUAL LOCKING HUBS 7-21
   REMOVAL & INSTALLATION 7-21
AUTOMATIC LOCKING HUBS 7-24
   REMOVAL & DISASSEMBLY 7-24

INSPECTION 7-24
LUBRICATION 7-24
ASSEMBLY & INSTALLATION 7-24
SPINDLE BEARINGS 7-26
   REMOVAL, PACKING & INSTALLA-
     TION 7-26
AXLE SHAFT, BEARING AND SEAL 7-29
   REMOVAL & INSTALLATION 7-29
PINION SEAL 7-32
   REMOVAL & INSTALLATION 7-32
AXLE HOUSING UNIT 7-33
   REMOVAL & INSTALLATION 7-33
REAR AXLE 7-33
IDENTIFICATION 7-33
DETERMINING AXLE RATIO 7-33
AXLE SHAFT, BEARING AND SEAL 7-34
   REMOVAL & INSTALLATION 7-34
PINION SEAL 7-39
   REMOVAL & INSTALLATION 7-39
AXLE HOUSING UNIT 7-41
   REMOVAL & INSTALLATION 7-41
SPECIFICATIONS CHART
   FRONT DRIVE AXLE APPLICATION
     CHART 7-22

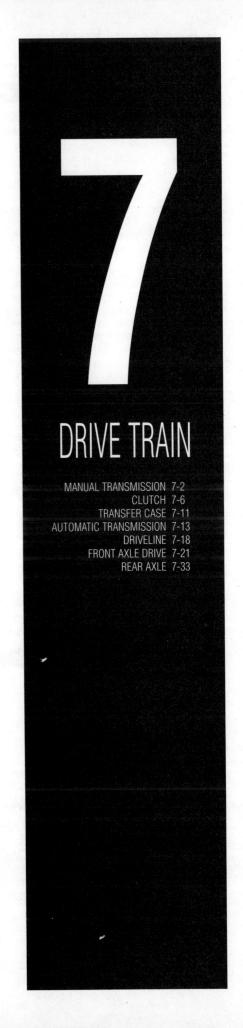

7
DRIVE TRAIN

MANUAL TRANSMISSION 7-2
CLUTCH 7-6
TRANSFER CASE 7-11
AUTOMATIC TRANSMISSION 7-13
DRIVELINE 7-18
FRONT AXLE DRIVE 7-21
REAR AXLE 7-33

DRIVE TRAIN

MANUAL TRANSMISSION

Understanding the Manual Transmission

Because of the way an internal combustion engine breathes, it can produce torque (or twisting force) only within a narrow speed range. Most overhead valve pushrod engines must turn at about 2500 rpm to produce their peak torque. Often by 4500 rpm, they are producing so little torque that continued increases in engine speed produce no power increases.

The torque peak on overhead camshaft engines is, generally, much higher, but much narrower.

The manual transmission and clutch are employed to vary the relationship between engine RPM and the speed of the wheels so that adequate power can be produced under all circumstances. The clutch allows engine torque to be applied to the transmission input shaft gradually, due to mechanical slippage. The vehicle can, consequently, be started smoothly from a full stop.

The transmission changes the ratio between the rotating speeds of the engine and the wheels by the use of gears. 4-speed or 5-speed transmissions are most common. The lower gears allow full engine power to be applied to the rear wheels during acceleration at low speeds.

The clutch driveplate is a thin disc, the center of which is splined to the transmission input shaft. Both sides of the disc are covered with a layer of material which is similar to brake lining and which is capable of allowing slippage without roughness or excessive noise.

The clutch cover is bolted to the engine flywheel and incorporates a diaphragm spring which provides the pressure to engage the clutch. The cover also houses the pressure plate. When the clutch pedal is released, the driven disc is sandwiched between the pressure plate and the smooth surface of the flywheel, thus forcing the disc to turn at the same speed as the engine crankshaft.

The transmission contains a mainshaft which passes all the way through the transmission, from the clutch to the driveshaft. This shaft is separated at one point, so that front and rear portions can turn at different speeds.

Power is transmitted by a countershaft in the lower gears and reverse. The gears of the countershaft mesh with gears on the mainshaft, allowing power to be carried from one to the other. Countershaft gears are often integral with that shaft, while several of the mainshaft gears can either rotate independently of the shaft or be locked to it. Shifting from one gear to the next causes one of the gears to be freed from rotating with the shaft and locks another to it. Gears are locked and unlocked by internal dog clutches which slide between the center of the gear and the shaft. The forward gears usually employ synchronizers; friction members which smoothly bring gear and shaft to the same speed before the toothed dog clutches are engaged.

Identification

♦ See Figure 1

All Dodge trucks have a transmission identification tag. This tag can identify your transmission by part number, model and build date, which are stamped on the tag. For a manual transmission an aluminum identification tag is secured by two bolts to the power take off cover. If you need to replace the cover do not discard of the tag. In other models, a blue ID tag is permanently attached to the left side of the transmission case, at the top, near the case cover.

Transmission types:
- New Process A–203 3–speed (1969–79)
- New Process A–250 3–speed (1969–74)
- New Process A–390 3–speed (1979)
- New Process A–745 4–speed (1967–68)
- New Process NP–420 4–speed (1967–68)
- New Process NP–435 4–speed (1967–87)
- New Process NP–445 4–speed (1967–78)
- New Process NP–2500 5–speed (1988)
- Borg-Warner T 87E 3–speed (1967–68)
- A–833 "Overdrive–4" 4–speed (1979–88)

Adjustments

SHIFT LINKAGE

A-230 and A-250

PICK-UPS

♦ See Figures 2 and 3

1. Adjust the length of the 2–3 shift rod so the position of the shift lever on the steering column will be correct.
2. Assemble the 1st-reverse and 2–3 shift rods, then place each in its normal position, secured with a clip. Loosen both swivel clamp bolts.
3. Move the 2–3 shift lever into 3rd position (this means moving forward lever forward). Move the steering column lever until it is about five degrees above the horizontal. Tighten the shift rod swivel clamp bolt, 125 inch lbs. (14 Nm).
4. Shift the transmission to neutral. Place a suitable tool between the crossover blade and the 2–3 lever at the steering column so that both lever pins are engaged by the crossover blade.
5. Set the 1st-reverse lever in neutral. Tighten the swivel clamp bolt, 125 inch lbs. (14 Nm).
6. Remove the tool from the crossover blade, and check all shifts for smoothness.

RAMCHARGER AND TRAIL DUSTER

1. Remove both shift rod swivels from the transmission shift levers. Make sure that the transmission shift levers are in the neutral position (middle detent).
2. Move the shift lever to align the locating slots in the bottom of the steering column shift housing and bearing housing.
3. Place a suitable tool between the crossover blade and the 2nd-3rd lever at the steering column, so that both lever pins are engaged by the crossover blade.
4. Set the 1st-reverse lever on the transmission to reverse position (rotate clockwise).
5. Adjust the 1st-reverse rod swivel by loosening the clamp bolt and sliding the swivel along the rod so it will enter the 1st reverse lever at the transmission. Install the washers and the clip. Tighten the swivel bolt.
6. Remove the gearshift housing locating tool, and shift the transmission into the neutral position.
7. Adjust the 2nd–3rd rod swivel by loosening the clamp bolt and sliding the swivel along the rod so it will enter the 2nd-3rd lever at the transmission. Install the washers and the clip. Tighten the swivel bolt.
8. Remove the tool from the crossover blade at the steering column and shift the transmission through all the gears to check the adjustment and crossover smoothness.

A–390

♦ See Figure 4

1. Loosen both shift rod swivels. Make sure that the transmission shift levers are in the neutral position (middle detent).

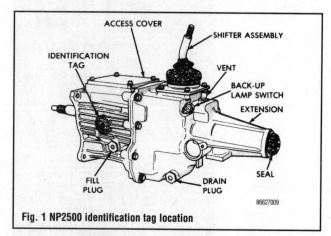

Fig. 1 NP2500 identification tag location

DRIVE TRAIN 7-3

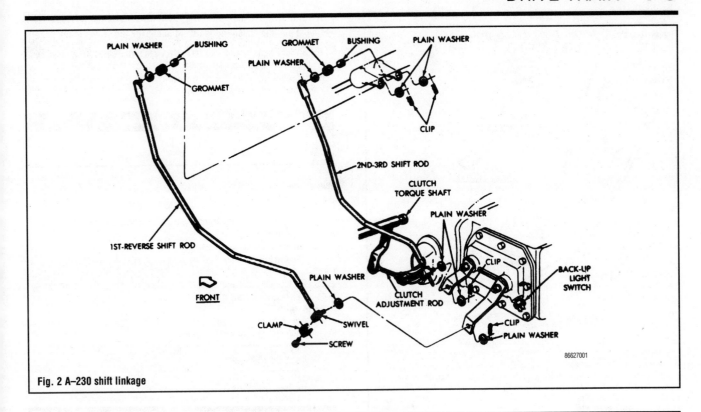

Fig. 2 A-230 shift linkage

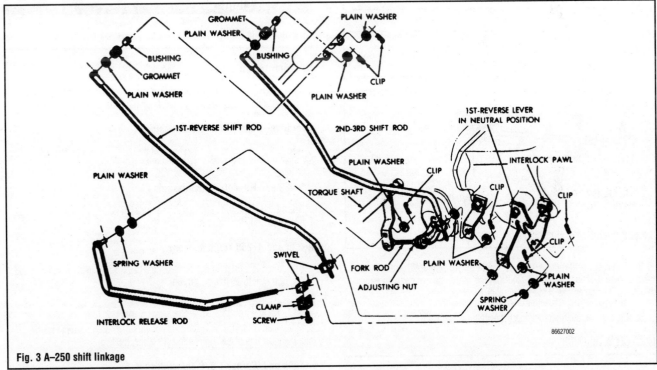

Fig. 3 A-250 shift linkage

2. Move the shift lever to align the locating slots in the bottom of the steering column shift housing and bearing housing. Install a suitable tool in the slot.

3. Place a suitable tool between the crossover blade and the 2nd-3rd lever at the steering column so that both lever pins are engaged by the crossover blade.

4. Tighten both rod swivel bolts, 125 inch lbs. (14 Nm). Remove the gearshift housing locating tool.

5. Remove the tool from the crossover blade at the steering column and shift the transmission through all gears to check adjustment and crossover smoothness.

6. Check for proper operation of the steering column lock in reverse. With the proper linkage adjustment, the ignition should lock in reverse only, with hands off the gearshift lever.

Overdrive-4

♦ See Figure 5

1. Place the floorshift lever in neutral. Insert a aligning tool to hold the levers in the neutral-crossover position.

2. Detach the shift rods. Make sure that the three transmission levers are in their neutral detents.

7-4 DRIVE TRAIN

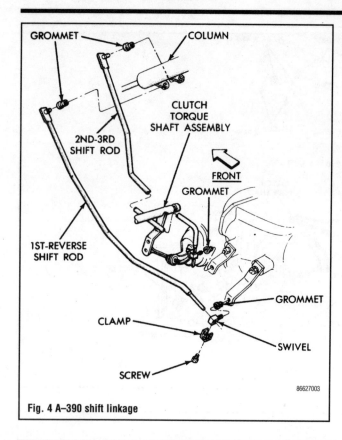

Fig. 4 A–390 shift linkage

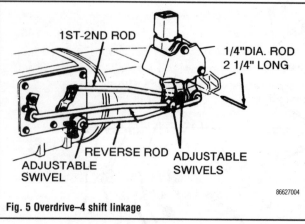

Fig. 5 Overdrive–4 shift linkage

3. Adjust the shift rods to make the length exactly right to fit into the transmission levers. Start with the 1st–2nd shift rod. It may be necessary to remove the clip at the shifter end of the rod to rotate this rod.
4. Replace the washers and the clips.
5. Remove the aligning tool check the shifting action.

CLUTCH INTERLOCK

A–250 3–Speed

This adjustment is required only on the A–250 3–Speed transmission. This is a top cover unit used only as base equipment on light duty six cylinder models. It has synchromesh only on 2nd and 3rd gears.
1. Disconnect the clutch rod swivel from the interlock pawl. Adjust the clutch pedal free-play.
2. Shift the transmission to neutral. Loosen the swivel clamp bolt and slide the swivel onto the rod until the pawl is positioned fully within the slot in the 1st-reverse lever. Install the washers and clips.
3. Hold the interlock pawl forward and tighten the swivel clamp bolt. The clutch pedal must be in full returned position during the adjustment.

➡ Do not pull the clutch rod rearward to engage the swivel in the panel.

4. Shift the transmission into 1st and reverse and release the clutch pedal while in either gear to check for normal clutch action. Next, shift halfway between neutral and either gear, then release clutch. The interlock should hold it to within one or two inches of the floor.

Shift Linkage

REMOVAL & INSTALLATION

Overdrive–4

1. Disconnect the battery ground cable.
2. Remove the retaining screws from the floor pan boot, then slide it up and off the shift lever.
3. Remove the shift lever itself.
4. Remove the retaining clips, washers and control rods form the shift unit levers.
5. Remove the bolts and washers that secure the shift unit to the mounting plate on the extension housing and remove the unit.

To install:
6. Fasten the two bolts and washers to the unit extension housing mounting plate and tighten to 30 ft. lbs. (41 Nm).
7. Install the shift rods, washers, and clips.
8. Install the shift lever.
9. Slide the boot over the shift lever and fasten to the floor pan.
10. Connect the battery cable.

Back-Up Light Switch

REMOVAL & INSTALLATION

NP–2500 Transmission

The switch is located on the left side of the transmission just below and behind the shifter. It screws into place. Tighten it to 15 ft. lbs. (20 Nm).

Overdrive–4 and A–745 Transmissions

The switch is located on the left side of the case, just behind the shift linkage housing. It screws into place. Tighten it to 15 ft. lbs. (20 Nm).

NP–435 and NP–445 Transmissions

The switch is located in the left side of the shift housing. It screws into place. Tighten it to 15 ft. lbs. (20 Nm).

A–230 and A–250 Transmissions

The switch is located in the left case, just below the shifters. It screws into place. Tighten it to 15 ft. lbs. (20 Nm).

A–390 Transmissions

The switch is located on the left side of the extension housing at the case end. It screws into place. Tighten it to 15 ft. lbs. (20 Nm).

NP–420 and Warner T–87E Transmissions

The switch is located on the left side of the case. It screws into place. Tighten it to 15 lbs. (20 Nm).

Extension Housing Seal

REMOVAL & INSTALLATION

A special tool is required for most transmission jobs. Read the procedure before starting to see if you need a special tool to do the job.

DRIVE TRAIN 7-5

A-230 and A-390 Transmissions

▶ See Figure 6

1. Place a drain pan under the yoke seal.
2. Disconnect the propeller shaft at the rear U-Joint. Matchmark both of the parts so installation is exactly in the same spot of removal. Carefully pull the shaft yoke out of the transmission extension housing.

➥Be very careful not to nick or scratch the surface on the sliding spline yoke during removal and installation of the shaft assembly.

3. Cut the boot end of the extension housing yoke seal, screw the tapered threaded end of seal remover into the seal. Turn the screw of the tool and remove the seal.

To install:

4. Position the new seal in the opening of the extension housing and drive it into the housing with tool C-3972 or a suitable seal installer.
5. Carefully guide the front U-Joint yoke into the extension housing and on the mainshaft splines. Connect the driveshaft to the rear axle pinion shaft yoke aligning the marks you made earlier in removal. Tighten the clamp screws to 15 ft. lbs. (20 Nm).
6. Fill the transmission to the level of the fill plug.

NP2500 and Overdrive-4 Transmissions

▶ See Figure 7

1. Place a drain pan under the yoke seal.
2. Disconnect the propeller shaft at the rear U-Joint. Matchmark both of the parts so installation is exactly in the same spot of removal. Carefully pull the shaft yoke out of the transmission extension housing.

➥Be very careful not to nick or scratch ground surface on the sliding spline yoke during removal and installation of the shaft assembly.

3. Remove the seal with tool C-3985, or any suitable seal remover.

To install:

4. Position the new seal in the opening of the extension housing and dive it into the housing with tool C-3972/3995, or a suitable tool.
5. Carefully guide the front U-Joint yoke into the extension housing and on the mainshaft splines. Connect the driveshaft to the rear axle pinion shaft yoke aligning the marks you made earlier in removal.
6. Fill the transmission to the level of the fill plug.

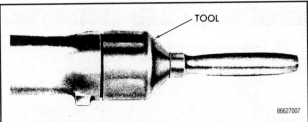

Fig. 6 A-230 installation of the extension housing seal with a special tool

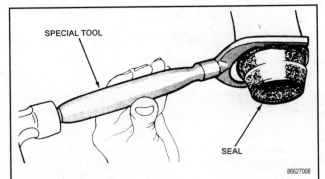

Fig. 7 NP2500 and Overdrive-4 removal of the extension housing seal

Transmission

REMOVAL & INSTALLATION

2-Wheel Drive Models

3-SPEED

1. Raise and support the vehicle.
2. Drain lubricant from the transmission.
3. Disconnect and matchmark the driveshaft. On the sliding spline type, disconnect driveshaft at the rear universal joint, then carefully pull the shaft yoke out of the transmission extension housing. Do not nick or scratch splines.
4. Disconnect the gearshift control rods and speedometer cable.
5. Remove the backup light switch, if so equipped.
6. Support the engine.
7. Remove the crossmember and rubber insulator on 1975 and later models with A-390 transmission. On all other models, unbolt the insulator or mount from the crossmember. Support the transmission with a jack.
8. Remove transmission-to-clutch housing bolts.
9. Slide transmission rearward until the pinion shaft clears the clutch completely, then lower the transmission from vehicle.

To install:

10. Before inserting transmission driveshaft into clutch, make sure the clutch housing bore, disc and face are aligned. Make sure you grease the inner end of the pinion shaft pilot bushing and the pinion bearing retainer pilot, for the clutch release sleeve using lubricant.
11. Slide the transmission forward until the pinion shaft enters the clutch completely, then push the transmission forward all the way.
12. Install the transmission-to-clutch housing bolts. Tighten the bolts to 50 ft. lbs. (67 Nm).
13. Install the crossmember and rubber insulator on 1975 and later models with A-390 transmission. On all other models, bolt the insulator or mount to the crossmember.
14. Install backup light switch if so equipped.
15. Connect gearshift control rods and speedometer cable.
16. Connect the driveshaft. On the sliding spline type, carefully slide the shaft yoke into the transmission extension housing. Do not nick or scratch splines. Connect the driveshaft at the rear universal joint.
17. Fill the transmission with lubricant.
18. Adjust shift linkage.
19. Lower the vehicle, then road test.

4-SPEED

1. Shift transmission into any gear.
2. Raise and support the vehicle with jack stands.
3. Disconnect universal joint matchmark parts, and loosen yoke retaining nut. Drain lubricant.
4. Disconnect the parking brake (if so equipped), along with the speedometer cables and back-up lamp switch at transmission.
5. Remove the lever retainer by pressing down, rotating retainer counterclockwise slightly, then releasing.
6. Remove the lever and its springs and washers.
7. Support the rear of the engine and remove the crossmember. Remove transmission to clutch bell housing retaining bolts and pull transmission rearward until drive pinion clears clutch, then remove transmission.

To install:

8. Place lubricant in the pinion shaft pilot bushing, taking care not to get any grease on flywheel face.
9. Align the clutch disc and backing plate with a spare drive pinion shaft or clutch aligning tool, then carefully install transmission.
10. Install the transmission to the bell housing with bolts, tightening to 50 ft. lbs. (67 Nm) torque. Replace the crossmember.
11. Install the gear shift lever, shift into any gear and tighten yoke nut to 95-105 ft. lbs. (128-142 Nm) torque.
12. Install the universal joint, speedometer cable and brake cable.
13. Adjust the clutch.
14. Install the transmission drain plug and fill transmission with lubricant. Make sure the truck is level.
15. Remove the jack stands and carefully lower the vehicle, then road test.

7-6 DRIVE TRAIN

5–SPEED

1. Raise and support the truck.
2. Remove the skid plate, if any. Drain lubricant from the transmission and transfer case.
3. Disconnect the speedometer cable.
4. Disconnect and matchmark the driveshaft. Suspend the shaft from a convenient place; do not allow it to hang free.
5. Disconnect the back-up light switch.
6. Support the engine.
7. Support the transmission.
8. Remove the transmission crossmember.
9. Remove the transmission-to-clutch housing bolts.
10. Slide the transmission rearward until the mainshaft clears the clutch disc.
11. Lower and remove the transmission.

To install:

12. The transmission pilot bushing in the end of the crankshaft requires high-temperature grease. Multipurpose grease should be used. Do not lubricate the end of the mainshaft, clutch splines, or clutch release levers.
13. Raise and position the transmission.
14. Slide the transmission forward until the mainshaft enters the clutch disc, then push it all the way forward.
15. Install the transmission-to-clutch housing bolts, then tighten to 50 ft. lbs. (67 Nm).
16. Install the transmission crossmember.
17. Connect the back-up light switch.
18. Connect the front driveshaft.
19. Connect the speedometer cable.
20. Install the skid plate, if any. Fill the transmission.
21. Lower the truck.

4WD Models

3 AND 4-SPEEDS

1. Raise and support the truck.
2. Remove the skid plate, if any. Drain lubricant from the transmission and transfer case.
3. Disconnect the speedometer cable.
4. Disconnect and matchmark the front and rear driveshafts. Suspend each shaft from a convenient place; do not allow them to hang free.
5. Disconnect the shift rods at the transfer case. On 4–speed transmissions, remove the shift lever retainer by pressing down and turning it counterclockwise. Remove the shift lever springs and washers.
6. Matchmark the driveshaft and rear U-joints then remove the driveshaft.
7. Support the transfer case.
8. Remove the extension-to-transfer case mounting bolts.
9. Move the transfer case rearward to disengage the front input shaft spline.
10. Lower and remove the transfer case.
11. Disconnect the back-up light switch.
12. Support the engine.
13. Support the transmission.
14. Remove the transmission crossmember.
15. Remove the transmission-to-clutch housing bolts.
16. Slide the transmission rearward until the mainshaft clears the clutch disc.
17. Lower and remove the transmission.

To install:

18. The transmission pilot bushing in the end of the crankshaft requires high-temperature grease. Multipurpose grease should be used. Do not lubricate the end of the mainshaft, clutch splines, or clutch release levers.
19. Raise and position the transmission.
20. Slide the transmission forward until the mainshaft enters the clutch disc, then push it all the way forward.
21. Install the transmission-to-clutch housing bolts, then tighten to 50 ft. lbs. (67 Nm).
22. Install the transmission crossmember.
23. Connect the back-up light switch.
24. Raise and position the transfer case.
25. Move the transfer case forwards to disengage the front input shaft spline.
26. Install the extension-to-transfer case mounting bolts, then tighten to 50 ft. lbs. (67 Nm).
27. Install the rear driveshaft.
28. Connect the shift rods at the transfer case. On 4–speed transmissions, install the shift lever retainer by pressing down and turning it clockwise. Install the shift lever springs and washers.
29. Connect the front driveshafts.
30. Connect the speedometer cable.
31. Install the skid plate, if any. Fill the transmission and transfer case.
32. Adjust the gearshift linkage on 3–speed transmissions.
33. Lower the truck.

CLUTCH

Understanding the Clutch

♦ **See Figure 8**

The purpose of the clutch is to disconnect and connect engine power at the transmission. A vehicle at rest requires a lot of engine torque to get all that weight moving. An internal combustion engine does not develop a high starting torque (unlike steam engines) so it must be allowed to operate without any load until it builds up enough torque to move the vehicle. To a point, torque increases with engine rpm. The clutch allows the engine to build up torque by physically disconnecting the engine from the transmission, relieving the engine of any load or resistance.

The transfer of engine power to the transmission (the load) must be smooth and gradual; if it weren't, drive line components would wear out or break

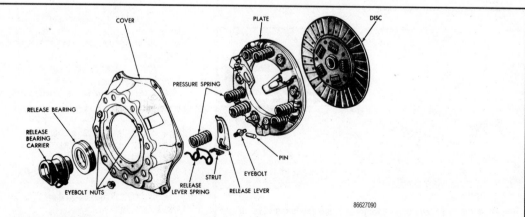

Fig. 8 Exploded view of a common clutch assembly

DRIVE TRAIN 7-7

quickly. This gradual power transfer is made possible by gradually releasing the clutch pedal. The clutch disc and pressure plate are the connecting link between the engine and transmission. When the clutch pedal is released, the disc and plate contact each other (the clutch is engaged) physically joining the engine and transmission. When the pedal is pushed in, the disc and plate separate (the clutch is disengaged) disconnecting the engine from the transmission.

Most clutch assemblies consists of the flywheel, the clutch disc, the clutch pressure plate, the throw out bearing and fork, the actuating linkage and the pedal. The flywheel and clutch pressure plate (driving members) are connected to the engine crankshaft and rotate with it. The clutch disc is located between the flywheel and pressure plate, and is splined to the transmission shaft. A driving member is one that is attached to the engine and transfers engine power to a driven member (clutch disc) on the transmission shaft. A driving member (pressure plate) rotates (drives) a driven member (clutch disc) on contact and, in so doing, turns the transmission shaft.

There is a circular diaphragm spring within the pressure plate cover (transmission side). In a relaxed state (when the clutch pedal is fully released) this spring is convex; that is, it is dished outward toward the transmission. Pushing in the clutch pedal actuates the attached linkage. Connected to the other end of this is the throw out fork, which hold the throw out bearing. When the clutch pedal is depressed, the clutch linkage pushes the fork and bearing forward to contact the diaphragm spring of the pressure plate. The outer edges of the spring are secured to the pressure plate and are pivoted on rings so that when the center of the spring is compressed by the throw out bearing, the outer edges bow outward and, by so doing, pull the pressure plate in the same direction — away from the clutch disc. This action separates the disc from the plate, disengaging the clutch and allowing the transmission to be shifted into another gear. A coil type clutch return spring attached to the clutch pedal arm permits full release of the pedal. Releasing the pedal pulls the throw out bearing away from the diaphragm spring resulting in a reversal of spring position. As bearing pressure is gradually released from the spring center, the outer edges of the spring bow outward, pushing the pressure plate into closer contact with the clutch disc. As the disc and plate move closer together, friction between the two increases and slippage is reduced until, when full spring pressure is applied (by fully releasing the pedal) the speed of the disc and plate are the same. This stops all slipping, creating a direct connection between the plate and disc which results in the transfer of power from the engine to the transmission. The clutch disc is now rotating with the pressure plate at engine speed and, because it is splined to the transmission shaft, the shaft now turns at the same engine speed.

The clutch is operating properly if:
1. It will stall the engine when released with the vehicle held stationary.
2. The shift lever can be moved freely between 1st and reverse gears when the vehicle is stationary and the clutch disengaged.

Adjustments

PEDAL FREE-PLAY

▶ See Figures 9, 10, 11, 12 and 13

The only adjustment required is pedal free-play. Adjust the clutch actuating fork rod by turning the self-locking adjusting nut to provide $FR3/32 in. (2.3mm) free movement at the end of the fork. This will provide the recommended 1½ in. (38mm) on most trucks or the recommended 1 in. (25mm) on Ramcharger, and Trail Duster free-play at the pedal.

Driven Disc and Pressure Plate

REMOVAL & INSTALLATION

Mechanical Linkage

▶ See Figures 14, 15, 16, 17 and 18

1. Support the engine on a suitable jack.
2. Remove crossmember.
3. Remove transmission. Remove transfer case, if equipped.
4. Remove clutch housing pan if so equipped.

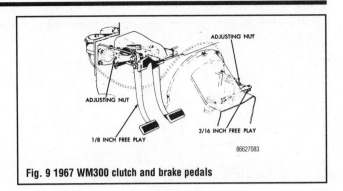

Fig. 9 1967 WM300 clutch and brake pedals

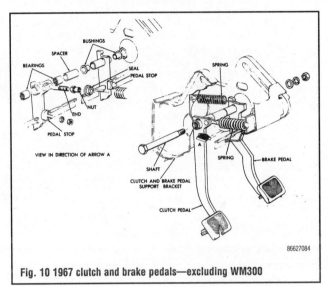

Fig. 10 1967 clutch and brake pedals—excluding WM300

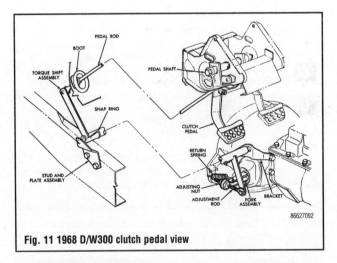

Fig. 11 1968 D/W300 clutch pedal view

5. Remove clutch fork, clutch bearing and sleeve assembly if not removed with transmission.
6. Matchmark clutch cover and flywheel. to assure correct reassembly.
7. Remove clutch cover retaining bolts, loosening them evenly so clutch cover will not be distorted.

✲✲ CAUTION

Clutch disc may contain asbestos. Do NOT use compressed air to clean components. Instead use a commercially available evaporative spray cleaner.

8. Pull the pressure plate assembly clear of flywheel and, while supporting the pressure plate, slide the clutch disc from between the flywheel and pressure plate.

7-8 DRIVE TRAIN

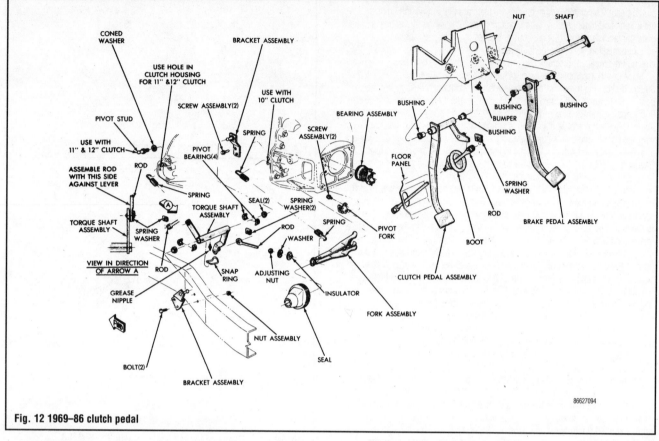

Fig. 12 1969–86 clutch pedal

To install:

9. Thoroughly clean all working surfaces of the flywheel and the pressure plate.
10. Grease radius at back of bushing.
11. Rotate clutch cover and pressure plate assembly for maximum clearance between flywheel and frame crossmember if crossmember was not removed during clutch removal.
12. Tilt the top edge of clutch cover and pressure plate assembly back and move it up into the clutch housing. Support the clutch cover and pressure plate assembly and slide clutch disc into position.
13. Position the clutch disc and plate against flywheel and insert spare transmission main drive gear shaft or clutch installing tool through clutch disc hub and into main drive pilot bearing.
14. Rotate the clutch cover until the punch marks on cover and flywheel align.
15. Bolt the cover loosely to flywheel. Tighten the cover bolts a few turns at a time, in progression, until tight. Then tighten bolts to 20 ft. lbs. (27 Nm) torque.

Fig. 13 1968 D/W100–200 clutch pedal setup

16. Apply grease to the release fork pads of the carrier. Lubricate the fork fingers and retaining spring at the pivot contact area points.
17. Engage the fork fingers under clutch carrier retaining springs while engaging the fork spring into the fork pivot. Be sure the groove of the dust seal is engaged on the seal opening flange in clutch housing.
18. Insert the threaded end of the fork rod assembly into the hole end of the release fork. Install the eye end of the fork rod on torque shaft lever pin and secure with spring washer.
19. Install the return spring to the clutch release fork and clutch housing.

➡ Do not lubricate the splines or pilot end of transmission drive pinon. when installing the transmission. These areas must be kept dry.

20. Install the transmission and transfer case, if so equipped.
21. Install the frame crossmembers and insulator, tighten all bolts.
22. Adjust clutch linkage.

Hydraulic Clutch

♦ See Figure 19

1. Remove the transmission. Remove transfer case, if equipped.
2. Remove the clutch housing.
3. Remove the clutch fork and release bearing assembly.
4. Mark the clutch cover and flywheel, with a suitable tool to assure correct reassembly.
5. Remove the pressure plate retaining bolts, loosening them evenly so the clutch cover will not be distorted.
6. Pull the pressure plate assembly clear of flywheel and, while the supporting pressure plate, slide the clutch disc from between flywheel and plate.

To install:

❈❈ CAUTION

Clutch disc may contain asbestos. Do NOT use compressed air to clean components. Instead use a commercially available evaporative spray cleaner.

DRIVE TRAIN 7-9

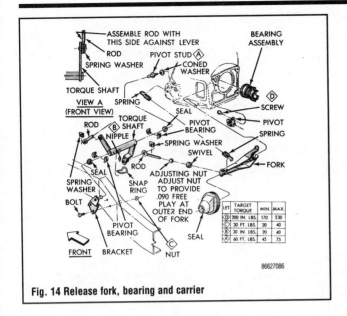

Fig. 14 Release fork, bearing and carrier

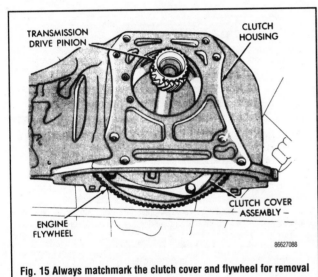

Fig. 15 Always matchmark the clutch cover and flywheel for removal and installation

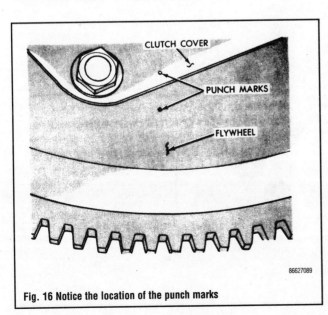

Fig. 16 Notice the location of the punch marks

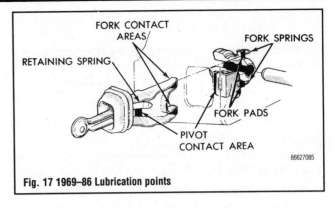

Fig. 17 1969–86 Lubrication points

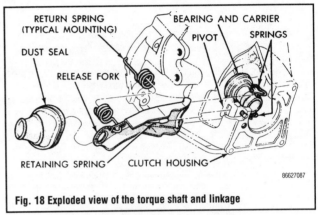

Fig. 18 Exploded view of the torque shaft and linkage

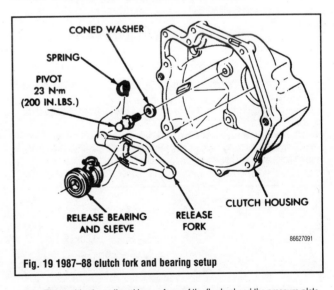

Fig. 19 1987–88 clutch fork and bearing setup

 7. Thoroughly clean all working surfaces of the flywheel and the pressure plate.
 8. Grease radius at back of bushing.
 9. Rotate clutch cover and pressure plate assembly for maximum clearance between flywheel and frame crossmember (if crossmember was not removed during clutch removal).
 10. Tilt top edge of clutch cover and pressure plate assembly back and move it up into the clutch housing. Support clutch cover and pressure plate assembly, then slide clutch disc into position.
 11. Position the clutch disc and the plate against the flywheel, then insert spare transmission main drive gear shaft or clutch installing tool through clutch disc hub and into main drive pilot bearing.
 12. Rotate clutch cover until the punch marks on cover and flywheel line up.
 13. Bolt the pressure plate loosely to flywheel. Tighten the bolts a few turns at a time, in progression, until tight. Then tighten bolts to:
  • 5/16 in. (8mm) bolts: 20 ft. lbs. (27 Nm)
  • 3/8 in. (9.5mm) bolts: 30 ft. lbs. (40 Nm)

7-10 DRIVE TRAIN

14. Install transmission.
15. Install frame crossmembers and insulator, tighten all bolts.

Clutch Master Cylinder and Slave Cylinder

The clutch master cylinder, remote reservoir, slave cylinder and connecting lines are all serviced as a complete assembly. The cylinders and connecting lines are sealed units. They are prefilled with fluid from the factory and cannot be disassembled or serviced separately.

REMOVAL & INSTALLATION

♦ See Figures 20 and 21

1. Disconnect the negative battery cable.
2. Raise the vehicle and support safely. On diesel models, remove the slave cylinder shield from the clutch housing.
3. Remove the nuts attaching the slave cylinder to the bell housing.
4. Remove the slave cylinder and clip from the housing.
5. Lower the vehicle. On diesel models, disconnect the clutch pedal interlock switch wires.
6. Remove the locating clip from the clutch master cylinder mounting bracket.
7. Remove the retaining ring, flat washer and wave washer that attach the clutch master cylinder pushrod to the clutch pedal. Slide the pushrod off of the pedal pin. Inspect the bushing on the pedal pin and replace if it is excessively worn.
8. Verify that the cap on the clutch master cylinder reservoir is tight so fluid will not spill during removal.
9. Remove the screws attaching the reservoir and bracket, if equipped, to the dash panel and remove the reservoir.
10. Pull the clutch master cylinder rubber seal from the dash panel.
11. Rotate the clutch master cylinder counterclockwise 45 degrees to unlock it. Remove the cylinder from the dash panel.
12. Remove the clutch master cylinder, remote reservoir, slave cylinder and connecting lines from the vehicle.

To install:

13. Verify that the cap on the fluid reservoir is tight so fluid will not spill during installation.
14. Position the components in the replacement kit in their places on the vehicle.
15. Insert the master cylinder in the dash. Rotate clockwise 45 degrees to lock in place.
16. Lubricate the rubber seal with a lubricant to ease installation. Seat the seal around the cylinder in the dash.
17. Install the fluid reservoir and bracket, if equipped, to the dash panel.
18. Install the master cylinder pushrod to the clutch pedal pin. Secure the rod with the wave washer, flat washer and retaining ring. Install the locating clip.

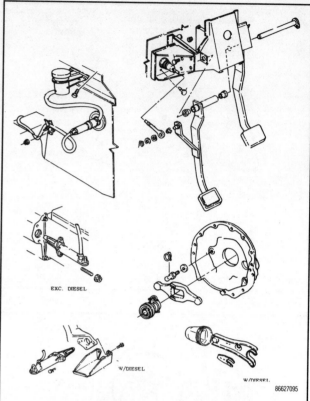

Fig. 20 Hydraulic clutch controls on all engines in 1988

Do not remove the plastic shipping stop from the pushrod until the slave cylinder has been installed.

19. Raise the vehicle and support safely.
20. Insert the slave cylinder pushrod through the opening and make sure the cap on the end of the pushrod is securely engaged in the release lever before tightening the attaching nuts. Torque the nuts to 22 ft. lbs. (2 Nm).
21. Install slave cylinder cover, if equipped. Lower the vehicle. Remove the plastic shipping stop from the master cylinder pushrod. Connect clutch pedal interlock switch wires.
22. Operate the clutch pedal a few times to verify proper system operation. The system will self-bleed any air in and vent through the reservoir.
23. Connect the negative battery cable and road test the vehicle.

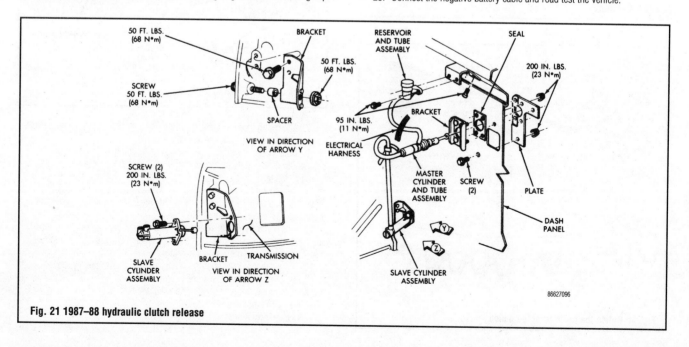

Fig. 21 1987–88 hydraulic clutch release

DRIVE TRAIN

TRANSFER CASE

Identification

There are a few different types of transfer cases on the Dodge trucks. Here are the ones that apply to the various years in this manual.

- New Process NP–200 1967–69
- New Process NP–201 1967–69
- New Process NP–203 1977–79
- New Process NP–205 1974–76 and 1980–88
- New Process NP–208 1980–87
- New Process NP–241 1988

Transfer Case Assembly

REMOVAL & INSTALLATION

Excluding New Process 203

1. Remove the skid plate, if any.
2. Drain the transfer case by removing the bottom bolt from the front output rear cover.
3. Disconnect the speedometer cable.
4. Matchmark, then disconnect the front and rear output shafts. Suspend these from a convenient location; do not allow them to hang free.
5. Disconnect the shift rods at the transfer case.
6. Support the transmission with a jack and remove the rear crossmember if necessary.
7. Disconnect the front and rear propeller shafts at the transfer case yokes. Secure the shafts with wire, do not allow them to hang.
8. Disconnect the parking brake cable guide from the pivot if necessary.
9. Remove the bolts attaching the exhaust pipe support bracket to the transfer case, if necessary.
10. Remove the adapter-to-transfer case mounting bolts and move the transfer case rearward to disengage the front input splines.
11. Remove any traces of gasket material from the rear of the transmission adapter housing.

To install:

12. Using a sealer, apply to both sides of the transfer case-to-transmission gasket, then position the gasket on the transmission.
13. Align and install the transfer case assembly to the transmission. Be sure the case input gear splines are aligned with the transmission output shaft.

➡ Do not install any of the transfer case attaching bolts until the transfer case is completely seated against the transmission.

14. Align and install the transfer case attaching bolts.
15. Install the rear crossmember, if removed, then remove the transmission support stand.
16. Install the exhaust pipe support bracket if removed, align and connect the propeller shafts.
17. Connect the parking brake cable guide to pivot bracket if removed.
18. Connect the speedometer cable.
19. Connect the shift rods onto the transfer case.
20. Make sure the drain plug is installed and fill transfer case with fresh fluid.
21. Replace the skid plate, if equipped.
22. Adjust the linkage. Lower the truck, test drive.

New Process 203

1. Raise and support the truck.
2. Drain the transfer case of fluid.
3. There are 4 skid plate attaching bolts, remove them.
4. Remove the 5 bolts attaching the front end of the skid plate to the transmission crossmember. Remove the skid plate.

➡ Some vehicles do not have a skid plate. Disregard steps 1 and 2 if your truck is not equipped.

5. Remove the bottom bolt from the output rear cover and allow the case to drain before proceeding.
6. Disconnect the speedometer cable.
7. Disconnect and secure the front and rear output shafts. Disconnect the shift rods at the transfer case.
8. Remove the adaptor-to-transfer case bolts. Move the case rearwards to disengage the front input spline.
9. With a 1 5/16 in. socket loosen and remove the rear output shaft yoke nut.
10. Remove the output shaft bearing retainer bolts. Remove the retainer and discard of the gasket.
11. With a hoist or suitable lifting devise lower the transfer case and remove from the truck.
12. Installation is reverse of removal.

ADJUSTMENTS

New Process Model T-200 De-Clutch and Shift Rod

▶ See Figure 22

1. Locate the shift lever in the HIGH SPEED position and the de-clutch lever in the DISENGAGED position.
2. Adjust the shift rod clevis until there is a clearance of approximately 1/2 in. (12mm) between the lever and the end of the floor slot.
3. Adjust the de-clutch rod clevis until there is a minimum clearance of 1/2 in. (12mm) between the protrusions on the shift and de-clutch levers.

※※ WARNING

A clearance of less than 1/2 in. (12mm) between the lever protrusions may cause the de-clutch lever to shift when applying the parking brake.

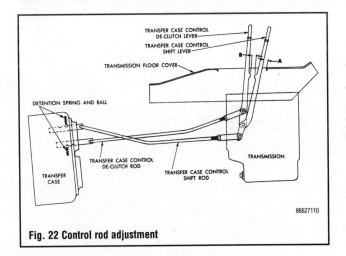

Fig. 22 Control rod adjustment

New Process Model NP–201 De-Clutch and Shift Rod

▶ See Figure 23

➡ All adjustments must be made with the front axle engaged and the transfer case in low range.

1. Disconnect the de-clutch and shift rods at the shift levers.
2. Adjust the de-clutch rod length until the lever clears the rear end of the slot in the cab underbody by 5/8 in. (15mm). Secure the adjusting yoke with a locknut.
3. Adjust the shift rod length until the distance between the protrusions on the shift and de-clutch levers is 1/4 in. (6mm). Secure the adjusting yoke with the locknut.
4. Connect the de-clutch and shift rods at the shift levers and then road test the vehicle.

7-12 DRIVE TRAIN

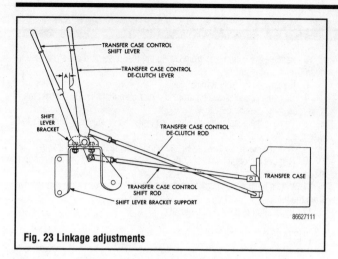

Fig. 23 Linkage adjustments

New Process Model NP-205

♦ See Figure 24

➡ Refer to the illustration for number reference.

1. Install the lower shift lever (3) to bracket (1).
2. Mount the bracket (1) loose to adapter.
3. Install the shift rod (4).
4. Position bracket (1) as far forward as possible and tighten bracket screw (2).
5. Cycle shift lever (3) to check for proper function.

NP208 and NP241

♦ See Figures 25 and 26

Please refer to the accompanying illustrations for adjustments on the NP208 and NP241 transfer cases.

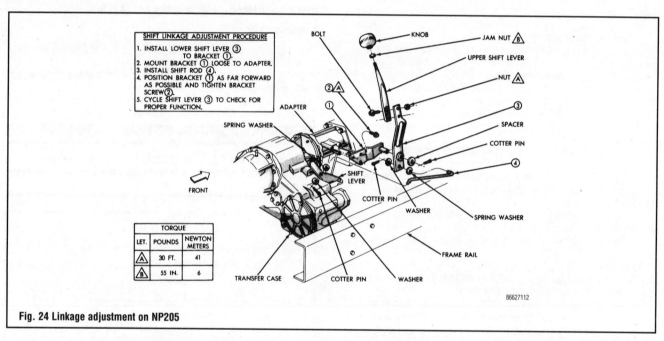

Fig. 24 Linkage adjustment on NP205

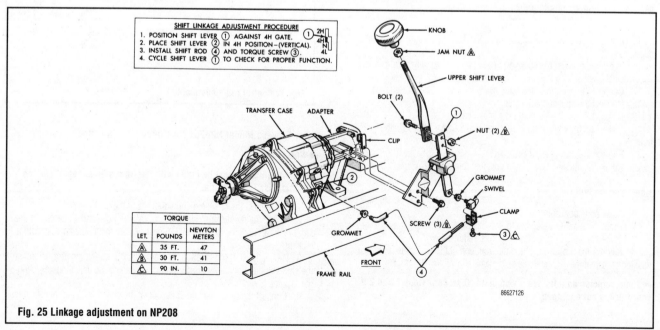

Fig. 25 Linkage adjustment on NP208

Drive Train 7-13

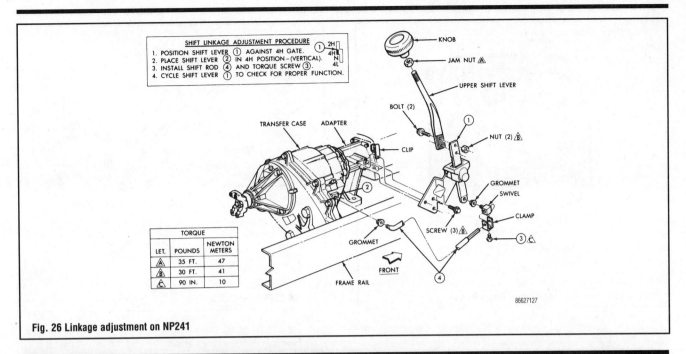

Fig. 26 Linkage adjustment on NP241

AUTOMATIC TRANSMISSION

Identification

An automatic transmission has a surface pad provided on the right side of the transmission case for identification.
Automatic Transmission Identification:
- New Process A–345 1974–76
- New Process A–727 1967–88
- New Process A–904T 1981–88
- New Process A–999 1981–88

Understanding Automatic Transmissions

The automatic transmission allows engine torque and power to be transmitted to the rear wheels within a narrow range of engine operating speeds. It will allow the engine to turn fast enough to produce plenty of power and torque at very low speeds, while keeping it at a sensible rpm at high vehicle speeds (and it does this job without driver assistance). The transmission uses a light fluid as the medium for the transmission of power. This fluid also works in the operation of various hydraulic control circuits and as a lubricant.

Adjustments

KICKDOWN BAND

A–727, A–904 and A–999

♦ See Figure 27

The kickdown band adjusting screw is located on the left-hand side of the transmission case near the throttle lever shaft.
1. Loosen the locknut and back it off about five turns. Be sure that the adjusting screw turns freely in the case.
2. Tighten the adjusting screw to 72 inch lbs. (97 Nm).
3. Back off the adjusting screw as follows:
   - 1967–72—2 turns
   - 1973–88 V8—2½ turns
   - 1973–84 6-cyl.—2 turns
   - 1985–88 6-cyl.—2½ turns
   - Diesel—2 turns
Tighten the Locknut as follows:
   - 1967–72—29 ft. lbs. (39 Nm)

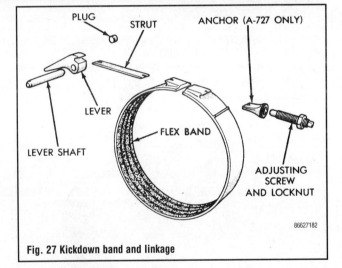

Fig. 27 Kickdown band and linkage

- 1973–75—35 ft. lbs. (47 Nm)
- 1976–88—30 ft. lbs. (40 Nm)

A–345

The kickdown band adjusting screw is located on the left-hand side of the transmission case near the throttle lever shaft.
1. Loosen the locknut and back it off about five turns. Be sure that the adjusting screw turns freely in the case.
2. Tighten the adjusting screw to 72 inch lbs. (8 Nm).
3. Back off the adjusting screw 2 full turns and tighten the locknut to 35 ft. lbs. (47 Nm).

LOW & REVERSE BAND

♦ See Figures 28 and 29

The pan must be removed from the transmission to gain access to the low and reverse band adjusting screw.
1. Remove the skid plate, if any. Drain the transmission fluid and remove the pan.

7-14 DRIVE TRAIN

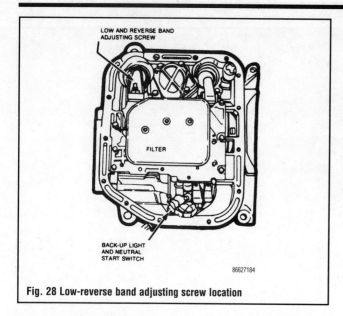

Fig. 28 Low-reverse band adjusting screw location

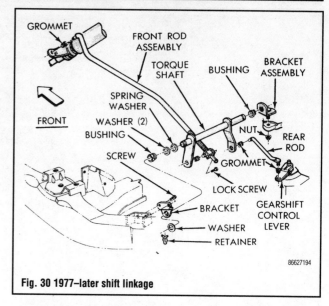

Fig. 30 1977–later shift linkage

2. Loosen the band adjusting screw locknut and back it off about five turns. Be sure that the adjusting screw turns freely in the lever.
3. Tighten the adjusting screw to 72 inch lbs. (8 Nm).
4. Back off the adjusting screw as follows:
- A–727—2 turns
- A–904T/A–999—4 turns
- A–345—5 turns

Keep the adjusting screw from turning, tighten the locknut to 30 ft. lbs. (40 Nm).

5. Use a new gasket and install the transmission pan. Tighten the pan bolts to 17 ft. lbs. (23 Nm). Refill the transmission with Dexron®III fluid.

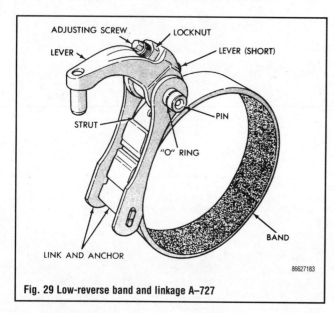

Fig. 29 Low-reverse band and linkage A–727

SHIFT LINKAGE

▶ See Figures 30 and 31

➡ To insure proper adjustment, it is suggested that new linkage grommets be installed.

1. Place the gearshift lever in Park position.
2. Move the shift control lever on the transmission all the way to the rear (in the Park detent).
3. Set the adjustable rod to an appropriate length that will not apply load in either direction. Tighten the swivel bolt to 90 inch lbs. (10 Nm).

4. The shift linkage must be free of binding and be positive in all positions.
5. Make sure that the engine can start only when the gearshift lever is in the Park or Neutral position.
6. Be sure that the gearshift lever will not jump into an unwanted gear.

THROTTLE KICKDOWN ROD

▶ See Figures 32, 33, 34 and 35

1967–69 Models

1. Warm the engine to operating temperature and adjust the idle speed to 550 rpm (6–cyl.) or 500 rpm (V8s).
2. Disconnect the transmission throttle rod at the bellcrank on the carburetor. Hold the transmission throttle rod forward so that the lever at the transmission is against its stop. Adjust the rod length so that the ball socket aligns with the bellcrank ball end and engage the ball and socket.
3. Disconnect the throttle rod at the other bellcrank. Adjust the rod length to produce a pedal angle of 115° and re–engage the bellcrank ball and socket.

1970–80 Models

▶ See Figures 36, 37 and 38

1. Warm the engine to operating temperature.
2. Block the choke plate fully open.
3. Remove the throttle return spring from the carburetor.
4. Remove the clip, washer and slotted throttle rod from the carburetor pin.
5. Rotate the threaded end of the rod so that the rear edge of the slot in the rod contacts the carburetor pin when the transmission throttle lever is held forward against its stop.
6. Install the washer and clip to retain the throttle rod to the carburetor.
7. Install the throttle rod return spring.
8. Check the transmission linkage for freedom of operation and unblock the choke plate.

1981–88 Models

▶ See Figure 39

1. Warm the engine up to normal operating temperature. Turn the engine OFF.
2. Disconnect the choke at the carburetor, or block the choke plate fully open.
3. Raise the truck on a hoist.
4. Loosen the adjusting swivel lockscrew.
5. To insure the proper alignment, the swivel must be free to slide along the flat end of the throttle rod so the preload spring action is not restricted. Clean the parts if necessary.
6. Hold the transmission lever firmly forward against the internal stop and tighten the swivel lockscrew to 100 inch lbs. (11 Nm). Linkage backlash will automatically be taken up by the preload spring.

DRIVE TRAIN 7-15

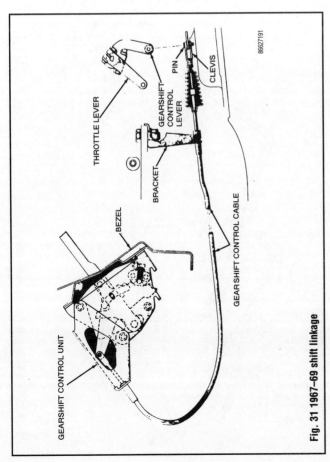

Fig. 31 1967–69 shift linkage

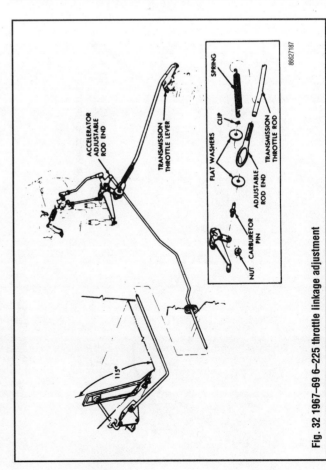

Fig. 32 1967–69 6-225 throttle linkage adjustment

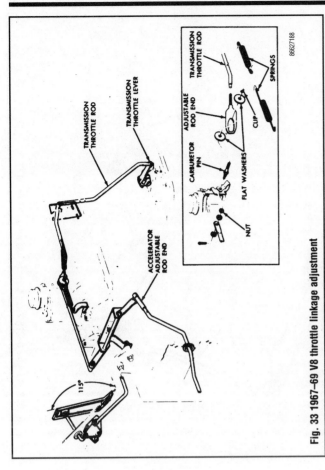

Fig. 33 1967–69 V8 throttle linkage adjustment

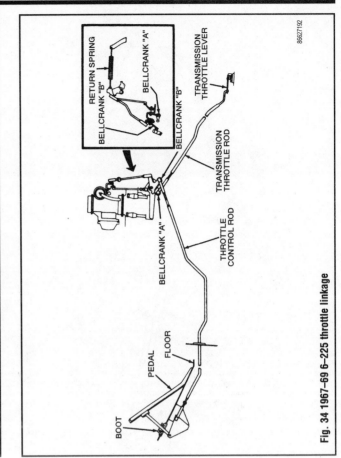

Fig. 34 1967–69 6-225 throttle linkage

7-16 DRIVE TRAIN

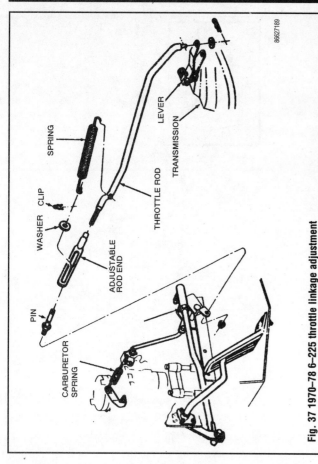

Fig. 37 1970-78 6-225 throttle linkage adjustment

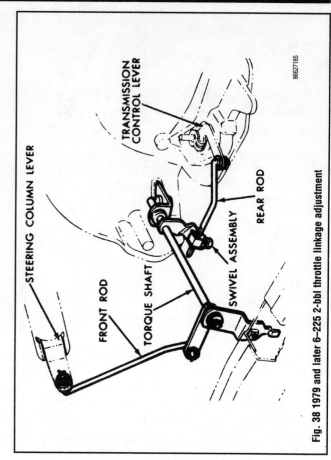

Fig. 38 1979 and later 6-225 2-bbl throttle linkage adjustment

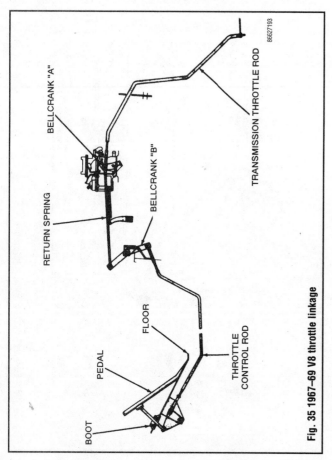

Fig. 35 1967-69 V8 throttle linkage

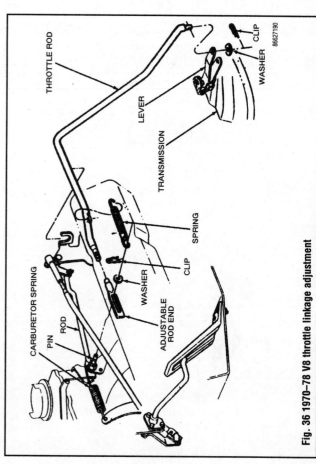

Fig. 36 1970-78 V8 throttle linkage adjustment

DRIVE TRAIN 7-17

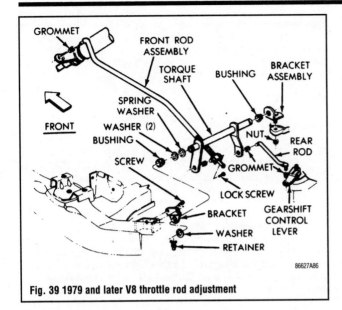

Fig. 39 1979 and later V8 throttle rod adjustment

7. Lower the truck, reconnect choke if disconnected, and test the linkage freedom. Move the throttle rod rearwards, slowly releasing it to confirm it will return fully forwards.

Neutral Safety Switch

REMOVAL & INSTALLATION

♦ See Figures 40 and 41

The neutral safety switch is thread mounted into the transmission case. When the gearshift lever is placed in either the Park or Neutral position, a cam, which is attached to the transmission throttle lever inside the transmission, contacts the neutral safety switch and provides a ground to complete the starter solenoid circuit.

The back–up light switch is incorporated into the neutral safety switch. The center terminal is for the neutral safety switch and the two outer terminals are for the back–up lamps.

There is no adjustment for the switch. If a malfunction occurs, the switch must be removed and replaced. To remove the switch:
1. Disconnect the negative battery cable.
2. Raise and support the vehicle on jackstands.

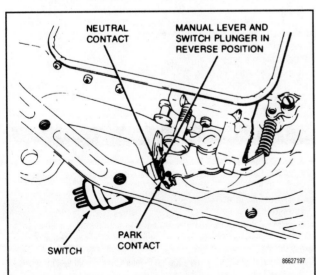

Fig. 40 Looking up at the neutral safety/backup light switch with the pan removed

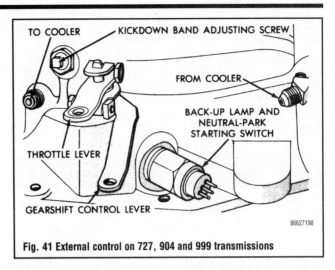

Fig. 41 External control on 727, 904 and 999 transmissions

3. Disconnect the electrical leads and unscrew the switch. Use a drain pan to catch the transmission fluid.

To install:
4. Using a new seal, install the new switch and torque it to 24 ft. lbs. (32 Nm).
5. Remove the jackstands and lower the vehicle.
6. Connect the negative battery cable.
7. Pour approximately four quarts of Dexron®III fluid through the filler tube.
8. Start the engine and idle it for at least 2 minutes.
9. Set the parking brake and move the selector through each position, ending in Park.
10. Add sufficient fluid to bring the level to the FULL mark on the dipstick. The level should be checked in Park, with the engine idling at normal operating temperature.

Extension Housing Seal

REMOVAL & INSTALLATION

1. Matchmark the yoke and driveshaft ends for reassembly.
2. Carefully pull shaft yoke out of the transmission extension housing.

➡Make sure you do not scratch or nick the surface on the sliding spline yoke during removal or installation of the shaft assembly.

3. Cut the boot end of the extension housing yoke seal then screw the tapered thread tool C–748 into the seal. Turn the screw of the tool, to remove the seal.

To install:
4. Position the new seal in the opening of the extension housing, then drive it into the housing using a suitable seal installer or driver.
5. Carefully guide the universal joint yoke into the housing and on the mainshaft splines. Align the matchmarks and connect the driveshaft to the rear axle pinion shaft yoke.

Transmission

REMOVAL & INSTALLATION

It will be necessary to remove the transmission and converter as an assembly; otherwise the converter driveplate pump bushing and oil seal will be damaged. The driveplate will not support a load. Therefore, none of the weight of transmission should be allowed to rest on the plate during removal.
1. Disconnect the battery ground cable.
2. Some models will need for the exhaust system to be dropped for clearance reasons.
3. Remove the engine-to-transmission struts, if so equipped.
4. Disconnect and remove the cooler lines at the transmission.
5. Next, remove the starter and cooler line bracket.

7-18 DRIVE TRAIN

6. Remove the torque converter access cover. On early models equipped with a drain plug on the converter, this will aid in draining the system.

➡ A running production change was made in January, 1977 which eliminated the converter drain plug. This means that the transmission must be removed in order to drain the converter on models manufactured after this date.

7. Loosen the oil pan bolts, then tap the pan to loosen, allowing the fluid to drain.
8. Reinstall the oil pan on the vehicles.
9. Matchmark the torque converter and driveplate.

➡ The crankshaft flange bolt circle, inner and outer circle of holes in the driveplate, and the usually four tapped holes in the front face of the converter, all have offset. These parts will have to be installed in the original positions. This will maintain the balance of the engine and converter.

10. Rotate engine clockwise with a socket wrench on the vibration dampener bolt, then position the bolts that attach the torque converter to the driveplate, remove the bolts.
11. Matchmark the parts for reassembly, then disconnect the propeller shaft at the rear of the universal joint. Carefully pull the shaft assembly out of the extension housing.
12. Disconnect the wire connections to the backup light switch/neutral safety switch, along with the lock-up solenoid connector (if equipped).
13. Disassemble the gear shiftrod and torque shaft assembly from the transmission.

➡ When it is necessary to disconnect the linkage rods from the levers that use plastic grommets and retainers, the grommets should be replaced with new ones. A prytool will be needed to remove the grommet from the lever, then cut away the old grommet. Use pliers to snap the new grommet into the lever and rod into grommet.

14. Disconnect the throttle rod from left side of transmission. Remove the linkage at the bellcrank from the transmission, if equipped.
15. Disconnect the speedometer cable, then remove the oil filler tube.
16. Install engine support fixture to hold up the rear of the engine.
17. Raise transmission slightly with jack to relieve load and remove support bracket or crossmember. Remove all bolts that secure the transmission mount-to-crossmember and crossmember-to-frame, then remove the crossmember.
18. Remove all the bellhousing bolts. Carefully work the transmission and torque converter assembly rearwards off the engine block dowels and disengage the converter hub from the end of the crankshaft.

➡ Attach a small C-clamp to edge of bell housing to hold converter in place during transmission removal; otherwise the front pump bushing might be damaged.

19. Lower the transmission and remove from under the vehicle. To remove the torque converter, remove the C-clamp from the edge of the bell housing, then carefully slide the assembly out of the transmission.

To install:

➡ Install transmission and converter must be installed as an assembly. If this is not done the driveplate, pump bushing, and oil seal will be damaged. Do not allow weight of transmission to rest on the plate during installation.

20. Rotate pump rotors until the rotor lugs are vertical.
21. Carefully slide converter assembly over input shaft and reaction shaft. Make sure converter impeller hub slots are also vertical, fully engage front pump inner rotor lugs. Test for engagement by placing a straight edge on the face of the case. The surface of the converter front cover lug should be at least ½ in. (13mm) to the rear of the straight edge when the converter is pushed all the way into the transmission.
22. Use a C-clamp on edge of converter housing to hold converter in place during transmission installation.
23. Converter driveplate should be free of distortion and driveplate to crankshaft bolts tightened to 55 ft. lbs. (74 Nm). Make sure both dowel pins are in the engine block and they are protruding far enough to hold the transmission in alignment.
24. Make sure to coat the converter hub hole in the crankshaft with multipurpose grease. Using a jack, position transmission and converter assembly in alignment with engine. You may need to raise or tilt the transmission until the engine and transmission is aligned.
25. Rotate converter so mark on converter (made during removal) will align with the mark on the driveplate. The offset holes in plate are located next to the ⅛ in. (3mm) hole in inner circle of the plate. A stamped **V** mark identifies the offset hole in converter front cover. Carefully work transmission assembly forward over engine block dowels with converter hub entering the crankshaft opening.
26. After the transmission is in position, then install the converter housing-to-engine bolts and tighten to 30 ft. lbs. (41 Nm).
27. Install the crossmember-to-frame and lower the transmission to install the mount on the extension to the crossmember, then tighten all bolts.
28. Remove the engine support fixture. Install the oil filler tube and speedometer cable.
29. Connect the throttle rod to transmission lever, gearshift rod and torque shaft assembly to the transmission lever and frame.

➡ When it is necessary to disconnect the linkage rods from the levers that use plastic grommets and retainers, the grommets should be replaced with new ones. A prytool will be needed to remove the grommet from the lever, then cut away the old grommet. Use pliers to snap the new grommet into the lever and rod into grommet.

30. Place the wire connections on the backup light/neutral safety switch, along with connections to the lockup solenoid at the rear of the transmission case, if equipped.
31. Rotate the engine clockwise with a socket wrench on the vibration dampener bolt, as needed, so to install the torque converter drive plate bolts. Matchmark made earlier will help, then tighten to 270 inch lbs. (31 Nm).
32. Install the torque converter access cover. Install the starter and cooler line bracket.
33. Connect the cooler lines to the transmission fittings.
34. Install engine to transmission struts, if required. Install the transfer case if equipped.
35. Replace the exhaust system if it was disconnected previously.
36. Guide the sliding yoke into the extension housing and on the output shaft splines carefully. Align the marks made earlier, then connect the propeller shaft(s) to the axle pinion shaft yoke(s).
37. Adjust the throttle and gearshift linkage.
38. Refill the transmission on level ground with the correct amount and type of fluid used on your truck.

DRIVELINE

4-WD Front Driveshaft

REMOVAL & INSTALLATION

1. Raise and support the vehicle on jackstands.
2. Remove the four flange retaining bolts and lockwashers from the constant velocity U-joint at the transfer case. Matchmark the parts to reinstall them in the same position. To prevent the constant velocity joint from turning while removing the nuts, utilize a press bar.
3. Remove the nuts and lockwashers from the U-bolts at the differential flange and remove the U-bolts.
4. Support the driveshaft and separate the U-joint at the front the driveshaft yoke, pulling backward to clear the flange. The driveshaft should never be allowed to hang by either universal joint.
5. Remove the driveshaft.

To install:

6. Before installing the driveshaft, wipe the areas with a clean cloth and inspect the surfaces for scratches, nicks, dents or burrs. If there are any of these correct the problem before proceeding.
7. Support the driveshaft and slide the U-joint into the front the driveshaft yoke, pushing forward past the flange.

➡ Be sure to install remarked parts with the same orientation as before removal.

DRIVE TRAIN 7-19

8. Install the U-bolts, then tighten the nuts and lockwashers for the U-bolts at the differential flange.
9. With the marked parts reinstall them in the same position. Replace the four flange retaining bolts and lockwashers for the constant velocity U-joint at the transfer case.

Rear Driveshafts and U-Joints

REMOVAL & INSTALLATION

▶ See Figure 42

Ball and Trunnion Type

1. Raise the vehicle and support it on jackstands.
2. Matchmark the U-joint and pinion flange to ensure proper installation. Remove both rear U-joint roller and bearing assembly clamps from the pinion yoke. Do not disturb the retaining clamp used to hold the roller assemblies in place.
3. Disconnect the front U-joint from the transmission flange and remove the shaft from the vehicle.

To install:
4. Before installing the driveshaft, wipe the areas with a clean cloth and inspect the surfaces for scratches, nicks, dents or burrs. If there are any of these correct the problem before proceeding.
5. If necessary replace the seal.
6. Replace the shaft on the vehicle, and connect the front U-joint at the transmission flange.
7. With the matchmarks on the U-joint and pinion flanges in position, install both rear U-joint roller and bearing assembly clamps at the pinion yoke.
8. Lower the truck.

Cross and Roller Type

1967–69 MODELS

1. Raise and support the vehicle. Matchmark the U-joints and sliding yokes.
2. Remove the U-joint at the rear axle by removing the two strap bolts and straps.
3. Remove the two bushing and roller assemblies.
4. Remove the front U-joint in the same manner by removing the strap bolts and straps.
5. Remove the driveshaft from the vehicle.

To install:
6. Before installing the driveshaft, wipe the areas with a clean cloth and inspect the surfaces for scratches, nicks, dents or burrs. If there are any of these correct the problem before proceeding.
7. If necessary replace the seal.
8. Installation is the reverse of removal. Make sure to replace parts with the matchmarks made earlier. Coat the bushing rollers with short fiber grease and tap the bushings into the yoke on the cross bearing journals.

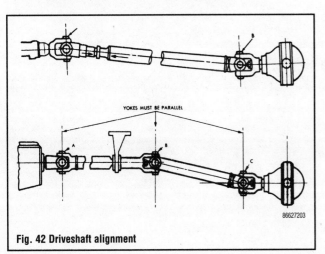

Fig. 42 Driveshaft alignment

1970–88 ONE-PIECE SHAFT

1. Raise and support the truck.
2. Matchmark the shaft and pinion flange to assure proper balance at installation.
3. Remove both rear U-joint roller and bushing clamps from the rear axle pinion flange. Do not disturb the retaining strap that holds the bushing assemblies on the U-Joint cross.

➡ Do not allow the driveshaft to hang during removal. Suspend it from the frame with a piece of wire. Before removing the driveshaft, lower the front end to prevent loss of fluid.

4. Slide the driveshaft from the truck.

To install:
5. Before installing the driveshaft, wipe the are with a clean cloth and inspect the surfaces for scratches, nicks, dents or burrs. If there are any of these correct the problem before proceeding.
6. Engage the yoke splines on end of the output shaft, be careful not to burr the splines.
7. Install the rear U-joint with roller bushings and seats of the drive pinion hub yoke, aligning the marks made during removal.
8. Install the bushing clamps and attaching screws. Tighten the $FR1/4–28 clamp screws to 19 ft. lbs. (26 Nm) and $FR5/16–24 clamp screws to 34 ft. lbs. (34 Nm).

1970–88 TWO–PIECE SHAFT

This driveshaft has a universal joint at either end, with a third universal joint and a support bearing at the center.

1. Matchmark the shaft and the rear axle pinion hub yoke. Matchmark the center support bearing spline and slip yoke.

➡ Do not allow the driveshaft to hang down during removal. Suspend it from the frame. Raise the rear of the truck to prevent loss of transmission fluid.

2. Remove both rear U-joint roller and bushing assembly clamps from the rear axle pinion yoke. Do not disturb the retaining strap used to hold the bushing assemblies on the U-joint cross.
3. Slide the rear half of the shaft off the front shaft splines at the center bearing. Remove the rear half.
4. At the transmission end of the front half, remove the bushing retaining bolts and clamps, after matchmarking. If there is a driveshaft brake, there will be flange nuts.
5. Unbolt the center support bearing mounting nuts and bolts, then remove the front half of the shaft.

To install:
6. Align the matchmarks at the transmission, then start all the bolts and nuts at the front U-joint and at the center support bearing.
7. Tighten ¼ in. (6.3mm) clamp bolts to 19 ft. lbs. (26 Nm) and 5⁄16 in. (8mm) bolts to 34 ft. lbs. (33 Nm). Tighten driveshaft brake flange nuts to 35 ft. lbs. (47 Nm). Leave the center bearing bolts just snug.
8. Align the rear shaft matchmarks and slide the yoke onto the front shaft spline.
9. Align the rear U-joint matchmarks and install the bushing clamps and bolts. Tighten the bolts to repeat retorque specs here.
10. Grease the joints and splines.
11. Jack up the rear wheels and drive the propeller shaft with the engine. The center support bearing will align itself.
12. Tighten the center support bearing bolts to 50 ft. lbs. (68 Nm).

U-JOINT OVERHAUL

Ball and Trunnion Type

1. Remove the driveshaft.
2. Straighten the tabs on the grease cover and remove the grease cover, then gasket.
3. Push the body back and remove the components from both ends of the trunnion pin.
4. Remove the clamps and loosen the dust cover. Remove and save the breather located between the driveshaft and rear end of the cover.

7-20 DRIVE TRAIN

5. Clean and examine the trunnion pin for wear. If wear in the body is noticeable, it should be replaced. A press is necessary to remove the pin.
6. Clean all parts in kerosene or a similar solvent.
7. When the trunnion pin and body have not been replaced, a new boot can be installed after coating all parts with U-joint grease. Stretch the boot over the pin and work it through the body into position on the shaft.
8. If removed the trunnion pin must be pressed into the driveshaft with a hydraulic press.
9. Install a thrust washer the rollers, ball, button spring, and thrust button on each end of the trunnion pin, then position the body over the pin.
10. Install the boot on the driveshaft with the breather parallel to the shaft. Install the clamp.
11. Position the boot on the U-joint body and install the retaining clamp.
12. Lubricate the U-joint with 2 oz. of U-joint grease applied evenly in both races.
13. Install the gasket on the cover, then install the cover on the body. Bend the tabs to retain the cover.
14. Install the driveshaft and U-joint assembly.

Lockring and Snapring Type

▶ See Figure 43

1. Hammer the bushings (roller caps) slightly inward to relieve pressure on the retainers. Remove the retainers.
2. Place the yoke in a vice with a socket bigger than the bushing on one side and one smaller than the bushing on the other side.
3. Apply pressure, forcing one bushing out into the larger socket.
4. Reverse the vise and socket arrangement to remove the other bushing and the cross.
5. On installation, press the new bushings in just far enough to install the retainers.

Strap Clamp Type (Rear Axle Yoke)

▶ See Figure 44

1. Unthread the strap bolts and remove straps, bushings, seals and washer retainers.

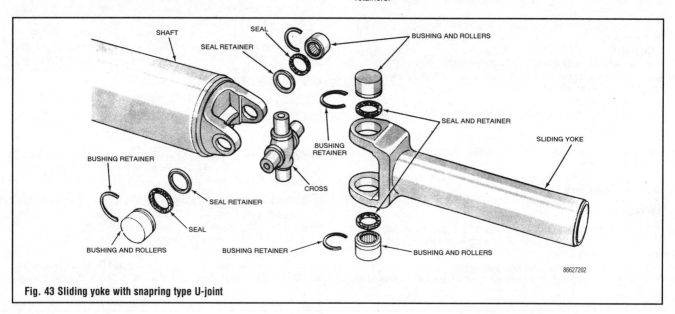

Fig. 43 Sliding yoke with snapring type U-joint

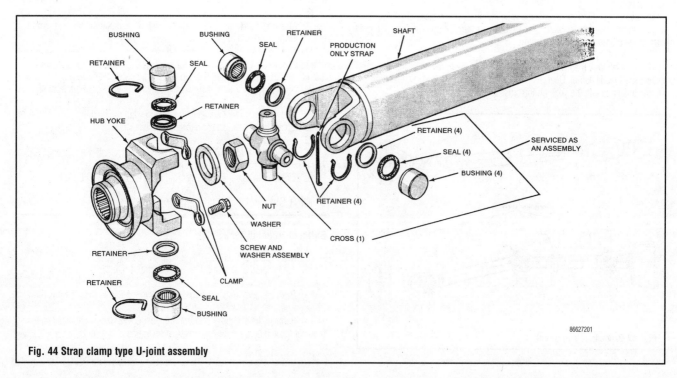

Fig. 44 Strap clamp type U-joint assembly

DRIVE TRAIN 7-21

2. Install new components as required.
3. Grease bearings when assembling. Install with grease fitting parallel to other fittings in the drive train.
4. Tighten strap bolts to 20 ft. lbs. (27 Nm).

Constant Velocity U–Joint

The constant velocity U-joint is the double universal joint used in the front driveshaft on four-wheel drive models. It can be are disassembled in the same way as the snapring type U-joint. Original equipment U-joints are held together by plastic retainers which shear when they are pressed out. The bearing cups in the center part of the joint should be pressed out before those in the yoke. Original equipment constant velocity joints cannot be re-assembled. Replacement part kits should have the bearing cups with grooves for retaining rings.

Slip Joints

When re–assembling slip joints, make sure that arrows stamped on each side are matched. This will assure proper universal joint alignment.

Center Support Bearing

When two or more driveshafts are used in tandem, a rubber–mounted center bearing supports the center portion of the drive line. The center bearing is mounted in rubber in a bracket which is bolted to the frame crossmember.

REMOVAL & INSTALLATION

♦ See Figure 45

1. Matchmark parts for installation, then remove driveshafts as described earlier.
2. Place the front shaft in a vise, then pull the bearing support and insulator away from the bearing.
3. Bend the slinger away from the bearing with a hammer for clearance to install a bearing puller.
4. Remove the bearing with a puller. Remove the slinger. Discard all parts. A replacement kit contains all necessary repair parts.

To install:

5. Place the new slinger, bearing assembly and retainer on the driveshaft. Each part is a press fit.
6. Use a strong tube or pipe which clears the shaft spline. Press or drive the parts forward into position.
7. If the seal on the rear slip yoke seal needs replacement, pry the cap from the yoke, then discard of seal and cap.
8. Place new seal cap and felt washer on center support bearing splines, to be assembled to yoke after driveshafts are installed.
9. Connect the two piece driveshaft and install.
10. Slide the seal and cap to the yoke, then crimp the cap tabs to the yoke.

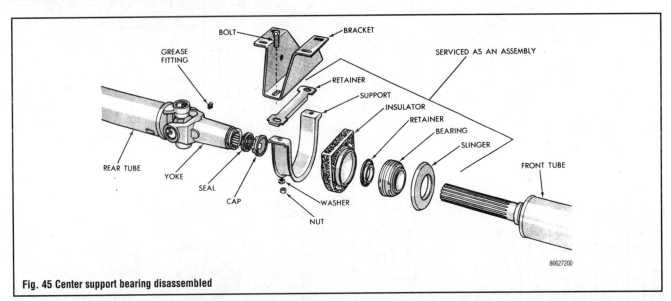

Fig. 45 Center support bearing disassembled

FRONT DRIVE AXLE

Manual Locking Hubs

REMOVAL & INSTALLATION

Warn Hubs

♦ See Figure 46

1. Straighten the locktabs and remove the six hub mounting bolts.
2. Tap the hub gently with a mallet to remove.
3. Separate the clutch assembly from the body assembly.
4. Remove the snapring from the rear of the body assembly, using snapring pliers. Slip the axle shaft hub out of the body from the front.
5. Remove the Allen screw from the inner side of the clutch, and remove the bronze dial assembly from the front side of the clutch housing assembly.
6. Remove the clutch assembly from the rear of the housing, complete with the twelve roller pins.

To install:

7. Coat the moving parts with a waterproof grease.
8. Slide the axle shaft hub into the body from the front, and replace the snapring.
9. Replace the bronze dial assembly and the inner clutch. Tighten the Allen screw and stake the edge of the screw with a center punch to prevent loosening.
10. With the dial it the free position, rotate the outer clutch body into the inner assembly until it bottoms in the housing. Back it up to the nearest hole and install the roller pins.
11. Position the hub and clutch assembly together with a new gasket in between.
12. Position the hub assembly over the end of the axle and replace the six hub mounting bolts and locktabs.
13. Torque the bolts to 35 ft. lbs. (47 Nm) and bend the locktabs to anchor the bolts.
14. Verify the operation by road testing.

Dana Front Locking Hubs

♦ See Figures 47 thru 56

1. Place the hub in the lock position. Remove the Allen head mounting bolts and washers.

7-22 DRIVE TRAIN

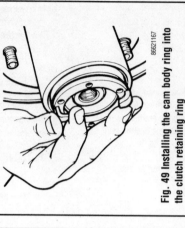

Fig. 47 Dana front drive locking hub

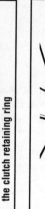

Fig. 49 Installing the cam body ring into the clutch retaining ring

Fig. 51 Axle shift sleeve, ring and inner clutch ring installation

Fig. 48 Removal of the locknut, lockring and adjusting nut

Fig. 50 Lubricating the selector knob

Front Drive Axle Application Chart

Axle	Model	Years
Dana 44-3F, 3HDF	W100, W200	1967–73
Dana 44-FBJ	W100, W150, W200	1974–79
	W150, W200, W250	1980–81
	Ramcharger, Trail Duster	1981
	W150, Ramcharger	1982–84
	W250	1982–84
	W350 w/131 in. & 149 in. WB	1982–84
Dana 44-8FD	W150, Ramcharger	1985–88
	W250	1985–88
	W350 w/131 in. & 149 in. WB	1985–88
Dana 60F	W200 opt.	1975–80
	W250 opt.	1981–88
	W300	1979–80
	W350	1981
	W350 w/135 in. & 149 in. WB	1982–88
Dana 70F	W200 opt.	1974
	W300	1967–74
Dana F-375	WM300	1967

opt.: optional equipment
WB: wheel base

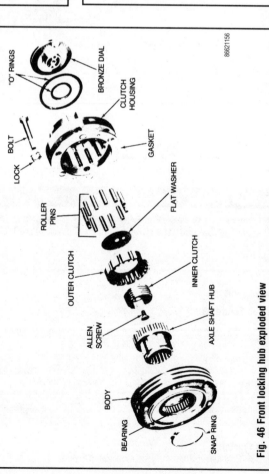

Fig. 46 Front locking hub exploded view

DRIVE TRAIN 7-23

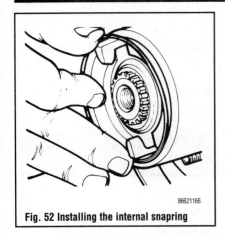
Fig. 52 Installing the internal snapring

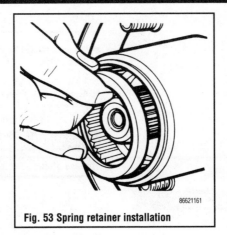
Fig. 53 Spring retainer installation

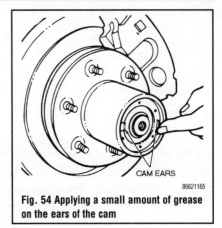
Fig. 54 Applying a small amount of grease on the ears of the cam

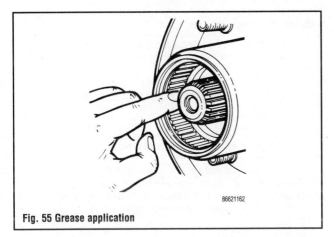
Fig. 55 Grease application

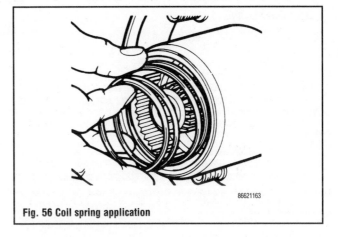
Fig. 56 Coil spring application

2. Carefully remove the retainer, O-ring seal and knob. Separate the knob from the retainer.
3. Remove the large internal snapring. Slide the retainer ring and cam from the hub.
4. While pressing against the sleeve and the ring assembly, remove the axle shaft snapring. Relieve the pressure, then remove the sleeve and ring, ring and bushing, spring and plate.
5. Inspect all parts for wear, nicks and burrs. Replace all of the parts which appear questionable.

To install:
6. Slide the plate and spring (large coils first) into the wheel hub housing.
7. Assemble the ring and bushing, sleeve and bushing. Slide the complete assembly into the housing.
8. Compress the spring, then install the axle shaft snapring.
9. Position the cam and retainer in the housing, then install the large internal snapring.
10. Place the small O-ring seal on the knob, lubricate with waterproof grease and install in the retainer at lock position.
11. Place the large O-ring seal on the retainer. Align the retainer and the retainer ring, then install the washers and the Allen head mounting screws.
12. Check operation.

Dualmatic Front Locking Hubs

♦ See Figure 57

1. Turn the knob to the ENGAGE position.
2. Apply pressure to the face of the knob and remove the 3 screws spaced 120° apart and nearest the flange.

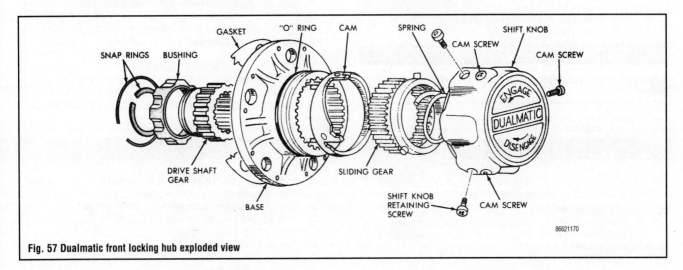
Fig. 57 Dualmatic front locking hub exploded view

7-24 DRIVE TRAIN

3. Pull outward and remove the knob from the mounting base.
4. Remove the snapring from the axle shaft.
5. Separate and remove the locking hub assembly from the rotor hub. Discard the gasket.
6. Clean all parts in a safe solvent. Replace any damaged parts.
7. Coat all parts with multi-purpose grease prior to assembly.
8. Place a new gasket and the locking hub on the rotor.
9. Install the capscrews and lockwasher and torque them to 30–40 ft. lbs. (41–54 Nm).
10. Install the snapring.
11. Position the shift knob on the mounting base. Align the splines by pushing inward and turning it clockwise to lock it in position.
12. Install and tighten the 3 shift knob retaining screws.

Automatic Locking Hubs

REMOVAL & DISASSEMBLY

♦ See Figures 58 thru 74

1. Remove the 5 Torx® screws securing the hub cover.
2. Remove the cover.
3. Remove the bearing race spring assembly.
4. Remove the sealing ring.
5. Remove the seal bridge retainer and bearing components.
6. Squeeze together the tangs of the wire retainer with needle-nosed pliers and pull the remaining components of the locking hub from the wheel.
7. If the hub was locked when removed, you must unlock it before proceeding:
   a. Hold the hub outer ring.
   b. Rotate the drag sleeve in either direction.
8. With the cover removed, turn the clutch gear until it drops, to engage the outer clutch housing.
9. Remove the retaining ring holding the drag sleeve to the hub sleeve.
10. Remove the spacer.
11. Lift and tilt the drag sleeve and detent to free the brake band tangs from the rectangular opening in the inner cage.
12. Remove the drag sleeve and detent, brake band assembly, or brake band retainer.

※※ WARNING

Never remove the brake band or band retainer from the drag sleeve and detent.

13. Remove the retaining ring from the outer clutch housing groove.
14. Using a small prybar, pry the plastic outer cage free from the inner cage and remove the inner cage.
15. Pry free all 5 lugs and remove the plastic outer cage from the outer clutch housing.
16. Remove the clutch gear and hub sleeve assembly from the outer clutch housing.
17. Compress the clutch gear return spring and remove the retaining ring from the clutch gear hub sleeve.

※※ CAUTION

To prevent injury, use a spring compressor to hold the spring securely.

18. Carefully release the spring tension, remove the spring support washer, return spring retainers and return spring from the hub sleeve.
19. Remove the C-ring from the hub sleeve.
20. Remove the clutch gear, spring and cam follower.

INSPECTION

1. Wash all parts in clean solvent.
2. Check all parts for wear or damage and replace any problem parts.
3. Examine the wire retaining ring for kinks, bends and diameter. Diameter range should be 0.088–0.094 in. (2 Nm).

LUBRICATION

➡ **The hubs should be lubricated every 24,000 miles, or, after being run in deep water.**

1. All parts except the bearing and race, brake band and drag sleeve, should be dipped in clean Dexron®III ATF prior to assembly.
2. Pack the bearing race with Mopar 4293040 lubricant, or equivalent.
3. Lubricate the brake band with 1.5 grams of the same lubricant.

※※ WARNING

The use of any other lubricant may cause hub failure.

ASSEMBLY & INSTALLATION

1. Snap the cam follower legs over the tooth gaps at the flat surfaces of the clutch gear.

➡ **Do not pry the legs of the cam apart.**

2. Compress and slide the conical spring into position between the cam follower and the clutch gear with the large diameter of the spring contacting the face of the clutch gear.
3. Install the assembled cam follower, conical spring and clutch gear assembly onto the hub sleeve with the teeth of the cam follower near the step at the end of the hub sleeve.
4. Position the C-ring between the clutch gear and the cam follower, then, snap it into place in the groove of the hub sleeve.
5. Place a spring retainer at the end of the return spring and position the spring and retainer over the clutch gear.
6. Install a spring retainer and the spring support washer on the remaining end of the return spring. Compress the return spring, install the retainer ring into the groove at the end of the hub sleeve. Clamp the spring securely.
7. Install the clutch gear and hub sleeve assembly into the outer clutch housing.
8. Install 3 of the clutch screws into the outer face of the clutch housing.
9. Position the plastic outer cage into the outerclutch housing, with the ramps of the plastic outer cage near the cam follower. Carefully work the outer cage into the outer clutch housing until the small external tabs of the plastic cage locate in the wide groove of the inner cage.
10. Install the steel inner cage into the outer cage, aligning the lug of the outer cage with the rectangular opening in the inner cage.
11. Install the retaining ring into the outer clutch housing groove to lock the outer cage in place.
12. Position one of the two brake band tangs on each side of the outer cage lug located at the rectangular opening of the steel inner cage. It may be necessary to tilt the drag sleeve while engaging the the brake band tangs. With the brake band tangs engaged, the drag sleeve teeth will be meshed with the teeth of the cam follower.
13. Remove the 3 recently installed screws from the clutch housing face.
14. Install the spacer and retaining ring to secure the drag sleeve in position.
15. Install the hub assembly on the axle.
16. Position the wire retaining ring in the groove machined in the outer clutch housing surface with the retaining ring tangs pointed away from the splines.
17. Hold the tangs together and assemble the seal bridge over the tangs, positioned in such a way that the bent-down tabs of the seal bridge clamp the wire tangs together.
18. Install the O-ring in the outer clutch housing groove and over the seal bridge.
19. Position the bearing over the inner race and lubricate it as described above. Install the bearing retaining clip in the inner race. The clip must be assembled on the bearing with the balls visible as shown in the accompanying illustration.
20. Install the bearing and retainer assembly into the end of the hub sleeve. Install the seal ring over the outer clutch housing.
21. Position the bearing race spring into the bore in the cover.
22. Install the spring and cover assembly, install the 5 screws and torque them to 50 inch lbs. (5.6 Nm).
23. The hub should turn freely.

DRIVE TRAIN 7-25

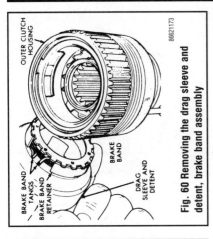

Fig. 60 Removing the drag sleeve and detent, brake band assembly

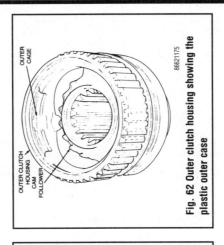

Fig. 62 Outer clutch housing showing the plastic outer case

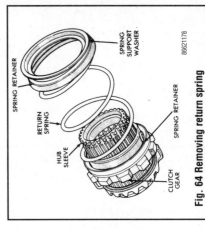

Fig. 64 Removing return spring

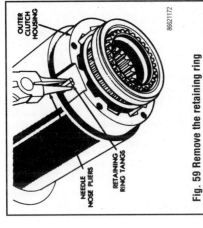

Fig. 59 Remove the retaining ring

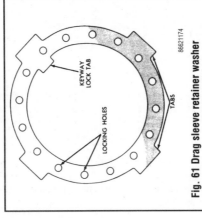

Fig. 61 Drag sleeve retainer washer

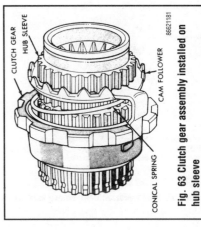

Fig. 63 Clutch gear assembly installed on hub sleeve

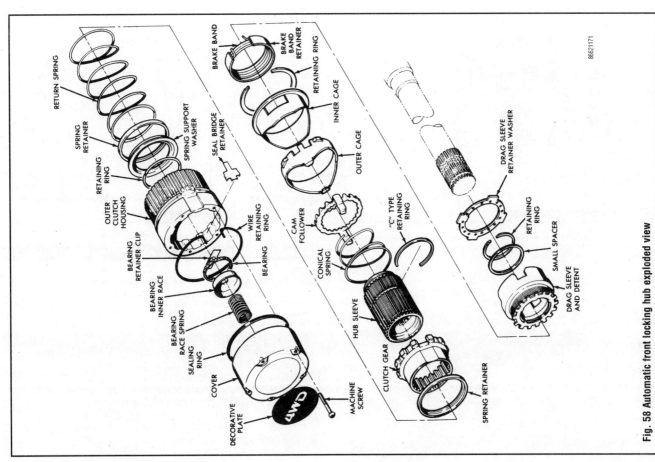

Fig. 58 Automatic front locking hub exploded view

7-26 DRIVE TRAIN

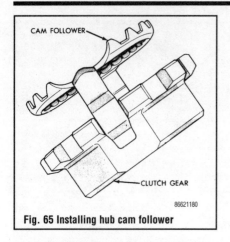

Fig. 65 Installing hub cam follower

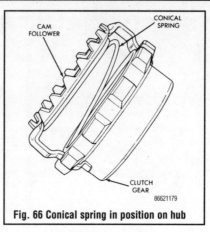

Fig. 66 Conical spring in position on hub

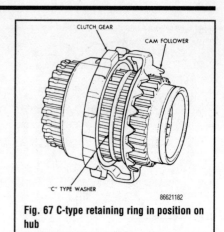

Fig. 67 C-type retaining ring in position on hub

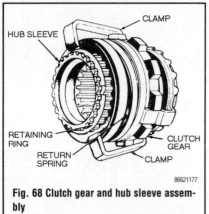

Fig. 68 Clutch gear and hub sleeve assembly

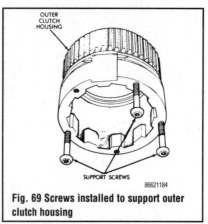

Fig. 69 Screws installed to support outer clutch housing

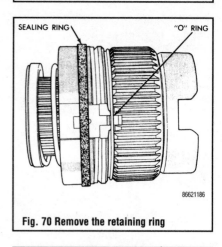

Fig. 70 Remove the retaining ring

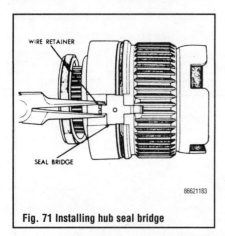

Fig. 71 Installing hub seal bridge

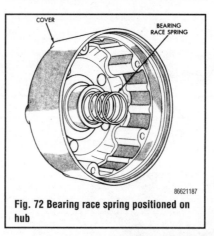

Fig. 72 Bearing race spring positioned on hub

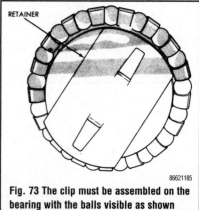

Fig. 73 The clip must be assembled on the bearing with the balls visible as shown

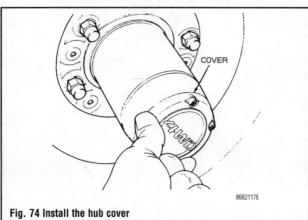

Fig. 74 Install the hub cover

Spindle Bearings

REMOVAL, PACKING & INSTALLATION

Before handling the bearings, there are a few things that you should remember to do and not to do.

Remember to DO the following:
- Remove all outside dirt from the housing before exposing the bearing.
- Treat a used bearing as gently as you would a new one.
- Work with clean tools in clean surroundings.
- Use clean, dry canvas gloves, or at least clean, dry hands.
- Clean solvents and flushing fluids are a must.
- Use clean paper when laying out the bearings to dry.
- Protect disassembled bearings from rust and dirt. Cover them up.
- Use clean rags to wipe bearings.

DRIVE TRAIN 7-27

- Keep the bearings in oil-proof paper when they are to be stored or are not in use.
- Clean the inside of the housing before replacing the bearing.

Do NOT do the following:
- Don't work in dirty surroundings.
- Don't use dirty, chipped or damaged tools.
- Try not to work on wooden work benches or use wooden mallets.
- Don't handle bearings with dirty or moist hands.
- Do not use gasoline for cleaning; use a safe solvent.
- Do not spin-dry bearings with compressed air. They will be damaged.
- Do not spin dirty bearings.
- Avoid using cotton waste or dirty cloths to wipe bearings.
- Try not to scratch or nick bearing surfaces.
- Do not allow the bearing to come in contact with dirt or rust at any time.

Dana 44 and 60 With Locking Hubs

♦ See Figure 75

1. Raise the vehicle and install safety stands.
2. Refer to Manual or Automatic Free Running Hub Removal and Installation and remove the hub assemblies.
3. Remove the wheel bearing locknut, using a hub nut wrench.
4. Remove the lockring from the bearing adjusting nut. This can be done with your finger tips or a screwdriver.

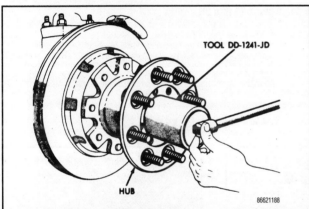

Fig. 75 Removing the outer locknut on Dana 60 or 70 front drive axle

5. Using a hub nut wrench remove the bearing adjusting nut.
6. Remove the caliper and suspend it out of the way. Please refer to the Section 9 of this manual.
7. Slide the hub and disc assembly off of the spindle. The outer wheel bearing will slide out as the hub is removed, so be prepared to catch it.
8. Lay the hub on a clean work surface. Carefully drive the inner bearing cone and grease seal out of the hub using a bearing driver.
9. Inspect the bearing cups for pits or cracks. If necessary, remove them with a drift. If new cups are installed, install new bearings.
10. Lubricate the bearings with wheel bearing grease. Clean all old grease from the hub. Pack the cones and rollers. If a bearing packer is not available, work as much lubricant as possible between the rollers and the cages.
11. Drive new cups into place with a driver, making sure that they are fully seated.
12. Position the inner bearing cone and roller in the inner cup and install the grease retainer.
13. Carefully position the hub and disc assembly on the spindle.
14. Install the outer bearing cone and roller, and the adjusting nut.

➡ The adjusting nut has a small dowel on one side. This dowel faces outward to engage the locking ring.

15. Using a hub nut wrench tighten the bearing adjusting nut to 50 ft. lbs. (67 Nm), while rotating the wheel back and forth to seat the bearings.
16. Back off the adjusting nut approximately 90°.
17. Install the lockring by turning the nut to the nearest hole and inserting the dowel pin.

➡ The dowel pin must seat in a lockring hole for proper bearing adjustment and wheel retention.

18. Install the outer locknut and tighten to 50–80 ft. lbs. (67–108 Nm). Final end-play of the wheel on the spindle should be 0.001–0.010 in. (0.025–0.250mm).
19. Assemble the hub parts.
20. Install the caliper.
21. Remove the safety stands and lower the vehicle.

Early Dana 44 Without Locking Hubs

♦ See Figure 76

1. Raise and support the front end on jackstands.
2. Remove the grease cap.
3. Remove the drive flange bolts and snapring.
4. Using a puller, remove the drive flange.

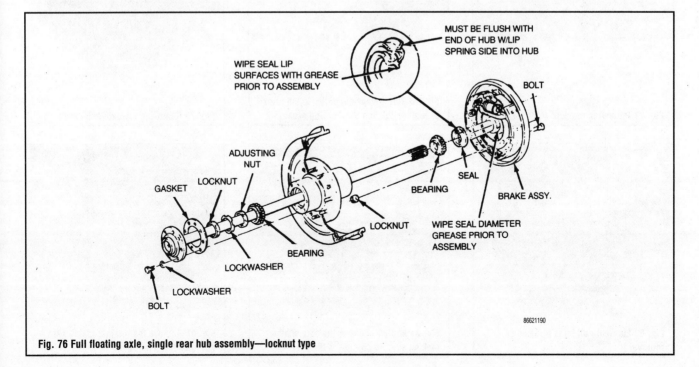

Fig. 76 Full floating axle, single rear hub assembly—locknut type

7-28 DRIVE TRAIN

5. Unbend the locktab and remove the outer locknut.
6. Remove the lockring and the bearing inner adjusting nut.
7. Remove the hub and drum assembly. Take care not to drop the outer bearing.
8. Lay the hub on a clean work surface. Carefully drive the inner bearing cone and grease seal out of the hub using a bearing driver.
9. Inspect the bearing cups for pits or cracks. If necessary, remove them with a drift. If new cups are installed, install new bearings.
10. Lubricate the bearings with wheel bearing grease. Clean all old grease from the hub. Pack the cones and rollers. If a bearing packer is not available, work as much lubricant as possible between the rollers and the cages.
11. Drive new cups into place with a driver, making sure that they are fully seated.
12. Position the inner bearing cone and roller in the inner cup and install the grease retainer.
13. Carefully position the hub and drum assembly on the spindle.
14. Install the outer bearing cone and roller, and the adjusting nut.

➡ **The adjusting nut has a small dowel on one side. This dowel faces outward to engage the locking ring.**

15. Using a hub nut wrench tighten the bearing adjusting nut to 50 ft. lbs. (67 Nm), while rotating the wheel back and forth to seat the bearings.
16. Back off the adjusting nut approximately 90°.
17. Install the lockring by turning the nut to the nearest hole and inserting the dowel pin.

➡ **The dowel pin must seat in a lockring hole for proper bearing adjustment and wheel retention.**

18. Install the outer locknut and tighten to 50–80 ft. lbs. (67–108 Nm). Final end-play of the wheel on the spindle should be 0.001–0.010 in. (0.025–0.250mm). Bend the locking tab over the nut.
19. Install the drive flange bolts and snapring.
20. Install the grease cap.
21. Remove the safety stands and lower the vehicle.

Dana F–375, Dana 70 Without Locking Hubs

1. Raise and support the front end on jackstands.
2. Remove the wheels.
3. Remove the brake drums. See Section 9.
4. Matchmark the drive flange and the hub.
5. Remove the nuts and lockwashers and install puller screws using the 2 threaded holes in the flange.
6. Pull the flange from the hub.
7. Remove the hub and bearings.
8. Thoroughly clean and inspect all parts.
9. Pack the wheel bearings and coat the inside of the hubs with wheel bearing grease.
10. Adjust the wheel bearings by turning the inner adjusting nut tightly, then backing it off 1/6 in. turn.
11. Install the lockring making sure that the pin on the inner nut enters one of the holes in the lockring. It's okay to move the inner nut **slightly** to position the pin.
12. Install the outer nut and torque it to 50 ft. lbs. (67 Nm).
13. Install the drive flange, using a new gasket.
14. Coat the flange and drum contact surfaces with anti-sieze compound and install the drum.
15. Install the wheel.

Full-Time 4–Wheel Drive

♦ See Figures 77 thru 86

1. Remove the wheel cover.
2. Remove the cotter pin and loosen the axle shaft nut.
3. Raise and support the front end on jackstands.
4. Remove the wheels.
5. Unbolt the caliper and support it out of the way. DO NOT DISCONNECT THE BRAKE LINE.
6. Remove the inboard brake pad.
7. Remove the axle shaft nut and washer.

Fig. 77 Removing the axle shaft nut

Fig. 78 Bolt the special puller to the rotor to remove the hub and bearing assembly.

Fig. 79 Removing the axle hub assembly

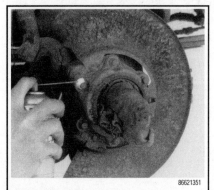
Fig. 80 Lubricate all bolts for ease of removal

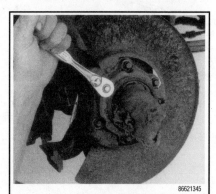
Fig. 81 Apply a rag over the axle shaft making sure no dirt enters the area

Fig. 82 Remove the retainer taking care not to disturb the rag

DRIVE TRAIN 7-29

Fig. 83 Scrap areas well of old gasket materials

Fig. 84 Insert a prybar though the U-joint and wedge the shaft inward as far as it will go. Make sure that it is wedged securely and can't be moved

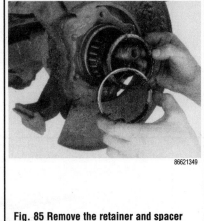

Fig. 85 Remove the retainer and spacer

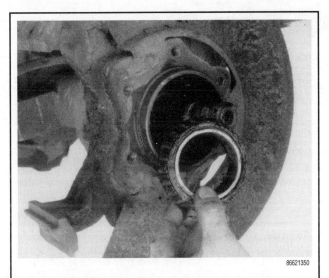

Fig. 86 Removing and inspecting the bearing

8. Some models have a hole provided through the rotor to remove the 6 retainer bolts. See your model for this type. If not proceed to step 9, if so remove the bolts first.
9. Position puller C–4358, or equivalent, over the wheel lugs and install the lug nuts. Tighten the main screw of the puller to remove the hub, bearings, retainer and outer seal as an assembly.
10. Spray lubricant on the retainer bolts to loosen them for easy removal. Apply a rag over the axle shaft making sure not dirt enters the area.
11. Remove the bolts on the retainer bolts
12. Make sure you scrape any traces of gasket and dirt from the retainer and mating area, clean well.
13. Insert a prybar though the U-joint and wedge the shaft inward as far as it will go. Make sure that it is wedged securely and can't be moved.
14. Remove the bearing spacer and retainer along with the bearing. Clean the retainer and spacer well and regrease them with fresh grease.

To install:
15. Take the bearing out and replace with a new one making sure you pack it with fresh grease. Scoop the bearing in the palm of your hand with the grease, making sure you have packed it well. All bearing specs must be filled with grease.
16. Install the hub, rotor and bearing assembly and torque the retainer bolts to 30 ft. lbs. (41 Nm) in a crisscross pattern.
17. Install the brake adapter. Torque the bolts to 85 ft. lbs. (115 Nm).
18. Remove the prybar from the U-joint.
19. Install the axle shaft nut and tighten it to 100 ft. lbs. (135 Nm), then continue tightening it to align the cotter pin holes. Install the cotter pin.
20. Using the lube fitting, fill the knuckle with NLGI, Grade 2, multi-purpose EP grease until the grease is seen flowing through the inner seal.

21. Install the inner brake pad and caliper. See Section 9.
22. Install the wheels and tighten the lug nuts to 110 ft. lbs. (135 Nm).

Axle Shaft, Bearing and Seal

REMOVAL & INSTALLATION

Early Dana 44 Without Locking Hubs

♦ See Figures 87 and 88

1. Raise and support the front end on jackstands.
2. Remove the grease cap.
3. Remove the drive flange bolts and snapring.
4. Using a puller, remove the drive flange.
5. Unbend the locktab and remove the outer locknut.
6. Remove the lockring and the bearing inner adjusting nut.
7. Remove the hub and drum assembly. Take care not to drop the outer bearing.
8. Remove the brake backing plate bolts and wire the plate up out of the way. DO NOT DISCONNECT THE BRAKE LINE.
9. Using a soft mallet, tap the spindle from the knuckle.
10. Pull the axle shaft from the housing. The axle shaft U-joint may be rebuilt in the same manner as a driveshaft U-joint, explained earlier in this Section.
11. Inspect the spindle bushing for wear and/or damage. Replace it if it looks bad.

To install:
12. Replace all seals.
13. Drive a new spindle bushing into place.
14. Lubricate the bushing and axle splines.
15. Carefully install the axle shaft into the housing, engaging the spline with the differential. Take care to avoid seal damage.
16. Install the spindle.
17. Install the backing plate. Torque the bolts to 30 ft. lbs. (40 Nm).
18. Carefully position the hub and drum assembly on the spindle.
19. Install the outer bearing cone and roller, and along with the adjusting nut.

➡ The adjusting nut has a small dowel on one side. This dowel faces outward to engage the locking ring.

20. Using a hub nut wrench tighten the bearing adjusting nut to 50 ft. lbs. (68 Nm), while rotating the wheel back and forth to seat the bearings.
21. Back off the adjusting nut approximately 90°.
22. Install the lockring by turning the nut to the nearest hole and inserting the dowel pin.

➡ The dowel pin must seat in a lockring hole for proper bearing adjustment and wheel retention.

23. Install the outer locknut and tighten to 50–80 ft. lbs. (68–108 Nm). Final end-play of the wheel on the spindle should be 0.001–0.010 in. (0.025–0.250mm). Bend the locking tab over the nut.

7-30 DRIVE TRAIN

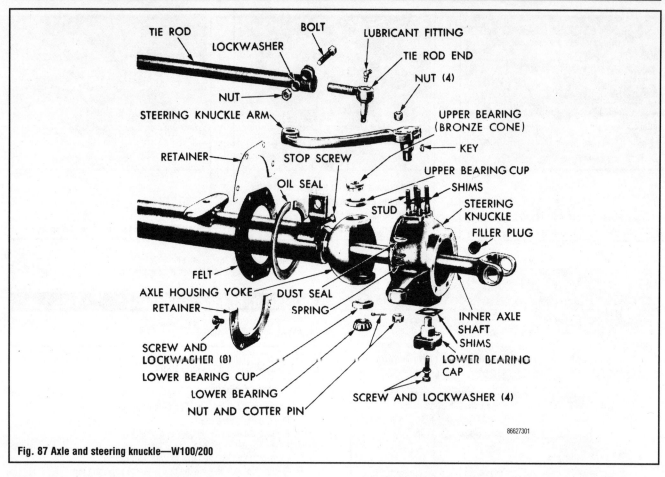

Fig. 87 Axle and steering knuckle—W100/200

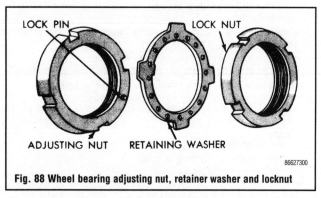

Fig. 88 Wheel bearing adjusting nut, retainer washer and locknut

24. Install the drive flange bolts and snapring.
25. Install the grease cap.
26. Remove the safety stands and lower the vehicle.

Dana 44 Models Through 1984 with Manual or Automatic Locking Hubs

1. Raise the vehicle and install safety stands.
2. Refer to Manual or Automatic Free Running Hub removal and installation and remove the hub assemblies.
3. Remove the wheel bearing locknut, using a hub nut wrench.
4. Remove the lockring from the bearing adjusting nut. This can be done with your finger tips or a screwdriver.
5. Using a hub nut wrench remove the bearing adjusting nut.
6. Remove the caliper and suspend it out of the way. Please refer to Section 9 of this manual.
7. Slide the hub and disc assembly off of the spindle. The outer wheel bearing will slide out as the hub is removed, so be prepared to catch it.

To install:
8. Carefully position the hub and disc assembly on the spindle.
9. Install the outer bearing cone and roller, along with the adjusting nut.

➡The adjusting nut has a small dowel on one side. This dowel faces outward to engage the locking ring.

10. Using a hub nut wrench tighten the bearing adjusting nut to 50 ft. lbs. (68 Nm), while rotating the wheel back and forth to seat the bearings.
11. Back off the adjusting nut approximately 90°.
12. Install the lockring by turning the nut to the nearest hole and inserting the dowel pin.

➡The dowel pin must seat in a lockring hole for proper bearing adjustment and wheel retention.

13. Install the outer locknut and tighten to 50–80 ft. lbs. (68–108 Nm). Final end-play of the wheel on the spindle should be 0.001–0.010 in. (0.025–0.250mm).
14. Assemble the hub parts.
15. Install the caliper.
16. Remove the safety stands and lower the vehicle.

1985–88 Dana 44 Models

LEFT SIDE AXLE SHAFT

◆ See Figures 89 and 90

1. Raise and support the front end on jackstands.
2. Remove the wheel.
3. Remove the caliper and support it up and out of the way. DO NOT DISCONNECT THE BRAKE LINE.
4. Remove the inboard brake pad.
5. Remove the hub/rotor assembly.
6. Unbolt, then remove the splash shield and spindle from the knuckle. It may be necessary to tap the spindle loose with a soft mallet.

DRIVE TRAIN 7-31

7. Disconnect the vacuum lines and wire at the disconnect housing on the axle.
8. Remove the disconnect housing cover, gasket and shield.
9. Carefully pull the intermediate shaft through the seal and out of the axle housing.
10. Remove the shift collar from the disconnect housing.
11. Drive out the inner axle shaft seal and remove it from the disconnect housing. Discard the seal.

➡ Some axles may have a seal guard. Replacement seal do not use a guard.

12. Remove the needle bearing from the intermediate shaft using tool D–330 or equivalent.
13. Remove the differential cover. Allow the oil to drain into a drain pan.
14. While pushing inward on the inner shaft, remove the C–lock from the groove on the shaft.
15. Remove the inner shaft with tools D–354–4 and adapter D–354–3.
16. Remove the bearing from the inner shaft with tools D–354–4, D–354–1 and C–637, or equivalents.
17. Thoroughly clean and inspect all parts. Replace any worn or damaged parts.

To install:

18. Using tools D–354–4, D–354–2 and C–637, install a new bearing on the inner shaft.
19. Position the inner shaft in the axle housing using tools D–354–4 and adapter D–354–3.
20. Carefully slide the shaft into position and install the C–lock.
21. Place a new axle shaft seal on tool 5041–1 and position the assembly in the disconnect housing. Screw threaded bar 5041–2 through the seal and into tool 5041–1. Place tool 5041–3 and the nut on the end of the bar and tighten the nut until the tool reaches the shoulder of the bar.
22. Install the shift collar onto the splined end of the inner shaft.
23. Using tool D–328 and handle C–4171, install the needle bearing into the intermediate shaft.
24. Coat the splined end of the intermediate shaft with multi–purpose chassis lube and install it through the inner axle seal. Avoid damage to the seal.
25. Install the disconnect housing cover and gasket. Make sure that the shift fork indexes the groove in the shift collar.
26. Torque the cover bolts to 10 ft. lbs. (13 Nm).
27. Connect the vacuum lines and wire. Install the clip securely around the 4–wheel drive indicator switch connector.
28. Install the splash shield and spindle. Use new nuts tightened to 30 ft. lbs. (40 Nm).
29. Install the hub and bearings.
30. Install the spacer, drive gear and snapring.
31. Apply RTV sealant on the mating edge of the cap and install it.
32. Install the inboard brake pad and caliper. See Section 9.
33. Thoroughly clean the carrier cover mating surfaces and install the cover using a bead of RTV sealant in place of a gasket. Torque the cover bolts to 40 ft. lbs. (54 Nm).
34. Fill the axle with fluid.
35. Install the wheel.

RIGHT SIDE AXLE SHAFT

♦ See Figure 91

1. Raise and support the front end on jackstands.
2. Remove the wheel.

3. Remove the caliper and support it up and out of the way. DO NOT DISCONNECT THE BRAKE LINE.
4. Remove the inboard brake pad.
5. Remove the hub/rotor assembly.
6. Unbolt, then remove the splash shield and spindle from the knuckle. It may be necessary to tap the spindle loose with a soft mallet.
7. Remove the caliper adapter from the knuckle.
8. Carefully pull the axle shaft from the housing.

To install:

9. Thoroughly clean and inspect all parts. Replace any worn or damaged parts. The axle U-joint can be rebuilt in the same manner as a driveshaft U-joint, explained above.
10. Install a new seal on the axle shaft stone shield with the lip facing the shaft splines.
11. Carefully slide the shaft into the housing, avoiding damage to the seal at the side gears.
12. Install the spindle and splash shield. Tighten the nuts to 30 ft. lbs. (40 Nm).
13. Install the hub/rotor assembly.
14. Install the spacer, drive gear and snapring.
15. Apply RTV sealant on the mating edge of the grease cap and install the cap.
16. Install the caliper adapter and torque the bolts to 85 ft. lbs. (115 Nm).
17. Install the inboard pad and caliper. Please refer to Section 9.
18. Install the wheels, lower the vehicle then, tighten the nuts to specification, refer to Section 8.

Models With Full–Time 4–Wheel Drive

1. Remove the wheel cover.
2. Remove the cotter pin and loosen the axle shaft nut.
3. Raise and support the front end on jackstands.
4. Remove the wheels.
5. Unbolt the caliper and support it out of the way. DO NOT DISCONNECT THE BRAKE LINE.
6. Remove the inboard brake pad.
7. Remove the axle shaft nut and washer.
8. Through the hole provided in the rotor, remove the 6 retainer bolts.
9. Position puller C–4358, or equivalent, over the wheel lugs and install the lug nuts. Tighten the main screw of the puller to remove the hub, bearings, retainer and outer seal as an assembly.
10. Remove the puller.
11. Remove the caliper adapter from the knuckle.
12. Place a prybar behind the inner axle shaft yoke and push the bearings out of the knuckle.
13. Some knuckles have an O-ring. If so, remove and discard it.
14. Carefully pull the axle shaft from the axle. Remove the seal and slinger from the shaft.
15. The U-joint can now be disassembled in the same manner as a driveshaft U-joint, explained earlier in this Section.

To install:

16. If you removed the brake dust shield, install it now. Torque the mounting bolts to 15 ft. lbs. (20 Nm).
17. Apply RTV silicone sealer to the sealing surfaces of the axle shaft.
18. Using a driver, install the slinger onto the shaft.
19. Install a new seal on the slinger with the lip towards the splines.

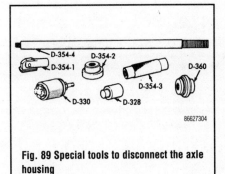

Fig. 89 Special tools to disconnect the axle housing

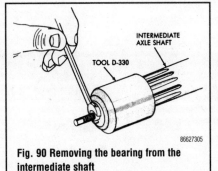

Fig. 90 Removing the bearing from the intermediate shaft

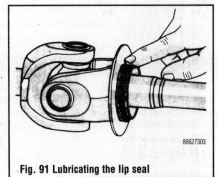

Fig. 91 Lubricating the lip seal

DRIVE TRAIN

20. Carefully insert the shaft into the axle housing, being careful to avoid damage to the differential side gear seal.
21. Insert a prybar though the U-joint and wedge the shaft inward as far as it will go. Make sure that it is wedged securely and can't be moved.
22. Using adapter tool C–4398–2 and driver, install the seal cup in the knuckle until it is bottomed. A small amount of wheel bearing grease on the adapter will help hold the cup in position. Leave the tool in position for the time being.
23. Apply a ¼ in. (6.3mm) bead of RTV sealant to the retainer face on the chamfer.
24. Carefully remove the seal installing tool so that the outer shaft remains centered.

➥If the shaft is touched, make sure that the seal lip is still riding inside the cup.

25. Position the bearing retainer on the knuckle so that the lube fitting is facing directly forward. **This is extremely important.**
26. Install the hub, rotor and bearing assembly, then torque the retainer bolts to 30 ft. lbs. (40 Nm) in a crisscross pattern.
27. Install the brake adapter. Torque the bolts to 85 ft. lbs. (115 Nm).
28. Remove the prybar from the U-joint.
29. Install the axle shaft nut and tighten it to 100 ft. lbs. (135 Nm), then continue tightening it to align the cotter pin holes. Install the cotter pin.
30. Using the lube fitting, fill the knuckle with multi–purpose EP grease until the grease is seen flowing through the inner seal.
31. Remove the grease gun and rotate the hub several times.
32. Install the grease gun and continue filling the knuckle until grease appears around at least 50% of the seal circumference.
33. Install the inner brake pad and caliper. Please refer to Section 9.
34. Install the wheels, lower the vehicle, then tighten the lug nuts to specification in Section 8.

Dana 60

1. Raise and support the front end on jackstands.
2. Remove the caliper from the knuckle and wire it out of the way.
3. Remove the locking hub.
4. Remove the front wheel bearing. See Section 1.
5. Remove the hub and rotor assembly.
6. Remove the spindle–to–knuckle bolts. Tap the spindle from the knuckle using a plastic mallet.
7. Remove the splash shield and caliper support.
8. Pull the axle shaft out through the knuckle.
9. Using a slide-hammer and bearing cup puller, remove the needle bearing from the spindle.
10. Clean the spindle bore thoroughly and make sure that it is free of nicks and burrs. If the bore is excessively pitted or scored, the spindle must be replaced.

To install:
11. Insert a new spindle bearing in its bore with the printing facing outward. Drive it into place with a driver. Install a new bearing seal with the lip facing away from the bearing.
12. Pack the bearing with waterproof wheel bearing grease.
13. Pack the thrust face of the seal in the spindle bore and the V–seal on the axle shaft with waterproof wheel bearing grease.
14. Carefully guide the axle shaft through the knuckle and into the housing. Align the splines and fully seat the shaft.
15. Place the bronze spacer on the shaft. The chamfered side of the spacer must be inboard.
16. Install the splash shield and caliper support.
17. Place the spindle on the knuckle and install the bolts. Torque the bolts to 50–60 ft. lbs. (67–81 Nm).
18. Install the hub/rotor assembly on the spindle.
19. Reinstall the caliper assembly on the knuckle.
20. Assemble the wheel bearings.
21. Assemble the locking hub.
22. Install the wheels, lower the vehicle, then tighten the lug nuts to specification in Section 8.

Dana 70 Dana F–375

1. Raise and support the front end on jackstands.
2. Remove the wheels.
3. Remove the brake drums. See Section 9.
4. Matchmark the drive flange and the hub.
5. Remove the nuts and lockwashers, then install puller screws using the 2 threaded holes in the flange.
6. Pull the flange from the hub.
7. Remove the hub and bearings.
8. Remove the attaching bolts and pull the brake supports from the knuckle. Wire them up and out of the way.
9. Using a soft mallet, tap the spindle from the knuckle.
10. Pull the short outer shaft and female section of the universal drive assembly from the axle housing.
11. Pull the male section and long inner shaft from the housing.
12. Discard all seals and seal bushings.

To install:
13. Thoroughly clean and inspect all parts.
14. Drive a new seal and bushing into the end of the housing. The seal lip should face inwards.
15. Pack the axle shaft U-joints with chassis lubricant. Install both the inner and outer axle shafts. Note that the shaft have numerical mating marks. Identical numbers should be mated during assembly.

➥On some axles the mating numbers are not identical. That's okay as long as the axle operates satisfactorily.

16. Position the spindle and brake supports on the knuckle. Install the bolts and lockwashers.
17. Pack the wheel bearings and coat the inside of the hubs with wheel bearing grease.
18. Adjust the wheel bearings by turning the inner adjusting nut tightly, then backing it off ⅙ turn.
19. Install the lockring making sure that the pin on the inner nut enters one of the holes in the lockring. It's okay to move the inner nut slightly to position the pin.
20. Install the outer nut and torque it to 50 ft. lbs. (68 Nm).
21. Install the drive flange, using a new gasket.
22. Coat the flange and drum contact surfaces with anti–seize compound and install the drum.
23. Install the wheels, lower the vehicle, then tighten the lug nuts to specification in Section 8.

Pinion Seal

REMOVAL & INSTALLATION

Dana 60, Dana 70, and Dana F–375

▶ See Figures 92, 93 and 94

➥A torque wrench capable of at least 300 ft. lbs. (406 Nm) is required for pinion seal installation.

1. Raise and support the truck on jackstands.
2. Allow the axle to hang freely.
3. Matchmark, then disconnect the driveshaft from the front axle.
4. Using a holding tool, secure the pinion flange while removing the pinion nut.
5. Using a puller, remove the pinion flange.
6. Use a puller to remove the seal, or drive the seal out using a pin punch.

To install:
7. Thoroughly clean the seal bore and make sure that it is not damaged in any way. Coat the sealing edge of the new seal with a small amount of 80W/90 oil and drive the seal into the housing using a seal driver.
8. Coat the inside of the pinion flange with clean 80W/90 oil and install the flange onto the pinion shaft.
9. Install the nut on the pinion shaft and tighten it to 250–300 ft. lbs. (338–406 Nm).
10. Connect the driveshaft.
11. Carefully lower the vehicle and remove the jackstands.

Dana 44

➥A torque wrench capable of at least 225 ft. lbs. (304 Nm) is required for pinion seal installation.

DRIVE TRAIN 7-33

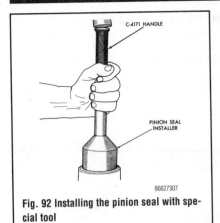

Fig. 92 Installing the pinion seal with special tool

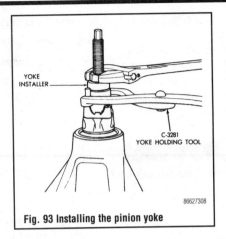

Fig. 93 Installing the pinion yoke

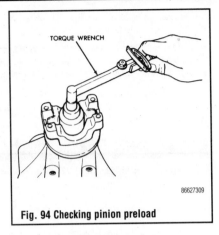

Fig. 94 Checking pinion preload

1. Raise and safely support the vehicle with jackstands under the frame rails. Allow the axle to drop to the rebound position for working clearance.
2. Mark the companion flanges and U-joints for correct reinstallation position.
3. Remove the driveshaft use a suitable tool to hold the companion flange. Remove the pinion nut and companion flange.
4. Use a slide-hammer and hook or sheet metal screw to remove the oil seal.

To install:

5. Install a new pinion seal after lubricating the sealing surfaces.
6. Use a suitable seal driver. Install the companion flange and pinion nut.
7. Tighten the nut to 200–220 ft. lbs. (271–298 Nm).

Axle Housing Unit

REMOVAL & INSTALLATION

1. Raise and support the front end on jackstands placed behind the springs.

2. Matchmark and disconnect the driveshaft at the axle flange.
3. On 1974 and later models, prop the brake pedal in the UP position.
4. On 1985 and later models, disconnect the vacuum lines and wire at the axle.
5. On the F–375, disconnect the steering arm at the left flange; on all other axles, disconnect the drag link at the knuckle.
6. Disconnect the shock absorbers from the axle.
7. Disconnect the sway bar.
8. Disconnect the brake line at the tee on the axle on the F–375; at the frame connector on all other axles.
9. Support the axle with a floor jack and remove the spring U-bolt nuts.
10. Lower the axle.
11. When installing the axle, lubricate all contact points with lithium grease, bleed the brakes, tighten the U-bolt nuts to 110 ft. lbs. (149 Nm); the shock absorbers to 55 ft. lbs. (74 Nm); the steering link to 60 ft. lbs. (81 Nm); the sway bar nuts to 200 ft. lbs. (271 Nm); the driveshaft nuts to 25 ft. lbs. (34 Nm).

➡ On castellated nuts, never back off the nut to align the cotter pin holes. Always us new cotter pins.

REAR AXLE

Identification

1967
- Chrysler semi-floating 8¾ in. ring gear—D100
- Dana 60 full-floating 9¾ in. ring gear—D200, W100 and W200
- Chrysler full-floating 9⅝ in. ring gear—WM300
- Dana 70 full-floating 10½ in. ring gear—D300 and W300

1968–71
- Chrysler semi-floating 8¾ in. ring gear—D100
- Dana 60 full-floating 9¾ in. ring gear—D200, W100 and W200
- Dana 70 full-floating 10½ in. ring gear—D300 and W300

1972–78
- Chrysler semi-floating 8⅜ in. ring gear—D100
- Chrysler semi-floating 8¾ in. ring gear—D100 and W100
- Chrysler semi-floating 9¼ in. ring gear—Ramcharger and Trail Duster
- Dana 60, 60HD full-floating 9¾ in. ring gear—D200 and W200
- Dana 70 full-floating 10½ in. ring gear—D300 and W300

1979
- Chrysler semi-floating 8⅜ in. ring gear—D100 and W100
- Chrysler semi-floating 9¼ in. ring gear—D100, W100, Ramcharger and Trail Duster
- Dana 60, 60HD full-floating 9¾ in. ring gear—D200 and W200
- Dana 70 full-floating 10½ in. ring gear—D300 and W300

1980
- Chrysler semi-floating 8⅜ in. ring gear—D150 and W100
- Chrysler semi-floating 9¼ in. ring gear—D150, W100, Ramcharger and Trail Duster
- Dana 60 full-floating 9¾ in. ring gear—D200 and W200
- Dana 70 full-floating 10½ in. ring gear—D300 and W300
- Dana 60HD full-floating 9¾ in. ring gear—D300

1981–83
- Chrysler semi-floating 8⅜ in. ring gear—D15 and, W150
- Chrysler semi-floating 9¼ in. ring gear—D150, W150, Ramcharger and Trail Duster
- Dana 60 full-floating 9¾ in. ring gear—D250 and W250
- Dana 70 full-floating 10½ in. ring gear—D350 and W350
- Dana 60HD full-floating 9¾ in. ring gear—D350

1984–88
- Chrysler semi-floating 8⅜ in. ring gear—D150 and W150
- Chrysler semi-floating 9$FR 1/4 in. ring gear—D150, W150, Ramcharger and Trail Duster
- Chrysler semi-floating 9¼ in. HD ring gear—D250 and W250
- Dana 60 full-floating 9¾ in. ring gear—D250 and W250
- Dana 70 full-floating 10½ in. ring gear—D350 and W350
- Dana 60HD full-floating 9¾ in. ring gear—D350

Determining Axle Ratio

An axle ratio is obtained by dividing the number of teeth on the drive pinion gear into the number of teeth on the ring gear. For instance, on a 4.11 ratio, the driveshaft will turn 4.11 times for every turn of the rear wheel. The most accurate way to determine the axle ratio is to drain the differential, remove the cover and count the number of teeth on the ring and pinion.

An easier method is to jack and support the vehicle so that both rear wheels are off the ground. Make a chalk mark on the rear wheel and the driveshaft. Block the front wheels and put the transmission in NEUTRAL. Turn the rear wheel one complete revolution and count the number of turns made by the driveshaft. The number of driveshaft rotations is the axle ratio. More accuracy

7-34 DRIVE TRAIN

can be obtained by going more than one tire revolution and dividing the result by the number of tire rotations.

➡ In order to rotate the driveshaft, 4wd vehicles must have their transfer cases set in Neutral or 2wd. On the full-time 4wd, you should raise and support the truck so all wheels are off the ground.

The axle ratio is also identified by the axle serial number prefix on the axle; the axle ratios are listed in dealer's parts books according to prefix number. Some axles have a tag on the cover.

Axle Shaft, Bearing and Seal

Before servicing any axle shafts, be sure to jack and support the truck so that both rear wheels are off the ground. This will ensure that the vehicle will not roll off the supports if the vehicle is equipped with a limited slip rear axle and one wheel is turned inadvertently.

REMOVAL & INSTALLATION

Chrysler 8¾ in. Axle

➡ Whenever this axle assembly is serviced, both the brake support plate gaskets and the inner axle shaft oil seal must be renewed.

1. Jack up the rear of the truck and remove the rear wheels.
2. Detach the clips which secure the brake drum to the axle shaft studs and remove the brake drum.
3. Remove the axle shaft retaining nuts through the access hole in the axle shaft flange. The right–side axle shaft has a threaded adjuster in the retainer plate and a lock under one of its studs which should be removed at this time.
4. Remove the parking brake strut.
5. Attach a suitable puller to the axle shaft flange and remove the axle shaft.
6. Remove the brake assembly from the axle housing.
7. Remove the axle shaft oil seal from the axle housing.

✴✴ WARNING

It is advisable to position some sort of protective sleeve over the axle shaft seal surface next to the bearing collar to protect the seal surface. Never use a torch or other heat source as an aid in removing any axle shaft components as this will result in serious damage to the axle assembly.

To install:

8. Wipe the axle housing seal bore clean. Install a new axle shaft oil seal.
9. Clean the axle shaft bearing cavity.
10. Grease and install the axle shaft bearing in the cavity. Be sure that the bearing is not cocked and that it is seated firmly against the shoulder.
11. Install the axle shaft bearing seal. It should be seated beyond the end of the flange face.
12. Insert the axle shaft, making sure that the splines do not damage the seal. Be sure that the splines are properly engaged with the differential side gear splines.
13. Install the C-locks in the grooves on the axle shafts. Pull the shafts outward so that the C-locks seat in the counterbore of the differential side gears.
14. Install the differential pinion shaft through the case and pinions. Install the lockscrew and secure it in position.
15. Clean the housing and gasket surfaces. Install the cover and a new gasket.
16. Install the wheels, lower the vehicle, then tighten the lug nuts to specification in Section 8.
17. Refill the axle with the specified lubricant.

➡ Replacement differential cover gaskets may not be available. The use of gel type, nonsticking sealant is recommended.

Chrysler 8⅜ in., 9¼ in. and 9¼ in. Heavy Duty Axles

▶ See Figures 95 thru 109

➡ There is no provision for axle shaft end-play adjustment on these axles.

1. Jack up the vehicle and remove the rear wheels.
2. Clean all dirt from the housing cover. Obtain a drain pan and place under rear axle.
3. Remove the fill plug and check to see if you need to replace it due to deterioration.
4. Loosen the few bottom bolts to drain some of the gear oil. Proceed by removing the housing cover completely.
5. Remove the brake drum.
6. Rotate the differential case until the differential pinion shaft lockscrew can be removed. Remove the lockscrew and pinion shaft.
7. Push the axle shafts toward the center of the vehicle and remove the C-locks from the grooves on the axle shafts.
8. Pull the axle shafts from the housing, being careful not to damage the bearing which remains in the housing.
9. Inspect the axle shaft bearings and replace any doubtful parts. Whenever the axle shaft is replaced, the bearings should also be replaced.
10. Remove the axle shaft seal from the bore in the housing, using the button end of the axle shaft.
11. Remove the axle shaft bearing from the housing. On the 8⅜ in. and 9¼ in. axle, use a slide hammer and adapter. On the 9¼ in. HD axle, use a puller such as C–4828. Do not reuse the bearing or the seal.
12. Check the bearing shoulder in the axle housing for imperfections. These should be corrected with a file.
13. Clean the axle shaft bearing cavity.

To install:

14. Grease and install the axle shaft bearing in the cavity. An installer tool is recommended, although a driver can be used. Be sure that the bearing is not cocked and that it is seated firmly against the shoulder.
15. Install the axle shaft bearing seal. It should be seated beyond the end of the flange face.
16. Insert the axle shaft, making sure that the splines do not damage the seal. Be sure that the splines are properly engaged with the differential side gear splines.
17. Install the C-locks in the grooves on the axle shafts. Pull the shafts outward so that the C-locks seat in the counterbore of the differential side gears.
18. Install the differential pinion shaft through the case and pinions. Install the lockscrew and secure it in position.
19. Clean the housing and gasket surfaces. Install the cover and a new gasket.
20. Install the wheels, lower the vehicle, then tighten the lug nuts to specification in Section 8.
21. Refill the axle with the specified lubricant.

➡ Replacement differential cover gaskets may not be available. The use of gel type nonsticking sealant is recommended.

Chrysler 9⅝ in. Axle

1. Jack up the vehicle and remove the rear wheels.
2. Remove the drum from the axle shaft.
3. Remove the axle shaft flange nuts.
4. Install puller screws in the threaded holes provided and tighten the screws to loosen the shaft.

➡ If threaded holes are not provided, rap the flange sharply with a soft mallet to loosen the shaft.

5. Pull the shaft from the housing.

To install:

6. Install the shaft into the housing.
7. Always use a new gasket coated with sealer.
8. Tighten the flange nuts to 30–35 ft. lbs. (40–47 Nm).
9. Install the brake drum.
10. Install the wheels, lower the vehicle, then tighten the lug nuts to specification in Section 8.

DRIVE TRAIN 7-35

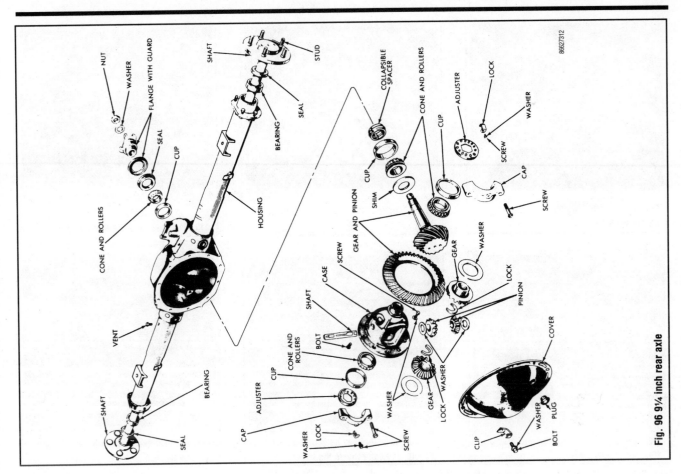

Fig. 96 9¼ inch rear axle

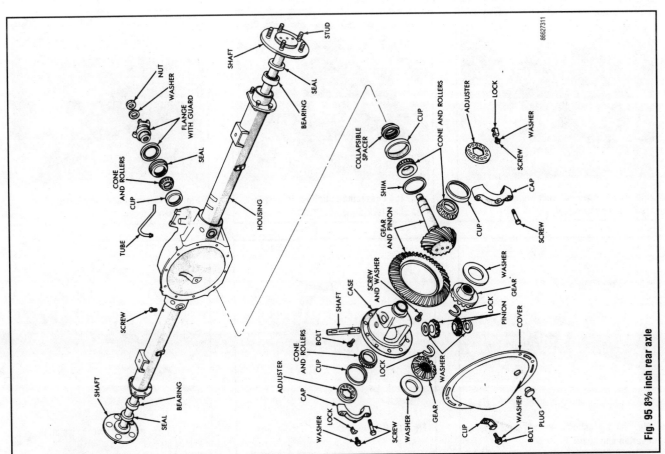

Fig. 95 8⅜ inch rear axle

7-36 DRIVE TRAIN

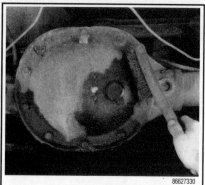
Fig. 97 Clean the outside of the cover before working

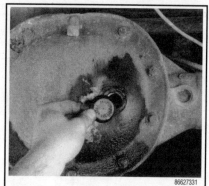
Fig. 98 Inspect the fill plug for deterioration

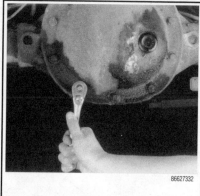
Fig. 99 Loosen the few lower bolts. . .

Fig. 100 . . . drain fluid, but make sure you have a pan ready

Fig. 101 Now that you have drained completely, you can remove the cover

Fig. 102 With the cover removed, the pinion and C-locks are now accessible

Fig. 103 You can use your fingers to remove the lockscrew

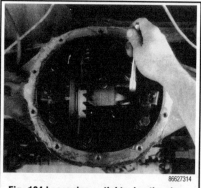
Fig. 104 Loosening or tightening the pinion shaft lockscrew

Fig. 105 Removal and installation of the axle shaft C-locks

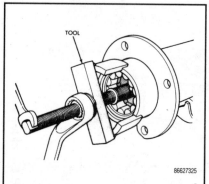
Fig. 106 9¼ inch HD removal of the axle bearing and seal

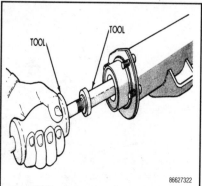
Fig. 107 Removing the axle bearing and seal

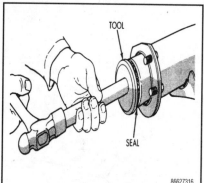
Fig. 108 Use a special tool to install the axle shaft seal

DRIVE TRAIN 7-37

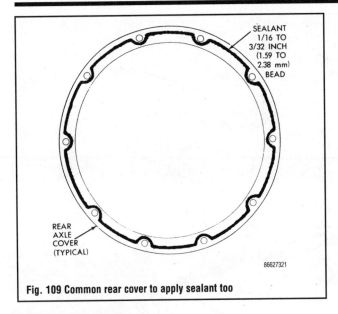

Fig. 109 Common rear cover to apply sealant too

Dana (Spicer) 60 and 70

1967–84 MODELS

♦ See Figures 110 and 111

1. Jack up the vehicle and remove the rear wheels.
2. Remove the drum from the axle shaft.
3. Remove the axle shaft flange nuts and washers.
4. Rap the axle shafts sharply in the center of the flange with a hammer to free the dowels.

To install:
5. Remove the tapered dowels and axle shafts. Some models are equipped with bolts rather than dowels.
6. Clean the gasket area with solvent and install a new flange gasket.

To install:
7. Install the axle shaft into the housing.
8. If the axle has an outer wheel bearing seal, install new gaskets on each side of the seal mounting flange.
9. Install the tapered dowels, lockwashers, and nuts. Tighten the nuts to 40–70 ft.lbs. (54–94 Nm) with 7/16 in. (11mm) studs and 65–105 ft.lbs. (88–142 Nm) with 1/2 in. (12mm). Some axles have bolts instead of studs and tapered dowels. Bolt torque is 45–75 ft.lbs. (61–101 Nm).
10. Install the brake drum.
11. Install the wheels, lower the vehicle, then tighten the lug nuts to specification in Section 8.

1985–88 MODELS

1. Jack up the vehicle and remove the rear wheels.
2. Remove the drum from the axle shaft.
3. Remove the axle shaft flange locknuts and washers, or bolts.
4. On axles with locknuts, rap the axle shafts sharply in the center of the flange with a hammer to free the dowels.
5. Remove the tapered dowels and/or axle shafts.

To install:
6. Clean the gasket area with solvent and install a new flange gasket.
7. Install the axle shaft into the housing.
8. If the axle has an outer wheel bearing seal, install new gaskets on each side of the seal mounting flange.
9. Install the tapered dowels, lockwashers, and nuts or Durlock® bolts. Tighten the 7/16–20 nuts to 40–70 ft. lbs. (54–94 Nm); the 1/2–20 nuts to 65–105 ft. lbs. (88–142 Nm) the Durlock® bolts to 60 ft. lbs. (81 Nm).
10. Install the brake drum.

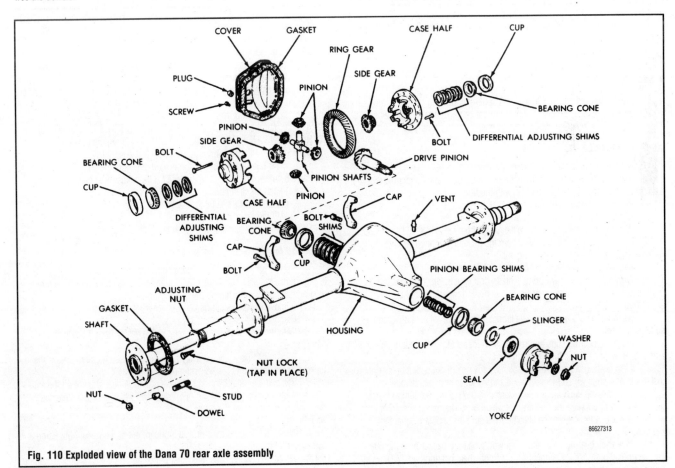

Fig. 110 Exploded view of the Dana 70 rear axle assembly

DRIVE TRAIN

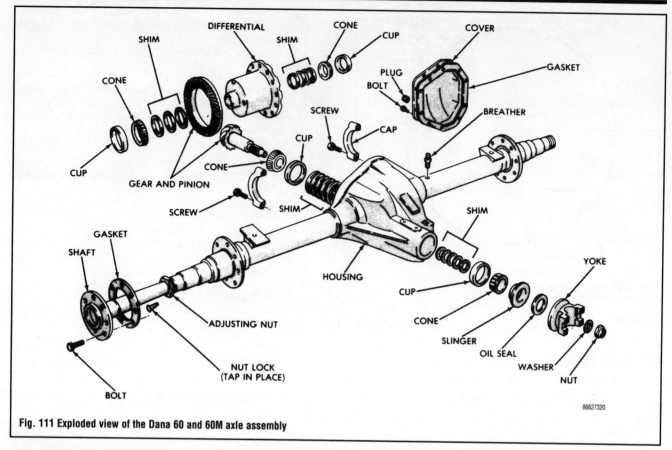

Fig. 111 Exploded view of the Dana 60 and 60M axle assembly

11. Install the wheels, lower the vehicle, then tighten the lug nuts to specification in Section 8.

Full-Floating Dana 60 and 70 Axles

♦ See Figures 112 and 113

The wheel bearings on the 200 and 300 series full floating rear axles are packed with wheel bearing grease. Axle lubricant can also flow into the wheel hubs and bearings, however, wheel bearing grease is the primary lubricant.

1967–84 MODELS

1. Set the parking brake and loosen the axle shaft bolts.
2. Raise the rear wheels off the floor and place jackstands under the rear axle housing so that the axle is parallel with the floor.
3. Remove the axle shaft bolts.
4. Remove the axle shaft and gaskets.
5. With the axle shaft out, remove the gasket from the axle shaft flange studs.
6. Bend the lockwasher tab away from the locknut, and then remove the locknut, lockwasher, and the adjusting nut.
7. Remove the outer bearing cone and pull the wheel straight off the axle.
8. With a piece of hardwood or a brass drift which will just clear the outer bearing cup, drive the inner bearing cone and inner seal out of the wheel hub.
9. Wash all the old grease or axle lubricant out of the wheel hub, using a suitable solvent.
10. Wash the bearing cups and rollers, then inspect them for pitting, galling, and uneven wear patterns. Inspect the roller for end wear.
11. If the bearing cups are to be replaced, drive them out with a brass drift. Install the new cups with a block of wood and hammer or press them in.
12. If the bearing cups are properly seated, a 0.0015 in. (0.038mm) feeler gauge will not fit between the cup and the wheel hub. The gauge should not fit beneath the cup. Check several places to make sure the cups are squarely seated.
13. Pack each bearing cone and roller with a bearing packer or in the manner previously outlined in Section 1 for the front wheel bearings on 2WD trucks. Use a multi-purpose wheel bearing grease.

14. Place the inner bearing cone and roller assembly in the wheel hub. Install a new inner seal in the hub with a seal installation tool.
15. Install the wheel.
16. Install the adjusting nut. For bearing adjustment proceed as followed:
    a. While rotating the wheel, tighten the adjusting nut until a slight drag is felt. Then, back off the nut ⅙ turn. This should give free rotation and little or no end-play.
    b. Install the lockring.
    c. Install the outer nut. MAKE SURE THAT THE ADJUSTING NUT DOES NOT TURN WHILE TIGHTENING THE OUTER NUT. Tighten the outer nut to 35–65 ft. lbs. (47–88 Nm).
    d. Bend one tab of the lockring inward to secure the adjusting nut and one tab outward to secure the outer nut. These tabs must be bent securely against a flat on each nut.
    e. Install the axle shaft and new gasket or seal.
17. Install the brake drum.
18. Remove the stands, lower the truck.

1985–88 MODELS

1. Set the parking brake and loosen the axle shaft bolts.
2. Raise the rear wheels off the floor and place jackstands under the rear axle housing so that the axle is parallel with the floor.
3. Remove the axle shaft bolts.
4. Remove the axle shaft and gaskets.
5. With the axle shaft removed, remove the gasket from the axle shaft flange studs.
6. Bend the lockwasher tab away from the locknut, and then remove the locknut, lockwasher, and the adjusting nut.
7. Remove the outer bearing cone and pull the wheel straight off the axle.
8. With a piece of hardwood or a brass drift which will just clear the outer bearing cup, drive the inner bearing cone and inner seal out of the wheel hub.
9. Wash all the old grease or axle lubricant out of the wheel hub, using a suitable solvent.
10. Wash the bearing cups and rollers, then inspect them for pitting, galling, and uneven wear patterns. Inspect the roller for end wear.

Drive Train 7-39

11. If the bearing cups are to be replaced, drive them out with a brass drift. Install the new cups with a block of wood and hammer or press them in.
12. If the bearing cups are properly seated, a 0.0015 in. (0.038mm) feeler gauge will not fit between the cup and the wheel hub. The gauge should not fit beneath the cup. Check several places to make sure the cups are squarely seated.
13. Pack each bearing cone and roller with a bearing packer or in the manner previously outlined for the front wheel bearings in Section 1 on 2WD trucks. Use a multi-purpose wheel bearing grease.
14. Place the inner bearing cone and roller assembly in the wheel hub. Install a new inner seal in the hub with a seal installation tool.
15. Install the wheel.
16. Install the adjusting nut. Proceed as follows to adjust the wheel bearings:
    a. While rotating the wheel, tighten the adjusting nut to 120–140 ft. lbs. (162–189 Nm).
    b. Back off the nut 1/3 turn (120°). This will provide 0.001–0.008 in. (0.02–0.20mm) end-play.
    c. Install the lockring onto the spindle keyway.
17. Install the axle shaft and new gasket.
18. Remove the stands, lower the truck.

Pinion Seal

REMOVAL & INSTALLATION

Chrysler 8¾ in. Axle

➡ An inch–pound torque wrench and a torque wrench capable of at least 200 ft. lbs. (271 Nm) are required for pinion seal installation.

1. Raise and safely support the vehicle with jackstands under the frame rails. Allow the axle to drop to the rebound position for working clearance.
2. Mark the companion flanges and U-joints for correct reinstallation position.
3. Remove the driveshaft.
4. Using an inch pound torque wrench and socket on the pinion yoke nut measure the amount of torque needed to maintain differential rotation through several clockwise revolutions. Record the measurement.

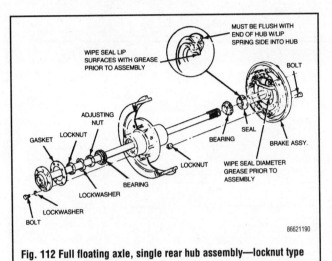

Fig. 112 Full floating axle, single rear hub assembly—locknut type

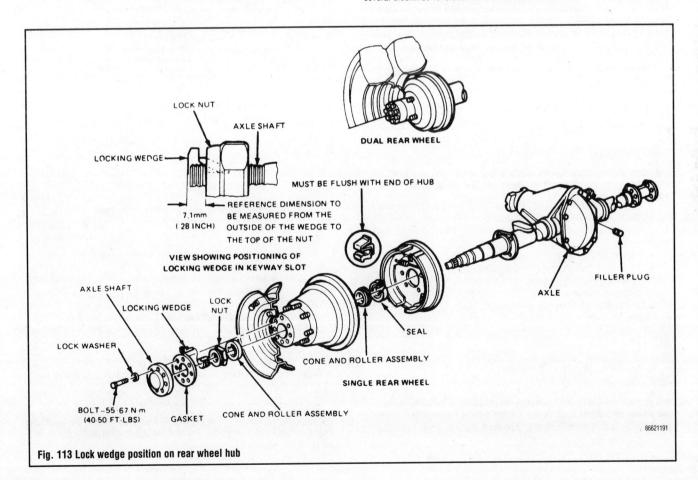

Fig. 113 Lock wedge position on rear wheel hub

DRIVE TRAIN

5. Use a suitable tool to hold the companion flange. Remove the pinion nut and washer.
6. Place a drain pan under the differential, clean the area around the seal, and mark the yoke–to–pinion relation.
7. Use a 2–jawed puller to remove the pinion.
8. Remove the seal with a small prybar.
9. Thoroughly clean the oil seal bore.

➡ If you are not absolutely certain of the proper seal installation depth, the proper seal driver must be used. If the seal is misaligned or damaged during installation, it must be removed and a new seal installed.

To install:
10. Drive the new seal into place with a seal driver. Coat the seal lip with clean, waterproof, wheel bearing grease.
11. Coat the splines with a small amount of wheel bearing grease and install the yoke, aligning the matchmarks. Never hammer the yoke onto the pinion.
12. Install a NEW nut on the pinion.
13. Secure the yoke with a holding tool. Tighten the pinion nut to 100 ft. lbs. (135 Nm). Take several readings using the inch–pound torque wrench. Continue tightening the nut until the original recorded preload reading is achieved.

➡ Under no circumstances should the preload be more than 5 inch lbs. (0.56 Nm) higher than the original reading.

14. Bearing preload should be uniform through several complete revolutions. If binding exists, the condition must be diagnosed and corrected. The assembly is unacceptable if the final pinion nut torque is below 170 ft. lbs. (230 Nm) or pinion bearing preload is not correct.

✳✳ WARNING

Under no circumstances should the nut be backed off to reduce the preload reading. If the preload is exceeded, the yoke and bearing must be removed and a new collapsible spacer must be installed. The entire process of preload adjustment must be repeated.

15. Install the driveshaft using the matchmarks. Tighten the nuts to 15 ft. lbs. (20 Nm).
16. Reinstall the rear brake drum. Install the wheels, then lower the vehicle.
17. Tighten the lug nuts to specification, refer to Section 8.

Chrysler 8⅜ in. and 9¼ in. Axles

▶ See Figures 114, 115 and 116

➡ An inch-pound torque wrench and a torque wrench capable of at least 250 ft. lbs. (338 Nm) are required for pinion seal installation.

1. Raise and safely support the vehicle with jackstands under the frame rails. Allow the axle to drop to the rebound position for working clearance.
2. Matchmark the companion flanges and U-joints for correct reinstallation position.
3. Remove the driveshaft.
4. Using an inch pound torque wrench and socket on the pinion yoke nut, measure the amount of torque needed to maintain differential rotation through several clockwise revolutions. Record the measurement.
5. Use a suitable tool to hold the companion flange. Remove the pinion nut and washer.
6. Place a drain pan under the differential, clean the area around the seal, and mark the yoke–to–pinion relation.
7. Use a 2–jawed puller to remove the pinion.
8. Remove the seal with a small prybar.
9. Thoroughly clean the oil seal bore.

➡ If you are not absolutely certain of the proper seal installation depth, the proper seal driver must be used. If the seal is misaligned or damaged during installation, it must be removed and a new seal installed.

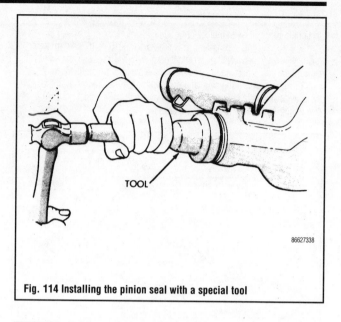

Fig. 114 Installing the pinion seal with a special tool

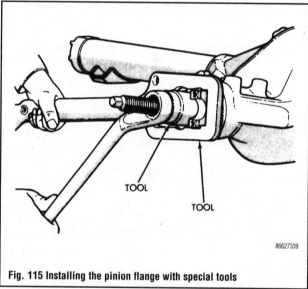

Fig. 115 Installing the pinion flange with special tools

To install:
10. Drive the new seal into place with a seal driver. Coat the seal lip with clean, waterproof wheel bearing grease.
11. Coat the splines with a small amount of wheel bearing grease and install the yoke, aligning the matchmarks. Never hammer the yoke onto the pinion.
12. Install a NEW nut on the pinion.
13. Secure the yoke with a holding tool. Tighten the pinion nut to 210 ft. lbs. (284 Nm). Take several readings using the inch–pound torque wrench. Continue tightening the nut until the original recorded preload reading is achieved.

➡ Under no circumstances should the preload be more than 5 inch lbs. (0.56 Nm) higher than the original reading.

14. Bearing preload should be uniform through several complete revolutions. If binding exists, the condition must be diagnosed and corrected. The assembly is unacceptable if the final pinion nut torque is below 210 ft. lbs. (284 Nm) or pinion bearing preload is not correct.

DRIVE TRAIN 7-41

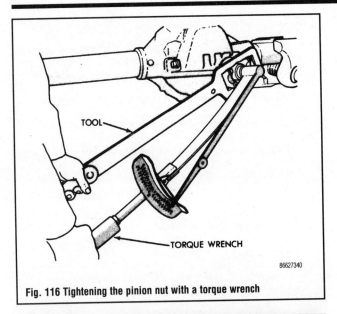

Fig. 116 Tightening the pinion nut with a torque wrench

✳✳ WARNING

Under no circumstances should the nut be backed off to reduce the preload reading. If the preload is exceeded, the yoke and bearing must be removed and a new collapsible spacer must be installed. The entire process of preload adjustment must be repeated.

15. Install the driveshaft using the matchmarks. Tighten the nuts to 15 ft. lbs. (20 Nm).
16. Reinstall the rear brake drum. Install the wheels, then lower the vehicle.
17. Tighten the lug nuts to specification, refer to Section 8.

Chrysler 9⅝ in. Axle

➡A torque wrench is capable of at least 350 ft. lbs. (474 Nm) which is required for the pinion seal installation.

1. Raise and safely support the vehicle with jackstands under the frame rails. Allow the axle to drop to the rebound position for working clearance.
2. Matchmark the companion flanges and U-joints for correct reinstallation position.
3. Remove the driveshaft.
4. Use a suitable tool to hold the companion flange. Remove the pinion nut and washer.
5. Place a drain pan under the differential, clean the area around the seal, and mark the yoke-to-pinion relation.
6. Use a 2-jawed puller to remove the pinion.
7. Remove the seal with a small prybar.
8. Thoroughly clean the oil seal bore.

➡If you are not absolutely certain of the proper seal installation depth, the proper seal driver must be used. If the seal is misaligned or damaged during installation, it must be removed and a new seal installed.

To install:
9. Drive the new seal into place with a seal driver. Coat the seal lip with clean, waterproof wheel bearing grease.
10. Coat the splines with a small amount of wheel bearing grease and install the yoke, aligning the matchmarks. Never hammer the yoke onto the pinion.
11. Install a NEW nut on the pinion.
12. Hold the yoke with a holding tool. Tighten the pinion nut to 325 ft. lbs. (440 Nm). Install a new cotter pin.

✳✳ WARNING

Under no circumstances should the nut be backed off to align the cotter pin hole.

13. Install the driveshaft using the matchmarks.
14. Reinstall the rear brake drum, install the wheels.
15. Lower the vehicle, then tighten the lug nuts to specification, refer to Chapter 8.

Dana (Spicer) 60 and 70

➡A torque wrench capable of at least 300 ft. lbs. (406 Nm) is required for pinion seal installation.

1. Raise and support the truck on jackstands.
2. Allow the axle to hang freely.
3. Matchmark and disconnect the driveshaft from the front axle.
4. Using a holding tool, secure the pinion flange while removing the pinion nut.
5. Using a puller, remove the pinion flange.
6. Use a puller to remove the seal, or punch the seal out using a pin punch.

To install:
7. Thoroughly clean the seal bore and make sure that it is not damaged in any way. Coat the sealing edge of the new seal with a small amount of 80W/90 oil and drive the seal into the housing using a seal driver.
8. Coat the inside of the pinion flange with clean 80W/90 oil and install the flange onto the pinion shaft.
9. Install the nut on the pinion shaft and tighten it to 250–300 ft. lbs. (338–406 Nm).
10. Connect the driveshaft.
11. Lower the vehicle.

Axle Housing Unit

REMOVAL & INSTALLATION

Chrysler 8⅜ in., 8¾ in., 9¼ in. and 9⅝ in. Axles

1. Raise and support the rear end on jackstands placed under the frame.
2. Prop the brake pedal in the UP position.
3. Remove the wheels and brake drums.
4. Disconnect the brake lines.
5. Disconnect the parking brake cables.
6. Matchmark the driveshaft and flange.
7. Disconnect the driveshaft at the flange and secure it out of the way.
8. Disconnect the shock absorbers at the axle.
9. Position a floor jack under the axle to take up the weight.
10. Remove the spring U-bolt nuts and lower the axle.

To install:
11. Raise the axle into position.
12. Install the spring U-bolt nuts.
13. Connect the shock absorbers at the axle. Tighten the nuts to 55 ft. lbs. (74 Nm).
14. Connect the driveshaft at the flange.
15. Connect the parking brake cables.
16. Connect the brake lines.
17. Install the wheels and brake drums.
18. Bleed the brakes.

Observe the following torques for U-bolt nuts:
- ½–20: 62–70 ft. lbs. (84–95 Nm)
- ¾–16: 175–225 ft. lbs. (237–304 Nm)
- 9⁄16–18: 120–130 ft. lbs. (162–176 Nm)
- ⅝–18: 175–200 ft. lbs. (237–271 Nm)

19. Lower the vehicle, tighten the lug nuts to specification, refer to Section 8.

Dana (Spicer) 60 and 70

1. Raise and support the rear end on jackstands placed under the frame.
2. Prop the brake pedal in the UP position.
3. Remove the axle shafts.
4. Remove the wheels and drums.
5. Disconnect the brake line and the flexible line connector.
6. Disconnect the parking brake cables.
7. Matchmark the driveshaft and flange.
8. Remove the driveshaft at the flange and position it out of the way.
9. Disconnect the shock absorbers at the axle.
10. Position a floor jack under the axle to take up the weight.
11. Remove the spring U-bolt nuts and lower the axle.

To install:

12. Raise the axle into position.
13. Install the spring U-bolt nuts. Tighten the nuts to 150–210 ft. lbs. (203–285 Nm).
14. Connect the shock absorbers at the axle. Tighten the nuts to 35–65 ft. lbs. (47–88 Nm).
15. Connect the driveshaft at the flange. Tighten the U-joint clamps to 170–200 inch lbs. (19–23 Nm).
16. Connect the parking brake cables.
17. Connect the brake lines.
18. Install the drums and wheels. On 60 series axles, torque the lug nuts to 225 ft. lbs. (305 Nm) for cone-shaped nuts; 325 ft. lbs. (440 Nm) for flanged nuts. On 70 series axles, torque the lug nuts to 400–450 ft. lbs. (542–609 Nm).
19. Remove the block from the brake pedal, and proceed to bleed the brakes.
20. Clean the axle gasket contact area. Installing a new flange gasket slide the axle shaft into the housing.
21. Install the tapered dowels, lockwashers and nuts. Tighten nuts to specifications.

Observe the following torques for tapered dowel nuts:
- 7/16–20: 40–70 ft. lbs. (54–95 Nm)
- 1/2–20: 65–105 ft. lbs. (88–142 Nm)

22. Refill the housing with fluid.
23. Install the wheels and brake drums.
24. Lower the vehicle, tighten the lug nuts to specification, refer to Section 8.

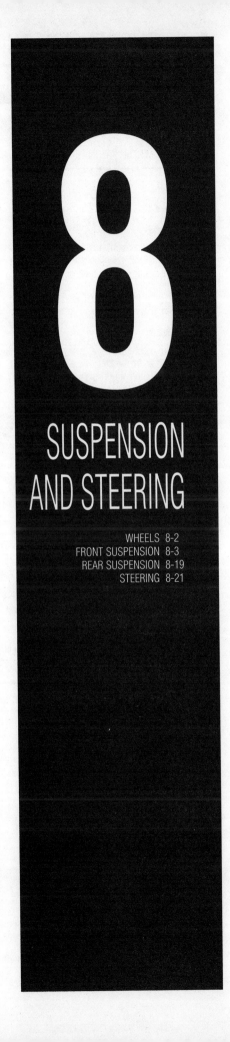

8 SUSPENSION AND STEERING

WHEELS 8-2
FRONT SUSPENSION 8-3
REAR SUSPENSION 8-19
STEERING 8-21

WHEELS 8-2
TIRES AND WHEELS 8-2
  REMOVAL & INSTALLATION 8-2
FRONT SUSPENSION 8-3
COIL SPRINGS 8-3
  REMOVAL & INSTALLATION 8-3
LEAF SPRINGS 8-4
  REMOVAL & INSTALLATION 8-4
SHOCK ABSORBER 8-5
  REMOVAL & INSTALLATION 8-5
  TESTING 8-7
UPPER BALL JOINT 8-8
  REMOVAL & INSTALLATION 8-8
LOWER BALL JOINT 8-8
  REMOVAL & INSTALLATION 8-8
SWAY BAR 8-9
  REMOVAL & INSTALLATION 8-9
UPPER CONTROL ARM 8-9
  REMOVAL & INSTALLATION 8-9
  CONTROL ARM BUSHING
    REPLACEMENT 8-9
LOWER CONTROL ARM 8-10
  REMOVAL & INSTALLATION 8-10
  CONTROL ARM BUSHING
    REPLACEMENT 8-10
LOWER CONTROL ARM STRUT 8-10
  REMOVAL & INSTALLATION 8-10
KNUCKLE AND SPINDLE—2WD 8-10
  REMOVAL & INSTALLATION 8-10
STEERING KNUCKLE AND BALL
  JOINTS—4WD 8-11
  REMOVAL & INSTALLATION 8-11
WHEEL ALIGNMENT 8-15
    CASTER 8-15
    CAMBER 8-15
    TOE 8-15
REAR SUSPENSION 8-19
LEAF SPRINGS 8-19
  REMOVAL & INSTALLATION 8-19
SHOCK ABSORBERS 8-20
  REMOVAL & INSTALLATION 8-20
  TESTING 8-21
STEERING 8-21
STEERING WHEEL 8-21
  REMOVAL & INSTALLATION 8-21
TURN SIGNAL SWITCH 8-22
  REMOVAL & INSTALLATION 8-22
IGNITION SWITCH 8-22
  REMOVAL & INSTALLATION 8-22
IGNITION LOCK CYLINDER 8-24
  REMOVAL & INSTALLATION 8-24
STEERING LINKAGE 8-24
  REMOVAL & INSTALLATION 8-24
MANUAL STEERING GEAR 8-26
    ADJUSTMENTS 8-26
    REMOVAL & INSTALLATION 8-28
POWER STEERING GEAR 8-30
    ADJUSTMENTS 8-30
    REMOVAL & INSTALLATION 8-31
POWER STEERING PUMP 8-31
  REMOVAL & INSTALLATION 8-31
SPECIFICATIONS CHARTS
WHEEL ALIGNMENT
  SPECIFICATIONS 8-17

8-2 SUSPENSION AND STEERING

WHEELS

Tires and Wheels

REMOVAL & INSTALLATION

Front Wheels

♦ See Figure 1

2WD MODELS

When changing a front wheel, place a jack under the inner edge of the lower control arm pivot bolt mounting bracket. Make sure the jack is centered for your safety. Before raising the tire off the ground, make sure you loosen the lug nuts. Raise the wheel off the ground, then remove the lug nuts and the wheel. Mount the spare wheel onto the axle and partially tighten the lug nuts (enough to keep the wheel on). Lower the truck and tighten the lug nuts to their specified torque.

4WD MODELS

When changing a front wheel, place a jack under the outside of the spring mounting bracket. Be certain the jack is centered under the axle. Before raising the tire off the ground, make sure you loosen the lug nuts. Raise the wheel off the ground, then remove the lug nuts and the wheel. Mount the spare wheel onto the axle and partially tighten the lug nuts (enough to keep the wheel on). Lower the truck and tighten the lug nuts to specified torque.

Rear Wheels

EXCEPT DUAL

On rear wheels, place the jack under the axle and next to the spring hanger. Before raising the tire off the ground make sure you loosen the lug nuts. Raise the wheel off the ground, then remove the lug nuts and the wheel. Mount the spare wheel onto the axle and partially tighten the lug nuts (enough to keep the wheel on). Lower the truck and tighten the lug nuts to their specified torque.

8-STUD DUAL REAR WHEELS WITH FLANGED WHEEL NUTS

♦ See Figures 2 and 3

These wheels have 4 equally spaced stud holes which are coined outwards, and 4 which are coined inwards. The outer wheel must be installed so the coined stud holes match the coined stud holes of the inner wheel.

There is a locating pin in the hub that will assist in correctly orienting the inner and outer wheels. The tires of both dual wheels must be completely off the

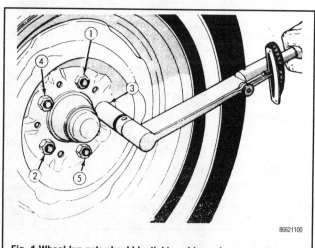

Fig. 1 Wheel lug nuts should be tightened in a crisscross pattern

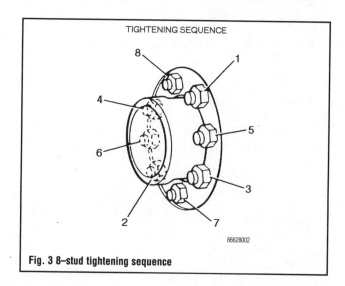

Fig. 3 8–stud tightening sequence

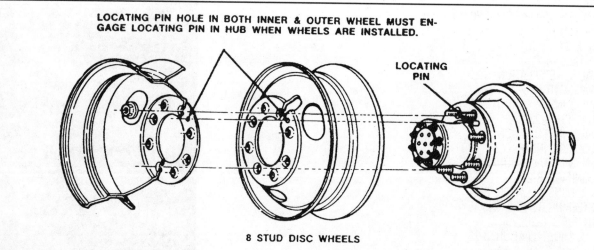

Fig. 2 8–stud dual wheels; notice the locating pin

SUSPENSION AND STEERING

ground when tightening to insure wheel centering and maximum wheel clamping.

Tighten these wheels as follows:
1. Tighten the lug nuts in the numbered order to a snug fit.
2. Retighten the lug nuts in the same sequence to the specified torque. Go through the sequence a second time to ensure the specific torque. Retighten to specifications at 100 miles (160 km), then again at 500 miles (800 km).

It is recommended that lug nuts be kept torqued to specifications at all times. Torque lug nuts to specifications at each lubrication interval. It is also advisable to keep a tire pressure gauge in your truck at all times, and to check the inflation pressure on a regular basis. For further information on tires and wheels, please refer to Section 1 of this manual.

Lug Nut Tightening Specifications:
- 1967: 65 ft. lbs. (89 Nm)
- 1968–69: 75 ft. lbs. (102 Nm)
- 1970–71: 80 ft. lbs. (109 Nm)
- 1972–74: 65–85 ft. lbs. (89–116 Nm)
- 1975–84: 85–125 ft. lbs. (116–170 Nm)
- 1985–88: 85–110 ft. lbs. (116–150 Nm)
- 1982–88 350 with H.D. axle (cone nut): 175–225 ft. lbs. (238–306 Nm)
- 1986–88 350 with H.D. axle (Flanged nut): 300–350 ft. lbs. (408–476 Nm)

FRONT SUSPENSION

Coil Springs

REMOVAL & INSTALLATION

1972–74 Models

1. Loosen the wheel lug nuts.
2. Raise the vehicle and safely support it with jackstands under the front ends of the frame rails.
3. Remove the wheel.

➡ It is advisable to spray the bolts and nuts with penetrating oil, then allow them to sit for a few minutes.

4. Remove the shock absorber and upper shock absorber bushing and sleeve.
5. If equipped, remove the sway bar.
6. Remove the lower control arm strut.
7. Install a spring compressor finger-tight.
8. Remove the cotter pins and ball joint nuts.
9. Install a ball joint breaker tool and turn the threaded portion of the tool to lock it against the lower stud.
10. Spread the tool to place the lower stud under pressure, then strike the steering knuckle sharply with a hammer to free the stud. Do not attempt to force the stud out of the steering knuckle with the tool.
11. Remove the tool. Slowly release the spring compressor until all tension is relieved from the spring.
12. Remove the spring compressor and spring.

To install:
13. Position the spring on the control arm and install the compressor.
14. Compress the spring until the ball joint is properly positioned.
15. Install the ball joint nuts and tighten them to 135 ft. lbs. (183 Nm) for 100 and 200 series; 175 ft. lbs. (237 Nm) for 300 series.
16. Install the strut. Tighten the mounting bolts to 85 ft. lbs. (115 Nm); the retainer nut to 50 ft. lbs. (68 Nm).
17. Connect the sway bar and tighten the link to 100 inch lbs. (11 Nm).
18. Remove the spring compressor.
19. Install the shock absorber. Tighten the upper end to 25 ft. lbs. (33 Nm); the lower end to 15 ft. lbs. (20 Nm).
20. Install the wheels.

1975–88 Models

▶ See Figure 4

1. Loosen the wheel lug nuts.
2. Block the brake pedal in the UP position.
3. Raise and safely support the front end on jackstands placed under the frame.
4. Remove the wheels.

➡ It is advisable to spray the bolts and nuts with penetrating oil, then allow them to sit for a few minutes.

5. Remove the brake calipers and suspend them out of the way. DO NOT DISCONNECT THE BRAKE LINE, AND DO NOT LET THE CALIPER HANG FROM THE HOSE!
6. Remove the hub/rotor assembly. Do not drag the seal or inner bearing over the steering knuckle thread, it will damage the parts.
7. Remove the brake splash shield.
8. Remove the shock absorbers.
9. Disconnect the sway bar.
10. Remove the lower control arm strut.
11. Install a spring compressor, such as tool DD-1278 or equivalent, finger-tighten the nut, then back it off ½ turn.
12. Remove the cotter pins and ball joint nuts.
13. Using ball joint separator C–3564–A, or equivalent, spread the tool against the lower joint just enough to exert pressure, then strike the knuckle sharply with a hammer to free the joint. NEVER ATTEMPT TO FORCE THE BALL JOINT OUT WITH TOOL PRESSURE ALONE! Remove the tool.
14. Slowly loosen the spring compressor until all tension is relieved from the coil.
15. Remove the compressor and spring.
16. Position the spring on the control arm and install the compressor.

To install:
17. Compress the spring until the ball joint is properly positioned.
18. Install the ball joint nuts and tighten them to 135 ft. lbs. (183 Nm) for 100 and 200 series vehicles; 175 ft. lbs. (237 Nm) for 300 series vehicles.
19. Install the strut. Tighten the mounting bolts to 85 ft. lbs. (115 Nm); the retainer nut to 50 ft. lbs. (58 Nm).
20. Connect the sway bar and tighten the link to 100 inch lbs. (11 Nm).
21. Remove the spring compressor.
22. Install the shock absorber. Tighten the upper end to 25 ft. lbs. (33 Nm); the lower end to 15 ft. lbs. (20 Nm).
23. Install the brake splash shield. Tighten the bolts to 15 ft. lbs. (20 Nm).
24. Install the rotor/hub assembly. Tighten the adjusting nut to 30–40 ft. lbs. (40–54 Nm) while rotating the rotor. Back off the nut to completely release bearing preload. Finger-tighten the nut, then install the locknut and new cotter pin.

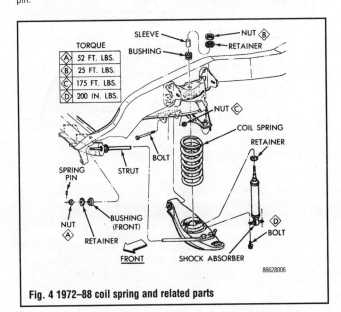

Fig. 4 1972–88 coil spring and related parts

8-4 SUSPENSION AND STEERING

25. Clean grease cap, lightly coat inside with wheel bearing lubricant, then install the cap.
26. Install the brake caliper.
27. Install the wheels.
28. Lower the vehicle, test drive operation.

Leaf Springs

REMOVAL & INSTALLATION

2WD Models

▶ See Figures 5 and 6

1. Raise and safely support the front end on jackstands placed under the frame. The wheels should still be on the ground, but the weight should be off of the springs.

➡ It is advisable to spray the bolts and nuts with penetrating oil, then allow them to sit for a few minutes.

2. Remove the nuts, lockwashers and U-bolts securing the spring to the axle.
3. Remove the spring shackle bolts, shackles and front eye bolt.
4. Remove the spring.

To install:
5. Position the spring in place and install the eye bolt and nut. Do not tighten the bolt yet.
6. Install the shackles and bolts. Tighten them just enough to make them snug.
7. Make sure that the spring center bolt enters the locating hole in the axle pad.
8. Install the U-bolts, lockwashers and nuts. Make them just snug for now.
9. Lower the truck to its normal position with the weight back on the springs. Now tighten all bolts and nuts as follows:
- 1/2–20 U-bolt nuts: 60–70 ft. lbs. (81–94 Nm)
- 3/4–16 U-bolt nuts: 175–225 ft. lbs. (237–304 Nm)
- 9/16–18 U-bolt nuts: 120–130 ft. lbs. (162–176 Nm)
- 5/8–18 U-bolt nuts: 175–200 ft. lbs. (237–271 Nm)
- 13/32–20 shackle bolts: 35–40 ft. lbs. (47–54 Nm)
- 7/16–20 shackle bolts: 45–50 ft. lbs. (61–67 Nm)
- Eye bolt: 150–175 ft. lbs. (203–237 Nm)

4WD Models

▶ See Figures 7 thru 12

1. Raise and safely support the front end on jackstands placed under the frame. The wheels should still be on the ground, but the weight should be off of the springs.

➡ It is advisable to spray the bolts and nuts you are working on with penetrating oil, then allow them to sit for a few minutes.

2. Remove the nuts, lockwashers and U-bolts securing the spring to the axle.
3. Remove the spring shackle bolts, shackles and front eye bolt.
4. Remove the spring.
5. Position the spring in place and install the eye bolt and nut. Do not tighten the bolt yet.
6. Install the shackles and bolts. Tighten them just enough to make them snug.
7. Make sure that the spring center bolt enters the locating hole in the axle pad.
8. Install the U-bolts, lockwashers and nuts. Make them just snug for now.
9. Lower the truck to its normal position with the weight back on the springs. Now tighten all bolts and nuts as follows:

1967–68 Models
- 1/2–20 U-bolt nuts: 60–70 ft. lbs. (81–94 Nm)
- 3/4–16 U-bolt nuts: 175–225 ft. lbs. (237–304 Nm)
- 9/16–18 U-bolt nuts: 120–130 ft. lbs. (162–176 Nm)
- 5/8–18 U-bolt nuts: 175–200 ft. lbs. (237–271 Nm)
- 13/32–20 shackle bolts: 35–40 ft. lbs. (47–54 Nm)
- 7/16–20 shackle bolts: 45–50 ft. lbs. (61–67 Nm)
- Eye bolt: 150–175 ft. lbs. (203–237 Nm)

1969–73 Models
- U-bolt nuts: 80 ft. lbs. (108 Nm)
- Upper shackle bolts: 100–150 ft. lbs. (135–203 Nm)
- Lower shackle bolts: 65–105 ft. lbs. (88–142 Nm)

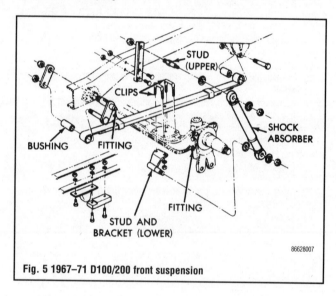

Fig. 5 1967–71 D100/200 front suspension

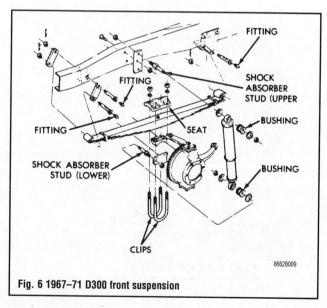

Fig. 6 1967–71 D300 front suspension

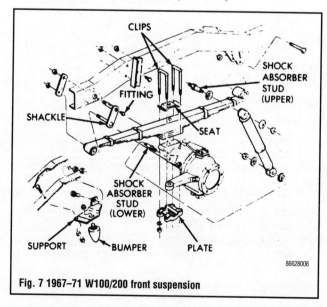

Fig. 7 1967–71 W100/200 front suspension

SUSPENSION AND STEERING 8-5

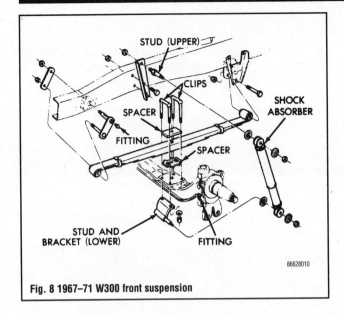

Fig. 8 1967–71 W300 front suspension

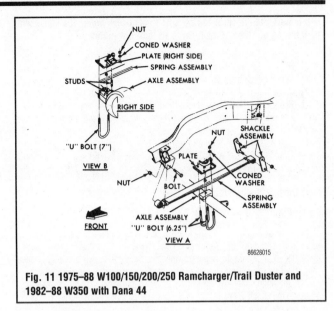

Fig. 11 1975–88 W100/150/200/250 Ramcharger/Trail Duster and 1982–88 W350 with Dana 44

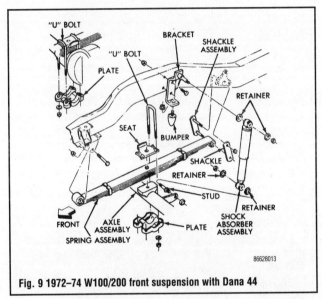

Fig. 9 1972–74 W100/200 front suspension with Dana 44

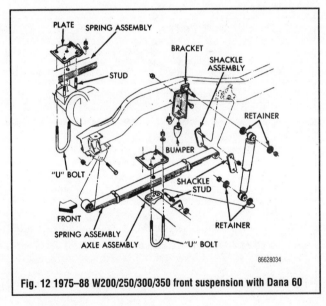

Fig. 12 1975–88 W200/250/300/350 front suspension with Dana 60

- Eye bolt:
- Except W300—65–105 ft. lbs. (88–142 Nm)
- W300—5–25 ft. lbs. (6–33 Nm)

1974–78 Models
- U-bolt nuts: 110 ft. lbs. (149 Nm)
- Shackle bolts: 80 ft. lbs. (108 Nm)
- Eye Bolt: 80 ft. lbs. (108 Nm)

1979–88 Models
- U-bolt nuts: 95 ft. lbs. (128 Nm)
- Shackle bolts: 80 ft. lbs. (108 Nm)
- Eye bolt: 80 ft. lbs. (108 Nm)

Shock Absorber

REMOVAL & INSTALLATION

Coil Spring Suspension

1. Loosen the wheel lug nuts.
2. Raise and safely support the vehicle with jackstands positioned at the extreme front ends of the frame rails.
3. Remove the wheel.

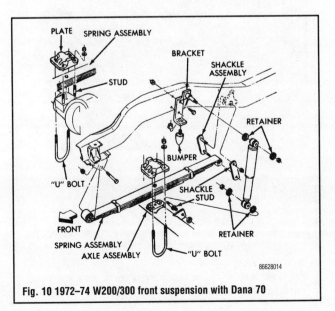

Fig. 10 1972–74 W200/300 front suspension with Dana 70

8-6 SUSPENSION AND STEERING

➡ It is advisable to spray the bolts and nuts which mount the shock with penetrating oil, then allow them to sit for a few minutes.

4. Remove the upper nut and retainer.
5. Remove the two lower mounting bolts.
6. Remove the shock absorber.

To install:

7. Replace the shock absorber with washers on the upper and lower bolts. Make sure the upper bushings are in the correct position, and replace any worn or cracked bushing.
8. Install the nuts.
9. Tighten the upper nut to 25 ft. lbs. (33 Nm). Then, tighten the lower bolts to 15 ft. lbs. (20 Nm).

Leaf Spring Suspension

♦ See Figures 13 thru 21

On most of the late model trucks covered by this manual, the shock absorber upper end is fastened to a removable bracket. Because this bracket may be easily damaged, it should be inspected whenever the shocks are removed. If necessary, this bracket is easily removed with the shock absorber for replacement.

1. Although not always necessary, removing the wheel will provide easier access to the shock. If this is desired, loosen the lug nuts before raising the vehicle.
2. Raise and safely support the truck.
3. If necessary, remove the wheel for access.

➡ It is advisable to spray the bolts and nuts which mount the shock with penetrating oil, then allow them to sit for a few minutes.

4. For late model vehicles on which the bracket is to be removed, loosen BUT DO NOT REMOVE, the bracket retainers at this time.
5. Remove the mounting nut and washer from the top of the shock.
6. Remove the lower nut, stud and washers from the bottom of the shock.
7. Remove the shock absorber from the vehicle.
8. If necessary on late model trucks, remove the fasteners which were loosened earlier and remove the shock upper mounting bracket from the truck.

To install:

9. Inspect the jounce bumper for wear or damage and replace, if necessary.
10. Replace any worn or cracked bushings, these should be supplied with the new shock absorber.
11. If removed on late model trucks, install the upper mounting bracket to the vehicle and tighten the retainers.
12. Position the shock absorber on the vehicle, then install the washers and nuts. Tighten the nuts to 50 ft. lbs. (67 Nm).

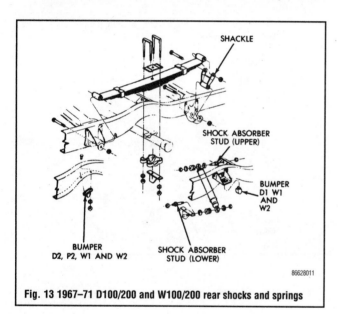

Fig. 13 1967–71 D100/200 and W100/200 rear shocks and springs

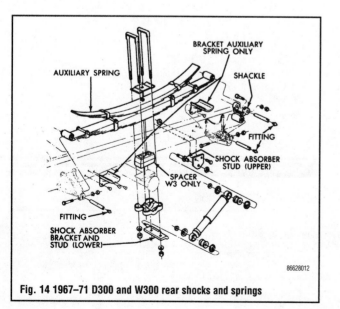

Fig. 14 1967–71 D300 and W300 rear shocks and springs

Fig. 15 Although not always necessary, removing the wheel makes access to the shock easier

SUSPENSION AND STEERING 8-7

➡ To help prevent possible damage to shock absorber bushings, always hold a movable stud (using a wrench on the rear nut or a flat on the stud itself) when tightening shock retainer.

13. If removed, install the wheel.
14. Remove the jackstands and carefully lower the vehicle.

TESTING

♦ See Figure 22

1. Remove the shock absorber from the truck.
2. To remove entrapped air from the cylinder, do the following:

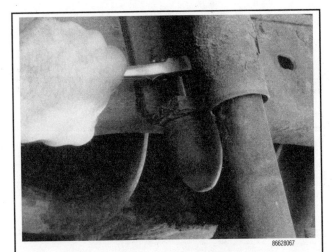

Fig. 16 The jounce bumper found on late model shock brackets may be easily replaced without removing the shock

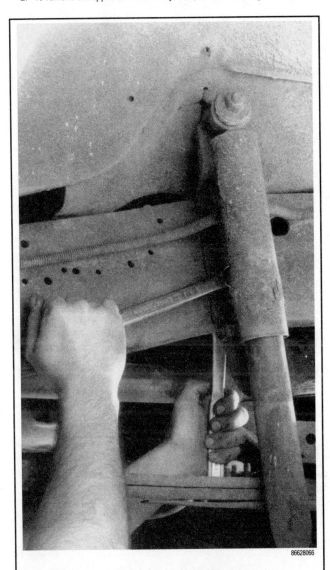

Fig. 18 If you are removing the upper bracket (on late model trucks), loosen the retainers before shock removal

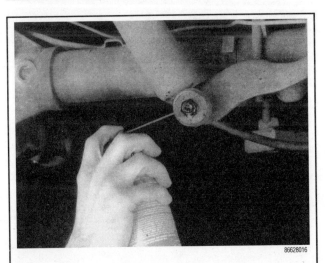

Fig. 17 Always spray fasteners with penetrating oil before you start a job—This will make the job much easier

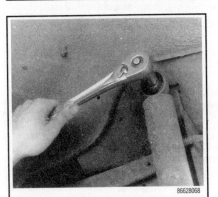

Fig. 19 Loosen the nut using a ratchet . . .

Fig. 20 . . . remove the nut and washer . . .

Fig. 21 . . . then remove the shock absorber

8-8 SUSPENSION AND STEERING

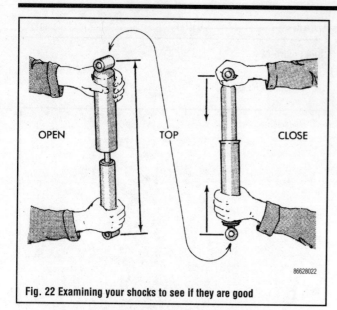

Fig. 22 Examining your shocks to see if they are good

    a. Hold the shock upright and open to its full extension.
    b. Invert the shock and slowly collapse until the piston bottoms.
    c. Repeat steps a and b several times.
  3. Clamp the lower end of the shock in a vise in the upright position.
  4. Open and close the shock several times.
  5. A good shock will have an even, steady resistance in both directions.
  6. If you have little or no resistance in your shocks, replace them.

Upper Ball Joint

REMOVAL & INSTALLATION

♦ See Figure 23

  1. Loosen the wheel lug nuts.
  2. Install a jack under the outer end of the lower control arm and raise the vehicle.
  3. Remove the wheel.

➡ It is advisable to spray the bolts and nuts you are working on with penetrating oil, then allow them to sit for a few minutes.

  4. Remove the ball joint nuts. Using a ball joint breaker, loosen the upper ball joint.

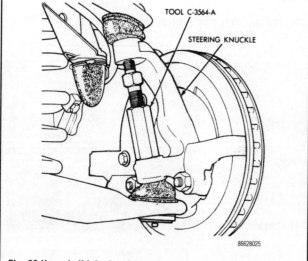

Fig. 23 Use a ball joint breaker tool to loosen the upper ball joint

  5. Unscrew the ball joint from the control arm.
To install:
  6. Screw a new ball joint into the control arm and tighten to 125 ft. lbs. (169 Nm). Be sure the ball joint is seated fully against the arm.
  7. Install the new ball joint seal, using a 2 in. socket. Be sure that the seal is seated on the ball joint housing.
  8. Insert the ball joint into the steering knuckle and install the ball joint nuts. Tighten the nuts to 135 ft. lbs. (183 Nm) for all but the 1972–74 300 series. On 1972–74 300 series, the torque is 175 ft. lbs. (237 Nm). Install the cotter pins.
  9. Install the wheel, then lower the truck to the ground.

Lower Ball Joint

REMOVAL & INSTALLATION

♦ See Figures 24 and 25

  1. Remove the lower control arm.
  2. Remove the ball joint seal.
  3. Using tool C–4212 or an arbor press and a sleeve, press the ball joint from the control arm.

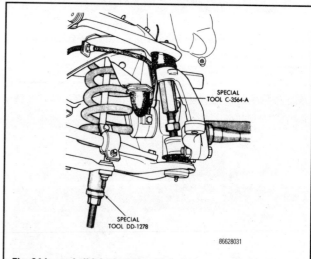

Fig. 24 Lower ball joint breaker with spring compressor tools installed

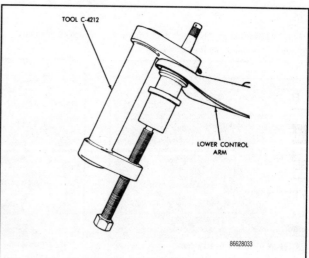

Fig. 25 The lower ball joint can be pressed in and out of the control arm using special tools

SUSPENSION AND STEERING

To install:

4. Press the new ball joint into the lower control arm using the tool C-4212 or equivalent.
5. Place a new seal over the ball joint, if necessary, with adapter tool C-4034.
6. Press the retainer portion of the seal down onto the ball joint housing until it is secure.
7. Install the lower control arm. Be sure to install the ball joint cotter pins.

Sway Bar

REMOVAL & INSTALLATION

▶ See Figure 26

1. Disconnect the bar at each end link.
2. Remove the bolts from the frame mounting brackets.
3. Remove the sway bar.

To install:

4. Position the bar on the frame mounting brackets.
5. Tighten the frame bracket bolts to 23 ft. lbs. (31 Nm); the end links to 100 inch lbs. (11 Nm).

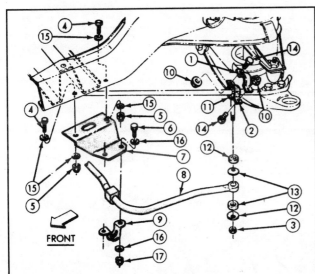

1. Retainer
2. Link assembly
3. Nut
4. Bolt
5. Lock nut
6. Bolt
7. Bracket
8. Shaft assembly
9. Retainer
10. Nut
11. Insulator
12. Retainer
13. Insulator
14. Bolt
15. Coned washer
16. Coned washer
17. Lock nut

Fig. 26 Sway bar and related parts

Upper Control Arm

REMOVAL & INSTALLATION

▶ See Figure 27

➡ Any time the control arm is removed, it is necessary to align the front end.

1. Loosen the wheel lug nuts.
2. Raise and safely support the vehicle with jackstands under the frame rails.
3. Remove the wheel.

➡ It is always advisable to spray the bolts and nuts your working on with penetrating oil and allow it to sit for a few minutes.

4. Remove the shock absorber as well as the upper bushing and sleeve.
5. Install a spring compressor and finger-tighten it, then back off ½ turn.
6. Remove the cotter pins and ball joint nuts.
7. Install a ball joint breaker C-3564-A, or equivalent, then turn the threaded portion of the tool, locking it securely against the upper stud. Spread the tool enough to place the upper ball joint under pressure, then strike the steering knuckle sharply to loosen the stud. Do not attempt to remove the stud from the steering knuckle with the tool.
8. Remove the tool.
9. Remove the eccentric pivot bolts, after marking their relative positions in the control arm.
10. Remove the upper control arm.

To install:

11. Install the upper control arm.
12. Install the pivot bolts and finger-tighten them for now.
13. Position the spring on the control arm and install the compressor.
14. Compress the spring until the ball joint is properly positioned.
15. Install the ball joint nuts and tighten them to 135 ft. lbs. (183 Nm) for all except 1972-74 300 series trucks. For 1972-74 300 series trucks, the torque is 175 ft. lbs. (237 Nm).
16. Install new cotter pins.
17. Remove the spring compressor.
18. Install the shock absorber. Tighten the upper end to 25 ft. lbs. (33 Nm); the lower end to 15 ft. lbs. (20 Nm).
19. Install the wheels.
20. Lower the truck to the ground.
21. Tighten the pivot bolts to 70 ft. lbs. (94 Nm).
22. Have the front end alignment checked.

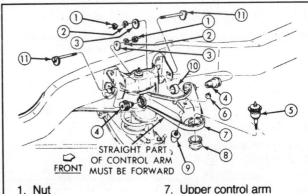

1. Nut
2. Lockwasher
3. Cam
4. Bushing assembly
5. Ball joint
6. Lock nut
7. Upper control arm
8. Upper ball joint
9. Bumper assembly
10. Sleeve
11. Cam and bolt assembly

Fig. 27 Exploded view of the upper control arm components—1972-88 vehicles

CONTROL ARM BUSHING REPLACEMENT

▶ See Figure 28

1. Remove the upper control arm.
2. Place the control arm in a vise and assemble tool C-3952 and adapter SP-3953 or equivalent, over the bushing, then press the bushing out of the arm.
3. When installing the new bushing, be sure the control arm is supported squarely at the point where the bushing is being pressed in.

➡ Do not use grease or oil to aid in installation.

8-10 SUSPENSION AND STEERING

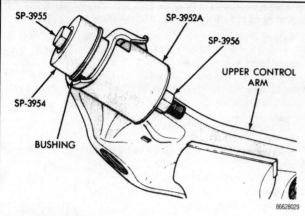

Fig. 28 The control arm bushing can be pressed in or out of the arm using special tools

4. Position the flange of the new bushing in tool C-3962 or equivalent, then support the arm and press the bushing into the control arm from the outside. Do this until the tapered portion seats on the arm.
5. Install the control arm on the truck.

Lower Control Arm

REMOVAL & INSTALLATION

♦ See Figure 29

1. Remove the coil spring, as described earlier in this section.

➡It is advisable to spray the bolts and nuts you are working on with penetrating oil, then allow them to sit for a few minutes.

2. Remove the mounting bolt from the crossmember.
3. Remove the lower control arm from the vehicle.

To install:

4. Install the lower control arm.
5. Fasten the crossmember bolt finger-tight.
6. Install the coil spring assembly.
7. After the vehicle has been lowered to the ground, tighten the mounting bolt to specifications.

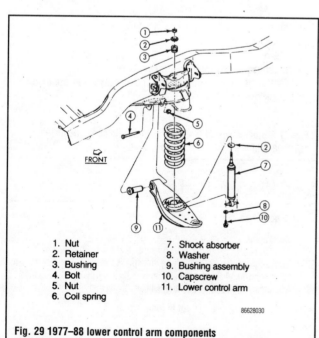

1. Nut
2. Retainer
3. Bushing
4. Bolt
5. Nut
6. Coil spring
7. Shock absorber
8. Washer
9. Bushing assembly
10. Capscrew
11. Lower control arm

Fig. 29 1977–88 lower control arm components

CONTROL ARM BUSHING REPLACEMENT

1. Removing the lower control arm.
2. Using an arbor press and a suitable sleeve, press out the old bushing.
3. Position the new bushing using the arbor press and suitable sleeve. Make sure it is fully seated.
4. Install the lower control arm in the truck.

Lower Control Arm Strut

REMOVAL & INSTALLATION

♦ See Figure 30

1. Raise and safely support the front end on jackstands.
2. Using a small drift and hammer, drive out the spring pin from the front end of the strut.

➡It is advisable to spray the bolts and nuts you are working on with penetrating oil, then allow them to sit for a few minutes.

3. Remove the nut, retainer and bushing.
4. Remove the rear mounting bolts, along with the jounce bumper and bracket.

To install:

5. Install the strut arm, along with the mounting bolts, nuts, retainer, bushing, bumper and bracket.
6. Install a new spring pin.
7. Torque the mounting bracket bolts to 85 ft. lbs. (115 Nm) for 1972–76 models; 95 ft. lbs. (128 Nm) for 1977–88 models.
8. Torque the retainer nut to 50 ft. lbs. (67 Nm).

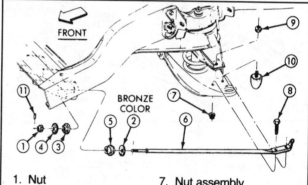

1. Nut
2. Rear retainer
3. Front bushing
4. Front retainer
5. Rear bushing
6. Strut
7. Nut assembly
8. Bolt
9. Nut
10. Bumper assembly
11. Spring pin

Fig. 30 1972–88 lower control arm strut

Knuckle and Spindle—2WD

REMOVAL & INSTALLATION

Drum Brakes

WITH LEAF SPRINGS

1. Support the brake pedal in the UP position.
2. Loosen the wheel lug nuts.
3. Raise and safely support the front end on jackstands.
4. Remove the wheels.
5. Remove the brake drum/hub.

SUSPENSION AND STEERING 8-11

6. Remove the brake backing plate bolts.
7. Lift the entire backing plate/brake shoe assembly off the knuckle and wire it out of the way. DO NOT DISCONNECT THE BRAKE LINE!
8. Separate the knuckle and knuckle arm.
9. Remove the pivot pin locking screw(s) or pin.

➡ Some models have two locking screws.

10. Remove the upper pivot pin oil seal plug (steel disc) and drive the pivot pin down, forcing the lower seal plug out. The pivot thrust bearing can now be removed.
11. Install the knuckle assembly on the axle, then install the backing plate and new dust seal. Install the upper plate mounting bolts and torque them to 55 ft. lbs. (74 Nm) on 100 and 200 series; 85 ft. lbs. (115 Nm) on 200 HD and 300 series.
12. Install the lower mounting bolts and torque them to 210 ft. lbs. (284 Nm) on 100 and 200 series; 225 ft. lbs. (305 Nm) on 200 HD and 300 series.
13. Install the hub/drum assembly and adjust the wheel bearings.
14. Install the wheels.
15. Lower the vehicle.

WITH COIL SPRINGS

1. Support the brake pedal in the UP position.
2. Loosen the wheel lug nuts.
3. Raise and safely support the front end on jackstands.
4. Remove the wheels.

➡ It is advisable to spray the bolts and nuts you are working on with penetrating oil, then allow them to sit for a few minutes.

5. Remove the brake drum/hub.
6. Support the lower control arm with a floor jack.
7. Disconnect the tie rod from the knuckle.
8. Remove the brake backing plate bolts.
9. Lift the entire backing plate/brake shoe assembly off the knuckle and wire it out of the way. DO NOT DISCONNECT THE BRAKE LINE!
10. Install and tighten the lower backing plate mounting bolts in the steering knuckle and knuckle arm.
11. Disconnect the ball joints from the knuckle and knuckle arm.
12. Separate the knuckle and knuckle arm.

To install:

13. Install the knuckle assembly to the control arms, then install the backing plate and new dust seal. Install the upper plate mounting bolts and torque them to 55 ft. lbs. (74 Nm) on 100 and 200 series; 85 ft. lbs. (115 Nm) on 200 HD and 300 series.
14. Install the lower mounting bolts and torque them to 210 ft. lbs. (284 Nm) on 100 and 200 series; 225 ft. lbs. (304 Nm) on 200 HD and 300 series.
15. Connect the ball joints. Torque the nuts to 135 ft. lbs. (183 Nm) on 100 and 200 series. On 300 series, the torque is 175 ft. lbs. (237 Nm). Always use new cotter pins.
16. Connect the tie rod end and torque the nut to 45 ft. lbs. (61 Nm) on the 100 and 200 series; 55 ft. lbs. (74 Nm) on the 300 series. Install a new cotter pin.
17. Install the hub/drum assembly and adjust the wheel bearings.
18. Install the wheels.
19. Lower the vehicle.

Disc Brakes

1. Support the brake pedal in the UP position.
2. Loosen the wheel lug nuts.
3. Raise and safely support the front end on jackstands.
4. Remove the wheels.
5. Remove the brake calipers and suspend them out of the way. DO NOT DISCONNECT THE BRAKE LINE! Remove the inner brake pad.
6. Remove the hub/rotor assembly. Carefully slide it off, making sure you do not drag the seal or inner bearing against the knuckle threads.
7. Remove the brake splash shield.
8. Support the lower control arm with a floor jack.
9. Disconnect the tie rod from the knuckle.
10. Separate the ball joints from the knuckle.
11. Unbolt the brake adapter from the knuckle.

To install:

12. Position a new dust seal on the knuckle.
13. Install the splash shield and new dust seal. Torque the bolts to 220 inch lbs. (25 Nm).
14. Install the adapter on the knuckle. Torque the bolts to 100 ft. lbs. (135 Nm).
15. Align the knuckle arm and the knuckle. Torque the mounting bolts to 215 ft. lbs. (291 Nm).
16. Install the knuckle assembly on the control arms and connect the ball joints. Torque the nuts to 135 ft. lbs. (183 Nm). On 1972–74 300 series, the torque is 175 ft. lbs. (237 Nm). Always use new cotter pins.
17. Connect the tie rod end and torque the nut to 55 ft. lbs. (75 Nm). Install a new cotter pin.
18. Carefully install the hub/rotor assembly and adjust the wheel bearings.
19. Install the caliper and pads.
20. Install the wheels.
21. Lower the vehicle.

Steering Knuckle and Ball Joints—4WD

The ball joints should be replaced if there is any looseness or end-play. The steering knuckle and ball joint must be removed to replace the ball joint.

REMOVAL & INSTALLATION

Dana 44

MODELS THROUGH 1984

♦ See Figures 31, 32, 33 and 34

1. Loosen the wheel lug nuts.
2. Raise and safely support the vehicle, then remove the wheel hub and bearings as detailed in Section 7 of this manual.
3. Refer to the Axle Shaft Removal and Replacement, for the detailed removal of the hub and bearings.
4. Remove and discard the O-ring from the steering knuckle.
5. Remove the capscrews from the brake splash shield. On models with disc brakes, remove the brake disc adapter from the steering knuckle.
6. Disconnect the tie rod from the steering knuckle. On the left side, disconnect the drag link from the steering knuckle arm.
7. Using a punch and hammer, remove the inner oil seal from the rear of the steering knuckle.
8. Carefully slide the outer and inner axle shaft (complete with the U-joint) from the axle housing.
9. On the left side, remove the steering knuckle arm by tapping it to loosen the tapered dowels.
10. Remove the cotter pin from the upper ball joint nut. Remove the upper and lower ball joint nuts and discard the lower nut.
11. Separate the steering knuckle from the axle housing yoke with a brass drift and hammer. Remove and discard the sleeve from the upper ball joint yoke on the axle housing.
12. Position the steering knuckle upside down in a vise equipped with soft jaws and remove the snapring from the lower ball joint.
13. Press the lower and upper ball joints from the steering knuckle individually.

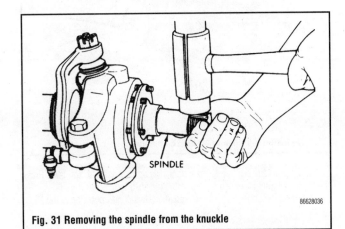

Fig. 31 Removing the spindle from the knuckle

8-12 SUSPENSION AND STEERING

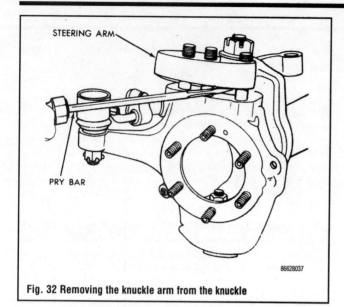

Fig. 32 Removing the knuckle arm from the knuckle

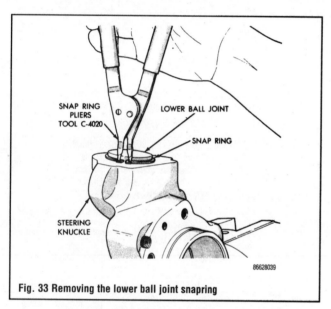

Fig. 33 Removing the lower ball joint snapring

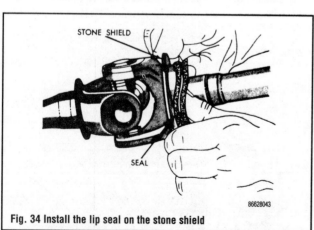

Fig. 34 Install the lip seal on the stone shield

14. Position the steering knuckle right side up in a vise with soft jaws. Press the lower ball joint into position and install the snapring.
15. Press the upper ball joint into position. Install new boots on both ball joints.

16. Screw a new sleeve into the upper ball joint yoke on the axle housing, leaving about two threads showing at the top.

To install:

17. Install the steering knuckle on the axle housing yoke, then install a new lower ball joint nut and tighten it to 80 ft. lbs. (108 Nm).
18. Tighten the sleeve in the upper ball joint yoke to 40 ft. lbs. (54 Nm). Install the upper ball joint nut and tighten it to 100 ft. lbs. (135 Nm). Align the cotter pin hole in the stud with the slot in the castellated nut and install the cotter pin. Do not loosen the nut to align the holes.
19. **On the left side only**, position the steering knuckle arm over the studs on the steering knuckle. Install the tapered dowels and nuts. Tighten the nuts to 90 ft. lbs. (122 Nm). Install the drag link on the steering arm. Install the nut and tighten it to 60 ft. lbs. (81 Nm). Install the cotter pin.
20. Install the tie rod end on the steering knuckle. Tighten the nut to 45 ft. lbs. (61 Nm) and install the cotter pin.
21. Install the lip seal on the stone shield with the lip towards the axle spline.
22. Install the axle shaft into the housing. Install the brake splash shield and tighten the screws to 13 ft. lbs. (17 Nm). On models with disc brakes, install the brake disc adapter and tighten the bolts to 85 ft. lbs. (115 Nm).
23. Install a new O-ring in the steering knuckle.
24. Clean any rust from the axle shaft splines.
25. Carefully slide the hub, rotor and retainer, and bearing onto the axle shaft, and start the shaft into the housing. Install, but do not tighten, the axle shaft nut.
26. Align the retainer with the steering knuckle flange. Install the retainer screws and tighten them in a crisscross pattern to 30 ft. lbs. (40 Nm).
27. Tighten the axle shaft nut to 100 ft. lbs. (135 Nm). Tighten the nut until the next slot in the nut aligns with the hole in the axle shaft. Install the cotter pin.
28. On models with disc brakes, install the inboard brake shoe on the adapter with the shoe flanges in the adapter ways. Install the caliper in the adapter and over the disc. Align the caliper on the machined ways of the adapter. Be careful not to pull the dust boot from its grooves as the piston and boot slide over the inboard shoe.
29. Install the anti-rattle springs and retaining clips. Torque to 16–17 ft. lbs. (21–23 Nm). The inboard shoe anti-rattle spring must always be installed on top of the retainer spring plate.
30. Install the wheel, and locking hub, then lower the truck. Lubricate all fittings.

1985–88 MODELS

♦ See Figure 25

➡The ball joints should be replaced if there is any looseness or end-play. The steering knuckle and ball joint must be removed to replace the ball joint.

1. Loosen the wheel lug nuts.
2. Raise and safely support the vehicle, them remove the rotor hub and bearings, as described in Section 7 of this manual.
3. After removing all necessary brake parts, remove the caliper adapter from the steering knuckle. Remove the six nuts and washers which fasten the spindle to the steering knuckle. Remove the splash shield. Using a soft hammer, hit the spindle lightly to break it free from the steering knuckle. Examine the bronze spacer and needle bearing. The left spindle does not have needle bearings. Replace any worn parts.
4. Remove the axle shaft assembly; make sure to remove and discard the old seal.
5. Disconnect the tie rod ends from the steering knuckles. **On the left side**, disconnect the drag link from the steering knuckle arm.
6. **On the left side only**, remove the nuts and washers from the steering knuckle arm. Tap the steering arm to loosen it from the knuckle. Remove the arm.
7. Remove the cotter pin from the upper ball joint nut. Remove the upper and lower ball joint nuts. Use a brass drift and hammer to separate the knuckle from the axle yoke. Remove and discard the sleeve from the upper ball joint yoke.
8. Position the steering knuckle upside down in a vise. Remove the snapring from the lower ball joint with a pair of snapring pliers. Press the lower ball joint first, then the upper from the steering knuckle.

SUSPENSION AND STEERING 8-13

To install:

9. Clean all parts and examine for wear. Replace any worn parts.
10. Press the lower ball joint into position and install the snapring. Press in the upper ball joint. Install new boots on both ball joints.
11. Position the steering knuckle into position on the axle housing yoke. Install the lower ball joint nut and tighten to 80 ft. lbs. (108 Nm).
12. Install the sleeve into the upper ball joint yoke and tighten to 40 ft. lbs. (40 Nm). Install the upper ball joint nut, tighten to 100 ft. lbs. (135 Nm). Align the nut with the hole in the ball joint stud and insert a new cotter pin.
13. Position and install the steering arm on the left knuckle, and tighten to 90 ft. lbs. (122 Nm). Install drag link, and tighten to 60 ft.lbs. Install the tie rod ends, and tighten to 45 ft.lbs. (61 Nm). Align and install new cotter pins.
14. Install the axle shaft assembly, using a new seal.
15. Install the splash shield, then attach the spindle to the steering knuckle.
16. Install the caliper adapter pad, and any brake parts which were removed.
17. Install the rotor hub and bearings, as described in Section 7.
18. Install the wheel and lower the vehicle.

Dana 60

♦ See Figures 25, 35 and 36

➡ For this job you'll need a torque wrench with a capacity of at least 600 ft. lbs. (813 Nm).

1. Raise and support the front end on jackstands.
2. Remove the caliper and pads.
3. Remove the axle shafts.
4. Alternately and evenly remove the 4 bolts that retain the spindle cap to the knuckle. This will relieve spring tension.
5. When spring tension is relieved, remove the bolts.
6. Remove the spindle cap, compression spring and retainer. Discard the gasket.
7. Remove the 4 bolts securing the lower kingpin and retainer to the knuckle. Remove the lower kingpin and retainer.
8. Remove the tapered bushing from the top of the upper kingpin.
9. Remove the knuckle from the axle yoke.
10. Remove the upper kingpin from the axle yoke with a piece of ⅞ in. (22mm) hex-shaped case hardened metal bar stock, or with a ⅞ in. (22mm) hex socket. Discard the upper kingpin and seal.

➡ The upper kingpin is tightened to 500–600 ft. lbs. (677–813 Nm).

11. Using a 2-jawed puller and step plate, press out the lower kingpin grease retainer, bearing cup, bearing and seal from the axle yoke lower bore. Discard the grease seal and retainer, as well as the lower bearing cup.

To install:

12. Coat the mating surfaces of a new lower kingpin grease retainer with RTV silicone sealer.
13. Install the retainer in the axle yoke bore, so that the concave portion of the retainer faces the upper kingpin.
14. Using a bearing driver, drive a new bearing cup in the lower kingpin bore until it bottoms against the grease retainer.

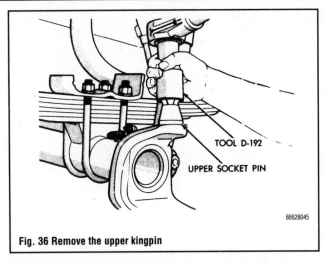

Fig. 36 Remove the upper kingpin

15. Pack the lower kingpin bearing and the yoke bore with waterproof wheel bearing grease.
16. Using a driver, drive a new seal into the lower kingpin bore.
17. Install a new seal and upper kingpin into the yoke using tool D–192 or equivalent. Tighten the kingpin to 500–600 ft. lbs. (677–813 Nm).
18. Install the knuckle on the yoke.
19. Place the tapered bushing over the upper kingpin in the knuckle bore.
20. Place the lower kingpin and retainer in the knuckle and axle yoke. Install the 4 bolts and tighten them, alternately and evenly, to 90 ft. lbs. (122 Nm).
21. Place the retainer and compression spring on the tapered bushing.
22. Install a new gasket on the knuckle. Position the spindle cap on the gasket and knuckle. Install the 4 bolts and tighten them, alternately and evenly, to 90 ft. lbs. (122 Nm).
23. Install the axle shafts and lubricate the upper kingpin through the fitting and the lower fitting through the flush fitting. The lower fitting may be lubricated with Alemite adapter No. 6783, or equivalent.

Dana 70

♦ See Figure 37

1. Loosen the wheel lug nuts.
2. Raise and support the front end on jackstands.
3. Remove the wheel.
4. Remove the hub and drum.
5. Remove the brake support.
6. Remove the spindle.
7. Remove the axle shaft.
8. Disconnect the tie rod ends from the knuckles.
9. **On the left side only**, disconnect the drag link from the knuckle arm. Remove the steering knuckle felt and oil seal retainers.
10. Remove the bolts from the lower bearing cap, then remove the cap and shims.
11. Record the thickness of the shims for later use.
12. Remove the nuts from the top of the knuckle arm or upper bearing cap.
13. Using a vise, remove the arm from the knuckle and bronze bearing. Discard the Woodruff key. Collect and record thickness of the shims.
14. Remove the knuckle housing, felt and oil seal.
15. Remove the upper and lower bearing cones.
16. Clean and inspect all parts thoroughly. Replace any worn or damaged parts.
17. Remove damaged bearing cups with a brass drift.

To install:

18. Place new felt and a new oil seal over the end of the axle housing.
19. Install the knuckle arm or upper bearing cap and the original shim pack on the knuckle housing, then tighten the retaining nuts or bolts.

➡ If a new shim pack is used, it must be 0.060 in. (1.5mm) thick.

20. Coat the bronze cone with multi-purpose chassis lube and press it into place on the upper bearing pivot. Make sure that the cone is properly positioned on the key.
21. Seat the bearing cups in the yokes of the axle housing. Slide the knuckle over the yoke and position the bronze bearing cone in its cup.

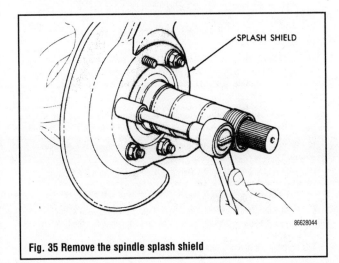

Fig. 35 Remove the spindle splash shield

8-14 SUSPENSION AND STEERING

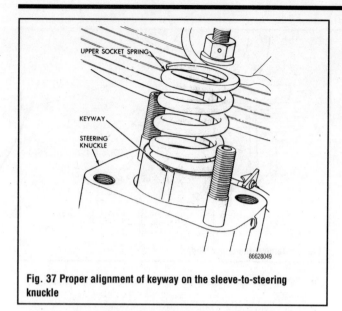

Fig. 37 Proper alignment of keyway on the sleeve-to-steering knuckle

22. Pack the lower bearing cone with multi-purpose chassis lube. Tilt the bottom of the knuckle outward and insert the lower cone into its cup. Return the knuckle to its proper position, then install the lower bearing cap and original shims. Tighten the bolts.

➡ If a new shim pack is used, it must be 0.055 in. (1.4mm) thick.

23. Using a torque wrench on the outer, upper bearing retainer nut, check the bearing preload. It should be 15–35 ft. lbs. (20–47 Nm) with the knuckle turning. If not, add or subtract shims, as necessary.
24. Attach the oiled felt and oil seal to the knuckle housing with the retainers and screws.
25. Connect the tie rod ends and drag link.
26. Install the axle shaft, spindle and brake support.
27. Install the hub with a new gasket. Install the drum and wheel.
28. Fill the knuckle with SAE 140 lubricant to the level of the fill plug. Lower the vehicle.
29. Have the front end alignment checked.

F–375

♦ See Figures 38, 39, 40, 41 and 42

1. Loosen the wheel lug nuts.
2. Raise and safely support the front end on jackstands.
3. Remove the wheels.
4. Remove the brake drums. See Section 9.

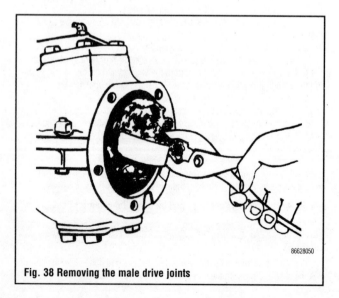

Fig. 38 Removing the male drive joints

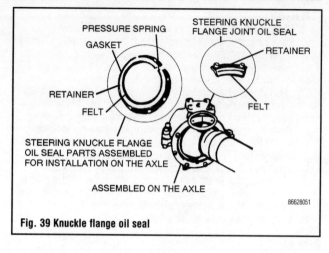

Fig. 39 Knuckle flange oil seal

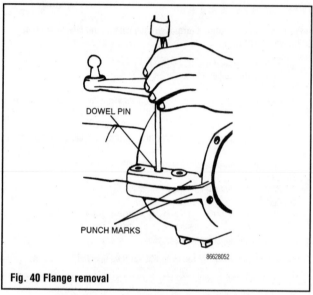

Fig. 40 Flange removal

5. Matchmark the drive flange and the hub.
6. Remove the nuts and lockwashers, then install puller screws using the 2 threaded holes in the flange.
7. Pull the flange from the hub.
8. Remove the hub and bearings.
9. Remove the attaching bolts and pull the brake supports from the knuckle. Wire them up and out of the way.
10. Using a soft mallet, tap the spindle from the knuckle.
11. Pull the short outer shaft and female section of the universal drive assembly from the axle housing.
12. Pull the male section and long inner shaft from the housing.
13. Discard all seals and seal bushings.
14. Disconnect the tie rod from the knuckle flange arm.
15. Remove the steering knuckle flange oil seal assembly.
16. If the left knuckle is being removed, disconnect the drag link from the steering arm.

➡ Before disassembling either knuckle, matchmark the upper and lower halves. They are not interchangeable from side to side.

17. Remove the dowel pins and bolts securing the knuckle halves, then remove the knuckle halves from the axle housing.
18. Remove the bearing cones from the axle housing trunnion pins.
19. Disconnect the steering arm from the left knuckle flange.
20. Remove the upper bearing cap from the right knuckle.
21. Fasten the steering knuckle flange bearing shims for each knuckle to either the steering arm or bearing cap to facilitate adjustment of the bearings during assembly.
22. Remove the flange lower bearing cap and gasket.

SUSPENSION AND STEERING　　8-15

To install:

23. Clean all parts thoroughly in a safe solvent. Inspect all parts for wear and/or damage, and replace any defective parts. Replace all seals and gaskets. Replace any bushing that shows signs of wear.

24. Drive a new seal and bushing into the end of the housing. The seal lip should face inwards.

25. Install the Woodruff key into the housing upper trunnion pins.

26. Coat the bearing cones with chassis grease, then install the bronze cone on the upper trunnion pin and the roller bearing on the lower trunnion pin.

27. Install the upper and lower knuckle halves on the housing, then install the dowel pins and bolts.

➡ **Don't tighten the bolts and nuts until the dowel pins are in place.**

28. Install the flange lower bearing caps and gaskets.

29. Place the bearing adjusting shims on the top of the steering knuckle flange assemblies.

30. Attach the steering arm to the left side and the bearing cap to the right side.

31. Adjust the knuckle flange bearings. This adjustment is always done with the axle shafts removed. To adjust the bearings:
   a. Place a torque wrench on one of the bearing caps or a steering arm bolt.
   b. Move the knuckle through its turning range until the bearings roll smoothly. Note the torque reading during the knuckle travel. The reading should be 25–27½ ft. lbs. (33–37 Nm).
   c. If necessary, correct the adjustment by adding or removing shims. Shims are available in thicknesses of 0.005 in. (0.12mm), 0.007 in. (0.17mm) and 0.020 in. (0.5mm).

32. Install the knuckle flange oil seal using new felt and gaskets.

33. Install the pressure spring in the oil retainer end.

34. Saturate the felt with clean oil and install it in the retainer ends flush with the retainer.

35. Connect the tie rod and drag link to the knuckles.

36. Pack the axle shaft U-joints with chassis lubricant. Install both the inner and outer axle shafts. Note that the shafts have numerical mating marks. Identical numbers should be mated during assembly.

➡ **On some axles, the mating numbers are not identical. That's okay as long as the axle operates satisfactorily.**

37. Position the spindle and brake supports on the knuckle. Install the bolts and lockwashers.

38. Pack the wheel bearings and coat the inside of the hubs with wheel bearing grease.

39. Adjust the wheel bearings by turning the inner adjusting nut tightly, then backing it off ⅙ turn.

40. Install the lockring, making sure that the pin on the inner nut enters one of the holes in the lockring. It's okay to move the inner nut **slightly** to position the pin.

41. Install the outer nut and torque it to 50 ft. lbs. (68 Nm).

42. Install the drive flange, using a new gasket.

43. Coat the flange and drum contact surfaces with anti–seize compound and install the drum.

44. Install the wheel, then lower the vehicle.

Wheel Alignment

If the tires are worn unevenly, if the vehicle is not stable on the highway or if the handling seems poor, the wheel alignment should be checked. If an alignment problem is suspected, first check for improper tire inflation and other possible causes. These can be worn suspension or steering components, accident damage or even unmatched tires. If any worn or damaged components are found, they must be replaced before the wheels can be properly aligned. Wheel alignment requires very expensive equipment and involves minute adjustments which must be accurate; it should only be performed by a trained technician. Take your vehicle to a properly equipped shop.

Following is a description of the alignment angles which are adjustable on most vehicles and how they affect vehicle handling. Although these angles can apply to both the front and rear wheels, usually only the front suspension is adjustable.

CASTER

♦ See Figure 43

Looking at a vehicle from the side, caster angle describes the steering axis rather than a wheel angle. The steering knuckle is attached to the axle yoke through ball joints or king pins. The wheel pivots around the line between these points to steer the vehicle. When the upper point is tilted back, this is described as positive caster. Having a positive caster tends to make the wheels self-centering, increasing directional stability. Excessive positive caster makes the wheels hard to steer, while an uneven caster will cause a pull to one side. Overloading the vehicle or sagging rear springs will affect caster, as will raising the rear of the vehicle. If the rear of the vehicle is lower than normal, the caster becomes more positive.

CAMBER

♦ See Figure 44

Looking from the front of the vehicle, camber is the inward or outward tilt of the top of wheels. When the tops of the wheels are tilted in, this is negative camber; if they are tilted out, it is positive. In a turn, a slight amount of negative camber helps maximize contact of the tire with the road. However, too much negative camber compromises straight-line stability, increases bump steer and torque steer.

TOE

♦ See Figure 45

Looking down at the wheels from above the vehicle, toe angle is the distance between the front of the wheels relative to the distance between the back of the wheels. If the wheels are closer at the front, they are said to be toed-in or to have negative toe. A small amount of negative toe enhances directional stability and provides a smoother ride on the highway.

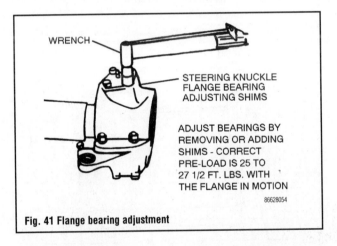

Fig. 41 Flange bearing adjustment

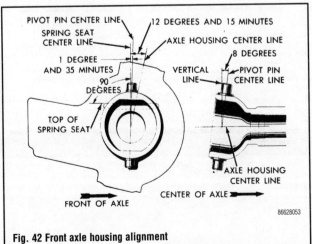

Fig. 42 Front axle housing alignment

8-16 SUSPENSION AND STEERING

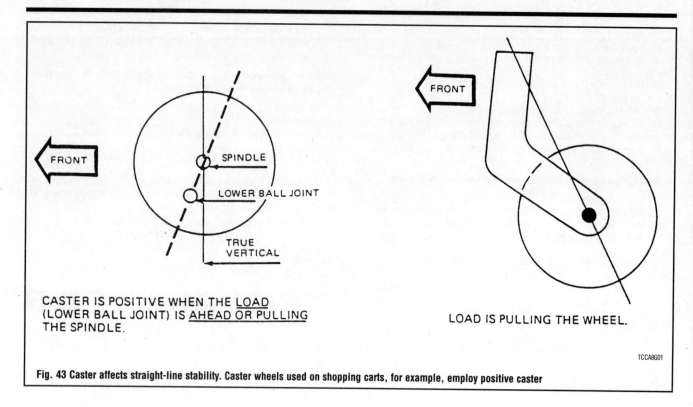

Fig. 43 Caster affects straight-line stability. Caster wheels used on shopping carts, for example, employ positive caster

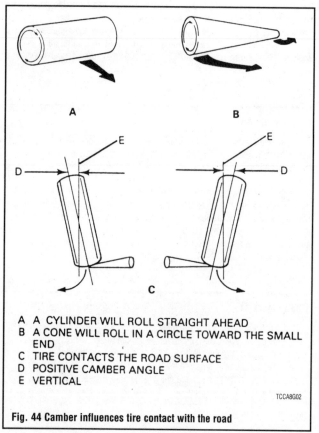

A A CYLINDER WILL ROLL STRAIGHT AHEAD
B A CONE WILL ROLL IN A CIRCLE TOWARD THE SMALL END
C TIRE CONTACTS THE ROAD SURFACE
D POSITIVE CAMBER ANGLE
E VERTICAL

Fig. 44 Camber influences tire contact with the road

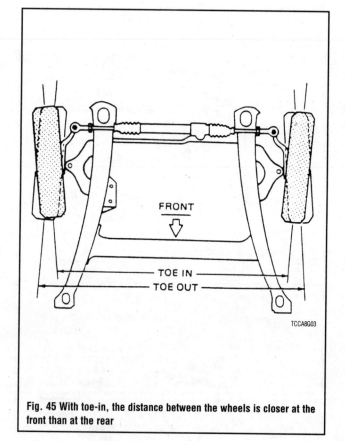

Fig. 45 With toe-in, the distance between the wheels is closer at the front than at the rear

WHEEL ALIGNMENT SPECIFICATIONS

Years	Models	Caster (deg.) Range	Caster (deg.) Pref.	Camber (deg.) Range	Camber (deg.) Pref.	Toe-in (in.)	Front Wheel Angle (deg.)
1967	D100*	3½P to 4P	3¾P	1¼P to 1¾P	1½P	0–1/8	37
	D200*	3½P to 4P	3¾P	①	②	0–1/8	37
	D300*	2¾P to 3¼P	3P	1¾P–2¼P	2P	0–1/8	39
	W100	2¾P to 3¼P	3P	1¼P–1¾P	1½P	0–1/8	29
	W200	2¾P to 3¼P	3P	1¼P–1¾P	1½P	0–1/8	29
	W300	3¼P to 3¾P	3½P	1¼P–1¾P	1½P	0–1/8	29
	WM300	¼P to ¾P	½P	1¼P–1¾P	1½P	0–1/8	30
1968	D100*	3½P to 4P	3¾P	1¼P to 1¾P	1½P	0–1/8	37
	D200*	3½P to 4P	3¾P	①	②	0–1/8	37
	D300*	2¾P to 3¼P	3P	1¾P–2¼P	2P	0–1/8	39
	W100	2¾P to 3¼P	3P	1¼P–1¾P	1½P	0–1/8	29
	W200	2¾P to 3¼P	3P	1¼P–1¾P	1½P	0–1/8	29
	W300	3¼P to 3¾P	3½P	1¼P–1¾P	1½P	0–1/8	29
	WM300	¼P to ¾P	½P	1¼P–1¾P	1½P	0–1/8	30
1969–71	D100*	3¼P to 3¾P	3½P	1¼P to 1¾P	1½P	1/16–3/16	37
	D200*	3½P to 4P	3¾P	①	②	1/16–3/16	37
	D300*	3½P to 4P	3¾P	1¾P–2¼P	2P	1/16–3/16	37
	W100	2¾P to 3¼P	3P	1¼P–1¾P	1½P	0–1/8	29
	W200	2¾P to 3¼P	3P	1¼P–1¾P	1½P	0–1/8	29
	W300	3¼P to 3¾P	3½P	1¼P–1¾P	1½P	0–1/8	29
1972–74	D100*	0 to 1P	½P	0 to 1¼P	⅛P	1/16–1/8	33
	D200*	0 to 1P	½P	0 to 1¼P	⅛P	1/16–1/8	33
	D300*	0 to 1P	½P	0 to 1¼P	⅛P	1/16–1/8	33
	W100 AW100 PW100	2¾P to 3¼P	3P	1¼P–1¾P	1½P	0–1/8	37
	W200	2¾P to 3¼P	3P	1¼P–1¾P	1½P	0–1/8	③
	W300	2¾P to 3¼P	3P	1¼P–1¾P	1½P	0–1/8	29
1975–76	D100	0 to 1P	½P	¼P to ¾P	½P	1/16–1/8	33
	D200*	0 to 1P	½P	¼P to ¾P	½P	1/16–1/8	33
	D300*	0 to 1P	½P	¼P to ¾P	½P	1/16–1/8	33
	W100 AW100 PW100	2¾P to 3¼P	3P	1¼P–1¾P	1½P	3/32–11/32	④
	W200	2¾P to 3¼P	3P	1¼P–1¾P	1½P	0–1/8	④
	W300	2¾P to 3¼P	3P	1¼P–1¾P	1½P	0–1/8	④

86628B55

WHEEL ALIGNMENT SPECIFICATIONS

Years	Models	Caster (deg.) Range	Caster (deg.) Pref.	Camber (deg.) Range	Camber (deg.) Pref.	Toe-in (in.)	Front Wheel Angle (deg.)
1977–78	D100* D150	0 to 1P	½P	¼P to ¾P	½P	1/16–1/8	33
	D200*	0 to 1P	½P	¼P to ¾P	½P	1/16–1/8	33
	D300*	0 to 1P	½P	¼P to ¾P	½P	1/16–1/8	33
	W100 AW100 PW100	2¾P to 3¼P	3P	1¼P–1¾P	1½P	3/32–11/32	④
	W200	2¾P to 3¼P	3P	1¼P–1¾P	1½P	0–1/8	④
	W300	2¾P to 3¼P	3P	1¼P–1¾P	1½P	0–1/8	④
1979	D100* D150*	0 to 1P	½P	0 to ½P	¼P	1/16–1/8	33
	D200*	0 to 1P	½P	0 to ½P	¼P	1/16–1/8	33
	D300*	0 to 1P	½P	0 to ½P	¼P	1/16–1/8	33
	W100 AW100 PW100	2¾P to 3¼P	3P	1¼P–1¾P	1½P	3/32–11/32	④
	W200	2¾P to 3¼P	3P	1¼P–1¾P	1½P	0–1/8	④
	W300	2¾P to 3¼P	3P	1¼P–1¾P	1½P	0–1/8	④
1980	AD100* D150*	0 to 1P	½P	0 to ½P	¼P	1/16–1/8	33
	D200*	0 to 1P	½P	0 to ½P	¼P	1/16–1/8	33
	D300*	0 to 1P	½P	0 to ½P	¼P	1/16–1/8	33
	W150 AW150 PW150	2¾P to 3¼P	3P	1¼P–1¾P	1½P	3/32–11/32	④
	W200	2¾P to 3¼P	3P	1¼P–1¾P	1½P	0–1/8	④
	W300	2¾P to 3¼P	3P	1¼P–1¾P	1½P	0–1/8	④
1981	AD100* D150*	0 to 1P	½P	0 to ½P	¼P	1/16–1/8	33
	D200*	0 to 1P	½P	0 to ½P	¼P	1/16–1/8	33
	D300*	0 to 1P	½P	0 to ½P	¼P	1/16–1/8	33
	W150 AW150 PW150	2¾P to 3¼P	3P	1¼P–1¾P	1½P	3/32–11/32	④
	W200	2¾P to 3¼P	3P	1¼P–1¾P	1½P	0–1/8	④
	W300	2¾P to 3¼P	3P	1¼P–1¾P	1½P	0–1/8	④

86628C55

WHEEL ALIGNMENT SPECIFICATIONS

Years	Models	Caster (deg.) Range	Caster (deg.) Pref.	Camber (deg.) Range	Camber (deg.) Pref.	Toe-in (in.)	Front Wheel Angle (deg.)
1982	AD150* D150*	0 to 1P	½P	0 to ½P	¼P	1/16–⅛	33
	D250*	0 to 1P	½P	0 to ½P	¼P	1/16–⅛	33
	D350*	0 to 1P	½P	0 to ½P	¼P	1/16–⅛	33
	W150 AW150 PW150	2¾P to 3¼P	3P	1¼P–1¾P	1½P	3/32–11/32	⑤
	W250	2¾P to 3¼P	3P	1¼P–¾P	1½P	0–⅛	⑤
	W250 W350 w/Dana 60	2¾P to 3¼P	3P	¼P–¾P	½P	0–⅛	⑤
1983	AD150 D150	½N to 1½P	½P	0 to 1P	½P	1/16–3/16	33
	D250	½N to 1½P	½P	0 to 1P	½P	1/16–3/16	33
	D350	½N to 1½P	½P	0 to 1P	½P	1/16–3/16	33
	W150 AW150 PW150	½P to 3½P	2P	½P–1½P	1P	⅛–⅜	⑤
	W250	½P to 3½P	2P	½P–1½P	1P	⅛–⅜	⑤
	W250 W350 w/Dana 60	½P to 3½P	2P	½P–1½P	1P	⅛–⅜	⑤
1984	AD150 D150	½N to 1½P	½P	0 to 1P	½P	1/16–3/16	33
	D250	½N to 1½P	½P	0 to 1P	½P	1/16–3/16	33
	D350	½N to 1½P	½P	0 to 1P	½P	1/16–3/16	33
	W150 AW150 PW150	½P to 3½P	2P	½P–1½P	1P	⅛–⅜	⑤
	W250	½P to 3½P	2P	½P–1½P	1P	⅛–⅜	⑤
	W250 W350 w/Dana 60	½P to 3½P	2P	½P–1½P	1P	⅛–⅜	⑤
1986	AD150 D150	½N to 1½P	½P	0 to 1P	½P	1/16–3/16	33
	D250	½N to 1½P	½P	0 to 1P	½P	1/16–3/16	33
	D350	½N to 1½P	½P	0 to 1P	½P	1/16–3/16	33
	W150 AW150 PW150	½P to 3½P	2P	½P–1½P	1P	⅛–⅜	⑤
	W250	½P to 3½P	2P	½P–1½P	1P	⅛–⅜	⑤
	W250 W350 w/Dana 60	½P to 3½P	2P	½P–1½P	1P	⅛–⅜	⑤

86628D55

WHEEL ALIGNMENT SPECIFICATIONS

Years	Models	Caster (deg.) Range	Caster (deg.) Pref.	Camber (deg.) Range	Camber (deg.) Pref.	Toe-in (in.)	Front Wheel Angle (deg.)
1987	AD150 D150	½N to 1½P	½P	0 to 1P	½P	1/16–3/16	33
	D250	½N to 1½P	½P	0 to 1P	½P	1/16–3/16	33
	D350	½N to 1½P	½P	0 to 1P	½P	1/16–3/16	33
	W150 AW150 PW150	½P to 3½P	2P	½P–1½P	1P	⅛–⅜	⑤
	W250	½P to 3½P	2P	½P–1½P	1P	⅛–⅜	⑤
	W250 W350 w/Dana 60	½P to 3½P	2P	½P–1½P	1P	⅛–⅜	⑤
1988	AD150 D150	½N to 1½P	½P	0 to 1P	½P	1/16–3/16	33
	D250	½N to 1½P	½P	0 to 1P	½P	1/16–3/16	33
	D350	½N to 1½P	½P	0 to 1P	½P	1/16–3/16	33
	W150 AW150 PW150	½P to 3½P	2P	½P–1½P	1P	⅛–⅜	⑤
	W250	½P to 3½P	2P	½P–1½P	1P	⅛–⅜	⑤
	W250 W350 w/Dana 60	½P to 3½P	2P	½P–1½P	1P	⅛–⅜	⑤

*Loaded

① Except Crew Cab: 1¼P to 1¾P
Crew Cab: 1¾P to 2¼P

② Except Crew Cab: 1½P
Crew Cab: 2P

③ 7.00 x 16 tires: right 30; left 37
7.50 x 16 tires: right 25; left 37
8.00 x 16.5 tires: right 33; left 37
8.75 x 16.5 tires: right 30; left 37
9.50 x 16.5 tires: right 27; left 37
Extra Equipment: 29 left or right

④ Left wheel, W100: 37
Left wheel, W200: 35
Left wheel W200 w/Extra Equipment and W300: 34
Right wheel:
7.00 x 15 load range C & D tires—27
10 x 15 load range B tires—27 w/man. strg.; 24 w/pwr.strg.
6.50 x 16 load range C tires—27
7.00 x 16 load range C tires—26
7.50 x 16 load range C & D tires—24
8.00 x 16.5 tires—29
8.75 x 16.5 tires—26
9.50 x 16.5 tires—24

⑤ Left wheel W150, AW150: 37
Left wheel, W250 w/Dana 44FBJ: 35
Left wheel, W250 w/Dana 60 and W350: 34
Right wheel:
7.00 x 15 load range C & D tires—27
10 x 15 load range B tires—27 w/man. strg.; 24 w/pwr.strg.
6.50 x 16 load range C tires—27
7.50 x 16 load range C & D tires—24
8.00 x 16.5 tires—29
8.75 x 16.5 tires—26
9.50 x 16.5 tires—24
P235/75R15 tires—29
P255/70R15 tires—29
LR60-15 tires—29

86628E55

SUSPENSION AND STEERING 8-19

REAR SUSPENSION

➡ The fasteners on most suspension components will rust into place over time. When working on many of these suspension parts it is advisable to first spray the mounting bolts and nuts with penetrating oil, then allow it to work into the threads for a few minutes. Heavily corroded fasteners may even need to sit overnight.

Leaf Springs

REMOVAL & INSTALLATION

◆ See Figures 46, 47, 48, 49 and 50

1. Raise the truck and safely support the rear with jackstands under the frame. Be sure that the front wheels are chocked and that the parking brake is set. The wheels should be touching the floor, but the weight must be off of the springs.
2. Remove the nuts, lockwashers and U-bolts that hold the axle to the springs.
3. Remove the front pivot bolt.
4. Disconnect and remove the outer shackle and bolt assembly from the hanger, then remove the spring.

To install:

5. Position the spring in place, then install the eye bolt and nut. Do not tighten the bolt yet.
6. Install the shackles and bolts. Tighten them just enough to make them snug.
7. Make sure that the spring center bolt enters the locating hole in the axle pad. On headless-type spring bolts, install the bolts with the lock groove lined up with the lockbolt hole in the bracket. Install the lockbolt and tighten the lockbolt nut. Install the lubrication fittings.
8. Install the U-bolts, lockwashers and nuts. Make them just snug for now. Align the auxiliary spring parallel with the main spring.
9. Lower the truck to its normal position with the weight on the springs.
10. Tighten all bolts and nuts to specification with the truck's weight on the suspension.

1967–68
- ½–20 U-bolt nuts: 60–70 ft. lbs. (81–94 Nm)
- ¾–16 U-bolt nuts: 175–225 ft. lbs. (237–305 Nm)
- 9/16–18 U-bolt nuts: 120–130 ft. lbs. (162–176 Nm)
- 5/8–18 U-bolt nuts: 175–200 ft. lbs. (237–271 Nm)
- 13/32–20 shackle bolts: 35–40 ft. lbs. (47–54 Nm)
- 7/16–20 shackle bolts: 45–50 ft. lbs. (61–67 Nm)
- Eye bolt: 150–175 ft. lbs. (203–237 Nm)

1969–73
- U-bolt nuts:
- D100—50–80 ft. lbs. (67–108 Nm)
- All others—100–150 ft. lbs. (135–203 Nm)
- Shackle bolts:
- D100—65–105 ft. lbs. (88–142 Nm)
- All others—125–175 ft. lbs. (169–237 Nm)
- Eye bolt:
- D100—65–105 ft. lbs. (142 Nm)
- All others—125–175 ft. lbs. (169–237 Nm)

1974
- U-bolt nuts:
- 100 series—85 ft. lbs. (115 Nm)
- 200/300—115 ft. lbs. (155 Nm)
- Shackle bolts: 80 ft. lbs. (108 Nm)
- Eye Bolt: 80 ft. lbs. (108 Nm)

1975–78
- U-bolt nuts:
- ½–20 nuts—65 ft. lbs. (88 Nm)

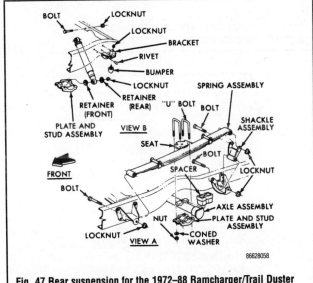

Fig. 47 Rear suspension for the 1972–88 Ramcharger/Trail Duster D100/150 and W100/150

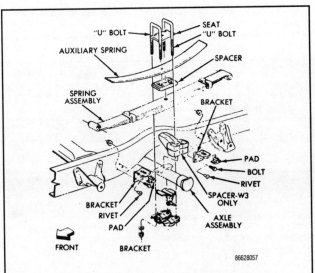

Fig. 46 Rear suspension with auxiliary spring—1972–78 trucks

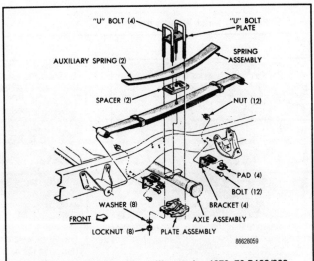

Fig. 48 Rear suspension with auxiliary spring 1972–78 D100/200 and 1979–88 D100/150

8-20 SUSPENSION AND STEERING

- 9/16–18 nuts—110 ft. lbs. (149 Nm)
- Shackle bolts and eye bolts:
- 1/2–20—93 ft. lbs. (126 Nm)

- 5/8–18—160 ft. lbs. (216 Nm)
- 3/4–16—200 ft. lbs. (271 Nm)

1979–88
- U-bolt nuts:
- 1/2–20 nuts—65 ft. lbs. (88 Nm)
- 9/16–18 nuts—110 ft. lbs. (149 Nm)
- Shackle bolts and eye bolts:
- 1/2–20—95 ft. lbs. (128 Nm)
- 5/8–18—125 ft. lbs. (169 Nm)
- 3/4–16—155 ft. lbs. (210 Nm)

Shock Absorbers

REMOVAL & INSTALLATION

♦ See Figures 51 thru 56

1. Raise and safely support the truck, on jackstands.
2. Remove the nut from the stud or bolt at the upper end. Remove the stud or bolt from the upper end.
3. Remove the lower nut at the bushing end.
4. Pivot the shock absorber and washers on the lower stud.
5. Remove the shock absorber and washers from the lower stud.
6. Installation is the reverse of removal. Purge the new shock of air by extending it in its normal position and compressing it while inverted. Do this several times. It is normal for there to be more resistance to extension than to compression. Torque the nuts to 60 ft. lbs. (81 Nm).

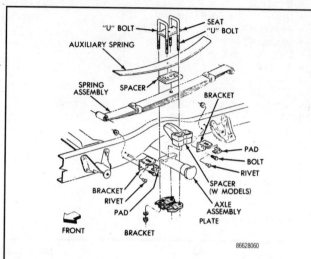

Fig. 49 Rear suspension with auxiliary spring for D250/W250, D300/W300 and D350/W350

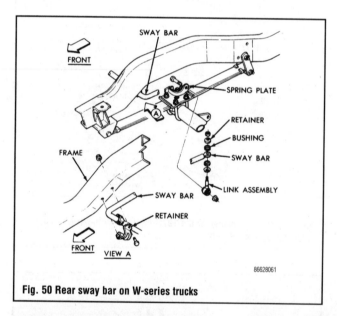

Fig. 50 Rear sway bar on W-series trucks

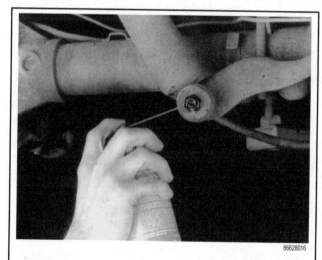

Fig. 51 To free parts, spray all fasteners with penetrating oil before you start a job

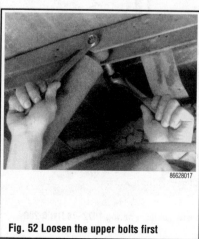

Fig. 52 Loosen the upper bolts first

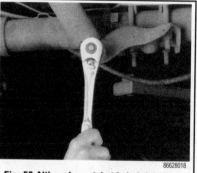

Fig. 53 Although a ratchet is helpful when removing the nuts, a backup wrench should be normally used to prevent damage to the shock bushing

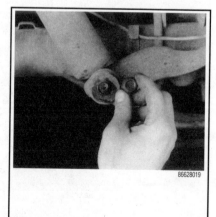

Fig. 54 Remove the nut . . .

SUSPENSION AND STEERING   8-21

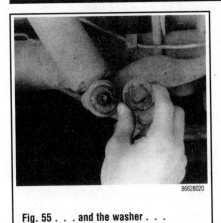

Fig. 55 . . . and the washer . . .

Fig. 56 . . . then you can remove the shock

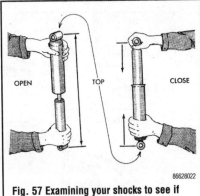

Fig. 57 Examining your shocks to see if they are good

TESTING

♦ See Figure 57

1. Remove the shock from the truck.
2. To remove the entrapped air from the cylinder, do the following:
   a. Hold the shock upright and open to its full extension.
   b. Invert the shock and slowly collapse until the piston bottoms.
   c. Repeat steps a and b several times.
3. Clamp the lower end of the shock in a vise in the upright position.
4. Open and close the shock several times.
5. A good shock will have an even, steady resistance in both directions.
6. If you have little or no resistance in your shocks, replace them.

STEERING

Steering Wheel

REMOVAL & INSTALLATION

1967 Models

1. Disconnect the battery ground cable.
2. Rotate the horn button ¼ turn counterclockwise, then remove the button, rubber grommet and horn contact ring.
3. Disconnect the horn wire.
4. Remove the three screws and spacers that attach the horn button housing to the column, then remove the horn button and housing.
5. Matchmark the steering wheel hub and column.
6. Remove the nut from the end of the steering shaft.
7. Remove the steering wheel with a puller.

To install:

8. Position the matchmarks and install the steering wheel. Install the nut on the end of the shaft and tighten.
9. Install the horn button and housing, replacing the mounting screws.
10. Reconnect the horn wire. Install the horn ring and grommet.
11. Tighten the nut to 24 ft. lbs. (32 Nm).
12. Connect the battery ground cable.

1968–71 Models

♦ See Figure 58

1. Disconnect the battery ground cable.
2. Pull the horn button off its spring clips.
3. Disconnect the horn wire.
4. Remove the 3 screws and lift out the horn switch.
5. Matchmark the steering wheel and shaft.
6. Remove the steering wheel retaining nut from the shaft.
7. Using a puller, remove the steering wheel.
8. Installation is the reverse of removal. When installing the steering wheel, align the matchmarks and torque the nut to 27 ft. lbs. (36 Nm).
9. Connect the battery ground cable.

1972–77 Models

1. Disconnect the battery ground cable.
2. Remove the horn button after unfastening the two screws from underneath.

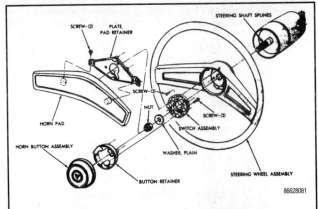

Fig. 58 Exploded view of a common steering wheel mounting on 1967–77 trucks

3. Disconnect the horn wire from the horn switch terminal.
4. Remove three screws, then lift out the horn switch and button or pad retainer assembly.
5. Back the steering wheel retaining nut off the top of the shaft.
6. Install a steering wheel puller and draw the steering wheel from the steering shaft splines.
7. Remove the steering wheel nut and pull the steering wheel off the steering shaft.
8. Installation is the reverse of removal. After replacing steering wheel and associated parts, tighten the nut to 27 ft. lbs. (36 Nm).
9. Connect the battery ground cable.

1978–88 Models

♦ See Figures 59, 60, 61, 62 and 63

1. Disconnect the battery ground cable.
2. Working through the access holes in the back of the wheel, push the horn pad off. DO NOT PRY THE PAD OFF!
3. Disconnect the horn wire.
4. Matchmark the steering wheel and shaft.
5. Remove the steering wheel retaining nut.
6. Using a puller, remove the steering wheel from the shaft. NEVER HAMMER THE SHAFT TO FREE THE WHEEL!

8-22 SUSPENSION AND STEERING

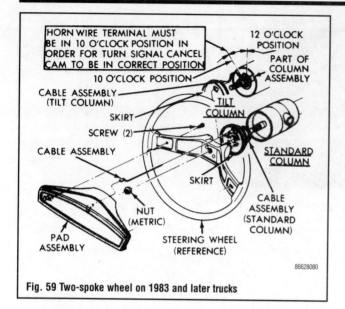

Fig. 59 Two-spoke wheel on 1983 and later trucks

7. Installation is the reverse of removal. After replacing steering wheel and associated parts, tighten the nut to 60 ft. lbs. on 1978–84 models; 45 ft. lbs. (61 Nm) on 1985–88 models.
8. Connect the battery ground cable.

Turn Signal Switch

REMOVAL & INSTALLATION

1967 Models

1. Remove the steering wheel.
2. Unscrew the turn signal lever.
3. Remove the column tube upper spring and spacer.
4. Disconnect the turn signal wires at the lower connector.
5. Remove the 2 switch hold-down screws, then pull the switch and wiring from the column.

To install:
6. Push the wiring of the switch into the column opening, then tighten the two screws to hold down the switch.
7. Attach the turn signal wires to the lower connector.
8. Install the column tube upper spring and spacer.
9. Bolt down the turn signal lever.
10. Install the steering wheel.

1968–88 Models

STANDARD COLUMNS

♦ See Figure 64

1. Remove the steering wheel.
2. Remove the turn signal lever retaining screw and remove the lever.
3. Detach the turn signal switch wiring at the lower connector.
4. Remove the wiring cover.
5. Remove the snapring from the upper end of the shaft.
6. Remove the screws retaining the turn signal switch and upper bearing.
7. Lift out the turn signal switch and wiring.

To install:
8. Push the wiring of the switch into the column opening. Replace the snapring, then tighten the screws that retain the switch and upper bearing.
9. Attach the turn signal wires to the connector.
10. Install the wiring cover for the upper end of the shaft.
11. Bolt down the turn signal lever.
12. Install the steering wheel.

TILT COLUMNS

♦ See Figures 65, 66 and 67

1. Remove the steering wheel.
2. Depress the lock plate with tool C-4156, or equivalent, just enough to remove the retaining ring, then pry the retaining ring out of the groove.
3. Remove the lock plate and upper bearing spring.
4. Place the turn signal switch in the right turn position.
5. Remove the screw which attaches the link between the turn signal switch and wiper/washer switch pivot.
6. Remove the screw which attaches the hazard switch knob.
7. Remove the 3 screws securing the turn signal switch.
8. Gently pull the switch and wiring from the column.
9. Installation is the reverse of removal.

Ignition Switch

REMOVAL & INSTALLATION

Standard Columns

♦ See Figures 68, 69, 70, 71 and 72

1. Remove the steering wheel.
2. Remove the turn signal switch.
3. Unfasten the two screws that release the buzzer switch (if equipped), then remove the switch.
4. Remove the retaining screw and lift the ignition lock cylinder lamp out of the way.

Fig. 60 Use a ratchet to loosen and remove the nut

Fig. 61 Unscrew the horn wire assembly

Fig. 62 Using a puller to free the wheel

SUSPENSION AND STEERING 8-23

Fig. 63 After disconnecting all of the retainers, remove the steering wheel from the truck

Fig. 64 The steering wheel must be removed in order to access the column components

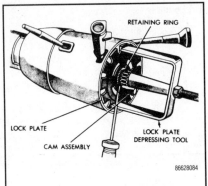

Fig. 65 Depressing the lock plate using a special tool

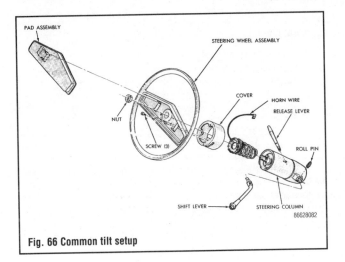

Fig. 66 Common tilt setup

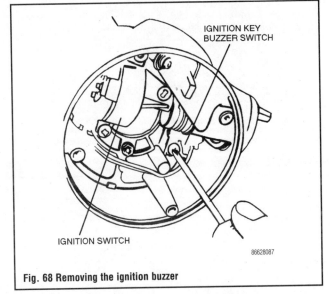

Fig. 68 Removing the ignition buzzer

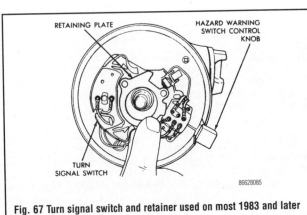

Fig. 67 Turn signal switch and retainer used on most 1983 and later vehicles

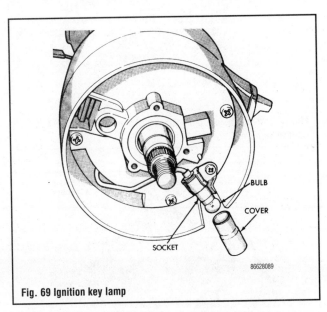

Fig. 69 Ignition key lamp

    5. Remove the bearing housing.
    6. Detach the coil spring.
    7. Remove the lock plate from the shaft.
    8. Unfasten the 2 retaining screws and lift the lock lever guide plate to expose the lock cylinder release hole.
    9. Insert the key and place the lock cylinder in the **LOCK** position. Remove the key.
    10. Insert a thin punch into the lock cylinder release hole and push inward to release the spring-loaded lock retainer. At the same time, pull the lock cylinder out of the column.
    11. Remove the 3 retaining screws and lift out the ignition switch.

To install:
    12. Position the ignition switch in the center detent position (OFF).
    13. Place the shift lever in PARK.
    14. Feed the wires down through the space between the housing and jacket. Position the switch in the housing and install the 3 retaining screws.
    15. Place the lock cylinder in the LOCK position, and press it into place in the column. It will snap into position.
    16. The remainder of assembly is the reverse of disassembly.

8-24 SUSPENSION AND STEERING

Tilt Columns

1. Remove the steering wheel.
2. Remove the tilt lever and turn signal lever.
3. If equipped, remove the cruise control lever.
4. Remove the turn signal switch.
5. Using the key, place the lock cylinder in the **LOCK** position. Remove the key.
6. Insert a thin punch in the slot next to the switch mounting screw boss, and depress the spring latch at the bottom of the slot. Hold the spring latch depressed and pull the lock cylinder out of the column.

7. Place the ignition switch in the **ACCESSORY** position and remove the mounting screws. Lift off the switch. The **ACCESSORY** position is the one opposite the spring-loaded end position.

To install:

8. Install the lock cylinder. Place the cylinder in the **LOCK** position and push it into the housing. It will snap into place.
9. Rotate the lock cylinder to the **ACCESSORY** position.
10. Fit the actuator rod in the slider hole and position the switch on the column. Insert the mounting screws, but don't tighten them yet.
11. Push the switch gently down the column to remove all lash from the actuator rod. Tighten the mounting screws. Make sure that you didn't take the switch out of the **ACCESSORY** detent!
12. The remainder of installation is the reverse of removal.

Ignition Lock Cylinder

REMOVAL & INSTALLATION

Standard Columns

1. Remove the steering wheel.
2. Disconnect the turn signal switch.
3. Unfasten the retaining screw and lift the ignition lock cylinder lamp out of the way.
4. Remove the bearing housing.
5. Remove the coil spring.
6. Disconnect the lock plate from the shaft.
7. Unfasten the 2 retaining screws and lift the lock lever guide plate to expose the lock cylinder release hole.
8. Insert the key and place the lock cylinder in the **LOCK** position. Remove the key.
9. Insert a thin punch into the lock cylinder release hole and push inward to release the spring-loaded lock retainer. At the same time, pull the lock cylinder out of the column.
10. When installing the lock cylinder, make sure it is in the **LOCK** position. Press it into the column; it will snap into place.
11. Install the lock lever guide plate and mount with screws. Attach the coil spring.
12. Install and fasten the bearing housing, and the ignition lamp.
13. Install the turn signal switch, and the steering wheel.

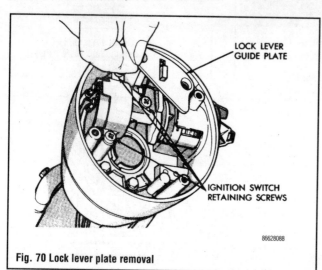

Fig. 70 Lock lever plate removal

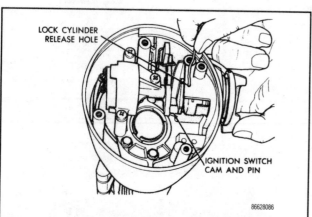

Fig. 71 Depress the lock plate which will expose the lock cylinder release hole

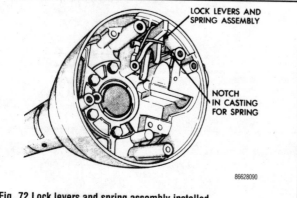

Fig. 72 Lock levers and spring assembly installed

Tilt Columns

1. Remove the steering wheel.
2. Remove the tilt lever and turn signal lever.
3. If equipped, remove the cruise control lever.
4. Remove the turn signal switch.
5. Using the key, place the lock cylinder in the **LOCK** position. Remove the key.
6. Insert a thin punch in the slot next to the switch mounting screw boss, and depress the spring latch at the bottom of the slot. Hold the spring latch depressed and pull the lock cylinder out of the column.
7. Place the lock cylinder in the **LOCK** position and press it into place in the column. It will snap into position.
8. Install the turn signal switch.
9. If equipped, install the cruise control lever.
10. Install the tilt lever and turn signal lever.
11. Install the steering wheel.

Steering Linkage

▶ See Figures 73, 74 and 75

REMOVAL & INSTALLATION

Pitman Arm

1. Place the wheels in a straight-ahead position.
2. Disconnect the drag link at the Pitman arm. You'll need a puller such as a tie rod end remover.

SUSPENSION AND STEERING 8-25

3. Remove the Pitman arm-to-gear nut and washer.
4. Matchmark the Pitman arm and gear housing for installation purposes.

5. Using a 2-jawed puller, remove the Pitman arm from the gear.
6. Installation is the reverse of removal. Align the matchmarks when installing the Pitman arm.
7. Torque the Pitman arm nut to 175 ft. lbs. (237 Nm); torque the drag link ball stud nut to 40 ft. lbs. (54 Nm), advancing the nut to align the cotter pin hole. Never back off the nut to align the hole.

Tie Rod Ends

2WD (WITH SOLID FRONT AXLE) AND 1967–74 4WD

1. Spray a penetrating oil on the bolts and nuts you are about to work on; they are probably rusty or very hard to loosen.
2. Remove the cotter pin and loosen the nut.
3. Using a tie rod end separator, free the tie rod end from the knuckle.
4. Unfasten the nut, then remove the tie rod end from the knuckle.
5. Count the exact number of threads visible between the tie rod end and the sleeve. Loosen the clamp bolts and unscrew the tie rod end.

To install:
6. Screw the end into the sleeve until exact number of threads originally noted is showing.
7. Tighten the clamp bolts to 40–70 ft. lbs. (54–94 Nm) and the tie rod end nut to the appropriate figure:
   - ½–20: 40–80 ft. lbs. (54–108 Nm)
   - ⅝–18: 50–90 ft. lbs. (67–121 Nm)
   - 9/16–18: 50–90 ft. lbs. (67–121 Nm)
   - ⅞–18: 60–110 ft. lbs. (81–149 Nm)

1972–88 INDEPENDENT FRONT SUSPENSION

1. Raise and safely support the front end on jackstands.
2. Spray a penetrating oil on the bolts and nuts you are about to work on; they are probably rusty or very hard to loosen.
3. Remove the cotter pin and nut from the tie rod end.
4. Using a separator, free the tie rod end from the knuckle arm or center link.
5. Count the exact number of threads visible between the tie rod end and the sleeve. Loosen the clamp bolts and unscrew the tie rod end.

To install:
6. Screw the end into the sleeve until the exact number of threads originally noted is showing.
7. Connect the tie rod end to the knuckle arm and center link. Tighten the tie rod end nut to 40–45 ft. lbs. (54–61 Nm).
8. Position the clamp onto the sleeve, and tighten the clamp bolts to 150–175 inch lbs. (16–19 Nm) on 100 and 200 series, or 20–30 ft. lbs. (27–40 Nm) on 300 series.

Tie Rod and Drag Link

♦ See Figures 76 and 77

1. Place the wheels in a straight-ahead position.
2. Remove the cotter pins and nuts from the drag link and tie rod ball studs.
3. Install puller tool C–4150 or equivalent, then apply pressure to free the link from the knuckle arm and steering gear arm.
4. Remove the drag link from the truck.

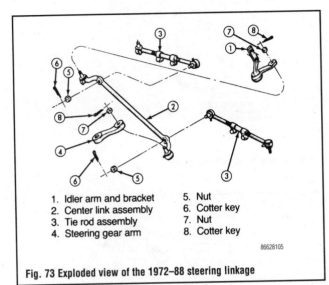

1. Idler arm and bracket
2. Center link assembly
3. Tie rod assembly
4. Steering gear arm
5. Nut
6. Cotter key
7. Nut
8. Cotter key

Fig. 73 Exploded view of the 1972–88 steering linkage

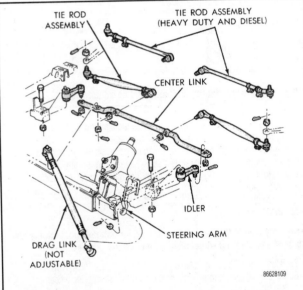

Fig. 74 If your truck has a center link the steering linkage should look like this

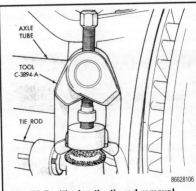

Fig. 75 Positioning the tie rod removal tool

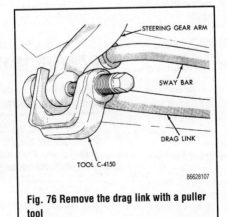

Fig. 76 Remove the drag link with a puller tool

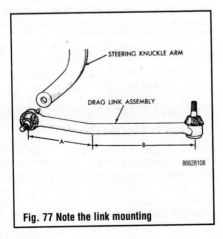

Fig. 77 Note the link mounting

8-26 SUSPENSION AND STEERING

To install:

5. Position the drag link as illustrated, so that the short segment (A) is mounted to the steering knuckle arm and the long end (B) is mounted to the steering gear arm.
6. Seat the studs in the tapered hole before tightening the nuts. This will avoid wrap-up of the rubber grommets during tightening of the nuts.
7. Install the new cotter pins. Torque the nuts to 40 ft. lbs. (54 Nm).
8. Have the front end alignment checked.

Connecting Rod

1. Raise and safely support the front end on jackstands.
2. Place the wheels in the straight-ahead position.
3. Detach the connecting rod from the drag link by removing the nut and separating the two with a tie rod end remover.
4. Loosen the bolts on the adjusting sleeve clamps. Count the number of turns it takes to remove the connecting rod from the adjuster sleeve, then remove the rod.
5. Install the connecting rod the exact number of turns noted during removal.
6. Tighten the mounting bolts by torquing the nuts to 40 ft. lbs. (54 Nm).
7. Lower the vehicle.
8. Have the front end alignment checked.

Manual Steering Gear

ADJUSTMENTS

1967–68 Saginaw 525D

♦ See Figures 78 and 79

There are two possible adjustments: the worm bearing preload, along with the ball nut and sector mesh. The worm bearing preload must be adjusted first.

You can check the steering gear adjustment without removing the gear from the truck as follows:

1. Place the wheels in a straight ahead position.
2. Matchmark and disconnect the Pitman arm from the gear shaft.
3. Remove the horn button and spring.
4. Make sure that there is no binding in the steering column.
5. Place an inch pound torque wrench on the steering wheel nut.
6. Turn the steering shaft with the torque wrench 2 full turns to either side of center, and check the torque necessary to turn the shaft back over the center point. If the torque (preload) is 5–9 inch lbs. (0.56–1.00 Nm) the gear is properly adjusted.

WORM BEARING PRELOAD

1. The Pitman arm must be removed.
2. Loosen the sector shaft adjuster locknut and back out the adjuster screw 2 turns.
3. Turn the steering wheel 2 complete turns to either side of center.

❋❋ WARNING

Never turn the steering wheel hard against either stop with the Pitman arm disconnected. Damage to the gear will result!

4. With an inch pound torque wrench, turn the steering shaft at least 1 turn toward center and note the turning torque. The torque should be 5–9 inch lbs. (0.56–1.00 Nm). If not, turn the adjuster screw clockwise to increase, or counterclockwise to decrease, the preload.
5. Hold the adjuster screw and torque the locknut to 85 ft. lbs. (115 Nm).
6. Recheck the preload. If the preload has changed, redo the adjustment.

BALL NUT AND SECTOR GEAR MESH

1. Complete the worm bearing preload adjustment first.
2. Turn the steering wheel gently from one lock to the other. Count the number of turns. Turn the wheel back exactly to the midpoint of its travel.
3. Loosen the sector shaft adjuster locknut. Turn the sector shaft adjusting screw, which is located on the housing cover, clockwise until there is no lash present between the ball nut and sector teeth. Tighten the locknut to 24 ft. lbs. (32 Nm).

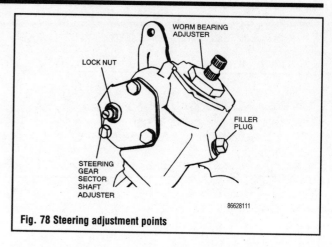

Fig. 78 Steering adjustment points

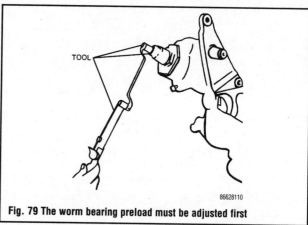

Fig. 79 The worm bearing preload must be adjusted first

4. Using an inch pound torque wrench on the steering shaft nut, rotate the steering wheel one-quarter turn away from the center. Note the torque required to turn the wheel through center. The reading should be 10–18 inch lbs. (1–2 Nm). Turn the sector shaft adjustment screw, if required, to obtain the correct preload. Hold the adjusting nut and tighten the locknut to 24 ft. lbs. (32 Nm).
5. Recheck the torque load. If the load has changed, redo the adjustment.
6. Once the adjustments are completed, straighten the front wheels and install the Pitman arm.

➡ Not only should the front wheels be straight-ahead, but both the steering gear and steering wheel should be centered, as well.

7. Tighten the Pitman arm securing nut to 175 ft. lbs. (237 Nm).
8. Install the horn button, ring, or trim pad on the steering wheel.

1967–68 Gemmer B–60 and Y5 and 375

WORM BEARING PRELOAD

1. The Pitman arm must be removed.
2. Loosen the sector shaft adjuster locknut and back out the adjuster screw 2 turns.
3. Turn the steering wheel 2 complete turns to either side of center.

❋❋ WARNING

Never turn the steering wheel hard against either stop with the Pitman arm disconnected. Damage to the gear will result!

4. With an inch pound torque wrench, turn the steering shaft through the center point and note the turning torque. The torque should be 7–14 inch lbs. (0.78–1.5 Nm). If not, add or remove shims beneath the lower worm bearing cover. Shims are available in 0.0025 in. (0.063mm), 0.0055 in. (0.139mm) and 0.010 in. (0.25mm) thicknesses.
5. Tighten the worm bearing cover bolts to 20 ft. lbs. (27 Nm).
6. Recheck the preload. If the preload has changed, redo the adjustment.

SUSPENSION AND STEERING 8-27

CROSS-SHAFT GEAR OR ROLLER-TO-WORM MESH

1. Disconnect the Pitman arm.
2. Counting the number of complete turns, turn the steering wheel completely from one lock to the other. Turn it GENTLY!
3. Turn the wheel back from either stop, ½ the total number of turns.
4. Loosen the cross-shaft adjusting screw locknut, and turn the adjusting screw in until all lash is removed. Tighten the locknut.
5. Turn the steering wheel 1 turn off of center.
6. Using an inch pound torque wrench on the steering wheel nut, measure the torque needed to rotate the wheel over center. The torque reading should be 20–27 inch lbs. (2.3–3 Nm). If not, turn the adjusting screw until the correct torque id obtained.
7. When the adjustment is complete, hold the adjusting screw and tighten the locknut to 20 ft. lbs. (27 Nm).
8. Recheck the adjustment. If the load has changed, redo the adjustment.
9. Install the Pitman arm and torque the nut to 250 ft. lbs. (338 Nm).

1969–73 Ross 24J

▶ See Figure 80

The worm bearing preload adjustment is performed with the gear out of the truck. The gear shaft adjustment can be performed with the gear in the truck. The worm bearing adjustment must be performed first, however.

Worm bearing preload can be checked with the gear in the truck as follows:
1. Place the wheels in a straight-ahead position.
2. Matchmark and disconnect the Pitman arm from the gear shaft.
3. Remove the horn button and spring.
4. Make sure that there is no binding in the steering column.
5. Place an inch pound torque wrench on the steering wheel nut.
6. Turn the steering shaft with the torque wrench 2 full turns to either side of center, and check the torque necessary to turn the shaft back over the center point. If the torque (preload) is 5–10 inch lbs. (0.56–1.10mm), the gear is properly adjusted.

WORM BEARING PRELOAD

1. The Pitman arm must be removed.
2. Loosen the cross-shaft adjuster locknut, then back out the adjuster screw 2 turns.
3. Turn the steering wheel 2 complete turns to either side of center.

✱✱ WARNING

Never turn the steering wheel hard against either stop with the Pitman arm disconnected. Damage to the gear will result!

4. With an inch pound torque wrench, turn the steering shaft through the center point and note the turning torque. The torque should be 5–10 inch lbs. (0.56–1.10 Nm). If not, add or remove shims beneath the wormshaft cover. Shims are available in 0.0025 in. (0.063mm), 0.0055 in. (0.139mm) and 0.010 in. (0.25mm) thicknesses.
5. Tighten the worm shaft cover bolts to 20 ft. lbs. (27 Nm).
6. Recheck the preload. If the preload has changed, re-do the adjustment.

GEAR SHAFT (CROSS-SHAFT)

1. Disconnect the Pitman arm.
2. Counting the number of complete turns, turn the steering wheel completely from one lock to the other. Turn it GENTLY!
3. Turn the wheel back from either stop, ½ the total number of turns.
4. Loosen the cross-shaft adjusting screw locknut, then turn the adjusting screw in until all lash is removed. Tighten the locknut.
5. Turn the steering wheel 1 turn off of center.
6. Using an inch pound torque wrench on the steering wheel nut, measure the torque needed to rotate the wheel over center. The torque reading should be 7–11 inch lbs. (0.78–1.2 Nm) more than the worm bearing preload. If not, turn the adjusting screw until the correct torque is obtained.
7. When the adjustment is complete, hold the adjusting screw and tighten the locknut to 20 ft. lbs. (27 Nm).
8. Recheck the adjustment. If the load has changed, redo the adjustment.
9. Install the Pitman arm and torque the nut to 95–145 ft. lbs. (128–196 Nm).

1969–77 Ross 376 (35J)

▶ See Figure 81

WORM BEARING PRELOAD

1. The Pitman arm must be removed.
2. Loosen the cross-shaft adjuster locknut, then back out the adjuster screw 2 turns.
3. Turn the steering wheel 2 complete turns to either side of center.

✱✱ WARNING

Never turn the steering wheel hard against either stop with the Pitman arm disconnected. Damage to the gear will result!

4. With an inch pound torque wrench, turn the steering shaft through the center point and note the turning torque. The torque should be 7–14 inch lbs. (0.78–1.5 Nm). If not, add or remove shims beneath the wormshaft cover. Shims are available in 0.0025 in. (0.063mm), 0.0055 in. (0.139mm) and 0.010 in. (0.25mm) thicknesses.
5. Tighten the worm shaft cover bolts to 20 ft. lbs. (27 Nm).
6. Recheck the preload. If the preload has changed, re-do the adjustment.

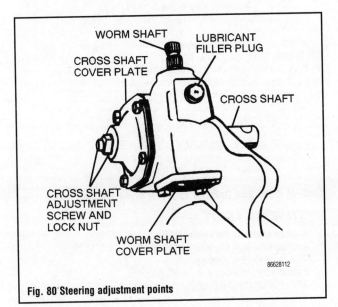

Fig. 80 Steering adjustment points

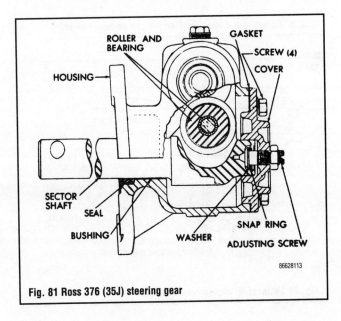

Fig. 81 Ross 376 (35J) steering gear

8-28 SUSPENSION AND STEERING

SECTOR SHAFT GEAR OR ROLLER-TO-WORM MESH

1. Disconnect the Pitman arm.
2. Counting the number of complete turns, turn the steering wheel completely from one lock to the other. Turn it GENTLY!
3. Turn the wheel back from either stop, ½ the total number of turns.
4. Loosen the cross-shaft adjusting screw locknut, then turn the adjusting screw in until all lash is removed. Tighten the locknut.
5. Turn the steering wheel 1 turn off of center.
6. Using an inch pound torque wrench on the steering wheel nut, measure the torque needed to rotate the wheel over center. The torque reading should be 20–27 inch lbs. (2.2–3 Nm). If not, turn the adjusting screw until the correct torque is obtained.
7. When the adjustment is complete, hold the adjusting screw and tighten the locknut to 20 ft. lbs. (27 Nm).
8. Recheck the adjustment. If the load has changed, redo the adjustment.
9. Install the Pitman arm and torque the nut to 135 ft. lbs. (182 Nm).

1974–88 Saginaw 525

♦ See Figures 82 and 83

WORM BEARING PRELOAD

1. The Pitman arm must be removed.
2. Loosen the sector shaft adjuster locknut and back out the adjuster screw 2 turns.
3. Remove the horn pad and spring.
4. Turn the steering wheel to the right stop, then turn it back ½ turn.

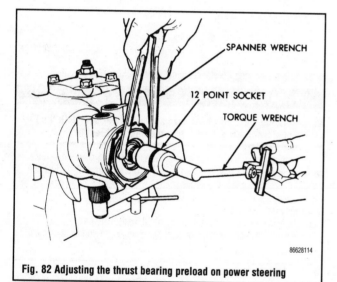

Fig. 82 Adjusting the thrust bearing preload on power steering

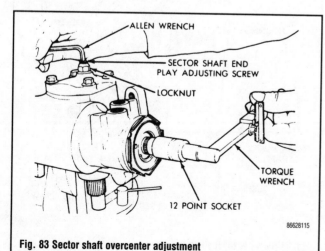

Fig. 83 Sector shaft overcenter adjustment

✱✱ WARNING

Never turn the steering wheel hard against either stop with the Pitman arm disconnected. Damage to the gear will result!

5. With an inch pound torque wrench, turn the steering shaft at least 1 turn toward center and note the turning torque. The torque should be 4–6 inch lbs. (0.44–0.67 Nm). If not, turn the adjuster screw clockwise to increase, or counterclockwise to decrease, the preload.
6. Hold the adjuster screw and torque the locknut to 85 ft. lbs. (115 Nm).
7. Recheck the preload. If the preload has changed, re-do the adjustment.

BALL NUT AND SECTOR GEAR MESH

♦ See Figure 84

1. Complete the worm bearing preload adjustment first.
2. Turn the steering wheel gently from one lock to the other. Count the number of turns. Turn the wheel back exactly to the midpoint of its travel.
3. Loosen the sector shaft adjuster locknut. Turn the sector shaft adjusting screw, which is located on the housing cover, clockwise until there is no lash present between the ball nut and sector teeth. Tighten the locknut to 24 ft. lbs. (32 Nm).
4. Using an inch pound torque wrench on the steering shaft nut, rotate the steering wheel ¼ turn away from the center. Note the torque required to turn the wheel through center. The reading should be 14 inch lbs. (1.5 Nm). Turn the sector shaft adjustment screw, if required, to obtain the correct preload. Hold the adjusting nut and tighten the locknut to 24 ft. lbs. (32 Nm).
5. Recheck the torque load. If the load has changed, redo the adjustment.
6. Once the adjustments are completed, straighten the front wheels and install the Pitman arm.

➡ Not only should the front wheels be straight-ahead, but both the steering gear and the steering wheel should be centered, as well.

7. Tighten the Pitman arm securing nut to 180 ft. lbs. (243 Nm).
8. Install the horn button, ring, or trim pad on the steering wheel.

REMOVAL & INSTALLATION

1967–68 D100/W100, D200/W200, and D300 With Saginaw 525D Recirculating Ball-Type

1. Raise and safely support the front end on jackstands.
2. Place the wheels in a straight ahead position.
3. Matchmark the Pitman arm and steering gear.
4. Disconnect the arm from the gear.
5. Remove the gear-to-frame bolts.
6. Support the gear and remove the wormshaft-to-steering shaft coupling bolt.
7. Matchmark the wormshaft and steering shaft.
8. Tap the coupling upward with a soft mallet until it is free, then remove the gear.
9. Installation is the reverse of removal. When installing the gear, make sure that the gear shaft is centered. To find the center, rotate the gear shaft from lock-to-lock with a ratchet and socket, counting the total number of revolutions necessary. Turn the shaft back from either lock, ½ the total number of lock-to-lock turns. Make sure that all matchmarks are aligned.

Tighten the coupling bolt to 30 ft. lbs. (40 Nm). Tighten the Pitman arm-to-gear nut to 175 ft. lbs. (237 Nm).

Tighten the steering gear mounting bolts as follows:
- ⁷⁄₁₆–20: 40–70 ft. lbs. (54–94 Nm)
- ½–20: 65–105 ft. lbs. (88–142 Nm)
- ⁹⁄₁₆–18: 90–140 ft. lbs. (122–189 Nm)

1967–68 W300 With Gemmer Y5D–375 Worm and Sector Gear

WITH LONG WORM SHAFT

1. Disconnect the battery ground cable.
2. Place the wheels in a straight ahead position.
3. Remove the steering wheel.
4. Disconnect all wiring at the steering column.
5. Disconnect the shift linkage at the column.

SUSPENSION AND STEERING 8-29

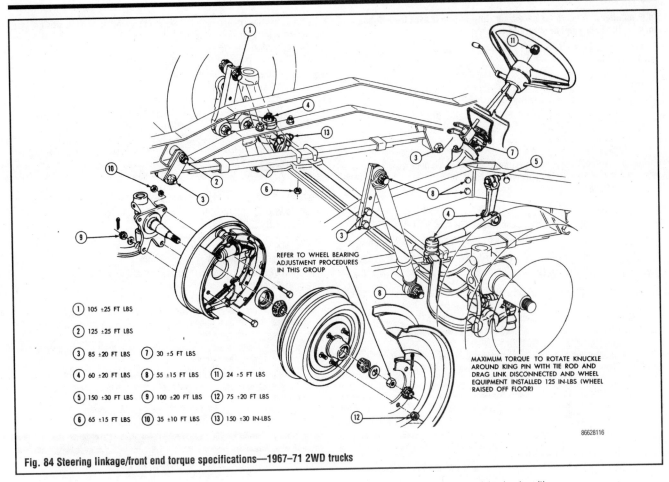

Fig. 84 Steering linkage/front end torque specifications—1967-71 2WD trucks

6. Remove the column-to-instrument panel clamp.
7. Matchmark the Pitman arm and steering gear.
8. Disconnect the drag link from the Pitman arm.
9. Disconnect the Pitman arm from the gear.
10. Remove the transmission shift linkage.
11. Support the gear and remove the mounting bolts.
12. Lower the gear and jacket tube assembly from the truck.

To install:

➡ Make sure that the gear shaft is centered. To find the center, rotate the gear shaft from lock-to-lock with a ratchet and socket, counting the total number of revolutions necessary. Turn the shaft back from either lock, ½ the total number of lock-to-lock turns.

13. Guide the jacket tube through the floor panel and position the gear on the frame.
14. Install the mounting bolts. Don't tighten them yet.
15. Install and tighten the column-to-instrument panel bolts.
16. Tighten the gear to frame bolts as follows:
- 7/16–20: 40–70 ft. lbs. (54–94 Nm)
- ½–20: 65–105 ft. lbs. (88–106 Nm)
- 9/16–18: 90–140 ft. lbs. (121–189 Nm)
17. Tighten the coupling bolt to 30 ft. lbs. (40 Nm). Loosen the column-to-instrument panel bolts. If the column tube shifted when the bolts were loosened, reposition the column bracket. Tighten the bolts.
18. Connect all wiring.
19. Install the steering wheel.
20. Connect and adjust the shift linkage.
21. Install the Pitman arm. Tighten the nut to 175–245 ft. lbs. (237–332 Nm). Connect the drag link. Torque the nut to 40 ft. lbs. (54 Nm). Install a new cotter pin.

WITH SHORT WORM SHAFT

1. Disconnect the battery ground cable.
2. Raise and safely support the front end on jackstands.
3. Place the wheels in a straight-ahead position.
4. Matchmark the steering shaft coupling and wormshaft.
5. Remove the coupling bolt.
6. Disconnect the battery ground cable.
7. Move the steering column upwards to free the coupling from the wormshaft. Refer to the steering column removal and installation procedure.
8. Matchmark the Pitman arm and gear.
9. Disconnect the Pitman arm from the gear shaft.
10. Unfasten the 3 mounting bolts and remove the gear.
11. Installation is the reverse of removal. Make sure that the gear shaft is centered. To find the center, rotate the gear shaft from lock-to-lock with a ratchet and socket, counting the total number of revolutions necessary. Turn the shaft back from either lock, ½ the total number of lock-to-lock turns. Tighten the steering shaft coupling bolt to 30 ft. lbs. (40 Nm); the Pitman arm clamp bolt to 170 ft. lbs. (230 Nm); the Pitman arm nut to 245 ft. lbs. (332 Nm).

1967–68 W300 With Gemmer B–60 Worm and Sector Gear

WITH LONG WORM SHAFT

1. Disconnect the battery ground cable.
2. Place the wheels in a straight-ahead position.
3. Remove the steering wheel.
4. Disconnect all wiring at the steering column.
5. Disconnect the shift linkage at the column.
6. Remove the column-to-instrument panel clamp.
7. Matchmark the Pitman arm and steering gear.
8. Disconnect the drag link from the Pitman arm.
9. Disconnect the Pitman arm from the gear.
10. Remove the transmission shift linkage.
11. Support the gear and remove the mounting bolts.
12. Lower the gear and jacket tube assembly from the truck.

To install:

➡ Make sure that the gear shaft is centered. To find the center, rotate the gear shaft from lock-to-lock with a ratchet and socket, counting the

8-30 SUSPENSION AND STEERING

total number of revolutions necessary. Turn the shaft back from either lock, ½ the total number of lock-to-lock turns.

13. Guide the jacket tube through the floor panel and position the gear on the frame.
14. Install the mounting bolts. Don't tighten them yet.
15. Install and tighten the column-to-instrument panel bolts.
16. Tighten the gear-to-frame bolts as follows:
- ⁷⁄₁₆–20: 40–70 ft. lbs. (54–94 Nm)
- ½–20: 65–105 ft. lbs. (88–106 Nm)
- ⁹⁄₁₆–18: 90–140 ft. lbs. (121–189 Nm)
17. Tighten the coupling bolt to 30 ft. lbs. (40 Nm). Loosen the column-to-instrument panel bolts. If the column tube shifted when the bolts were loosened, reposition the column bracket. Tighten the bolts.
18. Connect all wiring.
19. Install the steering wheel.
20. Connect and adjust the shift linkage.
21. Install the Pitman arm. Tighten the nut to 175–245 ft. lbs. (237–332 Nm). Connect the drag link. Torque the nut to 40 ft. lbs. (54 Nm). Install a new cotter pin.

WITH SHORT WORM SHAFT

1. Disconnect the battery ground cable.
2. Raise and safely support the front end on jackstands.
3. Place the wheels in a straight ahead position.
4. Matchmark the steering shaft coupling and wormshaft.
5. Remove the coupling bolt.
6. Move the steering column upwards to free the coupling from the wormshaft. Refer to the steering column removal and installation procedure.
7. Matchmark the Pitman arm and gear.
8. Disconnect the Pitman arm from the gear shaft.
9. Unfasten the 3 mounting bolts and remove the gear.
10. Installation is the reverse of removal. Make sure that the gear shaft is centered. To find the center, rotate the gear shaft from lock-to-lock with a ratchet and socket, counting the total number of revolutions necessary. Turn the shaft back from either lock, ½ the total number of lock-to-lock turns. Tighten the steering shaft coupling bolt to 30 ft. lbs. (40 Nm); the Pitman arm clamp bolt to 170 ft. lbs. (230 Nm); the Pitman arm nut to 245 ft. lbs. (332 Nm).

1969–73 D100/W100, D200/W200 and D300 With Ross 24J Worm and Roller-Type

1. Place the wheels in a straight-ahead position.
2. Loosen the bolts at the steering column support bracket.
3. Remove the floor plate bolts.
4. Remove the bolt from the wormshaft coupling.
5. Matchmark the wormshaft and coupling.
6. Matchmark the Pitman arm and gear shaft.
7. Remove the Pitman arm.
8. Tap the coupling assembly and column upwards with a soft mallet until the coupling is free of the wormshaft.
9. Support the gear and remove the 3 mounting bolts. Remove the gear.
10. Installation is the reverse of removal. When installing the gear, make sure that the gear shaft is centered. To find the center, rotate the gear shaft from lock-to-lock with a ratchet and socket, counting the total number of revolutions necessary. Turn the shaft back from either lock, ½ the total number of lock-to-lock turns. Align the matchmarks. Tighten the coupling bolt to 30 ft. lbs. (40 Nm). Tighten the Pitman arm to:
- ⁷⁄₈–14 nut: 95–145 ft. lbs. (128–196 Nm)
- 1–14 nut: 175–245 ft. lbs. (237–332 Nm)

Tighten the steering gear mounting bolts to:
- ⁷⁄₁₆–20: 40–70 ft. lbs. (54–94 Nm)
- ½–20: 65–105 ft. lbs. (88–142 Nm)
- ⁹⁄₁₆–18: 90–140 ft. lbs. (121–189 Nm)

1969–77 W300 With Ross 376 Worm and Roller Type

1. Place the wheels in a straight ahead position.
2. Remove the wormshaft coupling bolt.
3. Matchmark the wormshaft and coupling.
4. Disconnect the turn signal and horn wire connectors at the column.
5. Loosen the column bracket bolts and move the column upwards until the coupling is free of the wormshaft.
6. Matchmark the Pitman arm and gear shaft.
7. Remove the Pitman arm from the gear shaft.
8. Support the gear and remove the 3 mounting bolts. Remove the gear.
9. When installing the gear, make sure that the gear shaft is centered. To find the center, rotate the gear shaft from lock-to-lock with a ratchet and socket, counting the total number of revolutions necessary. Turn the shaft back from either lock, ½ the total number of lock-to-lock turns. Align all matchmarks. Tighten the coupling bolt to 30 ft. lbs. (40 Nm). On pot-type joints, the steering shaft should be centered in the joint to ensure adequate travel. Tighten the gear shaft clamp bolt to 85 ft. lbs. (115 Nm); the Pitman arm nut to 135 ft. lbs. (183 Nm).

1974–77 D100/W100, D200/W200 and D300, as well as All 1978–88 Models With Saginaw 525 Recirculating Ball-Type

1. Place the wheels in a straight-ahead position.
2. Matchmark the wormshaft coupling.
3. Remove the 2 wormshaft coupling bolts.
4. Matchmark the Pitman arm and gear shaft.
5. Remove the Pitman arm.
6. Support the gear, unfasten the mounting bolts and remove the gear.
7. Position the gear-to-frame and install the mounting bolts.
8. Install the Pitman arm and place the wheels in the straight-ahead position.
9. Place the steering wheel in the straight ahead position. Install the worm shaft to the column coupling bolts.
10. Install the coupling bolts. Tighten the coupling bolts to 30 ft. lbs. (40 Nm); the Pitman arm nut to 180 ft. lbs. (244 Nm); the steering gear mounting bolts to 55 ft. lbs. (74 Nm) for 1974–77, or 100 ft. lbs. (135 Nm) for 1978–88 models.

Power Steering Gear

Models through 1972 use a Thompson-type power cylinder system to turn a conventional steering gear. The steering gear application is the same as for trucks with manual steering, and gear removal is the same as with manual steering.

1973–88 models use a type 708 integral power steering gear.

ADJUSTMENTS

No adjustments are possible on the Thompson-type power cylinder system.

Preliminary Checks

1. Remove the gear from the truck.
2. Rotate the gear several times through its travel to expel all fluid from the gear.
3. Place a ¾ in. (19mm) 12–point socket on the stub shaft. Using an inch pound torque wrench, check the torque ½ turn off the right stop, then ¼ turn off the left stop. Record these figures.
4. Center the gear and check the torque ½ turn to each side of center. Record these figures.
5. Turn the gear 90° to the right of center and turn the gear in a 180° arc to the left of center. Record the reading.

Worm Thrust Bearing

1. Remove the adjuster plug locknut.
2. Turn the adjuster plug in until the plug and thrust bearing are fully bottomed. This takes about 20 ft. lbs. (27 Nm) of torque.
3. Matchmark the housing and one of the holes in the plug.
4. Measure counterclockwise ¼ in. (6mm) from that mark and make another mark on the housing.
5. Rotate the plug counterclockwise until the marked hole aligns with the second housing mark.
6. Install the locknut and, while holding the adjuster plug, tighten the locknut securely.

SUSPENSION AND STEERING 8-31

7. Using an inch pound torque wrench on the stub shaft, turn the shaft to the right stop, then back ¼ turn. Note the reading. The reading should be 4–10 inch lbs. (0.44–1.1Nm). If not:
   a. Loosen the sector shaft preload adjuster screw locknut and turn the screw 1½ turns counterclockwise. If the screw bottoms, turn it back ½ turn.
   b. Retighten the locknut while holding the screw.
   c. Loosen the adjuster plug locknut.
   d. Turn the plug 1 turn counterclockwise.
   e. Turn the stub shaft to the right stop, then back ¼ turn. Record the torque reading.
   f. Bottom the adjuster plug firmly with 20 ft. lbs. (27 Nm) torque, then back it off until the stub shaft rotational torque is 3–4 inch lbs. (0.33–0.44 Nm) more than the total torque reading with the adjuster plug tightened.
   g. Tighten the adjuster plug locknut securely.

➡ Preload torque tends to drop off when the locknut is tightened. Even so, the torque reading must be rechecked with the locknut tight, and the torque must still be 3–4 inch lbs. (0.33–0.44 Nm) more than the total.

Sector Shaft Overcenter

1. Center the gear shaft.
2. Loosen the sector shaft adjusting screw locknut, then tighten the sector shaft adjusting screw.
3. Tighten the locknut and, using an inch pound torque wrench, rotate the sector shaft 90° to either side of center, noting the torque reading over center. The highest reading is what counts.
4. Continue adjusting and checking the preload until the preload is 4–8 inch lbs. (0.44–0.89 Nm) for a new gear, do not exceed 18 inch lbs. (2 Nm). For a gear having more than 400 miles, the preload should be 4–5 inch lbs. (0.44–0.56 Nm) do not exceed 14 inch lbs. (1.5 Nm).

REMOVAL & INSTALLATION

1973–88 Models

1. Place the wheels in a straight-ahead position.
2. Remove the Pitman arm.
3. Place a drain pan under the gear and disconnect the hoses at the gear.
4. Matchmark and disconnect the gearshaft coupling.
5. Support the gear and remove the mounting bolts. Remove the steering gear.
6. Installation is the reverse of removal. Torque the Pitman arm nut to 175 ft. lbs. (237 Nm); the mounting bolts to 85 ft. lbs. (115 Nm) on models through 1977 or 100 ft. lbs. (135 Nm) on 1978–88 models.

Power Steering Pump

REMOVAL & INSTALLATION

Thompson Pump

◆ See Figure 85

1. Loosen the pump mounting and locking bolts, then remove the drive belt.
2. Disconnect and plug both hoses.
3. Remove the mounting and locking bolts, then remove the pump.

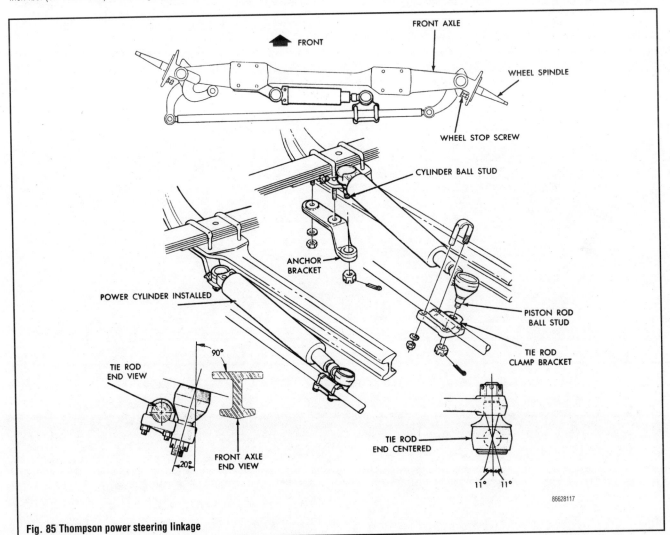

Fig. 85 Thompson power steering linkage

8-32 SUSPENSION AND STEERING

To install:

4. Position the pump on the engine, then install the mounting and locking bolts.
5. Install and adjust the drive belt. Tighten the mounting bolts to 30 ft. lbs. (40 Nm).
6. Connect the pressure and return hoses. Route the hoses in the same manner as they were prior to removal. They should be routed smoothly with no sharp bends. Tighten the pump end hose fitting to 30 ft. lbs. (40 Nm) on models through 1974, or 35 ft. lbs. (47 Nm) for 1975 and later. Tighten the gear end fitting to 19 ft. lbs. (25 Nm) on models through 1974, or 25 ft. lbs. (33 Nm) for 1975 and later. The hoses should remain at least 1 in. (25mm) away from the pulleys, battery case, and brake lines, and at least 2 in. (50mm) away from exhaust manifolds. If equipped, the protective sponge sleeves should be used to protect the hoses from contact with other parts.
7. Fill the pump with the specified power steering fluid or its equivalent.
8. Start the engine and turn the steering wheel lock-to-lock several times to bleed the system. Check for leaks and recheck the fluid level.

Saginaw Pump

1. If the pump is to be replaced or disassembled, remove the pulley nut before removing the belt.
2. Remove the belt.
3. Place a drain pan under the pump and disconnect both hoses from the pump.
4. Remove the mounting and adjusting bolts, then lift out the pump.

To install:

5. Mount the pump and install the bolts.
6. Reconnect the hoses and install the belt.
7. Install the pulley nut, then adjust the belt tension.
8. Torque the bolts to 30 ft. lbs. (40 Nm). Make sure that the hoses are routed at least 1 in. (25mm) from all surfaces, and at least 2 in. (51mm) from the exhaust manifold.

HYDRAULIC BRAKING SYSTEM 9-2
BASIC OPERATING PRINCIPLES 9-2
    DISC BRAKES 9-2
    DRUM BRAKES 9-2
ADJUSTMENTS 9-3
    DRUM BRAKES 9-3
BRAKE LIGHT SWITCH 9-3
    REMOVAL & INSTALLATION 9-3
    ADJUSTMENT 9-3
MASTER CYLINDER 9-4
    REMOVAL & INSTALLATION 9-4
POWER BOOSTER 9-5
    REMOVAL & INSTALLATION 9-5
HYDRO-BOOST 9-6
    REMOVAL & INSTALLATION 9-6
HYDRAULIC VALVES 9-6
    REMOVAL & INSTALLATION 9-6
    CENTERING THE PROPORTIONING VALVE 9-7
BRAKE HOSES AND PIPES 9-7
    REMOVAL & INSTALLATION 9-8
BLEEDING THE BRAKES 9-8
    MASTER CYLINDER 9-8
    WHEEL CYLINDERS & CALIPERS 9-8
FRONT DRUM BRAKES 9-9
BRAKE DRUMS 9-9
    REMOVAL & INSTALLATION 9-9
    INSPECTION 9-9
BRAKE SHOES 9-9
    REMOVAL & INSTALLATION 9-9
WHEEL CYLINDERS 9-10
    REMOVAL, INSTALLATION & OVERHAUL 9-10
FRONT DISC BRAKES 9-11
APPLICATION 9-11
DISC BRAKE PADS 9-11
    INSPECTION 9-11
    REMOVAL & INSTALLATION 9-11
DISC BRAKE CALIPERS 9-14
    REMOVAL & INSTALLATION 9-14
    OVERHAUL 9-15
BRAKE DISC (ROTOR) 9-16
    REMOVAL & INSTALLATION 9-16
    INSPECTION 9-16
REAR DRUM BRAKES 9-16
BRAKE DRUM 9-16
    INSPECTION 9-16
    REMOVAL & INSTALLATION 9-17
BRAKE SHOES 9-17
    REMOVAL & INSTALLATION 9-17
WHEEL CYLINDERS 9-20
    REMOVAL & INSTALLATION 9-20
PARKING BRAKE 9-20
CABLES 9-20
    REMOVAL & INSTALLATION 9-20
    ADJUSTMENT 9-22
SPECIFICATIONS CHARTS
    BRAKE SPECIFICATIONS 9-24

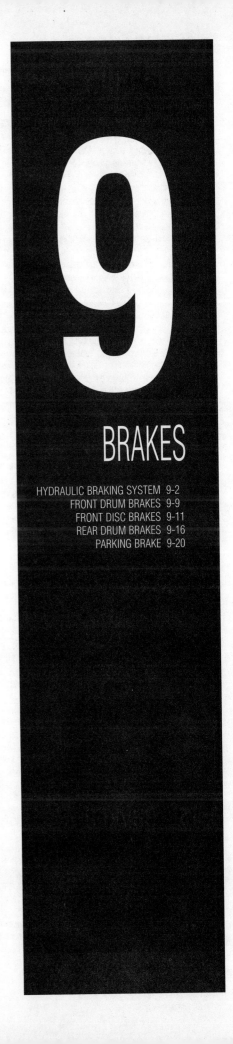

9
BRAKES

HYDRAULIC BRAKING SYSTEM 9-2
FRONT DRUM BRAKES 9-9
FRONT DISC BRAKES 9-11
REAR DRUM BRAKES 9-16
PARKING BRAKE 9-20

HYDRAULIC BRAKING SYSTEM

Basic Operating Principles

Hydraulic systems are used to actuate the brakes of all modern automobiles. The system transports the power required to force the frictional surfaces of the braking system together from the pedal to the individual brake units at each wheel. A hydraulic system is used for two reasons.

First, fluid under pressure can be carried to all parts of an automobile by small pipes and flexible hoses without taking up a significant amount of room or posing routing problems.

Second, a great mechanical advantage can be given to the brake pedal end of the system, and the foot pressure required to actuate the brakes can be reduced by making the surface area of the master cylinder pistons smaller than that of any of the pistons in the wheel cylinders or calipers.

The master cylinder consists of a fluid reservoir along with a double cylinder and piston assembly. Double type master cylinders are designed to separate the front and rear braking systems hydraulically in case of a leak. The master cylinder coverts mechanical motion from the pedal into hydraulic pressure within the lines. This pressure is translated back into mechanical motion at the wheels by either the wheel cylinder (drum brakes) or the caliper (disc brakes).

Steel lines carry the brake fluid to a point on the vehicle's frame near each of the vehicle's wheels. The fluid is then carried to the calipers and wheel cylinders by flexible tubes in order to allow for suspension and steering movements.

In drum brake systems, each wheel cylinder contains two pistons, one at either end, which push outward in opposite directions and force the brake shoe into contact with the drum.

In disc brake systems, the cylinders are part of the calipers. At least one cylinder in each caliper is used to force the brake pads against the disc.

All pistons employ some type of seal, usually made of rubber, to minimize fluid leakage. A rubber dust boot seals the outer end of the cylinder against dust and dirt. The boot fits around the outer end of the piston on disc brake calipers, and around the brake actuating rod on wheel cylinders.

The hydraulic system operates as follows: When at rest, the entire system, from the piston(s) in the master cylinder to those in the wheel cylinders or calipers, is full of brake fluid. Upon application of the brake pedal, fluid trapped in front of the master cylinder piston(s) is forced through the lines to the wheel cylinders. Here, it forces the pistons outward, in the case of drum brakes, and inward toward the disc, in the case of disc brakes. The motion of the pistons is opposed by return springs mounted outside the cylinders in drum brakes, and by spring seals, in disc brakes.

Upon release of the brake pedal, a spring located inside the master cylinder immediately returns the master cylinder pistons to the normal position. The pistons contain check valves and the master cylinder has compensating ports drilled in it. These are uncovered as the pistons reach their normal position. The piston check valves allow fluid to flow toward the wheel cylinders or calipers as the pistons withdraw. Then, as the return springs force the brake pads or shoes into the released position, the excess fluid reservoir through the compensating ports. It is during the time the pedal is in the released position that any fluid that has leaked out of the system will be replaced through the compensating ports.

Dual circuit master cylinders employ two pistons, located one behind the other, in the same cylinder. The primary piston is actuated directly by mechanical linkage from the brake pedal through the power booster. The secondary piston is actuated by fluid trapped between the two pistons. If a leak develops in front of the secondary piston, it moves forward until it bottoms against the front of the master cylinder, and the fluid trapped between the pistons will operate the rear brakes. If the rear brakes develop a leak, the primary piston will move forward until direct contact with the secondary piston takes place, and it will force the secondary piston to actuate the front brakes. In either case, the brake pedal moves farther when the brakes are applied, and less braking power is available.

All dual circuit systems use a switch to warn the driver when only half of the brake system is operational. This switch is usually located in a valve body which is mounted on the firewall or the frame below the master cylinder. A hydraulic piston receives pressure from both circuits, each circuit's pressure being applied to one end of the piston. When the pressures are in balance, the piston remains stationary. When one circuit has a leak, however, the greater pressure in that circuit during application of the brakes will push the piston to one side, closing the switch and activating the brake warning light.

In disc brake systems, this valve body also contains a metering valve and, in some cases, a proportioning valve. The metering valve keeps pressure from traveling to the disc brakes on the front wheels until the brake shoes on the rear wheels have contacted the drums, ensuring that the front brakes will never be used alone. The proportioning valve controls the pressure to the rear brakes to lessen the chance of rear wheel lock-up during very hard braking.

Warning lights may be tested by depressing the brake pedal and holding it while opening one of the wheel cylinder bleeder screws. If this does not cause the light to go on, substitute a new lamp, make continuity checks, and, finally, replace the switch as necessary.

The hydraulic system may be checked for leaks by applying pressure to the pedal gradually and steadily. If the pedal sinks very slowly to the floor, the system has a leak. This is not to be confused with a springy or spongy feel due to the compression of air within the lines. If the system leaks, there will be a gradual change in the position of the pedal with a constant pressure.

Check for leaks along all lines and at wheel cylinders. If no external leaks are apparent, the problem is inside the master cylinder.

DISC BRAKES

Instead of the traditional expanding brakes that press outward against a circular drum, disc brake systems utilize a disc (rotor) with brake pads positioned on either side of it. An easily-seen analogy is the hand brake arrangement on a bicycle. The pads squeeze onto the rim of the bike wheel, slowing its motion. Automobile disc brakes use the identical principle but apply the braking effort to a separate disc instead of the wheel.

The disc (rotor) is a casting, usually equipped with cooling fins between the two braking surfaces. This enables air to circulate between the braking surfaces making them less sensitive to heat buildup and more resistant to fade. Dirt and water do not drastically affect braking action since contaminants are thrown off by the centrifugal action of the rotor or scraped off the by the pads. Also, the equal clamping action of the two brake pads tends to ensure uniform, straight line stops. Disc brakes are inherently self-adjusting. There are three general types of disc brake:

1. A fixed caliper.
2. A floating caliper.
3. A sliding caliper.

The fixed caliper design uses two pistons mounted on either side of the rotor (in each side of the caliper). The caliper is mounted rigidly and does not move.

The sliding and floating designs are quite similar. In fact, these two types are often lumped together. In both designs, the pad on the inside of the rotor is moved into contact with the rotor by hydraulic force. The caliper, which is not held in a fixed position, moves slightly, bringing the outside pad into contact with the rotor. There are various methods of attaching floating calipers. Some pivot at the bottom or top, and some slide on mounting bolts. In any event, the end result is the same.

DRUM BRAKES

Drum brakes employ two brake shoes mounted on a stationary backing plate. These shoes are positioned inside a circular drum which rotates with the wheel assembly. The shoes are held in place by springs. This allows them to slide toward the drums (when they are applied) while keeping the linings and drums in alignment. The shoes are actuated by a wheel cylinder which is mounted at the top of the backing plate. When the brakes are applied, hydraulic pressure forces the wheel cylinder's actuating links outward. Since these links bear directly against the top of the brake shoes, the tops of the shoes are then forced against the inner side of the drum. This action forces the bottoms of the two shoes to contact the brake drum by rotating the entire assembly slightly (known as servo action). When pressure within the wheel cylinder is relaxed, return springs pull the shoes back away from the drum.

Most modern drum brakes are designed to self-adjust themselves during application when the vehicle is moving in reverse. This motion causes both shoes to rotate very slightly with the drum, rocking an adjusting lever, thereby causing rotation of the adjusting screw. Some drum brake systems are designed to self-adjust during application whenever the brakes are applied. This on-board adjustment system reduces the need for maintenance adjustments and keeps both the brake function and pedal feel satisfactory.

BRAKES

Adjustments

DRUM BRAKES

♦ See Figure 1

The drum brakes are self-adjusting and require a manual adjustment only after the brake shoes have been replaced, or when the length of the adjusting screw has been changed while performing some other service operation, as i.e., taking off brake drums.

To adjust the brakes, follow the procedures given below:

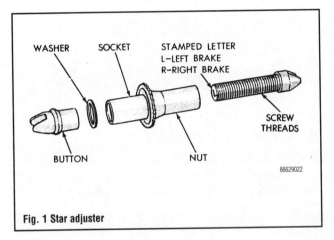

Fig. 1 Star adjuster

Drum Installed

♦ See Figures 2, 3 and 4

1. Raise and support the rear end on jackstands.
2. Remove the rubber plug from the adjusting slot on the backing plate.
3. Insert a brake adjusting spoon into the slot and engage the lowest possible tooth on the starwheel. Move the end of the brake spoon downward to move the starwheel upward and expand the adjusting screw. Repeat this operation until the brakes lock the wheels.
4. Insert a small prytool or piece of firm wire (coat hanger wire) into the adjusting slot and push the automatic adjusting lever out and free of the starwheel on the adjusting screw and hold it there.
5. Engage the top-most tooth possible on the starwheel with the brake adjusting spoon. Move the end of the adjusting spoon upward to move the adjusting screw starwheel downward and contract the adjusting screw. Back off the adjusting screw starwheel until the wheel spins freely with a minimum of drag. Keep track of the number of turns that the starwheel is backed off, or the number of strokes taken with the brake adjusting spoon.
6. Repeat this operation for the other side. When backing off the brakes on the other side, the starwheel adjuster must be backed off the same number of turns to prevent side-to-side brake pull.
7. Remove the safety stands and lower the vehicle. Road test the vehicle.
8. When the brakes are adjusted make several stops while backing the vehicle, to equalize the brakes at both of the wheels.

Drum Removed

※※ CAUTION

Brake shoes contain asbestos, which has been determined to be a cancer causing agent. Never clean the brake surfaces with compressed air! Avoid inhaling any dust from any brake surface! When cleaning brake surfaces, use a commercially available brake cleaning fluid.

1. Make sure that the shoe-to-contact pad areas are clean and properly lubricated.
2. Using an inside caliper check the inside diameter of the drum. Measure across the diameter of the assembled brake shoes, at their widest point.
3. Turn the adjusting screw so that the diameter of the shoes is 0.030 in. (0.76mm) less than the brake drum inner diameter.
4. Install the drum.

Brake Light Switch

REMOVAL & INSTALLATION

♦ See Figure 5

The brake light switch is located on the brake pedal bracket assembly, underneath the dash and steering column.

1. Disconnect the negative battery cable.
2. Disengage any connections from the switch.
3. Loosen the switch bracket.
4. Release the switch by sliding it away from the pedal arm.

To install:

5. Position a new switch to the bracket and secure any connections.
6. Adjust the switch.
7. Connect the negative battery cable and verify proper switch operation.

ADJUSTMENT

Without Speed Control

1. Loosen the switch-to-pedal bracket screw and slide the switch away from the pedal arm.
2. Push the pedal down by hand and allow it to return on its own to the free-hanging position. Do not pull it back!
3. Slide the switch towards the pedal until there is a gap of 0.140 in. (3.5mm) between the plunger and pedal arm.

Fig. 2 Remove the plugs located in the rear of the backing plate, this will allow for adjustment

Fig. 3 Use a brake spoon to adjust the brakes through the hole provided

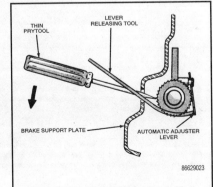

Fig. 4 Cut-way view of brake shoe adjustment

9-4 BRAKES

➥ **The pedal must not move when measuring the gap.**

4. Tighten the switch screw to 82 inch lbs. (9 Nm). Recheck the gap.

With Speed Control

1. Push the switch through the clip in the mounting bracket until it is seated against the bracket. The pedal will move forward slightly.
2. Gently pull back on the pedal as far as it will go. The switch will ratchet backwards to the correct position.

Master Cylinder

REMOVAL & INSTALLATION

▶ See Figures 6, 7, 8 and 9

Except 1979–82 Aluminum Master Cylinder

1. Use penetrating oil to help loosen the brake lines, then use an open end wrench (preferably a line-wrench) to disconnect them from the master cylinder.

※※ WARNING

Cap or plug all openings to prevent system contamination and to minimize fluid loss.

2. Except on vehicles equipped with power assist brakes, disconnect the master cylinder pushrod from the pedal linkage. On most vehicles you will have to loosen the nut and remove the retaining bolt.
3. Loosen the master cylinder retaining nuts, then support the cylinder and remove the nuts from the studs.
4. Remove the master cylinder from the vehicle. Be careful not to drip brake fluid on any painted surfaces.

To install:

➥ **Before installing a brake master cylinder it should be bench bled. Plug the ports and refill the master cylinder reservoir(s), then carefully bleed the master cylinder bore of air.**

5. Position the master cylinder over the mounting studs. On master cylinders equipped with external piston linkage, guide the pushrod carefully into position.
6. Install the master cylinder mounting nuts, then tighten to 10 ft. lbs. (13 Nm) for 1967–72 vehicles or to 16 ft. lbs. (21 Nm) for 1973 and later trucks.
7. If applicable, connect the pushrod to the pedal linkage and secure.
8. Remove the plugs and quickly thread the brake tubes to the master cylinder ports. Tighten the fittings sufficiently to begin the brake bleeding procedure.
9. Bleed the master cylinder and the entire hydraulic brake system.
10. Verify that a firm pedal has been obtained before attempting to move the truck.
11. Bleed the brake system.

1979–82 Aluminum Master Cylinder

WITHOUT POWER BRAKES

1. Use penetrating oil to help loosen the brake lines, then use an open end wrench (preferably a line-wrench) to disconnect them from the master cylinder.

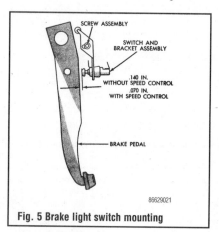

Fig. 5 Brake light switch mounting

Fig. 6 Use penetrating oil to help loosen the hydraulic line fittings on the master cylinder

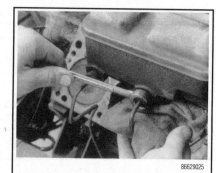

Fig. 7 Whenever possible, use a line wrench to prevent stripping the brake line fittings

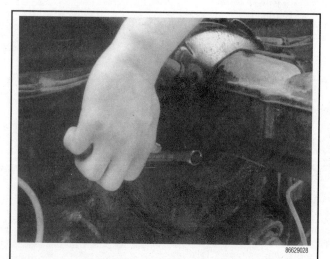

Fig. 8 You can loosen the master cylinder nuts using a box wrench, but a socket and torque wrench will be necessary for installation.

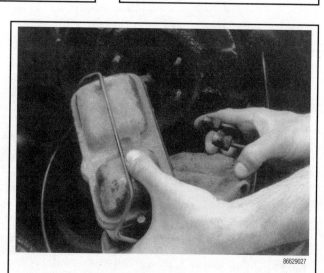

Fig. 9 Once all connections, nuts and fittings are removed, carefully withdraw the master cylinder from its mounting

BRAKES 9-5

⚠️ WARNING

Cap or plug all openings to prevent system contamination and to minimize fluid loss.

2. Disconnect the stop lamp switch bracket and allow the switch to hang out of the way.
3. Pull the brake pedal backwards to disengage the pushrod from the master cylinder piston. This will require at least 50 lbs. of force. It will also destroy the retention grommet.
4. Remove the master cylinder mounting nuts.
5. Slide the master cylinder straight away from the firewall. Remove all traces of the old grommet.

To install:

➥ Before installing a brake master cylinder it must be bench bleed.

6. When installing the master cylinder, tighten the nuts to 16 ft. lbs. (21 Nm). Moisten a new grommet with water, align the pushrod with the piston and, using the brake pedal, push the pushrod into the piston until it is fully seated. Install the boot.
7. Connect the stop lamp switch, adjust the switch, bleed the brake system.

WITH POWER BRAKES

1. Use penetrating oil to help loosen the brake lines, then use an open end wrench (preferably a line-wrench) to disconnect them from the master cylinder.

⚠️ WARNING

Cap or plug all openings to prevent system contamination and to minimize fluid loss.

2. Loosen the master cylinder retaining nuts, then support the cylinder and remove the nuts from the studs.
3. Remove the master cylinder from the vehicle. Be careful not to drip brake fluid on any painted surfaces.

To install:

➥ Before installing a brake master cylinder it should be bench bled. Plug the ports and refill the master cylinder reservoir(s), then carefully bleed the master cylinder bore of air.

4. Position the master cylinder over the mounting studs, then install the mounting nuts and tighten to 16 ft. lbs. (21 Nm).
5. Remove the plugs and quickly thread the brake tubes to the master cylinder ports. Tighten the fittings sufficiently to begin the brake bleeding procedure.
6. Bleed the master cylinder and the entire hydraulic brake system.
7. Verify that a firm pedal has been obtained before attempting to move the truck.

Power Booster

REMOVAL & INSTALLATION

♦ See Figures 10, 11, 12 and 13

1. Remove the master cylinder.
2. Disconnect the vacuum hose from the power booster.
3. Disconnect the pushrod from the brake pedal.
4. Remove the power booster attaching nuts and remove the booster.

To install:

5. Position the booster onto the mounting plate. Install and tighten the mounting nuts, tighten them to 16 ft. lbs. (21 Nm).
6. Connect the pushrod to the pedal. Coat the eyelet with Lubriplate® or equivalent.
7. Connect the vacuum hose to the check valve and check operation.

⚠️ CAUTION

Do not attempt to dissemble the brake booster as this unit has to be serviced by the Manufacture or a qualified service station.

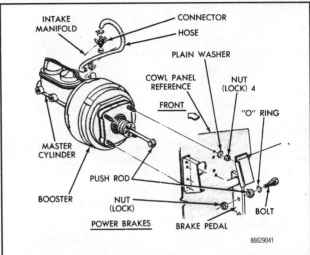

Fig. 10 Brake booster mounting—all models through 1976 and all 1977 models equipped with V8–440 engines

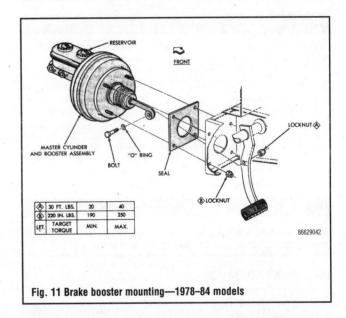

Fig. 11 Brake booster mounting—1978–84 models

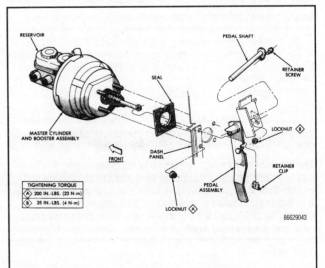

Fig. 12 Brake booster mounting—1985–88 vehicles

9-6 BRAKES

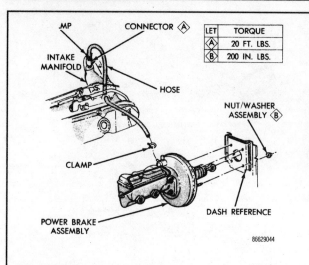

Fig. 13 Brake booster mounting/specifications—1977 models equipped with V8–318 or 360 engines

Hydro-Boost

Unlike gasoline engines, diesel engines have little vacuum available to power brake booster systems.

A hydraulically powered brake booster is used on diesel models. The power steering pump provides the fluid pressure to operate both the brake booster and the power steering gear.

The hydro-boost assembly contains a valve which controls pump pressure while braking, a lever to control the position of the valve and a boost piston to provide the force to operate a conventional master cylinder attached to the front of the booster. The hydro-boost also has a reserve system, designed to store sufficient pressurized fluid to provide at least 2 brake applications in the event of insufficient fluid flow from the power steering pump. The brakes can also be applied unassisted if the reserve system is depleted.

※※※ WARNING

Before removing the hydro-boost, discharge the accumulator by making several brake applications until a hard pedal is felt.

REMOVAL & INSTALLATION

※※※ CAUTION

Do not depress the brake pedal with the master cylinder removed!

1. Remove the master cylinder from the Hydro-Boost unit. DO NOT disconnect the brake lines from the master cylinder or the entire system will have to be bled! Instead, position the master cylinder out of the way, being careful not to kink or damage the hydraulic lines.
2. Disconnect the 3 hydraulic lines from the Hydro-Boost unit.
3. Disconnect the pushrod from the brake pedal.
4. Remove the booster mounting nuts and lift the booster from the firewall.

※※※ CAUTION

The booster should never be carried by the accumulator. The accumulator contains high pressure nitrogen and can be dangerous if mishandled! If the accumulator is to be disposed of, do not expose it to fire or other forms of incineration! Gas pressure can be relieved by drilling a 1/16 in. (1.6mm) hole in the end of the accumulator can. Always wear safety goggles during the drilling!

To install:
5. Position the booster on the vehicle, then install and tighten the booster mounting nuts to 30 ft. lbs. (40.6 Nm).
6. Connect the pushrod and tighten nuts to 30 ft. lbs. (40.6 Nm). Remove the plugs from the hydraulic lines and connect them to the respective ports. Tighten the tube nuts to 34 ft. lbs. (46 Nm).
7. If removed, connect the brake pedal return spring.
8. Connect the 3 hydraulic lines to the Hydro-Boost unit.
9. Install the master cylinder to the booster and secure using the mounting nuts.
10. Refill and bleed the booster as follows:
   a. Fill the pump reservoir with Dexron®II ATF.
   b. Disconnect the coil wires and crank the engine for several seconds.
   c. Check the fluid level and refill, if necessary.
   d. Connect the coil wires and start the engine.
   e. With the engine running, turn the steering wheel lock-to-lock twice. Shut off the engine.
   f. Depress the brake pedal several times to discharge the accumulator.
   g. Start the engine and repeat Step e.
   h. If foam appears in the reservoir, allow the foam to dissipate.
   i. Repeat Step e as often as necessary to expel all air from the system.

➡ The system is, in effect, self-bleeding and normal truck operation will expel any further trapped air.

Hydraulic Valves

▶ See Figure 14

Models with front and rear drum brakes are equipped with a brake warning light switch mounted in a housing on the frame rail. The front and rear brake lines are connected to the housing and a moving valve inside the housing reacts to changes in hydraulic pressure, warning the driver of excessively low pressure in either or both systems.

Models with front disc brakes incorporate the safety switch with either a metering valve or combination metering/proportioning valve

Fig. 14 Common proportioning valve assembly

REMOVAL & INSTALLATION

▶ See Figures 15, 16, 17 and 18

1. Raise and support the front end on jackstands.
2. Remove the splash shield.
3. Disconnect the wiring at the warning light switch.
4. Disconnect the brake lines at the valve.
5. Unbolt and remove the valve from the frame.

To install:
6. Install the valve, then connect the lines and wiring.
7. Properly bleed the brake system.
8. Install the splash shield.
9. Remove the jackstands and carefully lower the vehicle.

Brakes 9-7

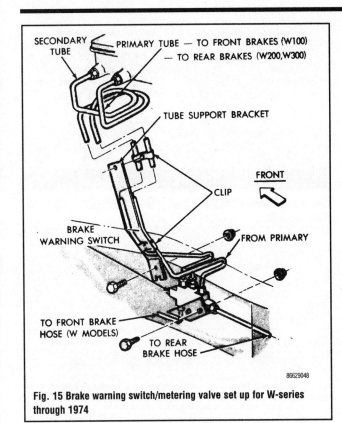

Fig. 15 Brake warning switch/metering valve set up for W-series through 1974

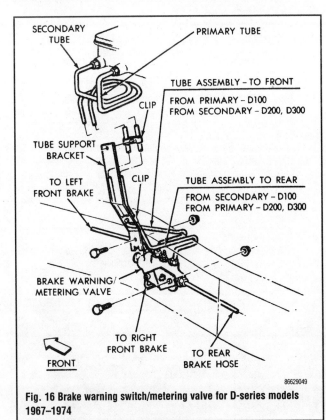

Fig. 16 Brake warning switch/metering valve for D-series models 1967–1974

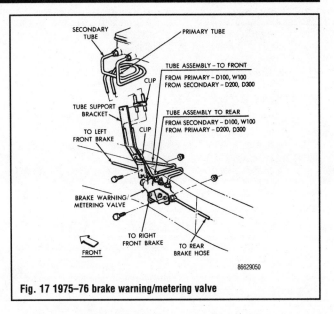

Fig. 17 1975–76 brake warning/metering valve

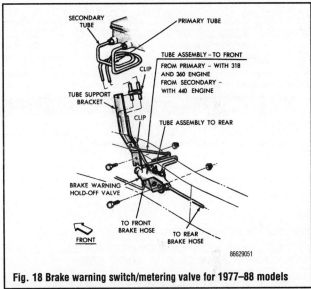

Fig. 18 Brake warning switch/metering valve for 1977–88 models

1. Raise and support the front end on jackstands.
2. Remove the splash shield.
3. Turn the ignition switch to **ON**.
4. Crack a front bleeder screw, have an assistant apply the brakes to produce a front failure condition. The warning light will come on and stay on.
5. Bleed the rear brakes, then the front brakes.
6. After bleeding both front and rear brakes apply moderate force to the brake pedal. This will hydraulically recenter the proportioning valve and turn off the warning light.
7. Refill the master cylinder.
8. Check the brake pedal for any air left in the system, if needed repeat the bleeding procedure until a good pedal is obtained.
9. Lower the vehicle and test drive.

Brake Hoses and Pipes

Metal lines and rubber brake hoses should be checked frequently for leaks and external damage. Metal lines are particularly prone to crushing and kinking under the vehicle. Any such deformation can restrict the proper flow of fluid and therefore impair braking at the wheels. Rubber hoses should be checked for cracking or scraping; such damage can create a weak spot in the hose and it could fail under pressure.

Any time the lines are removed or disconnected, extreme cleanliness must be observed. Clean all joints and connections before disassembly (use a stiff bris-

CENTERING THE PROPORTIONING VALVE

After the brake system has been opened for any reason, the warning light will remain ON until the proportioning valve is centralized. All proportioning valves are self-centering after the brakes are properly bled.

9-8 BRAKES

tle brush and clean brake fluid); be sure to plug the lines and ports as soon as they are opened. New lines and hoses should be flushed clean with brake fluid before installation to remove any contamination.

REMOVAL & INSTALLATION

▶ See Figures 19, 20, 21 and 22

1. Disconnect the negative battery cable.
2. Raise and safely support the vehicle on jackstands.
3. Remove any wheel and tire assemblies necessary for access to the particular line you are removing.
4. Thoroughly clean the surrounding area at the joints to be disconnected.
5. Place a suitable catch pan under the joint to be disconnected.
6. Using two wrenches (one to hold the joint and one to turn the fitting), disconnect the hose or line to be replaced.
7. Disconnect the other end of the line or hose, moving the drain pan if necessary. Always use a back-up wrench to avoid damaging the fitting.
8. Disconnect any retaining clips or brackets holding the line and remove the line from the vehicle.

➡ If the brake system is to remain open for more time than it takes to swap lines, tape or plug each remaining clip and port to keep contaminants out and fluid in.

To install:

9. Install the new line or hose, starting with the end farthest from the master cylinder. Connect the other end, then confirm that both fittings are correctly threaded and turn smoothly using finger pressure. Make sure the new line will not rub against any other part. Brake lines must be at least 1/2 in. (13mm) from the steering column and other moving parts. Any protective shielding or insulators must be reinstalled in the original location.

✺✺ WARNING

Make sure the hose is NOT kinked or touching any part of the frame or suspension after installation. These conditions may cause the hose to fail prematurely.

10. Using two wrenches as before, tighten each fitting.
11. Install any retaining clips or brackets on the lines.
12. If removed, install the wheel and tire assemblies, then carefully lower the vehicle to the ground.
13. Refill the brake master cylinder reservoir with clean, fresh brake fluid, meeting DOT 3 specifications. Properly bleed the brake system.
14. Connect the negative battery cable.

Bleeding the Brakes

When any part of the hydraulic system has been disconnected for repair or replacement, air may get into the lines and cause spongy pedal action (because air can be compressed and brake fluid cannot). To correct this condition, it is necessary to bleed the hydraulic system after it has been properly connected to be sure that all air is expelled from the brake cylinders and lines.

If air has been introduced at the start of the system (the master cylinder reservoir is allowed to approach empty and introduce air or the cylinder fittings are disconnected), then the system must be thoroughly purged of air beginning with the master cylinder. Once the master cylinder has been thoroughly bled, you should bleed one brake cylinder at a time, beginning at the cylinder with the longest hydraulic line (farthest from the master cylinder). Keep the master cylinder reservoir filled with brake fluid during bleeding operation.

Of course, if no air was introduced early in the system, only the cylinder(s) AFTER the point where the lines were disconnected must be bled. If you are only servicing a single caliper or wheel cylinder, that should be the only bleeding point necessary.

✺✺ WARNING

Never use brake fluid that has been drained from the hydraulic system, no matter how clean it is.

It may be necessary to centralize the proportioning valve after a brake system failure has been corrected and the hydraulic system has been bled.

The primary and secondary hydraulic brake systems are individual systems and are bled separately. During the entire bleeding operation, do not allow the reservoir to run dry. Keep the master cylinder reservoirs filled with brake fluid.

MASTER CYLINDER

1. Fill the master cylinder reservoirs.
2. Place absorbent rags under the fluid lines at the master cylinder.
3. Have an assistant depress and hold the brake pedal.
4. With the pedal held down, slowly crack open the hydraulic line fitting, allowing the air to escape. Close the fitting and have the pedal released.
5. Repeat Steps 3 and 4 for each fitting until all the air is released.

WHEEL CYLINDERS & CALIPERS

▶ See Figure 23

1. Clean all dirt from around the master cylinder fill cap, remove the cap and fill the master cylinder with brake fluid until the level is within 1/4 in (6.3mm) of the top of the edge of the reservoir.
2. Clean off the bleeder screws at the wheel cylinders and calipers.
3. Attach a length of rubber hose over the nozzle of the bleeder screw at the wheel to be done first. Place the other end of the hose in a plastic or glass jar, submerged in brake fluid.
4. Open the bleed screw valve 1/2–3/4 turn.
5. Have an assistant slowly depress the brake pedal. Close the bleeder screw valve and tell your assistant to allow the brake pedal to return slowly. Continue this pumping action to force any air out of the system. When bubbles cease to appear at the end of the bleeder hose, close the bleed valve and remove the hose.
6. Check the master cylinder fluid level and add fluid accordingly. Do this after bleeding each wheel.
7. Repeat the bleeding operation at the remaining 3 wheels, ending with the one closest to the master cylinder. Fill the master cylinder reservoir.

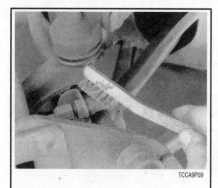

Fig. 19 Use a brush to clean the fittings of any debris

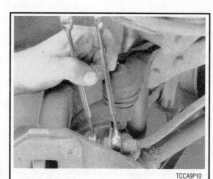

Fig. 20 Use two wrenches to loosen the fitting. If available, use flare nut type wrenches

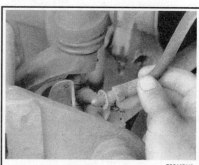

Fig. 21 Any gaskets/crush washers should be replaced with new ones during installation

BRAKES 9-9

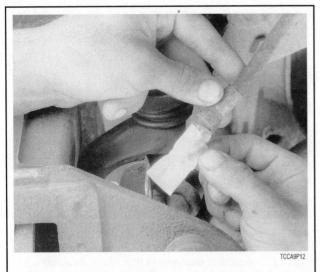

Fig. 22 Tape or plug the line to prevent contamination

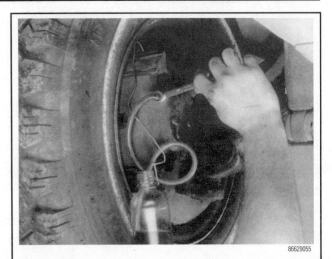

Fig. 23 For safety, use a plastic container to hold fluid during bleeding

FRONT DRUM BRAKES

※※ CAUTION

Brake shoes may contain asbestos, which has been determined to be a cancer causing agent. Never clean the brake surfaces with compressed air! Avoid inhaling any dust from any brake surface! When cleaning brake surfaces, use a commercially available brake cleaning fluid.

There are two types of front drum brakes used on Dodge and Plymouth trucks, a servo type with single anchor, and a Bendix Duo-Servo type. The servo type was used exclusively from 1967 to 1970, and the Bendix Duo-Servo was added sometime in 1970 and was used occasionally from then on. The Bendix Duo-Servo type can be identified by the brake shoes which are marked **Pri** (Primary) and **Sec** (Secondary) and "This Side Out", for easy identification.

Brake Drums

REMOVAL & INSTALLATION

Servo Type With Single Anchor

1. To aid in brake drum removal, loosen the brake adjusting star wheel.
2. If the wheel is going to be removed from the drum, loosen the lug nuts at this time.
3. Jack and support the vehicle.
4. Insert a thin prytool into the adjusting hole after removing the plug. Push the adjusting lever away from the adjuster.
5. Release the brake adjustment by prying down against the star wheel with a brake adjusting spoon.
6. If you are removing the wheel from the drum, remove the lug nuts, then remove the wheel at this time.
7. Remove the grease cap, cotter pin, lock, adjusting nut, and outer wheel bearing. Once the bearing is removed, you are free to pull the drum from the spindle.

To install:

8. Install the drum. Reinstall the outer bearing.
9. Insert the adjusting nut, a new cotter pin, and the grease cap.
10. If removed from the drum, install the wheel.
11. Adjust the wheel bearings and readjust the brakes.
12. Remove the jackstands and lower the vehicle, then make sure the lug nuts are properly tightened.

Bendix Duo-Servo

1. Raise and support the truck on jackstands.
2. Remove the wheel and tire.
3. Remove the dust cover, cotter key, nut, locknut, washer, and outer bearing.
4. Carefully remove the drum.
5. If there is interference between the brake shoes and drum, release the brake shoes by applying a brake adjusting spoon to the star wheel adjuster.
6. Installation is the reverse of removal. Adjust the wheel bearings and then the brakes.

INSPECTION

1. Drum run out (out of round) and diameter should be measured. Each drum should be marked with its diameter. Drum diameter cannot exceed specification by more than 0.020 in. (0.5mm) and run out cannot exceed 0.006 in. Do not reface a drum more than 0.060 in. (1.5mm) over its standard diameter.
2. Check the drum for large cracks and scores. Replace the drum if necessary.
3. If the brake linings are wearing more on one edge than the other then the drum may be "bell" shaped and will have to be replaced and resurfaced.

Brake Shoes

REMOVAL & INSTALLATION

▶ See Figures 24, 25 and 26

Servo Type With Single Anchor

Remove the wheel and brake drum as outlined above, then proceed in the following manner:

1. Take off the shoe return springs. Detach the adjusting cable eye from the anchor and unhook the other end from the lever. Withdraw the cable, overload spring, and anchor plate.
2. Detach the adjusting lever from the spring and separate the spring from the pivot. Take the spring completely off from the secondary shoe web and unfasten it from the primary shoe web.
3. Remove the retainer springs and pins from the shoe. Extract both shoes from the pushrods and lift them out. Withdraw the star wheel assembly from the shoes.

9-10 BRAKES

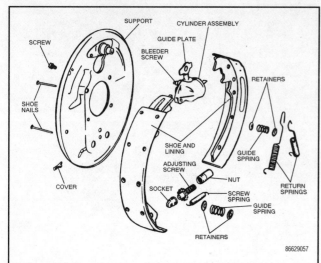

Fig. 24 Single anchor servo with fixed anchor pin front brake—1967 D200/W200 and D300/W300

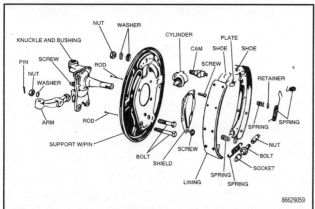

Fig. 25 Single anchor servo with adjustable front brakes—1967 D200/W200 and D300/W300

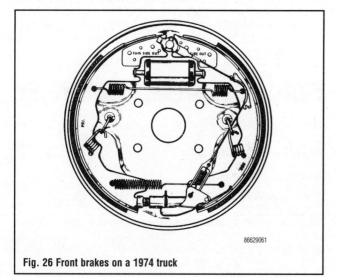

Fig. 26 Front brakes on a 1974 truck

To install:

4. Lightly lubricate the shoe tab contact area at six points on the support plate. Match both the primary and secondary brake shoes with each other.

5. Before installation in the truck, fit the star wheel assembly between the shoes, with the star wheel next to the secondary shoe. The star wheels are stamped with an **L** or **R** to mark their location. Spread the anchor ends of the shoes apart to keep the star wheel assembly positioned.

6. Place the assembly on the support plate while attaching the shoe ends to the pushrods.

7. Install the shoe retaining pins, springs, and retainers. Place the anchor plate over the anchor.

8. Place the adjustment cable eye over the anchor so that it rests against the anchor plate. Attach the primary shoe return spring shoe web and fit the other end over the anchor.

9. Place the cable guide in the secondary shoe web and fit the end over the anchor. Hold this in position while engaging the secondary shoe return spring, through the guide and into the web. Put its other end over the anchor.

➡ See that the cable guide stays flat against the web and that the secondary shoe return spring overlaps that of the primary.

10. Squeeze the ends of the spring loops, using pliers, until they are parallel, around the anchor.

11. The adjustment cable should be threaded over the guide and the end of the overload spring should be hooked into the lever.

➡ The eye of the adjuster cable must be tight against the anchor and parallel with the guide.

12. Install the drum as detailed above. Adjust the brakes.

Bendix Duo-Servo

1. Unhook and remove the adjusting lever return spring.
2. Remove the lever from the lever pivot pin.
3. Unhook the adjuster lever from the adjuster cable.
4. Unhook the upper shoe-to-shoe spring.
5. Unhook and remove the shoe hold-down springs.
6. Disconnect the parking brake cable from the parking brake lever.
7. Remove the shoes with the lower shoe-to-shoe spring and star wheel as an assembly.
8. The pivot screw and adjusting nut on the left side have left-hand threads and right hand threads on the right side.
9. Lubricate and assemble the star wheel assembly. Lubricate the guide pads on the support plates.
10. Assemble the star wheel, lower shoe-to-shoe spring, and the primary and secondary shoes. Position this assembly on the support plate.
11. Install and hook the hold-down springs.
12. Install the upper shoe-to-shoe spring.
13. Install the cable and retaining clip.
14. Position the adjuster lever return spring on the pivot (green springs on left brakes and red springs on right brakes).
15. Install the adjuster lever. Route the adjuster cable and connect it to the adjuster.
16. Install the brake drum and adjust the brakes.

Wheel Cylinders

REMOVAL, INSTALLATION & OVERHAUL

♦ See Figure 27

When the brake drums are removed, carry out an inspection of the wheel cylinder boots for cuts, tears, cracks, or leaks. If any of these are present, the wheel cylinder should have a complete overhaul performed.

➡ Preservative fluid is used during assembly; its presence in small quantities does not indicate a problem.

To remove and overhaul the wheel cylinders, proceed in the following manner:

1. Remove the brake shoes and check them. Replace them if they are soaked with grease or brake fluid.
2. Detach the brake hose.
3. Unfasten the wheel cylinder attachment bolts and slide the wheel cylinder off its support.
4. Pry the boots from either end of the wheel cylinder and withdraw the pushrods. Push **in** one of the pistons, to force out the other piston, its cup, the spring, the spring cup, and the piston, itself.

BRAKES 9-11

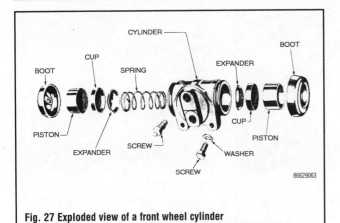

Fig. 27 Exploded view of a front wheel cylinder

6. Inspect the cylinder bore wall for signs of pitting, scoring, etc. If it is badly scored or pitted, the entire cylinder should be replaced. Light scratches or corrosion should be cleaned up with crocus cloth.

➡ Disregard the black stains from the piston cups that appear on the cylinder wall; they will do no damage.

Assembly and installation are performed in the following manner:

7. Dip the pistons and the cups in clean brake fluid. Replace the boots with new ones, if they show wear or deterioration. Coat the wall of the cylinder bore with clean brake fluid.
8. Place the spring in the cylinder bore. Position the cups in either end of the cylinder with the open end of the cups facing inward (toward each other).
9. Place the pistons in either end of the cylinder bore with the recessed ends facing outward (away from each other).
10. Install the boots over the ends of the cylinder and push down until each boot is seated, being careful not to damage either boot.
11. Install the wheel cylinder on its support.
12. Attach the jumper tube to the wheel cylinder. Install the brake hose on the frame bracket. Connect the brake line to the hose. Connect the end of the brake hose. Connect the end of the brake hose through the end of the stand-off. Attach the jumper tube to the brake hose and attach the hose to the stand-off.
13. Bleed the brake system.

5. Wash the pistons, the wheel cylinder housing, and the spring in fresh brake fluid, or in denatured alcohol, and dry them off using compressed air.

✽✽ CAUTION

Do not use a rag to dry them since the lint from it will stick to the surfaces.

FRONT DISC BRAKES

✽✽ CAUTION

Brake pads may contain asbestos, which has been determined to be a cancer causing agent. Never clean the brake surfaces with compressed air! Avoid inhaling any dust from any brake surface! When cleaning brake surfaces, use a commercially available brake cleaning fluid.

Application

Until 1975, only 2WD trucks came equipped with disc brakes. The brake system used was the Chrysler Sliding Caliper type. The D100 had a 11.75 in. rotor and the D200 and 300 had a 12.82 in. rotor.

On 1975–88 models, the D100/150, W100/150, Ramcharger and Trail Duster series used the Chrysler Sliding Caliper with 11.75 in. rotor; the D200/250, D300/350 and W200/250 w/Dana 44 axle used the Chrysler Sliding Caliper with 12.82 in. rotor; the W200/250 and W300/350 with the Dana 60 axle used a Bendix Sliding Caliper with 12.88 in. rotor.

Disc Brake Pads

INSPECTION

Remove the brake pads as described later in this section and measure the thickness of the lining. If the lining at ANY point on the pad assembly is less then specification, or there is evidence of the lining having been contaminated by brake fluid or oil, replace the brake pad. For light duty brakes the lining should be at least 1/16 in. (1.5mm) thick above the backing plate or rivets (as applicable). Heavy duty brakes should allow a minimum lining thickness of 1/32 in. (0.8mm).

Of course, many states have their own standards for safety. When in doubt, check with local authorities or an official inspection station for local safety inspection standards.

REMOVAL & INSTALLATION

➡ NEVER REPLACE THE PADS ON ONE SIDE ONLY! ALWAYS REPLACE PADS ON BOTH WHEELS AS A SET!

Chrysler Sliding Caliper

◆ See Figures 28 thru 37

1. Raise and support the front end on jackstands.
2. Remove the wheels.
3. Remove the caliper retaining clips and anti-rattle springs.
4. Remove the caliper from the disc by slowly sliding the caliper and brake pad assembly out and away from the disc. Do not damage the flexible brake hose.
5. Drain some of the fluid from the master cylinder.
6. Remove the outboard pad from the caliper by prying between the pad and the caliper fingers. Remove the inboard pad from the caliper support by the same method. DO NOT depress the brake pedal with the pads removed!
7. Push the pistons to the bottom of their bores. This may be done with a large C-clamp or a pair of large pliers by placing a flat metal bar against the

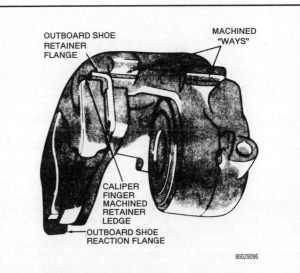

Fig. 28 Finger and shoe retainer flange locations

9-12 BRAKES

Fig. 29 The wheel must be removed for access to the front brake components

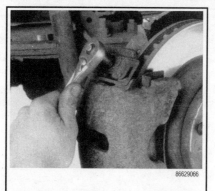
Fig. 30 Loosen the retaining clip bolt with the proper size socket

Fig. 31 After loosening, unthread the bolt and place it where it will be easily found for installation

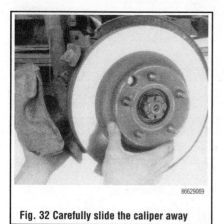
Fig. 32 Carefully slide the caliper away

Fig. 33 Once the caliper is free of the rotor and mounting, the brake pads may be removed

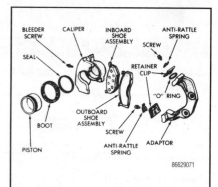
Fig. 34 Exploded view of a sliding caliper assembly

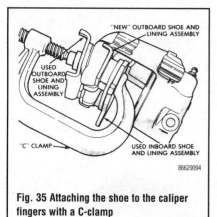
Fig. 35 Attaching the shoe to the caliper fingers with a C-clamp

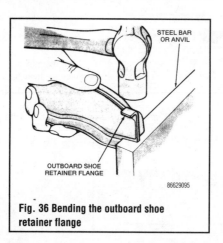
Fig. 36 Bending the outboard shoe retainer flange

Fig. 37 Install the retaining clip with the pads and caliper in position—now where did you put the bolt?

pistons and depressing the pistons with a steady force. This operation will displace some of the fluid in the master cylinder.

8. Slide the new pads into the caliper and caliper support. The ears of the pad should rest on the bridges of the caliper.
9. Install the caliper on the disc and install the caliper retaining clips, pins and anti-rattle springs. Pump the brake pedal until it is firm.
10. Check the fluid level in the master cylinder and add fluid as needed.
11. Install the wheels.
12. Road test the truck. Although the vehicle may pull to one slightly, the pull should disappear shortly as the pads wear in.

Bendix Sliding Caliper

▶ See Figures 38 thru 46

1. Remove and discard some of the fluid from the master cylinder without contaminating the contents to avoid overflow later on.
2. Support the vehicle on jackstands. Remove the wheels.
3. Put an 8 in. (203mm) C-clamp over the caliper and use it to push the outer pad in and pull the caliper out. This bottoms the caliper piston in its bore.
4. Remove the key retaining screw. Drive the caliper support key and spring out toward the outside, using a brass drift.
5. Push the caliper down and rotate the upper end up and out. Support the caliper, so as not to damage the brake hose.
6. Remove the outer pad from the caliper. You may have to tap it to loosen it. Remove the inner pad, removing the anti-rattle clip from the lower end of the shoe.

To install:

7. Thoroughly clean the sliding contact areas on the caliper and spindle assembly.
8. Put the new anti-rattle clip on the lower end of the new inner pad. Put the pad and clip in the pad abutment with the clip tab against the abutment and the loop-type spring away from the disc. Compress the clip and slide the upper end of the pad into place.

Brakes 9-13

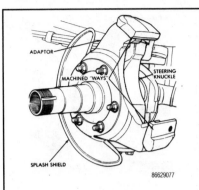

Fig. 38 Bendix caliper adapter, steering knuckle adaptor

Fig. 39 Before removing the caliper, use a C-clamp to carefully bottom the piston in its bore

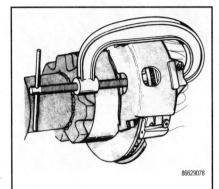

Fig. 40 Use a C-clamp to carefully bottom the piston

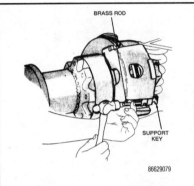

Fig. 41 Use a hammer and brass drift to tap out the support key and spring

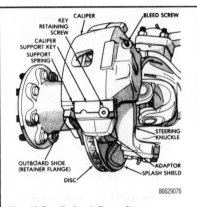

Fig. 42 Bendix front disc unit

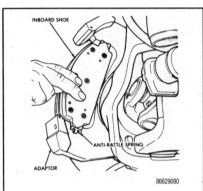

Fig. 43 Removal of the inner pad from the adapter

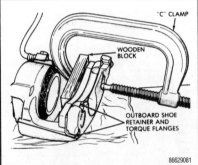

Fig. 44 Press the outboard pad onto the caliper, but make sure you protect the pad with a wooden block

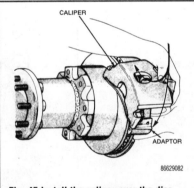

Fig. 45 Install the caliper over the disc into the upper mating groove

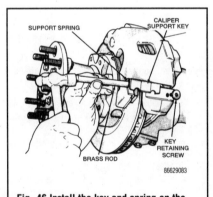

Fig. 46 Install the key and spring on the caliper

9. If the caliper piston isn't bottomed, bottom it with a C-clamp.
10. The replacement outer pad may differ slightly from the original equipment. Put the outer pad in place and press the tabs into place with your fingers. You can press the tabs in with a C-clamp, but be careful of the lining.
11. Position the caliper on the spindle assembly by pivoting it around the upper mounting surface. Be careful of the boot.
12. Use a prytool to hold the upper machined surface of the caliper against the support assembly. Drive a new key and spring assembly into place with a plastic mallet. Install the retaining screw and tighten to 12–20 ft. lbs. (16–27 Nm).
13. Replace the wheels and tires and lower the truck to the floor. Fill the master cylinder as specified in Section 1. Depress the brake pedal firmly several times to seat the pads on the disc. Don't drive until you get a firm pedal.

Chrysler Floating Caliper

1. Raise the vehicle and remove the wheel.
2. Remove the guide pins, positioners, and anti-rattle spring.
3. Slowly slide the caliper assembly away from the rotor.

➡ Support the caliper to prevent damage to brake hose.

4. Remove the disc pads, guide pin bushings, and positioners, discard of the bushings and positioners.

To install:

5. Check the piston seal for leaks and inspect the dust boot for damage.
6. Inspect the piston for damage or corrosion.

9-14 BRAKES

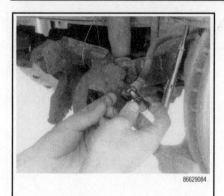
Fig. 47 Remove the hose connected to the caliper

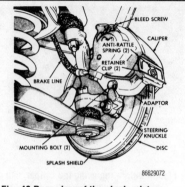
Fig. 48 Rear view of the single piston Chrysler sliding caliper—2WD trucks

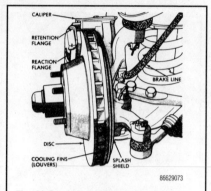
Fig. 49 Front view of the single piston Chrysler sliding caliper—2WD trucks

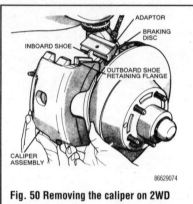
Fig. 50 Removing the caliper on 2WD trucks

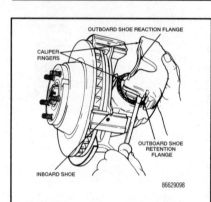
Fig. 51 Outboard shoe removal—4WD trucks

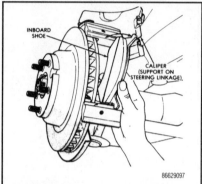
Fig. 52 Inboard shoe removal—4WD trucks

7. Check for corrosion or rust on the mating surfaces of the caliper and anchor plate.
8. Install new guide pin bushings with flanged end toward outside of vehicle.
9. Bottom piston into cylinder bore and install pads.

➡ Be sure the metal portion of pad is fully seated in recess of caliper and anchor plate.

10. Carefully slide caliper assembly into position over rotor.
11. Install new positioners over guide pins with open ends towards outside and stamped arrows pointing up.
12. Align guide pin holes in caliper and anchor plate, install guide pin assemblies.
13. Bleed the brake system.
14. Install the wheel, lower the vehicle and tighten lug nuts.

Disc Brake Calipers

REMOVAL & INSTALLATION

▶ See Figures 47 thru 53

Chrysler Sliding Caliper

1. Loosen the lug nuts slightly before you jack up the front of the truck and support it with jackstands.
2. Remove the wheels.
3. Disconnect the rubber brake hose from the tubing at the frame mount. If the pistons are to be removed from the caliper, leave the brake hose connected to the caliper. Check the rubber hose for cracks or chafed spots.
4. Plug the brake line to prevent loss of fluid.
5. Remove the retaining screw, clip and anti-rattle spring that attach the caliper to the adaptor.
6. Carefully slide the caliper out and away from the disc. Check the pads to be sure that they are reinstalled in the same position.

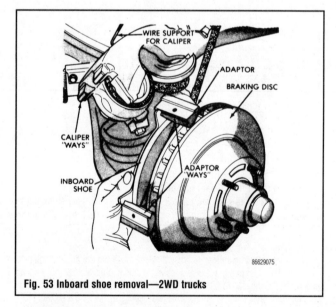
Fig. 53 Inboard shoe removal—2WD trucks

To install:
7. Position the outboard shoe in the caliper. The shoe should not rattle in the caliper. If it does, or if any movement is obvious, bend the shoe tabs over the caliper to tighten the fit.
8. Install the inboard shoe.
9. Slide the caliper into position on the adaptor and over the rotor.

✱✱ WARNING

Take great care to avoid dislodging the piston dust boot!

Brakes 9-15

10. Install the anti-rattle springs and retaining clips and tighten the retaining screws to 16 ft. lbs. (21 Nm).

➡ The inboard shoe must always be installed on top of the retainer spring plate.

11. Fill the system with fresh fluid and bleed the brakes.
12. Lower the truck.

Bendix Sliding Caliper

1. Loosen the lug nuts slightly before you jack up the front of the truck and support it with jackstands. Remove the front wheel.
2. Disconnect the brake hose. Cap the hose and plug the caliper.
3. Remove the key retaining screw and drive the key out with a brass drift.
4. Rotate the key end of the caliper out and slide the other end out.
5. Thoroughly clean the sliding areas.

To install:

6. Position the caliper rail into the slide on the support and rotate the caliper onto the rotor. Start the key and spring by hand. The spring should be between the key and caliper and the spring ends should overlap the key. If necessary, use a prytool to hold the caliper against the support assembly.
7. Drive the key and spring into position, aligning the correct notch with the hole in the support. Install the key retaining screw and tighten to 12–20 ft. lbs. (16–27 Nm).
8. Bleed the system of air. Replace the wheel and tire and lower the truck to the floor.

Chrysler Floating Caliper

1. Raise the vehicle and remove the wheel.
2. Remove guide pins, positioners, and anti-rattle spring.
3. Slowly slide caliper assembly out and away from rotor.
4. Disconnect the brake hose.
5. Inspect for any corrosion on mating surfaces of the caliper and anchor plate.

To install:

6. Install the caliper with new guide pin bushings, the flanged end faces towards the outside of vehicle.
7. Carefully slide the caliper assembly into position over rotor.
8. Install new positioners over guide pins with open ends towards outside and stamped arrows pointing up.
9. Align guide pin holes in caliper and anchor plate, install guide pin assemblies.
10. Bleed the brake system.
11. Install the wheel, lower the vehicle and tighten lug nuts.

OVERHAUL

♦ See Figures 54 thru 59

➡ Some vehicles may be equipped dual piston calipers. The procedure to overhaul the caliper is essentially the same with the exception of multiple pistons, O-rings and dust boots.

1. Remove the caliper from the vehicle and place on a clean workbench.

✹✹ CAUTION

NEVER place your fingers in front of the pistons in an attempt to catch or protect the pistons when applying compressed air. This could result in personal injury!

➡ Depending upon the vehicle, there are two different ways to remove the piston from the caliper. Refer to the brake pad replacement procedure to make sure you have the correct procedure for your vehicle.

2. The first method is as follows:
   a. Stuff a shop towel or a block of wood into the caliper to catch the piston.
   b. Remove the caliper piston using compressed air applied into the caliper inlet hole. Inspect the piston for scoring, nicks, corrosion and/or

Fig. 54 For some types of calipers, use compressed air to drive the piston out of the caliper, but make sure to keep your fingers clear

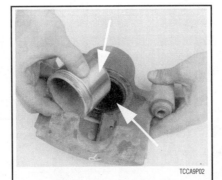

Fig. 55 Withdraw the piston from the caliper bore

Fig. 56 Use a prytool to carefully pry around the edge of the boot . . .

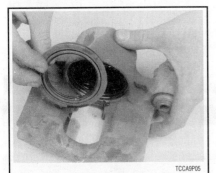

Fig. 57 . . . then remove the boot from the caliper housing, taking care not to score or damage the bore

Fig. 58 Use extreme caution when removing the piston seal; DO NOT scratch the caliper bore

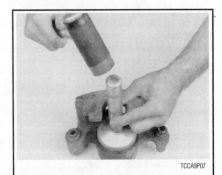

Fig. 59 Use the proper size driving tool and a mallet to properly seal the boots in the caliper housing

9-16 BRAKES

worn or damaged chrome plating. The piston must be replaced if any of these conditions are found.

3. For the second method, you must rotate the piston to retract it from the caliper.
4. If equipped, remove the anti-rattle clip.
5. Use a prytool to remove the caliper boot, being careful not to scratch the housing bore.
6. Remove the piston seals from the groove in the caliper bore.
7. Carefully loosen the brake bleeder valve cap and valve from the caliper housing.
8. Inspect the caliper bores, pistons and mounting threads for scoring or excessive wear.
9. Use crocus cloth to polish out light corrosion from the piston and bore.
10. Clean all parts with denatured alcohol and dry with compressed air.

To assemble:
11. Lubricate and install the bleeder valve and cap.
12. Install the new seals into the caliper bore grooves, making sure they are not twisted.
13. Lubricate the piston bore.
14. Install the pistons and boots into the bores of the calipers and push to the bottom of the bores.
15. Use a suitable driving tool to seat the boots in the housing.
16. Install the caliper in the vehicle.
17. Install the wheel and tire assembly, then carefully lower the vehicle.
18. Properly bleed the brake system.

Brake Disc (Rotor)

REMOVAL & INSTALLATION

▶ See Figures 60 and 61

1. Loosen the lug nuts slightly before you jack up the front of the truck and support it with jackstands. Remove the front wheel.

Fig. 60 The truck must be raised and the wheel must be removed for access to the brake rotor

Fig. 61 ALWAYS replace a used cotter pin with a new one

2. Remove the caliper assembly and attach it to the frame with a piece of wire without disconnecting the brake fluid hose.
3. Remove the grease cap, cotter pin, locknut, thrust washer and outer wheel bearing.
4. Pull the hub and rotor assembly off the spindle.

To install:
5. Slide the disc and hub assembly onto the spindle.
6. Install the outer bearing, thrust washer and outer nut.
7. Tighten the bearing adjusting nut down to 90 inch lbs. (10 Nm) while rotating the rotor and hub. Recheck the disc run out.
8. Back off the adjusting nut to release all preload, and retighten the nut finger-tight.
9. Install the locknut on the nut with one pair of slots in line with the cotter pin hole.
10. Install a new cotter pin. NEVER use a old cotter pin.
11. Clean and recoat the grease cap inside with bearing grease, not filling the cap, install the cap. Make sure the disc is completely clean of any dirt or grease. Use a suitable solvent.
12. Install the caliper.

INSPECTION

If the rotor is deeply scarred or has shallow cracks, it may be refinished on a disc brake rotor lathe. Also, if the lateral run-out exceeds 0.010 in. (0.25mm) within a 6 in. (152mm) radius when measured with a dial indicator, with the stylus 1 in. (25mm) in from the edge of the rotor, the rotor should be refinished or replaced.

A maximum of 0.020 in. (0.5mm) of material may be removed equally from each friction surface of the rotor. If the damage cannot be corrected when the rotor has been machined to the minimum thickness shown on the rotor, it should be replaced.

The finished braking surfaces of the rotor must be parallel within 0.007 in. (0.17mm) and lateral run-out must not be more than 0.003 in. (0.07mm) on the inboard surface in a 5 in. (127mm) radius.

REAR DRUM BRAKES

▶ See Figure 62

✳✳ CAUTION

Brake shoes contain asbestos, which has been determined to be a cancer causing agent. Never clean the brake surfaces with compressed air! Avoid inhaling any dust from any brake surface! When cleaning brake surfaces, use a commercially available brake cleaning fluid.

Brake Drum

INSPECTION

▶ See Figure 63

Check that there are no cracks or chips in the braking surface. Excessive bluing indicates overheating and a replacement drum is needed. The drum can be

Brakes 9-17

machined to remove minor damage and to establish a rounded braking surface on a warped drum. Never exceed the maximum oversize of the drum when machining the braking surface. The maximum inside diameter is stamped on the rim of the drum.

REMOVAL & INSTALLATION

Servo With Single Anchor

1. Jack and support the truck.
2. Remove the plug from the brake adjustment access hole.
3. Insert a thin bladed prytool through the adjusting hole and hold the adjusting lever away from the star wheel.
4. Release the brake by prying down against the star wheel with a brake spoon.
5. Remove the rear wheel and clips from the wheel studs. Remove the brake drum.
6. If there is a little trouble releasing the drum from the axle, you may tap around on the drum in an even manner to loosen it.

To install:
7. Install the drum and retaining clips.
8. Install the wheel and tire assembly.
9. Adjust the brakes.

Bendix Duo-Servo

1. Raise and support the vehicle.
2. Remove the rear wheel and tire.
3. Remove the axle shaft nuts, washers and cones. If the cones do not readily release, tap the axle shaft sharply in the center.
4. Remove the axle shaft.
5. Remove the outer hub nut.
6. Straighten the lockwasher tab and remove it along with the inner nut and bearing.
7. Carefully remove the drum.

To install:
8. Position the drum on the axle housing.
9. Install the bearing and inner nut. While rotating the wheel and tire, tighten the adjusting nut until a slight drag is felt.
10. Back off the adjusting nut 1/6 turn so that the wheel rotates freely without excessive end-play.
11. Install the lockrings and nut. Place a new gasket on the hub and install the axle shaft, cones, lockwashers and nuts.
12. Install the wheel and tire.
13. Road test the truck.

Brake Shoes

REMOVAL & INSTALLATION

Servo Type With Single Anchor

♦ See Figures 64 thru 78

1. Raise and support the vehicle.
2. Remove the rear wheel, drum retaining clips and the brake drum.
3. Remove the brake shoe return springs, noting how the secondary spring overlaps the primary spring.

Fig. 62 Most rear drums are easily removed once the wheel is out of the way

Fig. 63 Diameter is usually stamped on the outer edge of the drum

Fig. 64 Always leave the brakes on one side of the assembled as a reference, just remember it is a mirror image of the opposite side

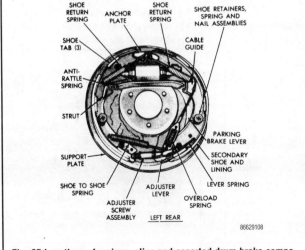

Fig. 65 Locations of springs, clips and assorted drum brake components

Fig. 66 Removing your return springs

9-18 BRAKES

Fig. 67 Check the springs for excessive rust or brittleness

Fig. 68 Using brake tools will save time and knuckles, but still be careful around springs

Fig. 69 Remove the spring, retainer and pin, but make sure you do not loose them

Fig. 70 Remove the cable, guide . . .

Fig. 71 . . . automatic adjuster lever . . .

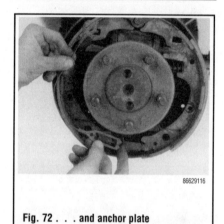
Fig. 72 . . . and anchor plate

Fig. 73 Remove the shoes as an assembly with the star adjuster connected

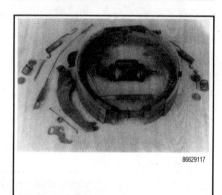
Fig. 74 Exploded view of the drum brake components

Fig. 75 Pad/backing plate lubricant is usually not supplied with the shoes, be sure to buy some before starting the job

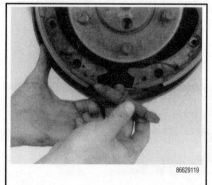
Fig. 76 Star adjusters are stamped with an L and R for replacement

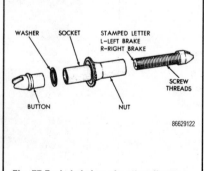
Fig. 77 Exploded view of a star adjuster assembly

Fig. 78 The adjuster cable eye is easily installed

Brakes 9-19

4. Remove the brake shoe retainer, springs and pins.
5. Disconnect the automatic adjuster cable from the anchor and unhook it from the lever. Remove the cable, cable guide, and anchor plate.
6. Remove the spring and lever from the shoe web.
7. Spread the anchor ends of the primary and secondary shoes and remove the parking brake spring and strut.
8. Disconnect the parking brake cable and remove the brake assembly.
9. Remove the primary and secondary brake shoe assemblies and the star adjuster as an assembly. Block the wheel cylinders to retain the pistons.
10. Measure the drum as described under "Front Brakes".
11. Apply a thin coat of lubricant to the support platforms.

To install:

12. Attach the parking brake lever to the back side of the secondary shoe.
13. Place the primary and secondary shoes in their relative positions on a workbench.
14. Lubricate the adjuster screw threads. Install it between the primary and secondary shoes with the star wheel next to the secondary shoe. The star wheels are stamped with an **L** (left) and **R** (right).
15. Overlap the ends of the primary and second brake shoes and install the adjusting spring and lever at the anchor end.
16. Hold the shoes in position and install the parking brake cable into the lever.
17. Install the parking brake strut and spring between the parking brake lever and primary shoe.
18. Place the brake shoes on the support and install the retainer pins and springs.
19. Install the anchor pin plate.
20. Install the eye of the adjusting cable over the anchor pin and install the return spring between the anchor pin and primary shoe.
21. Install the cable guide in the secondary shoe and install the secondary return spring. Be sure that the primary spring overlaps the secondary spring.
22. Position the adjusting cable in the groove of the cable guide and engage the hook of the cable in the adjusting lever.
23. Install the brake drum and retaining clips. Install the wheel and tire.
24. Adjust the brakes and road test the truck.

Bendix Duo-Servo

♦ See Figures 79 thru 86

1. Unhook and remove the adjusting lever return spring.
2. Remove the lever from the lever pivot pin.

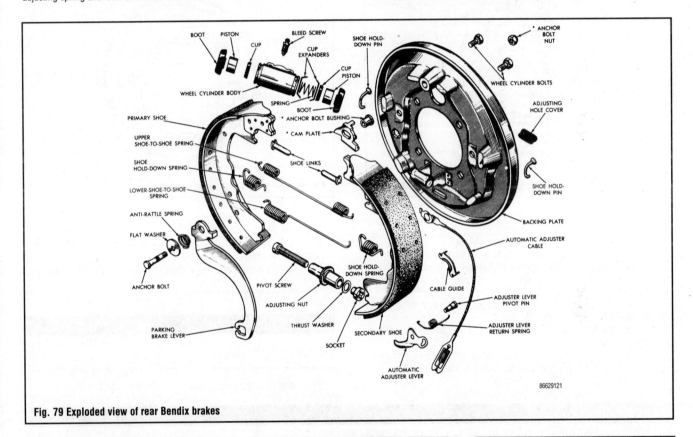

Fig. 79 Exploded view of rear Bendix brakes

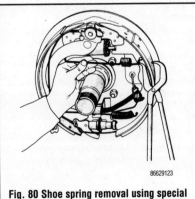

Fig. 80 Shoe spring removal using special brake tools

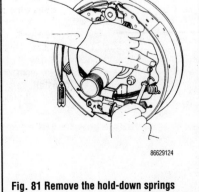

Fig. 81 Remove the hold-down springs

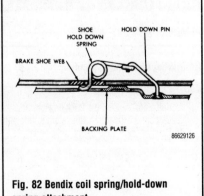

Fig. 82 Bendix coil spring/hold-down spring attachment

9-20 BRAKES

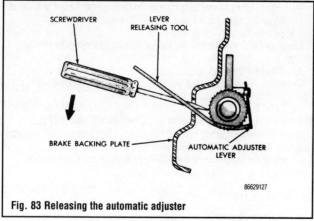

Fig. 83 Releasing the automatic adjuster

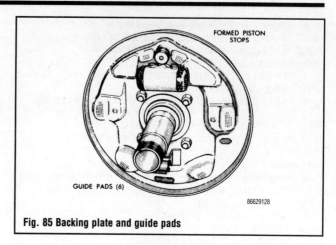

Fig. 85 Backing plate and guide pads

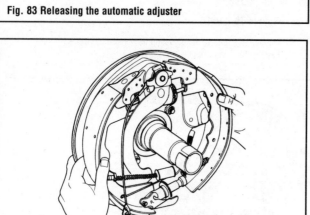

Fig. 84 On Bendix brakes remove the rear shoes as an assembly

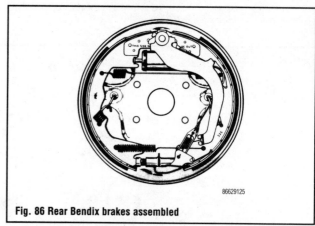

Fig. 86 Rear Bendix brakes assembled

3. Unhook the adjuster lever from the adjuster cable.
4. Unhook the upper shoe-to-shoe spring.
5. Unhook and remove the shoe hold-down springs.
6. Disconnect the parking brake cable from the parking brake lever.
7. Remove the shoes with the lower shoe-to-shoe spring and star wheel as an assembly.

To install:
8. The pivot screw and adjusting nut on the left side have left-hand threads and right hand threads on the right side.
9. Lubricate and assemble the star wheel assembly. Lubricate the guide pads on the support plates.
10. Assemble the star wheel, lower shoe-to-shoe spring, and the primary and secondary shoes. Position this assembly on the support plate.
11. Install and hook the hold-down springs.

12. Install the upper shoe-to-shoe spring.
13. Install the cable and retaining clip.
14. Position the adjuster lever return spring on the pivot (green springs on left brakes and red springs on right brakes).
15. Install the adjuster lever. Route the adjuster cable and connect it to the adjuster
16. Install the brake drum and adjust the brakes.

Wheel Cylinders

REMOVAL & INSTALLATION

Please refer to the front drum brake section for this procedure.

PARKING BRAKE

Cables

REMOVAL & INSTALLATION

Rear Wheel Internal Expanding

1967–72 FRONT

1. Raise and support the truck on jackstands.
2. Disconnect the front cable return spring at the equalizer.
3. Remove the adjusting nut at the equalizer.

4. Disconnect the cable housing at the lower anchor point and remove the cable and housing from the bracket.
5. Remove the bolt from the cable housing anchor clip at the parking brake lever.
6. Remove the clevis pin at the lever.
7. Remove the anchor clip from the cable housing.
8. Remove the housing grommet from the firewall and cable assembly by pushing the grommet forward, towards the engine.

To install:
9. Install the housing grommet in the firewall.
10. Install the anchor clip on the cable housing.
11. Install the clevis pin at the lever.

Brakes 9-21

12. Install the bolt from the cable housing anchor clip at the parking brake lever.
13. Install the cable and housing at the bracket. Connect the cable housing at the lower anchor point.
14. Install the adjusting nut at the equalizer.
15. Connect the front cable return spring at the equalizer.
16. Adjust the parking brake.

1973–88 FRONT

▶ See Figures 87 and 88

1. Raise and support the rear end on jackstands.
2. Remove the adjusting nut at the equalizer.
3. Disengage the cable housing at the lower anchor point and remove the cable and housing from the bracket.
4. Remove the cable housing anchor clip at the parking brake lever.
5. Remove the anchor clip from the lever.

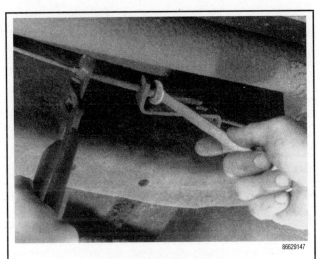

Fig. 87 Hold the threaded cable end steady while loosening the adjusting nut

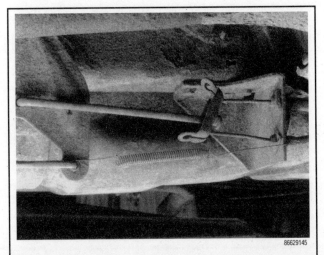

Fig. 88 Most equalizer assemblies divide the front/intermediate cable load across the 2 rear cables

6. Remove the housing grommet from the floor board.

To install:
7. Install the cable and housing through the floor pan and install the housing grommet.
8. Install the anchor clip on the cable housing.
9. Connect the cable at the adjusting link by installing the adjusting nut.
10. Adjust the parking brake.
11. Adjust the brakes.

1979–83 INTERMEDIATE CABLE

1. Raise and support the vehicle enough to gain access to the equalizer and cable adjustment.
2. Release parking brake.
3. Remove the adjusting nut at the adjusting link.
4. Disengage the rear end of the cable from the ratio lever and remove the cable.
5. Remove the ratio lever pivot bolt nut and bolt.
6. Disengage the front of the ratio lever rod from ratio lever assembly.
7. Remove the rod from the equalizer.

To install:
8. Install the rod to the equalizer.
9. Engage the front of the ratio lever rod to the ratio lever assembly.
10. Reinstall the ratio lever pivot bolt nut and bolt.
11. Replace the cable and engage the rear end of the cable to the ratio lever.
12. Install the adjusting nut at the adjusting link.
13. Adjust the brakes.
14. Lower the vehicle, test the parking brake system.

1984–88 INTERMEDIATE CABLE

1. Raise and support the vehicle enough to gain access to the equalizer and cable adjustment.
2. Release parking brake.
3. Remove the adjusting nut at adjusting link.
4. Disengage the rear end of cable from the ratio lever or cable equalizer and remove.

To install:
5. Replace the rear end of cable onto the ratio lever or equalizer.
6. Insert the adjusting nut onto link.
7. Adjust the brakes. Lower the vehicle.
8. Test the brake system.

1967–72 REAR CABLE

1. Raise and support the vehicle.
2. Release the brake and remove the rear wheels.
3. Remove the brake drum.
4. Remove the brake shoe return springs.
5. Remove the brake shoe retaining springs.
6. Remove the brake shoes, strut and spring from the support plate.
7. Disconnect the brake cable from the operating arm.
8. Compress the retainers on the end of the brake cable housing and remove the cables from the brake support plate.
9. Remove the retaining bolt and nut from the brake cable bracket and clips at the front bracket.
10. Disconnect the brake cable at the equalizer bar.
11. Remove the cable assembly.
12. Installation is the reverse of removal. Adjust the brakes.

1973–88 REAR CABLE

1. Raise and support the rear end on jackstands.
2. Remove the rear wheels.
3. Remove the drums.
4. Remove the brake shoe return springs.
5. Remove the brake shoe retaining springs.
6. Remove the shoes, strut and spring from the support plate.

9-22 BRAKES

7. Disconnect the cable from the operating arm.
8. Compress the retainers on the end of the cable housing and remove the cable from the support plate.
9. Move the retaining clip out at the crossmember.
10. Disconnect the brake cable from the equalizer.

To install:

→Before installing the new brake cable lubricate it with short fiber grease at all contact points.

11. Insert the cable and housing into the crossmember, and install the retaining clip.
12. Insert the brake cable and housing into the brake support plate making sure the housing retainers lock the housing firmly into place.
13. Holding brake shoes (and the strut, if equipped) in place on the support table. Engage the brake cable into the brake shoe operating lever.
14. Install the brake shoe retaining springs, and return springs.
15. Insert the front cable into the equalizer. Install the drum and wheel.
16. Adjust the brakes and parking cable.

ADJUSTMENT

Wheel Mounted

1. Adjust the service brakes by making a few stops in reverse.
2. Raise and support the rear end on jackstands.
3. Release the parking brake lever and loosen the cable adjusting nut to be sure that the cable is slack.
4. Tighten the cable adjusting nut until a slight drag is felt while rotating the wheels.
5. Loosen the cable adjusting nut until the wheels can be rotated freely, then back off the cable adjusting nut two turns.
6. Apply the parking brake several times, then release it and check to be sure that the rear wheels rotate freely.

Transmission/Transfer Case Mounted

EXTERNAL CONTRACTING

1. Check the free play between the anchor bracket on the band and the anchor. Free play should not exceed 0.005 in. (0.12mm). If it does, remove the anchor bracket and compress it in a vise. Install it and recheck. Keep at it until you get it right.
2. Place the parking brake lever in the fully released position.
3. Adjust the anchor bolt to give a clearance of 0.015–0.020 in. (0.38–0.50mm) between the lining and the drum.
4. Install a lockwire on the anchor bolt, but don't pull it tight.
5. Adjusting the guide bolt adjusts the lower half of the band; adjusting the nut adjusts the upper half. Adjust each until there is equal drag on both the lower and upper half with each having equal clearance.
6. To adjust the cable, loosen the locknut, remove the clevis pin and turn the yoke until all slack is removed from the cable.

INTERNAL EXPANDING

→If the adjustment is not performed correctly, shifting of the transmission will be affected.

1. Place the shift lever in NEUTRAL.
2. Fully release the parking brake.
3. Disconnect the driveshaft at the drum.
4. Remove the adjusting screw cover plate.
5. Loosen the brake cable clamp bolt and back off the cable adjusting nut.
6. Turn the nut to increase drag on the drum until a slight drag is felt, then, back off the nut one full notch.

→Make sure that the two raised shoulders on the adjusting nut are seated in the grooves on the adjusting sleeve.

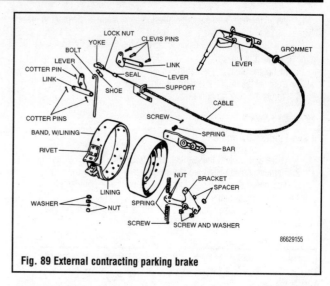

Fig. 89 External contracting parking brake

7. The cable length adjusting nut should be positioned against the cable housing so that there is 0.005–0.010 in. (0.12–0.25mm) clearance between the operating lever and the brake shoe cable.
8. To lock the adjustment, tighten the cable housing clamp securely.
9. Tighten the cable adjusting nut against the housing.
10. Check the parking brake lever travel.
11. Install the cover plate.
12. Connect the driveshaft.
13. Apply the parking brakes several times, then release and test to see if the rear wheels are rotating freely without dragging.

Brake Band Replacement

EXTERNAL CONTRACTING

♦ See Figure 89

1. Raise and support the front end on jackstands.
2. Disconnect the parking brake cable.
3. Unscrew and remove the adjusting nut.
4. Remove the guide bolt adjusting locknuts.
5. Remove the anchor adjusting screw.
6. Pull the band assembly away from the transmission and off the driveshaft.
7. Installation is the reverse of removal. Adjust the brake.

INTERNAL EXPANDING

♦ See Figures 90 and 91

1. Disconnect the driveshaft at the transmission.
2. Remove the companion flange nut, lockwasher and flatwasher.
3. Install a puller on the companion flange and remove the flange and drum. You'll have to devise a method of holding the unit to keep it from turning while pulling the drum.
4. Disengage the cable from the operating lever.
5. Separate the shoes at the bottom, allowing the shoe adjusting nut screws and sleeve to drop out and release the shoes.
6. Pry the brake shoe return spring up and over to the right and pry the brake shoe inward.
7. Remove the spring from the assembly.
8. Pry out the brake shoe retaining washer and remove the outer guide.
9. Slide each shoe out from under the guide spring. As the shoes are removed, the operating lever will drop out of place.
10. Separate the operating lever from the right shoe by removing the nut, lockwasher and bolt.

Brakes 9-23

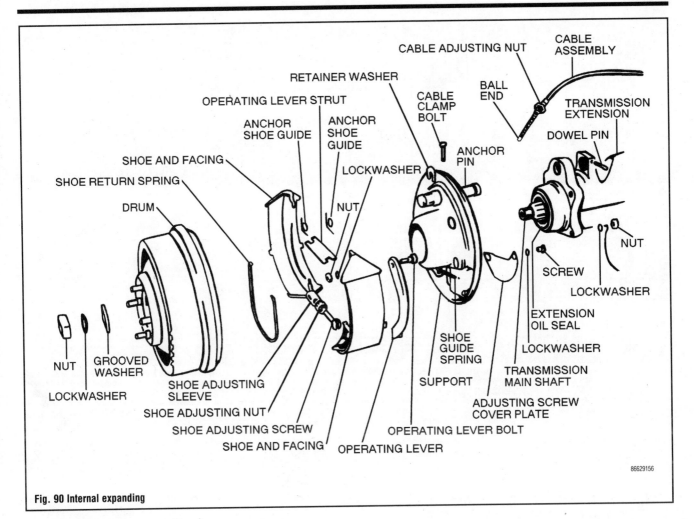

Fig. 90 Internal expanding

To assemble:
11. Assemble the operating lever on the right shoe.
12. Slide the right and left shoes under the guide.
13. Spread the shoes and insert the operating lever.
14. Work the return spring under the guide and upward to engage the retaining pin on the left shoe.
15. Force the other end of the return spring upward and over the retaining pin on the right shoe.
16. Spread the shoes apart at the bottom and install the adjusting nut, screw and sleeve.
17. Place the anchor guide over the anchor and secure the shoes with the retaining washer.
18. Turn the brake shoe adjusting nut until the shoes are in a released position and install the brake drum.
19. Make sure that the brake shoes are centered on the backing plate and are free to move.
20. Install the brake drum, washers and nut. Tighten the nut to 35 ft. lbs. (47 Nm).
21. Adjust the shoes and cable..

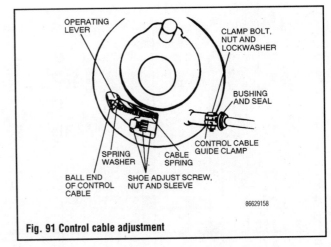

Fig. 91 Control cable adjustment

9-24 BRAKES

BRAKE SPECIFICATIONS
All specifications in inches.

Years	Models	Master Cyl. Bore	Brake Disc Minimum Thickness	Brake Disc Maximum Run-out	Brake Drum Orig. Inside Dia.	Brake Drum Max. Wear Limit	Wheel Cyl. or Caliper Bore Front	Wheel Cyl. or Caliper Bore Rear
1967-68	D100	1.000	—	—	11.000	11.060	1.125	0.937
	D200	1.125	—	—	12.125	12.185	1.125	1.125
	W100	1.125	—	—	12.125	12.185	1.125	1.125
	W200	1.125	—	—	12.125	12.185	1.125	1.125
	D300	1.125	—	—	F12.125 R13.000	12.185 13.060	1.125	1.250
	W300	1.125	—	—	F14.125 R13.000	14.185 13.060	1.375	1.000
	WM300	1.125	—	—	14.125	14.185	1.375	1.375
1969-71	D100	1.000	—	—	11.000	11.060	1.125	0.937
	D200	1.125	—	—	12.000	12.060	1.125	1.125
	W100	1.125	—	—	12.000	12.060	1.125	1.125
	W200	1.125	—	—	12.000	12.060	1.125	1.125
	D300	1.125	—	—	F12.000 R13.000	12.060 13.060	1.125	1.250
	W300	1.125	—	—	F14.125 R13.000	14.185 13.060	1.375	1.000
1972-74	D100	1.030	1.220	0.005	10.000	10.060	3.10	0.875
	D200 w/base GVW	1.125	1.160	0.005	12.000	12.060	3.10	0.875
	D200 w/Dana 60	1.125	1.160	0.005	12.000	12.060	3.10	1.000
	D300	1.125	1.160	0.005	12.000	12.060	3.10	1.000
	W100	1.000	—	—	11.000	11.060	1.125	0.938
	W200	1.125	—	—	12.000	12.060	1.125	0.875
	W300	1.125	—	—	12.000	12.060	1.375	1.000
1975-76	D100	1.030	1.220	0.005	10.000	10.060	3.10	0.875
	AW100	1.030	1.220	0.005	10.000	10.060	3.10	0.875
	PD100	1.030	1.220	0.005	10.000	10.060	3.10	0.875
	PW100	1.030	1.220	0.005	10.000	10.060	3.10	0.875
	D100 w/9¾ in. axle	1.130	1.220	0.005	11.000	11.060	3.10	0.938
	W100	1.030	1.220	0.005	11.000	11.060	3.10	0.938
	D200	1.125	1.160	0.005	12.000	12.060	3.10	1.000
	D300	1.125	1.160	0.005	12.000	12.060	3.10	1.000
	W200	1.125	1.160	0.005	12.000	12.060	3.10	1.000
	W200 w/Dana 60	1.125	1.160	0.005	12.000	12.060	3.38	1.000
	W300	1.125	1.160	0.005	12.000	12.060	3.10	1.000

BRAKE SPECIFICATIONS
All specifications in inches.

Years	Models	Master Cyl. Bore	Brake Disc Minimum Thickness	Brake Disc Maximum Run-out	Brake Drum Orig. Inside Dia.	Brake Drum Max. Wear Limit	Wheel Cyl. or Caliper Bore Front	Wheel Cyl. or Caliper Bore Rear
1977-80	AD100	1.125	1.220	0.005	10.000	10.060	3.10	0.938
	AW100	1.125	1.220	0.005	10.000	10.060	3.10	0.938
	PD100	1.125	1.220	0.005	10.000	10.060	3.10	0.938
	PW100	1.125	1.220	0.005	10.000	10.060	3.10	0.938
	D150	1.125	1.220	0.005	10.000	10.060	3.10	0.938
	W150	1.125	1.220	0.005	10.000	10.060	3.10	0.938
	D200 w/3300 lb. front axle	1.125	1.220	0.005	12.000	12.060	3.10	1.000
	D200 w/4000 lb. front axle	1.125	1.160	0.005	12.000	12.060	3.10	0.875
	W200 w/Dana 44	1.125	1.160	0.005	12.000	12.060	3.10	1.000
	D300	1.125	1.160	0.005	12.000	12.060	3.10	1.000
	W200 w/Dana 60	1.125	1.160	0.005	12.000	12.060	3.38	1.000
	W300	1.125	1.160	0.005	12.000	12.060	3.38	1.000
1981-88	AD150	1.125	1.160	0.005	11.000	11.060	3.10	0.938
	AW150	1.125	1.220	0.005	11.000	11.060	3.10	0.938
	D150	1.125	1.220	0.005	11.000	11.060	3.10	0.938
	AD150	1.125	1.220	0.005	11.000	11.060	3.10	0.938
	W150	1.125	1.220	0.005	11.000	11.060	3.10	0.938
	D250 w/3300 lb. front axle	1.125	1.220	0.005	12.000	12.060	3.10	1.000
	D250 w/4000 lb. front axle	1.125	1.160	0.005	12.000	12.060	3.10	1.000
	W250 w/Dana 44	1.125	1.160	0.005	12.000	12.060	3.10	1.000
	D350	1.125	1.160	0.005	12.000	12.060	3.10	1.125
	W250 w/Dana 60	1.125	1.160	0.005	12.000	12.060	3.38	1.125
	W350	1.125	1.160	0.005	12.000	12.060	3.38	1.125

EXTERIOR 10-2
DOORS 10-2
    ADJUSTMENT 10-2
HOOD 10-2
    ADJUSTMENT 10-2
LIFTGATE 10-2
    REMOVAL & INSTALLATION 10-2
TAILGATE 10-2
    REMOVAL & INSTALLATION 10-2
GRILLE 10-3
    REMOVAL & INSTALLATION 10-3
OUTSIDE MIRRORS 10-4
    REMOVAL & INSTALLATION 10-4
ANTENNA 10-4
    REMOVAL & INSTALLATION 10-4
SUNROOF 10-5
    REMOVAL & INSTALLATION 10-5
SUNROOF SEAL 10-5
    REMOVAL & INSTALLATION 10-5
ROOF VENT 10-5
    REMOVAL & INSTALLATION 10-5
INTERIOR 10-6
CONSOLE 10-6
    REMOVAL & INSTALLATION 10-6
DOOR PANELS 10-6
    REMOVAL & INSTALLATION 10-6
MANUAL DOOR LOCKS 10-6
    REMOVAL & INSTALLATION 10-6
POWER DOOR LOCKS 10-7
    REMOVAL & INSTALLATION 10-7
MANUAL DOOR GLASS AND
  REGULATOR 10-8
    REMOVAL & INSTALLATION 10-8
POWER DOOR GLASS AND REGULATOR
  MOTOR 10-9
    REMOVAL & INSTALLATION 10-9
INSIDE REAR VIEW MIRROR 10-9
    REMOVAL & INSTALLATION 10-9
WINDSHIELD AND FIXED GLASS 10-10
    REMOVAL & INSTALLATION 10-10
    WINDSHIELD CHIP REPAIR 10-10

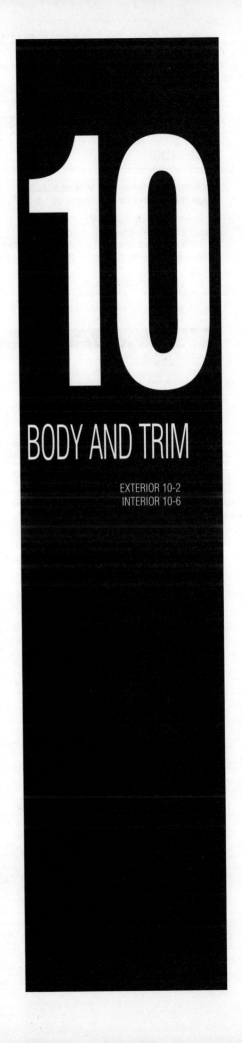

10
BODY AND TRIM

EXTERIOR 10-2
INTERIOR 10-6

10-2 BODY AND TRIM

EXTERIOR

Doors

ADJUSTMENT

➡ Loosen the hinge-to-door bolts for lateral adjustment only. Loosen the hinge-to-body bolts for both lateral and vertical adjustment.

1. Determine which hinge bolts are to be loosened and back them out just enough to allow movement.
2. To move the door safely, use a padded pry bar. When the door is in the proper position, tighten the bolts to 24 ft. lbs. (32 Nm) and check the door operation. There should be no binding or interference when the door is closed and opened.
3. Door closing adjustment can also be affected by the position of the lock striker plate. Loosen the striker plate bolts and move the striker plate just enough to permit proper closing and locking of the door.

Hood

ADJUSTMENT

♦ See Figures 1 and 2

1967–71 Models

1. Open the hood, then matchmark the hinge and latch positions.
2. Loosen the hinge-to-hood bolts just enough to allow movement of the hood.
3. Remove the hood lock striker from the grille support and loosen the stabilizer fork screws.
4. Close the hood and move it so that you have a 3/16 in. (5mm) clearance between the back of the hood and the cowl.
5. Raise the hood no more than 30° and tighten the hood-to-hinge bolts.
6. Install the lock striker, then check the engagement of the lock and striker.
7. Adjust the lock laterally and the striker vertically, as necessary, for a positive lock. Tighten the stabilizer fork screws.

1972–88 Models

1. Open the hood and matchmark the hinge and latch positions.
2. Loosen the hinge-to-hood bolts just enough to allow movement of the hood.
3. Loosen the hood lock at the grille support.
4. Close the hood and move it so that you have a 3/16 in. (5mm) clearance between the back of the hood and the cowl.
5. Raise the hood no more than 30° and tighten the hood-to-hinge bolts.
6. Tighten the latch, then lower the hood and check for even pressure at the fender pads. Open the hood and, using something like modeling clay, apply the substance to the top side of the primary latch striker arm.
7. Close the hood and make sure it is fully latched.
8. Open the hood and check the latch imprint in the clay.

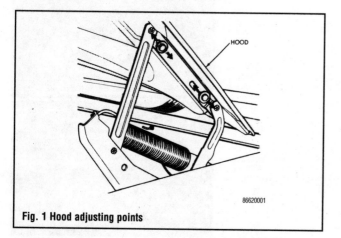

Fig. 1 Hood adjusting points

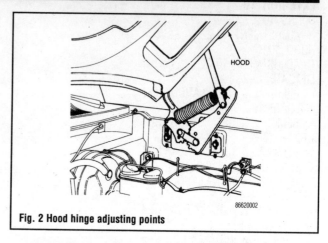

Fig. 2 Hood hinge adjusting points

9. A properly adjusted latch will show a centered imprint on the striker. If not, adjust the hood latch.

Liftgate

REMOVAL & INSTALLATION

Ramcharger and Trail Duster

2–PIECE LIFTGATE—UPPER HALF

♦ See Figure 3

1. Open the liftgate.
2. Remove the plug from the upper section of the liftgate.
3. Remove the hinge-to-gate bolts.
4. Remove the stud from the lower roof section.
5. Remove the liftgate and lift rod from the truck.

To install:

6. Install the liftgate rod into the liftgate. Place the liftgate in position.
7. Insert the stud into the lower roof section.
8. Install the hinge-to-gate bolts.
9. Insert the plug into the upper section of the liftgate.
10. Adjust the liftgate.

2–PIECE LIFTGATE—LOWER HALF

The lower half of the 2-piece liftgate found on some Ramchargers and Trail Dusters is removed and installed in the same manner as the Pick-Up truck tailgate. Please refer to that procedure found later in this section.

1–PIECE LIFTGATE

1. Open the liftgate.
2. Remove the hinge-to-liftgate bolts.
3. Remove the liftgate rod studs from the roof.
4. Remove the liftgate and rods from the truck.

To install:

5. Install the upper lift rod stud to the roof panel.
6. Install the lower stud to the liftgate.
7. Check the lift rod and liftgate for proper functions. Adjust the fit.

Tailgate

REMOVAL & INSTALLATION

♦ See Figures 4 and 5

The lower half of the 2-piece liftgate found on some Ramchargers and Trail Dusters is removed and installed in the same manner as the Pick-Up truck tailgate. In all cases, remove the tailgate as follows:

BODY AND TRIM

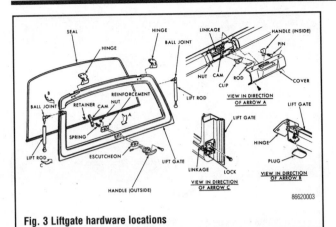

Fig. 3 Liftgate hardware locations

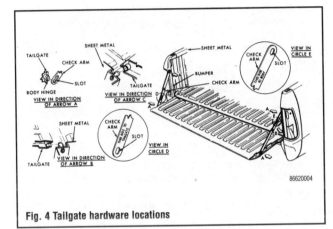

Fig. 4 Tailgate hardware locations

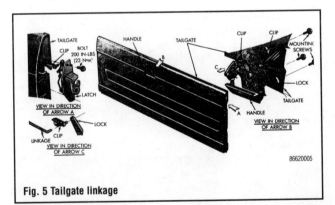

Fig. 5 Tailgate linkage

1. Open the tailgate.
2. Angle the gate so the slot in the check arm lines up with the body hinge.
3. Slip the check arm away from the hinge.
4. Remove the bottom of the gate from the slot in the lower hinge on the right side, facing the gate.
5. Remove the left side of the gate by sliding it out of the lower hinge.

To install:

6. Slide the gate into the left lower hinge.
7. Place the right side into the slotted hinge.
8. Install the check arms to the gate, noting the correct position of the arm and body.
9. Bring the gate up until the top of the check arm slotted section slips onto the hinge.

Grille

REMOVAL & INSTALLATION

1967–73 Models

1. Remove both headlight bezels.
2. Remove the grille extension.
3. Unplug the headlight wires.
4. Remove the grille attaching screws at each end and in the center, then lift off the grille.

To install:

5. Insert the new grille with its attaching bolts.
6. Plug the headlight wires in, then install the grille extensions.
7. Install the headlight bezels.

1974–76 Models

1. Remove both headlamp bezels.
2. Remove the grille upper screws.
3. Remove the grille lower screws.
4. Remove the attaching screws at each end of the grille.
5. Remove the grille-to-extension screws.
6. Remove the screws at each end of the extension.

To install:

7. Place the extensions in position and loosely insert all mounting screws for them.
8. Insert the center grille and place all screws in place. Tighten them all once the grille is aligned.
9. Install the headlamp bezels.

1977–88 Models

♦ See Figures 6, 7 and 8

1. Remove the grille upper screws.
2. Unfasten the grille lower screws.
3. Remove the attaching screws at each end of the grille.
4. Unfasten the screws at each end of the extension.

Fig. 6 The upper grille screws must be removed first

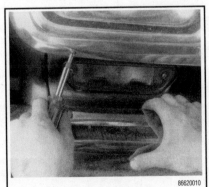

Fig. 7 The lower grille screws are easily accessible

Fig. 8 Watch your fingers when removing the grille—the edges may be sharp

10-4 BODY AND TRIM

5. Remove the grille.
To install:
6. Place the grille extensions in position, then install all the screws loosely.
7. Center the grille extensions and tighten the screws.
8. Place the grille in the opening and center it, then install and tighten all the screws.

Outside Mirrors

REMOVAL & INSTALLATION

Manual

1. Remove the mounting screws, then lift off the mirror and gasket.
To install:
2. Install by placing the gasket onto the bottom of the mounting area of the mirror.
3. Insert the mirror with the screws and tighten down.

Power

♦ See Figure 9

1. Remove the door trim panel and weathershield.
2. Reach inside the door and detach the wiring at the connector for the mirror.
3. Remove the mounting bracket cover screw, and slide the cover up onto the mirror stem.
4. Remove the three mounting nuts.
5. Pull the mirror loose from the door, feeding the wiring harness out through the hole in the outer door panel.
To install:
6. Connect the new mirror onto the harness, then feed the wire through the panel.
7. Insert the mirror on the mounting bracket, then install and tighten the nuts.
8. Install the mounting cover, replace the trim panel and weathershield.

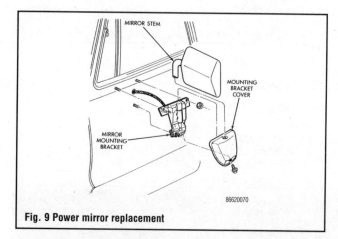

Fig. 9 Power mirror replacement

Antenna

REMOVAL & INSTALLATION

1967–72 Models

♦ See Figure 10

1. Unplug the antenna wire from the radio.
2. Remove the antenna wire from the clips on the cowl plenum panel, pedal support and stop bracket.

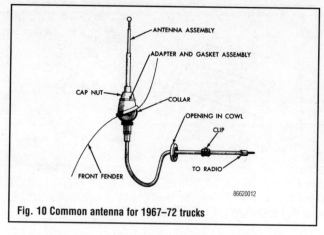

Fig. 10 Common antenna for 1967–72 trucks

3. Remove the cap nut from the antenna.
4. Remove the antenna assembly from under the fender opening.
To install:
5. Insert the antenna into the fender opening, then install the cap nut and tighten.
6. Install the wire clips onto the cowl plenum.
7. Insert the antenna wire jack into the rear of the radio.

1973–88 Models

♦ See Figure 11

1. Disconnect the battery ground cable.
2. Remove the glove box.
3. Reach behind the instrument panel and unplug the antenna lead from the radio.
4. Reach through the glove box opening and pull the antenna lead out of the retainer clip.
5. Open the right door and remove the cable grommet from the A-pillar.
6. Pull the cable from the A-pillar.
7. Loosen, but do not remove, the antenna mast.
8. Loosen the cap nut on the adapter.
9. Hold the antenna mast in one hand and remove the cap nut with the other.
10. Lower the antenna far enough to gain access to the antenna body.
11. While holding the antenna body, remove the antenna mast.
12. Pull the antenna body and cable from the fender.
13. Remove the adapter from the fender.
To install:
14. Route the antenna cable between the fender and firewall to the A-pillar.
15. Insert the mast through the hole in the fender and screw it into the antenna body.

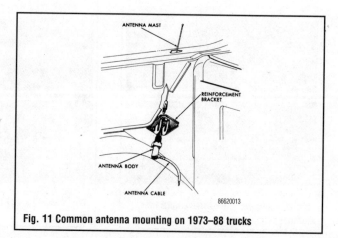

Fig. 11 Common antenna mounting on 1973–88 trucks

BODY AND TRIM 10-5

16. Pull the assembly into position and hold it there.
17. Install the adapter, then index the tab with the opening in the fender and antenna body.
18. Install the cap nut and tighten it securely.
19. Insert the cable through the opening in the A-pillar.
20. From inside the glove box opening, pull the cable in far enough to snap the grommet into place.
21. Route the cable through the clip and plug it into the radio.
22. Install the glove box.
23. Connect the battery ground cable.

Sunroof

REMOVAL & INSTALLATION

♦ See Figure 12

1. Unlatch the front bayonet mounts.
2. Unlatch the rear handle.
3. Unlatch the catch retainer by pushing the slide bar, then remove the handle from the retainer.
4. Lift the glass from the opening.

To install:

5. Center the glass into the opening.
6. Install the handle into the catch retainer.
7. Latch the handle and the bayonet mounts.

Sunroof Seal

REMOVAL & INSTALLATION

♦ See Figure 13

1. Remove the sunroof glass.
2. Remove the glass seal from the frame; it is glued in.

To install:

3. Clean the area of all dirt and glue deposits, on the frame and surrounding areas.
4. Using a weatherstrip cement, install the seal. Be sure the crown of the seal is into the corners of the frame for correct seating.
5. Install the sunroof glass. Allow to cure, then test with water.

Roof Vent

REMOVAL & INSTALLATION

♦ See Figure 14

Roof Vent

1. Open the cover, then drill the upper rivet head from the cover/handle assembly.
2. Remove the vent cover hinge. Remove the cover.

To install:

3. Install the cover, then attach the hinge.
4. Install the handle to the cover using a 2.125x187 inch rivet or equivalent.

Vent Cover Seal

1. Open the cover, then remove the cover hinge.
2. Remove the cover seal from the frame.
3. Clean the seal area of the frame well.

To install:

4. Using a weatherstip cement, install the seal.
5. Install the cover hinge, then water test the vent.

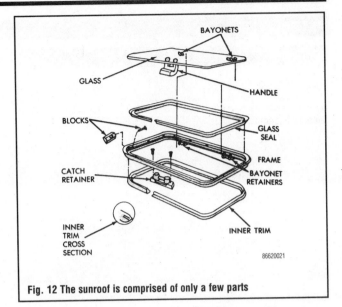

Fig. 12 The sunroof is comprised of only a few parts

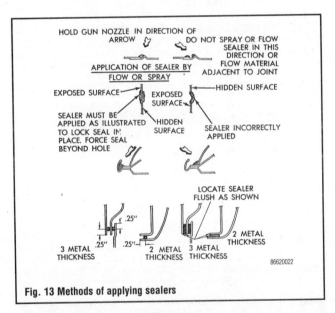

Fig. 13 Methods of applying sealers

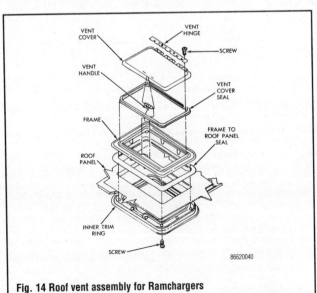

Fig. 14 Roof vent assembly for Ramchargers

10-6 BODY AND TRIM

INTERIOR

Console

REMOVAL & INSTALLATION

Console Assembly

♦ See Figure 15

1. Open the console door and remove the liner assembly.
2. Unfasten the screws in the bottom of the console which are mounted to the underbody.
3. Remove the console.

To install:
4. Place the console in position on the truck and secure with the mounting screws.
5. Insert the liner, then close the console door.

Lock

1. Open the console door and remove the mounting screws.
2. Remove the lock from the door.

To install:
3. Place the new lock into position, then secure with screws.
4. Close the door and check the lock cylinder operation.

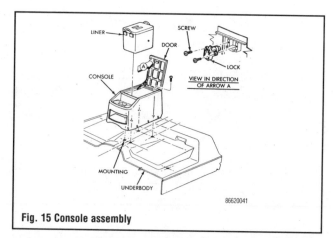

Fig. 15 Console assembly

Door Panels

REMOVAL & INSTALLATION

♦ See Figures 16, 17 and 18

1. Remove the armrest.
2. Remove the door handle screw, then pull off the handle.
3. On models with manual windows, remove the window regulator handle screw and pull off the handle. On models with power windows, remove the power window switch housing.
4. On models with manual door locks, remove the door lock control. On models with power door locks, remove the power door lock switch housing.
5. On models with electric outside rear view mirrors, remove the power mirror switch housing.
6. Using a flat tool, insert it carefully behind the panel and slide it along to find the push-pins. When you encounter a pin, pry the pin outward slowly and carefully. Do this until all the pins are out. NEVER PULL ON THE PANEL TO REMOVE THE PINS!

To install:
7. Install the door panel carefully by pushing the pins into the door trim holes.
8. Install the electric mirror if equipped, along with the lock control switch.
9. Install the window regulator handle or power switch housing.
10. Attach the arm rest.

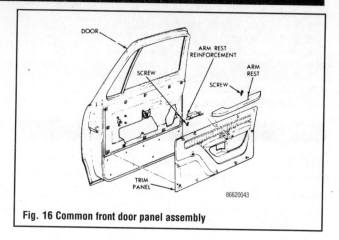

Fig. 16 Common front door panel assembly

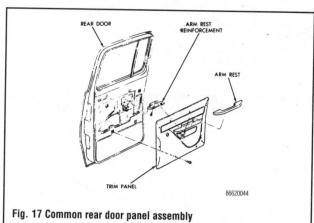

Fig. 17 Common rear door panel assembly

Fig. 18 Push the pins into the door panel carefully; you could damage the trim panel if you're not careful

Manual Door Locks

REMOVAL & INSTALLATION

Front Door Latch

ALL MODELS

♦ See Figures 19 and 20

1. Raise the glass to the full **UP** position.
2. Remove the door trim panel and watershield.

BODY AND TRIM   10-7

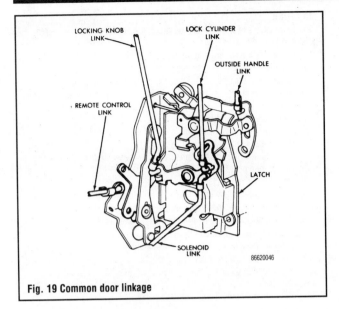

Fig. 19 Common door linkage

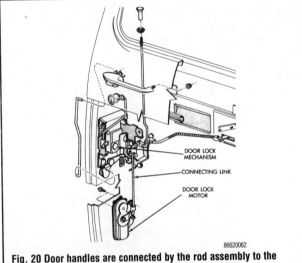

Fig. 20 Door handles are connected by the rod assembly to the latching mechanism—power door lock model shown

3. Disconnect the rods from the handle and lock cylinder, and from the remote control assembly.
4. Remove the latch assembly attaching screws and remove the latch from the door.

To install:

5. Install the latch with the mounting screws.
6. Connect the lock cylinder rods to the cylinder assembly. Attach the handle rods.
7. Install the watershield trim panel, as well as any other accessories.
8. Raise and lower the glass slowly to ensure that there is no interference.

Rear Door Latch

CREW CAB

1. Raise the glass to the full **UP** position.
2. Remove the door trim panel and watershield.
3. Disconnect the rods from the handle and lock cylinder, and from the remote control assembly.
4. Remove the latch assembly attaching screws and remove the latch from the door.

To install:

5. Attach the latch assembly, then install the rod assemblies. Install the attaching screws for the latch.

6. Install the trim panel and watershield.
7. Connect any outer trim pieces, then lower the window and make sure that there is no interference.

Door Lock Cylinder

♦ See Figure 21

1. Place the window in the **UP** position.
2. Remove the trim panel and watershield.
3. Disconnect the actuating rod from the lock control link clip.
4. Slide the retainer away from the lock cylinder.
5. Pull the cylinder from the door.
6. Installation is the reverse of removal.

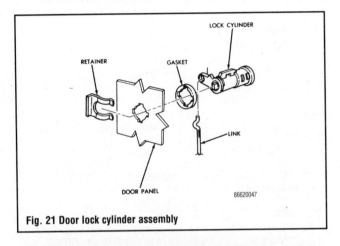

Fig. 21 Door lock cylinder assembly

Power Door Locks

REMOVAL & INSTALLATION

Actuator Motor

♦ See Figure 22

1. Raise the glass to the full UP position.
2. Remove the door handle, window regulator handle, if so equipped, and door trim panel.
3. Roll the door watershield away from the lower rear corner of the door to reveal the inside panel access opening.
4. Disconnect the motor from the door latch.

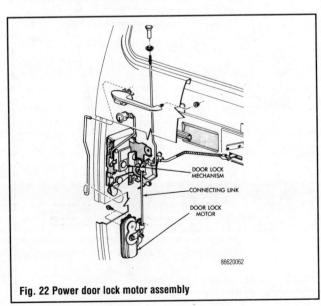

Fig. 22 Power door lock motor assembly

10-8 BODY AND TRIM

5. Remove the motor and swivel bracket from the door by drilling out the pop rivet.
6. Disconnect the wiring harness.

To install:
7. Attach the mounting bracket to the door inside panel and screws.
8. Attach the link to the motor rod and connect the wires.
9. Reset the watershield at the lower rear corner of the door.
10. Install the window regulator handle, if so equipped, as well as the door inside release lever handle and door trim panel.

Manual Door Glass and Regulator

REMOVAL & INSTALLATION

♦ See Figures 23 and 24

1967–76 Models

1. Remove the door trim panel and watershield.
2. Lower the glass completely.
3. On models equipped with stereo, remove the lower trim panel and speaker.
4. On models with a stationary glass panel in the door, remove the panel as follows:
    a. Remove the division channel attaching screws, then remove the channel.
    b. Move the glass and weatherstripping forward and out of the opening.
5. Remove the inner weatherstripping.
6. Remove the vent window lower support attaching screw.
7. Locate the vent window retaining clip screw through the weatherstripping and remove the screw.
8. Lower the door glass and tilt the vent window assembly rearward.
9. Remove the vent window.
10. Raise the door glass until the regulator connectors are visible.
11. Slide the window glass forward and remove the rear regulator connector from the guide.
12. Lower the regulator and tilt the glass upward to remove the front regulator connector.
13. Tilt the glass rearward and remove it from the door.

To install:
14. Slide the glass and regulator assembly into the door and connect the regulator arms in the guides.
15. Install a new retaining clip on the vent window assembly.
16. Install the vent window assembly into the door.
17. Install the lower vent window attaching screw. Don't tighten it yet.
18. Press the vent window retaining clip into the upper door frame with the palm of your hand.
19. Tighten the lower screw.
20. Install the inner weatherstripping.
21. On models with a stationary glass panel:
    a. Position the glass and weatherstripping in the window opening and insert it into the upper frame.
    b. Insert the division channel run into the channel.
    c. With the door glass in the down position, insert the division channel in the door and move it firmly against the stationary glass weatherstripping.
    d. Install, but don't tighten, the upper and lower attaching screws.
    e. Adjust the door glass in the channel.
    f. Tighten the channel against the stationary glass and check for a good seal.
22. Raise the door glass to the full up position.
23. If applicable, install the stereo speaker and lower trim.
24. Install the watershield and door trim panel.

1977–88 Models

1. Remove the door trim panel and watershield.
2. Lower the glass fully.
3. On models equipped with stereo, remove the lower trim panel and speaker.
4. On models with a stationary glass panel in the door, remove the panel as follows:
    a. Remove the division channel attaching screws and remove the channel.
    b. Move the glass and weatherstripping forward and out of the opening.

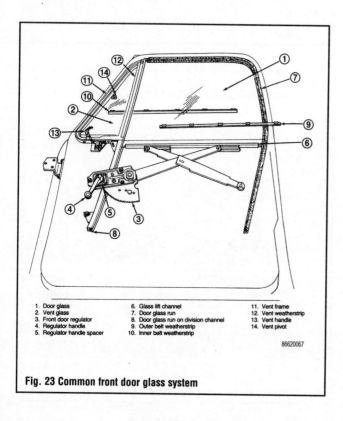

1. Door glass
2. Vent glass
3. Front door regulator
4. Regulator handle
5. Regulator handle spacer
6. Glass lift channel
7. Door glass run
8. Door glass run on division channel
9. Outer belt weatherstrip
10. Inner belt weatherstrip
11. Vent frame
12. Vent weatherstrip
13. Vent handle
14. Vent pivot

Fig. 23 Common front door glass system

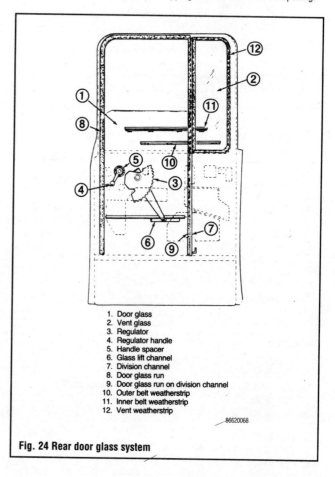

1. Door glass
2. Vent glass
3. Regulator
4. Regulator handle
5. Handle spacer
6. Glass lift channel
7. Division channel
8. Door glass run
9. Door glass run on division channel
10. Outer belt weatherstrip
11. Inner belt weatherstrip
12. Vent weatherstrip

Fig. 24 Rear door glass system

5. Remove the inner weatherstripping.
6. Pull back the upper glass run 8–10 in. (20–25cm), then remove the upper and lower vent window attaching screws.
7. Remove the vent window.
8. Slide the window glass forward off the regulator arms and remove the glass from the door.
9. Drill out the regulator mounting rivets and remove the regulator assembly from the door.

To install:
10. Position the regulator in the door.
11. Using ¼-20 screws and nuts in place of the rivets, torque the regulator mounting screws to 90 inch lbs. (10 Nm).
12. Slide the glass onto the regulator arms and into the rear glass run.
13. Install the plastic nut and U-nut on the vent window assembly.
14. Install the vent window assembly into the door.
15. Install the upper and lower vent window attaching screws. Don't tighten them yet.
16. Move the glass run back to the vent window by placing the run adjacent to the door channel and pressing it into the channel using a wide-bladed chisel or similar tool. Press in both corners to ensure the hidden lip engages the channel.
17. Install the inner weatherstripping.
18. Raise or lower the vent window to maintain a 0.062 in. (1.6mm) fore-aft glass free-play. Then, with the glass up, tighten the upper screws.
19. Hold the vent against the glass, with the glass down, and tighten the lower screws.
20. On models with a stationary glass panel:
    a. Position the glass and weatherstripping in the window opening and insert it into the upper frame.
    b. Insert the division channel run into the channel.
    c. With the door glass in the down position, insert the division channel in the door and move it firmly against the stationary glass weatherstripping.
    d. Install, but don't tighten, the upper and lower attaching screws.
    e. Adjust the door glass in the channel.
    f. Tighten the channel against the stationary glass and check for a good seal.
21. Raise the door glass to the full up position.
22. If applicable, install the stereo speaker and lower trim.
23. Install the watershield and door trim panel.

Power Door Glass and Regulator Motor

REMOVAL & INSTALLATION

♦ See Figure 25

1. Remove the door trim panel.
2. Lower the glass fully.
3. On models equipped with stereo, remove the lower trim panel and speaker.
4. Remove the down stop bumper bracket.
5. On models with a stationary glass panel in the door, remove the panel as follows:
    a. Remove the division channel attaching screws and remove the channel.
    b. Move the glass and weatherstripping forward and out of the opening.
6. Remove the inner weatherstripping.
7. Pull back the upper glass run 8–10 in. (20–25cm), then remove the upper and lower vent window attaching screws.
8. Remove the vent window.
9. Lower the glass fully.
10. Slide the window glass forward off the regulator arms and remove the glass from the door.
11. Drill out the regulator mounting rivets and remove the regulator assembly from the door.

To install:
12. Position the regulator in the door.

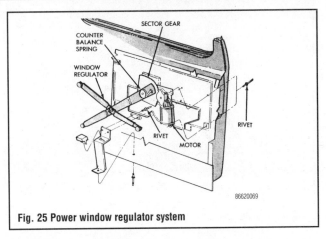

Fig. 25 Power window regulator system

13. Using ¼-20 screws and nuts in place of the rivets, torque the regulator mounting screws to 90 inch lbs. (10 Nm).
14. Slide the glass onto the regulator arms and into the rear glass run.
15. Install the plastic nut and U-nut on the vent window assembly.
16. Install the vent window assembly into the door.
17. Install the upper and lower vent window attaching screws. Don't tighten them yet.
18. Move the glass run back to the vent window by placing the run adjacent to the door channel and pressing it into the channel using a wide-bladed chisel or similar tool. Press in both corners to ensure the hidden lip engages the channel.
19. Install the inner weatherstripping.
20. Raise or lower the vent window to maintain a 1.6mm fore-aft glass free-play. Then, with the glass up, tighten the upper screws.
21. Hold the vent against the glass, with the glass down, and tighten the lower screws.
22. On models with a stationary glass panel:
    a. Position the glass and weatherstripping in the window opening and insert it into the upper frame.
    b. Insert the division channel run into the channel.
    c. With the door glass in the down position, insert the division channel in the door and move it firmly against the stationary glass weatherstripping.
    d. Install, but don't tighten, the upper and lower attaching screws.
    e. Adjust the door glass in the channel.
    f. Tighten the channel against the stationary glass and check for a good seal.
23. Raise the door glass to the full up position.
24. Install the down stop bumper.
25. If applicable, install the stereo speaker and lower trim.
26. Install the watershield and door trim panel.

Inside Rear View Mirror

REMOVAL & INSTALLATION

♦ See Figure 26

➡The mirror is held in place on a backing with a single setscrew. Though the mirror is easily removed or installed from the backing, the same cannot be said for the backing and glass. Should be backing come loose, you should purchase a mirror backing adhesive repair kit and follow its instructions.

1. Loosen the screw and lift the mirror off the button.

To install:
2. Slide the mirror over the button, then carefully tighten the set screw.

➡Do not overtighten the screw; it will strip and you will run into problems. Repair kits for damaged mirrors are available at many auto parts stores.

10-10 BODY AND TRIM

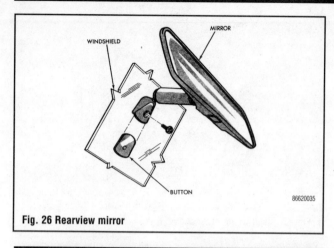

Fig. 26 Rearview mirror

Windshield and Fixed Glass

REMOVAL & INSTALLATION

If your windshield, or other fixed window, is cracked or chipped, you may decide to replace it with a new one yourself. However, there are two main reasons why replacement windshields and other window glass should be installed only by a professional automotive glass technician: safety and cost.

The most important reason a professional should install automotive glass is for safety. The glass in the vehicle, especially the windshield, is designed with safety in mind in case of a collision. The windshield is specially manufactured from two panes of specially-tempered glass with a thin layer of transparent plastic between them. This construction allows the glass to "give" in the event that a part of your body hits the windshield during the collision, and prevents the glass from shattering, which could cause lacerations, blinding and other harm to passengers of the vehicle. The other fixed windows are designed to be tempered so that if they break during a collision, they shatter in such a way that there are no large pointed glass pieces. The professional automotive glass technician knows how to install the glass in a vehicle so that it will function optimally during a collision. Without the proper experience, knowledge and tools, installing a piece of automotive glass yourself could lead to additional harm if an accident should ever occur.

Cost is also a factor when deciding to install automotive glass yourself. Performing this could cost you much more than a professional may charge for the same job. Since the windshield is designed to break under stress, an often life saving characteristic, windshields tend to break VERY easily when an inexperienced person attempts to install one. Do-it-yourselfers buying two, three or even four windshields from a salvage yard because they have broken them during installation are common stories. Also, since the automotive glass is designed to prevent the outside elements from entering your vehicle, improper installation can lead to water and air leaks. Annoying whining noises at highway speeds from air leaks or inside body panel rusting from water leaks can add to your stress level and subtract from your wallet. After buying two or three windshields, installing them and ending up with a leak that produces a noise while driving and water damage during rainstorms, the cost of having a professional do it correctly the first time may be much more alluring. We here at Chilton, therefore, advise that you have a professional automotive glass technician service any broken glass on your vehicle.

WINDSHIELD CHIP REPAIR

♦ See Figures 27 and 28

➡Check with your state and local authorities on the laws for state safety inspection. Some states or municipalities may not allow chip repair as a viable option for correcting stone damage to your windshield.

Although severely cracked or damaged windshields must be replaced, there is something that you can do to prolong or even prevent the need for replacement of a chipped windshield. There are many companies which offer windshield chip repair products, such as Loctite's® Bullseye™ windshield repair kit. These kits usually consist of a syringe, pedestal and a sealing adhesive. The syringe is mounted on the pedestal and is used to create a vacuum which pulls the plastic layer against the glass. This helps make the chip transparent. The adhesive is then injected which seals the chip and helps to prevent further stress cracks from developing

➡Always follow the specific manufacturer's instructions.

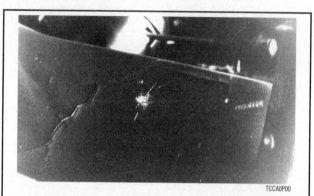

Fig. 27 Small chips on your windshield can be fixed with an aftermarket repair kit, such as the one from Loctite®

Fig. 28 Most kits use a self-stick applicator and syringe to inject the adhesive into the chip or crack

GLOSSARY

AIR/FUEL RATIO: The ratio of air-to-gasoline by weight in the fuel mixture drawn into the engine.

AIR INJECTION: One method of reducing harmful exhaust emissions by injecting air into each of the exhaust ports of an engine. The fresh air entering the hot exhaust manifold causes any remaining fuel to be burned before it can exit the tailpipe.

ALTERNATOR: A device used for converting mechanical energy into electrical energy.

AMMETER: An instrument, calibrated in amperes, used to measure the flow of an electrical current in a circuit. Ammeters are always connected in series with the circuit being tested.

AMPERE: The rate of flow of electrical current present when one volt of electrical pressure is applied against one ohm of electrical resistance.

ANALOG COMPUTER: Any microprocessor that uses similar (analogous) electrical signals to make its calculations.

ARMATURE: A laminated, soft iron core wrapped by a wire that converts electrical energy to mechanical energy as in a motor or relay. When rotated in a magnetic field, it changes mechanical energy into electrical energy as in a generator.

ATMOSPHERIC PRESSURE: The pressure on the Earth's surface caused by the weight of the air in the atmosphere. At sea level, this pressure is 14.7 psi at 32°F (101 kPa at 0°C).

ATOMIZATION: The breaking down of a liquid into a fine mist that can be suspended in air.

AXIAL PLAY: Movement parallel to a shaft or bearing bore.

BACKFIRE: The sudden combustion of gases in the intake or exhaust system that results in a loud explosion.

BACKLASH: The clearance or play between two parts, such as meshed gears.

BACKPRESSURE: Restrictions in the exhaust system that slow the exit of exhaust gases from the combustion chamber.

BAKELITE: A heat resistant, plastic insulator material commonly used in printed circuit boards and transistorized components.

BALL BEARING: A bearing made up of hardened inner and outer races between which hardened steel balls roll.

BALLAST RESISTOR: A resistor in the primary ignition circuit that lowers voltage after the engine is started to reduce wear on ignition components.

BEARING: A friction reducing, supportive device usually located between a stationary part and a moving part.

BIMETAL TEMPERATURE SENSOR: Any sensor or switch made of two dissimilar types of metal that bend when heated or cooled due to the different expansion rates of the alloys. These types of sensors usually function as an on/off switch.

BLOWBY: Combustion gases, composed of water vapor and unburned fuel, that leak past the piston rings into the crankcase during normal engine operation. These gases are removed by the PCV system to prevent the buildup of harmful acids in the crankcase.

BRAKE PAD: A brake shoe and lining assembly used with disc brakes.

BRAKE SHOE: The backing for the brake lining. The term is, however, usually applied to the assembly of the brake backing and lining.

BUSHING: A liner, usually removable, for a bearing; an anti-friction liner used in place of a bearing.

CALIPER: A hydraulically activated device in a disc brake system, which is mounted straddling the brake rotor (disc). The caliper contains at least one piston and two brake pads. Hydraulic pressure on the piston(s) forces the pads against the rotor.

CAMSHAFT: A shaft in the engine on which are the lobes (cams) which operate the valves. The camshaft is driven by the crankshaft, via a belt, chain or gears, at one half the crankshaft speed.

CAPACITOR: A device which stores an electrical charge.

CARBON MONOXIDE (CO): A colorless, odorless gas given off as a normal byproduct of combustion. It is poisonous and extremely dangerous in confined areas, building up slowly to toxic levels without warning if adequate ventilation is not available.

CARBURETOR: A device, usually mounted on the intake manifold of an engine, which mixes the air and fuel in the proper proportion to allow even combustion.

CATALYTIC CONVERTER: A device installed in the exhaust system, like a muffler, that converts harmful byproducts of combustion into carbon dioxide and water vapor by means of a heat-producing chemical reaction.

CENTRIFUGAL ADVANCE: A mechanical method of advancing the spark timing by using flyweights in the distributor that react to centrifugal force generated by the distributor shaft rotation.

CHECK VALVE: Any one-way valve installed to permit the flow of air, fuel or vacuum in one direction only.

CHOKE: A device, usually a moveable valve, placed in the intake path of a carburetor to restrict the flow of air.

CIRCUIT: Any unbroken path through which an electrical current can flow. Also used to describe fuel flow in some instances.

CIRCUIT BREAKER: A switch which protects an electrical circuit from overload by opening the circuit when the current flow exceeds a predetermined level. Some circuit breakers must be reset manually, while most reset automatically.

COIL (IGNITION): A transformer in the ignition circuit which steps up the voltage provided to the spark plugs.

COMBINATION MANIFOLD: An assembly which includes both the intake and exhaust manifolds in one casting.

GLOSSARY

COMBINATION VALVE: A device used in some fuel systems that routes fuel vapors to a charcoal storage canister instead of venting them into the atmosphere. The valve relieves fuel tank pressure and allows fresh air into the tank as the fuel level drops to prevent a vapor lock situation.

COMPRESSION RATIO: The comparison of the total volume of the cylinder and combustion chamber with the piston at BDC and the piston at TDC.

CONDENSER: 1. An electrical device which acts to store an electrical charge, preventing voltage surges. 2. A radiator-like device in the air conditioning system in which refrigerant gas condenses into a liquid, giving off heat.

CONDUCTOR: Any material through which an electrical current can be transmitted easily.

CONTINUITY: Continuous or complete circuit. Can be checked with an ohmmeter.

COUNTERSHAFT: An intermediate shaft which is rotated by a mainshaft and transmits, in turn, that rotation to a working part.

CRANKCASE: The lower part of an engine in which the crankshaft and related parts operate.

CRANKSHAFT: The main driving shaft of an engine which receives reciprocating motion from the pistons and converts it to rotary motion.

CYLINDER: In an engine, the round hole in the engine block in which the piston(s) ride.

CYLINDER BLOCK: The main structural member of an engine in which is found the cylinders, crankshaft and other principal parts.

CYLINDER HEAD: The detachable portion of the engine, usually fastened to the top of the cylinder block and containing all or most of the combustion chambers. On overhead valve engines, it contains the valves and their operating parts. On overhead cam engines, it contains the camshaft as well.

DEAD CENTER: The extreme top or bottom of the piston stroke.

DETONATION: An unwanted explosion of the air/fuel mixture in the combustion chamber caused by excess heat and compression, advanced timing, or an overly lean mixture. Also referred to as "ping".

DIAPHRAGM: A thin, flexible wall separating two cavities, such as in a vacuum advance unit.

DIESELING: A condition in which hot spots in the combustion chamber cause the engine to run on after the key is turned off.

DIFFERENTIAL: A geared assembly which allows the transmission of motion between drive axles, giving one axle the ability to turn faster than the other.

DIODE: An electrical device that will allow current to flow in one direction only.

DISC BRAKE: A hydraulic braking assembly consisting of a brake disc, or rotor, mounted on an axle, and a caliper assembly containing, usually two brake pads which are activated by hydraulic pressure. The pads are forced against the sides of the disc, creating friction which slows the vehicle.

DISTRIBUTOR: A mechanically driven device on an engine which is responsible for electrically firing the spark plug at a predetermined point of the piston stroke.

DOWEL PIN: A pin, inserted in mating holes in two different parts allowing those parts to maintain a fixed relationship.

DRUM BRAKE: A braking system which consists of two brake shoes and one or two wheel cylinders, mounted on a fixed backing plate, and a brake drum, mounted on an axle, which revolves around the assembly.

DWELL: The rate, measured in degrees of shaft rotation, at which an electrical circuit cycles on and off.

ELECTRONIC CONTROL UNIT (ECU): Ignition module, module, amplifier or igniter. See Module for definition.

ELECTRONIC IGNITION: A system in which the timing and firing of the spark plugs is controlled by an electronic control unit, usually called a module. These systems have no points or condenser.

END-PLAY: The measured amount of axial movement in a shaft.

ENGINE: A device that converts heat into mechanical energy.

EXHAUST MANIFOLD: A set of cast passages or pipes which conduct exhaust gases from the engine.

FEELER GAUGE: A blade, usually metal, or precisely predetermined thickness, used to measure the clearance between two parts.

FIRING ORDER: The order in which combustion occurs in the cylinders of an engine. Also the order in which spark is distributed to the plugs by the distributor.

FLOODING: The presence of too much fuel in the intake manifold and combustion chamber which prevents the air/fuel mixture from firing, thereby causing a no-start situation.

FLYWHEEL: A disc shaped part bolted to the rear end of the crankshaft. Around the outer perimeter is affixed the ring gear. The starter drive engages the ring gear, turning the flywheel, which rotates the crankshaft, imparting the initial starting motion to the engine.

FOOT POUND (ft. lbs. or sometimes, ft.lb.): The amount of energy or work needed to raise an item weighing one pound, a distance of one foot.

FUSE: A protective device in a circuit which prevents circuit overload by breaking the circuit when a specific amperage is present. The device is constructed around a strip or wire of a lower amperage rating than the circuit it is designed to protect. When an amperage higher than that stamped on the fuse is present in the circuit, the strip or wire melts, opening the circuit.

GEAR RATIO: The ratio between the number of teeth on meshing gears.

GENERATOR: A device which converts mechanical energy into electrical energy.

HEAT RANGE: The measure of a spark plug's ability to dissipate heat from its firing end. The higher the heat range, the hotter the plug fires.

GLOSSARY 10-13

HUB: The center part of a wheel or gear.

HYDROCARBON (HC): Any chemical compound made up of hydrogen and carbon. A major pollutant formed by the engine as a byproduct of combustion.

HYDROMETER: An instrument used to measure the specific gravity of a solution.

INCH POUND (inch lbs.; sometimes in.lb. or in. lbs.): One twelfth of a foot pound.

INDUCTION: A means of transferring electrical energy in the form of a magnetic field. Principle used in the ignition coil to increase voltage.

INJECTOR: A device which receives metered fuel under relatively low pressure and is activated to inject the fuel into the engine under relatively high pressure at a predetermined time.

INPUT SHAFT: The shaft to which torque is applied, usually carrying the driving gear or gears.

INTAKE MANIFOLD: A casting of passages or pipes used to conduct air or a fuel/air mixture to the cylinders.

JOURNAL: The bearing surface within which a shaft operates.

KEY: A small block usually fitted in a notch between a shaft and a hub to prevent slippage of the two parts.

MANIFOLD: A casting of passages or set of pipes which connect the cylinders to an inlet or outlet source.

MANIFOLD VACUUM: Low pressure in an engine intake manifold formed just below the throttle plates. Manifold vacuum is highest at idle and drops under acceleration.

MASTER CYLINDER: The primary fluid pressurizing device in a hydraulic system. In automotive use, it is found in brake and hydraulic clutch systems and is pedal activated, either directly or, in a power brake system, through the power booster.

MODULE: Electronic control unit, amplifier or igniter of solid state or integrated design which controls the current flow in the ignition primary circuit based on input from the pick-up coil. When the module opens the primary circuit, high secondary voltage is induced in the coil.

NEEDLE BEARING: A bearing which consists of a number (usually a large number) of long, thin rollers.

OHM: (Ω) The unit used to measure the resistance of conductor-to-electrical flow. One ohm is the amount of resistance that limits current flow to one ampere in a circuit with one volt of pressure.

OHMMETER: An instrument used for measuring the resistance, in ohms, in an electrical circuit.

OUTPUT SHAFT: The shaft which transmits torque from a device, such as a transmission.

OVERDRIVE: A gear assembly which produces more shaft revolutions than that transmitted to it.

OVERHEAD CAMSHAFT (OHC): An engine configuration in which the camshaft is mounted on top of the cylinder head and operates the valve either directly or by means of rocker arms.

OVERHEAD VALVE (OHV): An engine configuration in which all of the valves are located in the cylinder head and the camshaft is located in the cylinder block. The camshaft operates the valves via lifters and pushrods.

OXIDES OF NITROGEN (NOx): Chemical compounds of nitrogen produced as a byproduct of combustion. They combine with hydrocarbons to produce smog.

OXYGEN SENSOR: Use with the feedback system to sense the presence of oxygen in the exhaust gas and signal the computer which can reference the voltage signal to an air/fuel ratio.

PINION: The smaller of two meshing gears.

PISTON RING: An open-ended ring with fits into a groove on the outer diameter of the piston. Its chief function is to form a seal between the piston and cylinder wall. Most automotive pistons have three rings: two for compression sealing; one for oil sealing.

PRELOAD: A predetermined load placed on a bearing during assembly or by adjustment.

PRIMARY CIRCUIT: the low voltage side of the ignition system which consists of the ignition switch, ballast resistor or resistance wire, bypass, coil, electronic control unit and pick-up coil as well as the connecting wires and harnesses.

PRESS FIT: The mating of two parts under pressure, due to the inner diameter of one being smaller than the outer diameter of the other, or vice versa; an interference fit.

RACE: The surface on the inner or outer ring of a bearing on which the balls, needles or rollers move.

REGULATOR: A device which maintains the amperage and/or voltage levels of a circuit at predetermined values.

RELAY: A switch which automatically opens and/or closes a circuit.

RESISTANCE: The opposition to the flow of current through a circuit or electrical device, and is measured in ohms. Resistance is equal to the voltage divided by the amperage.

RESISTOR: A device, usually made of wire, which offers a preset amount of resistance in an electrical circuit.

RING GEAR: The name given to a ring-shaped gear attached to a differential case, or affixed to a flywheel or as part of a planetary gear set.

ROLLER BEARING: A bearing made up of hardened inner and outer races between which hardened steel rollers move.

ROTOR: 1. The disc-shaped part of a disc brake assembly, upon which the brake pads bear; also called, brake disc. 2. The device mounted atop the distributor shaft, which passes current to the distributor cap tower contacts.

10-14 GLOSSARY

SECONDARY CIRCUIT: The high voltage side of the ignition system, usually above 20,000 volts. The secondary includes the ignition coil, coil wire, distributor cap and rotor, spark plug wires and spark plugs.

SENDING UNIT: A mechanical, electrical, hydraulic or electro-magnetic device which transmits information to a gauge.

SENSOR: Any device designed to measure engine operating conditions or ambient pressures and temperatures. Usually electronic in nature and designed to send a voltage signal to an on-board computer, some sensors may operate as a simple on/off switch or they may provide a variable voltage signal (like a potentiometer) as conditions or measured parameters change.

SHIM: Spacers of precise, predetermined thickness used between parts to establish a proper working relationship.

SLAVE CYLINDER: In automotive use, a device in the hydraulic clutch system which is activated by hydraulic force, disengaging the clutch.

SOLENOID: A coil used to produce a magnetic field, the effect of which is to produce work.

SPARK PLUG: A device screwed into the combustion chamber of a spark ignition engine. The basic construction is a conductive core inside of a ceramic insulator, mounted in an outer conductive base. An electrical charge from the spark plug wire travels along the conductive core and jumps a preset air gap to a grounding point or points at the end of the conductive base. The resultant spark ignites the fuel/air mixture in the combustion chamber.

SPLINES: Ridges machined or cast onto the outer diameter of a shaft or inner diameter of a bore to enable parts to mate without rotation.

TACHOMETER: A device used to measure the rotary speed of an engine, shaft, gear, etc., usually in rotations per minute.

THERMOSTAT: A valve, located in the cooling system of an engine, which is closed when cold and opens gradually in response to engine heating, controlling the temperature of the coolant and rate of coolant flow.

TOP DEAD CENTER (TDC): The point at which the piston reaches the top of its travel on the compression stroke.

TORQUE: The twisting force applied to an object.

TORQUE CONVERTER: A turbine used to transmit power from a driving member to a driven member via hydraulic action, providing changes in drive ratio and torque. In automotive use, it links the driveplate at the rear of the engine to the automatic transmission.

TRANSDUCER: A device used to change a force into an electrical signal.

TRANSISTOR: A semi-conductor component which can be actuated by a small voltage to perform an electrical switching function.

TUNE-UP: A regular maintenance function, usually associated with the replacement and adjustment of parts and components in the electrical and fuel systems of a vehicle for the purpose of attaining optimum performance.

TURBOCHARGER: An exhaust driven pump which compresses intake air and forces it into the combustion chambers at higher than atmospheric pressures. The increased air pressure allows more fuel to be burned and results in increased horsepower being produced.

VACUUM ADVANCE: A device which advances the ignition timing in response to increased engine vacuum.

VACUUM GAUGE: An instrument used to measure the presence of vacuum in a chamber.

VALVE: A device which control the pressure, direction of flow or rate of flow of a liquid or gas.

VALVE CLEARANCE: The measured gap between the end of the valve stem and the rocker arm, cam lobe or follower that activates the valve.

VISCOSITY: The rating of a liquid's internal resistance to flow.

VOLTMETER: An instrument used for measuring electrical force in units called volts. Voltmeters are always connected parallel with the circuit being tested.

WHEEL CYLINDER: Found in the automotive drum brake assembly, it is a device, actuated by hydraulic pressure, which, through internal pistons, pushes the brake shoes outward against the drums.

MASTER INDEX

ADJUSTMENT (VALVE LASH)   2-21
   GASOLINE ENGINES   2-21
ADJUSTMENTS (AUTOMATIC TRANSMISSION)   7-13
   KICKDOWN BAND   7-13
   LOW & REVERSE BAND   7-13
   SHIFT LINKAGE   7-14
   THROTTLE KICKDOWN ROD   7-14
ADJUSTMENTS (CLUTCH)   7-7
   PEDAL FREE-PLAY   7-7
ADJUSTMENTS (ELECTRONIC IGNITION)   2-16
   1972-83 MODELS   2-16
   1984 V8 ENGINES WITH DUAL PICKUP AND VACUUM ADVANCE   2-18
   1984-88 V8 ENGINES WITH DUAL PICKUP AND NO VACUUM ADVANCE   2-18
ADJUSTMENTS (HYDRAULIC BRAKING SYSTEM)   9-3
   DRUM BRAKES   9-3
ADJUSTMENTS (MANUAL TRANSMISSION)   7-2
   CLUTCH INTERLOCK   7-4
   SHIFT LINKAGE   7-2
AIR CLEANERS   1-12
   REMOVAL & INSTALLATION   1-12
AIR CONDITIONING COMPONENTS   6-14
   REMOVAL & INSTALLATION   6-14
AIR CONDITIONING SYSTEM   1-23
   PREVENTIVE MAINTENANCE   1-24
   SYSTEM INSPECTION   1-24
   SYSTEM SERVICE & REPAIR   1-23
AIR INJECTION SYSTEM   4-4
   COMPONENT TESTING   4-5
   OPERATION   4-4
   REMOVAL & INSTALLATION   4-5
ALTERNATOR   3-3
   ALTERNATOR PRECAUTIONS   3-3
   BELT TENSION ADJUSTMENT   3-5
   REMOVAL & INSTALLATION   3-4
   TESTING   3-4
ANTENNA   10-4
   REMOVAL & INSTALLATION   10-4
ANTENNA MAST   6-16
   REMOVAL & INSTALLATION   6-16
APPLICATION (FRONT DISC BRAKES)   9-11
AUTOMATIC IDLE SPEED (AIS) MOTOR   5-40
   REMOVAL & INSTALLATION   5-40
AUTOMATIC LOCKING HUBS   7-24
   ASSEMBLY & INSTALLATION   7-24
   INSPECTION   7-24
   LUBRICATION   7-24
   REMOVAL & DISASSEMBLY   7-24
AUTOMATIC TRANSMISSION   7-13
AUTOMATIC TRANSMISSION (FLUIDS AND LUBRICANTS)   1-31
   DRAIN AND REFILL   1-31
   FLUID RECOMMENDATIONS   1-31
   LEVEL CHECK   1-31
AUXILIARY (IDLER) SHAFT   3-43
   REMOVAL & INSTALLATION   3-43
AVOIDING THE MOST COMMON MISTAKES   1-2
AVOIDING TROUBLE   1-2
AXLE HOUSING UNIT (FRONT DRIVE AXLE)   7-33
   REMOVAL & INSTALLATION   7-33
AXLE HOUSING UNIT (REAR AXLE)   7-41
   REMOVAL & INSTALLATION   7-41
AXLE SHAFT, BEARING AND SEAL (FRONT DRIVE AXLE)   7-29
   REMOVAL & INSTALLATION   7-29
AXLE SHAFT, BEARING AND SEAL (REAR AXLE)   7-34
   REMOVAL & INSTALLATION   7-34
AXLES   1-12
BACK-UP LIGHT SWITCH   7-4
   REMOVAL & INSTALLATION   7-4
BASIC ELECTRICAL THEORY   6-2

HOW DOES ELECTRICITY WORK: THE WATER ANALOGY 6-2
OHM'S LAW 6-2
BASIC FUEL SYSTEM DIAGNOSIS 5-2
BASIC OPERATING PRINCIPLES 9-2
    DISC BRAKES 9-2
    DRUM BRAKES 9-2
BATTERY (ENGINE ELECTRICAL) 3-6
    REMOVAL & INSTALLATION 3-6
BATTERY (ROUTINE MAINTENANCE) 1-16
    BATTERY FLUID 1-16
    CABLES 1-17
    CHARGING 1-18
    GENERAL MAINTENANCE 1-16
    PRECAUTIONS 1-16
    REPLACEMENT 1-18
BELTS 1-18
    ADJUSTMENTS 1-19
    INSPECTION 1-18
    REMOVAL & INSTALLATION 1-20
BLEEDING THE BRAKES 9-8
    MASTER CYLINDER 9-8
    WHEEL CYLINDERS & CALIPERS 9-8
BLOWER MOTOR 6-8
    REMOVAL & INSTALLATION 6-8
BODY LUBRICATION AND MAINTENANCE 1-38
    CARE OF YOUR TRUCK 1-38
    HOOD LATCH AND HINGES 1-38
    TAIL GATE AND DOOR HINGES 1-39
BOLTS, NUTS AND OTHER THREADED RETAINERS 1-5
BRAKE DISC (ROTOR) 9-16
    INSPECTION 9-16
    REMOVAL & INSTALLATION 9-16
BRAKE DRUM (REAR DRUM BRAKES) 9-16
    INSPECTION 9-16
    REMOVAL & INSTALLATION 9-17
BRAKE DRUMS (FRONT DRUM BRAKES) 9-9
    INSPECTION 9-9
    REMOVAL & INSTALLATION 9-9
BRAKE HOSES AND PIPES 9-7
    REMOVAL & INSTALLATION 9-8
BRAKE LIGHT SWITCH 9-3
    ADJUSTMENT 9-3
    REMOVAL & INSTALLATION 9-3
BRAKE MASTER CYLINDER 1-36
    FLUID RECOMMENDATIONS 1-36
    LEVEL CHECK 1-36
BRAKE SHOES (FRONT DRUM BRAKES) 9-9
    REMOVAL & INSTALLATION 9-9
BRAKE SHOES (REAR DRUM BRAKES) 9-17
    REMOVAL & INSTALLATION 9-17
BRAKE SPECIFICATIONS 9-24
BREAKER POINTS AND CONDENSER 2-9
    DWELL ADJUSTMENT 2-10
    GENERAL INFORMATION 2-9
    INSPECTION 2-10
    REMOVAL & INSTALLATION 2-10
CABLES 9-20
    ADJUSTMENT 9-22
    REMOVAL & INSTALLATION 9-20
CAMSHAFT AND BEARINGS 3-43
    CAMSHAFT BEARING REPLACEMENT 3-46
    INSPECTION 3-45
    REMOVAL & INSTALLATION 3-43
CAMSHAFT SPECIFICATIONS 3-14
CAPACITIES 1-44
CARBURETED ENGINES 2-22
    ALL 1967 MODELS 2-22
    ALL 1967-76 MODELS AND 1977 CALIFORNIA MODELS 2-23

CARTER BBD CARBURETOR 2-26
CARTER THERMO-QUAD CARBURETOR 2-29
HOLLEY 1945 CARBURETOR 2-34
HOLLEY 2210 CARBURETOR 2-32
HOLLEY 2245 CARBURETOR 2-33
HOLLEY 2280/6280 CARBURETOR 2-25
HOLLEY 6145 CARBURETOR 2-23
ROCHESTER QUADRAJET CARBURETOR 2-30
CARBURETED FUEL SYSTEM 5-2
CARBURETOR 5-4
    ADJUSTMENTS FOR CARTER AFB 5-4
    ADJUSTMENTS FOR CARTER BBD 5-6
    ADJUSTMENTS FOR CARTER THERMO-QUAD 5-8
    ADJUSTMENTS FOR CARTERBBS 5-5
    ADJUSTMENTS FOR HOLLEY 1945 5-12
    ADJUSTMENTS FOR HOLLEY 2210 5-13
    ADJUSTMENTS FOR HOLLEY 2245 5-14
    ADJUSTMENTS FOR HOLLEY 2280 5-16
    ADJUSTMENTS FOR HOLLEY 2300G 5-14
    ADJUSTMENTS FOR HOLLEY 4150G 5-18
    ADJUSTMENTS FOR HOLLEY 6145 5-18
    ADJUSTMENTS FOR HOLLEY 6280 5-20
    ADJUSTMENTS FOR ROCHESTER QUADRAJET 5-22
    ADJUSTMENTS FOR STROMBERG WW3 5-25
    REMOVAL & INSTALLATION 5-26
CARBURETOR APPLICATION: 5-2
    1967 MODELS 5-2
    1968 MODELS 5-2
    1969-72 MODELS 5-2
    1973-74 MODELS 5-2
    1975-77 MODELS 5-2
    1978-79 MODELS 5-2
    1980-81 MODELS 5-2
    1982 MODELS 5-2
    1983 MODELS 5-3
    1984 MODELS 5-3
    1985-87 MODELS 5-3
    1988 MODELS 5-3
CENTER SUPPORT BEARING 7-21
    REMOVAL & INSTALLATION 7-21
CHASSIS GREASING 1-37
    AUTOMATIC TRANSMISSION LINKAGE 1-38
    PARKING BRAKE LINKAGE 1-38
    STEERING LINKAGE 1-38
CHECKING ENGINE COMPRESSION 3-12
    DIESEL ENGINES 3-12
    GASOLINE ENGINES 3-12
CIRCUIT BREAKERS 6-26
    RESETTING AND/OR REPLACEMENT 6-26
CIRCUIT PROTECTION 6-24
CLOCK 6-20
    REMOVAL & INSTALLATION 6-20
CLUSTER MASK AND LENS 6-20
    REMOVAL & INSTALLATION 6-20
CLUTCH 7-6
CLUTCH MASTER CYLINDER AND SLAVE CYLINDER 7-10
    REMOVAL & INSTALLATION 7-10
COIL SPRINGS 8-3
    REMOVAL & INSTALLATION 8-3
COMBINATION MANIFOLD 3-25
    REMOVAL & INSTALLATION 3-25
COMPONENTS 2-18
    1984-88 CARBURETED ENGINES 2-18
    1988 FUEL INJECTED ENGINES 2-19
CONSOLE 10-6
    REMOVAL & INSTALLATION 10-6
CONTROL CABLES 6-13
    REMOVAL & INSTALLATION 6-13

MASTER INDEX

CONTROL UNIT 6-14
    REMOVAL & INSTALLATION 6-14
COOLING SYSTEM 1-22
    DRAINING & REFILLING THE SYSTEM 1-23
    FLUID RECOMMENDATIONS 1-23
    FLUSHING & CLEANING THE SYSTEM 1-23
    INSPECTION 1-22
CRANKCASE VENTILATION SYSTEM 4-2
    COMPONENT TESTING 4-3
    OPERATION 4-2
    REMOVAL & INSTALLATION 4-3
CRANKSHAFT AND CONNECTING ROD SPECIFICATIONS 3-14
CYLINDER HEAD 3-28
    INSPECTION 3-31
    REMOVAL & INSTALLATION 3-28
    RESURFACING 3-32
CYLINDER LINERS AND SEALS 3-52
    INSPECTION 3-52
    INSTALLATION 3-52
    REMOVAL 3-52
DESCRIPTION (ENGINE MECHANICAL) 3-10
DESCRIPTION AND OPERATION (ELECTRONIC IGNITION) 2-11
    1972-83 MODELS 2-11
    1984 V8 ENGINES WITH DUAL PICKUP DISTRIBUTORS AND VACUUM ADVANCE 2-12
    1987-88 ENGINES WITH SINGLE PICKUP DISTRIBUTORS AND NO VACUUM ADVANCE; 1984-88 ENGINES WITH DUAL PICKUP DISTRIBUTORS AND ON VACUUM ADVANCE 2-12
DETERMINING AXLE RATIO 7-33
DIAGNOSIS AND TESTING (ELECTRONIC IGNITION) 2-12
    1972-83 MODELS 2-12
    1984 V8 ENGINES WITH DUAL PICKUP DISTRIBUTORS AND VACUUM ADVANCE 2-12
    1987-88 ENGINES WITH SINGLE PICKUP DISTRIBUTORS AND NO VACUUM ADVANCE; 1984-88 ENGINES WITH DUAL PICKUP DISTRIBUTORS AND ON VACUUM ADVANCE 2-15
DIESEL FUEL SYSTEM 5-41
DIESEL MAINTENANCE INTERVALS SPECIFICATIONS 1-43
DIRECT DRIVE STARTER DIAGNOSIS 3-7
DISC BRAKE CALIPERS 9-14
    OVERHAUL 9-15
    REMOVAL & INSTALLATION 9-14
DISC BRAKE PADS 9-11
    INSPECTION 9-11
    REMOVAL & INSTALLATION 9-11
DISTRIBUTOR 3-3
    INSTALLATION IF TIMING WAS LOST 3-3
    REMOVAL & INSTALLATION 3-3
DO'S 1-4
DON'TS 1-5
DOOR PANELS 10-6
    REMOVAL & INSTALLATION 10-6
DOORS 10-2
    ADJUSTMENT 10-2
DRIVE AXLES 1-34
    DRAIN AND REFILL 1-34
    FLUID RECOMMENDATIONS 1-34
    LEVEL CHECK 1-34
DRIVELINE 7-18
DRIVEN DISC AND PRESSURE PLATE 7-7
    REMOVAL & INSTALLATION 7-7
ELECTRIC FUEL PUMP 5-36
    REMOVAL & INSTALLATION 5-36
ELECTRICAL COMPONENTS 6-2
    CONNECTORS 6-4
    GROUND 6-3
    LOAD 6-4
    POWER SOURCE 6-2

PROTECTIVE DEVICES 6-3
SWITCHES & RELAYS 6-3
WIRING & HARNESSES 6-4
ELECTRONIC CARBURETOR SYSTEM 4-8
    GENERAL INFORMATION 4-8
ELECTRONIC ENGINE CONTROLS 4-8
ELECTRONIC IGNITION 2-11
EMISSION CONTROLS 4-2
EMISSIONS MAINTENANCE REMINDER LIGHT 4-8
    RESETTING 4-8
ENGINE (ENGINE MECHANICAL) 3-16
    REMOVAL & INSTALLATION 3-16
ENGINE (FLUIDS AND LUBRICANTS) 1-27
    OIL AND FILTER CHANGE 1-28
    OIL LEVEL CHECK 1-28
ENGINE (SERIAL NUMBER IDENTIFICATION) 1-9
ENGINE ELECTRICAL 3-2
ENGINE IDENTIFICATION SPECIFICATIONS 1-10
ENGINE MECHANICAL 3-10
ENGINE OVERHAUL TIPS 3-10
    INSPECTION TECHNIQUES 3-11
    REPAIRING DAMAGED THREADS 3-11
    TOOLS 3-11
EQUIPMENT IDENTIFICATION PLATE 1-9
EVAPORATIVE CANISTER 1-15
    SERVICING 1-15
EVAPORATIVE EMISSION CONTROLS 4-3
    COMPONENT TESTING 4-4
    OPERATION 4-3
EXHAUST GAS RECIRCULATION SYSTEM 4-7
    COMPONENT TESTING 4-8
    OPERATION 4-7
EXHAUST MANIFOLD 3-24
    REMOVAL & INSTALLATION 3-24
EXHAUST SYSTEM 3-57
EXTENSION HOUSING SEAL (AUTOMATIC TRANSMISSION) 7-17
    REMOVAL & INSTALLATION 7-17
EXTENSION HOUSING SEAL (MANUAL TRANSMISSION) 7-4
    REMOVAL & INSTALLATION 7-4
EXTERIOR 10-2
FASTENERS, MEASUREMENTS AND CONVERSIONS 1-5
FIRING ORDERS 2-8
FLUID DISPOSAL 1-27
FLUIDS AND LUBRICANTS 1-27
FLYWHEEL AND RING GEAR 3-57
    REMOVAL & INSTALLATION 3-57
4-WD FRONT DRIVESHAFT 7-18
    REMOVAL & INSTALLATION 7-18
FOUR WHEEL DRIVE INDICATOR 6-20
    REMOVAL & INSTALLATION 6-20
FRONT COVER AND SEAL 3-38
    REMOVAL & INSTALLATION 3-38
FRONT DISC BRAKES 9-11
FRONT DRIVE AXLE 7-21
FRONT DRIVE AXLE APPLICATION CHART 7-22
FRONT DRUM BRAKES 9-9
FRONT HEADER PIPES, CATALYTIC CONVERTER AND INLET PIPES 3-59
FRONT SUSPENSION 8-3
FRONT WHEEL BEARINGS 1-39
    REMOVAL, REPACKING, & INSTALLATION 1-39
FUEL AND ENGINE OIL RECOMMENDATIONS 1-27
    DIESEL ENGINES 1-27
    GASOLINE ENGINES 1-27
FUEL FILTER 1-13
    REMOVAL & INSTALLATION 1-13
FUEL FITTINGS 5-38
    REMOVAL & INSTALLATION 5-38

MASTER INDEX

FUEL INJECTED ENGINES 2-36
    MINIMUM IDLE SPEED ADJUSTMENT 2-36
FUEL INJECTION 4-9
    GENERAL INFORMATION 4-9
FUEL INJECTORS 5-39
    REMOVAL & INSTALLATION 5-39
FUEL PRESSURE REGULATOR 5-39
    REMOVAL & INSTALLATION 5-39
FUEL SYSTEM PRESSURE TESTING 5-36
FUEL TANK 5-43
FUSE LINK 6-27
FUSES 6-24
    REPLACEMENT 6-24
GENERAL ENGINE SPECIFICATIONS 3-13
GENERAL INFORMATION (EXHAUST SYSTEM) 3-57
GENERAL INFORMATION (IGNITION TIMING) 2-20
GRILLE 10-3
    REMOVAL & INSTALLATION 10-3
HEADLIGHT SWITCH 6-21
    REMOVAL & INSTALLATION 6-21
HEADLIGHTS 6-21
    ADJUSTING & AIMING 6-21
    AIMING RECOMMENDATIONS 6-21
    REMOVAL & INSTALLATION 6-21
HEAT RISER 1-22
    SERVICING 1-22
HEATER AND AIR CONDITIONER 6-8
HEATER CORE 6-9
    REMOVAL & INSTALLATION 6-9
HOOD 10-2
    ADJUSTMENT 10-2
HOSES 1-21
    REMOVAL & INSTALLATION 1-21
HOW TO USE THIS BOOK 1-2
HYDRAULIC BRAKING SYSTEM 9-2
HYDRAULIC CLUTCH RESERVOIR 1-37
HYDRAULIC VALVES 9-6
    CENTERING THE PROPORTIONING VALVE 9-7
    REMOVAL & INSTALLATION 9-6
HYDRO-BOOST 9-6
    REMOVAL & INSTALLATION 9-6
IDENTIFICATION (AUTOMATIC TRANSMISSION) 7-13
IDENTIFICATION (MANUAL TRANSMISSION) 7-2
IDENTIFICATION (REAR AXLE) 7-33
IDENTIFICATION (TRANSFER CASE) 7-11
IDLE SPEED AND MIXTURE
  ADJUSTMENTS 2-22
IGNITION COIL 3-2
    REMOVAL & INSTALLATION 3-2
IGNITION LOCK CYLINDER 8-24
    REMOVAL & INSTALLATION 8-24
IGNITION MODULE 3-2
    REMOVAL & INSTALLATION 3-2
IGNITION SWITCH 8-22
    REMOVAL & INSTALLATION 8-22
IGNITION TIMING 2-20
INJECTION PUMP 5-41
    INJECTION TIMING 5-42
    REMOVAL & INSTALLATION 5-41
    TESTING 5-41
INJECTORS 5-42
    REMOVAL & INSTALLATION 5-42
    TESTING 5-43
INSIDE REAR VIEW MIRROR 10-9
    REMOVAL & INSTALLATION 10-9
INSTRUMENT CLUSTER 6-18
    REMOVAL & INSTALLATION 6-18
INSTRUMENTS AND SWITCHES 6-18

INTAKE MANIFOLD 3-23
    REMOVAL & INSTALLATION 3-23
INTERIOR 10-6
JACKING 1-41
KNUCKLE AND SPINDLE—2WD 8-10
    REMOVAL & INSTALLATION 8-10
LEAF SPRINGS (FRONT SUSPENSION) 8-4
    REMOVAL & INSTALLATION 8-4
LEAF SPRINGS (REAR SUSPENSION) 8-19
    REMOVAL & INSTALLATION 8-19
LIFTGATE 10-2
    REMOVAL & INSTALLATION 10-2
LIGHTING 6-21
LOWER BALL JOINT 8-8
    REMOVAL & INSTALLATION 8-8
LOWER CONTROL ARM 8-10
    CONTROL ARM BUSHING REPLACEMENT 8-10
    REMOVAL & INSTALLATION 8-10
LOWER CONTROL ARM STRUT 8-10
    REMOVAL & INSTALLATION 8-10
MAINTENANCE AND LUBRICATION CHARTS 1-42
MAINTENANCE INTERVALS SPECIFICATIONS 1-43
MAINTENANCE OR REPAIR? 1-2
MANUAL DOOR GLASS AND REGULATOR 10-8
    REMOVAL & INSTALLATION 10-8
MANUAL DOOR LOCKS 10-6
    REMOVAL & INSTALLATION 10-6
MANUAL LOCKING HUBS 7-21
    REMOVAL & INSTALLATION 7-21
MANUAL STEERING GEAR 8-26
    ADJUSTMENTS 8-26
    REMOVAL & INSTALLATION 8-28
MANUAL TRANSMISSION 7-2
MANUAL TRANSMISSION (FLUIDS AND LUBRICANTS) 1-29
    DRAIN AND REFILL 1-30
    FLUID RECOMMENDATIONS 1-29
    LEVEL CHECK 1-30
MANUAL TRANSMISSIONS (SERIAL NUMBER IDENTIFICATION) 1-12
MASTER CYLINDER 9-4
    REMOVAL & INSTALLATION 9-4
MECHANICAL FUEL PUMP 5-3
    REMOVAL & INSTALLATION 5-3
    TESTING 5-3
MINIMUM IDLE SPEED ADJUSTMENT 5-36
MUFFLER AND OUTLET PIPES 3-58
    REMOVAL & INSTALLATION 3-58
NEUTRAL SAFETY SWITCH 7-17
    REMOVAL & INSTALLATION 7-17
1967-69 MODELS 1-41
1970 AND LATER MODELS 1-41
OIL PAN 3-35
    REMOVAL & INSTALLATION 3-35
OIL PUMP 3-37
    REMOVAL & INSTALLATION 3-37
OUTSIDE MIRRORS 10-4
    REMOVAL & INSTALLATION 10-4
OXYGEN SENSOR 4-8
    OPERATION 4-8
    REMOVAL & INSTALLATION 4-8
PARKING BRAKE 9-20
PINION SEAL (FRONT DRIVE AXLE) 7-32
    REMOVAL & INSTALLATION 7-32
PINION SEAL (REAR AXLE) 7-39
    REMOVAL & INSTALLATION 7-39
PISTON AND RING SPECIFICATIONS 3-15
PISTON RING AND PIN REPLACEMENT 3-48
    CLEANING & INSPECTION 3-49
    HONING 3-50

INSTALLATION 3-51
  ROD BEARING REPLACEMENT 3-51
  SELECTING NEW PISTONS 3-49
PISTONS AND CONNECTING RODS 3-46
  REMOVAL & INSTALLATION 3-46
POINT TYPE IGNITION 2-9
POSITIVE CRANKCASE VENTILATION SYSTEM 1-14
  REPLACEMENT 1-15
  TROUBLESHOOTING 1-15
POWER BOOSTER 9-5
  REMOVAL & INSTALLATION 9-5
POWER DOOR GLASS AND REGULATOR MOTOR 10-9
  REMOVAL & INSTALLATION 10-9
POWER DOOR LOCKS 10-7
  REMOVAL & INSTALLATION 10-7
POWER STEERING GEAR 8-30
  ADJUSTMENTS 8-30
  REMOVAL & INSTALLATION 8-31
POWER STEERING PUMP (FLUIDS AND LUBRICANTS) 1-35
  FLUID RECOMMENDATIONS 1-35
  LEVEL CHECK 1-35
POWER STEERING PUMP (STEERING) 8-31
  REMOVAL & INSTALLATION 8-31
PUSHING 1-41
PUSHING AND TOWING 1-41
RADIATOR 3-26
  REMOVAL & INSTALLATION 3-26
RADIO 6-15
RADIO UNIT 6-15
  ANTENNA LEAD CONNECTIONS 6-15
  REMOVAL & INSTALLATION 6-15
  TRIMMER ADJUSTMENT 6-16
REAR AXLE 7-33
REAR DRIVESHAFTS AND U-JOINTS 7-19
  REMOVAL & INSTALLATION 7-19
  U-JOINT OVERHAUL 7-19
REAR DRUM BRAKES 9-16
REAR MAIN SEAL 3-52
  BREAK-IN PROCEDURE 3-57
  CLEANING & INSPECTION 3-55
  COMPLETING THE REBUILDING PROCESS 3-57
  CRANKSHAFT AND MAIN BEARINGS 3-53
  INSPECTION & REPLACEMENT 3-55
  REMOVAL & INSTALLATION 3-52
  REMOVAL & INSTALLATION 3-54
REAR SUSPENSION 8-19
REDUCTION GEAR STARTER DISGNOSIS 3-7
REGULATOR 3-5
  ADJUSTMENTS 3-5
  REMOVAL & INSTALLATION 3-5
RELIEVING FUEL SYSTEM PRESSURE 5-36
ROCKER ARM (VALVE) COVER 3-19
  REMOVAL & INSTALLATION 3-19
ROCKER ARMS/SHAFTS 3-20
  REMOVAL & INSTALLATION 3-20
ROOF VENT 10-5
  REMOVAL & INSTALLATION 10-5
ROUTINE MAINTENANCE 1-12
SAFETY PRECAUTIONS 3-58
  COMPONENT REPLACEMENT 3-58
SENDING UNITS AND SENSORS 3-9
  REMOVAL & INSTALLATION 3-10
SERIAL NUMBER IDENTIFICATION 1-7
SERVICE PRECAUTIONS 5-36
SERVICING YOUR VEHICLE SAFELY 1-4
SHIFT LINKAGE 7-4
  REMOVAL & INSTALLATION 7-4

SHOCK ABSORBER (FRONT SUSPENSION) 8-5
  REMOVAL & INSTALLATION 8-5
  TESTING 8-7
SHOCK ABSORBERS (REAR SUSPENSION) 8-20
  REMOVAL & INSTALLATION 8-20
  TESTING 8-21
SIGNAL AND MARKER LIGHTS 6-22
  REMOVAL & INSTALLATION 6-22
SNOW PLOW TOGGLE SWITCH 6-20
  REMOVAL & INSTALLATION 6-20
SPARK PLUG WIRES 2-4
  REMOVAL & INSTALLATION 2-4
  TESTING 2-4
SPARK PLUGS 2-2
  HEAT RANGE 2-2
  INSPECTION & GAPPING 2-3
  REMOVAL & INSTALLATION 2-2
SPECIAL TOOLS 1-4
SPECIFICATION CHARTS
  BRAKE SPECIFICATIONS 9-24
  CAMSHAFT SPECIFICATIONS 3-14
  CAPACITIES 1-44
  CRANKSHAFT AND CONNECTING ROD SPECIFICATIONS 3-14
  DIESEL MAINTENANCE INTERVALS SPECIFICATIONS 1-43
  DIRECT DRIVE STARTER DIAGNOSIS 3-7
  ENGINE IDENTIFICATION SPECIFICATIONS 1-10
  FRONT DRIVE AXLE APPLICATION CHART 7-22
  GENERAL ENGINE SPECIFICATIONS 3-13
  MAINTENANCE INTERVALS SPECIFICATIONS 1-43
  PISTON AND RING SPECIFICATIONS 3-15
  REDUCTION GEAR STARTER DISGNOSIS 3-7
  TORQUE SPECIFICATIONS (ENGINE AND ENGINE OVERHAUL) 3-15
  TORQUE SPECIFICATIONS, ADDITIONAL (ENGINE AND ENGINE OVERHAUL) 3-62
  TUNE-UP SPECIFICATIONS 2-5
  VALVE SPECIFICATIONS 3-13
  WHEEL ALIGNMENT SPECIFICATIONS 8-17
SPEEDOMETER 6-20
  REMOVAL & INSTALLATION 6-20
SPEEDOMETER CABLE 6-20
SPINDLE BEARINGS 7-26
  REMOVAL, PACKING & INSTALLATION 7-26
STANDARD AND METRIC MEASUREMENTS 1-7
STARTER 3-6
  REMOVAL & INSTALLATION 3-8
  SOLENOID & BRUSH REPLACEMENT 3-9
  TESTING 3-8
STEERING 8-21
STEERING GEAR 1-34
  FLUID RECOMMENDATIONS 1-34
  LEVEL CHECK 1-35
STEERING KNUCKLE AND BALL JOINTS—4WD 8-11
  REMOVAL & INSTALLATION 8-11
STEERING LINKAGE 8-24
  REMOVAL & INSTALLATION 8-24
STEERING WHEEL 8-21
  REMOVAL & INSTALLATION 8-21
SUNROOF 10-5
  REMOVAL & INSTALLATION 10-5
SUNROOF SEAL 10-5
  REMOVAL & INSTALLATION 10-5
SWAY BAR 8-9
  REMOVAL & INSTALLATION 8-9
SYSTEM DESCRIPTION (THROTTLE BODY FUEL INJECTION SYSTEM) 5-36
TAILGATE 10-2
  REMOVAL & INSTALLATION 10-2

10-20 MASTER INDEX

TANK ASSEMBLY 5-43
    REMOVAL & INSTALLATION 5-43
    SENDING UNIT 5-44
TEST EQUIPMENT 6-5
    JUMPER WIRES 6-5
    MULTIMETERS 6-5
    TEST LIGHTS 6-5
TESTING 6-6
    OPEN CIRCUITS 6-6
    RESISTANCE 6-7
    SHORT CIRCUITS 6-6
    VOLTAGE 6-6
    VOLTAGE DROP 6-7
THERMOSTAT 3-22
    REMOVAL & INSTALLATION 3-22
    TESTING 3-23
THROTTLE BODY 5-38
    REMOVAL & INSTALLATION 5-38
THROTTLE BODY FUEL INJECTION SYSTEM 5-36
THROTTLE BODY TEMPERATURE SENSOR 5-40
    REMOVAL & INSTALLATION 5-40
THROTTLE POSITION SENSOR 5-40
    REMOVAL & INSTALLATION 5-40
TIMING 2-20
    INSPECTION AND ADJUSTMENT 2-20
TIMING CHAIN AND SPROCKETS 3-40
    CHECKING TIMING CHAIN SLACK 3-41
    REMOVAL & INSTALLATION 3-40
TIMING GEARS 3-42
    REMOVAL & INSTALLATION 3-42
TIRES AND WHEELS (ROUTINE MAINTENANCE) 1-24
    INFLATION & INSPECTION 1-25
    TIRE DESIGN 1-25
    TIRE ROTATION 1-25
    TIRE STORAGE 1-25
TIRES AND WHEELS (WHEELS) 8-2
    REMOVAL & INSTALLATION 8-2
TOOLS AND EQUIPMENT 1-2
TORQUE 1-6
    TORQUE ANGLE METERS 1-6
    TORQUE WRENCHES 1-6
TORQUE SPECIFICATIONS (ENGINE AND ENGINE OVERHAUL) 3-15
TORQUE SPECIFICATIONS, ADDITIONAL (ENGINE AND ENGINE OVERHAUL) 3-62
TOWING 1-41
    COOLING 1-41
TRAILER WIRING 6-24
TRANSFER CASE 7-11
TRANSFER CASE (FLUIDS AND LUBRICANTS) 1-32
    DRAIN AND REFILL 1-33
    FLUID RECOMMENDATIONS 1-32
    LEVEL CHECK 1-33
TRANSFER CASE (SERIAL NUMBER IDENTIFICATION) 1-12
TRANSFER CASE ASSEMBLY 7-11
    ADJUSTMENTS 7-11
    REMOVAL & INSTALLATION 7-11
TRANSMISSION (AUTOMATIC TRANSMISSION) 7-17
    REMOVAL & INSTALLATION 7-17
TRANSMISSION (MANUAL TRANSMISSION) 7-5
    REMOVAL & INSTALLATION 7-5
TROUBLESHOOTING ELECTRICAL SYSTEMS 6-6
TUNE-UP PROCEDURES 2-2

TUNE-UP SPECIFICATIONS 2-5
TURN SIGNAL AND HAZARD FLASHER LOCATIONS 6-26
TURN SIGNAL SWITCH 8-22
    REMOVAL & INSTALLATION 8-22
UNDERSTANDING AND TROUBLESHOOTING ELECTRICAL SYSTEMS 6-2
UNDERSTANDING AUTOMATIC TRANSMISSIONS 7-13
UNDERSTANDING THE CLUTCH 7-6
UNDERSTANDING THE MANUAL TRANSMISSION 7-2
UPPER BALL JOINT 8-8
    REMOVAL & INSTALLATION 8-8
UPPER CONTROL ARM 8-9
    CONTROL ARM BUSHING REPLACEMENT 8-9
    REMOVAL & INSTALLATION 8-9
VACUUM DIAGRAMS 4-12
VALVE GUIDES 3-35
    REMOVAL & INSTALLATION 3-35
VALVE LASH 2-21
VALVE SEATS 3-35
    REMOVAL & INSTALLATION 3-35
VALVE SPECIFICATIONS 3-13
VALVE STEM SEALS 3-32
    REMOVAL & INSTALLATION 3-32
VALVE TIMING 3-42
    ADJUSTMENT 3-42
VALVES AND SPRINGS 3-32
    INSPECTION 3-35
    REMOVAL & INSTALLATION 3-32
VEHICLE IDENTIFICATION NUMBER (VIN) 1-7
    1967-69 MODELS 1-7
    1970-73 MODELS 1-7
    1974-79 MODELS 1-8
    1980-88 MODELS 1-8
WATER PUMP 3-27
    REMOVAL & INSTALLATION 3-27
WHEEL ALIGNMENT 8-15
    CAMBER 8-15
    CASTER 8-15
    TOE 8-15
WHEEL ALIGNMENT SPECIFICATIONS 8-17
WHEEL CYLINDERS (FRONT DRUM BRAKES) 9-10
    REMOVAL, INSTALLATION & OVERHAUL 9-10
WHEEL CYLINDERS (REAR DRUM BRAKES) 9-20
    REMOVAL & INSTALLATION 9-20
WHEELS 8-2
WHERE TO BEGIN 1-2
WINDSHIELD AND FIXED GLASS 10-10
    REMOVAL & INSTALLATION 10-10
    WINDSHIELD CHIP REPAIR 10-10
WINDSHIELD WIPER SWITCH 6-20
    REMOVAL & INSTALLATION 6-20
WINDSHIELD WIPERS 1-24
    ELEMENT (REFILL) CARE & REPLACEMENT 1-24
WINDSHIELD WIPERS AND WASHERS 6-16
WIPER ARM 6-16
    REMOVAL & INSTALLATION 6-16
WIPER LINKAGE 6-17
    REMOVAL & INSTALLATION 6-17
WIPER MOTOR 6-16
    REMOVAL & INSTALLATION 6-16
WIRE AND CONNECTOR REPAIR 6-8
WIRING DIAGRAMS 6-28

Don't Miss These Other Important Titles From NP/CHILTON'S

TOTAL CAR CARE MANUALS
The ULTIMATE in automotive repair manuals

Features:
- Based on actual teardowns
- Each manual covers all makes and models (unless otherwise indicated)
- Expanded photography from vehicle teardowns
- Actual vacuum and wiring diagrams—not general representations
- Comprehensive coverage
- Maintenance interval schedules
- Electronic engine and emission controls

ACURA
Coupes and Sedans 1986-93
PART NO. 8426/10300

AMC
Coupes/Sedans/Wagons 1975-88
PART NO. 14300

BMW
Coupes and Sedans 1970-88
PART NO. 8789/18300
318/325/M3/525/535/M5 1989-93
PART NO. 8427/18400

CHRYSLER
Aspen/Volare 1976-80
PART NO. 20100
Caravan/Voyager/Town & Country 1984-95
PART NO. 8155/20300
Caravan/Voyager/Town & Country 1996-99
PART NO. 20302
Cirrus/Stratus/Sebring/Avenger 1995-98
PART NO. 20320
Colt/Challenger/Conquest/Vista 1971-89
PART NO. 20340
Colt/Vista 1990-93
PART NO. 8418/20342
Concorde/Intrepid/New Yorker/LHS/Vision 1993-97
PART NO. 8817/20360
Front Wheel Drive Cars-4 Cyl 1981-95
PART NO. 8673/20382
Front Wheel Drive Cars-6 Cyl 1988-95
PART NO. 8672/20384
Full-Size Trucks 1967-88
PART NO. 8662/20400
Full-Size Trucks 1989-96
PART NO. 8166/20402
Full-Size Vans 1967-88
PART NO. 20420
Full-Size Vans 1989-98
PART NO. 8169/20422
Neon 1995-99
PART NO. 20600
Omni/Horizon/Rampage 1978-89
PART NO. 8787/20700
Ram 50/D50/Arrow 1979-93
PART NO. 20800

FORD
Aerostar 1986-96
PART NO. 8057/26100
Aspire 1994-97
PART NO. 26120
Contour/Mystique/Cougar 1995-99
PART NO. 26170
Crown Victoria/Grand Marquis 1989-94
PART NO. 8417/26180
Escort/Lynx 1981-90
PART NO. 8270/26240
Escort/Tracer 1991-99
PART NO. 26242
Fairmont/Zephyr 1978-83
PART NO. 26320
Ford/Mercury Full-Size Cars 1968-88
PART NO. 8665/26360
Full-Size Vans 1961-88
PART NO. 26400
Full-Size Vans 1989-96
PART NO. 8157/26402
Ford/Mercury Mid-Size Cars 1971-85
PART NO. 8667/26580
Mustang/Cougar 1964-73
PART NO. 26600
Mustang/Capri 1979-88
PART NO. 8580/26604
Mustang 1989-93
PART NO. 8253/26606
Mustang 1994-98
PART NO. 26608
Pick-Ups and Bronco 1976-86
PART NO. 8576/26662
Pick-Ups and Bronco 1987-96
PART NO. 8136/26664
Pick-Ups/Expedition/Navigator 1997-00
PART NO. 26666
Probe 1989-92
PART NO. 8266/26680
Probe 1993-97
PART NO. 8411/46802
Ranger/Bronco II 1983-90
PART NO. 8159/26686
Ranger/Explorer/Mountaineer 1991-97
PART NO. 26688
Taurus/Sable 1986-95
PART NO. 8251/26700
Taurus/Sable 1996-99
PART NO. 26702
Tempo/Topaz 1984-94
PART NO. 8271/26720
Thunderbird/Cougar 1983-96
PART NO. 8268/26760
Windstar 1995-98
PART NO. 26840

GENERAL MOTORS
Astro/Safari 1985-96
PART NO. 8056/28100
Blazer/Jimmy 1969-82
PART NO. 28140
Blazer/Jimmy/Typhoon/Bravada 1983-93
PART NO. 8139/28160
Blazer/Jimmy/Bravada 1994-99
PART NO. 8845/28862
Bonneville/Eighty Eight/LeSabre 1986-99
PART NO. 8423/28200
Buick/Oldsmobile/Pontiac Full-Size 1975-90
PART NO. 8584/28240
Cadillac 1967-89
PART NO. 8587/28260
Camaro 1967-81
PART NO. 28280
Camaro 1982-92
PART NO. 8260/28282
Camaro/Firebird 1993-98
PART NO. 28284
Caprice 1990-93
PART NO. 8421/28300
Cavalier/Sunbird/Skyhawk/Firenza 1982-94
PART NO. 8269/28320
Cavalier/Sunfire 1995-00
PART NO. 28322
Celebrity/Century/Ciera/6000 1982-96
PART NO. 8252/28360
Chevette/1000 1976-88
PART NO. 28400
Chevy Full-Size Cars 1968-78
PART NO. 28420
Chevy Full-Size Cars 1979-89
PART NO. 8531/28422
Chevy Mid-Size Cars 1964-88
PART NO. 8594/28440
Citation/Omega/Phoenix/Skylark/XII 1980-85
PART NO. 28460
Corsica/Beretta 1988-96
PART NO. 8254/ 28480
Corvette 1963-82
PART NO. 28500
Corvette 1984-96
PART NO. 28502
Cutlass RWD 1970-87
PART NO. 8668/28520
DeVille/Fleetwood/Eldorado/Seville 1990-93
PART NO. 8420/ 28540
Electra/Park Avenue/Ninety-Eight 1990-93
PART NO. 8430/28560
Fiero 1984-88
PART NO. 28580
Firebird 1967-81
PART NO. 28600
Firebird 1982-92
PART NO. 8534/28602
Full-Size Trucks 1970-79
PART NO. 28620
Full-Size Trucks 1980-87
PART NO. 8577/28622
Full-Size Trucks 1988-98
PART NO. 8055/28624
Full-Size Vans 1967-86
PART NO. 28640
Full-Size Vans 1987-97
PART NO. 8040/28642
Grand Am/Achieva 1985-98
PART NO. 8257/28660
Lumina/Silhouette/Trans Sport/Venture 1990-99
PART NO. 8134/28680
Lumina/Monte Carlo/Grand Prix/Cutlass Supreme/Regal 1988-96
PART NO. 8258/28682
Metro/Sprint 1985-99
PART NO. 8424/28700
Nova/Chevy II 1962-79
PART NO. 28720
Pontiac Mid-Size 1974-83
PART NO. 28740
Chevrolet Nova/GEO Prizm 1985-93
PART NO. 8422/28760
Regal/Century 1975-87
PART NO. 28780
Chevrolet Spectrum/GEO Storm 1985-93
PART NO. 8425/28800
S10/S15/Sonoma Pick-Ups 1982-93
PART NO. 8141/ 28860
S10/Sonoma/Blazer/Jimmy/Bravada Hombre 1994-99
PART NO. 8845/28862

HONDA
Accord/Civic/Prelude 1973-83
PART NO. 8591/30100
Accord/Prelude 1984-95
PART NO. 8255/30150
Civic, CRX and del SOL 1984-95
PART NO. 8256/30200

HYUNDAI
Coupes/Sedans 1986-93
PART NO. 8412/32100
Coupes/Sedans 1994-98
PART NO. 32102

ISUZU
Amigo/Pick-Ups/Rodeo/Trooper 1981-96
PART NO. 8686/36100
Cars and Trucks 1981-91
PART NO. 8069/36150

JEEP
CJ 1945-70
PART NO. 40200
CJ/Scrambler 1971-86
PART NO. 8536/40202
Wagoneer/Commando/Cherokee 1957-83
PART NO. 40600
Wagoneer/Comanche/Cherokee 1984-98
PART NO. 8143/40602
Wrangler/YJ 1987-95
PART NO. 8535/40650

MAZDA
Trucks 1972-86
PART NO. 46600
Trucks 1987-93
PART NO. 8264/46602
Trucks 1994-98
PART NO. 46604
323/626/929/GLC/MX-6/RX-7 1978-89
PART NO. 8581/46800
323/Protege/MX-3/MX-6/626 Millenia/Ford Probe 1990-98
PART NO. 8411/46802

MERCEDES
Coupes/Sedans/Wagons 1974-84
PART NO. 48300

MITSUBISHI
Cars and Trucks 1983-89
PART NO. 7947/50200
Eclipse 1990-98
PART NO. 8415/50400
Pick-Ups and Montero 1983-95
PART NO. 8666/50500

NISSAN
Datsun 210/1200 1973-81
PART NO. 52300
Datsun 200SX/510/610/710/810/Maxima 1973-84
PART NO. 52302
Nissan Maxima 1985-92
PART NO. 8261/52450
Maxima 1993-98
PART NO. 52452
Pick-Ups and Pathfinder 1970-88
PART NO. 8585/52500
Pick-Ups and Pathfinder 1989-95
PART NO. 8145/52502

2P1VerB

Total Car Care, continued

Sentra/Pulsar/NX 1982-96
PART NO. 8263/52700
Stanza/200SX/240SX 1982-92
PART NO. 8262/52750
240SX/Altima 1993-98
PART NO. 52752
Datsun/Nissan Z and ZX 1970-88
PART NO. 8846/52800

RENAULT
Coupes/Sedans/Wagons 1975-85
PART NO. 58300

SATURN
Coupes/Sedans/Wagons 1991-98
PART NO. 8419/62300

SUBARU
Coupes/Sedan/Wagons 1970-84
PART NO. 8790/64300
Coupes/Sedans/Wagons 1985-96
PART NO. 8259/64302

SUZUKI
Samurai/Sidekick/Tracker 1986-98
PART NO. 66500

TOYOTA
Camry 1983-96
PART NO. 8265/68200
Celica/Supra 1971-85
PART NO. 68250
Celica 1986-93
PART NO. 8413/68252

Celica 1994-98
PART NO. 68254
Corolla 1970-87
PART NO. 8586/68300
Corolla 1988-97
PART NO. 8414/68302
Cressida/Corona/Crown/MkII 1970-82
PART NO. 68350
Cressida/Van 1983-90
PART NO. 68352
Pick-ups/Land Cruiser/4Runner 1970-88
PART NO. 8578/68600
Pick-ups/Land Cruiser/4Runner 1989-98
PART NO. 8163/68602
Previa 1991-97
PART NO. 68640

Tercel 1984-94
PART NO. 8595/68700

VOLKSWAGEN
Air-Cooled 1949-69
PART NO. 70200
Air-Cooled 1970-81
PART NO. 70202
Front Wheel Drive 1974-89
PART NO. 8663/70400
Golf/Jetta/Cabriolet 1990-93
PART NO. 8429/70402

VOLVO
Coupes/Sedans/Wagons 1970-89
PART NO. 8786/72300
Coupes/Sedans/Wagons 1990-98
PART NO. 8428/72302

SELOC MARINE MANUALS

OUTBOARDS
Chrysler Outboards, All Engines 1962-84
PART NO. 018-7(1000)
Force Outboards, All Engines 1984-96
PART NO. 024-1(1100)
Honda Outboards, All Engines 1988-98
PART NO. 1200
Johnson/Evinrude Outboards, 1.5-40HP, 2-Stroke 1956-70
PART NO. 007-1(1300)
Johnson/Evinrude Outboards, 1.25-60HP, 2-Stroke 1971-89
PART NO. 008-X(1302)
Johnson/Evinrude Outboards, 1-50 HP, 2-Stroke 1990-95
PART NO. 026-8(1304)
Johnson/Evinrude Outboards, 50-125 HP, 2-Stroke 1958-72
PART NO. 009-8(1306)
Johnson/Evinrude Outboards, 60-235 HP, 2-Stroke 1973-91
PART NO. 010-1(1308)
Johnson/Evinrude Outboards, 80-300 HP, 2-Stroke 1992-96
PART NO. 040-3(1310)
Mariner Outboards, 2-60 HP, 2-Stroke 1977-89
PART NO. 015-2(1400)

Mariner Outboards, 45-220 HP, 2 Stroke 1977-89
PART NO. 016-0(1402)
Mercury Outboards, 2-40 HP, 2-Stroke 1965-91
PART NO. 012-8(1404)
Mercury Outboards, 40-115 HP, 2-Stroke 1965-92
PART NO. 013-6(1406)
Mercury Outboards, 90-300 HP, 2-Stroke 1965-91
PART NO. 014-4(1408)
Mercury/Mariner Outboards, 2.5-25 HP, 2-Stroke 1990-94
PART NO. 035-7(1410)
Mercury/Mariner Outboards, 40-125 HP, 2-Stroke 1990-94
PART NO. 036-5(1412)
Mercury/Mariner Outboards, 135-275 HP, 2-Stroke 1990-94
PART NO. 037-3(1414)
Mercury/Mariner Outboards, All Engines 1995-99
PART NO. 1416
Suzuki Outboards, All Engines 1985-99
PART NO. 1600

Yamaha Outboards, 2-25 HP, 2-Stroke and 9.9 HP, 4-Stroke 1984-91
PART NO. 021-7(1700)
Yamaha Outboards, 30-90 HP, 2-Stroke 1984-91
PART NO. 022-5(1702)
Yamaha Outboards, 115-225 HP, 2-Stroke 1984-91
PART NO. 023-3(1704)
Yamaha Outboards, All Engines 1992-98
PART NO. 1706

STERN DRIVES
Marine Jet Drive 1961-96
PART NO. 029-2(3000)
Mercruiser Stern Drive Type 1, Alpha, Bravo I, II, 1964-92
PART NO. 005-5(3200)
Mercruiser Stern Drive Alpha 1 Generation II 1992-96
PART NO. 039-X(3202)
Mercruiser Stern Drive Bravo I, II, III 1992-96
PART NO. 046-2(3204)
OMC Stern Drive 1964-86
PART NO. 004-7(3400)
OMC Cobra Stern Drive 1985-95
PART NO. 025-X(3402)

Volvo/Penta Stern Drives 1968-91
PART NO. 011-X(3600)
Volvo/Penta Stern Drives 1992-93
PART NO. 038-1(3602)
Volvo/Penta Stern Drives 1992-95
PART NO. 041-1(3604)

INBOARDS
Yanmar Inboard Diesels 1988-91
PART NO. 7400

PERSONAL WATERCRAFT
Kawasaki 1973-91
PART NO. 032-2(9200)
Kawasaki 1992-97
PART NO. 042-X(9202)
Polaris 1992-97
PART NO. 045-4(9400)
Sea Doo/Bombardier 1988-91
PART NO. 033-0(9000)
Sea Doo/Bombardier 1992-97
PART NO. 043-8(9002)
Yamaha 1987-91
PART NO. 034-9(9600)
Yamaha 1992-97
PART NO. 044-6(9602)

"...and even more from CHILTON"

General Interest / Recreational Books

ATV Handbook
PART NO. 9123
Auto Detailing
PART NO. 8394
Auto Body Repair
PART NO. 7898
Briggs & Stratton Vertical Crankshaft Engine
PART NO. 61-1-2
Briggs & Stratton Horizontal Crankshaft Engine
PART NO. 61-0-4
Briggs & Stratton Overhead Valve (OHV) Engine
PART NO. 61-2-0
Easy Car Care
PART NO. 8042

Motorcycle Handbook
PART NO. 9099
Snowmobile Handbook
PART NO. 9124
Small Engine Repair (Up to 20 Hp)
PART NO. 8325

Total Service Series

Automatic Transmissions/Transaxles Diagnosis and Repair
PART NO. 8944
Brake System Diagnosis and Repair
PART NO. 8945
Chevrolet Engine Overhaul Manual
PART NO. 8794
Engine Code Manual
PART NO. 8851
Ford Engine Overhaul Manual
PART NO. 8793
Fuel Injection Diagnosis and Repair
PART NO. 8946

COLLECTOR'S SERIES HARD-COVER MANUALS
Chilton's Collector's Editions are perfect for enthusiasts of vintage or rare cars. These hard-cover manuals contain repair and maintenance information for all major systems that might not be available elsewhere. Included are repair and overhaul procedures using thousands of illustrations. These manuals offer a range of coverage from as far back as 1940 and as recent as 1997, so you don't need an antique car or truck to be a collector.

MULTI-VEHICLE SPANISH LANGUAGE MANUALS
Chilton's Spanish language manuals offer some of our most popular titles in Spanish. Each is as complete and easy to use as the English-language counterpart and offers the same maintenance, repair and overhaul information along with specifications charts and tons of illustrations.

TOTAL SERVICE SERIES / SYSTEM SPECIFIC MANUALS
These innovative books offer repair, maintenance and service procedures for automotive related systems. They cover today's complex vehicles in a user-friendly format, which places even the most difficult automotive topic well within the reach of every Do-It-Yourselfer. Each title covers a specific subject from Brakes and Engine Rebuilding to Fuel Injection Systems, Automatic Transmissions and even Engine Trouble Codes.

For the titles listed, visit your local Chilton® Retailer
For a Catalog, for information, or to order call toll-free: 877-4CHILTON.

 1020 Andrew Drive, Suite 200 • West Chester, PA 19380-4291
www.chiltonsonline.com